LEGEN...AND...
The Ame...

Halifax

Massachusetts map:

Concord River

Bedford

Woburn

Stoneham

Concord Lexington

Lynn

M A S S A C H U S E T T S

Lincoln

Medford

Malden

Menotomy

Chelsea

Bunker Hill *Breed's Hill*

Sudbury

Waltham

Cambridge Charlestown

East Sudbury Weston

Watertown **Boston**

Charles River

Brookline

Roxbury

Boston Harbor

0 Miles 5
0 Kilometers 5

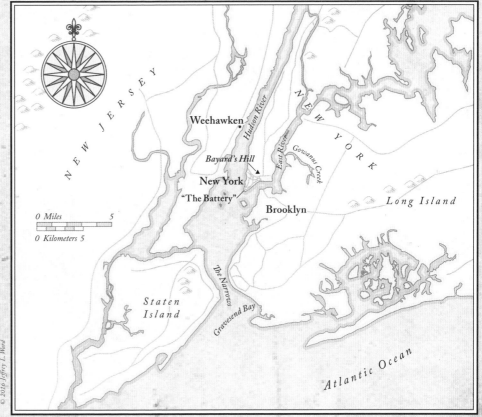

New York map:

N E W   J E R S E Y

N E W   Y O R K

Weehawken

Hudson River

Bayard's Hill

East River

Gowanus Creek

New York

"The Battery"

Brooklyn

Long Island

0 Miles 5
0 Kilometers 5

Staten
Island

The Narrows

Gravesend Bay

Atlantic Ocean

© 2016 Jeffrey L. Ward

BILL O'REILLY'S

BILL O'REILLY'S

LEGENDS & LIES

The Patriots

WRITTEN BY DAVID FISHER

Henry Holt and Company
New York

Henry Holt and Company, LLC
Publishers since 1866
175 Fifth Avenue
New York, New York 10010
www.henryholt.com

Henry Holt® and ⓗ® are registered trademarks of Henry Holt and Company, LLC.
Copyright © 2016 by Warm Springs Productions, LLC and Life of O'Reilly Productions
All rights reserved.
Distributed in Canada by Raincoast Book Distribution Limited

Library of Congress Cataloging-in-Publication Data is available.

ISBN: 978-1-62779-789-4

Henry Holt books are available for special promotions and premiums.
For details contact: Director, Special Markets.

First Edition 2016

Designed by Nancy Singer
Endpaper map by Jeffrey L. Ward
Photo research by Liz Seramur of Selected Shots Photo Research, Inc. with
assistance from Nancy Singer and Olivia Croom

Printed in the United States of America

1 2 3 4 5 6 7 8 9 10

CONTENTS

Having just finished writing another *O'Reilly Factor* script, I am thinking about the people who made my program possible: the American revolutionaries. This day the Factor is packed with opinion and robust debate that would be unthinkable on television in, say, China and many other countries.

Having lived in Boston for some years, I immersed myself in New England history. Back in the mid-eighteenth century, life was hard in the Massachusetts Bay Colony. Few people had any luxuries at all—they lived week to week trying to feed their families and ward off fatal disease.

The climate was harsh and the labor hard.

Thus many British subjects living in the colonies were in no mood to share what little they had with a corrupt king thousands of miles away. As King George's financial demands grew, so did rebellion and sedition against the Crown. It was almost all about money.

The leaders of the rebellion were a very mixed crew. Led by tough working-class guys, the Sons of Liberty roughed up the king's men and eventually sent an unforgettable message by dumping English tea, the source of a hated tax, into the cold, murky waters of Boston Harbor. Others, like John Hancock, were patricians who had a lot to lose by defying London but did so anyway because they believed in freedom and fairness.

The actual American Revolution began soon after the Tea Party and is filled with thrilling stories of bravery and deceit, brilliance and stupidity.

This book will bring some of those stories to life while telling the reader the truth about Benjamin Franklin, George Washington, John and Samuel Adams, and other American icons.

Along the way, we debunk some of the lies attached to the legends, which I always find fascinating. As a former high school history teacher,

I am often shocked to find that some Americans know virtually nothing about the origins of the place where they currently live and therefore believe most anything.

How many of us know the story of the Francis Marion—the Swamp Fox? What a guy he was—a fearsome fighter who used the thickets of South Carolina to terrorize British forces. Marion's guys were tough outdoorsmen who openly mocked the king's men dressed in their elaborate "red coats."

The Swamp Fox used guile and guerrilla tactics to hammer a much more powerful opponent. He exemplifies the true American spirit; self-sacrifice and goal oriented.

How much more opposite could Francis Marion be from, say, Benjamin Franklin, the crafty inventor turned diplomat who guided the Independence movement? Talk about two different worlds: Franklin at home in the salons of Paris; Marion camping out in desolate backwaters!

This book chronicles both men, demonstrating the diversity that was present in colonial America, even as it is today in modern times.

My life has been directly affected by those who forged rebellion against England and won freedom. I have made my living for over forty years by using my freedom of speech and working in a free press. No other country on earth has so many liberties in the marketplace of ideas in which I traffic every working day.

So I owe the original patriots a deep debt and hope to repay it by writing the truth about them and bringing their courageous deeds to millions of readers. It is a mission that is worthy and necessary in this age of declining knowledge about how America became the land of the free.

As always in my books of history, there is no political message other than stating the facts. The American revolutionaries were men and women of differing opinions, united against what they saw as an unbearable oppressor—King George.

But not every colonial was a rebel. About half the population, called Tories, did not want separation from the Crown. That caused a bitter divide that lasted for decades after independence was finally won. In fact, if you travel to Cambridge, Massachusetts, today, you can visit Brattle Street and see some of the large homes that colonists loyal to the king inhabited. To this day, that neighborhood is called "Tory Row."

So what side would you have taken? Most of us now would most likely say "the patriots!" But back in 1775, the decision was not an easy one. Few thought George Washington and his ill-equipped army could defeat the powerful, well-trained British regulars. And the Brits were vengeful—the lives of all rebels were definitely on the line, as they say.

Still, the allure of freedom intoxicated many colonists. But it was the extraordinary leadership provided by the subjects of this book that made our present freedoms possible.

Their stories demand to be told accurately. We don't need false legends or propaganda. The truth is simply too compelling.

Hopefully, you will enjoy the following pages and visualize the intense struggle that gave all contemporary Americans a chance at living a free and worthwhile life. Reading this book will be educational and enjoyable; my favorite formula. We write for you, the reader, in a fast-paced, action-packed way. But please don't forget how important these stories really are as you get caught up in the drama.

So let's go, and thanks for taking the time to learn about the patriots.

Bill O'Reilly

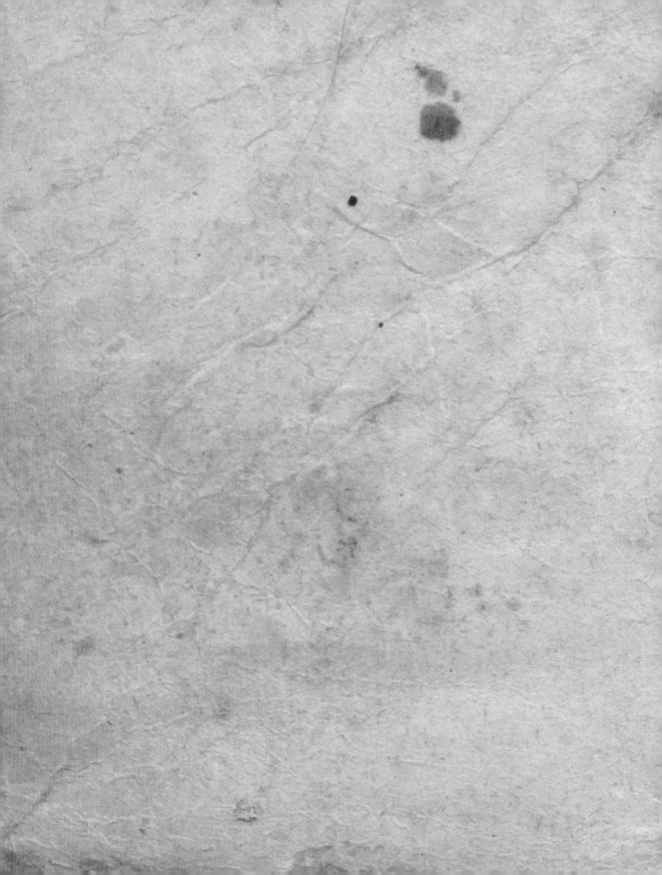

INTRODUCTION

It took slightly more than four decades from the first rumblings of discontent for the thirteen loosely aligned colonies comprising New England to be transformed into one of the largest and most prosperous nations on earth. It started with a simple idea, that all men deserve to be treated equally, and became the great experiment that would change the world.

The American Revolution was born in the town meetings of Massachusetts, when ordinary people stood up and spoke passionately to their neighbors about their common interests. It did not begin as a quest for freedom but rather as citizens' simple desire to have their rights respected. It was a war of ideas as much as a fight over economics.

When the first shots were fired at Lexington and Concord, it is probable that the British believed this was more of a nuisance than a war. Would the colonies really dare fight the greatest military power ever assembled? The British army was well equipped, well trained, and highly professional. The British navy controlled the oceans. The colonials had no army and no navy, just poorly equipped and untrained local militias.

At first the British tried to contain the revolt within Massachusetts, believing they might end it by occupying Boston. That strategy failed at Bunker Hill, when the redcoats were stunned by the ferocity of the colonists' defense. When the cannons Washington had retrieved from abandoned Fort Ticonderoga put the British troops in jeopardy, the British withdrew to Canada to reinforce their army. It was time to take this uprising seriously.

No man did more for the cause of American freedom than George Washington, who was, wrote Henry Lee, "First in war, first in peace and first in the hearts of his countrymen." At top, his celebrated entry into New York City in November, 1883. Below, General Horatio Gates accepts the surrender of General Burgoyne at Saratoga, New York, in October 1777, marking the turning point of the war.

In 1776 the largest military offensive in history captured New York, forcing Washington to retreat. The colonial army had been reduced to only six thousand men when Washington launched an extraordinary Christmas Night attack on the Hessians in Trenton, providing the colonies with a great military victory—and hope.

A year later the strategy changed once more; this time the British intended to isolate the northern colonies. To accomplish this, they split their army in half—and were stunned when five thousand troops were captured at the Battle of Saratoga. The war had become incredibly costly, causing many people in England—and Parliament—to question the value of continuing the fight.

Everything changed when France entered the war on the colonial side in 1778, forcing the British to protect their possessions scattered around the world. Once again the British objectives had changed, and they launched an invasion of the American south, where they expected to be supported by Loyalists. At the beginning of 1780 there were more than sixty thousand British and German troops fighting Washington's twelve-thousand-man army. While at first the southern strategy worked and the British successfully captured South Carolina, the attempt to move north was defeated by small, highly mobile guerrilla bands using hit-and-run tactics. The result was that Lord Cornwallis's army was trapped at Yorktown, Virginia, by American and French forces and ultimately surrendered, effectively ending the fighting in America.

The colonies won the war. The question became: What kind of nation would emerge from the victory? The founding fathers battled over lofty ideals and harsh realities, and slowly a new form of government was carefully molded. It was tested in numerous and unexpected ways, but, with the Louisiana Purchase, a vast new democratic nation was born.

What follows is not a complete retelling of the war and its aftermath but rather an investigation into the truth behind many of the legendary stories from the time, the stories of the heroes and the traitors, the leaders and the ordinary soldiers, who together forged one of the most exciting narratives in all of history.

David Fisher
January 2016

The midnight rides of Paul Revere, William Dawes, and others alert colonists that British troops are marching
ᛃ

After more repressive laws are passed, Samuel Adams begins organizing the colonies
ᛃ

The shots heard round the world are fired at Lexington and Concord
ᛃ

Washington's army suffers several devastating defeats and is in jeopardy of being disbanded
ᛃ

The first British troops are sent to Boston

1768

The Second Continental Congress meets and appoints George Washington commander in chief
ᛃ

The British army is defeated at Saratoga
ᛃ

The Marquis de Lafayette arrives
ᛃ

British Parliament passes the Sugar and Currency Acts
ᛃ

The Boston Tea Party and similar antitax protests are held throughout New England

The Battle of Bunker Hill is the first major conflict of the war
ᛃ

The Continental army settles in Valley Forge for the winter; Baron von Steuben arrives and begins training Washington's troops

The first Committees of Correspondence are formed

Lord Dunmore offers freedom to slaves who fight for the British

1764

1773

1775

1777

1770

1776

The protests turn violent with the Boston Massacre

Henry Knox completes an amazing journey carrying cannons from Fort Ticonderoga to Boston
ᛃ

1774

The British army evacuates Boston
ᛃ

1778

1765

Parliament imposes the Intolerable Acts
ᛃ

The Declaration of Independence is signed
ᛃ

France enters the war
ᛃ

Parliament imposes the Stamp Act on the colonies
ᛃ

The First Continental Congress meets in Philadelphia

British troops capture New York
ᛃ

British troops withdraw from Philadelphia

In Massachusetts, the Sons of Liberty are formed

Washington inspires the colonies by crossing the Delaware River on Christmas Night to capture more than a thousand Hessians in Trenton

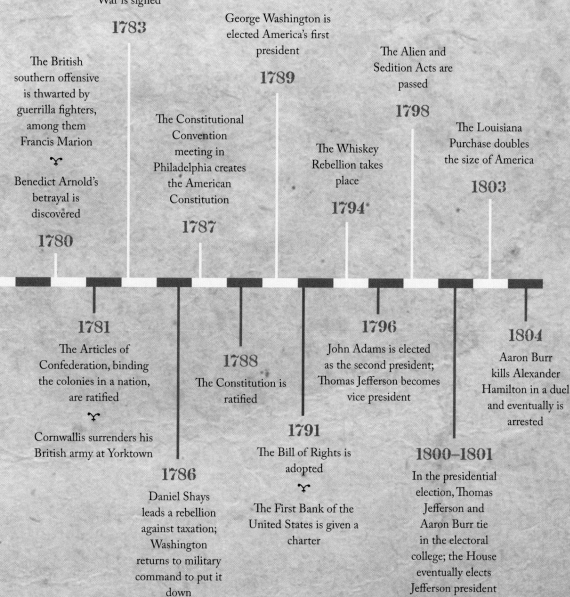

The Treaty of Paris ending the Revolutionary War is signed

1783

George Washington is elected America's first president

1789

The Alien and Sedition Acts are passed

1798

The British southern offensive is thwarted by guerrilla fighters, among them Francis Marion

Benedict Arnold's betrayal is discovered

1780

The Constitutional Convention meeting in Philadelphia creates the American Constitution

1787

The Whiskey Rebellion takes place

1794

The Louisiana Purchase doubles the size of America

1803

1781

The Articles of Confederation, binding the colonies in a nation, are ratified

Cornwallis surrenders his British army at Yorktown

1786

Daniel Shays leads a rebellion against taxation; Washington returns to military command to put it down

1788

The Constitution is ratified

1796

John Adams is elected as the second president; Thomas Jefferson becomes vice president

1791

The Bill of Rights is adopted

The First Bank of the United States is given a charter

1800–1801

In the presidential election, Thomas Jefferson and Aaron Burr tie in the electoral college; the House eventually elects Jefferson president

1804

Aaron Burr kills Alexander Hamilton in a duel and eventually is arrested

CHAPTER 1

Samuel Adams AND Paul Revere

THE REBELLION BEGINS

The flame that would ignite the American Revolution was lit on a Thursday morning, February 22, 1770, when, according to the *Boston Gazette*, "a barbarous murder . . . was committed on the body of a young lad of about eleven years of age."

Earlier that morning Christopher Seider and a crowd of young men had marched defiantly through Boston's cobblestone streets to the merchant Theophilus Lillie's shop. In addition to a cart overflowing with rotten fruit, they carried painted papier-mâché figures of Lillie and three other importers who refused to respect the colonists' boycott on all British goods. As the protesters stained the shop windows with rubbish, the greatly despised customs collector Ebenezer Richardson tried to stop them. Richardson, described by the *Gazette* as "a person of a most abandoned character," had been forced to leave the Massachusetts town of Woburn after impregnating his sister-in-law and blaming the local minister. Richardson tried to knock down the rioters' papier-mâché figures. When his attempt was thwarted, he threatened to "blow a lane through this mob" until finally retreating the hundred paces to his own home.

The Boston Massacre, March 5, 1770.

The growing crowd, numbering as many as sixty boys, turned its whole attention to him. The morning was dark. More nasty words were exchanged. "By the eternal God," Richardson swore, "I will make it too hot for some of you before night." At first only rubbish was thrown into Richardson's yard and was thrown back by Richardson and his wife, Kezia, but soon rocks were being hurled and the Richardsons retreated into their secure home. Windows were shattered as the barrage grew in intensity. Seconds after an egg or a stone struck his wife, Ebenezer Richardson appeared defiantly at a second-story window, holding high a musket loaded with swan shot.

He fired once. It was intended to be a warning, he later swore, but two boys were struck. Sammy Gore was wounded in both thighs and his hand but would survive. Christopher Seider was hit in his breast and abdomen by eleven pieces of shot "the bigness of large peas."

"The child fell," reported the *Boston Evening-Post*, "but was taken up and carried into a neighboring house, where all the surgeons within call were assembled, and speedily determined the wounds mortal, as they indeed proved about 9 o'clock that evening."

Richardson and his alleged accomplice, George Wilmot, were taken to Faneuil Hall. As more than a thousand people stood watching, they told their story to three magistrates. Richardson was charged with murder. The crowd pressed forward, its intentions clear, and, as the newspapers reported, "had not gentlemen of influence interposed, they would never have reached the prison." There is reason to believe one of those gentlemen may well have been Samuel Adams, who by then was well established as a leader of the protests.

The whole of Boston was invited to attend the boy's funeral, "when all the friends of Liberty may have an opportunity of paying their last respects to the remains of this little hero and first martyr to the noble cause." More than two thousand of the city's approximately twenty thousand citizens marched in an extraordinary procession, which caused John Adams to write in amazement, "My eyes never beheld such a funeral. The procession extended further than can be well imagined."

The fervor in the city continued to grow until a few days later it finally exploded in battle between the colonists and British soldiers. To the English this was called the Incident on King Street, but Americans have always known it simply as the Boston Massacre.

The names and events of the American Revolution are the foundation on which this great nation is built. But contrary to what is often believed, it did not begin as a quest for freedom but rather as a protest to ensure that colonists enjoyed their rights as citizens of the British Empire. How had relations between Great Britain and the colonists come to this kind of violence? Until the early 1760s, the estimated two million free white men and women living in America—or "the best poor man's country," as it was known to Europeans—enjoyed

News was interpreted by artists and published in newspapers and pamphlets, which often served as propaganda.

a mostly peaceful and prosperous relationship with Great Britain. While each of the thirteen colonies was mostly self-governed by elected assemblies that made and enforced laws, controlled land ownership, and levied taxes, the cultural, economic, and political ties to the empire remained strong. While some colonists had risked their lives crossing the ocean for personal or religious freedom, many more of them had come for the economic opportunity; the colonies were known as a place where a hardworking man could eventually lay claim to his own piece of land or establish a business.

While colonists proudly called themselves Americans, even those people born in North

America remained loyal to the Crown. Their goal was not to become an independent nation. The first sign of trouble came on November 16, 1742, when riots erupted in the streets of Boston after Royal Navy sailors impressed, or kidnapped, forty-six men, intending to force them to serve aboard British naval ships in the long war against France. While impressment was common in other parts of the world, until that night both tradition and the law had protected Massachusetts's men. The riots lasted three days; the city was paralyzed and colonists took several British naval officers hostage, then attempted to storm the State House.

The commodore of the British fleet anchored in Boston Harbor ordered his ships to load twenty-four cannons and threatened to bombard the city. He never had to make good on his threat, as Governor William Shirley soon arranged a trade of the impressed men for hostages held by the rioters. A day later the fleet sailed.

But the seeds of discontent had taken root. A pamphlet signed by "Amicus Patriae," an

anonymous American patriot, was distributed during the crisis. This "Address of the Inhabitants of the Province of Massachusetts" defended the "natural right" of the people to be free in the streets and band together for defense against impressment if necessary. Evidence suggests that the author of that pamphlet was a young brewer named Samuel Adams.

By that point in his life, Samuel Adams had proved to be a remarkably unsuccessful businessman. After being dismissed from his first job at a countinghouse, he borrowed a small fortune from his father to open his own merchant business, which failed. He then began working in the family's successful malt business, becoming known somewhat derisively as "Sam the maltster." His problem, according to historian Pauline Maier, was that he was "a man utterly uninterested in either making or possessing money." His true passion was politics, and that perhaps was his greatest inheritance: his father, Samuel Adams Sr., was a wealthy merchant, church deacon, and a leader in Boston politics, eventually being elected to the Massachusetts House of

Representatives. Samuel Adams Jr. entered politics in 1747, being elected to the post of clerk in the Boston market. He also served as the local tax collector—and failed miserably at that job, too. According to British law, he was personally responsible for taxes he failed to collect. To settle that debt, the sheriff announced an auction of Adams's property, including the family brewery. Adams's reputation, and perhaps the fact that he threatened to sue any purchaser, allowed him to keep his property. In 1748 Adams joined several men to found a newspaper, the *Independent Advertiser*, and wrote in its first issue, "Liberty can never exist without equality." It was an attack on both the wealthy mercantile class and the growing threats on individual freedom from England.

By 1760, 130 years after being founded by the Puritans, Boston was a thriving, growing seaport. While in theory its commerce was regulated by British navigation and trade laws called the Navigation Acts, in fact those laws were rarely strictly enforced. Instead, a system of common laws had developed based on the local practices that had served to encourage business. That changed in 1761, when London ordered its customs officials in Boston to begin aggressively cracking down on smugglers who were depriving the government of taxes needed to finance the Seven Years' War or, as it was known in America, the French and Indian War. Suddenly the Navigation Acts, so long ignored, were to be enforced. It seemed only fair that the Americans should help pay for the ten thousand British troops who were protecting them from the French. But rather than reducing the flow of smuggled goods, these duties had the opposite effect, enticing more people to take risks.

To assist the tax collectors, the newly appointed chief justice of the Massachusetts Superior Court, Thomas Hutchinson, issued writs of assistance, warrants that allowed the taxmen to enter any premises in the city without cause in order to search for smuggled goods and seize whatever they found. Years later Samuel Adams would write that it was in Hutchinson's courtroom that "the child independence was then and there born" as the men of Boston were "ready to take up arms against writs of assistance."

Behind the power of these laws, English customs agents ransacked homes and businesses searching for smuggled goods. Angry colonists joined together and formed raucous political parties to fight these new laws. They didn't demand independence from Great Britain; the colonists simply wanted to be treated with respect and have a voice in their own government. As Samuel Adams wrote, "If taxes are laid upon us in any shape without our having a legal representation . . . are we not reduced . . . to the miserable state of tributary slaves? . . . We claim British rights, not by charter only; we are born to them."

Several leaders emerged from this turmoil, among them John Adams and John Hancock. John Adams was the wealthy second cousin of Samuel Adams, who had drawn him into the cause. He and his cousin were said to be a curious sight when walking together, the wealthy

Stylized portraits like
these of John Adams (top)
and John Hancock were
intended to convey a
strong unemotional image.

This 1774 anti-British engraving of Samuel Adams, which appeared in the short-lived *Royal American* magazine, showed Parliament trampling on the colonists rights.

John Adams turned out as a proper gentleman while his admittedly poorer cousin reflecting the manners of a lesser class. By all accounts John was arrogant and cantankerous; he was also respected for his powerful intellect and was happy to lecture at length about his opinions. A fifth-generation descendant of Puritans who had settled in the Massachusetts Bay Colony in 1632, he was the first member of his family not to join the militia, instead becoming a lawyer. Under the pseudonym Humphrey Ploughjogger, in 1763 he began publishing essays supporting the legal rights of Americans.

John Hancock was only seven years old when his father died and he was sent to live with his wealthy uncle, the revered shipping tycoon Thomas Hancock. John was raised a child of great privilege, and after graduating from Harvard he traveled to Britain to attend the coronation of twenty-two-year-old King George III. When his uncle died, the then twenty-six-year-old Hancock took control of his import-export empire and became the second-richest man in the colonies. He was known as a generous man who gave easily and often to causes and friends, among them Samuel Adams—and would eventually become one of the primary financiers of the freedom movement. But he also was impossibly vain with the expected arrogance of the very wealthy, and at times his ambition seemed to extend farther than his capabilities. But like the other towering figures who would join with him to found the United States of America, he also had the extraordinary courage to risk his life and his fortune for a cause in which he deeply believed.

These men were brought into the fight in the early 1760s, when the British Parliament began passing new and more onerous trade laws. The British victory in the Seven Years' War had been costly; England's national debt had almost doubled to 145 million pounds, and the government was desperate for increased revenue. In 1764, the Sugar Act modified an existing but rarely enforced law and added new goods—including sugar, certain wines, coffee, and calico—to the growing list of taxable items, as well as limiting exports of lumber and iron. The Currency Act completely banned the New England colonies from issuing their own paper currency. These new restrictions crippled the colonial economies. But it was the widely vilified Stamp Act that finally led to rebellion.

The Stamp Act imposed a duty on all legal and commercial documents, newspapers, almanacs, liquor licenses, college diplomas, playing cards, and even pairs of dice. Essentially every printed document, except books, was taxed. Harsh penalties were in store for those who defied this act; in addition to large fines, people caught counterfeiting stamps "shall be adjudged a felon, and shall suffer death as in cases of felony without the benefit of clergy." This was the first attempt by Parliament to impose a direct tax on all of the colonies. And it was not at all prepared for the reaction.

For the first time, colonists began actively resisting British rule. In Boston the group that eventually became known as the Sons of Liberty was formed. Led by shoemaker Ebenezer McIntosh, it consisted of shopkeepers, workingmen, students, and artisans, including the noted silversmith Paul Revere—every one of them affected by this tax—and eventually numbered as many as two thousand people.

It was not long before their peaceful protests erupted into violence. Lieutenant Governor Hutchinson had arranged for his brother-in-law, Andrew Oliver, to be appointed to the lucrative post of stamp tax collector. On the morning of August 14, 1765, these Sons of Liberty hung an effigy of Oliver from "the Liberty Tree," a large elm tree at the corner of Essex and Washington Streets, steps from the Boston Common. Hutchinson ordered the sheriff to cut it down, but a crowd gathered in front of the tree to prevent him from doing so. This was among the very first public acts of defiance against the king. The day grew into a celebration as the colonists felt the first surge of their power. When night fell, the mob cut down the effigy and marched with it to the South End wharves, where they destroyed a brick building that had been built to distribute the stamps. They marched with timbers from that building to Oliver's grand home. In a bonfire fueled by those timbers they beheaded Oliver's effigy, then ransacked his home and stable house. The next day Oliver resigned his post.

Twelve days later a group of emboldened colonists attacked Hutchinson's home, venting years of frustration at being casually dismissed by the wealthy classes as "rabble," and within hours they had reduced the mansion to rubble. Hutchinson offered a $300 reward, several years' income for many of these people, to anyone providing information that would help convict the leaders of the attack. Although their identities were well known, no one stepped forward to claim that reward. McIntosh and several other rioters were indicted and jailed, but they were quickly released when angry crowds gathered in front of the jail.

The spirit of protest spread rapidly to the other colonies, from Newport, Rhode Island, to "Charlestown," South Carolina (as it was then spelled). A rudimentary communications network developed, creating new, stronger links among the colonies. Crowds marched through cities along the Eastern Seaboard shouting, "Liberty and no stamps!" In Virginia's House of Burgesses Patrick Henry introduced seven resolutions demanding repeal of the Stamp Act. Sons of Liberty groups were formed; the specter of what happened in Boston caused stamp agents to resign, convinced local tradesmen to ignore the Stamp Act, and led to an effective boycott of British goods. Four days after Hutchinson's house was destroyed, New York City's stamp distributor, merchant James McEvers, also resigned, fearing his "house would have been pillaged, my person abused and His Majesty's revenue impaired."

Smugglers flourished throughout the colonies; among those men accused of that crime was the New Haven merchant Benedict Arnold, who was accused by a hired deckhand of failing to pay duty on goods brought in from the West Indies. There was little sympathy for informers. Arnold responded by organizing a mob that tied his accuser to a whipping post and gave him forty lashes. After being fined 40 shillings for disturbing the peace, Arnold hanged the judge in effigy! Parliament, caught off guard, did not know how to respond. But something had to be done—the colonial boycott of imported English goods had rippled through the British economy, causing considerable unemployment and unrest. British citizens were demanding an end to this disruption. Benjamin Franklin of Pennsylvania sailed to London and warned the House of Commons that any attempt to use troops to enforce the Stamp Act would lead to a violent rebellion. England saw no sense in sending troops across the Atlantic, as the act had been passed to pay for the troops already there. Repealing the act seemingly would reward the protesters and encourage increased defiance in the future. But there was little alternative. In March 1766 Parliament repealed the Stamp Act.

An unintended movement had been born from the protests. "The people have become more attentive to their liberties," wrote John Adams in his diary, ". . . and more determined to defend them. Our presses have groaned, our pulpits have thundered, our legislatures have resolved, our towns have voted; the crown officers have everywhere trembled."

Speaking to Parliament in 1767, the statesman and philosopher Edmund Burke

Boston, May 17, 1766.

AT a Meeting of the Sons of Liberty, held last Evening in Hanover-Square, it was unanimously Voted,

1. That their Exhibition of Joy on the Repeal of the Stamp Act be on the Common.

2. That the Fire-Works be play'd off from a Stage to be erected near the Work-House Gates.

3. That there be an Advertisement published on Monday next, of the intended Exhibition, the Place where, and the Time when it will end.

I do therefore notify the Friends of Liberty, that an authentic Account of the Repeal of the Stamp Act is arrived, and the Gentlemen Select-Men of Boston, have fix'd upon This Evening for the public Rejoicing, at whose Desire, will be exhibited on the Common, an OBELISK — A Description of which is engraved by Mr. Paul Revere; and is now selling by Edes and Gill. —— The Signal of its Ending will be firing a Horizontal Wheel on the Top of the Obelisk, when its desired the Assembly would retire. By Order of the Committe,

May 19, 1766. (Signed) M. Y. Secretary.

The repeal of the Stamp Act in 1766 marked a significant colonial victory and, as the *Boston Gazette* (bottom) announced, was celebrated with "public rejoicing." It also was celebrated with the publication of *The Repeal or the Funeral of Miss Americ-Stamp*, which was widely reprinted and became one of the best-known satirical cartoons of the entire period.

acknowledged that a movement had been started and no one might predict the eventual outcome, saying ruefully, "The Americans have made a discovery that we mean to oppress them;
we have made a discovery that they intend to raise a rebellion against us. We know not how
to advance; they know not how to retreat."

Parliament failed to pay heed to Burke's warnings, instead passing new duties on glass,
lead, paints, paper, and tea. They believed that these Townshend Acts—as they were known
because they were proposed by the chancellor of the exchequer, Charles Townshend—would
be acceptable because they were indirect taxes. This time they were not going to allow mob
actions to force their hand; instead British commander in chief Lieutenant General Thomas
Gage ordered many of the soldiers who had been fighting the French in rural outposts to the
coastal cities, and with additional troops now sent from England, eventually two regiments
of redcoats were posted in Boston to maintain order.

Townshend was wrong. The colonists were fighting not only against the cost of these new
laws but even more so against the principle that the government in England had the right to
levy taxes on them without their consent. Boston, the main port of entry for British goods,
remained the center of this growing resistance to British rule. Samuel Adams, now forty-six
years old and clerk of the Massachusetts House, emerged as the leader of the opposition. It
was becoming increasingly obvious to him that the colonists, if they didn't want to be treated
as second-class British citizens, would eventually have to strike out on the incredibly risky
and seemingly impossible path to independence.

The taxes devastated the local economy. Silversmith Paul Revere, for example, turned to
performing dental work to make up for some of the losses he had suffered. Among his patients
was the highly respected and debonair physician Joseph Warren, who had become well known
in the city for bravely opening an inoculation hospital during the smallpox epidemic of 1763.
Both men had joined the Sons of Liberty, and their relationship would prove to be vital in the
ensuing years. Among Revere's accomplishments was the creation of a younger generation of
patriots called the Liberty Boys, several of whom conveniently served as apprentices in his shop.

As the situation deteriorated, the colonies looked at the bonds that had tied them to
"Mother England" for so long and now only saw chains. In the early spring of 1768 Lord
Hillsborough, the brusque cabinet officer responsible for the colonies, ordered the colonial
assemblies to be dissolved. Once again the American people took to the streets, attacking
customs agents. Parliament responded by ordering additional troops to Boston. Even more
ominous, their officers were granted permission to take whatever actions deemed necessary.

Under the protection of these soldiers, previously cowed customs agents began strictly
enforcing the Townshend laws. In June, John Hancock's small sloop, the *Liberty*, arrived in

port carrying a cargo of Madeira wine. Traditionally, shipowners and customs agents negotiated an accommodation, resulting in only part of a cargo being declared and taxed. It was mutually beneficial: the owner profited from the untaxed portion and the agent received some remuneration for his goodwill. But this time, the customs agent insisted that duty be paid on every bottle aboard the *Liberty*. The sloop's captain responded by locking the customs agent Samuel Adams in the brig while the entire cargo was unloaded. The next day the British navy seized the ship. As it was being towed out of Boston Harbor by the fifty-gun warship HMS *Romney*, a mob gathered on the dock; colonists beat two customs agents badly and vandalized their homes. When John Hancock was accused of smuggling, he hired lawyer John Adams to defend him; the charges were dropped but Hancock was not able to recover his sloop.

While Adams had attempted to raise a force to meet the arriving redcoats, there was still no appetite for direct, organized conflict. The reasons were not just sentimental—few

Independent groups known as the Sons of Liberty fomented revolution in colonial cities using any possible means: demonstrations, petitions, speeches, handbills, and, when necessary, violence. In this popular engraving, John Lamb is stirring up more than two thousand New York Sons of Liberty in December 1773 to prevent two shiploads of tea from landing.

colonists were foolish enough to believe that an untrained and poorly armed militia could resist the powerful British army.

The 1765 Quartering Act forced colonists to shelter British troops in both public buildings and unoccupied houses and barns—but not private homes, although the Colonial government was required to pay for all food and drink. The British army was no longer in America to protect the colonists; it had become an occupying force. Eventually it proved impossible to find appropriate housing for all of the troops that been marched into the city, and tents were set up in the very heart of the city, on the Boston Common.

The presence of a thousand redcoats in the city made an impression. In 1768, alarmed Boston merchants voted to boycott British goods. To their surprise, other colonies did not immediately join them. Only after Boston merchants voted to suspend trading with colonies that refused to participate did New York, Philadelphia, and others reluctantly join the boycott. A popular ditty titled "The Mother Country. A Song," which is often attributed to Ben Franklin and was written at some point during this period, explained the colonists' stance:

> We have an old Mother that peevish is grown,
> She snubs us like Children that scarce walk alone;
> She forgets we're grown up and have sense of our own;
> Which nobody can deny deny; Which nobody can deny.
>
> If we don't obey orders, whatever the case;
> She frowns, and she chides, and she loses all patience,
> and sometimes she hits us a slap in the face,
> Which nobody can deny deny; Which nobody can deny.
>
> Her orders so odd are, we often suspect
> That age has impaired her sound intellect:
> But still an old Mother should have due respect,
> Which nobody can deny deny; Which nobody can deny.

But should any nation question the colonists' loyalty to the Crown, Franklin concluded:

> Know too, ye bad neighbours, who aim to divide
> The sons from the Mother, that still she's our Pride;
> And if ye attack her we're all of her side,
> Which nobody can deny deny; Which nobody can deny.

The boycott was sustained with some difficulty for almost two years; while patriots were expected to avoid British-made goods, merchants needed the trade in British products to survive. But those merchants—men like Theophilus Lillie, who refused to honor the boycott—were publicly ridiculed and, in a few cases, physically attacked. Meanwhile, the women of the city organized into a group called the Daughters of Liberty. To reduce the demand for British textiles, they threw spinning and weaving parties and wore homespun clothing as a symbol of their devotion to the growing protest movement.

Members of Parliament were divided on how to handle this dissent among the colonists. Some demanded harsh penalties for Americans who defied the legal authority of the Crown and wanted to bring their leaders to England for trial, while others pushed to reestablish the traditional relationship that had long benefited both sides. "There is the most urgent reason to do what is right, and immediately," wrote Secretary of War Lord Barrington in 1767, "but what is right and who is to do it?"

The uneasy peace, enforced by the redcoats when necessary, lasted until 1770. The boycott agreement among the colonies was set to expire that January. Many merchants, whose storehouses were overstocked with British-made goods, were pleased to see it end. But when they finally offered those goods for sale, many colonists organized protests and began threatening them.

Those protests turned deadly on the twenty-second of February when Ebenezer Richardson shot eleven-year-old Christopher Seider. The boy's funeral became a great political event in which leaders of the Sons of Liberty attempted to rally the people of Boston to their cause. The coffin was inscribed with phrases in Latin: "The serpent is lurking in the grass" and "innocence itself is nowhere safe." As the increasingly bitter lieutenant governor wrote, "If it had been in their power to have brought him to life again, [they] would not have done it but would have chosen the grand funeral, which brought many thousands together, and the solemn procession from Liberty Tree."

During the days following the funeral, numerous fights broke out between soldiers and bands of Liberty Boys. As one British officer later stated, "The insolence as well as utter hatred of the inhabitants to the troops increased daily." On March 2 an employee of rope maker John Gray asked an off-duty soldier if he wanted work; when the soldier said he did, the workman replied, "Well then go and clean my shithouse!" That soldier came back later with about a dozen men and a great brawl ensued. The next day, a British sergeant disappeared and was believed to have been murdered. The soldiers spread word that many of the colonists "carried weapons concealed under their clothes" and would use them with little provocation. A handbill warned that soldiers would defend themselves when attacked, and the wife of a grenadier was heard to say that soon the soldiers "would wet their swords or bayonets in New England people's blood."

Rumors spread like wildfire across the city, among them the warning that the British

In August 1765, angry colonists gathered at the Liberty Tree, a large elm near Boston Common, to protest the Stamp Act by hanging an effigy of the royal stamp distributor.

intended to cut down the Liberty Tree. On the night of March 5, less than two weeks after Seider had been buried, an angry, boisterous mob roamed through the streets taunting soldiers and pelting them with snowballs. Some of them may have enjoyed at least one merry pint. Men broke into two meetinghouses and began ringing the alarm bells usually rung to alert the citizenry of a fire. This time it was a call to assemble. The city was alive with danger. At eight o'clock that evening two British soldiers were attacked and beaten. A small group of colonists descended on the 29th Regiment barracks but was repulsed without bloodshed. A larger crowd, as many as two hundred strong and armed with clubs, gathered in Dock Square. Slightly more than an hour later the Boston Massacre began with the exchange of a few nasty words.

As with so many historic confrontations, the Boston Massacre is remembered quite differently from both sides. Americans view it as a cold-blooded slaughter; the English consider it a terrible accident that escalated into a tragedy, an accident they had taken great steps to avoid.

What is agreed is that it began on King Street when a wig maker's apprentice named Edward Garrick publicly accused a British officer named John Goldfinch of failing to pay a bill. Captain Goldfinch did not respond, but a lone sentry guarding the customhouse named Hugh White spoke up and said, "He is a gentleman, and if he owes you anything he will pay it." Garrick replied that there were no gentlemen left in the regiment, causing White to leave his post to stand up for the honor of the troops. White struck Garrick with the butt of his musket, knocking him to the ground. A crowd quickly gathered, "mostly lads," the newspapers reported, and some of them started hurling pieces of ice at the guard. White retreated to the safety of the customhouse.

British captain Thomas Preston led twelve men and a noncommissioned officer to the customhouse "to protect both the sentry and the King's money." About a hundred colonists armed with clubs and other weapons had gathered in front of the customhouse, Preston later testified at trial, and were threatening "to execute their vengeance" on White. A townsman had told him that the mob intended to carry White off and murder him. Preston claimed he had been desperate to avoid conflict, testifying that "so far was I from intending the death of any person that I suffered the troops to go to the spot where the unhappy affair took place without any loading in their pieces; nor did I ever give orders for loading them."

According to eyewitness reports, Preston lined his men by twos in a column and, with empty muskets but fixed bayonets, moved smartly across King Street to rescue the beleaguered sentry. After White fell into the ranks, Preston attempted to march the men back to the barracks, but the mob that now numbered as many as three hundred blocked their way. The soldiers formed a rough skirmish line, standing in a semicircle about a body length apart. The crowd continued screaming threats and bombarding the troops with snowballs, pieces of coal, ice, oyster shells, rocks, and sticks.

But the patriots' account was very different. As the *Boston Gazette* reported a week later, "Capt. Preston with a party of men with charged bayonets, came from the main guard to the commissioner's house, the soldiers pushing their bayonets, crying, make way! They took place by the custom house and, continuing to push to drive the people off, pricked some in several places, on which they were clamorous and, it is said, threw snow balls."

As Preston claimed, "The mob still increased and were more outrageous, striking their clubs or bludgeons one against another and calling out, 'Come on you rascals, you bloody backs . . . fire if you dare, G-d damn you, fire and be damned, we know you dare not.' At this time I was between the soldiers and the mob, endeavoring all in my power to persuade them to retire peacefully, but to no purpose. They advanced to the points of the bayonets, struck some of them and even the muzzles of the pieces, and seemed to be endeavoring to close with the soldiers." One of the crowd asked Preston if he intended to order his men to fire. No, he replied, pointing out that he was at that moment standing in front of his men's muskets and "must fall a sacrifice if they fired."

What happened next changed the course of history, but we'll never know the exact chain of events. As the crowd pressed closer, according to the *Boston Gazette*, "the Captain commanded them to fire; and as more snow and ice balls were thrown he again said, 'Damn you, fire, be the consequences what it will.' One soldier then fired, and a townsman with a cudgel struck him over the hands with such force that he dropped his firelock; and, rushing forward aimed a blow at the captain's head. . . . However, the soldiers continued to fire successively till seven or eight or, as some say, eleven guns were discharged."

Captain Preston's version of events was different. "One of the soldiers having received a severe blow with a stick, stepped a little on one side and instantly fired, and on turning to and asking him why he fired without orders, I was struck with a club on my arm. . . . A general attack was made on the men by a great number of heavy clubs . . . by which all our lives were in imminent danger, some persons at the same time from behind calling out, 'Damn your bloods—why don't you fire?' Instantly three or four of the soldiers fired, one after another, and directly after three more in the same confusion and hurry. On my asking the soldiers why they fired without orders, they said they heard the word fire and supposed it came from me. This might be the case as many of the mob called out fire, fire."

According to several accounts, a forty-seven-year-old mulatto sailor named Crispus Attucks, who may have been an escaped slave who had found freedom working on the oceans, grabbed the musket held by a soldier and knocked the man to the ground. The soldier, Hugh Montgomery, scrambled to his feet and shouted, "Damn you, fire!" and triggered a blast into the crowd. Seconds later the other soldiers began firing. Other reports claim Montgomery was "jostled" and, in panic, fired his musket aimlessly but other troops, hearing that shot and thinking they heard a command to fire, began shooting.

What slim chance there might have been of preserving the peace between England and the colonies disappeared in those few seconds. Crispus Attucks was struck by two bullets in his chest and thus became the first casualty of battle in the Revolutionary War. By the time the shooting ended, three colonists were dead. Two others would die later that night, and another six men were injured. In addition to Attucks, among the dead were Samuel Gray, "killed on the spot, the ball entering his head and beating off a large portion of his skull," James Caldwell, shot in the back, and two other seventeen-year-olds.

The entire confrontation lasted no more than twenty minutes, but it resonated throughout the colonies and the British Empire. No one knows for certain which leaders of the Sons of Liberty were in that crowd that night. There has long been speculation that Samuel Adams and

Paul Revere were among them, but this was a mob beyond the powers of any leader to control.

Adams and Revere, and certainly Dr. Warren, were on the scene immediately, as was Lieutenant Governor Hutchinson, who ordered Preston and his men to return to their barracks. In an effort to prevent further violence, Hutchinson then went to the Old State House to meet with Boston Council leaders, assuring them that he would see justice done. Finally, stepping out onto a balcony overlooking the still-bloody streets, the lieutenant governor asked for calm, promising, "Let the law have its course. I will live and die by the law."

Within hours a warrant was issued for the arrest of Captain Preston. Two justices interrogated him for more than an hour about the shooting, then removed him to jail, probably as much for his own security as for punishment regarding the events.

Under most circumstances, the deaths of these five men barely would have been noted, but the patriot leaders understood that they could be used to further their political aims. A massive funeral was held for the five men; an estimated twelve thousand Bostonians turned out for the

On March 5, 1770, sailor and former slave Crispus Attucks became the first casualty of the Revolution when outnumbered and frightened redcoats began shooting into a crowd in what has become known as the Boston Massacre.

In 1768, the Sons of Liberty commissioned
silversmith Paul Revere to create this bowl to
honor the courage of the Massachusetts House
in standing up to demands from Parliament.

solemn procession. They were buried in a large vault in the same burying ground on Tremont
Street as Christopher Seider. Samuel Adams erected a marker with the words "as a memento
to posterity to that horrid massacre," thereby giving it the name that has lived in history.

According to Adams, in the days following the funeral John Hancock called on patriots
to tell the story of the massacre to their children until "tears of pity glisten in their eyes, and
boiling passion shakes their tender frame."

Many of the events leading to revolution were celebrated in art by Paul Revere, who was
among the leading engravers and silversmiths of the time. In 1767, for example, to honor the
ninety-two legislators who defied King George and Parliament by refusing to rescind a letter
sent to the other colonies protesting the Townshend Acts, he created the beautiful Sons of
Liberty or Rescinders' Bowl. Decorated with symbols of liberty, the classic silver bowl became
a symbol of freedom to the colonists. When General Gage marched his newly arrived troops
in a show of force in 1768, Revere's engraving depicting this occupying army, titled *The Insolent
Parade*, was widely distributed. And within three weeks of the Boston Massacre Paul Revere
also created and sold an engraving titled *The Bloody Massacre in King Street, March 5, 1770*, an
effective propaganda piece that contributed significantly to the rising fervor for independence.

The storied engraving, which relied heavily on a drawing done by the uncredited artist
Henry Pelham, bears little resemblance to the actual facts of the event. Rather than a chaotic
scene on a snowy winter's night, Revere portrayed an orderly, taut line of redcoats firing in
unison into an unarmed crowd on a bright blue-sky-lit afternoon, apparently responding
to orders from an officer standing behind them. The blood of the patriots spurts from their
bodies; the sign BUTCHER'S HALL is affixed to the building behind the troops and a puff of
gun smoke makes it appear as if a sniper is firing from that building. Below the engraving is
a poem apparently written by Revere, which includes the lines: "While faithless P—n and his
savage bands, / With murd'rous rancor stretch their bloody hands; / Like fierce barbarians
grinning o'er their prey, / approve the carnage and enjoy the day."

The journey to independence had begun.

Paul Revere's sensationalized engraving *The Bloody Massacre in King Street*, considered one of the most effective pieces of propaganda in American history, went on sale only three weeks after the event.

CHAPTER 2

John Adams

Ready for War

The morning after the Boston Massacre, the city was reeling. Shops were closed and church bells tolled. Captain Preston and his men had been detained and were being held and closely guarded. One of their victims, Patrick Carr, an Irish immigrant about thirty years of age, lay mortally wounded. Samuel Adams, Hancock, Revere, and other leaders of the Sons of Liberty were meeting to prepare their demand that all British troops be immediately removed. The representatives of the Crown also were meeting, discussing ways to stem the violence. Many customs commissioners were packing their belongings and preparing to flee, now fearful for their lives. Coroner Thomas Dawes was preparing the bodies of the dead men for their funeral and burial. And thirty-four-year-old lawyer John Adams was at work in his office when a prosperous merchant named James Forest knocked on his door. "With tears streaming in his eyes," as Adams wrote years later, the Loyalist Forest asked Adams to defend Captain Preston and his men against the murder charges.

Protests against the Stamp Act, like this Boston rally in 1765, ignited the bonfires of revolution.

Forest admitted that Adams was not his first choice; he had tried to retain other lawyers, but none of them would risk their standing in the city to take the case. It was an extraordinary request, but it was natural that Forest eventually would come to him. Adams's legal career had begun twelve years earlier. His first year of practice was a struggle. He made errors in preparing the documents for his only case, representing a farmer suing for damages to his crops caused by a neighbor's loose horse, and lost. His practice had grown slowly after this initial defeat, and he had received great recognition in the city only a year before when he successfully defended four sailors who had killed a British naval officer.

In the case of *Rex v. Corbet*, the British frigate *Rose* had stopped the American cargo vessel *Pitt Packet* returning from Spain with a hold full of salt. British navy lieutenant Henry Panton and several sailors boarded the brig and found four seamen hiding in the cargo space. As Adams told the story years later, Michael Corbet and the three other men, fearing they were being impressed into British service, had armed themselves with a fish gig, a musket, a hatchet, and a harpoon. Corbet swore he had drawn a line of salt and warned Panton that if he crossed that line, it would be an admission that he intended to impress the men and he would resist "and by the Eternal God in Heaven, you are a dead man." When Panton took a step forward, Corbet plunged his harpoon into the lieutenant's jugular vein.

But a different story was told during the trial. In that testimony, supposedly a marine had fired his pistol in the crowded brig and during the fight that ensued, Corbet had thrown his harpoon and killed Panton.

It was John Adams's first murder trial. Corbet's fate was not all that was at stake—the case put the laws governing the relationship between England and her colonies on trial. No one disputed that Corbet had killed Panton. But larger issues had to be adjudicated: By what legal right had Panton boarded the *Pitt Packet*? And was Corbet acting in self-defense, believing he was to be impressed?

While other patriots, like Adams's cousin Samuel, John Hancock, and Paul Revere, were ready to take the fight for their rights to the streets, Adams made the intellectual argument for each man's natural rights. He was said to value logic and reason far above strength and cunning, and he believed rights might be won more easily in the courtroom. His essays had made him well known to the citizenry of pre-Revolutionary Boston.

A large crowd had turned out for the trial. After three days of testimony and questioning, John Adams rose for the defense. The question that must be resolved, he argued, "is, whether impresses in any cases, are legal." If they were not, then the sailors had the right to resist and therefore must be acquitted. He had spent several weeks researching his case and had found a

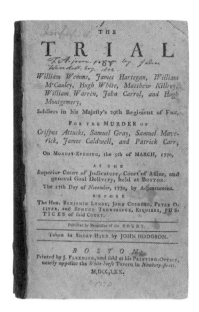

John Adams risked his reputation—and his life—to defend the British soldiers who had killed colonists at the Boston Massacre. The controversial trial resulted in the acquittal of the soldiers and proved that justice for all existed in the colonies.

statute specifically prohibiting British naval officers from impressing American seamen. But he had barely begun his argument when Lieutenant Governor and Chief Justice Hutchinson declared a recess. Adams was perplexed. When the trial resumed four hours later, Hutchinson announced a verdict of justifiable homicide and set the prisoners free.

No explanation was ever given for the abrupt decision, and Adams would wonder about it for the rest of his life. The most likely explanation is that rather than give Adams the opportunity to speak eloquently about the rights of man and further increase tensions between the Crown and the colonists, Hutchinson chose to end the trial quickly.

The verdict assured Adams's reputation as one of Boston's most respected lawyers and political leaders. So it was considered curious that he would now risk his reputation and perhaps even his own safety and that of his beloved wife, Abigail, and their young son John Quincy Adams, by agreeing to defend men who were seen as the cold-blooded killers of American patriots. And yet agree he did. His only stipulation was that his friend Josiah Quincy join him as cocounsel. Some historians believe the ambitious Adams took the case in exchange for an understanding that he would receive a seat in the Boston legislature when it became available. Indeed, three months after the trial, this is what happened. John Adams himself never directly explained why he had accepted this challenge. In his dotage he proudly described his defense of Preston and the other soldiers "one of the most gallant, generous, manly and disinterested actions of my whole life, and one of the best pieces of service I ever rendered my country." It might well have been a moral decision, based on his passion for equal justice for all under the law. His cousin, Samuel Adams, it was said, was not against his cousin defending the men—he expected him to give them a fine defense to show Boston's commitment to justice—after which all of the soldiers would be convicted.

But Samuel Adams was building a movement and undoubtedly saw the trial as an opportunity to gather greater support. Paul Revere's engraving of the massacre was widely circulated. When Patrick Carr died nine days later, his obituary, perhaps written by Samuel Adams, emphasized, "This is the fifth life that has been sacrificed by the rage of the soldiery, but it is feared it will not be the last" and was accompanied by a Paul Revere drawing of a coffin. A pamphlet titled "A Short Narrative of the Horrid Massacre in Boston," much of it written by Joseph Warren, was published several days after the event. Supposedly drawn from testimony given by ninety-six eyewitnesses, it described a cold-blooded, point-blank murder.

At the strong suggestion of General Thomas Gage, commander of British forces in North America, Hutchinson agreed to delay the trial for several months, giving Adams sufficient time to prepare his defense while allowing the colonists' white-hot anger to cool. Meanwhile, the British government took steps to calm the tension in the city. Within days, both of the regiments occupying the city were moved offshore to a fort on Castle Island in Boston Harbor—regiments that Parliament referred to sarcastically as the "Samuel Adams regiments." And less than two months later, in a decision that was as much economic as it was political, Parliament repealed the hated Townshend duties—with the exception of the tax on tea. It was estimated that the colonial boycott had cost British exporters as much as £700,000, while only £21,000 in duties had been collected, a staggering loss for those traders. Local merchants were pleased to resume selling imported British goods and even patriotic colonists were quite happy to buy them. Much of the unrest was slowly dissipating.

Five colonists died and six others were injured at the Boston Massacre, which became the rallying cry for colonists. This illustration, with the initials of the victims, accompanied reports of the funerals.

As he prepared for the trial, John Adams's defense was bolstered by the deathbed account of Patrick Carr, who lingered for several days before succumbing to his wounds. Carr told his doctor, Samuel Hemmingway, that the soldiers had shown great restraint and only after the mob began bombarding them with dangerous projectiles did they fire their muskets. He acknowledged that they acted in self-defense and told Dr. Hemmingway that he bore no malice to the man who had shot him. Adams knew this eyewitness testimony could possibly save his clients from the rope, but he also knew that the court might not admit the evidence. The prosecution would have no opportunity to cross-examine a dead man.

The trial of Captain Preston began on October 24 at Boston's new courthouse on Queen Street. Adams had successfully separated the officer's trial from that of his men. Josiah Quincy's Loyalist brother Samuel and patriot Robert Treat Paine prosecuted the case. Adams managed to seat a jury composed of men mostly from outside the city, and at least five of them were Tories, men who remained loyal to the Crown.

But it still would require all of Adams's legal skills to prove beyond a doubt that Captain Preston never ordered his men to fire their muskets. And doing so successfully would pit John Adams in direct opposition to his cousin and the patriotic movement. It is fair to assume that more than once Adams was asked to consider his loyalties, but it appears he remained steadfast in his commitment to justice above politics.

In his opening statement to the court, John Adams said, "I am for the prisoners at the bar, and shall apologize for it only in the words of the Marquis Beccaria: 'If I can but be the instrument of preserving one life, his blessing and tears of transport, shall be a sufficient consolation to me, for the contempt of all mankind. . . .' We are to look upon it as more beneficial, that many guilty persons should escape unpunished, than one innocent person should suffer. The reason is, because it's of more importance to community, that innocence should be protected, than it is, that guilt should be punished. . . . But when innocence itself, is brought to the bar and condemned, especially to die, the subject will exclaim, it is immaterial to me, whether I behave well or ill; for virtue itself, is no security. And if such a sentiment as this, should take place in the mind of the subject, there would be an end to all security what so ever."

Preston pleaded not guilty and Adams chose not to put him on the stand. The trial lasted six days, the first criminal trial in the colony's history to extend more than a single day. In a highly unusual step, the jury was sequestered for the duration of the trial. The prosecution presented fifteen witnesses, but several of them gave conflicting testimony. One, William Wyatt, for example, told the court, "I heard the officer say fire. The soldiers did not fire. His back was to me. I heard the same voice say fire. The soldiers did not fire. The officer then stamped and said Damn your bloods fire be the consequences what it will. Immediately the first gun was fired." But Theodore Bliss recalled, "I saw the people throw snow balls at the soldiers and saw a stick about 3 feet long strike a soldier upon the right. He sallied [moved forward] and then fired. . . . Then the other[s] fast after one another. . . . I know not whether he sallied on account of the stick or stepped back to make ready. I did not hear any order given by the captain to fire. I stood so near him I think I must have heard him if he had given an order to fire before the first firing."

Adams produced twenty-three witnesses to prove his contention that the soldiers had been provoked and Preston had not given an order to shoot. Newton Prince, a free black man who had responded to the ringing of the fire bells, swore, "The people whilst striking on the guns cried fire, damn you fire. I have heard no orders given to fire, only the people in general cried fire." A merchant, Richard Palmes, was close to Preston. "The gun which went off first had scorched the nap of my surtout [overcoat] at the elbow." Palmes testified that he said to Preston, "I hope you don't intend the soldiers shall fire on the inhabitants. He said by no means. The instant he spoke I saw something resembling snow or ice strike the grenadier on the captain's right hand. . . . He instantly stepped one foot back and fired the first gun. . . . After the gun went off I heard the word fire. . . . I don't know who gave the word fire."

After considerable deliberation, the jury found Captain Preston not guilty. He was released and awarded £200 in compensation. Then he sailed to England.

The trial of Preston's troops began on November 27. Apparently before it began, there was a heated debate between Adams and Josiah Quincy, who wanted to show that this terrible event was planned by patriots to drive British soldiers out of the city. Adams threatened to withdraw from the defense if Quincy insisted on employing that strategy. Rather than casting blame on the Sons of Liberty and perhaps antagonizing patriots on the jury, Adams suggested placing that blame on the distant and despised government in London, which had put these troops in an untenable position. Quincy finally agreed.

At trial they intended to show, in Adams's own words, that the soldiers had been attacked by "a motley rabble of saucy boys, negroes and mulattoes, Irish teagues [an epithet meaning a Roman Catholic] and outlandish jacktars [seamen] . . . throwing every species of rubbish they could pick up in the street" and therefore had the right to defend themselves. Admittedly they had fired their muskets, but only after being attacked and in fear for their safety.

Adams and Quincy kept residents of Boston off the jury. This trial lasted nine days. Samuel Adams was outraged that the court allowed jurors to hear the secondhand testimony of Patrick Carr, arguing that Carr's testimony was not to be trusted, as he was an Irish "papist" and a

Catholic, and this was his deathbed confession. Justice Peter Oliver told the jurors, "This Carr was not upon oath, it is true, but you will determine whether a man just stepping into eternity is not to be believed, especially in favor of a set of men by whom he lost his life." This notable exception to the inadmissibility of hearsay evidence has remained an important part of the American legal code.

Adams's brilliant summation lasted more than a day. He re-created the hectic scene of terrified soldiers under attack by a mob. How else could those soldiers respond, he wondered, "when the multitude was shouting and huzzaing, and threatening life, the bells all ringing, the mob whistle screaming and rending like an Indian yell, the people from all quarters throwing every species of rubbish they could pick up in the street, and some who were quite on the other side of the street throwing clubs at the whole party"?

Ironically, the person generally celebrated in American history as the first casualty of the Revolution, Crispus Attucks, is the person Adams blamed for inciting the soldiers to shoot. It was Attucks, Adams claimed, who "had hardiness enough to fall in upon them, and with one hand took hold of a bayonet, and with the other knocked the man down: this was the behavior of Attucks; to whose mad behavior, in all probability, the dreadful carnage of that night is chiefly to be ascribed."

And finally, Adams drew upon his own passion for the law, reminding jurors in a statement that has echoed throughout American courtrooms for longer than two centuries: "Facts are stubborn things; and whatever may be our wishes, our inclinations, or the dictates of our passions, they cannot alter the state of facts and evidence: nor is the law less stable than the fact; if an assault was made to endanger their lives, the law is clear, they had a right to kill in their own defense." It was not only the soldiers he was defending but the law itself, which had to remain free from shifting beliefs. Whatever politics or passions the jurors might hold, it is their sole job to uphold the law; as he told them, "The law, in all vicissitudes of government, fluctuations of the passions, or flights of enthusiasm, will preserve a steady undeviating course; it will not bend to the uncertain wishes, imaginations, and wanton tempers of men."

In instructing the jury, Judge Oliver addressed the complexities of the case when he told them, "If upon the whole ye are in any reasonable doubt of their guilt, ye must then . . . declare them innocent." It marked the first known time a judge had used the phrase "reasonable doubt" in an American courtroom.

The jury deliberated only two and a half hours before finding six of the soldiers not guilty. Only the two redcoats proved to have deliberately fired into the crowd were convicted of manslaughter. Adams pleaded for an ancient form of leniency by invoking an old tenet of

English law known as the "plea to clergy." Both men had an *M* for "murderer" branded on their thumbs, which meant they could never use that appeal again, then departed Boston with their entire regiment.

A satisfied Adams later wrote in his diary, "Judgment of death against those soldiers would have been as foul a stain upon this country as the execution of the Quakers or witches, anciently. As the evidence was, the verdict of the jury was exactly right."

When talk of a revolution against England began in earnest only a few years later, John Adams's defense of Preston and his troops served to give him credibility as the moral leader. Although the verdict was not received favorably by the patriots, he had emerged from the trial as a man of honor.

The king's government continued to make an effort to reduce the friction with the colonies, hoping to find a path to return to the respectful relationship, while contending with other challenges and opportunities across the ocean. Under the reign of George III, the debate over how far to extend the rights to free elections, freedom of the press, and free speech continued without resolution. In 1770, Captain James Cook sailed into Botany Bay and claimed Australia for Britain. In 1771 the "factory age" began when the first cotton mill was opened. A year later the abolitionist movement took hold, marking the first significant step toward outlawing slavery. New coal-powered inventions and canals were greatly improving transportation throughout the country.

A period of calm was interrupted in 1772 when the schooner HMS *Gaspee* ran aground in Rhode Island's Narragansett Bay. It had been chasing a small packet attempting to smuggle goods through customs. While the ship lay helpless in the shallows, members of the Providence Sons of Liberty boarded, wounded its captain, and burned the ship to the waterline. Lord Dartmouth ordered the royal governor of Rhode Island to identify and indict the men responsible. After an investigation, a commission of inquiry was set up to determine if there was enough evidence to arrest those men and send them to England to be tried for treason, an act that would deprive them of the right to trial by a jury of their peers.

In response to the *Gaspee* affair, as well as a rumor that the royal governor and superior court judges were to be paid directly by the royal treasury, making them less sensitive to local realities, Samuel Adams proposed the formation of a Committee of Correspondence in Boston with the stated purpose of determining other Massachusetts towns' sentiments toward the Crown. In fact, it was a desperately needed system to enable colonial leaders to communicate quickly and directly with each other. This first twenty-one-member committee was charged with determining "the rights of the colonists, and of this province in particular, as men, as

BURNING OF THE GASPEE SCHOONER.

In June 1772 the British customs ship *Gaspee* ran aground near Warwick, Rhode Island, while chasing smugglers. Patriots boarded the ship and looted and burned it.

Christians, and as subjects; to communicate and publish the same to the several towns in this province and to the world as the sense of this town." Six hundred copies of this document, titled *The Votes and Proceedings of the Freeholders and Other Inhabitants of the Town of Boston,* but more generally known as the "Boston Pamphlet," were printed and distributed to more than 250 towns. It enumerated twelve ways the British government was violating the colonists' rights, among them taxing and legislating without representation, the quartering of standing armies during peacetime, and enforcing trade policies that restricted economic growth. More than one hundred towns and villages formed their own committees and responded.

While the commission of inquiry eventually ruled that there was insufficient evidence to

In 1772, *The Votes and Proceedings of the Freeholders and Other Inhabitants of The Town of Boston, In Town Meeting assembled, According to Law* or as it became known, *The Boston Pamphlet*, described in detail how the rights of the colonists as English citizens were being violated.

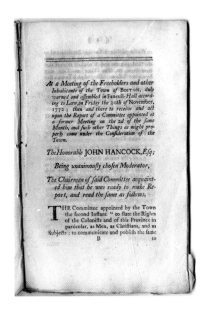

bring anyone to trial for the burning of the *Gaspee*, the Committee of Correspondence had become firmly entrenched. Eventually a single such committee representing the entire colony and chaired by Samuel Adams was formed. Other colonies followed that example and within two years a viable communications network was established. The patriot leaders had no great plan—there was not yet a strategy or even a stated goal—but the spirit of freedom had been born. In taverns and inns, in the safety of private homes, in churches, and in shops, newspapers, pamphlets, and broadsides were being distributed and debated, voices were being raised, sermons were being given, poems were read, and songs were sung. The idea that the colonies should be independent of England, an idea only a few years earlier too impossible to even imagine, had become real, and the fight was about to begin.

The job of transforming stirring words into actions began on the night of December 16, 1773. To save the financially troubled East India Company, Parliament had passed the Tea Act, which granted the failing company and its chosen distributors the exclusive rights to sell tea in America. The colonists, especially those merchants excluded from this monopoly, were furious—more by the haughty manner by which Parliament imposed its will than by the actual tax that, ironically, lowered the price of tea. But in paying that lesser price for tea, colonists would be accepting the right of Parliament to tax them.

Rather than facing the temptation of a favored beverage at a fine price, the colonies banded together to prevent the East India Company from landing its teas. In Boston, Philadelphia, and New York, tea-laden cargo ships were stopped from unloading. On December 16 an estimated seven thousand Bostonians gathered at the Old South Meeting House and resolved that the three vessels in the harbor, the *Dartmouth*, the *Eleanor*, and the *Beaver*—each carrying 114 chests of tea—be given safe passage to return to England with their cargoes intact. But when the king's customs collector refused to allow the ships to depart until the duty was paid, the colonists knew that it was time to show their grit.

That night, as thousands of people stood watching from the dock, approximately 116 men, most of them members of the Sons of Liberty, marched to Griffin's Wharf and boarded the ships. To protect their identities, they disguised themselves as Indians, wearing rudimentary war paint, cloths wrapped around their brows, and blankets around their shoulders, and they all carried hatchets and axes. The captains handed over the keys to their holds without fuss and the invaders smashed open every chest of tea and emptied the contents into the harbor waters. "The destruction of the tea," as it was called by the newspapers—it would not become celebrated as the Boston Tea Party for another fifty years—took about three hours. Contrary to the historical image of chaos, the raid was well organized and great care was taken to ensure that no one was hurt. There was no damage done to the ships, which actually were American-owned but carrying British cargo. The single lock broken by the patriots was replaced, and before departing the raiders took time to sweep the decks clean. Although there were several British warships in the harbor, no effort was made to stop the men. The financial loss was the equivalent of more than a million dollars.

The Sons of Liberty sent its best horseman, Paul Revere, to New York and Philadelphia to carry news of this rebellion. Eventually similar "tea parties," in which tea was dumped or burned, took place in New York, Annapolis, and Charlestown—and in March the Boston raid was repeated as sixty men tossed thirty chests into the water.

"This is the most magnificent movement of all," proclaimed John Adams. "This destruction of the tea is so bold, so daring, so firm, intrepid and inflexible, and it must have so important consequences, and so lasting, that I can't consider it but an epocha [momentous event] in history." And to demonstrate his support, Abigail Adams later reported, John Adams tossed all the tea in his cupboard into the fire.

This grave insult to the Crown demanded a response. "We are now to establish our authority," said Lord North, "or give it up entirely." The repercussions were harsh. Because Boston was acknowledged as the heart of colonial dissent, Parliament believed that by cracking down hard on that city, it would show the other colonies the potential consequences of their actions.

Americans throwing the Cargoes of the Tea Ships into the River, at Boston

The Destruction of the Tea at Boston Harbor depicts the 1773 Boston Tea Party, showing crowds on the docks cheering as the disguised patriots dump a British cargo into the bay.

The commander of the British army, General Thomas Gage, replaced Governor Hutchinson and immediately ordered his troops to occupy Boston. Parliament passed a series of new laws known collectively in England as the Coercive Acts, but became known in America as the Intolerable Acts. Under these new laws Boston Harbor was closed to all goods with the exception of food and firewood until the East India Tea Company was reimbursed. All town meetings and gatherings were prohibited, essentially eliminating self-government. Royal officials were granted increased authority, including the ability to force citizens to shelter soldiers in their homes. In defending these acts before the House of Commons, Lord North warned, "The Americans have tarred and feathered your subjects, plundered your merchants, burnt your ships, denied all obedience to your laws and authority. . . . Whatever may be the consequences, we must risk something; if we do not, all is over."

Virginia's Richard Henry Lee described the Intolerable Acts as nothing less than "a most wicked system for destroying the liberty of America." The meaning of these acts was clear to all the other colonies: the fate of any one colony foretells the future of all of them; they must stand together or fall separately. They immediately made preparations to send the necessary supplies—all of the vittles they would need to survive—to Massachusetts. And for the first time in a decade, representatives of twelve of the colonies agreed to meet in Philadelphia to debate a united resistance to continued British oppression. Only Georgia, which relied on its British soldiers for protection from hostile Cree Indians, did not send representatives.

At risk of being arrested for treason, Samuel and John Adams joined Thomas Cushing in representing Massachusetts at this First Continental Congress in Philadelphia. As the patriots passed through each town, the residents turned out to show support. Security along their route was provided by America's first intelligence network, Paul Revere's "Mechanics." Consisting of about thirty men drawn from the Sons of Liberty, the network had been created "for the purpose of watching British soldiers and gaining every intelligence on the movements of the Tories."

The Congress was called into session in Carpenter's Hall on September 5 and would meet through the end of October. This was the first time the colonies were attempting to form a united organization. But there was no common goal. There were as many representatives who wanted to negotiate a peaceful reconciliation with England, recommending the establishment of a continental parliament, as there were people who advocated a complete break from the Crown. What did become clear, though, was that should it become necessary, the other colonies would provide strong support for Massachusetts. In his diary of the First Continental Congress, John Adams wrote of being told that George Washington, a Virginia

Colonists believed the firm policies of British Prime Minister Lord North gave them no choice but to fight for their independence.

Clyde Osmar DeLands's romanticized 1911 oil painting shows delegates to the First Continental Congress outside Philadelphia's Carpenter's Hall in 1774.

earistocrat and planter who had gained renown for his courage during the French and Indian War, had vowed to the Virginia Convention that he "would raise 1,000 men, subsist them at my own expense, and march myself at their head for the relief of Boston." And on September 17, after the Congress had adopted a resolution basically renouncing allegiance to England so long as British troops remained in Boston, he added, "This day convinced me that America will support Massachusetts or perish with her."

The first links of unity were being forged. While this congress was unable to reach an acceptable compromise, on October 14 they did agree to send directly to the king, bypassing Parliament, a Declaration of Rights and Grievances. The inhabitants of the colonies "are entitled to life, liberty, and property," it read, "and they have never ceded to any sovereign power whatever, a right to dispose of either without their consent." After enumerating their rights, they threatened "to enter into a non-importation, non-consumption, and non-exportation agreement or association," a complete boycott of all British imports, if the Intolerable Acts were not repealed.

Following Boston's example, most of the cities and towns were by now being run by locally elected committees that made appointments, raised a militia, promoted trade, collected taxes, and administered the courts. There were some who were opposed to this development. Historically, political representatives had always come from the educated, wealthy class, and suddenly common folk were being appointed to important leadership positions. A wealthy South Carolina landowner complained bitterly about having to debate men who knew little more than "how to cobble a shoe" or "cut up a beast." The governor of Georgia was appalled by the fact that the great port city of Savannah was being run by a committee consisting of "a lowest parcel of people, chiefly carpenters, shoemakers, blacksmiths, etc., with a Jew at their head."

Change was inevitable and Parliament did not appear to know how to deal with it—other than by imposing its rule by force. The New England colonies began taking the next brave step toward independence: preparing for war. Massachusetts set out to train a twelve-thousand-man militia and requested the other colonies to provide an additional twenty thousand trained men. Under John Hancock's direction, Boston's Committee of Safety also formed an elite group known as the minutemen for their ability to respond to any provocation within minutes. Colonists hid muskets and balls in cellars and woodsheds and barns and carried out raids against British military stores; a hundred barrels of gunpowder and several cannons were captured at Portsmouth, New Hampshire, and forty-four pieces of artillery were taken at Newport, Rhode Island, and delivered to Providence.

As promised, throughout that winter the other colonies smuggled sufficient goods into Boston to avert starvation. When King George III was informed that the colonies had ignored his threats and were forming local governing assemblies, he ordered ports up and down the

American seaboard closed and forbade fishermen to cast their nets in the North Atlantic.

In March 1775, the Virginia Convention met in Richmond to consider raising its own militia. While many delegates to that convention urged patience, the matter was settled on March 23, when patriot Patrick Henry spoke eloquently about the many steps that had led them to this point, then concluded, "Is life so dear, or peace so sweet, as to be purchased at the price of chains and slavery? Forbid it, Almighty God! I know not what course others may take; but as for me, give me liberty, or give me death!" These precise words were not recorded, but those men inside St. John's Church who heard them said they could never forget them. They resulted in a resolution declaring the independence of the United Colonies from England. Henry himself was charged with building a militia.

The redcoats also began preparing for war. It is believed, though unproven, that early in 1775 Governor Gage issued warrants for the arrests of Samuel Adams and John Hancock, perhaps believing the rebellion could be stopped by containing its leadership. While that legal route proved tricky, another, more deadly solution was proposed: a plot to assassinate Adams, Hancock, and Dr. Warren. Although this story has never been completely proved, and the evidence remains sketchy, several hundred British soldiers reportedly volunteered to participate in the attempt. It was to be carried out on March 5 when thousands of Bostonians would be attending a rally at the Old South Meeting House to commemorate the fifth anniversary of the Boston Massacre.

As former governor Hutchinson wrote in his diary, he was told by Colonel James that about three hundred soldiers "were in the meeting to hear Dr. Warren's oration. If he had said anything against the King, etc., an officer was prepared, who stood near, with an egg to have thrown in his face, and that was to have been the signal to draw swords, and they would have massacred Hancock, Adams, and hundreds more; and he [Col. James] added he wished they had."

When the soldiers arrived at the meetinghouse, Adams asked the townsmen in the front rows to surrender their seats so as to reduce the tension, "inviting them into convenient seats," he wrote, "that they might have no pretense to behave ill." Warren concluded his remarks without incident, but when Adams rose to introduce the next speaker a soldier shouted, "Fire!" and the audience began fleeing the hall. People leaped from the windows and piled outside through the doors. The furious Adams and the soldier had to be held apart before order was restored. It was weeks later when the details of the plot were leaked. It failed, reported a newspaper, because "he who was deputed to throw the egg fell in going to the church, dislocated his knee, and broke the egg, by which means the scheme failed."

Boston was no longer a safe place for Samuel Adams and John Hancock. They secretly moved into the home of Reverend Jonas Clarke in the town of Lexington, twelve miles

This 1876 Currier & Ives lithograph captures the historic moment when Patrick Henry rose in the Continental Congress in 1775 and issued the call for freedom that has reverberated through the centuries: "Give me liberty, or give me death!"

outside Boston on the road to Concord. Meanwhile in London, Lord Dartmouth had decided to make a preemptive strike; he intended to end this rebellion before it could take root by seizing the rebels' arms, arresting their leaders, and reasserting royal authority. General Gage, told by Dartmouth to take whatever steps necessary to "re-establish government," ordered his troops to march to Concord to seize weapons and ammunition hidden there and "arrest and imprison the principle actors . . . in the Provincial Congress."

On the night of April 18, Joseph Warren learned from his spy network that as many as one thousand redcoats were preparing to march on Lexington and Concord. He knew that Samuel Adams and John Hancock were lodging in a tavern in Lexington and would be in grave danger. The source of the dashing Warren's intelligence may have been General Gage's winsome wife, Margaret Kemble Gage. Warren immediately summoned both Paul Revere and William Dawes, a tanner who was active in the militia, and sent them by different routes to give warning. Word of the redcoats' arrival spread rapidly throughout Boston, and numerous other riders were dispatched to alert the political leaders and the militias in the towns and villages surrounding the city. This British movement was not a surprise; in fact the militias had been preparing for a confrontation for months. They had been told exactly what to do, where to go, and whom to inform. In March, the Massachusetts Congress had declared that when Gage marched out of Boston with as many as five hundred armed troops, "it ought to be deemed a design to carry into execution by force the late acts of Parliament, the attempting of which . . . ought to be opposed." And, in response to warnings several days earlier, the cannons and powder had been moved out of the town. When the call to arms came, they were ready for it.

Few moments in American history are better known than "the midnight ride of Paul Revere." In preparation for this night, Revere had arranged a simple code for his men to use to relay information. When the troops began marching, they were to hang lanterns in the bell tower of the Old North Church, one lantern if the troops were proceeding by land from Boston Neck and two lanterns if they were rowing across the bay to march from Cambridge. After leaving

On April 18, 1775, Paul Revere was one of several patriots who risked their lives to warn that British troops were marching. This litho is as historically inaccurate as Longfellow's beloved poem about that night—it even appears that Revere is riding in sunny daylight.

The Midnight Ride of . . . Sybil Ludington?

While the concept of a lone man riding courageously through every Middlesex County village and farm warning colonists that the British are coming does make a wonderful story, the truth is that in addition to Revere, several other men and supposedly one legendary young woman rode through that April 18 night and several other nights to alert patriots that the British army was on the march. If Henry Wadsworth Longfellow had been slightly more accurate his classic poem, "The Midnight Ride of Paul Revere," actually would have read, "When the truth was known lamps were hung in the steeple, and the warning was spread by a large number of people." It was primarily due to Longfellow's poem that the patriot and master silversmith Revere emerged as the hero who aroused the countryside.

Best known among the other riders are William Dawes and Samuel Prescott. Like Revere, the tanner Dawes was sent by Dr. Joseph Warren to warn Hancock and John Adams to flee, and arrived in Lexington about a half hour behind the silversmith. Along the way Revere and Dawes met Prescott, who served as their guide, and after all three men were stopped by the British, Prescott became the only one of them to reach Concord.

Israel Bissell was a professional post rider, a postman, who may have made the longest journey, setting out along the Old Post Road on April 13 from Watertown, Massachusetts, and carrying a message from General Joseph Palmer 345 miles to Philadelphia in four days and six hours. Some historians believe he made it only to Hartford, where the news was passed to another post rider who continued the journey. But the oft-told story claims that along the way he warned militias and colonists that British troops had landed, announcing, "To arms, to arms, the war has begun." As General Palmer had published in a local newspaper to inform colonists that Bissell, who was mistakenly identified as Tryal Russell, was on a mission, "The Bearer, Tryal Russell, is charged to alarm the country quite to Connecticut and all persons are desired to furnish him with fresh horses as they may be needed."

But supposedly the most unusual person to make such a dangerous ride was sixteen-year-old Sybil Ludington. While this story has become firmly lodged in history, like many stories of the Revolution there is some doubt that it actually happened. According to legend, she made her forty-mile ride—twice the distance covered by Revere—from nine p.m. to dawn two years later, galloping through the rain on April 26, 1777, after her father, Colonel Henry Ludington, dispatched her to warn residents in Danbury, Connecticut, that the British were attacking. She carried a stick, which she used that night to prod her horse, beat upon closed doors, and defend herself when approached by a highwayman. The biography of her father, *Colonel Henry Ludington: A Memoir*, published in 1907, describes her ride: "Imagination only can picture what it was . . . on a dark night, with reckless bands of 'Cowboys' and 'Skinners' abroad in the land. But the child performed her task, clinging to a man's saddle, and guiding her steed with only a hempen halter, as she rode through the night, bearing the news of the sack of Danbury." According to the legend, while the four hundred men she roused arrived too late to save Danbury, which had been set on fire by men led by General William Tryon, at the Battle of Ridgefield they were able to drive the Loyalists back to Long Island Sound. In recognition of her effort, Alexander Hamilton wrote a letter of praise and General Washington visited the family mill to personally express his appreciation.

Several others risked their freedom to deliver warnings through those days of wartime. Nathaniel Baker, who was alerted by Revere and Dawes while visiting a lady friend, raced home spreading the alarm along his route. Samuel Prescott roused Sergeant Samuel Hartwell and requested he ride to inform Captain William Smith—instead his wife, Mary Hartwell, handed her five-month-old infant to a slave and took off down the road to tell the captain. Josiah Nelson was on alert, ready to spread the news throughout

Bedford when he heard men approaching. Assuming they were patriots, he shouted into the night asking if they had word that regulars were marching. Instead a British officer struck him in the head with a sword, opening a gash and making Nelson the first casualty of the war. After being bandaged by his wife, Nelson proceeded to Bedford to sound the alarm.

In reality there were dozens of brave men, and at least a few women, who rode to spread the word that "the British are coming!"

Two years after Revere's ride, sixteen-year-old Sybil Ludington rode twice the distance he covered to warn militiamen that the British were attacking Danbury, Connecticut. At left, William Dawes, who took a different route from Revere (bottom, right) that April night and avoided capture while raising the alarm.

Warren, Revere returned to his home to retrieve his boots and overcoat, then was rowed across the Charles River and waited for the signal. Two lanterns were hung in the tower and Revere took off on a borrowed horse to warn Adams and Hancock that the troops were coming by sea. It is said that as he passed each home on the road, he warned that the British were on the march.

As the British troops loaded into boats to be rowed to Cambridge, Revere rode the twelve miles to Lexington. As he neared Charlestown two redcoats on patrol tried to stop him, but he managed to escape at full gallop, and after chasing him three hundred yards, the redcoats returned to their post. He reached Clarke's home slightly before Dawes, and the sentry, Sergeant Monroe, cautioned him about making so much noise that he would wake everyone inside. Monroe later remembered that Revere responded, "Noise! You'll have noise enough before long! The regulars are coming out!"

While apparently John Hancock wanted to stay in Boston and join the fight, Samuel Adams convinced him that he would better serve the coming rebellion by going to Philadelphia, where the Second Continental Congress was scheduled to meet in just a few weeks.

Revere, joined by Dawes and Dr. Samuel Prescott, a doctor who had served as the liaison between Concord and the patriot leaders, set out to warn the militia in Concord. Riding into the dark night, they encountered a British scouting party. They split up, riding in different directions; Revere and Prescott were caught, and Dawes was said to have ridden into the yard of a home screaming that he was being pursued by two soldiers. Those redcoats, fearing an ambush, turned away. Prescott managed to escape his captors, disappearing into the forest, and continued on his mission until successfully reaching Lincoln and Concord.

Revere had previously carried many messages and had dealt with British patrols but, as he later recalled, he had never encountered such danger. "I saw four of them, who rode up to me with their pistols in their hands, said 'G-d d—n you, stop. If you go an inch further, you are a dead man.'" He was accused of being a spy and five different times the officers threatened to kill him; three times they promised to "blow your brains out." Revere identified himself and the officer in command recognized his name. Revere readily boasted that the warning had been spread and five hundred patriots were prepared to meet the British. The officer responded that fifteen hundred troops were marching. Four other men had been captured on the road, and they all rode as prisoners back toward Lexington. When they got close, they heard guns firing by the tavern. While the British assumed those shots meant the fight was beginning, later it was learned it was men emptying their muskets, as was tradition, before going into Buckman Tavern.

Revere and the others were released, although their horses were taken from them. After walking back to the house to retrieve papers left there by Hancock, Revere passed through fifty or sixty militia gathered on the green preparing to meet the British troops. As he did, he heard a commander telling his men, "Let the troops pass by, and don't molest them, without they begin first."

Paul Revere's night was done; the riders had raised the alert! Throughout Massachusetts, church bells rang, warning shots were fired, bonfires blazed, trumpets sounded, and drums were beaten. The minutemen were gathering in Lexington and Concord; the fight for freedom was about to begin.

No more than a hundred men awaited the British army on the common at Lexington.

Colonists fled from the green at Lexington when British troops fired "the shot heard round the world" on April 19, 1775 (above), but the patriots inflicted severe casualties on the confident British as they withdrew from Concord to Boston. (Following page) Seventy-three redcoats were killed, and 174 were wounded that day, causing British leader Lord Percy to proclaim, "Whoever looks upon them [the patriots] as an irregular mob will be much mistaken."

They were not blocking the road. Their commander, Captain John Parker, remained hopeful that the British would pass peacefully and, after discovering no cannons in Concord, would return to Boston. An advance guard of about 250 British regulars arrived in Lexington just before dawn. They made a rough attempt to surround the militia. While they maneuvered, Parker told his men, "Stand your ground; don't fire unless fired upon, but if they mean to have a war, let it begin here."

As Samuel Adams and John Hancock lay hidden in a nearby field, the redcoats and patriot militia confronted each other. A number of spectators stood to the side. An officer,

believed to be the commander of the British vanguard, Major John Pitcairn, rode forward waving his sword and ordering the patriots to disperse. Apparently Pitcairn also had ordered his troops not to fire. After a moment, Parker yelled to his men to go back to their homes. Some of the militia turned their backs and started moving away, but others didn't hear him.

Who fired the first shot, which has become known in history as "the shot heard round the world," has never been determined. Historians have identified several different men who might have fired that infamous first shot, but no one will ever know for certain that person's identity. Both sides believed the shots had come from the opposing force. A redcoat wrote

that there was no intention to attack the colonists, "but on our coming near them they fired on us two shots upon which our men without any orders, rushed upon them, fired and put them to flight." Yet in a deposition given, later signed by more than thirty men who had been there that morning, "whilst our backs were turned on the troops, we were fired on by them, and a number of our men were instantly killed and wounded, not a gun was fired by any person in our company on the regulars to our knowledge before they fired on us."

As Revere testified, "I saw, and heard, a gun fired, which appeared to be a pistol. Then I could distinguish two guns, and then a continued roar of musketry." Within seconds eight patriots suffered fatal wounds while another ten were wounded, while only one regular was slightly hurt. As these minutemen fled into the woods, the British continued their march toward Concord.

An estimated 250 men were waiting there for the British. When they finally arrived, the patriots' commander ordered his outnumbered men out of Concord, deciding to make the fight on his own terms. He would not give the British the static opponent they were trained

This political cartoon, titled *From Concord to Lexington of the Army of Wild Irish Asses Defeated by the Brave American Militia*, was published by a newspaper in London two months after the battle at Lexington and Concord as a means of criticizing the conduct of Prime Minister North's government.

to fight. While the British searched houses for weapons, setting on fire several houses and whatever contraband they found, reinforcements from villages and towns arrived and swelled the militia. There is some evidence that the soldiers actually helped put out the fires they had set to prevent the homes of completely innocent people from being destroyed. By the time the British were ready to leave Concord, the patriots had taken positions behind barricades and in the woods. Led by Major John Buttrick, a small force attacked the redcoats guarding the North Bridge. After fire from the regulars killed two of his men, Buttrick ordered, "Fire, fellow soldiers, for God's sake, fire!" Two soldiers were killed, the first British casualties of the war.

The British withdrew without finding the cannons and powder they had come to destroy. During much of the sixteen-mile march back to Boston, the militia army fired continually at the retreating British army, picking them off relentlessly, one by one, as more and more militiamen joined the force. The colonists let loose their anger and resentment on the retreating redcoats. When the British reached Lexington, the militiamen waiting for them there had their revenge.

The British regulars did not know how to contend with this Indian-like strategy and, enraged, broke into houses along their route, setting many of them on fire and shooting anyone they suspected of being a sniper. The militia attacks ceased only when reinforcements from Boston reached the redcoats. On this first day of war, 73 regulars were killed and as many as 250 more were wounded, while 49 minutemen were killed. It was an extraordinary victory for the colonists. The lessons learned that day about how to fight a superior force would become the patriots' hallmark throughout the Revolutionary War.

The leaders of the rebellion successfully avoided capture and made their way to Philadelphia. When the Second Continental Congress convened there on May 10, 1775, thousands of patriots had encircled Boston. While the British army could be supplied by sea, this overwhelming American force prevented them from breaking out. Among the first tasks facing the congress was turning that disorganized militia into an army. It is believed that John Adams was the one to nominate as its commander the gentleman farmer from Virginia, George Washington.

Washington was well respected, although his military experience was limited to success in frontier fighting during the French and Indian War. But he accepted the limitations of his military knowledge and the enormity of the task facing him, telling his fellow delegate from Virginia, Patrick Henry, "Remember Mr. Henry, what I now tell you: from the day I enter upon the command of the American armies, I date my fall, and the ruin of my reputation." He then purchased several books about organizing and commanding large forces and set off to Boston to take command.

—❦—

CHAPTER 3

Benjamin
FRANKLIN

Inventing America

When sixty-nine-year-old Benjamin Franklin landed in Philadelphia on May 5, 1775, he seemed to be a man without a country. He had spent most of the last two decades living on Craven Street in London, working to find ways to keep the colonies and England bound together. His son William, the governor of New Jersey, was an outspoken Loyalist. And as Franklin himself had written several years earlier, "Being born and bred in one of the countries, and having lived long and made many agreeable connections of friendship in the other, I wish all prosperity to both sides; but I . . . do not find that I have gained any point in either country except that of rendering myself suspected for my impartiality; in England, of being too much an American, and in America of being too much an Englishman."

☜ The brutality of the hand-to-hand fighting during the Battle of Bunker Hill is depicted in Alonzo Chappel's 1859 oil painting.

Franklin stepped off a ship into the Revolution. The first shots had been fired while he was still at sea. He immediately accepted an appointment as one of Pennsylvania's five delegates to the Second Continental Congress, becoming the oldest and most famous representative. This must have made him quite happy: Benjamin Franklin was noted for his appreciation of Benjamin Franklin. And, indeed, few men accomplished more in their lifetime than Ben Franklin. Historian Walter Isaacson described him as "the most accomplished American of his age and the most influential in inventing the type of society America would become."

The founding fathers arrived at the conclusion that a free and independent United States was a just cause worth dying for by following very different paths. But Franklin was the one who traveled the greatest distance to finally arrive at that point.

There was little in Franklin's early childhood to suggest that he would become such a towering figure. He was born in what was then the Massachusetts Bay Colony in 1705, the fifteenth child of candle maker Josiah Franklin. Although he had a limited formal education, he learned by reading every book or pamphlet he found. His lifetime of inventing began when he was eleven, when he devised a pair of swim fins that fit his hands. Among his many later inventions were bifocals, the heat-efficient Franklin stove, a musical instrument called the glass armonica, and the lightning rod. As a twelve-year-old he was apprenticed to his brother's print shop, where he worked for five years. When his brother refused to publish his writing, Ben wrote witty letters that appeared under the pseudonym Mrs. Silence Dogood, who introduced herself as a woman with "a natural inclination to observe and reprove the faults of others, at which I have an excellent faculty. I speak this by way of warning to all such whose offences shall come under my cognizance, for I never intend to wrap my talent in a napkin."

After leaving his brother's employ he settled in Philadelphia, where he formed a partnership to open a printing shop. He was quite successful and in 1729 he was elected the official printer for Pennsylvania. That same year he purchased the *Pennsylvania Gazette*, which eventually became the most successful newspaper in the colonies; it was also the paper that printed America's first political cartoon—naturally drawn by Franklin. He had a reputation as a ladies' man, and an affair resulted in the birth of his illegitimate son, William Franklin. He published his first *Poor Richard's Almanack* in 1732. In addition to containing all of the information expected in almanacs—a calendar, weather predictions, poems, recipes, sayings, and wisdom—he included serial stories and characters, one of them being poor Richard, to entice readers to purchase the following year's edition. Many of the well-known sayings attributed to Franklin, among them "a penny saved is a penny earned" and "early to bed, early to rise, makes a man healthy, wealthy and wise," first appeared in those pages. *Poor Richard's*

By 1745, as this scene outside his bookstore and print shop is dated, Benjamin Franklin had become one of Philadelphia's best known and most successful residents. By then he had been publishing his wildly popular *Poor Richard's Almanack* for more than a decade.

was widely popular and was published annually for twenty-five years, selling as many as ten thousand copies each year.

A man of infinite interests, Franklin soon delved into civic affairs. He created America's first lending library, the Pennsylvania Hospital, an early insurance company, an academy that would become the University of Pennsylvania, and the first fire company in Philadelphia. (His reminder, "An ounce of prevention is worth a pound of cure," was intended to remind people to take care when using candles or the fireplace.)

His small printing shop had become a substantial enterprise, which included a publishing company, a newspaper, and partial control of the postal system. The books he published ranged from Bibles to the first novel published in America, a reprint of Samuel Richardson's British bestseller, *Pamela, or, Virtue Rewarded*, a racy tale of lust and morality. By forming partnerships to open print shops in several cities, from Newport to Charlestown, he became a wealthy man and was able to retire when he was forty-two years old to pursue his interests in science and politics. He spent a decade experimenting with electricity and created terms including "battery," "conductor," and "electrician." In 1753 he performed one of history's best-known experiments, flying a kite with a key attached to it in a thunderstorm; he put his hand near the key—and felt a spark of static electricity; he had demonstrated that lightning was also an electrical spark and could be attracted with a conductor. That discovery led to his invention of the lightning rod, which he described as "upright rods of iron, made sharp as a needle and gilt to prevent rusting, and from the foot of those rods a wire down the outside of the building into the ground; . . . Would not these pointed rods probably draw the electrical fire silently out of a cloud before it came nigh enough to strike."

In 1736, long before his legendary capture of lightning, Franklin began serving in Pennsylvania's colonial legislature. He led Pennsylvania's delegation to the Albany Conference in 1754, a meeting of several colonies called to find ways of bettering relations with Native Americans and forming a common defense against the French. At that session he presented his Albany Plan of Union, one of the first serious attempts to unite the colonies around their common interests; while the plan was approved by the conference, it was rejected by colonial legislatures, which were not ready to cede any power to a central government. Franklin did manage to convince the Pennsylvania Assembly to fund a militia, and he led an expedition into the Lehigh Valley to build forts to enable settlers to defend themselves against the French and Indians.

By then one of Pennsylvania's most respected citizens, Franklin was sent to England in 1757 by the assembly to represent the interests of the colony—primarily against its proprietors, the Penn family. William Penn had been given the land in 1681 in payment of a royal debt. He had governed the territory in accordance with his Quaker heritage, and it had become a place that welcomed people of all religions and beliefs. Upon his death, his sons, Thomas and Richard Penn, inherited all the land that had not been sold. They remained in London and contributed very little toward the welfare or progress of the people who lived on those lands. Part of Franklin's mission was to petition the king to impose taxes on the family, to raise money desperately needed to help pay for the defense of the colony during the French and Indian War.

Franklin settled happily in London with his son William; his wife feared sea travel and remained at home. He fit easily into British society; like him, the English valued education and culture, celebrated provocative ideas, respected and understood science, and found joy in the theater and the arts. He traveled to several countries, meeting the most respected men of the time, including economist Adam Smith and philosopher David Hume. He met Samuel Johnson at least once and spent time with political satirist William Hogarth; he visited Joseph Priestley's laboratory; the Royal Society of London honored him as the first non-British citizen to receive its highest award; and, after being given an honorary degree by the

This oil painting by an unknown American artists portrays Franklin in his early forties. "Most people dislike vanity in others," he once wrote, "whatever share they have of it themselves; but I give it fair quarter wherever I meet with it, being persuaded that it is often productive of good to the possessor."

University of St. Andrews, he enjoyed the prestige of becoming the esteemed "Dr. Franklin." He also managed to make important connections in the government and secured for his son the post of royal governor of New Jersey. As to his initial mission, he enjoyed only limited success; while the concept of taxing a proprietor was accepted, the tax generated only a very small amount of money.

He returned to Pennsylvania in 1762 but pined for London. He wrote to Polly Stevenson, the daughter of his landlady on Craven Street, "I envy most its people. Why should that petty island, which compared to America is but like a stepping-stone in a brook, scarce enough of it above water to keep one's shoes dry; why, I say, should that little island enjoy in almost every neighborhood more sensible, virtuous and elegant minds than we can collect in ranging 100 leagues of our vast forests?"

Certainly to his delight, the assembly sent him back to London in 1764 to petition the king to allow Pennsylvania to be free of rule by the Penn family and become a royal colony. This was entirely in keeping with Franklin's own beliefs. "King George's virtue," he had written a year earlier when advocating this change in government, "and the consciousness of his sincere intentions to make his people happy, will give him firmness and steadiness in his measures . . . after a few of the first years, will be the future course of His Majesty's reign, which I predict will be happy and truly glorious." He believed that the British people had mostly goodwill toward the colonies. "The popular inclination here is to wish us well, and that we may preserve our liberties." He was certain that eventually Parliament would bow to the wishes of the people where the colonies were concerned.

It was a year later, when Parliament passed the Stamp Act, that Franklin was faced with having to choose between the England he had come to love and his American homeland. Although initially he argued forcefully against the Stamp Act, once it was clear that the king intended to impose it, he urged the colonists to be realistic, telling them, "A firm loyalty to the Crown . . . is the wisest choice."

Perhaps because it had been so long since he had truly lived in Philadelphia, Franklin wasn't aware of the hardening attitude toward the Crown. From his viewpoint in England, the alternatives to the tax were far more dangerous than the tax itself. At that time Franklin believed that the safest and wisest choice for America was to remain in the strong, sheltering arms of the greatest military power on earth. The British viewed the colonies as a single entity, but Franklin knew from his experience working on his Albany Plan how zealously each colony protected its independence. Getting them to agree on even the smallest point took great effort; trying to convince them to fight together for a seemingly impossible goal seemed, well, impossible. The colonists reacted to Franklin's words as might be expected, accusing him of betraying them to gain favor with the king, pointing out among other rewards he'd received his son's royal appointment. The seeds for John Adams's questions about where his loyalties lay had taken root. As the homes of customs collectors were being sacked in Boston and other cities, some talked of destroying Franklin's Philadelphia home.

When Franklin realized the depth of this anger, he quickly changed course and began fighting the Stamp Act, using all of the diplomatic tools he had mastered. He wrote against the act in British newspapers and argued against it at social occasions, warning British merchants that the effects of the threatened colonial boycott could be devastating. Appearing before the House of Commons, he answered more than 170 questions, arguing repeatedly that Parliament did not have the power to tax or legislate the colonies. A month after his appearance, the Stamp Act was repealed. Whether or not he actually influenced that decision, he received credit for it.

While officially the colonies had no ambassador to England, he emerged as their spokes-

A French admirer commissioned Joseph Siffred Duplessis to paint the seventy-year-old Franklin upon his arrival in Paris in 1776. Franklin was never constrained by age, pointing out, "We do not stop playing because we grow old, we grow old because we stop playing!"

person in Europe. Georgia, New Jersey, and, most important, Massachusetts appointed him to represent their interests in court. The Stamp Act had forced him to finally declare his allegiance; after British troops had taken control of Boston in 1768 and the Boston Massacre occurred two years later, he set out to erase any doubt, believing, as he later wrote, "Even peace may be purchased at too high a price." He fought valiantly against the Townshend Acts, warning Parliament that these "acts of oppression" would "sour the American tempers and perhaps hasten their final revolt." When the 1773 Tea Act was passed, he published several provocative essays, among them, "Rules by Which a Great Empire May Be Reduced to a Small One." His purpose, he wrote to one of his sisters, was to hold up "a looking-glass in which some ministers may see their ugly faces, and the nation its injustice."

At the same time he tried to convince the colonists to have patience. New leaders, "Friends of liberty" as he described them, were soon to be in power. "The ministry are not all of a mind," he wrote, "nor determined what are the next steps proper to be taken with us."

Among his final attempts to preserve the uneasy alliance was his decision to secretly forward inflammatory letters written by Royal Governor Thomas Hutchinson.

Just before the American-born Hutchinson had assumed his position in Massachusetts in 1769, he and his brother-in-law and aide, Andrew Oliver, had written to Prime Minister George Grenville's private secretary, urging Grenville to take drastic action to crush the rising spirit of rebellion in the colonies. "There must be an abridgment of what are called English liberties," he wrote in one of the letters, suggesting that if necessary, force should be used against the colonists. In another he stated, "I have been begging for measures to maintain the supremacy of Parliament."

Hutchinson and Franklin had worked together creating the Albany Plan. But that was long ago. These were incredibly damning letters. It has never been discovered how Franklin got hold of them. He sent six of them to Thomas Cushing, the leader of the Boston Assembly, in an attempt to prove to Massachusetts leaders that Parliament's harsh attitude hadn't been initiated in London but rather by an American living in Boston, who had been feeding bad advice to leading British politicians. These letters, Franklin wrote, "laid the foundation of most if not all our grievances."

Franklin asked Cushing not to make these letters public, but after Samuel and John Adams got hold of them they were published in the *Boston Gazette*. Bostonians were outraged. Hutchinson fled to England as quickly as possible. The assembly immediately petitioned the king to remove Hutchinson and Oliver from their positions. The king turned to his advisers, the Privy Council, for a decision.

In England, the publication of the letters was the great scandal of the day. The London newspapers gleefully reported every rumor speculating on the identity of the person who leaked them. Two ranking government officials each claimed the other was the source, and the argument became so bitter that they fought a duel. One of them was injured slightly and they agreed to fight again when the wounded man was sufficiently healed. Franklin decided he could not allow innocent men to risk death and wrote an editorial for the *London Chronicle* confessing his role. "I think it is incumbent on me to declare for the prevention of further mischief that I alone am the person who obtained and transmitted to Boston the letters in question." These letters had been written "by public officers to persons in public stations, on public affairs," he wrote in his own defense, and the policy they suggested would "incense the Mother Country against her colonies, and, by the steps recommended, to widen the breach." By forwarding those letters that revealed the source of animosity to responsible people in Boston, he had hoped to reduce the existing tension between England and the colonies.

In 1774, Franklin was ordered to appear before the highest ranking members of the British government, where he admitted to leaking secret incendiary letters to the Boston Assembly, destroying his well-earned reputation in England.

Franklin was summoned to appear before the Privy Council, where he was accused of illegally disclosing private correspondence. While these hearings were taking place, news of the Boston Tea Party reached England and Franklin bore the brunt of growing British anger toward the colonies. On January 29, 1774, he stood before thirty-four of the highest-ranking British government officials, including Lord North, in an area of Whitehall known as "the Cockpit" because years earlier cockfights had taken place there. In a dramatic conclusion, he was vilified by the council, while the king's solicitor general, Alexander Wedderburn, defended Hutchinson, claiming that Franklin was using an honest man's words to incite rebellion. According to Wedderburn, Franklin was the "actor and secret spring by which all the Assembly's motives were directed," and his actions had caused a "whole province set in flame." By the time the hearing was done, Franklin's reputation in England had been shattered. To Franklin, who cared so deeply for England and reveled in the respect he had earned there, this attack on his character was a huge personal insult. The one man who might have been able to find some common ground between England and her American colonies had been completely alienated. Within days he was fired as postmaster general of the colonies. A harshly worded letter sent from the king's ministers to American postal authorities warned ominously, "Fleets and troops are talked of, to be sent to America."

Dismissed by England, distrusted by Americans, Franklin sailed home. And while he was at sea the first shots were fired at Lexington and Concord.

Upon landing in Philadelphia Franklin soon began taking steps to demonstrate his commitment to the colonies in the coming war. But that necessitated terminating one of the most important relationships in his life. His beloved son William had stood proudly by his father's side throughout much of his career, through all his European travels, his scientific experiments, and his political work. In return Benjamin Franklin had supported his son, financially, emotionally, and politically. They grew to become not just father and son but good friends and confidants. When William Franklin produced his own illegitimate son, his father helped raise that child. And when Ben Franklin departed for England in 1764, he gave responsibility for the welfare of his family and his estate to his son. At every opportunity Benjamin Franklin had used his power to secure his son's future and had been rewarded when William was appointed royal governor of New Jersey. He assumed that his son would resign his own position in support of his father after his harsh treatment. And he was dismayed when William refused to do so.

In fact, William seemed to dismiss the damage that had been done to his father's reputation, describing the public humiliation at the Cockpit as a minor incident. He apparently believed it was a good time for his father to retire and spend the remaining years of his life at home with his family.

Rather than simply responding to his father's wishes, William Franklin reached his own conclusion: whatever the consequences, he would remain steadfast in his loyalty, a loyalty he had been taught by his father. At some point every colonist had to decide if they were to remain loyal to the Crown or support the independence movement. For many that was a difficult decision. The answer was not so clear then as it has become in history. Many of those, like William Franklin, stayed loyal to the Crown, not necessarily because they supported the clearly abusive actions but rather because they sincerely believed that it was the best course for the colonies. As William said, "You can never place yourself in a happier situation than in your ancient constitutional dependency on Great Britain. No independent state ever was or ever can be as happy as we have been, and might still be, under that government."

Before Franklin could prove his patriotism in the colonies, a small force commanded by General Benedict Arnold and militia leader Ethan Allen took Fort Ticonderoga in upstate New York on May 10, 1775, without a single shot being fired.

Father and son remained on amicable terms until the war broke out. After that there was no healing the rift between them. As Benjamin Franklin admitted, "Nothing has ever hurt me so much and affected me with such keen sensations, as to find myself deserted in my old age by my only son; and not only deserted, but to find him taking up arms against me, in a cause wherein my good fame, fortune and life were all at stake."

When William was imprisoned for two years in Connecticut during the war, his father did nothing at all to help him. William did not say a single cross word about him, but Benjamin Franklin never forgave his son. After the war they saw each other only once, to clear up some financial matters. William refused to renounce his wartime stance, claiming he was

Patriot leader Dr. Joseph Warren died providing covering fire for retreating soldiers on Breed's Hill. He was among the most respected men in the colonies, and had he lived would have become an honored founding father.

doing his duty as he saw it. In the year before his death Benjamin Franklin disinherited him, explaining, "The part he acted against me in the late war, which is of public notoriety, will account for my leaving him no more of an estate he endeavored to deprive me of."

Ben Franklin actually had little opportunity to prove his loyalty to the colonists after arriving in Philadelphia. There had been only sporadic fighting after Lexington and Concord.

In early May, the leader of the Committee of Safety, the patriots' quasi government, Joseph Warren, had ordered Colonel Benedict Arnold to seize British arms and stores at Fort Ticonderoga. To accomplish this mission, Arnold joined Ethan Allen and his Green Mountain Boys, a Vermont militia, to attack the British garrison at Fort Ticonderoga. In fact, Ticonderoga was lightly defended and in great disrepair, but inside its crumbling walls the British stored valuable cannons, mortars, howitzers, and ammunition. A surprise attack was launched at dawn on May 10. The only sentry on duty raised his musket, but when it misfired, he turned around and started running. The Green Mountain Boys poured into the fort, waking up its defenders by sticking guns in their faces. The commander surrendered his sword and no one was injured. This was the first colonial victory of the war, and the captured artillery would later prove vital.

Even after that there remained a slim hope that a war could be avoided, but that was extinguished on a small hill overlooking Boston on the night of June 16, 1775. The geography of Boston was different at that time from what it is today. It was a peninsula, connected to land by the narrow Roxbury Neck. While the city remained firmly in British control, Roxbury Neck, the only overland path out of the city, remained under the firm control of colonial general Artemas Ward. For more than a month militiamen had been arriving on horseback, by wagon, and on foot, ready to make a fight for the city. By mid-June Boston was surrounded by more than fifteen thousand men, while Royal Navy warships maintained control of the harbor and the sea. It was a classic stalemate.

Even after the colonial success at Lexington and Concord, the British generals too easily dismissed the colonists' military capability. They simply could not believe that this untrained, under-equipped, undisciplined army was a match for the well-supplied, superbly trained, and highly disciplined British regulars.

In early June, after reinforcements landed by the navy had brought his army to six thousand men, General Thomas Gage, the commander of all British forces in North America, and

This oil of the Honorable General Thomas Gage, Commander of the British Forces in North America, was painted at about the same time the war began in 1775. It was his decision to seize patriot munitions in April 1775 that led to the fighting at Lexington and Concord. He was replaced after the disastrous "victory" at Bunker Hill.

his staff began planning to break out of the city in order to open a vital overland supply line. They intended to smash the upstart army and put a quick end to this rebellion. But a colonial spy in the city reportedly overheard British commanders discussing the plan and alerted the Massachusetts Committee of Safety. General Ward ordered General Israel Putnam to organize a defense against the British, specifically telling him to fortify the tallest ground in the area, 110-foot-tall Bunker Hill. Putnam marched about twelve hundred men from Cambridge, but instead of making a stand as ordered on Bunker Hill, his men began setting up a defense on the smaller Breed's Hill. No one truly knows why this happened; it might well have been a simple mistake made in the dark of night. An eyewitness narrative prepared two weeks after the battle explained, "About 9 o'clock in the evening the detachment marched upon the design to Breed's Hill situated on the further part of the peninsula next to Boston, for by a mistake of orders this hill was marked out for the entrenchment instead of the other." However, some historians believe this was the intent, as Breed's Hill was thought to be more easily defensible and brought the city within range of the few cannons they had.

Under the command of Colonel William Prescott, the troops built a square redoubt, with six-foot-high dirt walls topped with fence rails, wheat, and stones with a raised platform inside enabling the soldiers to shoot over it. It was supported by a well-defended rail fence extending from one side down to the shore. Their presence was quickly detected and long before dawn the 128 guns aboard the three warships anchored in the harbor as well as additional cannons on land began bombarding the position. The barrage decapitated one man, causing several others to desert, but otherwise did little damage.

At first light in the morning, General Gage decided to launch an attack before the colonists could complete their preparations. While some of his officers suggested flanking the position, thus cutting the troops off from supplies and eventually starving them into surrender, General William Howe, who would lead the attack, argued for a frontal assault, explaining that the hill was "open and easy of ascent and in short . . . would be easily carried." Howe launched the attack on the flank, which was stopped on the beach, then launched his frontal assault on the rail fence.

Among the reinforcements who rushed to Breed's Hill that morning was Dr. Joseph Warren. Although he had been commissioned a major general by Washington two days earlier, he insisted on joining the infantry in the front lines. "Don't think I came to seek a place of safety," he supposedly told General Putnam, "but tell me where the onset will be the most furious." Warren, who had dispatched Paul Revere on his midnight ride, was a greatly admired local figure and was known for having told his mother after being grazed by a musket ball in the midst of the fighting at Concord, "Where danger is, dear mother, there must your

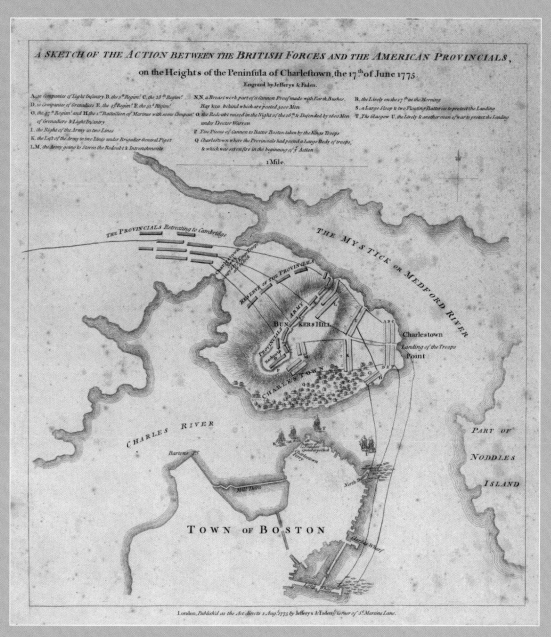

When war began, Charlestown was a peninsula with only a narrow bridge to land. This sketch, published in London, illustrates the course of the Battle of Bunker Hill.

son be. Now is no time for any of America's children to shrink from any hazard. I will set her free or die."

It was afternoon before the attack could be mounted. The British rowed to Moreton's Point, where they came under relentless sniper fire from Charlestown. In response, the big guns from the warships in the harbor began bombarding the city, setting it on fire. Soon afterward, according to the narrative, "flames and smoke were seen to arise in large clouds from the town of Charlestown which had been set on fire by a carcase fired from one some of the enemy's batteries with a design to favor their attack upon our lines by the smoke which as they imagined would have been blown directly [upon them] their way and covered them in their attack but the wind changing at this instant it was carried [beyond them] another way."

As townspeople in Boston watched from high points, church steeples, and rooftops, among them Abigail Adams and her son, John Quincy, and British general "Gentleman Johnny" Burgoyne, the battle began. Snipers fired down on the redcoats as they gathered in Charlestown. Then the British began the assault, marching across an open field in two long lines, each two men deep, with a separation between them, then up the hill in a ragged formation. Their march was slowed as they had to maneuver around fences, brick kilns, and other obstructions. It is said that one officer, so confident of victory, marched with a servant at his side, carrying a celebratory bottle of wine.

The colonists waited patiently, having been ordered to conserve ammunition and fire low. In legend, General Putnam gave the command, "Men, you are all marksmen; don't one of you fire until you see the white of their eyes," although in actuality there is no evidence he—or anyone else—said that. But it was hardly an original thought, as variations of that order had been reported through much of military history.

The colonials waited, they waited, they waited—and then the slaughter began. As the contemporary narrative reported, "The provincials in the redoubt and the lines reserved their fire till the enemy had come within about 10 or 12 yards and then discharged at once upon them. The fire threw their body into very great confusion, and all of them after having kept a fire for some time retreated in very great disorder." The colonists, many of them expert shots, aimed first at the officers, who were easily identified by their uniforms. After the officers fell, their dazed troops attacked without direction, sometimes bunching up to make even easier targets. At the conclusion of that initial attack, a colonial officer wrote, "The dead lay as thick as sheep in a fold."

At the bottom of the hill the British re-formed their lines, although some officers were seen "to push forward the men with their swords." This second attack had the same result;

Breed's Hill was littered with the bodies of the dead and wounded. The British retreated again.

By this time, though, the militia had expended much of its ammunition. There was little chance they could repulse a third attack, but rather than retreating, many of the men stayed in the redoubt to give others cover. Among them was Warren. Then the British began mounting an all-out attack. They were reinforced by troops who were rushed into the battle from Boston, and as many as two hundred wounded men rejoined the fight. The warships opened up on the hill with all their cannons. General Howe changed tactics, forming his men into carefully spaced columns rather than a single long line and attacked the redoubt opposite the rail fence.

The colonists fired the last of their ammunition. As Colonel Prescott recalled, their firing became sporadic, then "went out like a candle." When their guns were empty, they began throwing rocks, then fought hand to hand with the butts of their muskets as British troops came over the wall in waves and began bayoneting the defenders. The battle had become a deadly melee; British troops who had broken the line took their revenge. As British marine lieutenant John Waller described the scene, "I was with those two companies, who drove their bayonets into all that opposed them. Nothing could be more shocking than the carnage that followed the storming [of] this work. We tumbled over the dead to get at the living, who were crowding out of the gorge of the redoubt . . . the soldiers stabbing some and dashing out the brains of others." In fact, the greatest number of patriot casualties were suffered during this retreat, and it could have been much worse if brave men had not set up a line behind a fence and provided as much cover as possible to hold back British pursuit.

Among those who died in those last moments was Joseph Warren; he was swinging his musket like a club as he tried to fight his way out of the redoubt. He had successfully gotten out and was about sixty yards away when he was recognized by a British officer, who shot and killed him.

The battle lasted less than two hours. A total of 260 British soldiers were killed and another 828 wounded, a disproportionate number of them officers; the colonists lost about 140 men with an estimated 300 more wounded. But most devastating was the loss of Warren. As Abigail Adams said, "Not all the havoc and devastation they have made has wounded me like the death of Warren. We want him in the Senate; we want him in his profession; we want him in the field. We mourn for the citizen, the senator, the physician, and the warrior." His death was a terrible blow to the colonial army; British general Howe declared that Warren's life was worth the lives of five hundred other men.

Several historians claim that Warren's body was mutilated by the enraged British until it was no longer recognizable, and a day later his corpse was dug up and beheaded. What

The death of thirty-four-year-old Joseph
Warren in battle was a terrible blow to the
colonists. But they remembered his words,
"Our streets are filled with armed men; our
harbor is crowded with ships of war; but
these cannot intimidate us; our liberty must
be preserved, it is far dearer than life."

THE DEATH OF WARREN

is known for certain is that about ten months after the battle, his body was unearthed and
positively identified by Paul Revere, who found a false tooth he had fashioned and implanted.
While we can only speculate what great deeds Warren might have accomplished had he
lived, it is clear he would have been among the leaders of the new country, a signer of the
Declaration of Independence, and a man whose name would be celebrated by all Americans.

The Battle of Bunker Hill proved to be the bloodiest battle of the entire war. About
half of the British soldiers who marched so proudly into battle became casualties. While
General Burgoyne wrote, "The day ended with glory," the night in Boston was grim, as the
dead and wounded were taken off the boats that ferried them back to the city. As a local man
named Peter Oliver described the scene, "It was truly a shocking sight and sound, to see the
carts loaded with those unfortunate men and to hear the piercing groans of the dying and

those whose painful wounds extorted the sigh from the firmest mind." Among the British officers killed was John Pitcairn, the highly respected major whose loss greatly damaged British morale.

While Bunker Hill was considered a British victory, in reality the conduct and skill of the patriots shook British resolve. The path to victory had not been nearly as easy as they had anticipated. While publicly General Gage reported, "This action shows the superiority of the King's troops," in a private correspondence he admitted, "The trials we have had, show that the rebels are not the despicable rabble too many have supposed them to be. . . . In all their wars against the French, they never showed so much conduct, attention and perseverance as they do now." And in another letter pleading for more soldiers he confessed, "The loss we have sustained is greater than we can bear."

Other British officers remarked about the "ungentlemanly" tactics employed by the patriots. Just as they had at Concord, the colonists fought from behind barriers; they fired their weapons and were gone before feeling a response. These new Indian-like tactics concerned British commanders. As a result of this battle, General Gage was relieved of his command and ordered to return to England, and General Howe was given command.

News of the bloody battle shook the representatives' meeting in Philadelphia. They were especially infuriated by the burning of Charlestown, an unnecessarily brutal act. Ben Franklin, who sensed that he still had not gained the trust of John Adams or other leaders, saw his chance to prove his loyalty to the patriot cause. He wrote a letter to a friend in London, William Strahan, that apparently was left for Adams to find and read. "Mr. Strahan," it began, "You are a Member of Parliament, and one of that majority that has doomed my country to destruction. You have begun to burn our towns and murder our people. Look upon your hands, they are stained with the blood of your relations! You and I were long friends; you are now my enemy, and I am yours. B. Franklin."

That letter may simply have been a clever ploy; it was never mailed and Strahan never saw it. In fact, while Franklin and Strahan found themselves on opposite sides they somehow managed to maintain a friendship. A decade after the war ended and after America had won its independence, Franklin still signed his letters to Strahan, "I am ever, my dear friend, yours most affectionately."

However, the letter accurately stated Franklin's sentiment and convinced Adams and others that Franklin was an ally. In another letter, one that was mailed to the scientist Joseph Priestley, Franklin wrote, "America is determined and unanimous. . . . Britain, at the expense of three millions, has killed one hundred and fifty Yankees this campaign, which is about twenty thousand pounds a head; and at Bunker's Hill she gained a mile of ground. . . . During the same time sixty thousand children have been born in America. From these data his mathematical head [respected theologian and economist Dr. Richard Price] will easily calculate the time and expense necessary to kill us all, and conquer our whole territory."

As the Second Continental Congress set to work, Franklin was appointed to several committees. But his first official appointment for this new government was the first postmaster general of the United Colonies. Perhaps it was another jab at the British, who had fired him from that post, but he also was by far the best qualified.

History proves that the congress did do a fine job appointing the right people to vitally important posts, but none was more important than giving control of the army to George Washington. About two weeks after Bunker Hill, General Washington arrived in Cambridge to take command of this makeshift army. News of the fight had reached him along the way, and he was reportedly cheered by the bravery displayed by the patriots.

Washington's own bravery had been proved in 1755 during the Battle of Monongahela in the French and Indian War, when General Edward Braddock took twenty-six hundred troops to try to capture Fort Duquesne from the French. About ten miles from the fort, a smaller number of French and Indians ambushed a segment of Braddock's force. As the battle raged, most of the officers were killed—including General Braddock. The leaderless British troops were being decimated when George Washington, who had been serving as an aide-de-camp to Braddock, rode into the battle and took command. His display of courage caused the army to rally around him. During the bitter fighting two horses were shot from under him and four musket balls ripped through his coat. But he never wavered. His cool, efficient leadership enabled many soldiers to escape with their lives. While the British were defeated in that battle, Washington received a promotion to colonel, and several years later Washington successfully captured that fort.

Washington served under several British generals during the French and Indian War and learned lessons in military leadership from all of them. By the end of the war he had gained experience in commanding troops, delegating authority to subordinates, organizing equipment and supply lines, maintaining discipline and order in the ranks, and constructing forts and defensive positions—and obviously each of these skills would prove vital during the war he was about to fight.

The encampment in Cambridge could hardly be described as an army. While in sheer numbers, the estimated fifteen thousand volunteers actually outnumbered the ten thousand British troops occupying Boston, it was a motley assortment of poorly trained and ill-equipped militias from all thirteen colonies. There was little cohesion. The soldiers wore no standard uniforms; they carried the arms they brought with them; they were undernourished and poorly clothed. They were supposed to be paid by their local government, but those payments rarely arrived as scheduled. Morale was terrible. The pride and loyalty of each of these men was to the colony from which they'd come rather than to some abstract concept of a single united nation. What many of them were actually fighting for was relief from unjust taxation and harsh British regulation and the freedom to be left alone, rather than the dream of some new country.

Most of these militiamen knew about George Washington, though. These were hardened men—many of them depended on their hunting skills for survival—and they admired the general's mettle. Washington had proved himself in battle; he was the kind of man they didn't mind taking orders from. When he rode into the camp he made an impressive sight. At six-foot-two, he was almost seven inches taller than the average man of that time. As Dr. James Thacher reported, "His excellency was on horseback, in company with several military gentlemen. It was not difficult to distinguish him from all others. His personal appearance is truly noble and majestic, being tall and well proportioned. His dress is a blue coat with buff-colored facings, a rich epaulette on each shoulder, buff under-dress, and an elegant small sword; a black cockade in his hat. . . . He has been received here with every mark of respect, and addressed by our Provincial Congress in the most affectionate and respectful manner. All ranks appear to repose full confidence in him as commander-in-chief."

After reviewing his new command, Washington summed up this army with candor, "The abuses [problems] in this army, I fear, are considerable, and the new modeling of it [reorganization], in the face of an enemy, from whom we every hour expect an attack, is exceedingly difficult and dangerous."

Washington went to work immediately. On July 4, 1775, he issued one of his first General Orders, an attempt to turn the many disparate units into an army and to eliminate the suspicion and competition among them. "The Continental Congress having now taken all the troops of the several colonies which have been raised or which may be hereafter raised for the support and defense of the liberties of America into their pay and service, they are now the troops of the United Provinces of North America; and it is hoped that all distinctions of colonies will be laid aside, so that one and the same spirit may animate the whole, and the only contest be, who shall render, on this great and trying occasion, the most essential service to the great and common cause in which we are all engaged."

Among those men who soon visited Washington at Cambridge was none other than Benjamin Franklin, who wanted to know what supplies were most urgently needed. Everything,

This hand-painted Currier & Ives litho
portrays General George Washington
assuming command of the American
army in Cambridge, on July 3, 1775.

Washington apparently told him. But as important as provisions were weapons. The inventor Franklin urged that soldiers be armed with bows and arrows, pointing out that they were less expensive and easier to supply than muskets; four arrows could be fired in the time it took to fire and reload a musket, and a soldier struck by an arrow was out of combat until the arrow was removed. Both Washington and Franklin also wanted to equip their troops with fourteen-foot-long pikes and spears, which would be especially effective against cavalry, Washington noted, if they had "a spike in the butt end to fix them in the ground."

The patriot army was being created as the war began, and, looking at it realistically, even Washington and Franklin must have held doubts about the possibility of success.

The Liberty Bells

On the afternoon of July 4, 1776, the mammoth Liberty Bell in the tower belfry of Philadelphia's Independence Hall began ringing out loud and clear the long-awaited and glorious news throughout the city and countryside: independence had been declared! On that momentous day, a huge crowd, summoned by the rhythmic and resonant tolling of the one-ton bell, gathered in front of the Pennsylvania State House to hear Colonel John Nixon read the Declaration of Independence aloud for the first time.

It is a wonderful story, even if almost none of it is true. The Liberty Bell is among the most cherished symbols of freedom. Every schoolchild learns about the famous crack in the bell. The bell, its crack visible, has appeared on the reverse side of several half-dollar and silver dollar coins. America's Mercury astronauts named one of their capsules after it. Legendary frontiersman Davy Crockett was said to have gone to Washington and "patched up the crack in the Liberty Bell."

The State House Bell, as it was known until the late 1830s, certainly was not rung on July 4, and probably was not the bell that was rung four days later, the actual day the Declaration of Independence was read publicly. The wooden steeple in which it hung had been long neglected and was in such poor condition that it was feared it would topple if the bell was rung, so in all probability a considerably smaller backup bell enclosed in a second belfry "rang all day, and almost all night," according to John Adams.

The bell itself had been ordered by the Pennsylvania Provincial Assembly from London's famed Whitechapel Bell Foundry in 1751—the same company that made Big Ben a century later—to celebrate the fiftieth anniversary of William Penn's 1701 Charter of Privileges. It was finally delivered in September 1752; the copper and tin bell weighed almost a ton, was about twelve feet in circumference around the bottom and seven and a half feet at the crown, and cost £100. It was inscribed with a phrase from Leviticus 25:10, "Proclaim Liberty throughout all the land unto all the inhabitants thereof." It took six months to hang it; unfortunately, as a bell ringer named Isaac Norris wrote, "I had the mortification to hear that it was cracked by a stroke of the clapper without any other viollence [*sic*] as it was hung up to try the sound." It had cracked on the very first test stroke. Whitechapel later placed the blame on Pennsylvania, pointing out, "They did not appreciate that bell metal is brittle, and relies on this to a great extent for its freedom of tone."

Two experienced workers in a Philadelphia foundry, John Pass and John Stow, recast the bell for a fee of £36, adding copper to strengthen it and silver to sweeten its clanging tone. When it was hung for the second time and tested, the sound was so jarring that it was taken down and recast again by Pass and Stow. When the result proved no more agreeable, a second bell was ordered from Whitechapel Bell. That second bell was no more pleasing, so the original bell was left in the tower of the state house building—which years later was to become known as Independence Hall. It was hung in the attic and rung hourly to mark the time.

After the Pass and Stow bell was lowered into the brick portion of the belfry, it was used to call the Pennsylvania State Assembly together and alert citizens to special occasions and events. It announced the ascension to the throne of King George III in 1761, it summoned people for a debate about the Stamp Act—and later its repeal, it alerted them to the Battle at Lexington and Concord, and several years later was rung to mark the signing of the Constitution, George Washington's birthday, and the deaths, in turn, of founding fathers Franklin, Washington, Hamilton, and Jefferson.

During the Revolution, the bell was taken down and hidden in the floorboards of Zion's Reformed Church in Allentown, Pennsylvania. According to legend, this was done out of fear that the British would melt it down and turn it into cannons—which was highly unlikely as England's arms manufacturers were among the best in the world.

In fact, it wasn't until 1837 that it became known as the Liberty Bell, when it became a symbol for the abolitionist movement. The story that it rang out the news of independence was created by author George Lippard in an 1847 issue of the *Saturday Courier*. According to Lippard, an elderly bell ringer waiting anxiously in the steeple had begun to lose faith in the founding fathers when his grandson, who had pressed an ear to the door against the closed doors of Congress, shouted gleefully to him, "Ring, Grandfather, ring." And so the news was announced.

The news that the Declaration of Independence had been signed was actually spread by newspapers, being announced first on July 6 by the

"LIBERTY BELL."—[Sketched by Theo. R. Davis.]

By 1869, when this image was published in *Harper's Weekly*, the Pennsylvania State House bell had been cracked and recast and taken its place in American history as the Liberty Bell.

Pennsylvania Evening Post. It took more than a month for the news to reach England, as the *London Gazette* reported on August 10, "I am informed that the Continental Congress have declared the United Colonies free and independent states."

Incredibly, no one knows exactly when the crack in the Liberty Bell first appeared. Among the many stories was that it first cracked when celebrating the 1824 visit of Revolutionary War hero the Marquis de Lafayette to Philadelphia. Other stories claim it was damaged in 1835 during the funeral of Chief Justice John Marshall or in 1846 when it was rung to commemorate Washington's birthday. The original thin crack was intentionally widened to the expanse it is today during a repair effort that failed. It was silenced in 1846, as the *Philadelphia Public Ledger* reported, "The old Independence Bell rang its last clear note on Monday last in honor of the birthday of Washington and now hangs in the great city steeple irreparably cracked and dumb. . . . It gave out clear notes and loud, and appeared to be in excellent condition until noon, when it received a sort of compound fracture in a zig-zag direction through one of its sides which put it completely out of tune and left it a mere wreck of what it was."

The bell was put on display in 1852 and became a popular tourist attraction. In the 1880s it was brought to cities across the country to "proclaim liberty" and inspire patriotism. In 1915 it was displayed at San Francisco's Panama-Pacific International Exposition. While it never rang again, on very special occasions it is tapped. On D-day, June 6, 1944, for example, the dull sound of the bell being struck was broadcast on the radio to announce the Normandy invasion. And to commemorate its importance to the antislavery movement, each year it receives a gentle tap on Martin Luther King's birthday.

CHAPTER 4

GENERAL GEORGE WASHINGTON

Commanding Revolution

The situation was far worse than Washington had believed. Within months of taking command of the army he wrote, "Could I have foreseen what I have experienced and am likely to experience, no consideration upon earth should have induced me to accept this command." While these soldiers had courage and energy in abundance, they lacked discipline and the willingness to make sacrifices. Enlistments were brief, and many of the men in Cambridge would be done with it by the end of the year.

Washington immediately began trying to transform the scattershot militias into something resembling an army. As his General Orders issued on July 4 set forth:

> It is required and expected that exact discipline be observed, and due subordination prevail thro' the whole army, as a failure in these most essential points must necessarily produce extreme hazard, disorder and confusion; and end in shameful disappointment and disgrace.

General George Washington at Valley Forge in the winter of 1777, as engraved by Nathaniel Currier.

> The general most earnestly requires, and expects, a due observance of those articles of war, established for the government of the army, which forbid profane cursing, swearing and drunkenness; and in like manner requires and expects, of all officers, and soldiers, not engaged on actual duty, a punctual attendance on divine service, to implore the blessings of heaven upon the means used for our safety and defense.
>
> All officers are required and expected to pay diligent attention to keep their men neat and clean; to visit them often at their quarters, and inculcate upon them the necessity of cleanliness, as essential to their health and service. They are particularly to see, that they have straw to lay on, if to be had, and to make it known if they are destitute of this article. . . .
>
> It is strictly required and commanded that there be no firing of cannon or small arms from any of the lines, or elsewhere, except in case of necessary, immediate defense, or special order given for that purpose.

This army was desperate for the benefits of prayer, as they had little else. Among Washington's first directions was to make sure each man had at least one blanket. Feeding the army was to be a continuous problem that would get progressively worse. More immediately dangerous was the reality that the army was almost out of ammunition, possessing only thirty-six barrels of gunpowder. If the British attacked, it would be difficult to sustain a proper resistance. At one point, in fact, the commanding officer of each regiment was ordered to issue spears to thirty men who were "active, bold and resolute . . . in the defense of the line instead of guns."

Fortunately for Washington, the British were busy tending to their own needs. While the army General Howe took over was better trained and equipped than the rebels' army, it also was smaller and lacked sufficient food, as well as wood to keep its fires burning through the winter. Many of Howe's men were recovering from wounds or suffering from scurvy and smallpox. And although they had been victorious at Bunker Hill, the ferocity of the defense had been a great surprise. Gage's troops had expected to face a disorganized mob that would flee upon encounter; instead they had faced brave men who gave no quarter. This newfound respect for the rebels gave Howe pause. His army, he knew, was in no condition to launch an attack.

While few people questioned Washington's leadership, they did speculate about his tactical skill. In late August, he outlined a plan to launch a daring attack on Boston. He feared that a cold winter would make it difficult for his troops to maintain the siege. It certainly was something Howe would not expect. The element of surprise, he figured, might make up for the lack of supplies. In any case, supplies were shrinking, and if he let this time pass he might never again be sufficiently equipped to make such an attack. Washington argued for this plan passionately. His staff dissuaded him, pointing out that the British could still receive resupplies and reinforcements by sea; they suggested that he instead wait until the hardest part of the winter when the harbor would freeze. Washington agreed. But several months later, in preparation for this frontal assault, he was forced to send Henry Knox to Fort Ticonderoga to bring back the cannons, powder, and shells that had been left there after Ethan Allen and his Green Mountain Boys, along with Benedict Arnold, had captured the weapons and ammunition.

Meanwhile, Washington had to build his army, and to accomplish that, he knew, discipline was essential. Troops had to be taught to respect authority and respond to orders

In January 2005, this painting, Charles Willson Peale's *Washington at Princeton*, sold for $21.3 million, making it the most valuable Washington portrait in history. Peale produced eight copies, completing the first in 1779.

without question or complaint. "Discipline is the soul of an army," he wrote. "It makes small numbers formidable; procures success to the weak and esteem to all." He had significant work to do in order to build this discipline in his army. George Washington, the benevolent "Father of Our Country," the boy who was so honorable he would not lie about cutting down a cherry tree, was, by necessity, also a brutal disciplinarian who understood the value of fear. When appointed commander of the Virginia Regiment, the state militia, in 1755, he had imposed strict penalties: for swearing or uttering an oath of excretion a man received twenty-five lashes on the spot; for dereliction of duty or visiting an off-limits "tippling house or gin shop" he got fifty lashes. At one point, when soldiers were deserting, he erected a forty-foot-high gallows and sentenced fourteen men to hang. He chose that method of execution rather than a firing squad, he said, because "it conveyed much more terror to others." Eventually he relented and hanged only two men.

Maintaining order among as many as seventeen thousand poorly supplied, underfed men living in fetid conditions was almost impossible. Fights broke out almost daily. The oppression of the summer heat eventually gave way to the bitter cold of early winter snows. In November a company of fewer than a hundred riflemen arrived from the Virginia mountains and, according to a soldier named Israel Trask, their strange uniforms attracted attention: "Their white linen frocks, ruffled and fringed, excited the curiosity of the whole army, particularly the Marblehead [Massachusetts] regiment, who were always full of fun and mischief." Some pointed comments led to a snowball fight, which turned into a real fight "with biting and gouging on the one part, and knockdown on the other part . . . in less than five minutes more than a thousand combatants were on the field." Into the midst of the brawl, wrote Trask, "George Washington made his appearance, whether by accident or design I never knew. . . . With the spring of a deer, he leaped from his saddle . . . and rushed into the thickest of the melee, with an iron grip seized two tall, brawny, athletic, savage-looking riflemen by the throat, keeping them at arm's length, alternately shaking and talking to them. . . the belligerents caught sight of the general. Its effect on them was instantaneous flight at the top of their speed."

Washington moved into a grand mansion in Cambridge that had been abandoned by a Loyalist. He had brought with him from Virginia a considerable staff, including two cooks, his tailor, and several slaves, among them his aide, Billy Lee. Unlike many commanders, Washington believed in leading from the front and was often seen on the lines, and the troops got accustomed to seeing Washington and Billy Lee riding together.

After Washington's appointment as commander of the army, letters of congratulations from both the New York and Massachusetts legislatures addressed him formally as "Your

Excellency." While the title had royal connotations, he apparently accepted it, as he was addressed this way by his officers and men, and in official correspondence with Congress, for the rest of the war; and there is absolutely no evidence that he ever attempted to correct it.

Throughout the summer and into the fall the two sides skirmished. In late July the redcoats burned several houses in Roxbury. On August 2 an American rifleman was killed—his body was left hanging for the patriots to see. American sharpshooters spent the remainder of the day picking off British troops while losing only one additional man. On July 30, the British attempted to break out of the siege from the Boston Neck, but they were repulsed and ended up retreating, burning the popular George Tavern as they did. The following night, three hundred patriots rowed to Little Brewster Island and burned the lighthouse there while killing several troops and capturing twenty-three. Passage in and out of the city was possible with great care, so spies for both sides worked efficiently. Washington learned in late August from "various people who had just left Boston," that they [Howe's army] were preparing to "come out" through Charlestown. He sent one thousand men to prepare entrenchments and another fifteen hundred to protect them in case the British attacked. They dug through the night despite a continuous bombardment. Four men were killed, as Washington reported to Virginia's Richard Henry Lee; there was little to be done to prevent it, "not daring to make use of artillery on account of the consumption of powder, except with one nine-pounder placed on a point, with which we silenced, and indeed sunk, one of their floating batteries."

The British also had their spies, none more infamous than the supposed patriot Dr. Benjamin Church. Spy craft at the time was quite rudimentary, consisting of ciphers and simple codes, invisible inks—or "sympathetic stains"—other substances that could be materialized by exposure to heat, and masked letters in which the secret message could be read when a precut cover page was placed over the original letter. Documents were hidden in ordinary yet ingenious places; in addition to being sewn into clothing, messages might be slipped into the hollowed-out quill of a large feather or hidden in buttons. Benjamin Church was a respected patriot leader, a member of the Sons of Liberty, the Committees of Correspondence and Safety, a delegate to the Massachusetts Congress, and a liaison to the Continental Congress. Washington named him chief physician of the Continental army, essentially the surgeon general. While serving in those positions, Church was trusted with important information— which he apparently had been sharing with the British for several years. It is believed that he supplied at least some of the intelligence to General Gage regarding the captured cannons that were being kept in Concord, which prompted the British march that ended with the

While the traitorous act of Benedict
Arnold is well known, the treachery
of Benjamin Church might well
have caused far more damage. One
of Washington's most trusted aides,
Church supplied vital intelligence to
the British until he was caught—and
served less than a year in prison before
being pardoned.

shots heard round the world. But as has been the fate of spies through history, Benjamin
Church was undone by a woman.

Church's career began unraveling in August 1775, when a former mistress of Godfrey
Wainwood—a Newport, Rhode Island, baker—traveled from Cambridge to ask Wainwood
for his assistance in delivering a letter to a British official aboard a ship docked in the harbor. Wainwood was not told the contents of the letter, nor that the official was to hand it to
a Major Cane when this ship arrived in Boston. Wainwood's suspicion was raised by this
strange request and he eventually opened the letter—it was totally unintelligible, consisting
of cryptic Greek characters, numbers, letters, and symbols. Obviously it was a secret message.
Wainwood held on to it for another month or so, but when the young woman complained
that it hadn't been sent, he decided to take it to Washington's headquarters.

Henry Ward, a member of Rhode Island's assembly, wrote to Washington and warned
him that there was a spy in his inner circle and suggested he "take up the woman in so private
a way as to arouse no suspicion, and it is probable that rewards and punishments properly
placed before her will induce her to give up the author."

Washington heeded Ward's advice. "For a long time," Washington wrote to Congress,
"she was proof against every threat and persuasion to discover the author. However, at length
she was brought to a confession, and named Doctor Church." As it turned out, the woman

had been "kept" by Church. Church was immediately taken into custody. He admitted having written the letter but denied it contained important information, instead claiming that it was a note to his brother-in-law. But he steadfastly refused to decipher it. Within a few days two teams of men were able to break the code. The letter contained vital intelligence concerning the location of cannons in New York, troop strength in Philadelphia, details of a proposed attack on Canada, and, most important to Washington, an estimate of his ammunition stores.

Church claimed that he had intentionally exaggerated the army's situation in this letter, hoping to convince the British to make peace even at that late date. Although this was the only letter found, Washington surmised that Church might have passed other information that had caused unexpected failures in his strategy. In fact, the full extent of Church's betrayal wouldn't be discovered for decades. Oddly, there was no official mechanism in place for dealing with a spy. Church was sent to prison in Norwich, Connecticut, and forbidden to have pen, ink, or paper or speak with anyone at any time except the magistrate. He served less than a year, then was pardoned, supposedly because he was in poor health. He returned to Massachusetts and eventually received permission to travel to the West Indies; during that passage in 1780 his ship was lost and presumably he went down with it.

Fortunately, Church's deception was uncovered only months after Washington had assumed command of the army and long before his espionage could cause permanent damage.

The siege of Boston continued through the winter of 1776. While the winter at Valley Forge has become an important symbol of American courage, in this first winter of the war both armies suffered greatly. For the British army blockaded on the Boston Peninsula as well as Washington's troops, survival depended on the availability of wood, livestock, and plants—all of them in short supply. By November, Washington complained, "Different regiments were upon the point of cutting each other's throats for a few standing locusts near their encampments to dress their victuals with." In Boston, fences, houses, and even the Old North Meeting House were knocked down and used to fuel ovens and hearths—the famed Liberty Tree was cut down and provided fourteen cords of firewood. British soldiers joked openly about joining whatever army could provide fresh meat. One Boston fisherman wrote, "No language can paint the distress of the inhabitants, most of them destitute of wood and of provisions of every kind. . . . The soldiers . . . are uneasy to a great degree, many of them declaring they will not continue much longer in such a state, but at all hazards will escape." In fact, much of the fighting that took place in the winter months was a by-product of either getting supplies or keeping them from the enemy.

As winter settled in, Washington wrote to his wife, Martha Custis Washington, at their

This 1865 engraving depicts George and Martha Washington with their grandchildren, George Washington Parke Custis and Nelly Custis, looking at plans for the new American capitol named Washington, D.C. The servant at right may well be the renowned William Lee.

home in Mount Vernon, asking her to join him in Cambridge. While certainly he was concerned that the general's wife might be in jeopardy should there be fighting in Virginia, it's probably more accurate that he simply missed her. Martha was barely five feet tall, but she was a strong, smart woman, and the two of them formed an imposing pair. Apparently she had never before traveled outside Virginia, but after receiving his invitation she agreed to be inoculated for smallpox and then travel north. She brought with her on the three-week trip their two children and four slaves. As her coach passed through each town on her journey, people would turn out to cheer her, and an honor guard of Continental troops would escort her to the next town.

When she arrived in December, she apparently was shocked at the situation; a child of affluence, it is probable she had never been exposed to such harsh conditions. Supposedly she was stunned to see the circumstances under which the Continental army was living—many of the soldiers lacked sufficient clothing, and some didn't even have socks. Apparently she immediately went to work: She organized the women of the encampment into a sewing and knitting circle. She made socks and shirts, mended clothing for bachelor soldiers, visited the wounded in hospitals, changed bandages, and distributed food. The grateful troops began referring to her as Lady Washington. Most often she could be found sitting in the parlor, wearing a work apron and knitting. But she never forgot that she was in the middle of a war. As the cannons boomed around her she wrote, "To me that has never seen anything of war, the preparations are very terrible indeed, but I endeavor to keep my fears to myself as well as I can."

These winter hardships decimated Washington's army. The enlistment for thousands of his troops expired at the end of the year, and, rather than reenlisting, many of them were ready to go home, the lack of all supplies and necessities having, as Washington predicted, "an unhappy influence upon their enlisting." By the beginning of 1776 Washington found himself "weaker than I had any idea of," and warned Congress, "This army, if there comes a spell of rain or cold weather, must inevitably disperse." While his army still numbered ten thousand troops, in fact probably only half that number was fit for duty, and it wasn't clear that they had sufficient weapons even for those troops. As he wrote to a friend, "If I shall be able to rise superior to these and many other difficulties . . . I shall most religiously believe that the

Charles Willson Peale painted this portrait of sixty-four-year-old Martha Washington in 1795. George Washington told the artist his wife would be happy to pose for him, as "the temptation of looking well was too strong to be resisted."

finger of Providence is in it, to blind the eyes of our enemies; for surely if we get well through this month, it must be for want of their knowing the disadvantages which we labor under."

But the British government had made several significant mistakes. Among them was ordering the Royal Navy to burn patriot ships and seaports in retaliation for colonial attacks on British supply vessels. They had completely misjudged the consequences of that policy. Even after the first shots were fired at Lexington and Concord, considerable debate continued throughout the colonies about making a clean break with England; many people saw the fighting as Massachusetts's problem. In many cities, citizens' complaints focused on local enforcement of the laws and collection of the taxes, problems that might be resolved. But in October a British fleet commanded by Captain Henry Mowat anchored in the harbor of Falmouth (now Portland), Maine, as part of the plan to burn colonial ships and seaports. Falmouth certainly was not a hotbed of rebellion; in fact, there may have been as many Loyalists living there as patriots. Mowat gave the residents two hours to pack and evacuate, informing them that he had orders "to fire the town." Desperate town leaders tried to negotiate with him, but according to the newspapers he told them that "his orders were to set on fire all the seaport towns between Boston and Halifax, and then he expected New York was then burnt to ashes."

Ignoring the pleas, "in the morning he began to fire from the four armed vessels. . . . He continued firing till after dark that same day, which destroyed the large part of the town." Mowat also sent a raiding party ashore to set fire to those places the ships' guns couldn't reach. More than four hundred buildings and houses, as well as eleven ships, were destroyed. More than a thousand people were left homeless at the beginning of winter. The job done, the fleet then sailed for the next town.

The wanton attack and burning of the city was reported in newspapers in every colony. George Washington called the attack "an outrage exceeding in barbarity and cruelty every hostile act practiced among civilized nations." For many colonists this was the turning point. "Good God! What savage barbarity!" exclaimed Josiah Quincy, who had assisted John Adams in the Boston Massacre trials. "Let us no longer call ourselves Englishmen but free born Americans." Many other towns that were far from the fighting and had been protective of their independence and reluctant to become involved now opted to join the fight.

But even this renewed and expanding spirit could not substitute for a lack of supplies. Washington knew he could not maintain the blockade forever, but without sufficient guns and powder he couldn't risk an attack. The solution came through a remarkable display of courage and fortitude. On January 27, 1776, Henry Knox returned.

Henry Knox was a bookstore clerk when he witnessed the Boston Massacre. It is said that he had tried to intervene, beseeching the British soldiers to return to their barracks. Later, he testified at their trials. Knox had left school at the age of twelve and was apprenticed to a bookseller, where he developed an interest in engineering and the military. In 1771 he opened his own shop in Boston, the London Book Store. At the start of the rebellion, he aligned with the Sons of Liberty and might well have been one of the many unidentified colonists who participated in the Boston Tea Party. After war broke out, Knox and his wife of less than a year, Lucy, fled Boston. He joined the militia, helped erect fortifications, and even directed cannons during Bunker Hill. Although Knox had not yet received a commission, Washington quickly came to respect his talents—and perhaps his size. Knox was one of the few men taller than Washington—by an inch—and his weight was estimated at 280 pounds. When Knox suggested a mission to retrieve the cannons abandoned at Fort Ticonderoga in upstate New York, after the fort had been captured by General Benedict Arnold and Ethan Allen, Washington placed him in charge of the effort. "No trouble or expense must be spared to obtain them," he wrote, and authorized Knox to spend as much as £1,000—a substantial sum—if necessary. It turned out to be an epic journey.

Knox arrived at Fort Ticonderoga on December 5 with mild expectations. While at one time the fort had been well defended, Knox had no idea what he would find there now. Even if the artillery was still there, it had lain exposed without proper care for months. But Knox must have been stunned when he walked into the remains of the fort and discovered a treasure of British artillery. He eventually selected fifty-nine guns from the fort and the nearby bastion at Crown Point, consisting of forty-three brass and iron cannons, eight full-size mortars and six smaller coehorn mortars, and two howitzers—plus twenty-four boxes of ammunition and flint. He'd found more than sixty tons of weaponry, ranging in size from twenty-six iron guns weighing five thousand pounds each and capable of firing twenty-four pound cannon balls to portable coehorn mortars. And all he had to do was transport all of it three hundred miles through forests and narrow paths, across lakes, rivers, vast flatlands, and snow-covered mountains.

The incredible story of his struggle to get the cannons to Washington is equal to any tale of the Revolution. Knox's "noble train of artillery," as it became known, began by hauling the armament overland more than fifty miles until they reached Lake George. There the cannons were transferred onto large gundalows, flat-bottomed cargo transport ships built for use on shallow rivers, and the journey across the lake began. On the second day one of the boats hit a submerged rock, foundered, and sank. Knox feared its cargo was lost, but his brother, in command of the boat, managed to refloat it and land it at Fort George. There, Knox ordered built "42 exceeding strong sleds" and secured 160 oxen and horses "to drag them [over snow-covered ground] as far as Springfield [Massachusetts]." In slightly longer than two weeks, he wrote Washington quite optimistically, he hoped "to be able to present your Excellency a noble train of artillery."

Unfortunately, the ground was dry, making the sleds temporarily useless. Knox and his men and the hungry animals sat waiting for a week, until more than two feet of snow fell on Christmas Day. Then the deep and drifting snow made the roads impassable. The horses quit and the men had to leave the sleds "to undertake a very fatiguing march of about two miles in snow three feet deep, through the woods, there being no beaten path." When they finally reached Albany, General Philip Schuyler provided additional men, horses, oxen, and sleds, enabling them to slide on.

The quickest route to Cambridge required crossing the Hudson River four times. The first two passages over the frozen river were completed without difficulty. But when "the train" finally reached Albany, the weather turned and a "cruel thaw" made the ice too thin. Knox and his men, and probably some townspeople, cut holes in the ice and poured water into those holes to thicken and strengthen it; when the water froze, the ice in those places was strong enough to support the sleds. Most of them made it across successfully, but one sled fell through the ice at a place called Half Moon, a small outpost south of Saratoga. Again, Knox had chosen that spot because the river there was not especially deep, and his men were able to retrieve the cannons without too much difficulty. As Knox recorded in his diary on January 7: "Went on the ice about 8 o'clock in the morning & proceeded so carefully that before night we got over 23 sleds & were so lucky as to get the cannon out of the river, owing to the assistance the good people of the city of Albany gave. In return for which we christened her, the Albany."

This "train" climbed over the Berkshires, which he described as "mountains from which we might almost have seen all the kingdoms of the earth." When he reached Blandford, Massachusetts, his lead crew had had enough. The lack of snow and the steep descent to the Connecticut River were just too much. Knox hired more oxen and convinced his crew to persevere. By then news of this journey had reached townspeople along his route and they turned out to cheer and urge him onward. In the town of Westfield scores of people, most of whom had never seen large cannons up close, turned out to touch the guns. Knox gave them a treat; he loaded one of the large cannons and fired it.

It seemed like every day Knox was forced to deal with a new crisis. When he reached Springfield he was stalled by a second thaw. As the guns sat in the mud by the side of a road, several members of his crew from New York decided to return home, forcing him to find replacements. On the twenty-fifth, John Adams rode to Framingham to view the now celebrated train. Two days later, after fifty days of dragging, pushing, floating, and sliding, Knox arrived in Cambridge. The journey had cost exactly £520, 15 shillings, 8¾-pence, not an especially large sum in that day. But his arrival may have changed the outcome of the war. In addition to pikes and spears, Franklin's bows and arrows, and the dwindling supply of powder, General Washington had big guns.

In late January, when the waters between Roxbury and Boston had frozen, Washington considered launching a direct assault across the ice. His staff convinced him it would be disastrous. But the presence of the cannons offered another, more enticing plan.

Since the beginning of the siege, Washington had his eye on Dorchester Heights, an area overlooking Boston. General Howe, although certainly aware of its strategic value, had chosen not to occupy it. It had remained an intriguing no-man's-land through the New Year. Washington

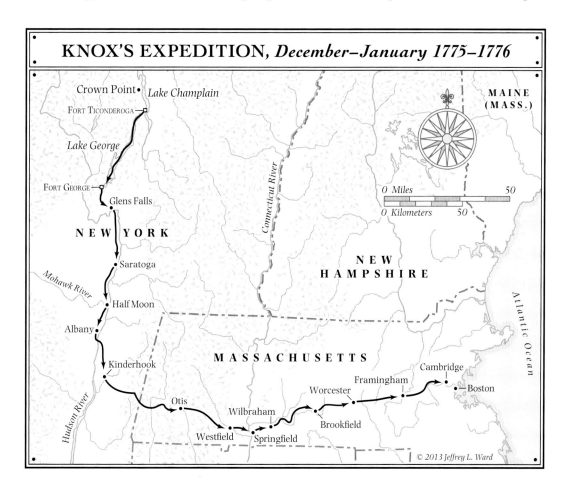

KNOX'S EXPEDITION, *December–January 1775–1776*

© 2013 Jeffrey L. Ward

KNOX ENTERING CAMP WITH ARTILLERY.

This 1855 litho depicts Henry Knox (on horseback) arriving in Cambridge with fifty-nine cannons, mortars, and howitzers after an incredible three-hundred-mile journey from Fort Ticonderoga across seemingly impassable terrain.

decided it was the perfect place from which his new artillery could rain down hell upon occupied Boston. His problem was that the frozen ground made it impossible to construct defensive earthworks, the absence of which would leave his soldiers unacceptably vulnerable. One of his soldiers suggested a relatively simple solution: construct a barrier of logs, hay bales, sticks, and rocks to offer protection from musket fire and grapeshot. Washington approved of the idea, but getting it built within range of that British musket fire and grapeshot would be more difficult. Undoubtedly Howe had learned the lesson of Breed's Hill, and as soon as he heard the sounds of building work in the night, he would organize an offensive. Washington, who of necessity rapidly was becoming a master of military improvisation, devised a plan to prevent that from happening.

Meanwhile, despite the hardships of the occupation, Howe seemed content to keep his army safely in Boston through the winter. As he wrote to Lord Dartmouth, "We are not under the least apprehension of an attack upon this place from the rebels, by surprise or otherwise." In fact, he boasted that he wished Washington would attack "and quit those strong entrenchments to which they may attribute their present safety." Apparently Howe planned to evacuate Boston in favor of New York, with its larger harbor and its proximity to the other colonies, but had decided to wait until more ships were available for transport and the weather was favorable. While the troops struggled in their barracks, the officers fared quite well. They passed the early days of 1776, wrote one officer, as agreeably as possible. "We had a theatre, we had balls, there is actually a subscription on foot for a masquerade."

Washington actually had similar thoughts as his adversary and completely understood Howe's intention, but he wanted to force Howe to fight. As he informed the council, "I am preparing to take post on Dorchester Heights, to try if the enemy will be so kind as to come out to us." Then he told Congress, "I should think, if anything will induce them to hazard an engagement, it will be our attempt to fortify these heights, as on that event taking place, we shall be able to command a great part of that town, and almost the whole harbor, and to make them rather disagreeable than otherwise."

In late February Washington received a shipment of three thousand pounds of desperately needed gunpowder from Rhode Island. While not as much as he had been hoping for, it was sufficient to allow him to put his plan into action. On February 27 he alerted his troops that the campaign was finally about to begin: "As the season is now fast approaching when every man must expect to be drawn into the field of action, it is highly necessary that he should prepare his mind." And he warned that any soldier who shirked his duty "will be instantly shot down as an example of cowardice."

Washington's message was clear: the gravity of the situation could not be overestimated.

As one of his officers noted in his diary, Washington "told the soldiery that on our present conduct depends the salvation of America." Washington had his troops prepare as much of the materials they would need as possible; wooden barricades, gunpowder, and cannons, as well as barrels filled with dirt and stones, were quietly moved into position below the heights. The barrels would be rolled down the hill if the British attacked to disrupt their formation. During the first days of March, Washington moved some of Knox's cannons into position on Lechmere's Point and Cobble Hill in Cambridge and Lamb's Den in Roxbury. On the night of March 2 these emplacements began firing on Boston, although they were too far from the city to cause much harm. The British returned fire, also to little effect. The following night Washington again began bombarding the city and again Howe returned fire. On the night of March 4, the cannons opened fire once more, and again Howe responded. But what Howe did not grasp was that this seemingly useless exchange actually was a means of providing cover while Washington's troops occupied Dorchester Heights.

Two thousand patriot troops under the command of General John Thomas marched up

The city of Boston in peacetime, 1793,
as seen from the Dorchester Heights.

the hill and began putting in place their previously built protective shield—with every sound drowned by the artillery battle in progress around them. While the British were "amused," or misled by the shelling, the patriots worked at a fever pitch through the night. They were hidden from view by a fog that covered the hilltop as well as smoke from the bombardment, but they could see by the light of a bright moon. General Howe's attention reportedly was distracted not just by the shelling but by a game of faro or, in some reports, the charms of a woman named Elizabeth Loring. By the time the sun rose the following morning, Washington's troops had put up a wall of timber and several levels of barriers in front of it, then fixed forty-three cannons and fourteen mortars in position.

Howe was stunned—and incredulous—when he woke in the morning and saw what had happened while his own guns were engaging the enemy. He was also surprised that Washington, who had not previously shown such impressive tactical ability, had somehow managed to pull off this feat. "The rebels have done more in one night," he supposedly commented, "than my whole army would have done in one month."

Howe's troops were equally astonished. One of his officers wrote that putting these cannons and entrenchments in place in one night was possible only "with an expedition equal to that of the genii belonging to Aladdin's wonderful lamp."

The success of the operation put the redcoats' continued presence in Boston in great jeopardy. The commander of the fleet informed Howe that his ships could not safely remain in the harbor. Howe ordered his own artillery to engage the guns on the heights. His cannons opened fire, but he watched helplessly as the shells fell well short of the top. They tried to elevate the guns by burying their rear wheels in the ground, but they still lacked sufficient range to reach Washington's entrenched and protected guns. Howe knew he could not remain in Boston with those guns towering above him. He had only two options: attack Washington's position in force and drive the rebels off the heights or abandon the city. The thought of giving up the town in which the rebellion had started to such an inferior force, to give them such a meaningful victory, was more than he was willing to accept. Leaving Boston for New York on his own terms and by his own timetable was an acceptable military maneuver; being forced from the city had very different ramifications. He decided to attack, and in such force that he would drive them off the hill and cause the patriot army to scatter. He gave orders for twenty-four hundred men to prepare to assault the American position that night.

Howe had taken the bait. Once again he had underestimated Washington. The rebel commander had never given up his plans to take back the city. He had about four thousand men and several floating batteries waiting on the banks of the Charles River for his signal to cross Back Bay and attack the town from three different places. When the British began their frontal assault on his positions on Dorchester Heights, he would surprise them by attacking from the rear. It was an audacious and risky maneuver, and failure could have broken his army. Once his troops landed there could be no retreat. This battle would be bigger, and bloodier, than Bunker Hill.

At the same time Washington sent additional troops to fortify the line on the heights. His troops there waited anxiously. When the assault began, they would continue to wait, until the British formation began marching up the hill. Then they would roll their dirt- and stone-filled barrels down the hill, completely disrupting the redcoats' order—and then they would let loose whatever powder they had left. There was a chance that the fate of the entire colonial uprising would be determined by Washington's bold gamble.

And then the winds began blowing.

Accurate weather forecasting did not exist at that time; predictions were as reliable as Franklin's Poor Richard could make them a year in advance. As the two armies prepared for battle, dark, ominous clouds blanketed the sky. By late afternoon the waters were so treacherous

As General Henry Lee said upon George Washington's death, he was "First in war, first in peace, and first in the hearts of his countrymen." This romanticized portrait shows him on Dorchester Heights, perhaps with the cannons carried by Knox behind him.

that no attack from the sea was possible. Howe's boats would be smashed on Dorchester's shore, while Washington's troops might be swept away. The winds continued increasing in strength; then it began raining. The "hurricane" raged into the night, forcing Howe to postpone his offensive. On the heights, Washington continued to reinforce and strengthen his barricades. The storm continued into the second day. There was nothing Howe could do but wait—and reconsider his strategy. In Boston the Reverend William Gordon had watched as the army prepared to attack. And then he wrote, "When I heard in the night how amazingly strong the wind blew (for it was such a storm as scarce any one remembered to have heard) and how it rained towards morning, I concluded that the ships could not stir, and pleased myself with the reflection that the Lord might be working deliverance for us and preventing the effusion of human blood."

By the time the storm finally ended, Howe had changed his mind. Rather than risking his army on a daring but dangerous attack, he decided to withdraw. Instead of sailing directly

General William Howe, 5th Viscount
Howe, served as Commander of the
British forces in North America from
1775 to 1778. Although Howe disagreed
publicly with Parliament's policy
concerning the colonies, he accepted the
command, explaining "he was ordered,
and could not refuse."

to New York, his army went north to Halifax, Nova Scotia, where a massive thirty-two-
thousand-man force was being assembled. When he attacked again, it would be with an
overwhelming number of troops. Munitions and property would be left behind but could
be replaced. The patriots occupied a superior position that was exceedingly dangerous to his
army and the ships in the harbor. It was better to withdraw to fight on better terms than to
lose an army in a futile effort.

On March 8, a signed letter from several Boston residents was delivered to Washington's
headquarters informing him that the British intended to make an orderly withdrawal from
the city by sea. "General Howe . . . has no intention of destroying the town, unless the troops
under his command are molested during their embarkation or at their departure. . . . If such
an opposition should take place, we have the greatest reason to expect the town will be exposed to entire destruction." The threat was clear: if Washington interfered with the British
withdrawal Howe would burn the city. To emphasize that point, Royal Navy ships moved
into position. Washington did not respond to these terms, as the letter did not come from
the British and it was not addressed to him by name or rank. But he understood its meaning.

The British army made preparations to abandon the city. This was not simply moving some troops to another post; this was a complete departure from what was essentially a military fortress. In addition to all of the troops and as much equipment as could be packed and carried to Halifax, those public officials and people who had remained loyal to the Crown throughout the occupation, and surely would suffer the consequences of that choice when the patriots returned, were offered passage with the army.

Taking no chances, Washington decided to move his troops closer. On the night of March 9 they occupied Nook's Hill, putting them in position even closer to the city. British artillery detected the movement and began a relentless shelling, but it had little effect. The following day colonists picked up more than seven hundred cannonballs.

The British spent the next few days packing the ships and destroying anything that had to be left that might benefit the enemy. The fort on Castle Island was set on fire and allowed to burn to embers. On March 10 Howe ordered all residents of Boston to hand over all the linen and woolen goods they possessed, warning that anyone who "secrets or keeps in his possession such articles, he will be treated as a favorer of the rebels"—in other words, a traitor. The cannons that could not be carried on board were spiked, their transport was smashed, and a large amount of ammunition was thrown into the harbor. Officers who had purchased goods anticipating a long stay destroyed and burned as much as they could. Loyalist looters, enraged at having to leave their homes, broke into shops and took what they wanted. As Reverend Gordon wrote, they went through the city, "carrying destruction wherever they went; what they could not carry away they destroyed." Howe did not condone this activity and, in fact, when he was informed that his troops were breaking into houses, he warned, "The first soldier who is caught plundering will be hanged on the spot." He also warned patriots that anyone found to be destroying or defacing pictures of the king or queen would be fined £50, for many people nearly a year's salary.

Days passed as British preparations progressed. The winds refused to assist a rapid departure. Meanwhile at sea, colonial privateers began intercepting inbound British merchants carrying military supplies and provisions—ships that had not been made aware of Howe's decision—and diverted them to ports under patriot control.

A wary Washington carefully watched this activity, ready to pounce should there be any signs that Howe had changed his mind. On March 16 Boston residents were warned to stay indoors to prevent harassment of the troops as they boarded their ships. But once again the winds shifted, preventing them from leaving, and they returned to their barracks. Washington was beginning to have his doubts about Howe's real intent. But on Sunday the seventeenth almost nine thousand troops, an additional thousand wives and children, and twelve hundred

Washington's success in fortifying Dorchester Heights with cannons brought from Fort Ticonderoga left Howe no choice but to withdraw from Boston. On March 17, 1776, more than eleven thousand troops sailed for Nova Scotia, a day still celebrated in Boston as Evacuation Day.

Loyalists—including Mrs. Loring—boarded more than 120 ships and sailed out of the harbor.

The evacuation of Boston was roundly criticized in England, and Howe's career was in jeopardy. It was a tremendous victory for George Washington, who had proved he was the strategic equal and perhaps even better than one of Great Britain's respected generals. Through a difficult winter he had transformed the assembly of colonial militias into an American army. His men had gained great confidence in his leadership abilities, which would prove vital as the war continued. Desperate to save his honor, Howe painted a very different picture: "The troops had evacuated Boston after having made every possible use of the town; they had left it voluntarily, and without any conversation between the king's and the rebel general. They were now gone to effect a matter of great consequence, to put Halifax in a state of safety." But that claim was intended to mask the enormity of this action.

As Washington's army watched the British fleet sail, they noticed that some sentries seemed to have been left behind on Bunker Hill to keep watch. Two scouts carefully moved forward, only to discover that the British had left wooden dummies dressed in uniforms. The colonial army went ahead and took possession of the once-bloodied battlefield. An advance force of about five hundred men commanded by General Putnam marched into Boston and claimed it, reported the *New England Journal,* "in the name of the thirteen United Colonies of North America . . . which the flower of the British army, headed by an experienced general, and supported by a formidable fleet of men-of-war, had but an hour before evacuated in the most precipitous and cowardly manner."

Not satisfied by seeing the British depart, Washington ordered his ships to harass the fleet. Among several ships captured by the patriots was one of the two carrying a vast amount of goods—including linen and woolens—stolen from the city.

Because there was an outbreak of smallpox in the city, Washington initially limited occupying troops to those who had suffered from it and therefore now had immunity. But days later his army marched in. And when they did, wrote a citizen, "the inhabitants appeared at their doors and windows . . . [and] manifested a lively joy at being liberated from their long confinement."

The end of the siege of Boston marked the beginning of a new and stronger relationship among the colonies. As historian Richard Frothingham wrote in 1850:

> The patriots now felt their strength. . . . When the siege of Boston commenced, the colonies were hesitating on the great measure of war, were separated by local interests, were jealous of each other's plans, and appeared on the field, each with its independent army under local colors: when the siege of Boston ended, the colonies had drawn the sword and nearly cast away the scabbard; . . . they had united in a political association; and the union flag of the thirteen stripes waved over a continental army. When the siege of Boston commenced, the great object and the general desire were for a work of restoration, for a return to the halcyon days of a constitutional connection to the mother country: when the siege of Boston ended, a majority of the patriots had irrevocably decided, that the only just and solid foundation for security and liberty was the creation of an independent American empire.

The Voyage
of the Turtle

When the Revolutionary War began in 1775, the vaunted Royal Navy had 131 ships of the line, although only 39 of them were considered battle ready. The colonists had no navy, although small sloops were used to harass British merchant vessels and privately owned schooners were granted letters of marque, essentially legal permission to engage and capture enemy ships. But the heavily outgunned colonists also utilized a remarkable device in an attempt to even the odds—history's first combat submarine.

The *Turtle*, as it was named by its inventor, David Bushnell, because it resembled "two upper tortoise shells of equal size," bound together side by side by iron hoops, was made of oak beams and hand "powered" by its single occupant. Bushnell, a Yale graduate, had previously invented the torpedo by proving that gunpowder could be detonated underwater. His plan was to attach this bomb to the hull of an enemy ship, but he lacked a reliable delivery system. The *Turtle* was his ingenious solution to that problem.

It was a fittingly revolutionary device. The *Turtle* was reportedly six feet in length and was the first submersible to contain its own breathing system, employ water as ballast for submerging or rising, and use a screw propeller—although it was maneuvered with a single oar. It was equipped with an extraordinary biological "lighting" system to enable the pilot to read his dials; called "foxfire," it was a luminescent blue-green fungus often found in decaying wood.

In a desperate attempt to break the British blockade of New York, the *Turtle* set out to attack Admiral Richard Howe's sixty-four-gun flagship, HMS *Eagle*, very early in the morning of September 7, 1776. Piloted by

Sergeant Ezra Lee, the craft carried one watertight wooden keg packed with gunpowder, a fuse, and a timing device attached near its top. Under the cover of darkness, Lee successfully maneuvered his craft beneath the *Eagle*'s keel without being spotted. He actually brushed against its stern and touched it before descending. As Lee began attempting to affix his time bomb to the *Eagle*, he could see British sailors on deck, completely oblivious of what was taking place just below their feet. According to the journal of Dr. James Thacher, he "struck, as he supposes, a bar of iron which passes from the rudder hinge. . . . Had he moved a few inches, which he might have done without rowing, there is no doubt he would have found wood where he might have fixed the screw. . . . But not being well skilled in the management of the vessel, in attempting to move to another place, he lost the ship." The iron sheathing had saved Howe's flagship.

This replica of the wooden *Turtle*, with barely enough room for its one-man crew, is in the Royal Navy Submarine Museum in Portsmouth, England.

Lee had no choice. He rowed away from the *Eagle* and after several minutes surfaced—into the first rays of the sunrise. There was no way to make a second attempt without being spotted. He aborted his mission and began moving as rapidly as possible toward shore. "As he passed near Governor's Island," Thacher continued, he "thought he was discovered by the enemy on the island. Being in haste, to avoid the danger he feared, he cast off the magazine, as he imagined it retarded him in the swell. . . . After the magazine had been cast off an hour, the time the internal apparatus was set to run, it blew up with great violence, throwing a vast column of water to an amazing height in the air, and leaving the enemy to conjecture whether the stupendous noise was produced by a bomb, a meteor, a water-spout, or an earthquake."

During the following week several additional attempts failed, as Lee had difficulty maneuvering in the harbor's swirling currents. The *Turtle* eventually was lost when the sloop transporting it was spotted and sunk

This nineteenth-century woodcut illustrates how inventor David Bushnell's submarine was hand-propelled and steered.

during the Battle of Fort Lee. The submersible did achieve a minor success when the unexplained explosion caused Admiral Howe to move his fleet to a less vulnerable position.

Bushnell made several additional—and unsuccessful—attempts to sink the British navy. In August 1778 one of his floating mines nearly sank the HMS *Cerberus* in Connecticut's Black Point Bay—but instead struck a small tender, killing four men and wounding several others. British troops, alerted to the threat, were ordered onshore and told to shoot at any floating pieces of wood. Several months later Bushnell launched several mines down the Delaware River in what became known as the Battle of the Kegs. These barrels of gunpowder failed to hit any ships, but one of them unfortunately exploded and killed two curious boys.

Washington recognized Bushnell's talents, referring to him in a letter to Jefferson as "a man of great mechanical powers, fertile in invention and a master of execution." In 1779 Washington appointed him commander of the Corps of Sappers and Miners, a predecessor of the Corps of Engineers. After the war, the father of submarine warfare spent time in France, perhaps working there with Robert Fulton, eventually returning and settling in Georgia where he worked as a physician.

CHAPTER 5

❖

THOMAS JEFFERSON

INDEPENDENCE DECLARED

Early in the morning of August 27, 1776, William Howard Jr. was asleep in his bedroom above his father's tavern, the Halfway House, in the city of Brooklyn. He was brusquely shaken awake and opened his eyes to see a British soldier holding a musket and bayonet inches from his head. The soldier led him downstairs, into the barroom. General William Howe, his uniform covered by a cloak, was standing by the bar, a drink in his hand. As young William would later remember, "I saw my father standing in one corner with three British soldiers before him with muskets and bayonets fixed. The army was then lying in the field in front of the house."

Howe engaged the tavern owner in calm conversation but eventually told him, "I must have some one of you to show me over the Rockaway Path." William Jr. immediately understood the gravity of the situation. There were three main roads to Brooklyn Heights where Washington's Continental army was entrenched; the passes at Gowanus, Bedford, and

🖎 A detail from John Trumbull's historically inaccurate *Declaration of Independence*. The men in this painting were never together in the same room. It was hung in the Capitol rotunda in 1826.

Flatbush were all strongly guarded. But there was one additional route, through Jamaica Pass, an old Indian trail that was little more than a narrow footpath. It was guarded by only five mounted troops. While a smaller force coming through the Gowanus Pass made a frontal assault on Washington's defenses, Howe intended to march ten thousand men through this little-used pass to launch a surprise attack on the flank.

The older Howard bravely stood his ground, saying defiantly, "We belong to the other side, General, and can't serve you against our duty."

"That is all right," the young man later recalled the general responding, "stick to your country or stick to your principles, but Howard, you are my prisoner and must guide my men over the hill." The tavern owner refused again, and Howe let him speak. But when he paused the general said coldly, "You have no alternative. If you refuse I shall shoot you through the head."

William Howard understood that he had no choice. He nodded acceptance. The Battle of Brooklyn was about to begin.

After the British evacuation of Boston, Washington had taken little time to savor his victory. He guessed that Howe would next mount a campaign to capture the much larger port city of New York, "a post of infinite importance" that was not nearly as committed to the patriot cause as Boston. While the British were boarding their ships in the harbor, Washington ordered troops under the command of Brigadier General James Sullivan to rush to New York to fortify the city's defenses before Howe could get there.

Washington didn't know that Howe had no intention of proceeding directly to New York and was instead sailing to Halifax, Nova Scotia. Howe knew he had underestimated the grit, daring, and courage of the colonists' citizen army—and its commander. That was not an error he would repeat; the next time he met Washington, Howe intended to show him the might of the British army. So he would pause in Halifax to wait for thousands of reinforcements that had set sail from Europe to join his army. Washington was right: they would fight in New York, but Howe would bring with him an overwhelming force and, he hoped, once and for all end this rebellion.

On April 4 Washington wrote to Richard Henry Lee that the British withdrawal was done—"The coast is now clear of them"—and began his journey to New York. Among those who marched with his army was the recently formed Commander-in-Chief's Guards, the "Life Guards," which were charged with protecting Washington, his official papers, and considerable cash.

The army faced an uncertain welcome in New York. While the royal governor, William Tryon, had fled and was living safely aboard the seventy-four-gun HMS *Duchess of Gordon*

In one of the greatest acts of courage in American military
history, at the Battle of Long Island in August 1776, troops from
Maryland and Delaware militias successfully covered the retreat
of Washington's army, suffering grievous casualties before
withdrawing under direct British fire, as pictured here.

docked in the harbor, many Loyalists still resided in the city. The war was devastating their business. In fact, tradesmen and merchants of the city had continued to supply the British ships anchored in the harbor. One of the first things Washington did upon arriving in New York on April 14 was send a note to the city's Committee of Safety, the ruling body, pointing out, "We are to consider ourselves either in a state of peace or war with Great Britain. If the former, why are our ports shut up, our trade destroyed, our property seized, our towns burnt, and our worthy and valuable citizens led into captivity and suffering the most cruel hardships? If the latter, my imagination is not fertile enough to suggest a reason in support of the intercourse." While such trade may well have been understandable in the past, he continued, it now constituted a real danger as "it also opens a regular channel of intelligence, by which they are from time to time made acquainted with the number and extent of our works, our strength, and all our movements; by which they are enabled to regulate their own plans to our great disadvantage and injury." But he was to soon learn that at that moment it was not the British whom he had to fear.

When Washington was settling on the southern part of Manhattan Island and preparing to reinforce his defenses, the representatives of the thirteen colonies were gathering in Philadelphia to make important political decisions. Among them was the tall and elegant thirty-three-year-old scholar from Virginia, Thomas Jefferson. Unlike the firebrands from Boston, Jefferson was the epitome of quiet reason. The word "gentleman" fit no one better than him. His father had been a planter and surveyor who had married into one of the wealthiest and most prominent Virginia families, and upon the death of his parents he had inherited a vast plantation and as many as two hundred slaves. A graduate of William and Mary College, where he had read the works of the great British philosophers, he had pursued law as a career before entering public life as a magistrate and then as a member of the House of Burgesses. While serving there he had been inspired by the stirring words of another delegate, Patrick Henry, who had responded, when accused of committing treason for comparing King George III to other tyrants, "If this be treason, make the most of it." Jefferson had laid out his own belief that Great Britain had no right to govern the colonies in his radical pamphlet, "A Summary View of the Rights of British America," which had been widely circulated and established him as a leader of the liberty movement.

When Jefferson arrived in Philadelphia, he immediately joined the debate about the future of the colonies. While many delegates wanted the congress to finally declare independence, others still held hope that they might find some way of reaching a peaceful resolution. Jefferson pointed out that it was the king who had insisted the colonies bow down to him; in fact Parliament had practically declared war by passing the Prohibitory Act of 1775, which

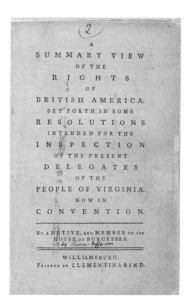

Virginia's Thomas Jefferson set down for posterity—but especially for that state's House of Burgesses—the British abuses that left colonists little choice but armed rebellion.

outlawed "all manner of trade and commerce" with the colonies and was now pressuring England's European allies to do the same.

Washington left debate to the politicians; if he was going to protect New York he needed more soldiers and equipment. His plan to defend the city required constructing earthwork fortifications in Manhattan, Brooklyn, and the Battery, the southern tip of Manhattan. At the north end of the island he reinforced Fort Washington. While these positions were strong, arming them had forced him to spread his army too thin. He stationed more than four thousand of his best men on the Brooklyn Heights, which left him woefully light in other places. Although he supposedly had twenty thousand troops, thousands of them were poorly trained, poorly equipped, or suffering from a camp illness.

In May he rode to Philadelphia, escorted by his Life Guards, to ask Congress for more troops and arms. By this point he had heard rumors that Howe was gathering a massive army in Halifax and that his brother, Admiral Howe, would join him for the attack. In fact, the king, furious after the defeat in Boston, had begun hiring seventeen thousand professional German soldiers, Hessians, to support the British army. Washington beseeched Congress: "We have not one-half the men absolutely required to hold this position; and what we have are poorly clad and equipped, and not half fed. Then we have reason to expect that the enemy will come with greater inhumanity to man, and that fire and sword will do a more fearful work than ever."

Congress eventually agreed to add twenty-three thousand men to his army. It was soon after Washington's return to New York that he discovered that he had been betrayed; Governor Tryon had somehow managed to infiltrate his closest circle, and there was a plot in progress to kill or kidnap him and his top commanders, then set fire to the city. It was, wrote future Massachusetts governor William Eustis, "the greatest and vilest attempt ever made against our country."

The Loyalists in New York had secretly remained quite active. Throughout May numerous Tories were arrested for assisting the enemy, many of them offering information to the British, but none of them had reached this level of infiltration. Governor Tryon had hatched and financed an incredibly audacious plot that, if carried out, might have ended the war. No one knows for sure how it was uncovered. In one story a woman approached Washington in mid-June and asked him for a private meeting, during which she confided in him that his life was in danger.

In another version, the daughter of tavern keeper Samuel Fraunces was working as Washing-

Long before we had a national flag, military units had their own banners. This one was created for Washington's Life Guards, the forerunner of the Secret Service, charged with protecting him.

Because the British army was fighting European enemies, Parliament hired thirty thousand German mercenaries, who fought under their own flags, commanded by their own officers. In this drawing, soldiers are departing from Hesse in 1776.

ton's housekeeper when she learned of a plan to poison his green peas with arsenic and confided in her father. Fraunces then exposed the plot to authorities. In 1785 Congress agreed that Fraunces was "instrumental in discovering and defeating" the plot and paid him a substantial sum.

What is certain is that a member of Washington's Life Guards, Thomas Hickey, was deeply involved. According to legend, Hickey was a British army deserter who had been selected to become part of this elite group in March. But after arriving in New York he had become less confident of an eventual patriot victory. At some point he had taken on a major role in this conspiracy; he was to be the assassin or the kidnapper, and after killing Washington or delivering him to Howe, he was to join others in spiking cannons in strategic locations and destroying ammunition stores.

Fortunately for Washington, on June 15 Hickey and one other member of the Guards were arrested for trying to pass counterfeit bills of credit and they were locked in custody. While awaiting trial, Hickey attempted to recruit another member of the Guards. He revealed the plot to a prisoner named Isaac Ketchum. Ketchum, who also had been caught passing counterfeit bills, reported this news to officers in an attempt to get a better deal for himself. In the following few days a small group of men loyal to Washington conducted a series of late-night raids in which more than forty people were placed under arrest, among them the mayor of New York, David Mathews, Washington's housekeeper, and an additional five or six members of his security guard. Washington himself led one of the raids. Apparently during questioning it was revealed that a woman General Washington was "especially fond of" and "maintained her genteelly" was also part of the conspiracy.

WASHINGTON AND THE GREEN PEAS.

In this 1877 wood engraving, housekeeper Phoebe Fraunces serves supposedly poisoned green peas to Washington, whom she had warned about the plot, while one of the would be assassins watches surreptitiously.

Less than two weeks later, Hickey was court-martialed, charged with "joining in a mutiny and sedition . . . and receiving pay from the enemies." He didn't deny his involvement but claimed he was only trying to make some money and ensure that if the British army were victorious, he would be safe. He was immediately declared guilty and was sentenced to be hanged. On June 28 an estimated twenty thousand people turned out to watch his execution. Intending "to make this a warning," Washington ordered every soldier not on duty to be there. At eleven a.m. Hickey was hanged, the first "American" soldier to be executed for treason.

The poisoned green peas story has been repeated for centuries, but there isn't much evidence that it's true. In the most popular versions, Phoebe Fraunces either grabbed the peas away from Washington at the very last second and threw them out the window, or warned him about them and he threw them out the window: in both, chickens ate the peas and died, proving the plot was real, and deadly.

While Washington was distracted by the conspiracy, events were taking place that would shape history. On June 8 the British fleet under the command of Admiral Lord Richard Howe had quietly slipped anchor at Halifax and sailed for New York. On the same day Hickey was hanged, the first four warships arrived off Staten Island. A lantern signal informed Washington that the British fleet had been spotted. By the next morning forty ships had assembled, and for the next several days they continued to arrive, until more than four hundred ships and transports carrying an estimated forty thousand soldiers—the largest expeditionary force in England's history—were ready to land their men and munitions. It would be more than 150 years, until World War II, that a larger naval invasion force was assembled. An American soldier wrote, "The whole bay was full of shipping as it ever could be . . . I thought all of London was afloat." On July 2 the British army landed unopposed on Staten Island. Washington had his men in place. There was nothing for him to do but wait for General Howe to attack.

Meanwhile, in the Second Continental Congress, the months of debate had finally narrowed down to one question: Would the colonies declare independence? The answer would not be reached easily. The representatives all understood that by taking this step, they would be committing high treason against the king, which had a clearly established penalty: A traitor was to be hanged by the neck but cut down while still alive, and his bowels were to be cut out and burned. Only then was his head to be cut off and his body cut into four pieces. Additionally, all of his property was to be forfeited and his family and immediate heirs were prohibited from owning property or conducting business.

On May 15 the Virginia Convention had committed itself to the path of independence, instructing its delegates "to propose to [the Congress] to declare the United Colonies free and independent States, absolved from all allegiance to, or dependence upon, the Crown or Parliament of Great Britain." On June 7 Richard Henry Lee stood up in Congress and offered the Lee Resolution, the official act of declaring independence. The following day debate began. As Jefferson wrote in his diary, some of the delegates had not yet received instructions from their legislatures and therefore could not vote. "That tho' they were friends to the measures themselves," he wrote, "and saw the impossibility that we should ever again be united with Gr. Britain, yet they were against adopting them at this time. . . . That the people of the middle colonies (Maryland, Delaware, Pennsylvania, the Jerseys and New York) were not yet ripe for bidding adieu to British connection but that they were fast ripening and in a short time would join in the general voice of America."

Other delegates, led by John Adams and Richard Lee, argued for an immediate declaration, pointing out, as Jefferson recorded, "that the question was not whether, by a declaration of independence, we should make ourselves what we are not; but whether we should declare a fact which already exists."

The opposition, led by the greatly respected John Dickinson of Pennsylvania, urged moderation, still believing that reconciliation was possible without bloodshed. A vote on Lee's resolution was postponed for three weeks to allow the delegates to receive instructions. But in anticipation of eventual approval, a Committee of Five—consisting of John Adams, Benjamin Franklin, Thomas Jefferson, Robert R. Livingston of New York, and Roger Sherman of Connecticut—was appointed to prepare a written declaration of independence. Initially they turned to John Adams, who refused, instead suggesting Jefferson. As Adams related in a letter, "Jefferson proposed to me to make the draft. I said, 'I will not,' 'You should do it. . . . Reason first, you are a Virginian, and a Virginian ought to appear at the head of this business. Reason second, I am obnoxious, suspected, and unpopular. You are very much otherwise. Reason third, you can write ten times better than I can.' 'Well,' said Jefferson, 'if you are decided, I will do as well as I can.' 'Very well. When you have drawn it up, we will have a meeting.'"

Jefferson drew up his document in only two or three days, but then spent another two weeks perfecting it, meeting occasionally and separately with "Doctor Franklin" and Adams, who apparently made very few suggestions. As Jefferson wrote years later to Henry Lee, "I did not consider it any part of my charge to invent new ideas altogether, and to offer no sentiment which had ever been expressed before. . . . This was the object of the Declaration of Independence. Not to find out new principles, or new arguments, never before thought of, not merely to say things which had never been said before; but to place before mankind the common sense of the subject."

In Alonzo Chappell's oil painting *Drafting the Declaration of Independence* (from left) Robert R. Livingston, Roger Sherman, John Adams (standing), Thomas Jefferson, and Benjamin Franklin create the most historic document in our nation's history.

Adams was delighted with its "high tone and the flights of oratory with which it abounded," although he knew parts of it would not survive congressional debate, especially a section Jefferson included "concerning negro slavery, which, though I knew his southern brethren would never suffer to pass in Congress, I certainly never would oppose." He also wondered whether it was necessary to refer to King George as a tyrant, considering it "too passionate, and too much like scolding, for so grave and solemn a document."

On June 28 Jefferson delivered his draft, titled "A Declaration by the Representatives of the United States of America, in General Congress assembled." That certainly was among the very first times the phrase "United States of America" was used in an official document.

Congress spent two days editing and revising the draft. As Adams knew, the mention of slavery was eliminated completely to retain the support of the southern states. Overall, as much as a third of the document was eliminated or changed. On July 1, the first vote was taken. Nine states voted to approve it, Pennsylvania and South Carolina voted against it, New York abstained to await further directions from the state assembly, and Delaware did not cast a vote because its two delegates were split.

On July 2, an official vote was taken on Richard Lee's resolution. There were twelve yea votes, with New York abstaining. The thirteen colonies had united to declare their independence from Great Britain. Two days later, after about eighty minor revisions to the text of the declaration, it, too, was adopted. Jefferson, who took great pride in his effort, was reportedly furious at the number of changes, but the Declaration of Independence as adopted—with all of its compromises—has served as a model for other nations around the world. Those brave fifty-six men who affixed their signatures knew it was substantially more than an official document; for them it was a death warrant. With their signatures, they were committing treason.

John Adams wrote to Abigail, "The second day of July 1776 will be the most memorable Epocha in the history of America. . . . It ought to be commemorated as the day of deliverance . . . solemnized with pomp and parade, with shows, games, sports, guns, bells, bonfires and illuminations from one end of this continent to the other."

It is not surprising that several myths swirl around the story of the signing of the most important document in American history. First, while in re-creations of the day, the founding fathers lined up to sign the declaration, in fact no one really knows who signed it when. It is generally agreed that John Hancock, president of the Congress, was the first to sign on July 4, most others signed a parchment copy on August 2, and a few others added their signatures in the ensuing weeks and even months. Supposedly, when signing in bold strokes, Hancock explained that he was writing so large so that "King George will be able to read that." There isn't any evidence that he actually said these words or anything close. Also, in legend, Hancock acknowledged that all the signers would hang together, to which Franklin replied, "We must indeed all hang together, or most assuredly we shall all hang separately." That quote appeared in print for the first time half a century after the signing.

After Congress voted its approval, an estimated two hundred copies of the document, bearing only the names of Hancock and the secretary of the Congress, Charles Thomson,

Signers of the Times

On the twenty-fifth anniversary of the signing of the Declaration of Independence, Dr. Benjamin Rush wrote to his close friend John Adams, "Do you recollect the pensive and awful silence which pervaded the house when we were called up, one after another, to the table of the President of Congress to subscribe to what was believed by many at that time to be our own death warrants? The silence and the gloom of the morning were interrupted, I well recollect, only for a moment by Colonel Harrison of Virginia, who said to Mr. Elbridge Gerry at the table, 'I shall have a great advantage over you, Mr. Gerry, when we are all hung for what we are now doing. From the size and weight of my body I shall die in a few minutes, but from the lightness of your body you will dance in the air an hour or two before you are dead.'"

The British had made it clear that affixing one's signature to the Declaration of Independence was a treasonous act, punishable by hanging. Each of the fifty-six delegates who signed it knew the risk he was taking, and doing so at a time when few people believed the colonies could defeat the mighty British army. And while the names of many of these founding fathers live in our history—men like John and Samuel Adams, John Hancock, Benjamin Franklin, Thomas Jefferson, and Richard Henry Lee—many others have been largely forgotten. But these were all men of substantial achievements, some of whom went on to make additional small marks in history, while others met a sadder fate.

Among the lesser-known signers was the thoroughly abrasive delegate from Maryland, Samuel Chase, who was known to his fellows as Old Bacon Face. Chase was a renowned orator of the time and credited with convincing

Maryland to vote for independence—although he personally did not sign the document until August 2. As a member of the Continental Congress, he was suspected of using inside information to corner the flour market and eventually lost his seat, but his tarnished reputation was restored when Washington appointed him to the Supreme Court. It was as an associate justice that he gained another kind of recognition—becoming the only Supreme Court justice to be impeached. The House claimed he allowed his political bias to affect several lower court decisions; but in fact this was a political maneuver by President Jefferson to remove Federalists from the bench. The effort failed when Chase was acquitted by the Senate, a result that many historians believe helped guarantee an independent judiciary.

Connecticut's Samuel Huntington has lived in history as the answer to a tricky trivia question: Who really was the first president of the United States? Huntington may have been the only delegate to the Continental Congress who had no formal education; he was raised on his family's farm and became a cooper, or barrel maker, and eventually a practicing attorney and judge. In 1779 he was elected president of the Congress and was serving in that position on March 1, 1781, when the Articles of Confederation were officially adopted, transforming the thirteen sovereign colonies into the United States of America. On that day his new title became president of the United States in

Samuel Huntington

Congress Assembled. While he did have a few powers as the leader of this new nation, in fact the executive office wasn't created until the Constitution was ratified in 1787.

It is probable that no delegate traveled a longer distance to independence, both literally and figuratively, than Pennsylvania's George Taylor. Born in Ireland, making him one of the eight foreign-born signers of the Declaration of Independence, he immigrated to Pennsylvania in 1736. He paid for his passage by becoming indentured, or bound, to a Philadelphia iron maker until he had worked off his debt. He rose from shoveling coal into the furnace to bookkeeper, and, when the iron maker died, he married the widow and took control of the business. He expanded the works and, as a successful businessman, was elected to the Pennsylvania Assembly. When five Loyalist representatives to the Continental Congress were forced to resign before the vote for independence, he was one of the men appointed to replace them. Signing the Declaration of Independence on August 2, 1776, may have been the first thing he did in Congress; seven months later he was replaced. But he did make one additional contribution to freedom: his furnaces produced grapeshot, cannons, and cannonballs, in addition to other weapons. He died at age sixty in 1781—before the war was won.

While none of the signers was punished by death for treason, Virginia's George Wythe was the only delegate to be murdered. Wythe was considered among the brightest and most respected members of the Congress; Jefferson

George Wythe

referred to him as "my second father" and "my faithful and beloved mentor in youth, and my most affectionate friend through life." He also was a leader in the debates about how best to respond to the British acts and was considered an important adviser to James Monroe, John Marshall, and Henry Clay. He, too, signed the Declaration of Independence in August, then left Congress to work with Jefferson in creating a constitutional system in Virginia. Accepting a job offer from the College of William and Mary, he is recognized as the nation's first law professor. In keeping with his commitment to human rights, he freed his own slaves, although two of them remained in his house to care for him in his dotage. Wythe had provided for both of them in his will, although his grand-nephew was to inherit the bulk of his estate. This grand-nephew also would inherit the bequest to the former slaves if they died before Wythe.

One morning Wythe's housekeeper saw this grand-nephew furtively throw a piece of paper in the fire and later that day, after drinking coffee,

Wythe and his two helpers were felled by terrible stomach pains. One of the former slaves died and Wythe lingered for weeks in terrible pain before finally crying out, "I am murdered" and dying. The grand-nephew was arrested for using arsenic to poison two people, disposing of the packet in the fire. Ironically, because black men and women were not legally permitted to bear witness against whites, the killer was acquitted. A legal technicality allowed Wythe's murderer to get away with his crimes, although he was disinherited.

Only a few men who signed the Declaration of Independence actually suffered because of it; among them were New Jersey delegates "Honest John" Hart and Richard Stockton. Hart was an uneducated New Jersey farmer admired for his common sense and plainspoken manner. After casting his vote for independence, he was elected the speaker of New Jersey's first assembly. In December 1776, as British troops approached his farm, the recently widowed Hart sent his children to live with friends, then escaped into nearby Sourland Mountain. According to legend, for the next few months the sixty-five-year-old Hart survived in the wild, sleeping in caves and snow-covered forests, for a time finding shelter in a natural rock formation known as the Rock House. When the patriots defeated the British at Princeton, they began to withdraw, allowing Hart to return. Although his home and lands had been plundered, he was able to rebuild and resume his position in the New Jersey legislature.

Richard Stockton was considerably less fortunate. Unlike Hart, Stockton was born into wealth—his father donated the land where Princeton University stands—and he became a well-known lawyer, horse breeder, and art collector. But he was as committed to the cause of freedom as Hart and drew up a plan that could have avoided the war by allowing America to become a self-governing British Commonwealth, like Australia. When his plan was rejected by the king and Parliament, he became more active in the fight, donating substantial sums to feed, supply, and arm Washington's soldiers. After signing the Declaration of Independence, Stockton returned to his family's palatial estate, known as Morven, which in later years served as the official residence of New Jersey's governor. When the British invaded the state, he remained there until every soldier in the area was safely gone before

Contrary to the legend in which the fifty-six signers of the Declaration lined up on July 4, 1776, and one-by-one risked death by affixing their names to it, many weeks passed before the document was finally signed.

fleeing with his family to stay with friends thirty miles away in Monmouth. But someone betrayed him and he was arrested by Loyalists, put in irons, and eventually imprisoned in New York. Congress passed a resolution urging Washington to take whatever steps necessary to secure Stockton's release; and while the legend is that he was freed in a prisoner exchange, there also is evidence that General Howe pardoned him after Stockton signed a document in which he swore allegiance to the king and agreed to cease involvement in the war. If he did sign such an agreement— and no one knows for certain what papers he signed—he was the only man who recanted his signature, but he did so only after suffering in prison. He returned home considerably weakened and was soon diagnosed with cancer. Those people who knew him well continued to support him, and after his death at age fifty in 1781, Washington wrote to his widow, "Be assured we can never forget our friend at Morven."

Ironically, among this group of lesser-known signers, Georgia's Button Gwinnett has gained the most fame. Gwinnett must have had quite a winning personality, because before entering politics he accomplished little other than borrowing considerable sums of money and losing it. He convinced various

Button Gwinnett

people to loan him money to immigrate to America from England—he was one of only two signers born in England—open a business in South Carolina, and buy a Georgia plantation, without ever repaying anyone. He also convinced Georgians to send him to the Continental Congress, where he voted for and signed the Declaration of Independence, and then, upon the death of the state's governor, to make him acting governor. A feud with Colonel Lachlan McIntosh, commander of Georgia's Continental Army militia, was settled with a duel, which resulted in Gwinnett's death from gangrene. But what has made Gwinnett so memorable, besides the several places in Georgia that bear his name, is not what he did but rather what he did not do—he did not sign his name to many documents other than the Declaration of Independence. In fact, only about fifty examples of his signature are known to exist, apparently most of them IOUs, making it the rarest and most expensive autograph of all the signers—and a great prize for collectors. Most of his autographs are owned by libraries and museums. A document he signed was sold in 2011 for $722,500—among the most valuable signatures in history.

The men who signed the Declaration of Independence were rich and poor; they were among the best educated and least educated people in the country; they were native born or immigrants from Europe; they were brave and . . . less brave; they were lawyers and ministers, farmers and coopers. Twenty-six-year-old Edward Rutledge was the youngest to sign and seventy-year-old Ben Franklin the oldest. In other words, they were as different as any group of more than fifty people might be. But one thing brought them together: the courage to risk their lives to declare America a free and independent nation.

were printed and distributed to newspapers throughout the thirteen colonies. Because sign-ing it was an act of treason, the names of the signers were kept secret until the following year. On July 8, the document was read publicly for the first time. On the ninth, George Wash-ington read it to many of his troops gathered in Bowling Green, Brooklyn, and ordered his brigade commanders to read it to those who could not attend; in response, his army pulled down an equestrian statue of King George III, ripped off its head, and carried it high atop a pole through the narrow streets of the city. That statue subsequently was melted down to provide more than forty-two thousand musket balls and bullets of "melted majesty," as one patriot described them. Similar acts of defiance took place in cities throughout the states as these newly anointed "Americans" celebrated by tearing down British signs, knocking over statues, ringing the bells of freedom, and lighting great bonfires.

The announcement that the Declaration had been signed was greeted by celebrations throughout the colonies. In this fanciful 1776 engraving, turbaned black men, presumably slaves, pull down a statue of King George III in Bowling Green, New York City.

And as the newly proclaimed nation celebrated, the massive British fleet began lifting anchor.

It took more than a month for news of the Declaration of Independence to reach England. On August 10 the *London Gazette* reported that a letter from General Howe read, "I am informed that the Continental Congress have declared the United Colonies free and independent states." By that point shots already had been fired in New York.

On July 12, Lord Richard Howe, or "Black Dick," as he was known, had dispatched the forty-four-gun *Phoenix* and twenty-four-gun *Rose* to probe American shore defenses along the Hudson River. The ships sailed several miles inland, to Tarrytown, as soldiers on land watched in awe. As they turned and began cruising back to New York, Lieutenant Alexander Hamilton, commander of a battery built on Bayard's Hill, the tallest point on Manhattan Island, ordered his men to fire on them. His gunners loaded and lit their nine-pounders. These were the first rounds ever to be fired in defense of the United States of America—and one of the cannons blew up. The misfire killed six of Hamilton's men. This was a disaster for the twenty-year-old Hamilton, whose excellent work had previously caught the attention of General Washington.

Alexander Hamilton was an unlikely American leader. He had been born on the West Indies island of Nevis, the illegitimate son of a Scottish merchant and a divorced young woman. He proved to be a brilliant student and at seventeen was sent to the colonies by several patrons to further his education. He settled finally at King's College, which is now Columbia University, in New York. In 1775, his passions aroused by the growing demands for freedom, he dropped out of school and organized his own volunteer militia unit. When the sixty-four-gun British man-of-war *Asia* sailed for Halifax in late August of that year, his unit was ordered to seize a battery of twenty-four cannons seemingly abandoned on the southern tip of Manhattan. In fact, the British had set up a clever ambush. As Hamilton's unit moved into the fort, redcoats waiting on a patrol barge floating just offshore opened fire on them with their muskets. The militia returned fire, killing one soldier. The *Asia* returned, letting loose a thirty-two-gun broadside. One shell went through the roof of the famed Fraunces Tavern. Hamilton proved his cool under fire, continuing to labor until he and the men with him successfully hauled away twenty-one cannons.

Hamilton's mathematical prowess earned him a reputation as an outstanding artillery officer, capable of plotting and adjusting the trajectory of his cannons. In March 1776, New York appointed him captain of its new artillery unit and allowed him to recruit twenty-five men. When Washington's army arrived to prepare the city for battle, Hamilton and his men constructed such a splendid fortification on Bayard's Hill that Washington praised them "for their masterly manner of executing the work." Hamilton clearly was a young officer to watch—until his cannon exploded. There were some reports that his men had been "at their cups," meaning their celebration had continued too long and they were drunk.

Whatever the truth of it, there was little Washington could do. A great army sitting offshore was preparing for battle and he needed every man. Earlier in the summer he had contemplated launching his own offensive on the British troops that had landed on Staten Island, catching them before their preparations were complete. Major General Lord Stirling apparently had drawn up a plan of attack, but a lack of able men and sufficient boats prevented him from going ahead.

On August 8, Washington put his army on twenty-four-hour watch, warning them, "The movements of the enemy and intelligence by deserters give the utmost reason to believe that the great struggle in which we are contending for everything dear to us and our posterity, is near at hand. . . . The fate of unborn millions will now depend, under God, on the courage and conduct of this army. . . . We have therefore to resolve to conquer or die."

The British kept their powder dry. While American history tends to portray them as ruthless aggressors, they actually made substantial efforts to prevent more bloodshed. Admiral Howe, who years earlier had become close with Benjamin Franklin and almost seemed sympathetic to the colonial cause, had tried to avoid this battle. Twice in July he had sent a letter addressed to George Washington, Esquire, in which he offered a basis for reconciliation, offering a pardon for everyone who professed loyalty to the king. Washington's aide, Colonel Joseph Reed, would not accept the letter, pointing out that it was improperly addressed and explaining that there was no such person in the camp of that name, the only Washington being His Excellency General George Washington. A second letter, this one addressed to "George Washington, Esquire and etc. etc." also was refused. Washington finally agreed to meet with Howe's adjutant, Colonel James Patterson, on July 20.

Patterson brought the letter with him. He regretted that General Howe was powerless to use that title because doing so meant he was endorsing the legitimacy of the rebellion. He suggested that "etc. etc." meant "everything" that would follow. Washington countered that it also could be construed to mean "anything." Patterson made the offer of pardons and again Washington corrected him, pointing out that Americans had done nothing wrong; they simply were defending their rights. Thus, as they had committed no crimes, they had no need of a pardon. Patterson continued to search for a means to resolve the conflict short of battle. Washington refused to relent. For a man facing an army of forty thousand professional soldiers supported by a great naval armada with less than half that number of men, it was a remarkable display of courage. The letter sat unopened.

In a final effort, while thousands of British troops were stepping ashore on Staten Island, Admiral Howe had a copy of the letter delivered to his friend Benjamin Franklin, who thanked him for the offer but rejected it respectfully, because it contained only "offers of pardon upon submission." Howe responded by claiming that he had the king's authority to negotiate "a lasting peace and reunion" if only the Americans would acknowledge the supremacy of the king.

Washington was a realist, yet the victory over a superior force in Boston must have emboldened him. In a letter to Hancock earlier in the summer he had written, "If our troops will behave well . . . [the British] will have to wade through much blood and slaughter before they can carry any part of our works, if they carry 'em at all."

Washington's commanders were not so certain. General Nathanael Greene, who commanded the troops on Long Island, proposed withdrawing the army and burning the city, depriving the British of its benefits, and saving the army to fight again under more favorable conditions. Washington admitted that he had considered that possibility but had decided to make his stand there.

By mid-August Howe's army had made camp on Staten Island. Watching this vast army prepare for battle, an American captain named Nathan Hale wrote to his brother, "For about six or eight days the enemy have been expected hourly, whenever the wind and tide in the least favored. . . . We hope, under God, to give a good account of the enemy whenever they choose to make the last appeal."

John Adams wrote Abigail, "The eyes of the world are upon Washington and Howe and their armies."

On August 22, Howe ferried twenty-two thousand troops and forty pieces of artillery across the Narrows from Staten Island to Gravesend Bay, in Brooklyn. They marched six miles inland, making camp at the village of Flatbush. Washington felt certain that the main assault would be made on Manhattan and that this was a bluff, intended to draw his troops out of their well-defended positions. He had put fewer than three thousand men and thirty-six cannons in Brooklyn, spread out in four shabbily constructed forts, connected by four miles of entrenchments. When he was notified that Howe's troops had landed there, he sent an additional fifteen hundred to join General Greene's forces.

All attempts at making peace had failed, and Howe prepared for battle. He would not repeat the mistakes he'd made in Boston. This time he would seize the offensive with an overwhelming army and continue fighting until the rebellion was crushed. On the night of August 27, he walked into William Howard's Halfway House, and sometime later he walked out with Howard and his son, who would guide his men through the night.

Howe's column was two miles long, led by guides followed by "pioneers," who were to saw down any trees that blocked the passage of cannons. His men had left their campfires burning to deceive any Americans who might be watching. Soon into their journey, five American guards, who mistakenly believed the approaching troops were friendly, were captured without a shot being fired.

Just before midnight on August 26, the first shots of a battle that was to become known as both the Battle of Brooklyn and the Battle of Long Island were fired. The British began the frontal assault through the Gowanus Pass, one of the four routes into Brooklyn. The Americans, occupying the high ground, fought back ferociously. Washington's strategy was to meet the initial assault, then have his men retreat into the fortifications on Brooklyn Heights—knowing that the British would pursue them right into his cannons. The superior position on top of the hill would give the Americans a strategic advantage.

At precisely 9:00 a.m. Howe fired his cannons, the signal that the flanking attack was about to begin. At that moment Hessian troops began a frontal assault on the center of Washington's defenses. At about the same time Washington accepted that he had been wrong, that this was the real attack, and ordered more troops to move quickly to Brooklyn. The Americans initially were able to blunt the attack, not yet aware of Howe's flanking maneuver. But as the battle raged, Howe's trap was revealed. The American troops were blocked on three sides, and the only possible escape was across the eighty-yard-wide Gowanus Creek. With no other option available, and some of his units now outnumbered by as much as ten to one, Washington ordered a retreat to the fortifications on Brooklyn Heights.

As the main elements of the American army desperately withdrew, Lord Stirling's 1st Maryland Regiment, known as the Maryland 400, held the line against the overwhelming British force for more than a half hour at a place known as the Old Stone House. The regiment made as many as six counterattacks on troops commanded by General Charles Cornwallis, trying to break through the lines. The Hessians took no prisoners, bayoneting even those men who threw down their muskets and surrendered. A British regular wrote in his diary, "We took care to tell the Hessians that the rebels had resolved to give no quarter to them in particular, which made them fight desperately, and put all to death that fell into their hands."

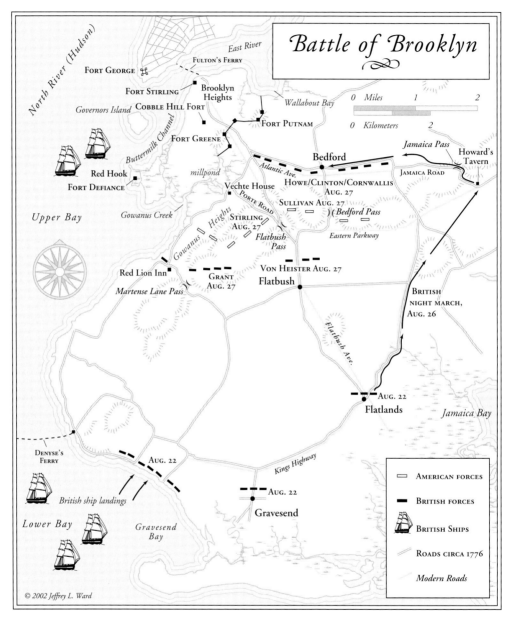

This map of the Battle of Brooklyn, also known as the Battle of Long Island, includes numerous details about the fighting in which the British conquered New York.

Watching this battle at a distance, General Washington remarked with great sadness to one of his commanders, General Putnam, "Good God, what brave fellows I must this day lose."

After more than 3,000 men had successfully escaped the trap, the surviving Marylanders made a break for it, trying to get across the creek. Many of them got bogged down in the mud and only 12 men made it safely back to American lines. More than 360 Americans died that day and another 1,100 were wounded or captured. Lord Stirling was surrounded and taken prisoner, but his courage and that of his men, who sacrificed themselves for this new country, had saved Washington's army. In reports of the battle one newspaper referred to him as "the bravest man in America."

The American losses had been catastrophic. According to General Howe's reports, the British had lost only 367 men.

With his victory assured, Howe made a fateful decision. The American fortification on Brooklyn Heights was about two miles across and one mile deep. A frontal assault would cost hundreds, perhaps thousands of lives. So rather than pressing his attack as his staff suggested, Howe ordered his army to halt. With his army in front of the entrenched Americans and the Royal Navy blocking the East River at their rear, there appeared to be no escape for the patriots. Howe ordered his cannons brought forward, stretched his lines to encircle Washington's troops, and settled in for a siege, confident that Washington's army must either surrender or die on the heights.

Once again, though, the weather intervened unexpectedly. A nasty rainstorm accompanied by unfriendly winds on the twenty-eighth made it impossible for the British fleet to sail up the East River, which separated Washington's troops in Brooklyn from the safety of Manhattan. While the British built earthworks in preparation for their eventual attack, Washington spent that day visiting camps and encouraging his men, trying to raise their battered morale. But as the toll of the battle became clearer to him, he accepted the vulnerability of his position. Somehow he had to get his men across the river directly under the watchful eyes of the enemy. To make that feat possible, he turned to Colonel John Glover and his "Marvelous Men from Marblehead," the 14th Continental Regiment, consisting almost entirely of Massachusetts fishermen.

John Glover had been serving in the militia since 1759. During the Siege of Boston, Washington had chartered Glover's schooner, the *Hannah*, to harass and raid British supply ships. The *Hannah* was the first privateer in the service of the Continental army, and it has been celebrated as the first ship of the United States Navy. Washington told Glover that somehow, in the dark of night, he and his men had to ferry the entire American army across

General Howe's victorious
army lands in New York in
September 1776, beginning
an occupation that was to last
seven years.

the river. An aide, Colonel Benjamin Tallmadge, later wrote of the situation in a letter: "To move so large a body of troops, with all their necessary appendages, across a river a full mile wide, with a rapid current, in the face of a victorious, well-disciplined army nearly three times as numerous . . . and a fleet capable of stopping the navigation so that not one boat could have passed over, seemed to present most formidable obstacles."

No one knows for certain how Glover was able to assemble his makeshift armada within a few hours. And yet he did it, pulling together a miniature fleet of rowboats, sailboats, one schooner, and numerous flat-bottomed craft capable of carrying horses and artillery.

In addition to somehow hiding this massive operation from the enemy, they had to overcome three natural factors: time, tides, and the wind—and any of them could prevent or end the operation. Washington was depending on the dark to conceal the evacuation, and the late August night was one of the shortest of the year. Any man left on shore at sunrise would be lost. Unfriendly tides might make rowing more difficult, and a lack of wind would make sailing impossible.

But Washington had no choice. Suspecting that spies in his camp would see Glover's boats gathering and give away his plans, he devised a clever ruse. He sent a message to General William Heath in Manhattan, advising him, "We have many battalions from New Jersey which are coming over this evening to relieve those here. You will please, therefore to order every flat-bottomed boat and other craft fit for transportation of troops down to New York as soon as possible." If that message was intercepted, as Washington thought it would be, Howe would believe the boats were to carry reinforcements to Long Island rather than ferry Washington's army to Manhattan. To get his men ready without disclosing the plan, he ordered his commanders to prepare them for a nighttime attack.

The storm remained stationary over the area, the thick, dark clouds blocking the moon and intermittent rain obscuring visibility for more than a few feet. One of the most unusual episodes of the Revolutionary War began at ten o'clock. The troops were told unit by unit that they were being relieved and sent back to Manhattan, so none knew that the whole army was retreating. They were ordered to leave their fires burning and their tents in place, cover their wagon wheels with rags to muffle their sounds, and then proceed briskly and silently to the river.

Glover had managed to assemble a fleet of oars and sail, manned by the seamen of Marblehead. For the first few hours the evacuation went well, and the cooperating winds and tides enabled the boats to make the two-mile round-trip without difficulty. But after midnight, with half the army still on Long Island, the winds shifted and an unusually strong ebb tide made the trip long and difficult for rowboats and sailing ships alike. The sailors struggled through the night, and a few hours before sunrise the winds shifted once again and caught the sails. It was an efficient operation, but as dawn approached Washington realized it had not been good enough. The rearguard was still waiting on the shore for transport and there were only minutes until the sun revealed their presence.

In many of his letters and diary entries during the war, Washington made reference to Providence, the hand of God or nature that had helped deliver his men. This certainly was one of those instances. As the sun rose on the morning of the twenty-ninth, a dense blanket of fog rolled in and covered the entire area, saving hundreds of men. It would take more than an hour before the sun would burn it off, and by then all nine thousand troops and almost all of the horses, supplies, powder, and cannons were safely across the river.

Washington and Colonel Benjamin Tallmadge were among the last men to leave. Tall-madge regrettably had to leave his favorite horse tied to a tree—but when he reached the

After being defeated in the Battle of Long Island, Washington successfully saved the remnants of his army with a daring retreat, pictured here, across the treacherous mile-wide East River. If Howe had been able to prevent this withdrawal, the revolution might have ended on the shores of Long Island.

other side he decided to go back and get it. "I called for a crew of volunteers to go with me," he wrote, "and guiding the boat myself, I obtained my horse and got off some distance into the river before the enemy appeared in Brooklyn."

Later that day the British fleet sailed up the East River, but the miraculous escape was a complete success. In only nine hours, Washington's army had been saved.

The question became what to do now. From the high points the British now occupied in Brooklyn, Howe's artillery could reach much of the city. Within hours they could reduce it to rubble or burn it to the ground. Washington did not believe either was likely. With so many Loyalists still living in the city, Howe would not dare destroy it, and his troops would need the houses and buildings through the winter months. He would have to attack, Washington knew, and drive the American army out of the city.

Perhaps more than anything else at that moment, Washington needed reliable intelligence. He needed to know what Howe intended to do and when he would strike. He needed to know the disposition of his forces and the level of his powder and supplies. What Washington needed was a reliable spy.

At the time, spies were considered men without honor or integrity. Most often they were civilians living behind enemy lines who would pass along intelligence because they believed in the cause, were paid, or were threatened. Washington had previously sent several spies on missions but had received only sketchy and somewhat dubious information from them. But he was desperate. With his army outnumbered, and soldiers deserting in growing numbers, his only chance for victory was to learn the enemy's plans. As he complained on September 6, "We have not been able to obtain the least information as to the enemy's plans."

Finally Washington turned to Thomas Knowlton, who, a month earlier, had been promoted to lieutenant colonel and authorized to form a small and select unit to carry out specialized reconnaissance missions. This consisted primarily of going out well in front of the army and observing enemy movements through a telescope. Knowlton's Rangers were America's first unit of elite troops. Knowlton himself had already distinguished himself on special missions. During the Siege of Boston, Washington had sent him into the city to burn the buildings at the base of Bunker Hill that provided cover for the redcoats and to capture a British guard for interrogation. Knowlton accomplished that mission without being detected.

Among the men Knowlton selected for his Rangers was a twenty-one-year-old schoolteacher named Nathan Hale. After graduating from Yale University, Hale had taken a position at a public school supported by "the gentlemen of New London, Connecticut." Like so many other young men, he shared the dream of freedom. He had already joined the local militia. Days after Lexington and Concord, he stood up at a meeting in church and proclaimed,

"Let us march immediately, and never lay down our arms until we obtain our independence." Hale was determined to finish the last few months of his contract at the school, but then he received a letter from his classmate and friend, Benjamin Tallmadge. "Was I in your condition," Tallmadge wrote, "I think the more extensive service would be my choice. Our holy religion, the honor of our God, a glorious country, and a happy constitution is what we have to defend." The next day Hale resigned his teaching position and accepted a commission as first lieutenant in the 7th Connecticut Regiment. He served loyally through the opening months of the war but saw no combat. When offered the opportunity to join Knowlton's unit—possibly because he was one of the few Yale graduates serving on the front lines—he accepted the challenge. He was put in command of a reconnaissance company watching the Westchester and Manhattan shorelines. It was important but tedious work.

In early September Washington had called upon Knowlton to find a volunteer willing to put on civilian clothes and go behind the English lines to gather intelligence. It isn't known if Washington found it necessary to remind the colonel that the ignoble penalty for spying was death by hanging. Knowlton gathered his officers and told them about this conversation, then asked if there was a volunteer. After several seconds of absolute silence, Nathan Hale spoke up, the only person to do so, volunteering, "I will undertake it."

Another classmate from the university, William Hull, tried to talk Hale out of what he believed to be a suicide mission. It was a dangerous job, Hull said, and Hale lacked the experience and the necessary tools. He had no training for the work, nor did he have the nature for it: Hale was "of too frank and open a temper to act successfully the part of a spy, or to face its dangers; he was too open to deceit and disguise, and it probably would lead to an ignominious death." Hull pleaded with him to "abandon the enterprise . . . for the love of country, for the love of kindred." The risk was too great. Live; and fight for the country!

Hale listened politely to his friend, then explained, "I wish to be useful, and every kind of service necessary to the public good becomes honorable by being necessary. If the exigencies of my country demand a peculiar service, its claims to perform that service are imperious." He had spent more than a year in service, and he had been paid, but had made no accomplishment worth mentioning. As he had wished, he finally was getting the opportunity to do something meaningful for his country.

While there is no official record of Nathan Hale meeting with General Washington, which is not surprising considering the highly secretive circumstances, the story has been told that they did indeed meet privately. And undoubtedly Washington praised his courage and outlined his needs for information. No one knows if Washington watched Hale depart.

Crossing the Delaware

German artist Emanuel Leutze's circa-1850 painting of George Washington crossing the ice-covered Delaware River may be the best-known image from the Revolutionary War. In this painting General Washington is standing nobly in the front of a small boat as oarsmen push large chunks of ice away, while other boats are slightly in the distance behind him. It is indeed a stirring image, although it bears little resemblance to what actually happened. The real story is far more heroic than the artist portrayed.

By the end of 1776 a series of defeats had pushed Washington's army out of New York and New Jersey. The once promising lamp of freedom had

Washington Crossing the Delaware, oil on canvas, Emanuel Leutze.

dimmed. It was becoming clear that this colonial army was no match for the haughty British and their Hessian allies. In late December the patriots were camped in Delaware with little hope of victory. The army was already weak and under-supplied and many men intended to go home when their enlistments expired at the end of the month. There was a small boost in morale in late December when Washington ordered Thomas Paine's stirring new pamphlet, "The American Crisis," read to his troops: "These are the times that try men's souls," Paine wrote. "The summer soldier and the sunshine patriot will, in this crisis, shrink from the service of his country; but he that stands it now, deserves the love and thanks of man and woman. Tyranny, like hell, is not easily conquered; yet we have this consolation with us, that the harder the conflict, the more glorious the triumph."

But Washington knew that far more than inspirational words were necessary. His men needed the hope that only a military victory could provide. While the enemy sat safe and secure in his winter headquarters, Washington knew that he had only one significant advantage: surprise. And so he planned one of the most audacious, difficult, and unexpected attacks in military history. It was a bold stroke and the outcome of the war might depend on his success. Under the cover of night he intended to row and pole thousands of troops across the swollen Delaware River to surprise the Hessian troops warmly encamped in Trenton. The password for attack was straightforward: "victory or death."

Washington's troops certainly must have been stunned that Christmas Day when informed at regular afternoon muster that they were about to embark on a secret mission. They marched silently to the river and waited till dark—and as they did the weather turned on them. The wind began to blow and it started snowing. Rather than the daylight crossing in fair weather depicted in Leutze's painting, the extraordinarily dangerous crossing was made during a raging storm in the night.

An estimated twenty-four hundred men, eighteen cannons and ammunition, and as many as seventy-five horses made the crossing, engineered by Colonel Henry Knox. Supposedly among them were future presidents James Monroe and James Madison, future Supreme Court justice John Marshall, and Alexander Hamilton and Aaron Burr. Rather than the shallow rowboat in the painting, they used flat-bottomed freight boats and almost definitely Washington remained seated; if he had attempted to stand up in a small boat while crossing an ice-filled river in a storm, the result most probably would have been disastrous.

Other details in the painting also are inaccurate, among them the fact that the flag being carried in the boat actually wouldn't exist for another six months and that chunks of ice did not clog the Delaware.

But the defiant spirit conveyed by Leutze is absolutely accurate. Washington certainly understood what he was risking that night. Three contingents were scheduled to cross the river, but only the largest group, led by Washington, successfully made the crossing. Washington decided to proceed with his mission, a direct attack on the Hessian camp at Trenton. One of the soldiers who made that crossing later wrote, "Our horses were then unharnessed and the artillery men prepared. We marched on and it was not long before we heard the out sentries of the enemy . . . retreated firing, and our army, then with a quick step pushing on upon both roads, at the same time entered the town. Their artillery taken, they resigned with little opposition, all Hessians, with 4 brass field pieces; the remainder crossing the bridge at the lower end of the town escaped."

While popular history infers that Washington caught the Hessians stuffed, drunk, and sleepy from a night of celebrations, respected historians report no evidence of that. In fact, fife player John Greenwood wrote, "I am certain not a drop of liquor was drunk during the whole night, nor, as I could see, even a piece of bread eaten, and I am willing to go upon oath that I did not see even a solitary drunken soldier belonging to the enemy."

The surprise attack had been a complete success, catching the enemy unprepared. The Hessians fought bravely but briefly before surrendering. A reported twenty-two Hessians were killed, eighty-three wounded, and almost nine hundred men captured, in addition to a substantial store of weapons and supplies. Two Americans died from frostbite because they had no shoes and eight others were injured in the fighting, among them future president James Monroe, who nearly bled to death. While the plan originally called for Washington's army to march on Princeton and New Brunswick after capturing Trenton, the failure of the other two elements to reach their objectives made that impossible. Washington wisely withdrew with his prisoners—and his victory.

While the capture of almost a thousand men surely was significant, the victory's greater value was in boosting morale. It demonstrated that ordinary Americans could defeat the previously feared Hessians. General Howe supposedly was stunned that his elite—and expensive—soldiers could be so easily captured by the rebels. Some historians believe the Battle of Trenton may have even marked the turning point of the war. Congress, greatly buoyed by the success, agreed to pay a $10 bonus to each man who agreed

This heroic portrait of Washington about to dismount and join his army in crossing the Delaware River was painted in 1819 by famed American portrait artist Thomas Sully.

to stay for an additional six weeks after his enlistment ended. As the soldier Elisha Bostwick recorded, "I engaged to stay that time and made every exertion in my power to make as many of the soldiers stay with me as I could, and quite a number did engage with me who otherwise would have went [*sic*] home."

The monumentally large romantic painting *Washington Crossing the Delaware* is twelve feet by twenty-one feet and was painted in Düsseldorf, Germany. When it was exhibited in 1851, more than fifty thousand people came to see it. It is now on display at the Metropolitan Museum of Art in New York.

CHAPTER 6

Benedict Arnold

American Traitor

General Howe's army had been settled in New York City for only a few days when the great fire began during the afternoon of September 21, 1776. It was believed to have been ignited near the Fighting Cocks Tavern, a bar and brothel in the lower part of the city not far from Whitehall Slip in the Battery. It raged throughout the night, spread by a southwest wind. By the time it burned itself out, more than five hundred buildings, as much as a quarter of the entire city, had been destroyed.

The British immediately suspected arson. Alarm bells had disappeared, handles had been cut off fire buckets, and many of the city's cisterns were mysteriously empty. Even as new fires appeared to spring up without cause, incensed soldiers raced through the city arresting—or killing—suspects. "Some of them were caught with matches and fire-balls about them," wrote an eyewitness to the Great Fire of New York, Ambrose Serle. "One man, detected in the act, was knocked down by a grenadier and thrown into the

☞ A mezzotint of Colonel Benedict Arnold, "who commanded the Provincial Troops sent against Quebec through the wilderness of Canada and was wounded in storming that city under General Montgomery," published in 1776, oddly, in London.

flames for his reward. Another, who was found cutting off the handles of water buckets to prevent their use, was first hung by the neck till he was dead and afterwards by the heels upon a signpost by the sailors. Many others were seized . . . and, but for the officers, most of them would have been killed by the enraged populace and soldiery."

Officially the cause of the fire was never determined. But the royal governor, William Tryon, blamed Washington, claiming, "Some officers of his army were found concealed in the city." Among them was Nathan Hale.

Disguised as a schoolteacher seeking employment, supposedly carrying his Yale diploma, Hale had spent several days behind British lines gathering information. His notes and hand-drawn maps were concealed in the soles of his shoes as he waited on the Brooklyn shores to meet the boat that would carry him to safety. It isn't known how Hale was captured. There were claims he was recognized and exposed by a Loyalist cousin, Samuel Hale. But most

This hand-colored French etching from about 1778 depicts the looting and violence that took place during the great fire that destroyed almost one quarter of New York only days after the British occupied the city.

likely he was caught by Robert Rogers, the founder of the legendary Rangers who had laid the foundation for modern-day special operations during the French and Indian War. Hale had attracted Rogers's curiosity and, after Rogers falsely professed to be a patriot spy to gain his confidence, admitted his mission.

Hale was arrested while smoke from the great fire was still rising over the city. No evidence was found that he was an arsonist. But he was caught up in the British fury over the fire. Several days earlier the Americans had caught a lieutenant colonel named Ledwitz, trying to sell information to the British; he claimed in a letter to Howe found on his person that he had joined Washington's army only to save himself and his family. While the penalty for treason was death, a military court-martial voted to spare his life. Nathan Hale was not so fortunate.

He was locked in the brig aboard the *Halifax* and transported to the city. On the afternoon of September 21 he was brought in front of General Howe. Apparently he identified himself and admitted his mission. Howe pronounced the only penalty permitted: Hale would be hanged the next morning. While dozens of men and women all over the city were being detained, arrested, or even killed on suspicion of being involved in the Great Fire, there is no indication that Howe believed Hale was involved.

Nathan Hale spent some of his last night alive with Howe's chief engineer, Captain John Montresor, who later remembered, "He was calm, and bore himself with gentle dignity, in the consciousness of rectitude and high intentions." At about eleven in the morning he was marched to a nearby apple orchard. A rope was thrown over a heavy branch and then placed around his neck. A small crowd gathered to watch the American spy hang, among them the engineer Montresor. Provost Marshal William Cunningham, known to be an especially hard and brutal man, asked Hale if he had any final words. And then Nathan Hale did or did not say the words that have been etched into history: "I only regret that I have but one life to lose for my country."

There is no actual record of Hale's final words. Apparently the day of the hanging, Howe sent Montresor to deliver a message to Washington. Traveling under the protection of a white flag, he met Hale's friend, William Hull, and informed him of what had happened, then quoted those last words. The statement actually was paraphrased from Joseph Addison's 1712 play, *Cato*: "What a pity it is / That we can die but once to serve our country." The well-educated Hale would have read the play or seen it performed. So it certainly is possible, but there are several other equally probable stories that quote far different words.

For example, British lieutenant Frederick MacKensie wrote in his diary that same day that he had been told by a witness, a farmer named Tunis Bogart, that Hale "behaved with great composure and resolution, saying, he thought it the duty of every good officer, to obey

On the night of September 22, 1776, General
Howe wrote in his orderly book: "A spy from the
enemy by his own full confession, apprehended
last night, was executed this day at 11 o'clock
in front of the Artillery Park"—thus coldly
recording the fate of the patriot Nathan Hale.

any orders given him by his commander in chief; and desired the spectators to be at all times prepared to meet death in whatever shape it might appear."

The first newspaper report of the hanging appeared less than a year later in the *Essex Journal*, which reported that his final words were, "You are shedding the blood of the innocent. If I had ten thousand lives, I would lay them all down, if called to it, in defense of my injured, bleeding country." And in 1781 the *Independent Chronicle and the Universal Advertiser* quoted another version of Hale's last words, closer to the ones that have been made famous. "I am so satisfied with the cause in which I have engaged, that my only regret is that I have not more lives than one to offer in its service."

Whatever his actual words, his patriotism could not be questioned. And because of that, Nathan Hale, a young man who failed to complete his only mission as a spy, has earned a place in American history.

After his execution his body was left hanging for three days, until it was cut down and buried in an unmarked grave. If that was intended to serve as a message to would-be spies, it failed.

Hale's death apparently caused barely a ripple among American troops. Few people knew him, much less his mission, and its impact seemed minor measured against the great events of those days: the burning of the city and Washington's fear of another British assault.

But Washington still had a desperate need for reliable information. Greatly outnumbered by better-trained and -equipped troops, his only hope for victory was to gain early knowledge of the enemy's plans and the disposition of his forces. To accomplish that, he turned to his aide, Colonel Benjamin Tallmadge, who had been a Yale classmate of Hale's. Tallmadge, who had been born on Long Island, had established a small spy network on the island and in New York that became known as the Culper Ring, consisting mostly of friends from schooldays and ordinary citizens committed to the Revolution. Using clever methods to relay information—for example, the female member of the ring, Anna Strong, would hang a black petticoat on her clothesline when there was a packet of documents to be picked up on her farm—the group was responsible for alerting Washington that Howe intended to attack newly arrived French troops at Newport, Rhode Island. It also detected a massive British counterfeiting operation. But the group's signature success was uncovering Major John André and General Benedict Arnold's plot to surrender the vitally important fort at West Point to General Howe.

Throughout all the wars of American history, few stories are as compelling, as complex, or as mystifying as that of Benedict Arnold, whose name was to become synonymous with betrayal. For a time, Benedict Arnold was a true hero; he began the war as a patriot and his courage and leadership in battle contributed significantly toward the eventual victory. But obviously heroism is not his legacy.

Most Americans know the end of the story—Benedict Arnold's betrayal of Washington. But what is it that would cause a man of proven courage and honor to give up his most closely held beliefs and betray those people closest to him?

Nothing in Benedict Arnold's early life suggested that he would become the most notorious traitor in American history. Like so many military officers of that time, Arnold was born into privilege. His father was a wealthy Connecticut businessman who sent his son to prestigious schools in Canterbury in the expectation that eventually he would attend Yale. He was considered to be smart and clever and his path seemed laid out nicely for him. But when three of his sisters died of yellow fever, his father began drinking excessively, which led to financial ruin. Benedict's life changed quickly and drastically; his father had lost the family fortune and, with it, his son's future. Rather than head to the leafy walks of Yale, Arnold was withdrawn from secondary school and apprenticed to his cousin's successful apothecary business. As a sixteen-year-old, he took a brief leave from the business to join the Connecticut militia in the French and Indian War, but returned within weeks without being involved in any action.

Those who have looked for reasons why Arnold chose to betray his country often begin with this sudden change of circumstances. But at first he appeared to have adjusted well, and even prospered. After concluding his seven-year apprenticeship, he opened his own apothecary and bookstore in New Haven with his only surviving sister. That shop was so successful that he eventually purchased a share in three merchant ships carrying goods from the West Indies. Arnold had learned life's hard lessons and had a reputation as a tough man who would not back down. He was reputed to be an excellent shot and a strong and relentless fighting man. He often commanded one of his ships and supposedly once challenged a British captain named Croskie to a duel after being insulted as a "damned Yankee, destitute of any good manners or those of a gentleman." He wounded his opponent, who apologized after Arnold threatened to kill him.

When the British trade acts drove him into debt, Arnold became a skillful smuggler. Once again he was threatened with losing everything that mattered to him. But his aptitude for business eventually enabled him to prosper, and he became one of New Haven's most successful and respected merchants. He owned ships, wharves, shops, and even slaves and servants. He lived with his wife and their three children in what was described as one of the finest mansions in the city.

But like so many colonists, Arnold became angrier with each British slight. He was trading in the Caribbean when news of the Boston Massacre reached him. Knowing only the most basic facts, he reportedly was stunned that the British had started shooting protesters. As he wrote to a merchant friend, "Good God! Are Americans all asleep and tamely giving up their glorious liberties, or are they all turned philosophers that they don't take immediate vengeance on such miscreants?"

In response Arnold became active in the Sons of Liberty and was elected a captain of the militia. As politics moved seemingly inevitably toward war, he spoke publicly for liberty from the British oppressors and prepared his men to fight. Few men so openly challenged British rule.

After news of the battle at Lexington and Concord reached New Haven, the citizens voted narrowly to stay out of the fighting. But Arnold gathered about sixty men, who vowed to march to Boston to give support to the cause. The following morning he led his militia to the city's armory where the gunpowder was stored. When the commander of the local militia warned him that he was not permitted to hand over the keys without orders, Arnold reportedly responded, "Regular orders be damned and our friends and neighbors being mowed down by redcoats. Give us the powder or we'll take it!" When the commander continued to resist, Arnold warned, "None but the Almighty God shall prevent my marching!"

With their fill of powder, they marched to Boston and helped enforce the siege.

Samuel Adams and other colonial leaders believed General Gage would try to lift the siege by bringing troops down from Canada. If he was able to relieve his troops in Boston, Gage also might successfully isolate the New England colonies—those places stirring the pot of rebellion. The quickest way to get the British into the fight was to bring them down through Lake Champlain to Lake George and then to the Hudson River. There was at least one good way to prevent that—take Fort Ticonderoga.

Fort Ticonderoga—"Ticonderoga" was an Iroquois word meaning "between two waters" or "where the waters meet"—was strategically located between the western shores of Lake Champlain and Lake George, and offered access to the Hudson River. Originally known as Fort Carillon, it had been built by the French in 1755 and was considered "the gateway to the continent," the most heavily contested piece of land during the French and Indian War. The British suffered more than two thousand casualties in an unsuccessful attempt in 1758 to take the fort—the bloodiest battle of that war—although they did return and drive out the French a year later. But before the French withdrew, they blew up the fort's magazine. In the ensuing years, with the French no longer a threat, the fort fell into disrepair. But colonial leaders understood its potentially vital strategic location—and even more important, they had heard tantalizing stories that the British kept a large amount of artillery there.

Arnold had traveled extensively through the region and was aware that the fort was ideally located and lightly defended. He convinced the Massachusetts Committee of Safety to fund a secret mission to capture the fort. The committee commissioned him a colonel and authorized him to recruit as many as four hundred men to capture the fort and return with any materials that might prove useful.

Arnold was not the only person to recognize Ticonderoga's value. Ethan Allen—frontiersman, land speculator, homespun philosopher, writer, politician, and eventually a founder of Vermont—also knew those woods well. Years earlier he had raised a small militia, known as the Green Mountain Boys, to protect and defend disputed lands in an area known as the New Hampshire Grants—which were later to become Vermont. Ethan Allen and about a hundred Green Mountain Boys took off to capture the fort before Arnold and his men could get there.

Arnold and his Massachusetts militia caught up with Allen en route. The men argued about who had the right to take the fort: Arnold said he had been ordered by the legal authorities to capture it. Good for you, Allen told him; his Green Mountain Boys weren't taking orders from no fancy-pants. The two men reached an uneasy truce and agreed to lead the expedition together—and they rode side by side to make certain neither one of them looked to be in charge.

One of Allen's men had snuck into the fort disguised as a peddler. He reported that its walls were deteriorating, the garrison was undermanned, what powder they had was wet—and they were expecting reinforcements within days. The two commanders agreed to attack. In the early brush of sunrise on May 10, 1775, a small force warily approached the fort; by all reports, they were stunned by the British response.

The one guard watching the wide-open gate tried to fire his musket, but his powder was wet. He dropped his musket and ran. Allen's Green Mountain Boys walked uncontested into the fort and quickly rounded up the sleeping soldiers. They learned later that the British had neglected to inform this garrison that shots had been fired in Massachusetts, so the troops there were completely unprepared to resist. Supposedly, when the fort's commanding officer asked from behind a locked door what they were doing there, Allen responded that he had taken the fort, "in the name of the Great Jehovah and the Continental Congress," although another report claimed he simply said, "Come out, you old rat."

The greatest danger in the capture of Fort Ticonderoga came later, when Allen's men discovered and helped themselves to the liquor stores and almost came to battle with Arnold's troops.

This was Arnold's first victory. The artillery captured there would later force the British to abandon Boston. After Allen's men departed, Arnold set about rebuilding the fort's defenses, fully aware of its value. Within weeks Connecticut sent an estimated one thousand troops to prevent a British drive from the north. Apparently Arnold was furious when Colonel Benjamin Hinman arrived and tried to take command. He resisted until delegates from the Committee of Safety informed him that he was to serve under Colonel Hinman. In response Arnold resigned his commission, disbanded his militia, and went home.

Although both Allen and Arnold wrote extensive reports about the events for the Committee of Safety, it appears they received only Allen's glorified version, which barely mentioned Arnold. In fact, when Allen later published his memoir, he didn't even mention Arnold.

This was the beginning of a pattern that was to repeat itself several times. Benedict Arnold would take great risks for the cause in which he so fervently believed—and then his accomplishments would be ignored or he would be set aside. It's unclear why Arnold was regularly denied the credit he had earned. According to some descriptions, while he had substantial leadership skills, he had an abrasive personality, lacking the political charm that others used so well to gain prestige and power—sometimes beyond their actual accomplishments. This might well be the source of the bitterness that resulted in his turning. Remarkably, his talents allowed him to rise high in the ranks without his rancor being detected.

George Washington's respect for him began with Arnold's mission to Quebec. With each succeeding colonial success, it seemed more and more likely that British troops then in Canada would be summoned south to help end the rebellion. In July 1775, the Continental Congress authorized New York general Philip Schuyler to invade Quebec. Arnold, greatly disappointed that he was not put in command, went directly to Washington and proposed a second offensive aimed specifically at Quebec City. With Schuyler's support, Washington approved the plan—and commissioned Benedict Arnold a colonel in the Continental army.

Arnold marched north with eleven hundred men. The route through the Maine wilderness proved far more difficult than had been anticipated. The lack of food and supplies caused more than three hundred men to turn back, while about two hundred men died of disease and starvation, perished in the swamps, or were carried away in river rapids. This was still mostly an unsettled and unmapped country and men like Arnold risked their lives, facing unknown dangers day after day. By the end of this march, which turned out to be more than twice as long as originally anticipated, Arnold's men, as he wrote to Washington, "were almost naked and in want of every necessity." It was a substantially weakened force that finally made contact with General Richard Montgomery's troops outside Quebec City in late December. Montgomery's army had been far more successful, capturing Montreal on its march into Canada.

Although Arnold would not learn of it for several weeks, he'd been promoted to the rank of brigadier general.

Quebec City was well fortified, defended by about five hundred regular troops and an equal number from the local militias. The assault began in a snowstorm on December 31. It was a disaster. Montgomery was killed early in the battle, and Arnold suffered a serious leg wound. The British held the city, killing or capturing more than 350 Americans. Arnold was given command of Montreal. When the British finally began their advance in the summer and fall of 1776, Arnold distinguished himself in several battles that delayed the British long enough to allow an orderly patriot retreat. But he resented the way the war was being conducted. Complaining of the difficulties he faced as a commander, Arnold purportedly wrote to Continental Navy Captain David Hawley, "When you ask for a frigate, they give you a raft. Ask for sailors and they give you tavern waiters. And if you want breeches, they give you a vest."

The Last Portage of the Great Carrying Place depicts some of the hardships endured by Arnold's troops on their incredible 1775–1776 march to Quebec.

In the ensuing months Arnold once again was caught up in military politics as other officers, men he viewed as far less deserving, were promoted over him as the Congress attempted to balance the number of generals from each state. Arnold again threatened to resign. Washington was sympathetic and wrote to Congress in his behalf, and as a result Arnold received his promotion to major general—but not the seniority he strongly felt he deserved.

It was at the crucial Battle of Saratoga, in September 1777, that Benedict Arnold distinguished himself as an American military hero—and faced the greatest humiliation of his career. The previous June, General John Burgoyne had begun the British offensive from Canada, leading eight thousand troops armed with more than 130 artillery pieces from Quebec down the Hudson River toward Albany, where he was to link up with General Howe's troops moving north from New York. If this maneuver succeeded, New England would be isolated from the rest of the states and the war might rapidly be brought to an end. In July, "Gentleman Johnny" Burgoyne shocked the Continental Congress by successfully recapturing strongly fortified Fort Ticonderoga. As a result, Washington replaced Schuyler with General Horatio Gates as commander of the northern army.

Washington had seen far too much of officers who led from behind; to blunt the British offensive, he needed men who weren't afraid to fight, men who took the battle directly to the enemy, men like Arnold. At Washington's request, General Arnold withdrew his resignation and joined Gates at Saratoga in upstate New York. Initially the two men got along, but hostility set in when the first battle of Saratoga began on September 17. At Saratoga, the cautious Gates spread his ten thousand men across an area known as the Bemis Heights, overlooking the west bank of the Hudson River. Arnold was given command of the left flank.

Burgoyne decided to initiate his attack from that left flank, hoping to get behind Gates's army on the heights. In anticipation, Arnold requested permission to attack before Burgoyne was prepared. Gates refused; a former British officer, he still harbored great respect for that army and preferred to maintain his secure position. He would defend the heights. But he allowed Arnold to send out elements of his own division for reconnaissance. The advance units of both armies came together at Freeman's Farm. Both sides quickly sent reinforcements into the fighting—although Gates refused to commit his main force, certain Burgoyne would make a frontal assault. The battle raged through the afternoon; one of Arnold's men, Captain Ebenezer Wakefield, reported watching his commander, "in front of the line, his eyes flashing, pointing with his sword to the advancing foe, with a voice that rang clear as a trumpet and electrified the line." When the fighting was done for the day, Burgoyne's forces had won but had paid a terrible price. More than six hundred men were killed or wounded, almost twice the casualties suffered by Arnold. It turned out to be more than Burgoyne could afford.

Several days after the battle, Arnold confronted Gates in his tent. In addition to refusing to provide reinforcements, in the report of the fighting that Gates sent to Congress, he did not mention Arnold or his men. In legend Arnold slashed open Gates's tent with his sword. While that's probably apocryphal, he did storm into Gates's tent and confronted him. The two men screamed at each other, reportedly employing "high words and gross language." The imperious, infuriated Gates relieved Arnold of his command. Arnold responded by writing a note in which the first signs of his bitterness were revealed, claiming that despite the "ingratitude of my countrymen, every personal interest shall be buried in my zeal for the safety and happiness of my country." Arnold also requested permission from Gates to leave the camp and report to Washington. It was granted, but Arnold hesitated; the battle was about to be renewed and he intended to fight alongside his men.

When word of this confrontation spread to the troops, Arnold's men circulated a petition demanding that he be reinstated. But before Gates could respond, Burgoyne attacked.

The first battle of Saratoga had left Burgoyne in an untenable position. He had won, but he had lost whatever advantages he once had. He had no choice but to press the attack, to smash through Gates's line and get to Albany, but he lacked sufficient forces to properly support the effort. On October 7 Burgoyne marched two thousand men back to Freeman's Farm. When Arnold, who no longer had command authority, practically begged Gates to send a force to meet the attack, Gates told him, "General Arnold, I have nothing for you to do. You have no business here."

Benedict Arnold was not going to let Gates's hesitancy cost his men victory again. He rode into the battle. By the time he arrived, the Americans had counterattacked and were overrunning British lines. Arnold raced to the front. Screaming, "Come on brave boys, come on!" he led a charge into the center of the redcoats' position. Finding a gap in the line, he charged through it, then turned left to get behind the defenders. Bullets were whizzing by him. He was hit again in his left leg. His horse was hit and went down, crushing his already wounded leg. The battle continued all around him, as Burgoyne desperately withdrew his troops. That day more than eight hundred men had been killed, wounded, or captured. Burgoyne tried to make a stand in the town of Saratoga, but Gates encircled him. Burgoyne had no choice but to surrender his army.

Answering to Parliament at a later time, Burgoyne admitted he had expected Gates to defend his superior position, but "Arnold chose to give rather than receive the attack." While General Nathanael Greene credited Arnold and Major General Benjamin Lincoln for much

Only a month after the British had captured Philadelphia in September 1777, General Gates revived patriot morale by defeating General Burgoyne at Saratoga. Burgoyne's surrender, pictured here, convinced French king Louis XVI to provide support for the revolution.

of the success, a gold medal in Gates's honor was authorized by the Congress. As a direct result of the success at Saratoga, the French decided to enter the war to support the American army. For France, which had lost its foothold in the new country in the French and Indian War, this was a satisfying outcome.

Benedict Arnold spent months in the hospital; his leg was saved but was never again truly serviceable. When British general Henry Clinton was ordered to withdraw his troops from Philadelphia, Washington rewarded Arnold by appointing him military commander of that city. It was a safe and plum post that offered numerous possibilities to a man who understood business. And by this time, Arnold had experienced far too much to remain an idealist. For him this war was no longer about breaking the bonds of British tyranny. The fact was that Philadelphia would be a lucrative post for him.

Philadelphia was a place in turmoil. The patriots, who had left hurriedly when the British had taken control of the city in September 1777, now returned, while the Loyalists either fled or lived in fear of retribution. Washington ordered Arnold to provide equal "security to individuals of every class and description," but that proved a difficult task. When Arnold took the necessary steps to protect Loyalists and their property, he was viewed with suspicion by patriots who began to wonder about his true sympathies.

In the chaotic economic circumstances, a lively black market developed—and this was exactly the type of commerce Arnold understood. Years earlier in New Haven he had made his fortune in a similar situation. Not surprisingly, he began to prosper. Among other questionable activities, he was involved in the lucrative smuggling business and also profited from buying confiscated Loyalists' property at greatly reduced value, then selling for a substantial profit.

Finally away from the battlefields, Arnold found his pleasures in Philadelphia society. His first wife had died years earlier, so he was open to the charms of the most eligible women in the city, finally settling on eighteen-year-old Peggy Shippen, the lovely daughter of wealthy merchant, judge—and Loyalist—Edward Shippen. They married in April 1779. Peggy Shippen was young but not naive. During the British occupation she had found favor with British major John André, and even after the British had withdrawn from the city she had maintained contact with him. A Philadelphia shopkeeper, Joseph Stansbury, was known to carry messages between them.

It never has been determined precisely when or even why Benedict Arnold made his decision to betray his country. Certainly it may have been as simple as money: Life in Philadelphia with his lovely, much younger bride turned out to be far more expensive than Arnold had expected and once again he had fallen deeply into debt. His weakness for the gambling tables may have contributed to those losses. His wife was likely a factor. Peggy Shippen was said to be a sensual woman with expensive tastes; she also was a Loyalist with strong ties to her ex, André. She might easily have swayed her already bitter husband—and undoubtedly her already established contacts facilitated his betrayal. Or the repeated slights accumulated, culminating with being insulted by the man he most admired, George Washington.

Arnold's often-suspect business dealings eventually brought disfavor on him, and in 1779 he was charged with thirteen counts of profiteering, including the misuse of government property. Those charges infuriated Arnold, who already believed he had been robbed of much of the credit he had earned for his courage and leadership. He was court-martialed and wrote to Washington, "Having become a cripple in the service of my country, I little expected to meet

This 1778 pencil drawing by Major John André captures the beauty of eighteen-year-old Peggy Shippen, rumored to have been his paramour, who became Benedict Arnold's second wife—and may have led Arnold to betray his country.

[such] ungrateful returns." A Philadelphia diplomat named Silas Deane informed General Greene that General Arnold was embittered more by the "wounds his character has received, from base, and envious men, than those he received, in defense of his country." Although a court-martial acquitted him of eleven of those charges—he was convicted of two minor infractions—as part of his penalty Washington publicly rebuked him, writing in his General Orders on April 6, 1780, "The Commander in Chief would have been much happier in an occasion of bestowing commendations on an officer who has rendered such distinguished services to his country as Major General Arnold; but in the present case a sense of duty and a regard to candor oblige him to declare, that he considers his conduct in the instance of the permit as peculiarly reprehensible, both in a civil and military view, and . . . imprudent and improper." Arnold responded to Washington's censure by resigning his post in Philadelphia.

By that time, though, Arnold already had committed treason. It appears that at some point while awaiting his court-martial, Arnold had begun his correspondence with André, who by then had been placed in charge of British secret intelligence in America. John André

The nineteenth-century print *The Treason of Arnold* illustrates Benedict Arnold persuading
Major John André to conceal the plans for West Point in his boot. Had André remained
in uniform he would have been treated as a military prisoner when captured. Instead he
changed into civilian clothes and was hanged as a spy.

was an enlightened man. He was fluent in four languages and could draw, paint, sing, and write. During the occupation of Philadelphia he had become a favorite of high society. And undoubtedly he appreciated the value of turning a man like Benedict Arnold.

By May 1779, Arnold had made his intentions known to André, demanding payment and an equivalent rank in the British army in exchange for information. While André was the spymaster, decisions concerning Arnold were to be made by the commander in chief of North America, General Sir Henry Clinton. Clinton and André responded by offering Arnold fair payment and establishing the method of communication: Arnold would send seemingly ordinary letters through Stansbury, but they actually would include messages written in invisible ink, or transmitted by code and cipher. Blackstone's *Commentaries on the Laws of England* would serve as the key.

While negotiations continued over terms, Arnold proved his value by providing intelligence about troop dispositions and movements and the anticipated arrival of the French fleet—including six warships and six thousand troops—in Newport, Rhode Island. At some point André apparently suggested that Arnold approach Washington about assuming command of the fortifications at West Point. General Clinton was extremely interested in obtaining the plans and details about its defenses.

The importance of that strategic location to either the Americans or the British cannot be overstated. Sitting on a plateau in upstate New York, West Point commanded a critical choke point on the Hudson River. Its defenses included artillery batteries, an almost impregnable fortress manned by a full contingent of three thousand troops, and a five-hundred-yard-long sixty-five-ton iron chain stretching across the Hudson from West Point to Constitution Island to prevent ships from slipping through. Any ship trying to break through would inevitably be hung up on the chain—each link weighed 180 pounds—then blasted into smithereens by the artillery. Washington considered it his "most important post in America . . . first in magnitude and importance," and warned that if the British gained control they could "interrupt our easiest communication between the eastern and southern states, open a new source of supplies to them, and a new door to distress and disaffect the country."

It isn't known precisely why Washington decided to give Arnold command of that fortress. Obviously he had not lost respect for him after his conviction and continued to value his proven courage and leadership on the battlefield. In fact, he wrote to Arnold promising, "as far as it shall be in my power, I will myself furnish you with opportunities for regaining the esteem which you have formerly enjoyed." In 1780, when Washington began planning an assault on the British army entrenched in New York, he offered Arnold command of the left wing. It was the kind of prestigious position Arnold had been desperate for in the past, but the offer came much too late. Washington was quite surprised when Arnold turned down this offer, writing, "His countenance changed and he appeared to be quite fallen and instead of thanking me . . . never opened his mouth." Arnold later claimed that his injured left leg would not permit him to lead troops in battle. But eventually he did make a request of Washington; he would like to be put in command of West Point.

In fact, it made sense. It was a position that had to be held at all costs and Arnold long ago had proved himself. It was a stationary post, so Arnold's disability would not be a problem. And there was something else: starting earlier that year there had been persistent rumors that a British spy had infiltrated Washington's command. To try to identify him, Benjamin Tallmadge reactivated the Culper spy ring, which had been dormant for some time. While they kept few records, for obvious reasons, they must have enjoyed at least some success, because in June Tallmadge warned one of Washington's closest advisers, Jonathan Trumbull, of an insider plot to attack West Point. Assuming Washington also had knowledge of these rumors, it makes sense that he would put someone he trusted completely—like General Arnold—in charge.

In June, Arnold stopped at West Point on his way home to Connecticut to make a thorough inspection, and he prepared a detailed report of his visit. By then Arnold obviously was committed to this plot, as he arranged through friends in New York to begin transferring his assets to London. In early July, Arnold sent a message to Clinton that he was to be given command of the fortress, offering to provide "drawing of the works . . . by which you might take [West Point] without loss." The price for his betrayal, he wrote in a second letter, was £20,000, more than a million dollars today. On August 3, his appointment as commander of West Point, in addition to several other posts along the Hudson, was made official. Two weeks later he received a letter from André agreeing to most of his demands. The plot was put into action.

There is some evidence that by August Arnold's letters were being intercepted, although there is no hint that anyone could link them directly to him. What is known is that some of Arnold's letters never got to Clinton, that someone had tampered with at least one letter that did get through to make the message illegible, and that Tallmadge was becoming suspicious of Arnold.

After taking command, General Arnold immediately began weakening West Point's defenses. Needed repairs on the chain were postponed. The garrison was reduced by sending troops to other river posts or detailing them to Washington. Supplies of necessities were cut back so drastically that some of his officers wondered if he was selling them on the black market.

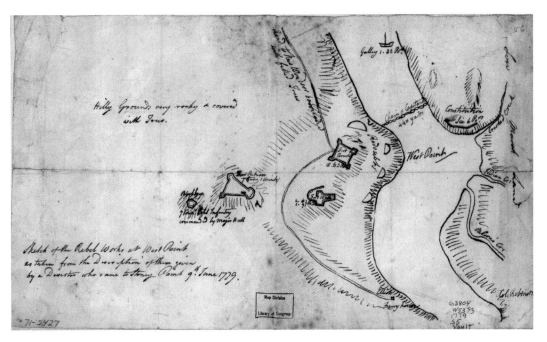

This 1779 sketch, made from a description provided by a deserter, shows the positions of the defenses at West Point.

General Clinton, meanwhile, began preparations to launch his attack on West Point. His plan was to sail up the river and land his army, knowing that Arnold would put up little more than a token defense before surrendering. Apparently Clinton already had in his hands a great deal of intelligence detailing the weakest points of the fort. Rather than risk an attack before all the pieces were in place, he decided to wait until André was able to coordinate a time and date with Arnold. While a meeting between the men was risky, the stakes were so high that it was worth it. Clinton was reluctant to permit André to meet with Arnold, and allowed the encounter only after the major agreed he would not take off his uniform, he would not go behind enemy lines, and he would not carry any incriminating documents. The first meeting, planned for September 11 near the town of Dobbs Ferry, was called off when British gunships mistakenly fired at the boat carrying André.

The second meeting, the final meeting, was scheduled for September 23. On the seventeenth, Arnold dined with Joshua Hett Smith, a New York businessman whom many people suspected of being a Loyalist but who also may have been for sale to either side. There is

A steel engraving made from a sketch provided by Major
Charles L'Enfant showing the fortress at West Point as it
looked in 1780, overlooking the Hudson River. West Point
was considered the most vital strategic position on the
river. Slightly more than a decade later, L'Enfant would
create the city plan for Washington, D.C.

some evidence that he was a double, or even a triple agent, and his involvement—whether intentional or not—led directly to the failure of the plot.

On the eighteenth Arnold met with Washington and came away confident that his superior harbored no suspicions. What Tallmadge knew, if anything, at this point is unclear. Most probably the unmasking of Arnold's deception was the result of chance, but if there had been a plan in place to foil Arnold's plan without divulging sources of information, it certainly could have proceeded this same way.

On the twentieth, the sloop HMS *Vulture* secretly carried Major André up the river. The following evening, at Arnold's request, Smith rowed to that ship and brought back a man identified to him as John Anderson. "Anderson" spent much of the following day meeting with General Arnold at Smith's home in West Haverstraw. Smith later claimed he had not been privy to any of their discussions. The *Vulture* was supposed to wait at anchor for André to return, but on the morning of the twenty-second, shore batteries opened fire and the ship was unable to wait for him.

In Smith's confession, which he made to Alexander Hamilton, he claimed he was suffering from "the fever and ague [shaking]," and was therefore unable to row "Anderson" back to the ship without making any reference to the shelling. But after the ship left, Smith rode with Anderson and put him on the road toward White Plains. He also testified that Anderson was wearing an officer's red coat and, at Arnold's request, he gave him civilian clothes to wear. This proved to be very important; the fact that André was caught behind enemy lines wearing civilian clothes identified him as a spy rather than a prisoner of war and therefore made him eligible to be hanged. For some never-disclosed reason, rather than showing "Anderson" the most direct route south, Smith instead took him north into American-patrolled territory. "The circuitous route . . ." André later said, "was imposed without alternative upon me." On the road they met several people and passed successfully through two checkpoints. They spent the night in a farmhouse. The next morning Smith left him at a fork near Tarrytown, telling him which path to take. "Anderson" obviously didn't trust him, instead taking the other path.

Gangs of bandits, highwaymen, and militiamen were known to roam those woods. Later that morning, as he got close to British lines, André was stopped by three men. They could have been bandits or militiamen; in any case, their allegiance was to the Americans. One of them was wearing a Hessian's coat and, because they were near a British camp, André initially identified himself as a British officer. When he realized his mistake he tried bargaining, showing them a pass written by Arnold; when that failed, he offered them his horse, his

CAPTURE OF ANDRE 1780.

A classic 1845 Currier & Ives print of the capture of Major John André. The papers in his boot have been discovered and he is now dressed as a civilian—sealing his doom.

watch, whatever he had to bargain with. When the men searched him they found six pages of maps, diagrams, and papers hidden in his boot. While only one of the men could read, they all certainly could recognize the plans for West Point. Rather than taking a substantial bribe or André's valuables, they decided to deliver him to the closest American post. Maybe it was loyalty, maybe it was because they believed they would receive a larger reward—or maybe there was a more complicated reason.

They delivered André to their local commander, Colonel John Jameson, who decided to send him back to Arnold under guard with a note explaining he had been caught carrying important papers. But he sent the "parcel of papers taken from under his stockings . . . of a very dangerous tendency" to Washington. At that moment, André probably figured he was safe.

Hours later Tallmadge learned of the events. When he saw the papers taken from André, who was traveling with a pass from Arnold, he knew he had identified his traitor. He ordered Jameson to send a fast rider to bring back André, but Jameson, fearing he was caught between two officers, insisted that his note be delivered to Arnold. There was nothing Tallmadge could do to prevent that.

Coincidently, Arnold was to host Washington for breakfast at West Point that very morning. He received Jameson's note shortly before the general was due to arrive. He went upstairs, kissed his wife, and fled. When Washington arrived and found Arnold was not there to greet him, he apparently was upset at the absence of proper military protocol. Most reports indicate he was still at West Point when Jameson's "parcel of papers" arrived. The following day Washington made Arnold's betrayal public, including in the General Orders, "Treason, of the blackest dye, was yesterday discovered. General Arnold, who commanded at West Point—lost to every sentiment of honor, of private and public obligation—was about to deliver up that important post into the hands of the enemy. Such an event must have given the American cause a deadly wound, if not a fatal stab."

Arnold's treachery actually served the American cause by inspiring a renewed anti-British fervor. Arnold was reviled throughout the states, and effigies of him were hanged and burned. The morale of the army, which had been lagging due to the long and inconclusive war, picked up substantially. Riflemen were said to take target practice on his image.

While General Arnold successfully escaped to New York, which was occupied by the British, André was convicted of being a spy. A board of officers, including fourteen generals, ordered that "Major André, Adjutant General to the British Army, ought to be considered as a spy from the enemy; and that, agreeable to the law and usage of nations, it is their opinion he ought to suffer death." Sir Henry Clinton beseeched Washington to spare him but reportedly refused when Washington offered to trade him for Arnold, explaining that doing so would prevent any man from ever again changing sides. At Clinton's request, Arnold threatened Washington if André was executed, writing, "I call heaven and earth to witness, that your Excellency will be justly answerable for the torrent of blood that may be spilt in consequence." During André's captivity, as was true during Nathan Hale's, André earned the respect of his enemy; Hamilton wrote, "Never perhaps did any man suffer death with more justice, or deserve it less."

André was hanged on October 2. Supposedly many witnesses cried. His last words, carefully recorded, were, "I pray you to bear me witness that I meet my fate like a brave man." Several decades later his remains were sent to England, where he was buried in Hero's Corner in Westminster Abbey.

Smith, whose role in this story remained murky, also was tried, but he was acquitted because of a lack of evidence. Peggy Arnold was never charged with any complicity and Washington permitted her to join her husband in New York.

Arnold received his promised commission in the British army and returned to the battlefield. American leaders had orders to hang him immediately if he was captured. He led an invasion force into Virginia and briefly held—and looted—Richmond, then attacked and burned New London, Connecticut, while his troops massacred captured militiamen. Even after British forces were defeated at Yorktown, he urged the king to renew attacks, with greater force, but the British never embraced him. While he served their objectives, his treason was never completely overlooked, and many people held him responsible for the execution of the revered major, John André. Arnold actually tried several times to rehabilitate his reputation, writing letters to newspapers in which he claimed that it was his conscience, not the monetary rewards, that motivated his actions.

Arnold spent the remainder of his life earning and losing fortunes, at one point owning more than thirteen thousand acres in Canada, but he was always looking for his next war. Ironically, while trading in the Caribbean he was captured by the French and presumed to be a British spy. In that instance he again escaped the noose, this time by squeezing through a cabin window and sliding down a rope to a raft, which he managed to row to a British warship. When he died in England in 1801, he was given a state funeral—but without the military honors he would have wished. His wife spent the last years of her life settling all of his debts—except the biggest one of all, to America, which could never be repaid.

Foreign Aides

George Washington must have truly despaired at dinner on the evening of August 5, 1777, when he was formally introduced to the nineteen-year-old Marquis de Lafayette. That morning he had been informed that 250 British ships, carrying as many as eighteen thousand troops, were en route to Philadelphia where his under-equipped, poorly trained, and dispirited army was on the verge of collapse. And yet he was forced to spend his evening entertaining this extremely wealthy teenager.

Marie-Joseph-Paul-Yves-Roch-Gilbert du Motier de La Fayette, one of the richest young men in France, had purchased his own boat, hired his own soldiers, and, against the explicit orders of King Louis XVI who did not want to threaten France's fragile peace with England, sailed to America. Some historians believe his purpose was to avenge the death of his father, who had been killed by British soldiers in the 1759 Battle of Minden. It was a ludicrous situation that might well have been imagined by the satirical novelist Henry Fielding; although Lafayette spoke almost no English and had no experience in battle, the Continental Congress had awarded him the rank of major general. The problem was that while the Congress intended the commission to be purely honorary, Lafayette had very different expectations: he was determined to fight the British.

Washington had no idea what to do with this pleasant but inexperienced and determined teenager. He wrote to Virginian Benjamin Harrison for advice, complaining, "What line of conduct I am to pursue, to comply with [Continental Congress's] design and his expectations, I know no more than the child unborn, and beg to be instructed."

Lafayette was only the latest of many Europeans who had come to America. Since the beginning of the war, American agents in Europe had been trying to recruit experienced military officers who could help transform the disparate militias into an army. Mostly they had succeeded in sending to Washington a series of nondescript counts, barons, chevaliers, and veteran military officers of low repute who desired to use this war for personal gain. At first, Lafayette appeared to be just another dilettante to be kept out of danger while he helped fund the patriotic cause.

But as Washington—and the world—would learn, Lafayette was one of a small group of extraordinary European soldiers—among them the Prussian baron Friedrich von Steuben, and Polish officers Tadeusz Kościuszko and Kazimierz Pulaski, whose courage and capabilities contributed significantly to the American victory and the birth of the revolutionary spirit that was to resonate across their own continent.

A letter of recommendation from Benjamin Franklin, who was in Paris trying to persuade the French to enter the war, convinced Washington to find a place on his staff for Lafayette. The young Frenchman began proving his value in early September at the Battle of Brandywine. When Washington's right flank was threatened, he sent Lafayette into battle with Major General John Sullivan's 3rd Pennsylvania Brigade. Although wounded in the calf, Lafayette distinguished himself by forsaking treatment in order to organize an orderly retreat. As a result, he was cited for bravery and given a command.

It was during the infamous winter of 1777–78 at Valley Forge that Lafayette proved his mettle to Washington. The two men became close friends and allies. As Lafayette wrote to his wife in France, Washington "finds in me a trustworthy friend in whom he can confide and who will always tell him the truth. Not a day goes by without his talking to me at length or writing long letters to me. And he is willing to consult me on most interesting points." Living and suffering through the coldest days of that bitter winter alongside the troops, Lafayette bought uniforms, weapons, and supplies for the army—but, more important, he continued to urge the French government to support the Revolution. Sent north in early February by the Congress to invade Canada so it might be returned to France, Lafayette abandoned that mission in Albany when more than half the troops and the supplies he had been promised failed to arrive, and he returned to Valley Forge.

Washington's confidence in Lafayette continued to grow. In May, Washington ordered him to take twenty-two hundred troops toward Philadelphia to try to ascertain British general William Howe's intentions. General Howe must have been quite pleased to learn of Lafayette's presence; capturing this aristocrat would send a strong message to the French government about the consequences of interfering in this conflict. Howe sent more than

Washington and the newly arrived twenty-year-old Marquis de Lafayette, pictured during the terrible winter at Valley Forge by John Ward Dunsmore.

twelve-thousand troops to trap Lafayette in an area called Barren Hill. Lafayette skillfully managed to escape, with his force suffering only minor casualties.

After serving at Washington's side in several other small battles, Lafayette sailed to France in 1779, creating a stir in Paris when he appeared in court wearing his Continental army uniform. But his reports helped convince the king to send the French fleet north from the Caribbean and commit six thousand troops and supplies to the war. Washington reported this success by his protégé to Congress, writing, "During the time he has been in France, he has uniformly manifested the same zeal in our affairs, which animated his conduct while he was among us; and he has been upon all occasions an essential friend to America."

Lafayette returned to America in 1781 and distinguished himself in a campaign against British forces led by the traitor General Benedict Arnold. In October, the French support he had helped muster made the difference in the climactic Battle of Yorktown: While five thousand American troops under Lafayette's command blocked Lord Cornwallis's escape routes, Washington's twenty-five hundred soldiers joined four thousand French troops and the

French fleet to completely encircle the British. After British efforts to relieve Cornwallis failed, the general finally agreed to surrender his eight thousand men and a strong naval force, marking the end of fighting on American soil. Lafayette stood with Washington to accept the British surrender.

At the conclusion of the war, Lafayette served nobly in the French Revolution. As commander of the French National Guard, he tore down the Bastille, sending the key to its west portal to Washington at Mount Vernon. Celebrated in America for his contributions, in 1824 the Marquis de Lafayette became the first foreign dignitary invited to address Congress, and upon his death a decade later John Quincy Adams said, "The name of Lafayette shall stand enrolled upon the annals of our race, high on the list of the pure and disinterested benefactors of mankind."

In contrast to the young and inexperienced Lafayette, forty-seven-year-old Friedrich Wilhelm Ludolf Gerhard Augustin von Steuben brought with him to America more than three decades of military experience in the Prussian army when he arrived in December 1777. After having served as quartermaster general and adjutant general on the personal staff of Frederick the Great, in 1764 he was made Baron von Steuben.

The American Revolution provided great opportunity for soldiers from several foreign countries. The British, whose armies were spread thinly throughout the world, hired as many as thirty thousand soldiers from Hesse-Cassel and other German states, paying the leaders of their principalities for their services. Veteran officers from other parts of Europe, left without a cause after the end of the Seven Years' War, also looked to America for employment. Among them was Baron von Steuben, who approached Franklin in Paris after failing to find a position with other foreign armies. When the Continental Congress would not provide any guarantees of pay, rank, or command, Steuben traveled to America and volunteered his services to Washington in exchange for his expenses. "The object of my greatest ambition is to render your country all the service in my power," he wrote, "and to deserve the title of a citizen of America by fighting for the cause of liberty."

The Continental army was in shambles when Steuben joined Washington at Valley Forge in late February 1778. In addition to lacking arms, ammunition, food, shelter, and morale, the army had no orderly military structure, no formal training system, and no organized administration procedures. The troops didn't even know how to march in formation. Steuben immediately began imposing the lessons he had learned in the Prussian military on the encampment, attempting to transform a willing but untrained assembly of militias into an army in a matter of months. The fact that he didn't speak English only made the already seemingly impossible task just a little more difficult.

Steuben attacked the problem by creating a model company of slightly more than a hundred men, then began drilling them in the full range of military skills from marching to fighting with a bayonet. Creating the prototype of the tough drill sergeant, he made his men relentlessly practice reloading and firing, reloading and firing, until the process became natural and efficient. He taught them basic tactics and simple maneuvers. As a veteran officer described Steuben's impact, "Discipline flourishes and daily improves under the indefatigable efforts of Baron Steuben—who is much esteemed by us." In addition to personally demonstrating these techniques, he spoke to Alexander

Due to a scarcity of paper, Baron von Steuben's command and drill manual was printed on blue paper. The fundamental principles explained in "The Blue Book," as it became known, have remained the foundation of the American military for more than two centuries. The model company he formed also remains in existence and is known as the The President's 100.

Hamilton and General Nathanael Greene in French and they translated his comments into English. When harsher language became necessary, he employed Captain Benjamin Walker to curse at the troops for him.

Once these men were sufficiently trained, they began passing along their knowledge to other groups, and the effect rippled through the entire army. This training regimen eventually was turned into the classic manual *Regulations for the Order and Discipline of the Troops of the United States*. The *Blue Book*, or *Steuben's Regulations*, served as the basic training program, manual of arms, and organizational structure for generations of American soldiers—and remains the foundation for the professional army.

Von Steuben also instituted strict sanitation regulations, introducing the novel concept of latrines to soldiers who had no understanding of sanitary conditions, then established a standard layout of the camp in which orderly rows of tents were separated from the kitchens and latrines. Within months of his arrival, Washington had named Steuben inspector general of the army with the rank of major general.

Almost single-handedly Steuben brought professionalism to the colonial army. His training began paying off during the Battle of Monmouth in June, when retreating colonial troops stopped and formed an orderly battle line and, for the first time in the entire war, fought the British to a draw in a static battle. In subsequent battles the colonists stunned the British with their rapid and orderly response to commands, their newfound ability to maneuver, and their deadly use of the bayonet. Washington eventually gained such confidence in Steuben that during the decisive Battle of Yorktown, he put Steuben in command of one of three American divisions.

After the victory Baron von Steuben became an American citizen, settling on sixteen thousand acres of land in upstate New York given to him by a grateful government.

Among the other idealistic Europeans who came to America to fight for human rights was the young Polish military engineer Andrzej Tadeusz Bonawentura Kościuszko. To an army lacking just about every form of military expertise, Kościuszko's arrival in the summer of 1776 proved incredibly fortuitous. Initially a volunteer paid by Benjamin Franklin, who recognized the importance of his unique skills, in October he was commissioned a colonel. His first challenge was building fortifications along the Delaware River to prevent a British advance toward Philadelphia. He attracted Washington's attention the following spring at Fort Ticonderoga when he urged General Arthur St. Clair to situate a battery on a nearby hilltop. Two months after St. Clair refused to act on his suggestion, British general Burgoyne installed artillery on that high point, forcing the Americans to abandon the fortress. As the American army retreated south, Kościuszko was ordered to somehow delay the enemy pursuit. By cutting down trees to block roads, destroying bridges, and damming streams to bog down the British army, Kościuszko gave St. Clair the time needed to successfully withdraw.

A greatly impressed General Gates assigned Kościuszko to find the best defensive position for his army to make a stand. Kościuszko finally found that place—an area overlooking the Hudson River called Bemis Heights, not too far from the town of Saratoga. He designed an almost impregnable array of battlements there—which later enabled Gates's army to repulse several British attacks and led directly to Burgoyne's surrender. Gates reported in admiration, "The great tacticians of the campaign were the hills and forests, which a young Polish engineer was skillful enough to select for my encampment."

Kościuszko designed the fortifications at West Point that Benedict Arnold sold to the British, and when Major John André was captured with those plans, it was Baron von Steuben who supervised his hanging, turning down André's request to face a firing squad.

Kościuszko later fought in the campaign in the south, selecting positions for both camps and ambushes that provided a natural advantage, fortifying bases, running an intelligence network, and even leading men into battle. At one point, during Cornwallis's frantic pursuit of General Nathanael Greene's retreating army through the forest and across the rivers of the Carolinas, Kościuszko's preparations proved instrumental in saving the southern army. At the end of the war Congress promoted him to brigadier general.

While traveling to join the army in South Carolina, Kościuszko had paused in Virginia to fulfill one of his greatest desires—meeting Thomas

Jefferson. He and Jefferson eventually became good friends and faithful correspondents and Jefferson once said about him with admiration, "He is as pure a son of liberty as I have ever known."

After the American victory was secured, Kościuszko returned to Poland to lead the fight for freedom in his native country, eventually leading an unsuccessful uprising against occupying Russian forces. For his valor he was awarded his country's highest military honor. He returned to America in 1797 and, before departing for the final time to join the French in their fight against the Russians, he named Jefferson the executor of his estate, which was to be used to purchase the freedom of black slaves—including Jefferson's—and to educate them so they might live as free men. It was a request Jefferson was unable to fulfill.

Some foreign soldiers gave their lives to the revolutionary cause, among them the Polish aristocrat Kazimierz Pulaski. After leading Polish forces in an unsuccessful attempt to free his country from Russian and Prussian influence, he was exiled to France, where Lafayette and Benjamin Franklin strongly recommended him to Washington. "Count Pulaski of Poland," Franklin wrote, "an officer famous throughout Europe for his bravery and conduct in defense of the liberties of his country against the three great invading powers of Russia, Austria and Prussia . . . may be highly useful to our service."

Pulaski was a fighting soldier, a skilled horseman who had earned great respect for leading the cavalry into battle. While awaiting his commission he wrote to Washington, "I came here, where freedom is being defended, to serve it, and to live or die for it." He gained Washington's respect in September 1777 at the Battle of Brandywine, when he led a charge into British lines that averted a disastrous defeat of the Continental army's cavalry—and may have saved the commander in chief's life.

Until that time Washington used his few hundred mounted troops mostly for scouting, but after Congress appointed Pulaski brigadier general in charge of the army's four horse regiments, they began engaging in battle. "The Father of the American Cavalry," as he became known, created the Pulaski Legion, the country's first trained cavalry corps, and employed classic tactics in a series of battles, twice courageously leading charges into British lines. At the Battle of White Horse Tavern, his men alerted Washington that Howe's army was on the march, allowing the colonists to take strong defensive positions to prevent the attack. Other officers considered him quarrelsome, but no one ever questioned his courage in battle. In October 1779, during the Siege of Savannah, he was struck by grapeshot while leading a full-scale cavalry charge into British fortifications—and became one of the few European officers to lose his life in the cause of freedom.

The soldiers of Europe joined the fight for independence for many reasons, but without their combined contributions both on land and at sea, the outcome of the Revolutionary War might well have been very different.

Washington with the soldiers from Europe who helped create the victorious army: Washington (at left); Major General Baron Johann de Kalb, who had arrived with Lafayette; Von Steuben; Pulaski; Kościuszko; Lafayette; and the Lutheran pastor American-born Peter "Teufel Piet" (Devil Pete) Muhlenberg, who had served briefly in the German dragoons.

CHAPTER 7

Francis Marion

American Guerrilla Fighter

In late August 1780, elements of His Majesty's 63rd and Prince of Wales Regiments settled in for the night on the overgrown grounds of Thomas Sumter's abandoned plantation at Great Savannah, keeping careful watch over the 150 colonial prisoners captured at the Battle of Camden. The next day they would take them down the Santee Road to the prison ships docked in Charlestown. They put out sentries but expected no difficulty; they were in friendly territory and the colonial army was in tatters. General Gates had been badly beaten at Camden, and Sumter's men had been decimated at Fishing Creek. The British were so confident, in fact, that many of the troops slept inside the manor house, leaving their weapons stacked outside. But all around them, Colonel Francis Marion's militia was moving unseen and unheard through the South Carolina woods. It's possible the redcoats may have heard the forest whistling a conversation, but, if so, they did not understand the meaning.

⌐ The elusive General Francis Marion relaxing in camp with his men. The Swamp Fox, whose guerrilla tactics confounded the British, prevented the enemy from securing gains in the Carolinas, thereby keeping a sizable number of troops in the south.

Marion's men slowly tightened their knot. They waited patiently for darkness. The night woods were their home; surprise was their ally. Marion detailed sixteen men to guard the escape route over Horse Creek. When a British sentry spotted them, he frantically fired a single warning shot. The alert sent the camp scurrying into action but it was too late; it was much too late. Marion's raiders, swinging swords and firing their muskets, raced out of the woods. Within minutes, twenty-two British regulars and two Loyalists had been killed or captured. One of Marion's riders had been mortally wounded and one prisoner had suffered a head wound.

The colonial prisoners were freed—but when asked if they wanted to join the raiders who had saved them, many of them looked warily at this ragged band of forest men and instead decided to take their chances in Charlestown. Francis Marion let them go. His men gathered the British weapons and supplies and faded back into the comfortable darkness of the woods.

Francis Marion, the Swamp Fox, is remembered today mostly by America's toughest and bravest warriors, who often honor him as the "Father of Special Operations." In a war that was fought mostly according to the traditional principles of battle—long static lines marching nobly into the battle—Francis Marion broke the rules. According to another redcoat who unsuccessfully pursued him, Lieutenant Colonel John W. T. Watson, Marion "would not fight like a gentleman or a Christian," and by doing so Marion introduced a new type of warfare.

With his small band of untrained and unpaid fighting men, who lived and fought in the swamps and forests of South Carolina, Marion successfully harassed the British army for almost three years, helping disrupt General Clinton's strategy of conquering and cutting off the southern states. Then the Swamp Fox moved north. Like American Robin Hoods, his men traveled like ghosts, appearing suddenly and creating havoc—and then just as quickly were gone.

The legend of the Swamp Fox was born in late 1780. After several encounters in which Marion's outnumbered forces humiliated British regulars at places like Blue Savannah, Black Mingo Creek, and Tearcoat Swamp in South Carolina—employing what decades later would be known as "guerrilla tactics"—Lord Cornwallis ordered Banastre "Bloody Ban" Tarleton to take his dragoons into the countryside and bring an end to Marion's shenanigans.

After several days the notorious "Tarleton's raiders" finally caught Marion's tracks. Although Marion was a daring and courageous man, this time too many men were pursuing him, and he fled. He and his men led the British on a spirited chase for more than seven hours, racing through as much as twenty-five miles of South Carolina wilderness. As the afternoon stretched into the early evening, Tarleton was forced to end his pursuit at Ox Swamp,

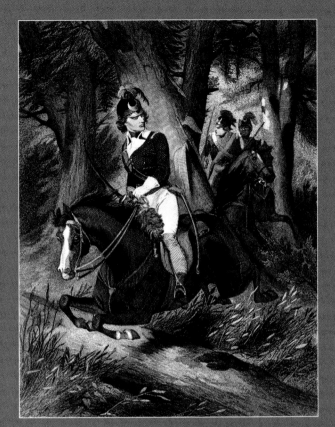

General Francis Marion (left), considered one of the fathers of guerrilla warfare, led his small band of patriots in the hit-and-run attacks that frustrated the imperious redcoats.

The despised British colonel Banastre Tarleton (at right) earned the nicknames "Bloody Ban" and "Butcher" after slaughtering surrendering troops at the Battle of Waxhaws. He pursued Marion through the Carolina swamps throughout 1780 without catching him, giving Marion the nickname by which he became known when he said, "as for this damned old fox, the devil himself could not catch him."

admitting bitterly that he had been unable to catch "that damned old fox," adding, "the devil himself could not catch him."

Renowned poet and journalist William Cullen Bryant would later celebrate the exploits of the Swamp Fox in his 1858 poem, "Song of Marion's Men":

> Our band is few, but true and tried,
>   Our leader frank and bold;
> The British soldier trembles
>   When Marion's name is told.
> Our fortress is the good greenwood,
>   Our tent the cypress-tree;
> We know the forest round us,
>   As seamen know the sea.
> We know its walks of thorny vines,
>   Its glades of reedy grass,
> Its safe and silent islands
>   Within the dark morass.

The battle for the south is often overlooked in history books, but it played a significant part in the outcome of the war. The British decision to maintain control of the southern colonies had drained them of soldiers and supplies that might have made a significant difference in the north, where George Washington's army was struggling. As Washington wrote despairingly in 1780, "We have been half our time without provision and are likely to continue so. We have no magazines, nor money to form them. And in a little while we shall have no men, if we had money to pay them. We have lived upon expedients till we can live no longer. In a word, the history of the war is a history of false hopes and temporary devices, instead of system and economy."

The British decision to greatly expand the war to the American south had been made two years earlier. After more than two years of battling the Continental army around the great northern cities of Boston, New York, and Philadelphia, in 1778 General Clinton switched tactics: he would attack those southern states that had a substantial Loyalist population and emancipated slaves, believing the men there would rise to his cause. Rather than chasing Washington's army through the states where the rebels enjoyed the fullest support, he would draw those soldiers south, where the population was far more favorable to the Crown. Once those states were subdued and again under Loyalist control, he would be free to turn his full attention to the north.

The British had launched this southern strategy by capturing the deep-water port of Savannah, Georgia, in December 1778, allowing them to safely land an army and all the necessary supplies. In late 1779, a fleet of ninety British ships carried fourteen thousand troops under the command of Generals Clinton and Cornwallis to Johns Island and Seabrook Island in South Carolina. General Clinton marched his troops overland across several rivers until he reached the south's largest port, Charlestown. The Siege of Charlestown lasted six months; in May 1780 patriot general Benjamin Lincoln surrendered the five thousand troops trapped there. But for an odd stroke of fate, one of them would have been Francis Marion.

One night in March 1780, Lieutenant Colonel Francis Marion, commander of the 2nd South Carolina Regiment, had joined his fellow officers in bitter revelry. Months earlier, when patriot general Benjamin Lincoln's offensive to retake Savannah had been repulsed with substantial losses, Marion had swallowed defeat for the first time. And now, as thousands of

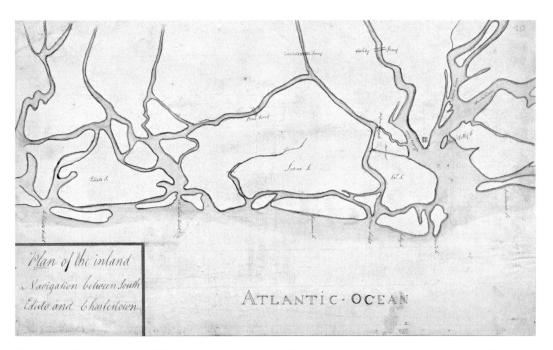

The inland waterways of South Carolina created a network of swamps and forests that served as barriers to the British but allowed local militia to move safely and secretly.

redcoats were moving to attack the city, he was in no mood for celebration. He had mostly declined to participate in the many rounds of toasts. Finally, his reluctance noted, he decided to leave. But in keeping with tradition, the doors had been locked—no one was permitted to go until the last glasses were raised. So Marion instead opened a window. He was on the second floor, but the drop to the ground didn't seem prohibitive. He eased himself out the window and fell awkwardly, badly damaging his ankle. The injury made him temporarily unfit for duty, so he went back to his farm outside Charlestown to heal. The city and its five thousand men fell while he was recuperating, leaving most of the Carolinas in British hands. It would be

many months, even years, before the American army could mount an effective offensive in the south. And so Marion began his own war, a war he was well suited to fight.

The details of Francis Marion's childhood are sketchy. He was born on a plantation near the town of Cordesville, South Carolina, hard on the banks of the Copper River, to Gabriel Marion Jr. and his wife, Esther. He was the last of seven children and was described as puny. One report said that as a baby he was smaller than a New England lobster and would fit easily into a cook pot. Apparently he had little formal schooling, spending much of his childhood hunting and fishing in the Low Country forests, swamps, and marshes. It was probably

Alonzo Chappel's engraving *Charleston: Siege 1780* depicts the beleaguered city from British lines.

during this time that he became especially close to a young slave named Oscar Marion, a boy about his own age who explored the woods with him. The great adventure of Francis Marion's life began at age fifteen, when he hired onto a merchant ship running the trade route to the West Indies. Just as in the stories of young lads trying to make their way in the world that Robert Louis Stevenson would write a century later, Marion's ship sank on his first voyage, supposedly after being struck by a whale. Six members of the crew managed to get into a lifeboat. Two men apparently died of exposure while praying to be rescued, and after a long week in the blazing sun the rest of them were saved. For the next decade Francis and his older brother, Job, managed the family plantation. But when the campaign against the Cherokee began in 1757, Captain John Postell recruited the brothers for the South Carolina militia.

The French and Indian War, or the Seven Years' War, as the British refer to it, matched the British colonies and their Indian allies against the French colonies and their Native American allies. Both nations committed regular military units to the fight for the natural riches of North America. Rather than the pitched battles common in European wars, much of the fighting was done in unsettled regions. To survive, Francis Marion had to learn how to mimic the Indian techniques: always moving rapidly in small forces, respecting the wilderness and living off its bounty, striking quickly and unexpectedly, and avoiding static battles against larger forces. The Cherokee lived in harmony with nature, and their ability to strike when and where they chose caused a fear in their enemies far greater than their actual numbers would have inspired, a lesson Marion learned well. By the time his war ended, Francis Marion had been promoted to lieutenant.

After the war he settled on his own plantation; it was on the Santee River and he named it Pond Bluff. He lived there peacefully with his wife and children, having seen enough of fighting in the French and Indian War. For a time, at least, he was far from the bickering taking place way up north. But in 1775 he was elected to the South Carolina Provincial Congress, where representatives were talking about wanting more independence from Parliament. For men like Marion, who had fought valiantly and loyally for the king only a few years earlier, this could not have been an easy decision to make. But when the fighting started in Massachusetts, the South Carolina Congress commissioned three state regiments and appointed him a captain. His allegiance was to the land he knew, South Carolina, rather than to a nation he had never seen.

Captain Marion spent the first years of the Revolution at Fort Sullivan, helping repulse the British attack on Charlestown in June 1776. With the exception of the ill-fated Siege of Savannah, he saw no more action—until the British captured Charlestown in May 1780.

The Liberty Flag, one of our first national flags, flew for the first time during the June 1776 siege of Sullivan's Island. By repulsing the attack, the small garrison inside Fort Moultrie successfully prevented the British fleet from capturing Charleston.

After the fall of the city, American reinforcements who had been on their way to assist the garrison there turned back. Some of them, however, were caught by British regulars led by Banastre Tarleton near Lancaster, South Carolina. There are many different reports about what actually happened in the Battle of Waxhaws, but the result was a massacre, as British troops, swinging their sabers, brutally murdered 113 patriots and severely wounded another 150. While Tarleton always insisted the massacre had taken place without his knowledge or authority, it gave rise to the expression "Tarleton's quarter," which meant that the victorious side would take no prisoners. "The loss of officers and men was great on the part of the Americans," Tarleton admitted, "owing to . . . a report amongst the [British] cavalry, that they had lost their commanding officer, which stimulated the soldiers to a vindictive asperity not easily restrained." In simpler words, his men believed he had been killed in the fighting and went crazy. Whatever the truth, the damage was done and many more men would die because of it.

In subsequent southern battles, countless wounded or surrendering soldiers were slaughtered in retribution. While the Waxhaws massacre was a military victory for the British, it proved to be a far more important rallying cry and propaganda victory for the Continental army.

Once General Clinton had secured Charlestown, he sent troops out into the countryside to apprehend separatist leaders. Marion, who would have spent the rest of the war sitting in a British prison if he had not fallen and injured his ankle, instead fled to General Horatio Gates's camp near Charlotte, North Carolina. He received a message there from the men from the Williamsburg district who had formed a militia and wanted him to lead them. At that time Gates had neither the men nor the supplies to sustain an offensive, so he ordered Marion and his Williamsburg men to attack British boats and communications on the Santee River.

Though clearly a man capable of inspiring others, Francis Marion did not look the part of a leader. While tall, impressive men like Washington were considered role models, Marion, according to Colonel Henry Lee, who fought at his side, was "in stature of the smallest size, thin as well as low. His visage was not pleasing, and his manners not captivating. He was reserved and silent, entering into conversation only when necessary, and then with modesty and good sense. He possessed a strong mind, improved only by his own reflections and observations, not by books or travels. His dress was . . . plain, regarding comfort and decency only. . . . He was sedulous and constant in his attention to the duties of his station, to which every other consideration yielded. . . . The procurement of subsistence for his men, and the contrivance of annoyance to his enemy, engrossed his entire mind." In other words, like most great leaders, he led by example: "Never avoiding danger," Lee continued, "he never rashly sought it; and acting for all around him as he did for himself, he risked the lives of his troops only when it was necessary." In fact, he apparently cared so little about his appearance that even after his leather regimental cap was partially burned, he continued to wear it.

Marion had fewer than one hundred men and limited supplies when he set out in the summer of 1780, but he did have one advantage: his men knew the land. This was their home. They had hunted these woods and fished the rivers; they had camped there and knew the dangers of the swamps. They knew the solid paths and they knew the soft bogs. And having grown up in those parts, they were well practiced with a long gun. In fact, while Marion often wore a sword when in battle, he was never known to use it. That turned out to be fortuitous. One day while cleaning his equipment, he tried to draw his sword—only to discover it was rusted to its scabbard.

At first, Marion's attacks were little more than irritants. His men disrupted supply lines, harassed troops, picked off stragglers. They barely accomplished enough to be noticed and were little more worrisome than the pesky mosquitoes that infested the southern swamps. Cornwallis's attention was focused on Gates, who commanded the last sizable Continental force in the Carolinas. Gates, perhaps emboldened by his prior success at Saratoga, began marching his four thousand men toward Charlestown. As much as possible, Marion and several other detachments softened their route. But Gates had little knowledge of the terrain or the elements or reliable intelligence about the enemy. The blistering hot weather, a lack of sufficient fresh water, dysentery, and even stomach ailments caused by green corn reduced his army by almost half. Among those men still able to fight were hundreds of untrained, terrified militia.

Cornwallis came out to meet Gates at Camden. When the first shots were fired, Gates's lines collapsed, as countless militia fled the battlefield. It quickly turned into a rout, and in less than an hour of fighting the Americans had suffered more than two thousand casualties. Gates himself had fled when his left flank crumbled. With the loss at Camden, the irregulars under the command of Lieutenant Colonel Francis Marion were about the last remnants of

Lord Charles Cornwallis by Thomas Gainsborough. After successfully capturing New York, Cornwallis was appointed commander of the British army in the south. Ordered to Yorktown, Virginia, by General Clinton with the promise he would be resupplied and reinforced there, he was forced to surrender his army to Washington when that assistance failed to arrive.

Washington's army left in South Carolina. They had no source of resupply, no safe havens to provide shelter, no hope of reinforcements. They were alone.

Washington, in fact, had little hope that Marion might accomplish anything of significance, yet he desperately needed him and other South Carolina militia to keep Cornwallis occupied to such an extent that he could not confidently move his army north without risking his southern base. As Washington wrote to John Rutledge, "[You] may rest assured that I am fully impressed with the importance of the southern states, and . . . the necessity of making every effort to expel the enemy from them. The late unlucky affair near Camden renders the situation more precarious. . . . Our endeavors in that quarter should be directed rather to checking the progress of the enemy by a permanent, compact, and well-organized body of men, than attempting immediately to recover the state of South Carolina by a numerous army of militia, who . . . are too fluctuating and undisciplined to oppose one composed chiefly of regular troops."

The Swamp Fox and his men moved like shadows through the countryside, cutting British lines of communications, disrupting shipping on the river, and continuing to harass Cornwallis's army. Marion began to focus his attention on Nelson's Ferry, where he embarrassed General Clinton by freeing 150 prisoners and capturing 22 men. Marion's first great victory came several days later. After handing over his 22 prisoners at Brittons Neck, his 52 men rode hard to make good their escape. More than a week later they ran into a much larger Loyalist force commanded by Major Micajah Ganey at Blue Savannah. In a brief skirmish that morning, Marion's band had routed Ganey's advance guard, but rather than pressing their luck, they had retreated into the countryside. Ganey wanted revenge and his whole force of two hundred men joined the pursuit. They raced through the afternoon, determined to punish the impudent Americans.

Marion watched contentedly as Ganey rode right into his trap. After Ganey's militia had raced past his position, he ordered his men to move in behind the much larger force. They stayed behind them until late in the afternoon, and when the pursuers paused to figure their position, Marion sprang his ambush. Ganey's men, exhausted and confused, panicked as volley after volley of shots came from all around them. As Colonel Peter Horry described the fighting years later, "In a moment the woods were all in a blaze. . . . Down tumbled the dead; off bolted the living; loud screamed the wounded; while far and wide, all over the woods, nothing was to be heard but the running of tories, and the snorting of wild bounding horses." They fled without any semblance of order into the swamps, suffering substantial casualties. Marion lost three men in the fighting.

That night the militia celebrated their victory with a rare large meal of roasted pigs, turkey, and "fine old peach brandy" that the British had been enjoying until attacked. "Ah, this brandy," Marion supposedly said, "was the worst foe these poor rogues ever had. But I'll take care it should be no foe to us."

The following morning Marion and his men moved into the swamps to round up any British survivors. As legend has it, they came upon the body of one of Ganey's men, but upon inspection they found no obvious wounds. They were mystified as to what had killed this soldier—until one of them saw a rattlesnake crawling into the undergrowth. One of them quickly raised his rifle to eliminate the threat, but another man stopped him, pleading for the reptile's life. They agreed to grant the snake a fair chance to live. A noose was fashioned and it was quickly captured. To decide its fate, they convened a court-martial. The snake was accused of the murder of a British soldier. There was a body of evidence to prove its guilt. But its defense attorney made a sensible plea: "If this creature is a murderer, then so are we all. This snake has killed one British soldier; we have killed many. This is not a murder, gentlemen. This is war!" The jury found the defendant not guilty, and it was released from captivity.

News of Marion's success spread rapidly through the South Carolina countryside. For the colonists this was the first bit of good cheer they had enjoyed in months. From that time forward they would seek Marion out, or his men, to inform him or warn him of British movements. For example, about a week after the victory at Blue Savannah, Marion was warned that a large force had made camp near Black Mingo Creek, outside the town of Hemingway. Rather than fading into the protection of the swamps, which was what he would be expected to do when facing a substantially larger force, Marion decided to attack. Perhaps he figured he would have the advantage of surprise. He led his men more than seventy miles through the countryside before finding Colonel John Cummins Ball and at least 150 Loyalists camped at Shepard's Ferry. Just before midnight Marion began his attack. Surprise was lost when a British sentry heard the lead horses crossing Willtown Bridge, which was north of the camp, and fired warning shots.

Marion never hesitated; he broke his men into three units and attacked from the center and both flanks, holding a substantial number in reserve. The British waited too long, until Marion's men were less than thirty yards away, then fired their first volley. Before they could reload, the militia was on them. When they came around the right flank, the Tories broke formation and ran for their lives. Ball's force broke apart. Three men were killed and an additional thirteen were wounded or taken prisoner. Two of Marion's men were killed, six were wounded. The skirmish had lasted no longer than fifteen minutes. The militia also captured as many as a hundred horses with new saddles and bridles, guns and powder, and even several fiddles and bows left by the fire. Among the horses was Colonel Ball's own mount; Marion claimed it for himself, named it Ball, and rode him through the next several months of the campaign. And another important lesson was learned: from that night forward Marion's men never crossed a bridge in the night until it had been covered with blankets to muffle the sound.

As was common, after this skirmish several members of the militia took leave and rode to their homes to tend to their personal affairs, while the rest of Marion's "Brigade," as it was being called, went back to their camp on Snow's Island, a desolate parcel of land in Florence County accessible only by boat. Its isolated location made it the perfect hideout for Marion's men between forays. No one could reach it without being spotted a great distance away. The number of men on Snow's Island at any particular time varied greatly as the size and the makeup of the militia were changing continually. There never was a steady number; volunteers came from far and wide. For example, after the fight at Black Mingo Creek five of Ball's men who had been captured volunteered to join the militia. With each success, country men would somehow find them and stay and fight awhile, then up and leave. Some returned; others did not. There was never a commitment asked or given. There was no discrimination among them; the militia consisted of black and white men, farmers and merchants, Irish immigrants and third-generation settlers, all brought together by their disgust for British intrusion into their lives. But among those men who stayed with Marion throughout his entire campaign was his slave, Oscar Marion.

To enlist slaves in the fight, especially in the south, in 1775 Lord Dunmore granted freedom to "all indentured servants, negroes, or others . . . that are able and willing to bear arms, they joining his majesty's troops."

Throughout the war Washington tried to walk the very narrow path between enlisting free black men and slaves, but the result was that African Americans in substantial numbers fought for both sides, in a great variety of roles in both the army and naval forces. And among them was Francis Marion's friend Oscar.

Oscar Marion was said to be Francis's aide, servant, chef, bugler, oarsman when necessary, and fighting man. As if they were writing a story of friendship that would be told centuries later, the two men fought side by side for seven years and, in fact, were depicted together in several noted paintings. In one painting, in which Oscar appears to be wounded, he and Marion are riding a white horse that has stopped for water at the Pee Dee River; in another he is shown hiding in the swamps with the rest of the brigade, and in still another he is rowing their boat. Perhaps the most famous painting, John Blake White's *General Marion Inviting a British Officer to Share His Meal*, which has hung in the US Senate since 1899, shows Oscar Marion in the background cooking a meal of sweet potatoes. According to the legend, a British officer under a white truce flag was brought blindfolded to the camp to discuss a prisoner exchange, and during that meeting he joined the rebels in a meal consisting solely of those roasted potatoes. When he returned to his lines, he resigned his commission, stating he could no longer engage in war against an enemy with the determination to keep fighting while having so little to eat. Or so the story goes.

At times the brigade was also joined by Marion's teenage nephew, Lieutenant Gabriel Marion, who had served in several of his uncle's campaigns. But that ended one terrible night in mid-November 1780. Marion had planned an attack on the village of Georgetown, a village on Winyah Bay, which was rich with needed supplies. While the main body waited in

John Blake White's 1820 painting *General Marion Inviting a British Officer to Share His Meal* depicts Marion with his slave, friend, and aide, Oscar Marion.

the swamps, he sent out two patrols to gather intelligence. Gabriel Marion was riding with Captain John Melton when they learned that Loyalists had made camp at a nearby place called "The Pens." As they passed through an overgrown swamp, they crossed paths with a Loyalist patrol. Both sides opened fire. In the melee Gabriel Marion was caught, and enemy soldiers started clubbing him with their muskets. As they beat him with the stocks of their long guns, Gabriel saw a familiar face, a man who before the war had often shared meals with his uncle. He ran to the man and threw his arms around him, beseeching him to help. There was nothing this man could do, although it is believed he spoke up on the young lieutenant's behalf. One of the Tories answered disgustedly that Gabriel "was one of the breed of that damned old rebel." His uncle's friend was warned to step off, or he would be killed, too. He had no choice. He moved away and Gabriel was shot through the chest.

Francis Marion was distraught when he learned of his nephew's death. Supposedly, in the next few days his killer was caught in another raid. Marion had promised that no harm was to come to him while in captivity. But when several prisoners were being moved across the swamps off the Black River, an officer rode right up to the man, lifted his weapon, and killed him on the spot. Marion was furious, ready to punish that deed; although he had been told that this Tory had murdered his nephew, "as a prisoner, his life ought to have been held most sacred; especially as the charge against him was without evidence, and, perhaps, no better than conjecture. As to my nephew, I believe he was cruelly murdered: but living virtuously, as he did, and then dying fighting for the rights of man, he is, no doubt, happy: and this is my comfort." The men who rode with Marion often said this was the only time they had seen him broken.

Francis Marion became a legend not only because of what he accomplished but by the way he accomplished it. Even though up north Ethan Allen and his Green Mountain Boys employed many of the same techniques as Marion's men, they were able to sustain their attacks for only a brief period of time. And eventually Ethan Allen was captured. The Swamp Fox was able to continue this mode of battle for many months, several times while large British forces were searching for him. In October Marion learned that Lieutenant Colonel Samuel Tynes had organized and was training a Loyalist militia consisting of many conscripted men in the hills near Tearcoat Swamp. The camp was established in the fork of the Black River; Tynes believed the swamp created an impassable natural barrier behind his men. Marion decided to attack and "break up the party, before its newly made converts should become confirmed in the principles they had unwillingly adopted."

Covered by the night, Marion's men silently crossed the river and set up an ambush on all three sides. At his signal the attack was launched. It ended in minutes; the Loyalists had suffered six dead, fourteen wounded, and twenty-three men captured. The raiders lost two horses. In addition to eighty muskets and horses captured, they gained several prisoners, who opted to join Marion's men.

In addition to these raids in force, groups of Marion's men continued pecking away at the Loyalists, taking small actions as much to keep the enemy off balance as to inflict real damage. As Marion once explained, "The destruction of all British stores . . . is of the greatest consequence to us, and only requires boldness and expedition." Operating from his island base, he sent out small detachments to harass the enemy. While one squad destroyed "a great quantity of valuable stores . . . at Manigault's Ferry," for example, Marion and other men raided a wagon convoy near Moncks Corner and destroyed fourteen wagonloads of soldiers' clothing and baggage while taking forty prisoners without absorbing any losses. He was relentless, inflicting the death of a thousand small stings.

Marion's unconventional tactics continued to confound his enemy. After crossing bridges, he would destroy them. He would approach an unwary enemy force or avoid potential ambush by fording streams at the deepest point rather than the shallowest, with his horse Ball almost always leading the way. His men moved under the cover of night and slept in the hottest part of the day. His scouts, who would remain hidden in tall trees for long periods, communicated by a shrill whistle. And to ensure complete secrecy, he never confided his plans to anyone else, even his officers; instead he led them to the point of attack. He picked his fights carefully; when confronted by an overwhelming force, he would scatter his men, only to reassemble them days later and a distance away. And as was written in celebration of his life in the early 1800s, "A swamp, right or left, or in his rear; a thicket beside him; any spot in which time could be gained . . . were all that he required, in order to secure a fit position for fighting in."

Furious at their inability to catch Marion, the British took out their frustration on the local population. Cornwallis told his officers, "All the inhabitants of this province . . . who had taken part in the revolt, should be punished with the greatest rigor; that they should be imprisoned and their whole property taken from them and destroyed." In early November Marion's relentless pursuer, Banastre Tarleton, devised a clever plan to finally bring an end to the Swamp Fox and his infernal attacks. His force was near Santee, camped on the plantation of rebel general Richard Richardson, who had died several weeks earlier and was buried on his land. Tarleton began spreading the rumor that the main body of his forces had returned to Camden, leaving only a small force behind. He was hoping that this opportunity would lure Marion into an attack against an overwhelming force. The plan might actually have worked, had Mary Richardson not dispatched one of her sons to warn Marion. When the Swamp Fox was informed that more than a thousand men were awaiting him, he sent his men home and faded safely into North Carolina's Great White Marsh.

When Tarleton learned from a prisoner who had escaped from his camp that Marion had eluded him again, he had a pleasant dinner with Mrs. Richardson and then, as Governor John Rutledge informed Congress, he "exceeded his usual barbarity, for having dined in her house, he not only burned it, after plundering it of everything it contained, but having driven into the barn a number of cattle, hogs, poultry, he consumed them, together with the barn, and the corn in it, in one general blaze." According to some historians, even that wasn't sufficient punishment. To ensure that General Richardson was dead and hadn't in fact escaped, Tarleton purportedly led or dragged Mary Richardson to her husband's grave and forced her to watch as his coffin was dug up and opened, then made her look at his decomposing remains.

Banastre once again pursued Marion, and once again without any success. To retaliate, as Cornwallis had ordered, his officers set fire to a huge swath of South Carolina, burning homes and farms over an area covering the seventy miles from Kingstree to Cheraw. They burned plantations, they burned crops, they killed livestock—especially sheep because their wool provided warm clothing—and they burned the churches. The result was quite different than Banastre expected; rather than being terrified by him, many of the radicalized colonists with nothing more to lose joined Marion's growing brigade.

Early in December 1780, only months after General Nathanael Greene had presided over the trial and execution of the spy Major John André, George Washington named Greene commander of the southern army, which at that time consisted of about a thousand irregulars, plus Marion's Brigade and similar militias under Thomas Sumter and Andrew Pickens.

In recognition of Marion's continued success, Greene promoted him to the rank of brigadier general of the South Carolina militia and put him in command of those troops in the eastern part of the state. More than that, though, Greene gave Marion reinforcements, sending Lieutenant Colonel Henry "Light Horse Harry" Lee and three hundred infantry and cavalry to support his efforts. At twenty-five, Henry Lee—whose son was Robert E. Lee—was about half as old as Marion and, in contrast to him, was said to be tall and handsome. But beginning in January, they made a fine team, as this larger force finally was able to take the offense.

Marion and Lee began by planning an attack on the two-hundred-man garrison at Georgetown. The Swamp Fox divided his force into three elements; in the middle of the night Captain Patrick Carnes and ninety men sailed down the Pee Dee River, taking cover in a swamp just across the river from the town, remaining there in hiding throughout the day. Meanwhile, Marion and Lee moved into place on either side of the town, waiting for

Nathanael Greene (above) began the war
as a militia private but rose to become
a major general in command of fighting
in the south and one of Washington's
most trusted aides; Colonel Henry
"Light Horse Harry" Lee (right) waged
a successful campaign in the south under
Greene—and was the father of Robert E.
Lee.

nightfall. After dark Carnes's commandos rowed across the river on flat-bottomed boats and captured the completely surprised British commander. Then they fired a signal shot to launch the attack. From either side of the village, Marion and Lee closed in.

After briefly trying but failing to make a fight of it, the garrison barricaded themselves inside secure bastions, choosing not to fight back. Marion and Lee walked into a completely calm town. There wasn't an enemy soldier to be seen. As they carried no tools for breaking down doors or windows, there was nothing they could do. The commander was granted parole, an honorable practice recognized by both sides, in which he was released with the understanding that he would no longer fight. More than twenty Loyalists were killed or wounded; Marion's men suffered no losses. Before dawn, the Swamp Fox and his men were again safely in the marshes.

In March, when General Greene attempted to lure Cornwallis into North Carolina, Lee temporarily rejoined his army, leaving Marion and his dwindling force on Snow's Island. Colonel Francis, Lord Rawdon, perceived this to be an opportunity to put an end to the Swamp

Fox. He planned to launch a frontal assault led by Lieutenant Colonel John Watson, and when the outnumbered Marion attempted to withdraw to North Carolina, he would be met by a second substantial force, waiting on the Pee Dee River to crush him.

Marion, who had been alerted that Watson was on the march, had his men prepare an ambush. They attacked him near Murrays Ferry, then lured him across the Santee River into the Wiboo Swamp. By the time Watson realized what was happening, his army was trapped on the wrong side of the river. For the next week they played a human chess game, two armies maneuvering for position. Meanwhile, Marion's sharpshooters picked off Watson's men, es-

William Ranney's circa 1850 painting *Francis Marion Crossing the Pee Dee* depicts the irregularly dressed militia in their most comfortable surroundings. Marion was so successful, Cornwallis complained "that there was scarcely an inhabitant between the Santee and the Peedee that was not in arms against us."

pecially his officers, one by one by one. Each time Watson attempted to break out, Marion would destroy the bridges he needed. Watson found himself trapped in the marshes and bogs between the Santee and Black Rivers, unable to move and running out of provisions. Watson finally made camp at the Cantey plantation, waiting, and hoping, for reinforcements that never arrived. When his men tried to forage for food, the sharpshooters were waiting for them. Watson finally was forced to stage a breakout, crossing the Sampit River under fire, then racing for the safety of Georgetown. His defeated army arrived there with wagonloads of casualties.

But Lord Rawdon had enjoyed one substantial success. While Marion had Watson's men pinned down, Rawdon's second force had landed unopposed on Snow's Island and burned the base there. All of Marion's supplies were destroyed, except what his men were carrying on their back. They were reduced to two rounds per man, not enough to repulse even a minor attack. Francis Marion had been fighting relentlessly for many months and now found himself without enough men, ammunition, supplies, or even a base. It was time, he understood, to consider disbanding his militia.

Before he could act on that notion, he received word that Light Horse Harry Lee was returning with Continental army reinforcements. The day after he arrived, on April 15, 1781, the combined force began a march on Fort Watson, a key point in the communications chain between North and South Carolina. Located just below the junction of the Congaree and Wateree Rivers, it was manned by 120 British troops and had been built on the highest point in the area, rising more than thirty feet above the plains. The land around it had been cut bare, making it impossible to move close under cover. The walls were steep and covered with three rows of sharpened stakes, which protruded from its sloping sides. Several weeks earlier the fort had successfully held out against an attack by Sumter's men, killing eighteen of them and suffering almost no losses. The fort seemed impenetrable.

But if Marion couldn't get in, he reasoned, the defenders couldn't get out. Freshwater ran into the fort from Scott's Lake. Marion's men dammed that source, shutting off the fort's water supply. Then they waited. The fort's resourceful commander responded by sinking a deep well, providing all the water the garrison would need.

The attack seemed blunted. The lack of cover prevented Marion's sharpshooters from getting close enough to the fort to keep the defenders off the walls. What followed was one of the most unusual events of the entire war. Colonel Hezekiah Maham proposed building their own fortification, a tower that protected Marion's riflemen as they sniped at the walls. Having no other solution, Marion agreed to try it. His men began cutting down green pine trees and carrying them closer to the fort. They laid them down as two long parallel trunks, but each level of two trunks crossed the last. It took five days to construct this thirty-foot-high rectangular tower, a Maham Tower, as it later came to be known. At its top they built a fully protected platform. In the dark night of the twenty-second, troops carried the tower into place.

When the sun rose on the morning of the twenty-third, the defenders were stunned to see a wooden tower in front of the fort. Sharpshooters inside the tower forced the defenders off the walls, allowing two "forlorn hope" teams—the leading attackers—to scale the walls without opposition. As an officer inside the fort later wrote, "cowardly and mutinous behavior of a majority of men, having grounded their arms and refused to defend the post any longer," caused the commander to surrender the fort. Marion lost two men and an additional three men were wounded, but he captured a vast amount of stores and ammunition. Two of the defenders were killed, six were wounded, and the thirty-six Loyalist militia were taken prisoner. The remaining troops were paroled. After the fort was emptied, it was pulled down, and an important link in the British chain of forts across South Carolina was gone.

General Greene's letter to General Marion about the victory remains one of the great tributes an officer has received from his commander:

> When I consider how much you have done and suffered, and under what disadvantage you have maintained your ground, I am at a loss which I admire most, your courage and fortitude, or your address and management. . . . History affords no instance wherein an officer has kept possession of a country under so many disadvantages as you have; surrounded on every side with a superior force, hunted from every quarter with veteran troops, you have found means to elude all their attempts, and to keep alive the expiring hopes of an oppressed militia, when all succor seemed to be cut off. To fight the enemy bravely, with a prospect of victory, is nothing; but to fight with intrepidity, under the constant impression of a defeat, and inspire irregular troops to do it, is a talent peculiar to yourself. . . . I shall miss no opportunity of declaring to Congress, and to the world in general, the great sense I have of your merit and your services.

The British attempt to bring South Carolina under their control had failed. Unlike those northern cities with large population centers, the geography and climate of the agrarian southern society and the already established tradition of fierce independence had presented obstacles Cornwallis had never truly understood, much less been able to conquer. Francis Marion's militia had provided the Continental army the time it needed to rebuild and return in force to the south. By early May, General Greene was finally prepared to meet the British at equal strength on a great battlefield—and drive them out of the Carolinas. In response, the British began fortifying the larger cities, such as Charlestown and Savannah.

As British forces withdrew into Charlestown, Marion's militia kept up its attacks. In late May, with Lee's Continental troops, they attacked Fort Motte, the main British supply depot between Charlotte and country outposts. The fort had been built around a large plantation house. Using bows and flaming arrows, the men set fire to the manor home, with all its supplies and the protection it offered. Attempts to douse the fire were met with cannon balls. The garrison had no choice but to surrender.

The once powerful line of British forts that stretched across the state fell like dominoes. Marion once again marched on Georgetown. This time, as he set up his siege lines, the redcoats boarded ships and sailed for Charlestown. His men marched in unopposed—and he celebrated by wearing a new uniform and taking two mules to carry his baggage.

In late August Washington and French general Rochambeau began marching seven thousand troops toward Cornwallis's army in Yorktown, Virginia, at the mouth of Chesapeake Bay. With British attention focused there, the battle for the south was nearing a conclusion. But the British had one more stand left in them. In September, the regular Continental forces and the various militias caught twenty-three hundred British troops camped by the Eutaw Springs in South Carolina. On the morning of September 8, a small Loyalist party out collecting yams encountered a colonial patrol. The Loyalists gave chase—right into Harry Lee's waiting ambush. Throughout the afternoon the fighting elevated into a pitched battle, with a British charge directly into patriot lines proving temporarily successful. It was an especially vicious battle at point-blank range and the blood was said to have been ankle-deep in places. The militias counterattacked, driving back the British—then actually settling into the redcoats' camp. Some men were finishing meals that had been left there by Loyalist troops when the British attacked—and a four-hour bloodbath ensued. It was a fury of death. And when the survivors left the battlefield, the outcome was ambiguous. While the British ended up holding the most territory, they had suffered grievous casualties: more than seven hundred men were killed, wounded, or captured. The patriots suffered, too, losing five hundred men killed, wounded, or captured. Many men were buried where they fell.

Neither side was left fit for more fighting. The British continued their retreat to Charlestown. And they prepared to move north to reinforce Cornwallis, who had stumbled into a trap at Yorktown. Washington surrounded Cornwallis's army with more than seventeen thousand French and Americans. Any escape over land was blocked by troops led by the Marquis de Lafayette; any attempt to flee by ship was blocked by the French fleet. On September 28, a massive and continuous bombardment began. For three weeks, day and night, infantry and naval artillery and cannons blasted the British position. Finally, on October 17, Cornwallis surrendered. For such a historic battle, the number of casualties actually was very light. Only 156 British men were killed, 326 wounded, and 70 men were missing. On the other side, 88 allied French and American men were killed and 301 wounded—considerably fewer than the mostly forgotten Battle at Eutaw Springs. Although the war continued for almost two more years, the victory at Yorktown marked the end of major combat in America.

There were repeated skirmishes as the war came slowly to an end. But Francis Marion, the Swamp Fox, had seen too much death. When told to attack a small British force gathering freshwater outside Charlestown, for example, he replied, completely in keeping with his character, "My brigade is composed of citizens, enough of whose blood has been

The bloody Battle of Eutaw Springs on September 8, 1781, was the last major engagement in the southern campaign. The outcome was indecisive: the British reported 85 men killed and 351 wounded, while the patriots lost an estimated 125 killed and 382 wounded. Afterward, the redcoats withdrew to Charlestown, unsuccessful in blunting the Americans, advance.

John Trumball's large painting *Surrender of Lord Wallis*, depicting the British laying down
their arms at Yorktown in October 1781, has hung in the Capitol rotunda since 1820.
Noticeably absent from that painting—as in real life—is General Cornwallis, who claimed
to be too ill to attend.

shed already. If ordered to attack, I shall obey; but with my consent, not another life shall be
lost. . . . Knowing, as we do, that the enemy are on the eve of departure, so far from offering
to molest, I would rather send a party to protect them."

With the fighting done, the men of his militia went home, most of them to peacefully
work their fields. In 1781 Marion was elected to the South Carolina Assembly, helping to
forge a peace between the remaining Loyalists and the victorious Americans. While others
cried for retribution, he championed conciliation, one time even stepping in to prevent the
lynching of a former Tory commander.

Marion rebuilt his own plantation, reportedly with Oscar, who had been wounded but
had healed. Eventually Francis Marion married his cousin and lived the remainder of his life
in peace and relative obscurity.

Valley Forge

The British army had proudly marched into Philadelphia in September 1777. The Continental Congress had fled to York, approximately one hundred miles away. After defeats at Brandywine and Germantown, the battered remnants of Washington's army had settled in for the long, cold winter of 1777–78 at Valley Forge, a strong defensive position on the Schuylkill River. It would be during this terrible winter at Valley Forge that Washington molded his army and brought hope to what at times had seemed like a hopeless fight for freedom.

Valley Forge has become symbolic of the terrible conditions that had to be overcome in the fight to create a new nation. As the French volunteer, the Chevalier de Pontgibaud, wrote upon arriving there in December:

> My imagination had pictured an army with uniforms, the glitter of arms, standards, etc., in short, military pomp of all sorts; instead of the imposing spectacle I expected, I saw, grouped together or standing alone, a few militiamen, poorly clad, and for the most part without shoes. . . . I also noticed soldiers wearing cotton nightcaps under their hats, and some having for cloaks or greatcoats coarse woolen blankets, exactly like those provided for the patients in our French hospitals. I learned afterwards that these were the officers and generals. Such, in strict truth, was, at the time I came amongst them, the appearance of this armed mob.

When Washington's twelve-thousand-man army made camp, they were short of every conceivable provision, including food, clothing, and medicine. It is difficult to imagine the deprivations his army faced: an estimated two out of three soldiers lacked shoes, and even blankets were scarce. Men injured in battle couldn't be properly treated and many of them died from their wounds. For a time many of the troops were forced to subsist on a mixture of water and flour known as a "firecake." At first there was little shelter from the cold and wet. As a result, scores of men left when their enlistment expired and others simply deserted in despair. General Washington pleaded to Congress: "It is more alarming than you will probably conceive. . . . For some days past, there has been little less, than a famine in camp. A part of the army has been a week, without any kind of flesh, and the rest for three or four days. Naked

In his General Orders of March 1, 1778, Washington paid tribute to the men who had suffered the Valley Forge winter with him, seen in this Tompkins H. Matteson painting, writing "to return his warmest thinks to the virtuous officers and soldiery of this army for persevering fidelity and zeal which they have uniformly manifested in all their conduct. Their fortitude . . . under the additional sufferings . . . clearly proves them worthy the inevitable privilege of contending for the rights of human nature, the Freedom and Independence of their Country."

and starving as they are, we cannot enough admire the incomparable patience and fidelity of the soldiery." Rather than facing these problems directly, the Congress discussed replacing Washington with a more aggressive leader.

Incredibly, while Washington's men lacked provisions, great numbers of them apparently had an abundance of spirit and fortitude. Meanwhile, only twenty miles away, the British army was warmly entrenched in Philadelphia, passing the winter in a safe and civilized manner, hosting formal dinners, attending theater, awaiting the spring thaw to finish this war, suffering few if any hardships. While the British celebrated Christmas with feasts by blazing fireplaces, the colonists dined on rice and vinegar, covering their freezing feet with rags. Yet at the end of the winter, it was the colonial army that emerged stronger and ready to do battle.

There were several reasons for this turnabout. For one thing, Congress had finally taken Washington seriously when he decried, "Unless some great and capital change suddenly takes place . . . this Army must inevitably . . . starve, dissolve, or disperse, in order to obtain subsistence in the best manner they can." Congress began spending the funds necessary to properly feed and equip the army. By February more than two thousand basic eighty-log cabins had been constructed and provisions were arriving daily at the encampment. In addition, the Prussian drill master Baron von Steuben had arrived and, with Washington's approval, began implementing uniform training procedures that would rapidly transform the troops into a well-drilled army. Wives and families, the "camp followers," had come to support their men, among them Martha Washington, who organized the women into sewing and nursing groups. Perhaps most important, the French government, inspired by the American victory at Saratoga the previous September and October, finally entered the war, agreeing to send both troops and the French fleet.

Washington celebrated the French decision by pardoning two men sentenced to hang for desertion, giving his troops a day off and proclaiming that he wanted "to set apart a day for gratefully acknowledging the divine goodness" and allotting each man one "gill of rum."

The toll taken by the winter was enormous. Of the twelve thousand men who began the winter, an estimated twenty-five hundred died of wounds; diseases including smallpox, dysentery, typhoid, and pneumonia that raced through the camp; or simply malnutrition. Another two thousand had finished their enlistment or deserted.

Although Washington's army had been reduced significantly in size, it had become a tougher, more resilient, properly trained, and highly motivated force. Having been tested and persevered, the colonial troops were now ready to take the fight to the enemy.

The British army, meanwhile, had lost its edge. By the time Washington marched his men out of Valley Forge, the strategic situation had changed drastically. Fearful of being cut off by the French fleet, General Howe decided to abandon Philadelphia and marshal his forces in New York. Continental troops reoccupied Philadelphia in June 1778. A week later, the Congress returned.

The colonial army took the offensive. As the British marched the hundred miles overland to New York, Washington ordered an attack on Howe's rear guard. The Americans caught the British at the Monmouth, New Jersey, courthouse. The Battle of Monmouth raged throughout the blistering hot day of June 28. As cold as it had been in the depths of December, temperatures on this day exceeded 100 degrees Fahrenheit. It was during this battle that the legend of Molly Pitcher was born. A woman named Mary Ludwig Hays was among the camp followers who served during the fighting by bringing water from a nearby spring to the fighting men to quench their thirst and cool their cannons. According to the story, when her husband, an artilleryman, was either wounded or had been killed she took his place and continued firing, and his gun crew mates began referring to her respectfully as "Molly Pitcher."

While the British rear guard achieved its aims by successfully protecting its withdrawing troops, the colonial army considered Monmouth a great victory. Washington's men had stood up to the full might of the British for the first time and fought them to a draw. The hard-won lessons learned during the winter at Valley Forge had made all the difference.

CHAPTER 8

FORGOTTEN
Heroes

Asilvery moon slipped out from behind a cloud, briefly illuminating the lone sentry. Forty-eight men, mostly from the 1st Rhode Island regiment, instantly fell silent in the shadows, watching and waiting. They were about to attempt one of the boldest raids of the war: they were going to kidnap British general Richard Prescott.

It was a seemingly impossible mission. Several months earlier Washington's second-in-command, General Charles Lee, had been captured. Military tradition of the time allowed officers of equal rank to be exchanged. When informers reported that General Prescott was staying in a farmhouse in Newport, Rhode Island, a daring raid was planned: a small party would row across Narragansett Bay, sneak onto the island, and, under the eyes of three thousand enemy soldiers, grab the general and return safely. "The

⌐ Prince Whipple, believed to be the African-American in this painting, became a legendary figure. Once, while carrying a substantial sum for his master, he was attacked by two highwaymen. He struck one with a whip, shot the other one, and delivered the money safely.

The slave Jack Sisson was credited with heroics in the successful raid to kidnap British general Richard Prescott.

enterprise will be attended with danger," the commander, Major William Barton, had warned when asking for volunteers, "and it is probable some of us may pass the shades of death before it is accomplished." The whole regiment stepped forward. Barton chose forty men; among them was an African American named Jack Sisson. Little is known of Sisson, beyond the fact that he was tall and broad and muscular, and he was a slave owned by Thomas Sisson, who had died that year. Major Barton must have had great confidence in him, though, as he picked him to steer the lead boat across the bay and participate in the actual raiding party.

With oars muffled, the five whale boats rowed three-quarters of a mile across open water; after landing, the raiding party moved quickly and quietly through fields and pastures more than half a mile to Mr. Overing's farmhouse. As they approached the house, the sentry called out, "Who comes there?" One of Barton's men responded, "Friends. Have you seen any deserters tonight?" As the cautious sentry waited for the proper countersign, Sisson raced forward and brought him down before he could raise a signal. He was quickly bound. Barton and Sisson went into the house; they climbed the stairway and found Prescott's door locked. According to the *Pennsylvania Evening Post*, Sisson banged his head against the door and "with his head, at the second stroke, forced a passage." The door flew open and the two men quickly hustled the startled general outside. In addition to Prescott, an aide and the sentry were taken back to the boats.

The raiding party was halfway back across the bay when the alarm was raised. Artillerymen fired cannons to alert the Royal Navy, but it was too late. The raid was a success and Prescott was exchanged for General Lee.

Jack Sisson was only one of the estimated nine thousand African Americans who fought and distinguished themselves in both the army and the navy in the war. The role of African Americans in the Revolution has been largely ignored, but black men actually fought on both sides and participated in just about all the major events of the war. Crispus Attucks is acknowledged as one of the first fatalities, being shot and killed in the Boston Massacre. At least nine black soldiers were among the minutemen who stood up to the British regulars

Newton Prince, an African American eyewitness to the shooting of Crispus Attucks at the Boston Massacre, reported, "I saw two or three strike with sticks on the guns. I was going off to the west of the soldiers and heard the guns fire and saw the dead carried off."

at Lexington and Concord, and among the wounded that day was Prince Estabrook, who is credited by many as being the first black combatant of the war.

Prior to the start of the war, both free and enslaved African Americans had served in many local and state militias, and saw action in battles against Indians. When war broke out the militias joined Washington's army, putting many African Americans in the uncomfortable position of fighting for a country that considered them property and deprived them of most of those rights they were fighting for. Among these soldiers was Salem Poor, a former slave who in 1769 had purchased his freedom for £27, about a year's salary, and married a freewoman. He enlisted in 1775 and soon found himself in the middle of the chaos on Breed's Hill. As British regulars overran the patriots' position, Salem Poor was one of the last men to abandon their redoubt, giving other soldiers the chance to get away. Historian Sarah Bailey wrote in 1880 that Poor saw Lieutenant Colonel James Abercrombie, commander of the elite grenadiers, "mount the redoubt and wave his arms in triumph; the colored lad aimed and fired, and then watched the British officer topple over." While there is limited historical record to support Bailey's specific claim, Poor's actions on Breed's Hill were so courageous that fourteen officers noted his heroism in a letter to the General Court of Massachusetts, writing, "The subscribers beg leave to report to your Honorable House (which we do in justice to the character of so brave a man), that, under our own observation, we declare that a negro man called Salem Poor of Col. Fryes regiment . . . behaved like an experienced officer, as well as an excellent soldier. To set forth particulars of his conduct would be tedious. We would only beg leave to say in the person of this negro centers a brave and gallant soldier."

Another African American hero of that bloody battle was Peter Salem, who had been given his freedom in 1775 to enlist in the Continental army. On Breed's Hill that bloody day he is credited by many historians with killing Marine major John Pitcairn. For his bravery that day he was acclaimed as a hero of battle. Men like Poor and Salem proved without doubt that African Americans were the equal of their white comrades in battle, but their presence posed a dilemma for Washington. Colonists were frightened that slaves who were given weapons might someday rise and turn those weapons against their owners, while slave owners knew that slaves who served in the military did so expecting their freedom. Washington was a slaveholder, but he also was an especially benevolent man and his opinion on the matter has never been clear. His own servant, Billy Lee, rode at his side throughout the war, according to historian Fritz Hirschfeld, "in the thick of battle, ready to hand over to the general a spare horse or his telescope or whatever else might be needed." As a valued aide to the beloved Washington, Lee became one of the best-known African Americans of the time.

In his 1887 book, *History of the Colored Race in America*, William Alexander wrote that at Bunker Hill, as seen in this lithograph, "Peter Salem, also a colored man, who so gallantly manned and defended the slight breastworks, shot dead Major Pitcairn, of the British Marines, who, in the final struggle, had scaled the redoubt and shouted 'The day is our own!'"

The question of what to do with African American soldiers aroused complex political issues. While the men were needed desperately, Washington could not risk alienating the colonies whose economy depended on slave labor. Finally, in July 1775, he ordered recruiters to stop enlisting "any stroller, negro, or vagabond," although permitting any African American already serving to remain in the ranks until his term of enlistment ended. As might have been predicted, the northern colonies objected. As Massachusetts's militia general John Thomas wrote to John Adams, "We have some negroes ... I look on them [as] equally serviceable with other men ... in action; many of them have proved themselves brave."

In response, the following November Virginia's royal governor, Lord Dunmore, offered slaves who volunteered to fight for the British their freedom: "I do hereby further declare all

John Trumbull's 1780 portrait of George Washington accurately portrays Washington's servant and slave Billy Lee at his side, where he served proudly throughout the war. In Washington's will the only slave he freed was the loyal Lee.

indentured servants, negroes, or others, [appertaining to Rebels,] free, that are able and willing to bear arms, they joining His Majesty's troops." Only a few hundred African Americans joined in the British ranks and, rather than being integrated into the ranks, they were formed into the specially created Ethiopian Regiment. The reality of runaway slaves fighting for the British—and their freedom—further complicated Washington's dilemma.

Finally, perhaps after a meeting with young Phillis Wheatley, the African American teenage poet, who became famous in both the colonies and England when her first volume was published in 1773, and whose work was read at the funerals of patriots, Washington informed Colonel Henry Lee, "We must use Negroes or run the risk of losing the war. . . . Success will depend on which side can arm the Negroes faster." The final resolution was that free African Americans who had served would be permitted to reenlist, but slaves would not be allowed to serve. Ironically, Dunmore's offer actually provided some benefit to his enemy, as southern plantation owners, somewhat ambivalent about being drawn into what many believed was a northern war, suddenly saw their way of life threatened and offered support to the American army.

The slaves themselves faced a very difficult choice with no guarantees, no matter what decision they made. When slave owner William Whipple enlisted in Washington's army, he took his servant, Prince Whipple, to war with him. Along the way he told Prince that should they be involved in combat, William expected him to acquit himself with courage to defend

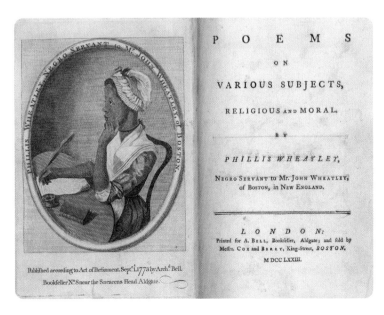

In 1773, eighteen-year-old slave Phillis Wheatley became the first black woman in America to have a collection of her poems published. The London publisher required the affirmation of eighteen important men, among them John Hancock, Reverend Samuel Mather, and royal governor Thomas Hutchinson that Wheatley actually was the author of these poems.

his country. The slave purportedly replied, "Sir, I have no inducement to fight; but if I had my liberty, I would endeavor to defend it to the last drop of my blood."

Hearing that, Captain Whipple freed him immediately. Prince Whipple enlisted in the army and eventually became an aide to George Washington. In fact, he is reputed to be the African American who is at Washington's side in the classic painting *Washington Crossing the Delaware.*

Only three colonies—Massachusetts, Connecticut, and Rhode Island—actively recruited African American soldiers, but there is no way of knowing precisely how many black soldiers were serving with the 1st Rhode Island Regiment at the Battle of Red Bank. Certainly it was a sizable contingent. One of them, it is known, was Jack Sisson. But whatever the number, the Continental troops made a historic and brave stand on October 22, 1777. After the British had conquered Philadelphia in September, Washington attempted to prevent them from being resupplied by blockading the Delaware River. He ordered two forts built downriver, Fort Mercer on the New Jersey side and Fort Mifflin on the opposite bank. As long as the Americans held those high points, no British shipping could reach the city. General Howe sent two thousand Hessian troops under the command of Colonel Carl von Donop to attack the four hundred men inside Fort Mercer. The colonel promised confidently, "Either the fort shall be called Fort Donop, or I shall have fallen."

Von Donop's prediction was accurate. The attack was repulsed by the courageous defenders of the fort and he was mortally wounded. In addition to 377 troops being killed during the battle, compared to 14 Americans, two British warships brought forward to support the attack ran aground and were set on fire and destroyed. It was the worst British defeat since Bunker Hill. Colonel James Varnum was so impressed by the courage displayed by his African American troops during the battle that he petitioned the Rhode Island Assembly to allow him to form an all-black regiment.

Varnum's timing was perfect. A shortage of troops had forced Washington to issue a quota to the states, allowing those states to determine who would be allowed to serve. The Rhode Island General Assembly permitted both free and enslaved African Americans to enlist, promising them that "every slave so enlisting shall, upon his passing muster before Colonel Christopher Greene, be immediately discharged from the service of his master or mistress, and be absolutely free." Their owners were to be paid the full market value, up to $400, for every slave who joined the fight. Eventually the 1st Rhode Island Regiment became the only majority African-American regiment in the Continental army.

The regiment first distinguished itself at the Battle of Rhode Island in late August 1778. This was planned to be the first battle in which colonial troops were supported by French

This Nathaniel Currier print features an unidentified black officer with Washington after he crossed the Delaware River. It is possible the soldier is supposed to be Prince Whipple or Washington's slave William Lee—or is simply intended to acknowledge the bravery of the black soldiers who fought in the Continental Army.

troops and the newly arrived French fleet. They were planning to attack the British garrison on Aquidneck Island, knowing that if they could capture the sixty-seven hundred soldiers there, General Clinton's position in New York would be desperate. But the French fleet was crippled by a storm and was unable to provide the promised assistance. General John Sullivan decided to press the attack and for several days the two sides traded artillery fire and met in occasional skirmishes. It became clear that without naval support Sullivan's army would not be able to advance. An orderly retreat began. Sullivan had to ferry more than five thousand troops across the Sakonnet River with six thousand enemy troops in pursuit. General Varnum's 1st Rhode Island was ordered to provide a defensive line across the island to prevent the British from attacking the retreating forces.

The battle raged through the day. The Hessians attacked the line three times and in hand-to-hand fighting were repulsed. As Samuel Greene Arnold wrote in his 1859 *History of the State of Rhode Island*:

> A third time the enemy, with desperate courage and increased strength, at-
> tempted to assail the redoubt, and would have carried it, but for the timely
> aid of two Continental battalions dispatched by Sullivan to support his
> almost exhausted troops. It was in repelling these furious onsets, that the
> newly raised black regiment . . . distinguished itself by deeds of desperate
> valor. Posted behind a thicket in the valley, three times they drove back the
> Hessians, who charged repeatedly down the hill to dislodge them; and so
> determined were the enemy in these successive charges that, the day after the
> battle, the Hessian colonel . . . applied to exchange his command . . . because
> he dared not lead his regiment again to battle, lest his men should shoot him
> for having caused so much loss.

Among the soldiers was an African American artillerist who was wounded in the arm. Rather than withdrawing, this soldier, whose name was not recorded, exchanged places with a white soldier, telling him, "I've got one arm to fight for my country." As he took his new position, he was shot and killed on the spot.

After their valiant stand on Aquidneck Island the 1st Rhode Island was sent to defend a position on the northern bank of New York's Croton River. On May 31, 1781, sixty caval-rymen and two hundred infantrymen of Colonel James DeLancey's Westchester Refugees launched a surprise attack on the camp. In the lightning raid, fourteen men of the 1st Rhode Island were killed, one hundred wounded, and thirty men were taken prisoner and later sold back into slavery in the West Indies. DeLancey's men suffered no casualties. Among the dead was the regiment's white commander, Colonel Christopher Greene, who was run through with a saber while still in his nightclothes, then thrown over a saddle and carried away. A contemporary account reported Greene's body was found about a mile away, cut and mangled "in a most shocking way." While there is no firm evidence to support it, the accepted belief at the time was that this raid was in retribution for Greene's fervent efforts in leading black soldiers against British troops.

While the 1st Rhode Island had suffered devastating losses it was rapidly reconstituted as a fighting force and within a few months was marching south under a new commander, Colonel Steven Olney.

The artist John Trumbull was an eyewitness to the Battle of Bunker Hill. This painting, circa 1820, depicts the death of General Warren. Trumbull became known for his painstaking research and visual accuracy. The African American on the right may have been Peter Salem or a slave belonging to the man in front of him, colonial officer Thomas Grosvenor.

Even among the numerous examples of extraordinary courage displayed by African American soldiers in combat, the actions of Jordan Freeman and Lambert Latham at the Battle of Groton Heights stands out. In September 1781, seventeen hundred British troops commanded by traitorous general Benedict Arnold landed near New London, Connecticut, and attacked lightly defended Fort Griswold. The estimated 185 patriots manning the fort, including both black and white soldiers, put up a spirited resistance, but had no chance of defeating the much larger force. As British troops led by Major William Montgomery scaled the walls, Jordan Freeman raced out to meet them. Out of ammunition, he bayoneted and killed Major Montgomery, then was himself killed.

After the fort had been taken, according to an eyewitness, a British captain demanded to know who had been in command of the fort. Colonel William Ledyard stepped forward, saying, "I did once. You do now." And then, according to an eyewitness, "at the same moment handing him his sword, which the unfeeling villain buried in his breast! Oh, the hellish spite and madness of a man that will murder a reasonable and noble-hearted officer, in the act of submitting and surrendering!"

In response, African American soldier Lambert Latham "retaliated upon the [British] officer by thrusting his bayonet through his body. Lambert, in return, received from the enemy thirty-three bayonet wounds, and thus fell, nobly avenging the death of his commander." The British response was to strike out against the survivors in what became known as the Fort Griswold Massacre. In fact, at the Battle of Yorktown, the Marquis de Lafayette purportedly led his men into battle with the war cry, "Remember Fort Griswold!"

The soldier at left in Jean Verger's 1780 watercolor featuring men who fought at Yorktown is a member of the 1st Rhode Island Regiment. While many colonials units were integrated, "the Black Regiment" is considered to be the first African American military force.

In addition to fighting on the front lines, many African Americans served in the Continental navy or filled a variety of other positions. Several men proved invaluable as spies, among them a slave named Pompey Lamb. In May 1779, Major General Sir Henry Clinton and forty-five hundred men captured the supply depot at Kings Ferry on the Hudson about twelve miles south of West Point, and the lightly defended forts at Stoney Point and Verplanck Point. It was an important position and he quickly reinforced it.

Clinton's plan was to try to draw Washington to him, but the colonial commander refused to take the bait. The problem was that these positions were almost impregnable; Stoney Point stood on a promontory about 150 feet above the Hudson River surrounded on three sides by the river and protected on the fourth side by a marsh. The British referred to it as "the Table on the Hill," and it could be reached only by traversing a causeway running through the marsh or by wading through the marshes at very low tide. A frontal assault would be close to suicidal; as Washington wrote to a friend, "An attempt to dislodge them . . . would require a greater force and apparatus than we are masters of." Rather than arms, he decided to use subterfuge. He sent several women to visit the position and their reports were disheartening; they saw no obvious weaknesses in the fortifications.

But when the British began using Stoney Point as a staging area for raids up and down the river, Washington knew he had to act. He assigned the task of taking the fortress to one of his bravest generals, "Mad Anthony" Wayne. Wayne commanded the Corps of Light Infantry, an elite group trained by Baron von Steuben to fight at close quarters, especially with a bayonet. The problem was getting close enough to the British troops to be able to use their bayonets.

The attack was planned for July 15. According to a now legendary story, one of the few people permitted regular passage into the fort was the slave Pompey, owned by a patriot known as Captain Lamb. Pompey would supply the garrison with locally grown berries, cherries, and vegetables. In early July, according to Wayne's plan, Pompey informed the soldiers that Captain Lamb needed him to work the fields during the day, but he would be pleased to make his delivery at night if he was given the password so he could get by the sentinels. The countersign on the night of the fifteenth was "The fort's our own." General Wayne was so pleased when he was informed of this that he made it the war cry of his attack.

Early that afternoon Wayne's men set out on a fourteen-mile march, reaching the fort after dark. This was to be a daring midnight attack made with bayonets, axes, and pikes. Muskets were not loaded. The attackers knew that if their approach was discovered before they reached the fort, they would be brutally cut down by British cannons. Fortunately, the weather was poor that night and clouds obscured the moon. The soldiers were each given a square of white paper to affix to their caps that would make them identifiable in the fighting. Wayne announced a bounty of as much as $500 to the first men to mount the breastworks. As the men prepared for what might be a suicide mission, many of them wrote final letters to their family; General Wayne wrote out his will.

Near midnight Pompey and two soldiers disguised as farmers, all of them carrying large baskets filled with fruits and vegetables, approached the first sentry on the far side of the causeway. After giving him the correct countersign, they were permitted to approach. As Pompey engaged the sentry in conversation, the soldiers seized and gagged him before he could sound a warning. They then proceeded to the causeway, taking the sentry with them. Several hundred men raced across the causeway while others waded through the marsh in water up to their chest. It was only as they approached the fort itself that pickets spotted them and raised the alarm, far too late for the deadly British artillery to be employed.

The battle began. It was brief but brutal, lasting only a half hour before the British surrendered. Some of Wayne's men had to make an extraordinarily difficult climb almost straight up the side of a cliff, but they made it. Wayne had lost 18 men, and 83 were wounded. Nineteen British soldiers were killed and 543 taken prisoner. Washington eventually abandoned the position because it required more men than he could spare to defend it, but before leaving, his army took a vast amount of stores and weapons.

It was in that same area, more than a year later, that an African American soldier supposedly helped foil the plot that might have changed the outcome of the war. On September 21, 1780, John Jacob "Rifle Jack" Peterson and a white soldier, Moses Sherwood, both members of the 2nd Regiment of New York, were stationed as lookouts at Croton Point. Peterson must have been recognized as a fine shot, as he carried a rifle rather than a musket. As they looked down upon the great Hudson River, they spotted a longboat carrying twenty-four men leave the British warship HMS *Vulture* and head directly for them. When the boat was close enough, the two men began firing, reportedly killing two soldiers. The boat turned around and hurried back to the ship. Within minutes the *Vulture* opened fire on Croton Point.

Peterson and Sherwood raced to nearby Fort Lafayette and reported the exchange. The commander of the fort dispatched two cannons and a howitzer to move within range of the ship. At dawn the next morning they opened fire, causing minor damage but forcing the *Vulture*'s captain to lift anchor and sail out of range—leaving behind the person it was there to collect, Major John André, who had just obtained from General Benedict Arnold the plans for West Point. Forced to return to New York on horseback, André was captured and then Arnold was revealed as a traitor.

Certainly one of the most important contributions made by an African American to the victory was the undercover work of James Armistead, a slave on the Armistead plantation in New Kent County, Virginia. By 1781 the war had moved to the south, and when General Lafayette's troops arrived in Virginia, James received permission from his master to join the Continental army. He eventually was assigned one of the most dangerous and difficult missions in the war—he was to become a double agent.

The details of his exploits remain sketchy, but there is no question about his courage or the results. Armistead successfully made his way into turncoat general Benedict Arnold's camp, claiming to be a runaway slave, and volunteered to work for the British. Supposedly he earned Arnold's trust by guiding his troops through the back roads of Virginia. African Americans were treated as invisible men in those days and officers didn't hesitate to speak freely in front of them. Armistead soaked up information, which was passed along to Lafayette. Eventually the British employed him as a spy, sending him back behind patriot lines—and he returned with false information given to him by Lafayette. When Arnold moved north, Armistead stayed in Virginia, talking his way into Lord Charles Cornwallis's headquarters. There he served as a waiter and, of course, passed along any intelligence he overheard to Lafayette. In the summer of 1781, Armistead learned that the British fleet was going to transport ten thousand troops to reinforce the garrison at Yorktown, Virginia, making it the center of their planned offensive. With this information, Admiral Comte de Grasse's French fleet got there first and successfully blocked the Chesapeake Bay, preventing British admiral Thomas Graves from delivering the vital reinforcements. Without those new troops, the outmanned Cornwallis eventually was forced to surrender.

While the Emancipation Act of 1783 freed slaves who had served as soldiers, because Armistead had been a spy, rather than a fighting man, he was returned to his owner. When Lafayette learned about this, he issued a testimonial, writing, "This is to certify that the bearer by the name of James has done essential services to me while I had the honour to command in this state. His intelligences from the enemy's camp were industriously collected and faithfully delivered. He perfectly acquitted himself with some important commissions I gave him and appears to me entitled to every reward his situation can admit of." As a result, in 1787 the Virginia General Assembly paid his owner for his freedom.

In appreciation James Armistead took the name Lafayette as his surname; he married, bought forty acres, and became a farmer. When the Marquis de Lafayette returned to the United States in 1824 at President James Monroe's invitation, he was honored in all twenty-four states. Huge crowds lined the streets to greet him. Supposedly, while in Virginia

This 1783 painting by Jean Baptiste Le Paon portrays the Marquis de Lafayette with his trusted spy, James Armistead, who successfully infiltrated Cornwallis's headquarters. It was intelligence provided by Armistead that enabled Washington to prevent the British from reinforcing Yorktown, leading to the colonists' historic victory.

to visit Washington's grave and give a speech to the House of Delegates, Lafayette ordered his carriage stopped when he saw Armistead Lafayette—a free man—standing among the crowd, and he got out and embraced him.

African Americans also fought bravely and successfully for the British. Historians estimate that as many as a hundred thousand slaves escaped their bondage during the war, but no one knows how many of them responded to Lord Dunmore's offer of freedom. Certainly the best-known—and feared—was Colonel Tye.

Titus Cornelius escaped from his owner in Monmouth County, New Jersey, in 1775, and eventually organized a guerrilla band of twenty-four mixed-race Loyalists known as the Black Brigade. While the British never formally commissioned black soldiers, rank was earned and bestowed out of respect for accomplishments. Colonel Tye first gained recognition in the 1778 Battle of Monmouth, when his band captured an officer of the Monmouth militia, but his real success began the following year when he launched a series of hit-and-run raids throughout that region. His brigade would appear suddenly, strike swiftly, then fade back into the safety of the county's swamps, rivers, and forests. These raids often targeted slave owners and were a lethal mix of revenge, military strategy, and commission—the British paid a bounty for each successful operation. His men struck throughout the summer of 1779; in July, for example, they attacked Tye's old town of Shrewsbury, capturing horses, cattle, and two men. That winter his men joined forces with the Queen's Rangers, an elite British guerrilla unit, to attack patriot strongholds around New York for desperately needed supplies.

Tye's attacks escalated the following summer, when the Black Brigade captured two New Jersey legislators, two militia leaders, and twelve of their men, rustled more than two hundred head of cattle, and began assassinating patriot leaders like Joseph Murray, who was known to brutally execute Loyalists. Tye became a local legend when in August 1780 he attacked a patriot named Joshua Huddy, in reprisal for Huddy's involvement in several hangings, at his tavern in Colts Neck. Huddy and a lady companion managed to hold off the band for several hours, firing preloaded muskets, until Tye's men set fire to the tavern. Huddy quickly surrendered in return for Tye's men putting out the fire and allowing his companion, Lucretia Emmons, to go safely.

Huddy was taken into custody but managed to escape the next morning when a patriot militia came upon Tye's band and opened fire. Either during the initial fighting or in this action, Tye was wounded in the wrist. While the wound itself was minor, over time it became infected and he died several weeks later. The death notice that appeared in a local paper described him as "justly to be more feared and respected than any of his brethren of a fairer complexion."

More than a year later, Huddy was captured by another African American Loyalist, a man known as Moses, and this time he was hanged.

The story of contributions made to the cause of American freedom by African American soldiers reaches a crescendo at the Battle of Yorktown, the climactic battle of the war. The arrival of the French fleet and fifty-five hundred well-trained and equipped troops under the command of the Comte de Rochambeau in the summer of 1780 had greatly bolstered Washington's army. At that time British forces were fighting on two fronts: General Clinton's troops were occupying New York while General Lord Cornwallis's southern army had successfully captured Charlestown and Savannah. Initially Washington planned to link up with Rochambeau to attack New York when the larger French fleet arrived. But when the fleet instead sailed south toward Chesapeake Bay, Washington changed his plans.

Under orders from Clinton to find a protected deep-water harbor for the British fleet in the lower Chesapeake Bay, Cornwallis had settled at Yorktown. Washington realized that Cornwallis had put himself in a precarious position, although it would take great luck, skill, and courage to exploit it. Rather than attacking Clinton, Washington would march south and trap Cornwallis's army. To ensure that Clinton stayed put in New York, Washington used subterfuge to convince him that he intended to attack New York. He had large brick bread ovens built, erected tents, and prepared false plans detailing the attack that spies carried into the city. Then, leaving a small force behind to show continued activity in the camp, Washington and Rochambeau marched to Virginia.

In early September the French fleet landed three thousand troops in the lower Chesapeake Bay, then fought off a British attack. When the British sailed back to New York, the French fleet established a blockade to prevent Cornwallis from being resupplied by sea. By the end of September, almost eighteen thousand American and French troops were only seventeen miles away from the eighty-three hundred British troops at Yorktown—among them more than a thousand escaped slaves. Cornwallis sent Clinton a message pleading for help. Clinton responded that a British fleet carrying five thousand soldiers would depart from New York in early October. Somehow Cornwallis had to hold out until those reinforcements arrived.

Cornwallis began establishing a secure defensive position, including ten redoubts, small enclosed artillery positions connected by trenches. On September 28, Washington's army arrived at Yorktown. They immediately began digging siege trenches eight hundred yards from the British line. When that digging was completed, artillery moved up and began a barrage that continued for nine days, knocking out much of Cornwallis's cannons.

It was sometime during that period that Cornwallis learned that Clinton had been delayed. The British fleet was not en route to relieve him. On October 11, Washington began digging a second trench, this one only four hundred yards from the British lines. But artillery fire from redoubts 9 and 10 prevented him from completing this second trench. As historian Samuel Greene Arnold wrote, "These were two very strong redoubts, in advance of their principal line, from which the British fire was most galling." Washington had no choice: he had to mount an assault directly into those guns. He and Lafayette determined that the French were to storm the stronghold to the left, while the reconstituted 1st Rhode Island Regiment—among them Jack Sisson—was to attack redoubt 10, on the right.

The attack began on the night of October 14. As Colonel Olney, later of the 1st Rhode Island, remembered:

> General Washington made a short address or harangue, admonishing us to act the part of firm and brave soldiers. . . . I thought then that His Excellency's knees rather shook, but I have since doubted whether it was not mine.
>
> The column marched in silence. . . . Many, no doubt, thinking, that less than one quarter of a mile would finish the journey of life with them. On the march, I had a chance to whisper to several of my men (whom I doubted,) and told them I had full confidence they would act the part of brave soldiers . . . and if their guns should be shot away, not to retreat, but take the first man's gun that might be killed.

The attack began when a small group raced forward to hack a path through the abatis, a line of fallen trees arranged so that their intertwined branches formed a sort of barbed-wire barricade. They came under intense British fire. As Olney wrote, "The enemy fired a full body of musketry. At this, our men broke silence and huzzaed; and as the order for silence seemed broken by every one, I huzzaed with all my power, saying, see how frightened they are. . . . We made out to crawl through or get over, and from the enemy's first fire, until we got possession of the redoubt, I think did not exceed ten minutes." Colonel Olney was shot and stabbed by a bayonet, but survived. The French took a full half hour to capture their objective, suffering fifteen deaths, while nine Americans died in the attack.

The second trench was completed the following day and, as Arnold wrote in his history, "The walls of Yorktown crumbled before the terrible fire of the besiegers. . . . The British fire slackened, their ammunition was nearly exhausted, and their artillery broken and dismounted." Cornwallis made a futile counterattack, which was repulsed, then attempted to escape by crossing the York River in small boats. But foul weather forced him to turn back. He had no choice but to ask for terms of surrender.

Four days later the British fleet arrived. When informed of the situation, the fleet returned to New York.

On October 19, 1781, American and French troops lined up facing each other on either side of a road, lines said to stretch more than a mile long. The British soldiers, drums muffled in black cloth, marched between them and laid down their weapons. Watching proudly were the men of the 1st Rhode Island, whose attack on redoubt 10 had played a vital role in the victory.

While the war continued for almost two more years, Yorktown was the last substantial battle on American soil. It would be poetic to claim that all of the African Americans who fought in the war then enjoyed their freedom, but that is far from reality. It is estimated by historians that only about a third of former slaves eventually lived as free men. Supposedly as many as twenty thousand African Americans sailed to England with the defeated redcoats, knowing that slavery had been outlawed there. Former soldiers also ended up in other parts of Europe, Canada, and the West Indies. Unfortunately, a substantial number appear to have once again been enslaved.

Several thousand men who had served in the British army were granted land in Nova Scotia, but when that acreage proved to have little value for farming, twelve hundred of them were transported to Africa, where they founded the aptly named community of Freetown, in the colony of Sierra Leone.

Yankee Doodle Dandy

❧

Yankee Doodle came to town,

riding on a pony,

Stuck a feather in his cap,

and called it Macaroni...

❧

Young Americans have been joyfully singing that playful verse— without knowing what it means—for more than 250 years. "Yankee Doodle" is certainly among the oldest and best-known songs in American history. In fact, it's difficult to even read those few words without the familiar tune bouncing in your head. But very little actually is known about the derivation of that song, and there probably are as many stories about it as there are verses.

The derivation of the word Yankee isn't even known, although the first known use of it in print was by British general James Wolfe, who referred to the colonists fighting alongside his troops in the Seven Years' War. While inside the United States it usually refers specifically to northerners, to the rest of the world it means all Americans.

The well-known tune is considerably older than the Revolutionary War lyrics, and some version of it is said to exist in work songs sung in the French vineyards; or Irish, Dutch, Hungarian, and English folk tunes, including the British ditty "Lydia Fisher's Jug." The first known sheet music was published in London in 1775, and was to be sung "thru the Nose, and in the West Country drawl and dialect." But most historians believe the "Yankee Doodle" lyrics apparently date back to the 1750s, when often-ragged colonial militiamen in their simply country clothing and tricornered hats joined the handsomely turned out, well-drilled redcoats to fight the French. The lyrics, supposedly written by British surgeon and musician Richard Schackburg, were intended to ridicule the American country bumpkins: A doodle was a foolish person, so a "Yankee Doodle" was a silly colonist. A dandy was a man who affected an overly elite persona in his dress, speech, and manners, a man pretending to be far more than he is in an effort to impress people.

Rather than being pasta, "macaroni" referred to an overly feminine style of dress and manners made popular in England by wealthy young men returning from Italy and France after completing what was then known as the "Grand Tour" of Europe. So the seemingly silly feather-in-the-hat line was meant to make fun of the naïve Americans, who supposedly were so silly that they thought simply by sticking an animal feather in their coonskin caps they could look like a sophisticated European.

The joke backfired. Rather than being insulted, the colonists adopted the tune and when the Revolution began added their own verses to it, often writing new stanzas to reflect the latest events of the war. When the colonists acquired new artillery, for example, someone wrote: "Every time they shoot it off, It takes a horn of powder; and makes a noise like father's gun, Only a nation louder."

Apparently both sides marched to it throughout the war. It was a tune easily played on a fife, and its often boisterous, colorful, and even risqué lyrics added to the flavor. One well-known British stanza told the story of a colonist named Thomas Ditson who was tarred and feathered for trying to purchase a musket: "Yankee Doodle came to town, For to buy a musket; We will tar and feather him, and so we will John Hancock!"

According to a Boston newspaper report, confident British troops apparently were singing a derogatory version of that song as they marched out of that city in April 1775 to relieve redcoats under attack at Lexington and Concord. And when they returned, having been stunned by both the ferocity and innovative tactics of the local militia, one soldier, when asked if he had changed his tune, replied, "D--n them, they made us dance it till we were tired."

It eventually became the most popular American song, and was adopted as the unofficial anthem. According to legend, when the British surrendered to Washington at Yorktown in 1781, they played the song "The World Turned Upside Down," while the victorious Americans avenged the slight from so many years earlier by responding with a lively version of "Yankee Doodle." If that were true it would make a perfect ending, though contrary to most reports it probably isn't.

A charcoal sketch by Norman Rockwell from his 1937 large mural *Yankee Doodle Came to Town.*

Tradition at that time allowed musicians from the surrendering army to play a march favored by the victors while its flags flew and troops walked forward and laid down their arms. But when General Benjamin Lincoln had surrendered to British general Clinton at Charlestown he was ordered to keep the American colors furled and prohibited from playing an English or German song. It was an insult Lincoln did not forget; when Washington chose him to negotiate the terms of the British surrender at Yorktown he insisted on including a clause reading, "The garrison of York will march out to a place to be appointed in front of his posts, at two o'clock precisely, with shouldered arms, colors cased, and drums beating a British or German march." And while records do appear to show that the victorious Americans played "Yankee Doodle" when General Burgoyne surrendered his 6,000-man army to General

Currier & Ives's 1862 hand-colored lithograph *Yankee Volunteers Marching into Dixie*, subtitled *Yankee Doodle Keep It Up, Yankee Doodle Dandy*, demonstrates the lasting popularity of the song.

Horatio Gates at Saratoga, there is no record of any music being played during the ceremony of surrender at Yorktown.

Rather than the popularity of the song ending with the conclusion of the war, as most wartime songs do, the ease with which new verses can be fit to it, as well as the seemingly nonsensical lyrics of the original version that have always appealed to children, have kept it popular. During the Civil War, for example, both Union and Confederate troops embraced it. While the Southerners pointed out in their song "Dixie Doodle," "Yankee Doodle had a mind, To whip the Southern Traitors; Because they didn't choose to live, on codfish and potatoes," the Northerners advised in the chorus of their version, "Yankee Doodle keep it up, Yankee Doodle dandy; Plant your bayonet on top, and with your gun be handy!"

The appeal of this simple song really has never ended.

A lobby card for the 1942 movie musical *Yankee Doodle Dandy*. James Cagney won the Academy Award as Best Actor for his starring role as the beloved entertainer George M. Cohan.

CHAPTER 9

President George Washington

FORGED IN CONFLICT

I n the winter of 1786, George Washington stood silently at a large window, looking out onto the sprawling fields of his beloved plantation, Mount Vernon, wondering if he would be able to retain it. As was the case with so many people in this new country, his debts were growing rapidly and it had become far more difficult to pay them. But he must have realized how fortunate he was that at least his storehouses were well stocked. His Excellency had led the colonies to one of the greatest military victories in history, but the peace that followed was proving far more painful than anyone could have imagined.

The Revolution was over. It had been a long and bloody war, but the colonies had won their freedom. Now different battles had to be fought, with words and ideas rather than with muskets, to determine the kind of country so many men had died to create. The states had united for battle; now they had to form a nation.

Jean Ferris's painting *John Paul Jones at the Constitutional Convention* depicts the American naval hero entering Constitution Hall with Benjamin Franklin and George Washington.

General Washington had resigned his commission in December 1783. He was regarded throughout the new country with such great favor that he might have remained in command with any title of his choosing—there were some who would not have been disappointed if he had accepted a king's crown—but instead he chose to return to his former life as a benevolent plantation owner. He owned many thousands of acres and was known to treat his slaves fairly. To mark his resignation he had invited his officers to meet with him one final time at Fraunces Tavern in New York City. These were the men with whom he had fought through the hardest winters and the bloodiest battles. At this meeting, wrote Colonel Benjamin Tallmadge:

> His emotions were too strong to be concealed which seemed to be recip-rocated by every officer present. After partaking of a slight refreshment in almost breathless silence the general filled his glass with wine and turning to the officers said, "With a heart full of love and gratitude I now take leave of you. I most devoutly wish that your latter days may be as prosperous and happy as your former ones have been glorious and honorable." . . . General Knox being nearest to him turned to the commander in chief who, suffused in tears, was incapable of utterance but grasped his hand when they em-braced each other in silence. In the same affectionate manner every officer in the room marched up and parted with his general in chief. Such a scene of sorrow and weeping I had never before witnessed and fondly hope I may never be called to witness again.

And then he went home, leaving to others, he thought, the job of molding the separate states into a country. Few people realized how difficult a task that would prove to be. The cost of waging war had been extraordinarily high; it had left the new nation with massive debts. The colonies had struggled to pay for the war using a variety of methods to raise revenue: To support its militia, each state printed its own currency, taxed its residents, and even imposed duties on goods brought in from other states. In addition, the Continental Congress printed its own money but it had very questionable worth, as there was almost nothing of real value to back it, giving rise to the phrase "Not worth a continental."

The new country was fighting a different kind of war, and one that struck hard at every citizen; post–Revolutionary War America was suffering a devastating economic depression. During the war people had done business with trust, credit, and barter, but that had changed; merchants were insisting on hard currency. To settle their own debts they needed real dollars,

Alonzo Chappel's *Washington's Farewell to His Officers* captures the dramatic scene on December 4, 1783, when Washington gathered his staff at New York's Fraunces Tavern and announced his resignation. Finally, the war was over. Freedom had been won.

Among the first orders of business—literally—for the new country was the creation of a national currency. Until this time varied forms of exchange were common, from commodities to state-issued money to foreign coins and bills. The continental currency seen here was essentially worthless by the end of the war because the Congress devalued it by over-printing.

backed by gold and silver, but their customers just didn't have it. The farmers and tradesmen had little money to buy products, and so fewer people were employed to make those products. The manufacturing industry collapsed. The once thriving export market had shrunk drastically; Britain still dominated international trade and kept its markets mostly closed to Americans, especially the valuable West Indies trade, while at the same time dumping its own cheap goods, mostly in the south. The French were demanding repayment for their war expenditures while also protecting their own ports. American merchants, increasingly desperate for those foreign markets to be reopened, wanted taxes to be raised to settle those war debts. At the center of the problem was the fact that the country lacked a strong central government that could impose the policies necessary to deal with this crisis. The states were still almost completely autonomous, bound together only by a weak document called the Articles of Confederation.

Passed by the Continental Congress in 1777 and finally ratified in 1781, this treaty was intended to loosely bind the states together in a "perpetual union." It was drafted with great difficulty, as the states wanted to gain the benefits of a union without surrendering any of their individual powers. It contained thirteen articles, the first one bestowing on this confederation a name: "The stile of this confederacy shall be 'The United States of America.'" The other twelve mostly acted to limit the powers of the central government: The second article, arguably the most important, specifically did that, stating, unequivocally, "Each state retains its sovereignty, freedom, and independence, and every power, jurisdiction, and right, which is not by this Confederation expressly delegated." The government was given no power to mediate disputes between states. Also each state, regardless of its size, was granted one vote in Congress—and as unanimous consent was required to make any changes to this agreement, each state had complete veto power.

While it did grant some limited powers to the central government—for example, Article 8 stated that the expenditures of the central government would be paid by funds raised by state governments—it provided no mechanism to raise that revenue or enforce penalties. As a result, the very weak central government was helpless to deal with the current economic situation.

As Henry Knox described the problem in a 1786 letter to Washington, "Our political machine constituted of thirteen independent sovereignties, have been perpetually operating against each other, and against the federal head, ever since the peace—The powers of Congress are utterly inadequate to preserve the balance between the respective States, and oblige them to do [t]hose things which are essential for their own welfare, and for the general good. . . . The machine works inversely to the public good in all its parts. . . . [S]omething is wanting, and something must be done or we shall be involved in all the horror of faction and civil war without a prospect of its termination."

To raise desperately needed revenue, states had begun imposing taxes on their citizens—in some instances, ironically, at rates even higher than the British had once demanded. When farmers were unable to pay their debts or their mortgages or satisfy their tax bills, their homes, fields, livestock, and other possessions were seized. In a few places farmers who couldn't pay their debts—men who had fought for their country—were imprisoned. The farmers pleaded with their state assembly for relief, asking specifically for the state to lower taxes and issue more paper currency, but the merchants who dominated the legislature knew that would hurt their own interests and refused to consider it. Before the war, debtors had despised the tax collectors—now, after years of fighting, the only difference was who ended up with their money or property.

Once again anger was simmering in New England. These people had risen once before and been successful, and the memory was still quite fresh. Before the Revolution John Adams had written many critical articles under the pseudonym Humphrey Ploughjogger, meaning "the farmers," and while this time it probably was not the work of Adams, "Plough Jogger"—as this note was signed—reappeared in a local newspaper. "I have been greatly abused," he wrote, "have been obliged to do more than my part in the war, been loaded with class rates, town rates, province rates, Continental rates and all rates . . . been pulled and hauled by sheriffs, constables and collectors, and had my cattle sold for less than they were worth. . . . I think it is time for us to rise and put a stop to it, and have no more courts, nor sheriffs, nor collectors nor lawyers."

And just as they had two decades earlier, the protesters began taking action. In Massachusetts and Connecticut, farmers met tax collectors with force, seizing back their property and hiding livestock and other possessions. They prevented local courts, which were issuing writs to enforce debt collection, from meeting, and broke debtors free from jail. In response, state governments called out the militia—although in some instances that militia consisted of many of the same men participating in the protests. A fearful James Warren wrote to Adams, "We are now in a state of anarchy and confusion bordering on a civil war." Adams, a champion of liberty and individual rights, claimed the British were instigating treason and helped pass legislation in the state assembly suspending habeas corpus, allowing leaders of this growing rebellion to be jailed without a trial.

This growing rebellion found a leader in a farmer named Daniel Shays. His followers called themselves Regulators and sometimes marched with pine needles in their hats symbolic of the liberty tree. Shays was a farmer who had served as a captain in the Massachusetts militia during the war, seeing action at Lexington, Bunker Hill, and Saratoga before being wounded. Like so many other patriots, he never received the promised pay for his service and so was unable to pay his debts. In 1780 he was given an ornamental sword for his service— which he sold in an unsuccessful effort to settle those debts. In August 1786, Shays and an estimated fifteen hundred protesters successfully prevented the Northampton County Court of Common Pleas from hearing foreclosure cases. A week later the Worcester County Court was similarly stopped from meeting. For three days in late September Shays and six hundred farmers occupied the Springfield courthouse to ensure the Supreme Judicial Court could not meet. The county militia was called out to respond, but sympathetic members of that force refused to take arms against their friends and neighbors. In desperation, Governor James Bowdoin authorized General Benjamin Lincoln to recruit a private twelve-hundred-man militia, paid for by merchants, to protect the courts.

Until then, Shays's protests had been peaceful, but the presence of an armed militia changed the situation. To meet this new challenge, Shays planned to overrun a new federal arsenal at Springfield and seize all the arms and ammunition his growing army would need. They believed the defenders would also be sympathetic and stand aside. On January 25, 1787, two thousand farmers marched on the arsenal. The twelve hundred defenders stood their

The 1787 satirical engraving
(top) gives some idea of all the
problems local, state, and federal
governments faced in establishing
an equitable system. While focused
on Connecticut politics, the wagon
being pulled from either side as it
sinks into the mud illustrated the
difficulty in getting anything done.
The woodcut (right) appeared on
the cover of a pamphlet supporting
Shay's Rebellion against economic
injustice.

This illustration from an 1884 edition of *Harper's* depicts followers of Daniel Shays taking control of the Northampton, Massachusetts, courthouse to prevent judges from enforcing orders confiscating land from debtors. To the left, the proclamation signed by Benjamin Franklin offering a reward for the leaders of the rebellion.

ground. When Shays's Regulators continued to press forward, the guards fired warning shots; when that failed to stop them, they opened fire with artillery. Four men were killed and another twenty were wounded. Shays's army scattered, with Lincoln's militia in pursuit. Lincoln caught up with Shays at Petersham, capturing some of the protesters and causing most of the rest to return to their farms. Shays and some other leaders escaped into the independent republic of Vermont. The rebellion was finished.

Shays and other leaders eventually were granted amnesty; and while their protests failed, they had made their voices heard. In the next election, Massachusetts governor Bowdoin was easily defeated by the more conciliatory John Hancock. The newly elected Massachusetts legislature quickly cut taxes and suspended debt payments. The country began to climb out of its depression.

But the Shays Rebellion had made obvious the need for a stronger central government. The Annapolis Convention, meeting the prior September, had agreed to a constitutional convention intended to strengthen the Articles of Confederation. This meeting convened in Philadelphia in May 1787. Rhode Island, which had remained so aloof at times that it was referred to as Rogue Island, was concerned that strengthening the government would be harmful to its sovereignty and refused to send representatives.

Initially George Washington did not want to attend, convinced the states were not prepared to cede power to a stronger central government and nothing of value would be accomplished. As he wrote to Henry Knox, "I believe that the political machine will yet be much tumbled and tossed, and possibly be wrecked altogether, before such a system . . . will be adopted." It's also possible that Washington knew he would be elected the leader and did not want to appear to be grasping for power. But Knox, James Madison, and Benjamin Franklin, among others, prevailed upon him to attend, recognizing that he was the only man capable of bringing together a convention with so many competing interests.

At the beginning of the convention Washington was unanimously elected its president and it was agreed that the proceedings would be kept completely secret—to prevent outside pressure from being brought upon the delegates, none of the debates would be printed or communicated. The doors and windows were closed and few notes were taken. While apparently Washington was not an especially active participant in the debates, his presence in the hall, seated at the front in an ornate chair with a rising sun carved into its back, added the necessary solemnity to the proceedings.

It was a remarkable event. These men were attempting to achieve something that had never before been done: form a central government with sufficient power to rise above the states when necessary, while making certain those states maintained their sovereignty and that the individual rights of each citizen were protected. At that moment most people were far more loyal to their state than to the union. Citizens awaited eagerly to learn what type of government the convention would propose. Some people anticipated Washington emerging from behind those doors as the first king of America.

The framework for the convention was drawn from history. The representatives based their conclusions on British law and tradition, on arguments made thousands of years earlier by Greeks and Romans when debating the role of the state, and by their contemporaries from Germany and Holland who only recently had wrestled with the same complex questions. The debates were said to be long and at times angry. The desire to form a stronger nation certainly existed, but the lack of trust among the states created a roadblock. Washington's frustration

Junius Brutus Stearns's *Washington as Statesman* depicts the Constitutional Convention.
Initially about the only thing on which the delegates could reach an agreement was the
election of war hero Washington as the presiding officer.

was obvious, as he wrote to Alexander Hamilton, "In a word, I almost despair of seeing a
favorable issue to the proceedings of the convention, and do therefore repent having had any
agency in the business."

While supposedly this convention had been called to amend the Articles of Confederation, one of the first accomplishments was an agreement that an entirely new document be
drafted, a document that would constitute the laws by which the united states would come
together as one country.

The most difficult issue to be solved was how power would be shared by the central
government and the states. Some representatives continued to insist that the rights of the
individual states had to remain superior to any central government, while others, like James

Madison, wanted a strong national government. Many delegates were concerned that a strong central government could eventually lead to the same type of tyranny they had spent so many years and lives to overcome. In Madison's personal notes, he quoted New York's John Lansing, who summed up the feelings of those representatives defending states' rights: "Is it to be thought that the people of America, so watchful over their interests, so jealous of their liberties, will give up their all, will surrender both the sword and the purse, to the same body, and that, too, not chosen immediately by themselves? They never will. They never ought. Will they trust such a body with the regulation of their trade, with the regulation of their taxes, with all the other great powers which are in contemplation?"

Madison responded, "It will be said that, if the people are averse to parting with power, why is it hoped that they will part with it to a national legislature? The proper answer is that in this case they do not part with power; they only transfer it from one set of immediate representatives to another set."

James Madison had been among the first to arrive in Philadelphia and, while awaiting the others, had drawn up a government structure that became known as the Virginia Plan. Proposed to the convention by Edmund Randolph, it consisted of fifteen resolutions that were based loosely on concepts created by the French political philosopher Montesquieu and the British philosopher John Locke. Basically, it proposed a government elected by the citizens consisting of three branches; a legislature, a judiciary, and an executive, each with its own powers and some ability to provide checks and balances over the others. The legislature was to be divided into two houses; members of the House of Representatives would be directly elected by the people to three-year terms, and senators would be elected by state legislatures to seven-year terms. The plan did not include any suggestion over the composition of the executive branch.

Tempers frayed in the heat of the Philadelphia summer. To counter the Virginia Plan, which granted more power to those states with larger populations, the smaller states supported the New Jersey Plan, in which every state had one vote in a single legislative body. For a time compromise seemed impossible. At one point in the debate Delaware's Gunning Bedford Jr. rose and warned that if the large states tried to impose this structure, to protect their rights, "the small ones would find some foreign ally of more honor and good faith, who will take them by the hand and do them justice."

The suggestion that a state might need to turn to foreign nations for protection, so soon after the Revolution, was denounced as practically traitorous. Unfortunately, two greatly respected men who might have brought more order to the proceedings, Thomas Jefferson and

John Adams, were both in Europe trying to settle national debts and establish better relations. As Jefferson in Paris wrote to his close friend Adams in London, "I have news from America as late as July 19. Nothing had then transpired from the federal convention." Adding that while he thought it had been an "abominable" mistake keeping the proceedings private, he did suggest "all their other measures will be good and wise" because "it is really an assembly of demigods."

Jefferson's "assembly of demigods" debated and argued and reasoned and pleaded into the summer, searching for some compromise that would be agreeable to both large and small states. The larger states insisted that because they would be contributing more to the nation's finances and defense, they should have greater influence; the smaller states remained concerned that they would have no voice and demanded equal representation. Connecticut's Roger Sherman finally proposed a solution; the Great Compromise, as eventually modified, created a national legislature composed of two houses. The lower house would consist of representatives based on each state's population, while in the upper house every state would have two senators. The plan did not please everyone, but the delegates were sensible enough to understand, as Massachusetts's Caleb Strong warned before the vote was taken, "If no accommodation takes place, the Union itself must soon be dissolved."

After extended debate on July 16, the convention finally considered the compromise. It passed by one vote, arguably the most important single vote in American history.

There was still one additional and very complex problem to be solved: How would the lower house be apportioned? The southern states wanted nonvoting slaves to be counted when determining their population; the northern states wanted to include only free men. The balance of power in the government depended on the resolution; counting slaves the equal of free men would almost double the number of representatives from the southern states in this Congress as well as in the body that would elect the executive, the electoral college. It would tilt the balance of power in their direction.

In a brutal turn of logic, Massachusetts's Elbridge Gerry wondered, why "should the blacks, who were property in the south, be in the rule of representation more than the cattle and horses of the north?" The antislavery contingent also feared that allowing slaves to be counted would provide an additional incentive for the southern states to import more slaves.

The delegates finally agreed to recognize the existence of the slaves without making them the equal of free men. After considerable negotiation—all manner of ratios were considered, from one-quarter to three-fourths—they eventually settled on the Three-Fifths Compromise. One reason the South finally accepted this provision is that the convention also tied taxation to population. As Madison wrote later in his Federalist Papers, "By extending the rule to both [taxation and representation], the states will have opposite interests, which will control and balance each other, and produce the requisite impartiality."

New York's Gouverneur Morris was asked to write the preamble. He was given a draft of the ideas to be included, which began, "We the people of the states of New-Hampshire, Massachusetts, Rhode-Island and Providence Plantations, Connecticut, New-York, New-Jersey, Pennsylvania" and after much thought changed it to the now-familiar, "We the people of the United States, in order to form a more perfect union."

Patrick Henry rejected those words, instead wondering, "Who authorized them to speak the language of 'We the People,' instead of 'We the States'?"

It was Madison who responded, pointing to the defining philosophy that has made this Constitution so unique: "This is derived from the superior power of the people."

After considerable haggling, the delegates finally agreed on the basic principles that would bind the colonies together into a nation. The purpose of the Constitution, Morris's preamble continued, was to "establish justice, insure domestic tranquility, provide for the common defense, promote the general welfare, and secure the blessings of liberty to ourselves and our posterity."

The final draft of the document was the result of numerous compromises that left many of the men who drafted it dissatisfied. Benjamin Franklin may well have been speaking for the majority when he said on September 17, at the final meeting of the convention, "I confess that there are several parts of this constitution which I do not at present approve, but I am not sure I shall ever approve them . . . when you assemble a number of men to have the advantage of their joint wisdom, you inevitably assemble with those men, all their prejudices, their passions, their errors of opinion, their local interests, and their selfish views. From such an assembly can a perfect production be expected? It therefore astonishes me, Sir, to find this system approaching so near to perfection as it does."

Of the fifty-five delegates, thirty-nine signed the Constitution that day. George Washington pointed out that the Constitution had been accepted by the delegates from eleven states and Alexander Hamilton—the only one of New York's three delegates who had not left the convention in disgust. Washington was the first to sign. As the rest of the delegates signed, one by one, it was Benjamin Franklin, once again, who found the right words: "I have often and often, in the course of the session . . . looked at that [sun] behind the president, without being able to tell whether it was rising or setting: but now at length, I have the happiness to know, that it is a rising, and not a setting sun."

The Constitution of the United States was written by Jacob Shallus, the clerk of the Pennsylvania General Assembly. It was handwritten over a single September 1787 weekend with quill and ink on parchment. No one knows for certain how many handwritten copies of the original document were produced.

As Franklin left Independence Hall that September afternoon, a crowd had gathered outside to learn the result of the months of deliberations. Rumors had circulated, but overall the founding fathers had done a fine job maintaining secrecy. According to the notes of Maryland delegate Dr. James McHenry, Franklin was approached by an otherwise unidentified woman named Mrs. Powell who asked, "Well, Doctor, what have we got, a republic or a monarchy?" Franklin barely hesitated before responding, "A republic, if you can keep it!"

Before the Constitution became binding, it had to be ratified by at least nine of the thirteen states. Five states quickly did so; the others showed reluctance. Ironically, it was not so much what the document said as what it did not say that raised considerable alarm. Massachusetts, the birthplace of the Revolution, refused to sign the Constitution because it failed to reserve to the states all the powers not specifically granted to the national government. It also did not guarantee the political rights that in the past had proved so important: the freedoms of speech, religion, assembly, and the press. Only after Massachusetts and several other states were assured that those and other amendments would immediately be taken up by the new Congress did they agree to sign the Constitution of the United States of America. On June 21, 1788, New Hampshire became the ninth state to ratify the Constitution.

It was agreed that the new government would meet for the first time in New York on March 4, 1789.

In January of that year, George Washington, running unopposed, was elected the first president of the United States, receiving all 43,782 popular votes and 69 electoral votes. John Adams was elected vice president. There were no political parties and Washington did not campaign for the office; in fact, he had to be convinced to come out of retirement and accept the post. As he said somewhat ruefully, "My movements to the chair of government will be accompanied with feelings not unlike those of a culprit who is going to the place of his execution."

One of the first decisions Washington had to make was how he should be addressed. The Senate proposed he be called His Highness the President of the United States of America and the Protector of Their Liberties, but he opted for the far more modest Mr. President.

Although Washington was one of the richest men in America, his wealth was tied up in land. To pay the expenses of his move from Mount Vernon to the first presidential residence, at 3 Cherry Street in New York City, he was forced to borrow a substantial amount of money. Becoming president, he said, forced him "to do what I never expected to be driven to—that is, to borrow money on interest." The founding fathers had failed to determine the president's salary. While Washington considered rejecting any payment, concerned about the ethics of being paid for public service, he eventually agreed to accept $25,000 annually—although he still found it necessary to use his own money to cover all the household expenses.

As Washington's carriage took him from Virginia to New York, crowds gathered to offer their respects and warm hurrahs. On April 30, 1789, he was sworn into office on the balcony of Federal Hall, where the First Congress was meeting.

Washington was well aware he was setting the precedent for the nation's highest office, and while he brought dignity to the office, he was especially careful to avoid any of the trappings of a monarchy—although some traditions proved impossible to eliminate. For example, he set aside every Tuesday afternoon from three p.m. to four p.m. to meet with male visitors in his residence. Each week a long line of people waited to be formally introduced to him, and rather than shaking hands, they would bow respectfully. Members of Congress and other government officials or dignitaries were often invited to Thursday evening dinner. Martha Washington hosted Friday night levees. Both men and women were invited to these much less formal social events. At these dinners, guests were served by George and Martha Washington's slaves.

The most familiar legend about Washington tells of him cutting down his father's favorite cherry tree with a hatchet when he was only six years old, and when asked by his father if he had done it, replying honestly, "I cannot tell a lie. I cut down that tree." In truth, though, Washington was a smart, shrewd politician. He knew how—and when—to use his power to achieve his aims. Unlike Madison, Jefferson, Adams, and Franklin, Washington's name isn't closely attached to the important documents of that period, but his influence and his philosophy are present in every one of them.

During Washington's first two years in office, the new Congress was debating the initial amendments to the Constitution. In September, Congress passed the Bill of Rights containing twelve amendments, although the states ratified only the first ten: The First Amendment guaranteed freedom of religion, speech, and the press. The Second Amendment guaranteed that a well-regulated militia would provide security "and the right of the people to keep and bear arms." The Fourth Amendment prohibited the unreasonable search and seizures that had been so common during the British occupation. To prevent legal authorities from misusing their powers, the Sixth Amendment guaranteed that anyone accused of a crime would be given a fair and speedy public trial, and the right to legal counsel and a trial by jury. And the Tenth Amendment answered Massachusetts's fears, reserving all rights not specifically granted to the central government to the states. The Bill of Rights was ratified on December 15, 1791.

1776

THE DEFENDER OF THE MOTHERS
PROTECTOR WILLBE OF THE DAUGHTERS

BARON STEUBEN. GOV. ARTHUR ST. CLAIR. SECRETARY SAMUEL A. OTIS. ROGER SHERMAN. GOV. GEORGE CLINTON.
CHANCELLOR ROBERT R. LIVINGSTON. GEORGE WASHINGTON. JOHN ADAMS. GEN'L HENRY KNOX.

WASHINGTON TAKING THE OATH AS PRESIDENT,
APRIL 30, 1789, ON THE SITE OF THE PRESENT TREASURY BUILDING, WALL STREET, NEW YORK CITY.

On the way to New York City's
Federal Hall in April 1789, where
he was to be inaugurated as the
first president of the United States
(at left) by Robert Livingston,
Washington stopped in many
towns—including (top) in Trenton,
New Jersey—to share in the joy of
this historic event.

The two amendments that were not ratified and so did not become part of the Bill of Rights prohibited a Congress in session from giving itself a pay raise and established a formula to be used to determine how representatives would be apportioned to the states. Incredibly, the amendment prohibiting Congress from raising its own salary did not have a termination date for ratification, so when a college student made that discovery in 1982 he began lobbying state legislatures—and eventually gained enough support to ratify it as the Twenty-Seventh Amendment.

Although there was no provision for it in the Constitution, Washington recruited a group of advisers to run various government departments for him. There was no official name for this group; it would be two decades before James Madison began referring to these advisers as his cabinet. Like the president, these first cabinet officials were building the foundation on which the future of the country would rest. They were making decisions that would resonate through the centuries, and a wrong choice could lead to ruin.

Alexander Hamilton, the first secretary of the Treasury, had to establish the economic policies for the new nation—while also handling the existing financial crisis. It was an especially difficult task, given that it had been England's repressive taxation that had ignited the Revolution. Hamilton advocated the creation of a central bank with the power to issue paper money. To gain support from the states, he proposed that this national bank assume the $25 million in war debts they were struggling to settle. To pay those debts, and finally put the United States on a sound financial footing, he proposed instituting excise taxes. It was a daring suggestion, especially when many Americans did not trust bankers. Benjamin Franklin argued that "the Colonies would gladly have borne the little tax on tea and other matters, had it not been the poverty caused by the bad influence of the English bankers on the Parliament, which has caused in the Colonies hatred of England and the Revolutionary War." And while Franklin may have feared the intrusion of bankers into the political arena, when the bank was chartered, he purchased one share or 0.01 percent ownership for $400 as a way of demonstrating his support. But many others fought against it.

Among the cabinet members who vehemently opposed Hamilton was the first secretary of state, Thomas Jefferson, who believed the creation of a national bank was unconstitutional—and the imposition of excise taxes had been the very reason the states had declared independence. As Jefferson remembered about those discussions, "Hamilton and myself were daily pitted in the cabinet like two cocks. . . . The president, on weighing the advice of all, is left free to make up an opinion for himself."

This was just one of many battles in the war between Hamilton and his followers, who believed in a strong central government, and Jefferson and his followers, who were wary of the tyranny of a too powerful national government. To gain support for his ideas, Hamilton had helped form the nation's first political party, the Federalists, in 1787.

Washington eventually supported Hamilton's proposal and the First Bank of the United States was chartered in February 1791. As a result, Jefferson began forming opposition parties, then known as Democratic-Republican Societies. While they existed under a variety of names—Democratic, Republican, True Republican, Constitutional, Patriotic, Political, Franklin, and Madisonian—they all supported strong state governments and were united as anti-Federalists. Basically, the Federalists consisted of northern businessmen, bankers, and merchants who believed that industry fueled the American economy, which in turn benefited everyone, whereas the Democratic-Republicans were mostly farmers and artisans who wanted government to just leave them alone. The founding fathers abhorred political parties. Washington warned against "factions" and Jefferson said, "If I could not go to heaven but with a party, I would not go there at all." But among their many extraordinary accomplishments was the creation of our current two-party political system.

Congress agreed to impose the first excise tax in American history, a tax "upon spirits distilled within the United States, and for appropriating the same." By far the most popular distilled beverage was whiskey, so this became known as the whiskey tax. The result was a very unusual event, the only time in American history that the president has led troops into a battle.

With the spirit of rebellion against a powerful government imposing burdensome taxes still very much in the air, farmers—especially those on the western frontier who had long been distilling their surplus corn, rye, and grain—strongly objected. While the owners of large distilleries, many of them in the east, could easily absorb this additional tax, it placed a terrible burden on smaller farmers who grew their own crops and operated their own small stills. In some places on the frontier, whiskey was used as a form of currency, making this essentially an income tax. For many of them it was proof they had been right to fight against giving up their rights to a government so far away.

At first, these angry citizens tried to fight the tax legally; they organized and sent petitions to the Pennsylvania State Assembly as well as Congress. As a result, the tax was reduced by a penny. That gesture wasn't sufficient and, just as had happened so many years earlier, the peaceful protests gradually became violent. In September 1791 protesters tarred and feathered a tax collector. When a court officer tried to serve assault warrants on the guilty people, he also was tarred and feathered. As a result of that and other threats, the tax was not collected for almost two years.

The resistance continued to escalate. More tax collectors were attacked. Letters written by "Tom the Tinker" threatening anyone who complied with the tax appeared in local newspapers. Hamilton began asking for military support to suppress the growing Whiskey Rebellion. It wasn't simply a matter of collecting unpaid taxes; it was a challenge to the right of the central government to enforce laws passed by Congress. Washington had no choice; he had to respond. Trying desperately to maintain peace, he issued a proclamation criticizing westerners for "tending to obstruct the operation of the laws of the United States" and calling it a "duty that every citizen owes to his country and to the laws, and of a nature dangerous to the very being of a government." He warned that if they refused to "refrain and desist . . . all lawful ways and means will be strictly put in execution for bringing to justice their infractors . . . and securing obedience."

Washington's threats were ignored. In July 1794, an estimated fifty armed men surrounded the home of John Neville, a wealthy distiller and the regional supervisor for tax collections in western Pennsylvania. They demanded that Neville resign his position and hand over all his tax records. There also is some speculation that a US marshal who had come to serve legal papers on several residents was hiding in Neville's house. It isn't known who fired the first shots, but one of the protesters was killed and four more were wounded.

The following day the farmers' army returned to Neville's house in force, this time bringing as many as six hundred men commanded by Revolutionary War veteran Major James McFarlane. Neville barricaded himself inside with several armed slaves and eleven soldiers from nearby Fort Pitt. After negotiations, several women and children were permitted to leave the house, and Neville himself managed to sneak out to safety. Then the shooting began. Eventually the rebels asked for a cease-fire—supposedly someone in the house had waved a white flag. But when McFarlane stepped out from behind cover he was shot and killed. In response the protesters burned the house, barns, slave quarters, and storage sheds. Several men died.

A violent protest army was gathering and becoming a serious threat to the new government. The anger was no longer confined to the whiskey tax but included other grievances against the government. As Washington later wrote in his diary, he was told "that it was not merely the excise law their opposition was aimed at, but to all law, and government, and to the officers of government." The leaders of this rebellion had taken the lessons of the Revolution to heart. In several towns Friends of Liberty groups were organized. Supposedly plans were being made to burn the homes of the wealthy. There were even rumors that western towns had approached representatives from France, England, and Spain for aid in organizing a

The spirit of rebellion was still alive in September 1791, when this group of Whiskey rebels tarred and feathered a tax collector and forced him from his burning home in western Pennsylvania.

separatist movement. In August, more than seven thousand people attended a rally at Braddock's Field in Pennsylvania, then marched toward Pittsburgh, destroying considerable private property before disbanding.

Finally, Supreme Court Justice James Wilson affirmed that western Pennsylvania was in an active state of rebellion, which permitted President Washington to legally call out the militia. In his proclamation Washington noted the stakes, "the contest being whether a small portion of the United States shall dictate to the whole Union, and at the expense of those who desire peace, indulge a desperate ambition." This was the first test of the supremacy of the central government over a state government. Militias from Virginia, Maryland, Penn-

Braddock's Field, Pennsylvania, where more than seven thousand protesters gathered to protest the whiskey taxes in August 1794 before marching nine miles to Pittsburgh.

sylvania, and New Jersey joined to create a 12,950-man force that was ordered to Carlisle, Pennsylvania. Washington decided to lead the army; Hamilton went with him, as he felt responsible for the situation. General Henry Lee, then governor of Virginia, was put in command of the troops.

The president joined his army in Carlisle. He created a stir wherever he went, as younger Americans wanted to see the hero of the Revolution, the president of the United States, in person. He certainly was the nation's greatest celebrity. There was at least one benefit to his participation; as his secretary wrote to Henry Knox, "As the president will be going . . . into the country of whiskey he proposes to make use of that liquor for his drink." In fact, it was a difficult situation for Washington. As Pennsylvania Congress member William Findley recalled, "He was anxious to prevent bloodshed, and at the same time to enforce due submission to the laws, with as little trouble as possible." On September 19, he became the only president ever to lead troops in the field when they began a monthlong march over the Allegheny Mountains to the town of Bedford.

By the time they got there, the rebellion was collapsing. The leaders were fleeing to avoid prosecution. The Whiskey rebels had lost their spirit, and the soldiers returned to their farms and homesteads. The crisis over, Washington went back to Philadelphia, leaving Lee in charge. By mid-November about 150 men had been arrested, including many of the leaders. But with Washington's approval, Lee issued a general pardon "in the wicked and unhappy tumults and disturbances lately existing"—with the exception of those who had committed crimes. A federal grand jury indicted 24 men for treason, but only 2 were found guilty. They were sentenced to hang, but Washington mercifully pardoned them. Several others were convicted of a variety of crimes, mainly assault and rioting, by the Pennsylvania state courts.

Washington's firm actions in putting down the rebellion proved popular throughout the country, and while there were still many battles to be fought in the creation of this nation, this established for the first time the right of the government to enforce federal laws in the individual states and the power of Congress to levy and collect taxes nationally. It marked the

Charles Willson Peale's 1782 portrait of General Henry "Light Horse Harry" Lee, who was appointed by Washington to lead the 1794 expedition against the Whiskey rebels, the first real test of the ability of the federal government to enforce its laws on the individual states.

beginning of a debate that would continue to resonate throughout history and would explode into the Civil War: How do the states and federal government share power?

George Washington served two terms as president and shepherded the nation through often difficult growing pains. There is considerable evidence that Washington actually had wanted to step down after his first term but was convinced to serve again because the bitterness between the Federalists and Democratic-Republicans threatened to rip the country apart. By the time he was truly ready to leave office, the nation was stable and there was a functioning government in place. But there remained one final precedent for Washington to set: the peaceful transition of power. While it is now taken for granted in America, it was not commonplace at that time. Most nations were still monarchies, governed by royals for their lifetimes. Rulers, whatever their title, rarely chose to give up their power. The Constitution did not limit the number of four-year terms an American president could serve. And there is no doubt that Washington easily could have won a third term.

But in September 1796 he published "The Address of General Washington To The People of The United States on his declining of the Presidency of the United States," or as it became known in history, "Washington's Farewell Address," in Philadelphia's *American Daily Advertiser*. It subsequently was reprinted in newspapers throughout the country. This thirty-two-page handwritten document announced, "I should now apprise you of the resolution I have formed, to decline being considered among the number of those out of whom a choice is to be made," and then proceeded to reveal his deepest feelings about the government he had been instrumental in creating. After explaining, often at great length, those things he had learned and what he believed, he concluded by suggesting, humbly, that "these counsels of an old and affectionate friend" might perhaps on occasion be looked to as a guide, "if I may even flatter myself that they may be productive of some partial benefit, some occasional good; that they may now and then recur to moderate the fury of party spirit, to warn against the mischiefs of foreign intrigue, to guard against the impostures of pretended patriotism."

As a result of his decision to step down, the first contested presidential election took place in 1796. Vice President John Adams was the Federalist candidate, and he ran against the Democratic-Republican Thomas Jefferson. The race set the tone for all future elections; in posters and handbills and at rallies Adams was portrayed as the candidate of the wealthy, "the champion of rank, titles, and hereditary distinctions," who would happily establish a titled monarchy if he could, while Jefferson was accused of everything from being an atheist, to displaying cowardice during the Revolution, and, it was whispered, having an affair with one of his female slaves! By three electoral votes John Adams was elected the second president of the United States.

Adams was inaugurated on March 4, 1797. George Washington received a great round of applause when he entered the hall and another when he left to return for the last time to his private life at Mount Vernon. There was no great clamor, no battles or coups. He simply handed to Adams the presidency. It was a remarkable moment, as he reinforced the unique concept that the power to rule this nation did not belong to a person but rather to the office— and it was the American people who would choose the occupant of that office.

Washington left Philadelphia that day to return to Mount Vernon, having fulfilled his constitutional obligations. He would live there for less than three more years, dying on December 14, 1799. His friend Richard Henry Lee delivered his eulogy, which had been written by John Marshall. George Washington, he said, was "first in war, first in peace, and first in the hearts of his countrymen, he was second to none in humble and enduring scenes of private life. Pious, just, humane, temperate, and sincere; uniform, dignified, and commanding; his example was as edifying to all around him as were the effects of that example lasting."

But perhaps James Monroe found a simpler way to characterize Washington, reminding Jefferson, "Be assured his influence carried this government."

CHAPTER 10

Alexander Hamilton AND Aaron Burr

DEADLY DIVISION

A large crowd was gathered in front of the Chester, South Carolina, tavern on that March afternoon in 1807. Those who were there that day recalled it being a happy time, with plenty of music and spirited dancing. They were so absorbed in their merrymaking that at first they didn't notice the nine men riding into town. It was an orderly procession; a bedraggled man in the center was surrounded on all sides by four men. The man had a scraggly beard and was wearing a baggy coat, homespun coarse pantaloons, and a floppy, once-white beaver hat; a tin cup and a knife hung from his cloth belt. Few people paid much heed to him until suddenly, as was reported, "He threw himself from his horse, and exclaimed in a loud voice, 'I am Aaron Burr, under military arrest, and claim the protection of the civil authorities.'"

🏴 Raising the American flag in Louisiana as the state declares its independence from France in 1803.

Their attention now riveted on the spectacle, they watched as a second man dismounted, drew two pistols, and ordered Burr back on his horse. "I will not!" the prisoner responded. Anything could have happened at that moment: Burr's daughter was married to a favored citizen of the state and the former vice president of the United States remained quite popular there. There was a good chance some of the men would take action on his behalf. The guard put down his pistols and, "seizing Burr around the waist with the grasp of a tiger, threw him into his saddle." Before the townspeople could recover from their confusion, "the whole party vanished from their presence."

The riders halted when they safely reached the outskirts of the town. And Burr then burst into tears. One of his guards, "seeing the low condition to which this conspicuous man was now reduced," also started crying. After a brief pause the party continued to Richmond, where the former vice president of the United States was to stand trial for treason.

In popular lore Aaron Burr is most remembered for killing Alexander Hamilton in a duel for honor, but in fact he played a far more important role in the creation of our institutions. He was one of the four remarkable men, along with Hamilton, John Adams, and Thomas Jefferson, whose passions, ambitions, and complex rivalries helped shape our history—and ensured that the fledgling country would survive.

Because of a quirk in our original election laws, Federalist president John Adams's vice president was Democratic-Republican Thomas Jefferson. This was the only time in our history when the president and vice president belonged to different political parties. While the two men had been close friends when serving as President Washington's ambassadors to England and France, their political beliefs had driven them far apart. And during Adams's administration few issues were more contentious than our relationships with those two countries. Britain and France had been at war since 1793, and in 1796 the French had begun raiding and seizing American merchant ships carrying goods to and from England. American sympathies were divided; while officially the country remained neutral, in fact Jefferson's Republicans supported France in gratitude for its assistance in the Revolution, while Adams's Federalists believed the French actions were unacceptable.

Adams dispatched three emissaries to France to try to restore relations, but France's foreign minister, the Marquis de Talleyrand, essentially ignored them, then set terms for peace and threatened to invade America unless Adams agreed to meet those terms. To fight this Quasi-War, as it was known, Congress authorized Adams to raise a ten-thousand-man army; Congress also gave him the "wooden walls" he requested, establishing a Navy Department and commissioning fifteen new cruisers. In June, Adams officially asked George Washington

Once friends, Thomas Jefferson and John Adams became
bitter political rivals. After serving as Adams's vice president,
Jefferson defeated him for the presidency in 1800. Years later
the wounds healed; incredibly they died on the same day,
July 4, 1826, and John Adams's last words were supposedly,
"Thomas Jefferson still survives."

to once again serve as the military's commander in chief, mostly because his name would aid
recruiting. Washington accepted, knowing he would never actually serve, and named Alexander Hamilton his second-in-command. While Adams opposed Hamilton's appointment,
he needed Washington's support, so he had no choice but to accept. In the shifting winds of
power and influence, this was a significant victory for Hamilton.

Perhaps more than anyone, Jefferson was appalled. He believed firmly that Hamilton
secretly had been maneuvering events to reach this outcome. Jefferson remained strongly opposed to taking military action against the French. Supposedly he financed a series of sordid
attacks in the press against Federalist leaders, many of them written by the well-known scandalmonger James Callender. Although Jefferson denied paying for these articles and cartoons,
he certainly appreciated them.

In 1797 Callender had revealed Treasury Secretary Hamilton's adulterous affair with a married woman—for which Hamilton apologized—but then also accused him of attempting to bribe the woman's husband with money and insider information. While Callender practiced the most salacious form of journalism, his explanation for it remained valid, pointing out: "The more that a nation knows about the mode of conducting its business, the better chance has that business of being properly conducted."

As the nation debated going to war against France, the political debate in the House of Representatives turned vicious. On September 30, 1798, Vermont Republican Matthew Lyon

American political debate has always been loud but only occasionally violent. This 1798 etching depicts the fight in the House between Federalist Roger Griswold and Republican Matthew Lyon. It is described in rhyme at the bottom: "He in a trice struck Lyon thrice / Upon his head, enrag'd sir, / Who seiz'd the tongs to ease his wrongs, / And Griswold thus engag'd, sir."

accused the members from Connecticut of putting their own financial interests ahead of the people of their state. That state's Federalist representative, Roger Griswold, responded by calling Lyon a coward, claiming he had been dishonorably discharged during the Revolution. Lyon answered by spitting tobacco juice in Griswold's eyes. The men had to be physically held apart. The members of the House then spent two weeks debating whether or not to expel Lyon for his "gross indecency," but the Federalists were not able to get the two-thirds vote necessary. When the House resumed regular business, Griswold immediately approached Lyon and began bashing him with his hickory stick. Lyon fell back, stunned. He grabbed a set of iron fireplace tongs and began swinging them, knocking the cane from Griswold's hand. Griswold tackled him and the two men crashed to the floor. Any lingering sense of decorum in the people's House was long gone. Other congressmen pulled them apart and held them tightly away from each other.

Their fight served as an apt metaphor for the anger, the bitterness, and the frustration that existed between the two political parties, both of them fully convinced the other was set upon destroying the precarious union. The hostility between the warring parties came to an ugly conclusion, at least temporarily, in what became known as the Alien and Sedition Acts.

Anticipating war with France, the Federalists passed a series of acts that made it far more difficult for immigrants to become voting citizens—for example, increasing the residency requirement from five years to fourteen years—and barred any immigration from "enemy nations." They also permitted the president to deport or imprison immigrants if they were found to be "dangerous to the peace and safety of the United States," especially during wartime. While nominally intended to prepare the country for the war, there was little doubt of the real reason for these new laws: these acts took direct aim at the Republican Party, as much of that party's support came from immigrants. As a Federalist congressman admitted, he saw no reason to "invite hordes of Wild Irishmen, nor the turbulent and disorderly of all the world, to come here with a basic view to distract our tranquility." While the Alien Acts were vaguely threatening, the Sedition Act was a direct challenge to the Bill of Rights. It specifically made it illegal for people to assemble "with intent to oppose any measure . . . of the government" or "print, utter, or publish . . . any false, scandalous and malicious writing . . . against the government." Incredibly, after the long and hard-fought battles for freedom had finally been won, this law made the free expression of thoughts or ideas illegal if they were deemed to be critical of the government, and it allowed the government to fine and imprison people—especially Republicans—who violated these laws.

Because the Federalists completely controlled the Supreme Court, the violation of the First Amendment didn't become a constitutional issue. And while President Adams never used the powers granted to him under the Alien Acts, he brutally applied the Sedition Act for political advantage. In what clearly was one of the darkest moments in our early history, fourteen men were eventually fined or imprisoned for expressing their political beliefs. Perhaps not surprisingly, the first person to be tried was Congressman Lyon, who was indicted in 1800 for an essay published in the *Vermont Journal* in which he had accused Adams's administration of "ridiculous pomp, foolish adulation, and selfish avarice." He was convicted, fined $1,000—a large sum at that time—and served four months in prison. He was reelected to Congress while serving his sentence and later returned to the House.

The scandalmonger Callender was fined $200 and sentenced to nine months for calling President Adams a "repulsive pedant, a gross hypocrite and an unprincipled oppressor," and his administration a "continued tempest of malignant passions."

Both Madison and Jefferson found these acts repugnant and secretly worked with the legislatures of Kentucky and Virginia to pass laws overturning them. As Jefferson said in protest, "Let the honest advocate of confidence read the Alien and Sedition Acts . . . and let him say what the government is, if it not be a tyranny." Madison's Virginia Resolution emphasized that Congress lacked the power to enact these laws, pointing out that enacting them gave Congress "a power not delegated by the Constitution, but on the contrary, expressly and positively forbidden by one of the amendments thereto." Jefferson's Kentucky Resolution argued that every state has the right to nullify, or disobey, federal laws it believes are unconstitutional. It was a strong argument for states' rights. The resolution also warned that the only answer to such repressive legislation was for that state to secede. It was an extraordinarily risky response by Jefferson; if it had become known that the vice president of the United States was calling openly for rebellion, he might well have been arrested for treason. Washington was so incensed by these resolutions that he warned that if those states pursued them it might be sufficient to "dissolve the Union."

Fortunately, it would be another half century before the issue of states' rights actually led to armed revolution—the Civil War. Rather than being settled on a battlefield, this crisis was solved at the ballot box. It turned out to be an amazing display of the power of the people to chart their own course.

In the bitterly fought election of 1800 President John Adams ran against Vice President Thomas Jefferson, the only time in our history that the president and vice president were pitted against each other. The most significant issues of the 1800 election were the Alien and Sedition Acts and a new tax levied to pay for the mobilization of the army and navy. Adams defended them; Jefferson attacked them. In its often-vicious tone, this election set a model for future elections. Among many other slurs, the Republicans attacked the president as a "hideous hermaphroditical character, which has neither the force and firmness of a man, nor the gentleness and sensibility of a woman." The Federalists were no better, calling Jefferson "a mean-spirited, low-lived fellow, the son of a half-breed Indian squaw, sired by a Virginia mulatto father." Even Martha Washington made her opinion known, perhaps intentionally being overheard telling a clergyman that Jefferson was "one of the most detestable of mankind."

The election appeared to be close; Jefferson had strong support in the south but needed to find at least some backing in the north. To appeal to New York's electoral voters, he chose that state's popular former assemblyman and US senator, Aaron Burr, to run with him as vice president. Ironically, Colonel Burr had been a Revolutionary War hero whose leadership during the retreat from New York City had saved an entire brigade—and among those soldiers was Alexander Hamilton.

The Republicans easily won the election, but a quirk in the new electoral voting system that allowed each elector to cast two votes for president led to an unexpected outcome: running mates Jefferson and Burr each received the same number of votes. (To ensure this never happened again, Congress passed the Twelfth Amendment, which created the electoral system still in use today.)

In fact, only a technicality prevented Burr from winning outright and becoming the third president. The election would be decided by the outgoing House of Representatives—in which Federalists held a majority. The votes of nine states were required; the Federalists, loath

John Vanderlyn's 1802 portrait of Aaron Burr, who served as vice president, almost became our third president, eventually was indicted for the killing of Alexander Hamilton, and may have planned a rebellion against the United States.

to put their bitter enemy, Jefferson, in the highest office, instead cast their ballots for Burr. During seven days of debate the House voted thirty-five times—and each time Jefferson fell one vote short of a majority, winning eight states. This stalemate might have continued considerably longer, but Federalist Alexander Hamilton began campaigning for Jefferson, considering him "by far not so dangerous a man" as Burr. Hamilton's disdain for Burr went back to the Revolution, when both men had served on Washington's staff, and had grown in the election of 1791, when Burr had defeated Hamilton's father-in-law, Philip Schuyler, for a seat in the Senate. As Jefferson later explained, "I never indeed thought him [Burr] an honest, frank-dealing man, but considered him as a crooked gun, or other perverted machine, whose aim or stroke you could never be sure of."

Jefferson also was working to ensure that the outcome was in his favor. Unlike most other states, Delaware was represented in the House by one man, James Bayard. Delaware's vote was Bayard's decision alone. Throughout the long impasse Bayard had persistently cast his vote for Burr. Although it was never proved, and Jefferson denied it, Bayard claimed later that Jefferson had made a deal with the Federalists; he agreed not to dismantle Hamilton's financial structure, reduce the size of the navy, or rid the government of Federalists.

Hamilton's efforts, perhaps aided by Jefferson's negotiating skills, eventually proved successful. While Bayard could not bring himself to vote for Jefferson, on the thirty-sixth vote he abstained, making Thomas Jefferson president. But this election also set Hamilton and Burr on a course that would end in disaster.

Among Jefferson's first acts in office was to pardon those men still imprisoned under the Sedition Act, and allow it and most of the Alien Acts to expire. Among those men pardoned was James Callender, who apparently expected to be rewarded for his efforts by being appointed postmaster of Richmond, Virginia. Jefferson, however, wanted nothing to do with him, admitting, "I am really mortified at the base ingratitude of Callender. It presents human nature in a hideous form." Although he refused him that post, Jefferson apparently did give Callender $50.

The furious Callender went to work for the Federalist newspaper, the *Richmond Recorder*, using its pages to attack Jefferson. He claimed that Jefferson had financially supported his efforts against Adams, which caused Abigail Adams to attribute to Jefferson "the blackest calumny and foulest falsehoods." Callender then went much farther, printing for the first time the rumor that has become part of the Jefferson mystique: that Thomas Jefferson had been living in sin for many years with his slave, Sally Hemings, "The African Violet." "By this wench," he wrote, "our president has had several children. There is not an individual in the neighborhood of Charlottesville who does not believe the story, and not a few who know it."

Had that story been printed before the election, it is probable it would have ended his campaign. Jefferson never responded, but historians continue to debate the story. What has been established is that Sally Hemings may have been a half sister of Jefferson's wife, Martha, as Martha's father had taken Sally's mother as his concubine—a not uncommon practice among southern slaveholders. Jefferson had married the widow Martha Wayles Skelton in January 1772, and in the decade they spent together she bore six children. Apparently they were truly devoted to each other and often spent evenings reading poetry together and playing duets, she on the harpsichord or pianoforte and he on the violin. When Martha Jefferson died in 1782 at age thirty-three, several months after giving birth, her husband inherited all of her property, including her five half siblings. And one of them was Sally.

The five Wayles-Hemings children were three-quarters white and one-quarter black. Jefferson never referred to them as his slaves but rather called them servants. In addition to Sally, he also became especially close with James Hemings, who served as his personal assistant and often traveled with him, and who eventually was given his freedom. Tests conducted more than two centuries later confirm that Sally Hemings's descendants share DNA with a male member of the Jefferson family. It would not have been at all unusual for the plantation owner and his servant to have had such a bond. While many historians accept the broad strokes of the story, though, the truth about Thomas Jefferson's relationship with Sally Hemings is likely to remain an unsolved American mystery.

With the Quasi-War with France ended and the American government now firmly in place, Jefferson looked west to see the future. He was aware of how vast the unsettled country was and became determined to expand the nation. His first opportunity came in the south, when Spain ceded the territory of Louisiana to France. Included in that grant was the port of New Orleans, which meant that the mouth of the great Mississippi River, the outlet for almost half of all the crops and goods produced in the western territories, would be controlled by Napoleon. For Jefferson, that was a very troubling situation, "the embryo of a tornado," he warned. As he wrote to the American minister to France, Robert R. Livingston, "Every eye in the U.S. is now fixed on this affair of Louisiana. Perhaps nothing since the Revolutionary War has produced more uneasy sensations through the body of the nation. . . . The day that France takes possession of New Orleans . . . we must marry ourselves to the British fleet and nation." To avoid a future confrontation, Jefferson ordered Livingston to discuss the purchase of "the island of New Orleans" with the French government. In 1803 he also dispatched James Monroe to France, authorizing him to work with Livingston and to offer as much as

$10 million for New Orleans and all or part of the Floridas. If that bid proved unsuccessful, Monroe was instructed to try to buy only New Orleans, supposedly for $6 million, and if that was impossible, he was to take whatever sensible steps necessary to secure permanent access to the port and the river. If the French refused all offers, Monroe was to proceed to London to negotiate an alliance. "All eyes, all hopes, are now fixed on you," Jefferson told Monroe, "for on the event of this mission depends the future destinies of this republic."

The day before Monroe's arrival, France made an extraordinary and completely unexpected counteroffer. Napoleon's adventures in the Americas were not proceeding well, and it appeared another round of war with England was likely. He was advised by his minister of finance, François de Barbé-Marbois, that the country could not afford—and probably would not win—a widespread war in America. Instead, Barbé-Marbois urged Napoleon to abandon his plan to restore the French empire on the North American continent and simply sell the entire Louisiana Territory to the United States.

The offer flabbergasted Monroe. It was far more than anyone had imagined possible. "The purchase of Louisiana in its full extent, tho' not contemplated," Monroe wrote to Livingston, "is received with warm, and in a manner universal approbation. The uses to which it may be turned, render it a truly noble acquisition. Under prudent management it may be made to do much good as well as to prevent much evil." The two men seized the opportunity, eventually agreeing to pay Napoleon $11,250,000 and to assume an additional $3,750,000 in claims American citizens had lodged against France. For $15 million Jefferson had purchased

President Jefferson sent James Monroe (in the engraving at right) to France to try to negotiate the purchase of New Orleans and all or part of Florida. Instead, Monroe successfully bought the entire Louisiana Territory, more than doubling the size of the country, and later became our fifth president in 1817.

Napoleon authorized the sale of the Louisiana Territory (at left) when it became clear France could not afford to restore its North American empire and likely would lose it in a war with England. (Below) John L. Boqueta de Woiseri's colored print of the city of New Orleans in 1803, as seen from a nearby plantation, was dedicated to Thomas Jefferson.

UNDER MY WINGS EVERY THING PROSPERS

828,000 square miles, or about 3 cents an acre, arguably the greatest real estate deal in American history. Stretching from the Gulf of Mexico in the south to the Hudson Bay basin in the north, from the Mississippi River in the east to the Rocky Mountains in the west, this acquisition would more than double the size of the United States. Eventually six states and large areas of three others, as well as smaller portions of two Canadian provinces, were carved out of the land. As Talleyrand admitted, "You have made a noble bargain for yourselves."

When the Louisiana Purchase Treaty was signed on April 30, 1803, Robert Livingston proudly declared, "From this day the United States take their place among the powers of the first rank."

Jefferson's reputation was greatly enhanced by this popular purchase. But among those people who did not share in the celebration was Jefferson's vice president, Aaron Burr. Since taking office, Burr had not been given any work of importance by Jefferson. His patronage suggestions were ignored and he was not consulted on policy decisions; as his political fortunes faded, his resentment grew. Only a few years earlier he had been one of the most respected men in the country, but he quickly had become little more than a shadow lurking in

the background of American politics. When he learned that Jefferson intended to replace him on the Republican ticket with New York governor George Clinton in the 1804 election, he decided to instead run as an Independent—for the governorship of New York. This powerful position, he believed, would allow him to revive his political career.

Alexander Hamilton was horrified by the prospect of Burr winning such an important election. Just as he had four years earlier, Hamilton worked vigorously against him. Burr was soundly defeated by Republican Morgan Lewis. Although it is doubtful that Hamilton's efforts had much impact on the outcome, Burr placed substantial blame on him for his loss. His

Raising the Colours for the Last Time, the Cessation of New Orleans in 1803 shows the French flag flying over the port for the final time before becoming an American possession.

contempt, his anger, and his frustration reached a peak shortly after the election when a letter from Dr. Charles Cooper to Philip Schuyler was published in the *Albany Register*. Relating conversation from a dinner party he had recently attended, Cooper wrote that Hamilton and other Republicans had agreed that Burr was a dangerous man who could not be trusted with "the reins of government." But then, Cooper added, Hamilton had continued ominously that if pressed, he could describe in detail "a still more despicable opinion" of Burr.

No attempt was made to further explain this "despicable opinion." Perhaps it was an allusion to Burr being a well-known womanizer who might have fathered a child out of wedlock. Whatever the inference, Burr took great offense. Whether it was only about this remark or a response to the accumulation of slights, Burr demanded "a prompt and unqualified acknowledgment or denial of the use of any expression which would warrant the assertion of Dr. Cooper."

This was not just an angry exchange of words; Burr had made it a matter of honor. In those days one's honor was not something to be taken lightly: a man's reputation was his greatest possession and needed to be protected, whatever the cost. Hamilton tried to defuse the issue, asserting that he was not responsible for Cooper's interpretation—although he did not deny that he had made the comment. He pointed out that there were "infinite shades" of the meaning of "despicable," an evasion that Burr considered insulting.

Burr persisted, continuing to demand an apology, writing, "Political opposition can never absolve gentlemen from the necessity of a rigid adherence to the laws of honor and the rules of decorum." Hamilton responded through an intermediary, claiming he had truly forgotten the particulars of that conversation "but to the best of his recollection it consisted of comments on the political principles and views of Colonel Burr, and the results that might be expected from them in the event of his election as governor, without reference to any particular instance of past conduct, or to private character."

After a further exchange of letters, Aaron Burr formally challenged Hamilton to a duel of honor. Hamilton had no choice but to accept; a refusal would have been considered an unsightly display of cowardice and likely would have ended his own political career. A secondhand insult had been elevated to a life-and-death confrontation. Duels were not at all uncommon; in fact, a New York newspaper described them as "much in fashion," but they rarely reached the point of gunplay. Most often it would end with an apology or satisfaction, meaning honor had properly been defended. Both men, being high-profile outspoken politicians, had been involved in numerous previous encounters. Hamilton, for example, had been a participant in ten previous duels, including either two or three with Burr—but none of them had ever resulted in a shot being fired. Even those few duels that did end up with two men facing each other with pistols at ten paces only rarely resulted in injury. Often the duelists would *delope*, or intentionally "throw away their fire," usually by shooting directly into the ground. Simply by engaging in the duel, honor was earned.

But Hamilton did fully understand the potentially tragic outcome of such a contest. Only three years earlier, his nineteen-year-old son, Philip, had been shot and killed defending his father's honor in a duel on the heights at Weehawken, New Jersey.

Historians have long speculated—without any resolution—why Hamilton and Burr allowed their feud to reach this point. Most agree that it was not about this last dispute. There are people who believe that Hamilton might have been suicidal, perhaps depressed about his son's death, while Burr required a clear victory over Hamilton to restore his battered reputation.

Whatever the reasons, early in the morning of July 11, 1804, Hamilton and Burr faced each other ten paces apart on the cliffs of Weehawken—on the same grounds where Philip Hamilton had been killed. They had rowed across the Hudson River because, while both New York and New Jersey had outlawed dueling, New Jersey rarely brought criminal action against surviving participants.

No one will ever know precisely what was in the minds of Hamilton and Burr as they faced each other. A week earlier the rivals had attended a Fourth of July reunion of officers who had fought in the Revolution, but there is no record of any conversation between them. A day earlier Hamilton had written his will, making certain all of his affairs were in order, although there is some conjecture that he never intended to fire at Burr but rather planned to retire from the field with both duelists having their honor restored. Only hours before the duel he wrote, "I have resolved, if . . . it pleases God to give me the opportunity, to reserve and throw away my first fire; and I have thoughts even of reserving my second fire."

Burr got there first. Hamilton arrived shortly thereafter. Both men were accompanied by their seconds, friends chosen to ensure that the duel was conducted honorably and to arrange a peaceful resolution if possible. The rules were explained. Considerable tradition dictated the conduct of a duel, and the participants and their seconds were careful to respect it. Hamilton and Burr loaded their .56-caliber dueling pistols. Their seconds measured the distance, ten full paces. Unexpectedly, Hamilton called for a pause. Everyone stopped, curious as to his intentions; he carefully adjusted his spectacles, sighted the barrel of his pistol, and then said he was ready to proceed. As the two seconds, Nathaniel Pendleton for Hamilton, William P. Van Ness for Burr, later agreed in a jointly written statement, "[Pendleton] then asked if they were prepared; being answered in the affirmative, he gave the word 'present,' as had been agreed on, and both parties presented and fired in succession. The intervening time is not expressed, as the seconds do not precisely agree on that point." That disagreement between the seconds is the stuff of history. Only the people on that bluff that morning knew the truth and they would never agree on it. In some tellings, Hamilton shot first, intentionally shooting wide and high into the air above Burr's head, but Burr, startled by the shot in the air rather than into the ground, fired directly at his opponent. Others believe that both men fired at about the same moment or that Burr fired first and his shot threw off Hamilton's aim. Whatever the truth of it, the result was the same, as both seconds agreed: "The fire of Colonel Burr took effect, and General Hamilton almost instantly fell. Colonel Burr then advanced toward General Hamilton with a manner and gesture that appeared to General Hamilton's friend to be expressive of regret, but without speaking, turned about and withdrew, being urged from the field by his friend, as has been subsequently stated, with a view to prevent his being recognized by the surgeon and bargemen, who were then approaching. No further communication took place between the principals, and the barge that carried Colonel Burr immediately returned to the city."

DUEL BETWEEN ALEXANDER HAMILTON AND AARON BURR.

The oft-depicted duel in which Aaron Burr killed Alexander Hamilton on the Weehawken Heights, July 11, 1804.

Hamilton was struck in the lower right abdomen, with the bullet lodging in his spine. His physician, Dr. David Hosack, ran to his aid and immediately understood the severity of the wound. Hamilton said, "This is a mortal wound, Doctor," and lost consciousness. Dr. Hosack later reported, "His pulses were not to be felt; his respiration was entirely suspended; and, upon laying my hand on his heart, and perceiving no motion there, I considered him as irrecoverably gone." Incredibly, though, he revived and in his few words emphasized, "I did not intend to fire at him."

Hamilton was taken back to New York and survived thirty-one hours. Burr, at least initially, seemed remarkably unmoved by the duel. After returning to New York he had breakfast with a relative—and never mentioned the fact that only hours earlier he had shot and presumably killed Alexander Hamilton. The response to the duel seemed to surprise him: rather than having his honor restored, as he had imagined, he was vilified. Any hope he might have had of reviving his political career ended that day. But even more dangerous for him, the New York coroner had convened a grand jury to investigate the shooting. Even though the duel had taken place in New Jersey, meaning New York had no legal jurisdiction, he was indicted in both states for murder. "There is a contention of a singular nature between the two states of New York and New Jersey," he wrote to his daughter. "The subject in dispute is, which shall have the honor of hanging the vice president." Burr never stood trial for the duel; several years later, New Jersey's charges were dismissed and New York failed to take any action to support its indictment.

Although Burr remained confident he had not committed any crimes, he left New York to stay with a friend on Saint Simons Island, Georgia, in order to avoid being arrested. So long as he did not return to New York or New Jersey, he was not in jeopardy. Incredibly, after a brief stay in Georgia he returned to the District of Columbia to complete his term as vice president. President Jefferson, perhaps aware that his own political fortunes might be tainted by any relationship with Burr, stated flatly, "There never had been an intimacy between us, and but little association."

The young nation was then treated to an odd spectacle: a vice president under indictment for murder presiding over the impeachment trial of a Supreme Court justice. Federalist Justice Samuel Chase was impeached by the House for judicial misconduct. Specifically he was accused of eight different articles of impeachment focusing on his conduct during three cases—one of them the Callender sedition trial. There was little question that Chase had remained politically active while sitting on the High Court, and some of his rulings seemed as much political as legal, but it was also clear that Justice Chase had become a problem for the Republicans and they wanted him removed. In his role as president of the Senate, Burr presided over the trial with—according to newspaper reports, "correctness and astonishing dignity." After hearing the testimony of more than fifty witnesses, the thirty-four senators acquitted Chase of all charges and he returned to the bench.

For Aaron Burr, this was to be the last great moment of his once promising career; after finishing his term, he left politics and became embroiled in one of the more curious episodes of early American history. It appears that Burr went west to try to create his own independent nation. Whether he intended to provoke a war with Mexico and annex Spanish territories, lead at least two states to declare independence, or simply develop territories he had already purchased isn't known, but he began traveling up and down both the Ohio and Mississippi Rivers, engaging in land speculation, negotiating to sell parts of the Louisiana Territory to England for half a million dollars, and becoming involved in several other questionable negotiations. In New Orleans he met with Mexican revolutionaries to plan a military expedition into Mexico that a newspaper described as an effort "to form a separate government." He met several times with the British minister to the United States, Anthony Merry, who reported that Burr had told him "the inhabitants of Louisiana . . . prefer having the protection and assistance of Great Britain . . . [and] their design is only delayed by the difficulty of obtaining previously an assurance of protection and assistance from some foreign power." And he met with Spain's minister to the United States, Carlos Martínez de Irujo y Tacón, and supposedly told him that his actual plan was to invade Washington, D.C., kidnap Jefferson and Vice President Chase, and capture the United States Treasury and its arsenal. As his activities grew even more bizarre, he began recruiting an army—it eventually included an estimated eighty men—and storing sufficient weapons and supplies for an invasion of no one was quite certain where.

Burr's primary coconspirator was General James Wilkinson, whom Jefferson had appointed governor of the Louisiana Territory. Wilkinson, who for a time had been commander of the United States Army, had previously tried to separate Kentucky and Tennessee from the Union. But among people who loaned money to Burr during this period was Andrew Jackson, later to be elected president, although there is no evidence that "Old Hickory" knew anything of these plans.

Apparently Jefferson had been informed in 1805 by Joseph Hamilton Daveiss, the federal district attorney in Kentucky, that Burr was "meditating the overthrow of your administration," and intended to foment a rebellion and form an independent nation in the southwest. Jefferson probably found the story difficult to believe, and he took no action. At some point, for unknown reasons, Wilkinson revealed the plot. As evidence, he sent Jefferson a letter he had received from Burr, which read in part, "I, Aaron Burr, have obtained funds and have actually commenced the enterprise. Detachments from different points and under different pretenses, will rendezvous on the Ohio, 1st November. Everything internal and external favors views; protection of England is secured. . . . Navy of the United States are ready to join, and final orders are given to my friends and followers; it will be a host of choice spirits." While the letter did not specifically state that Burr intended to attack New Orleans or set up an independent nation, it did seem to corroborate Wilkinson's story. Finally convinced that this plot was real, if far-fetched, Jefferson informed Congress, alerted federal authorities in

BURR'S TROOPS GOING DOWN THE OHIO.

An 1882 engraving showing Burr's hired troops leaving their camp in 1805 to begin an insurrection.

the west to keep a sharp watch for suspicious activities, and ordered the arrest of Aaron Burr.

Burr was completely unaware that the president was on to him. In November, sixty men and ten flatboats set out down the Ohio River for New Orleans, expecting to meet Wilkinson and a larger force there. Burr himself was two hundred miles away in Kentucky when this expedition was launched. Wilkinson, meanwhile, having completely turned on Burr, declared martial law in New Orleans and arrested most of Burr's followers. Burr was at Bayou Pierre, just outside Natchez, Mississippi, when he discovered he had been betrayed. Months earlier he had been the vice president of the United States; suddenly he was a fugitive on the run, accused of treason.

Apparently outraged by the accusations, Burr declared his innocence and invited the good people of Mississippi to search his boats. While nothing suspicious was found, nonetheless he was arrested. A grand jury found no reason to indict him, but the judge refused to allow him to leave the jurisdiction. Frustrated, Burr escaped. A $2,000 reward was posted for his capture and US marshals were put on his trail.

Abandoning his plans, Burr headed for Pensacola, Florida, purportedly intending to sail to Europe, where he might enlist the support of the British or French to seize Spanish territories in North America. With rumored assistance from Andrew Jackson, Burr made his way into Alabama. He wore old and common clothes, and later his former associates in New York, Philadelphia, and Washington would find great humor in the fact that this elegant man, who had always favored fancy dress and proper manners, would be arrested wearing the mismatched clothes of a bumpkin.

Late on the night of February 18, 1807, a man named Nicholas Perkins was standing outside Sheriff Theodore Brightwell's home in Washington County, then in the Mississippi Territory but eventually to become Huntsville, Alabama, when two men passed slowly. As Perkins, the federal land registrar, later testified, the first man kept his head down and said nothing; the second man paused to ask for directions to Major John Hinson's place. Perkins pointed the way but explained that Hinson wasn't there and besides, getting there meant crossing the creek at the high-water mark in the middle of the night, a very dangerous enterprise.

The man thanked him and the two went on their way. *Well, that's odd*, Perkins must have thought, wondering why they didn't stop to pass the night safely at the inn. It occurred to him that they might be robbers or, even more ominous, the fugitive Aaron Burr and a companion, who were said to be in the area. His suspicions were raised sufficiently for him to wake the sheriff.

They rode over to Hinson's and Sheriff Brightwell conversed with the two men. Something wasn't right about them, Perkins knew, and he galloped to Fort Stoddert to enlist help. He would later testify that Burr's "keen" glance gave away his true identity. Hours later

Perkins and the commandant, Lieutenant Edmund Pendleton Gaines, caught up with Burr and Sheriff Brightwell near the ferry crossing on the Tombigbee River. Apparently he readily admitted his identity and was arrested for the crime of treason against the United States of America. There is no mention of Perkins collecting the bounty.

Eight men escorted the prisoner up to Richmond, where he was to be tried. It was on that long ride that Burr made the Chester, South Carolina, escape attempt that ended in his tears.

Thousands of people from around the country crammed into Richmond in August to witness this spectacular treason trial, the majority of them common folk wearing home-spun clothes and buckskin coats. Those who couldn't afford lodging lived in their wagons or pitched tents. Burr was said to have borrowed as much as $1,000 to purchase his own elegant wardrobe and wore black silk garments throughout the trial; if this was to be Jefferson's show trial, he would show them a man of style and grace.

The former vice president of the United States was arrested in the Mississippi Territory on February 18, 1807, as he attempted to flee into Spanish territory in disguise.

Supreme Court Justice John Marshall was one of two judges presiding, and several of his decisions in this complex legal case set legal precedents that have been respected for two centuries. When picking the jury, it was reported, Burr's attorney selected those men most outwardly hostile to their client, appealing to their honor to render a just decision—but also showing great confidence in Burr's innocence.

Rather than a man on trial for his life, Burr was treated like a celebrity. He was invited to dinner with Justice Marshall at his attorney's home and was given three large rooms in the prison in which to receive visitors of both sexes, who arrived carrying gifts for him. Harman Blennerhassett, the wealthy lawyer and southern politician who had been indicted as a co-conspirator, wrote in his journal, "Burr lives in great style, and sees much company within his gratings, where it is as difficult to get an audience as if he really were an emperor."

The trial lasted several weeks. Justice Marshall and President Jefferson had long been at odds, so Marshall was not at all susceptible to political pressure. If anything, as a strong public supporter of Hamilton's, Marshall might have been accused of bias against Burr. But he insisted on a narrow and specific interpretation of the law. He also ruled that the president could be subpoenaed to provide evidence in his possession, making the important statement that even the president was not above the law. Jefferson rejected that opinion, citing the independent nature of the three branches of government and asking, "But would the executive be independent of the judiciary, if he were subject to the commands of the latter, and to imprisonment for disobedience." He did, however, turn over the requested document.

Wilkinson was the main prosecution witness and Burr's lawyers successfully turned his testimony, showing that his word could not be trusted and that he may well have collaborated with Spanish interests intending to invade Florida in return for the promise that he would lead the new country. The general was thoroughly raked in the media, and the foreman of the grand jury, Congressman John Randolph, colorfully described this very large man as "a mammoth of inequity" and a "most finished scoundrel." The legendary writer Washington Irving, reporting on the trial, described the general's entrance into the courtroom: "Wilkinson strutted into court and took his stand in a parallel line with Burr on his right hand. Here he stood for a moment, swelling like a turkey cock and bracing himself for the encounter of Burr's eye."

Marshall's key ruling was that committing treason required an overt act of war—real steps had to be openly taken—which had to be proved by evidence; intent was not nearly enough. His point was a vitally important one: talking about it, even plotting it, wasn't sufficient to prove guilt. The right of Americans to criticize the government was guaranteed by the Constitution. Burr's lawyers provided evidence that he had been hundreds of miles away when his so-called army left Ohio; as his attorney emphasized, he wasn't even there.

The foreman of the trial jury, Colonel Edward Carrington, read the verdict: "We of the jury say that Aaron Burr is not proved to be guilty under this indictment by any evidence submitted to us." Not guilty. A second trial on a lesser charge had the same result: not guilty. Jefferson, reportedly, was furious, but he had no recourse.

Justice Marshall, in fact, bore the brunt of criticism for the verdict. Jefferson denounced him as "a mountebank, a trickster, a corrupt judge, and worthy of impeachment." He was burned in effigy in Baltimore by Jefferson's supporters and criticized in many newspapers as being a monarchist. While Burr was judged not guilty, the stigma and controversy made it impossible for him to ever again have a normal life in America. He traveled with his schemes first to England, where he tried to find support to instigate revolution in Mexico; when he was ordered to leave that country, he moved throughout Europe to Sweden, Denmark, Germany, and eventually France, still hoping to convince Napoleon to back his dreams. His efforts left him penniless and he returned to America in 1812, rumored to be fleeing a British debtor's prison.

He returned to New York where the murder charges against him were dropped and he resumed his legal career under an assumed name. Eventually he married a wealthy widow, who sued for divorce only four months later when she discovered he was using her money for land speculation. Once the center of the trial of the nineteenth century, he lived out the rest of his life in obscurity.

Jefferson, after finishing his second term, returned to his home, his beloved Monticello. While his popularity at the time was waning, he had long ago assured his rightful place in history by helping to create a nation of laws—and then overseeing its inevitable expansion westward.

The founding fathers had somehow envisioned the possibilities of a great democracy, then gave us the tools necessary to bring that dream to fruition and make it work. But their time was coming to an end, as was Jefferson's. Washington was dead, Hamilton had been killed on that windy New Jersey bluff, and within a few years the rest of the founding fathers would be gone: Adams and Madison, the extraordinary Benjamin Franklin, John Hancock and John Jay, Thomas Paine, Paul Revere and Richard Henry Lee, men who had willingly risked their lives on battlefields time and again to fight for a new nation, a nation founded on a simple and inalienable principle—"that all men are created equal, that they are endowed by their Creator with certain unalienable Rights, that among these are Life, Liberty, and the pursuit of Happiness. That to secure these rights, Governments are instituted among Men, deriving their just powers from the consent of the governed."

Betsy Ross

AND THE

American Flag

On August 3, 1777, Fort Schuyler in upstate New York was besieged by almost two thousand British, Loyalist, and Indian troops commanded by General Barry St. Leger. This was a key battle in the British plan to capture the Mohawk Valley and divide the American colonies. The estimated seven hundred patriots trapped inside the fort waited desperately for reinforcements that might never arrive. At some point that morning, an unknown patriot raised a flag consisting of thirteen alternating red and white stripes with a blue field, or canton, with thirteen white stars. For the first time in history, the American flag had flown.

Ironically, reports that a large relief column led by none other than General Benedict Arnold was approaching caused the British to flee.

There certainly was neither pomp nor circumstance when the flag was raised that day. Nobody cheered with joy; it didn't inspire a surge of patriotism; by all reports few soldiers paid much attention to it if they even knew what it was. While the American flag has become the revered symbol of freedom throughout the world, it was considerably less important during the Revolution. In fact, the Stars and Stripes is considered to be only the third flag to represent a country; until then, most flags represented monarchs, royal families, or military units.

Several variations of American flags had flown before that one. On January 1, 1776, for example, General George Washington, in command of the troops surrounding Boston, ordered the Grand Union flag raised above his headquarters on Prospect Hill. The Continental Colors, as this flag also was known, consisted of thirteen alternating red and white stripes with the British Union Jack in its upper left-hand corner.

According to one of our most cherished legends, Philadelphia seamstress Betsy Ross sewed the first American flag. With her husband, Betsy Ross ran a small upholstery shop not far from the state house. Supposedly Washington would visit often to have his shirt ruffles embroidered and other alterations made. The story told almost a full century later by her family is that Washington and two members of Congress came into the shop on or about June 1, 1776, not long after Betsy Ross had been widowed when her husband was killed in a munitions explosion, and asked her to make a flag based on a pencil drawing they presented. It was said that her late husband's uncle, Colonel George Ross, had recommended her to Washington. She agreed to do it but suggested one change: the stars on the roughly drawn flag had six points and she suggested five-pointed stars. With their approval, she hand-sewed the first American flag.

It is an important story in our history, even if it most probably isn't true. It would be another year, in June 1777, before the Continental Congress would pass an act establishing an official American flag. "Resolved," it read, "that the flag of the thirteen United States be thirteen stripes alternate red and white; that the union be thirteen stars, white in a blue field, representing a new constellation." The resolution, one of many passed the same day, did not further describe the flag, so the actual placement and size of the elements were completely at the whim of the person crafting it. In different early versions of the flag, the stars are placed in a circle, in several stacked lines, or even arranged into a single large star.

Historians generally believe the claim made by New Jersey's Francis Hopkinson, a naval flag designer who had signed the Declaration of Independence, that he designed the basic flag we recognize today, probably adapting it from several different variations. He actually sent a letter and several bills to Congress, requesting a "quarter cask of the public wine" as payment for his work on the flag, the Great Seal of the United States,

Continental currency, and other projects, which was denied because he was a member of Congress and this was seen as part of his duties.

Washington explained the symbolism of the flag, saying, "We take the stars from heaven, the red from our mother country, separating it by white stripes, thus showing that we have separated from her, and the white stripes shall go down to posterity representing liberty." The thirteen stars, obviously, represented the thirteen original colonies. The flag flown in battle over Fort Schuyler apparently was made inside the fort; the white stripes came from soldiers' shirts, the red stripes were made from the red flannel petticoats of officers' wives, and the blue field was cut out of Captain Abraham Swartwout's blue cloth coat. We know for certain Swartwout gave up his coat because a record exists of Congress paying him for it.

But there is no record of who sewed the first flag or what happened to it. The only official mention of Betsy Ross during this period appears in the minutes of Pennsylvania's Navy Board, which paid her "fourteen pounds twelve shillings and two pence" for making the colors for Pennsylvania state ships. But at least three other Philadelphia seamstresses were paid about the same to produce a variety of unidentified standards at this same time. It is known that Ross did eventually sew many variations of the flag; in 1810, for example, she was paid for six eighteen-by-twenty-four-foot garrison flags

 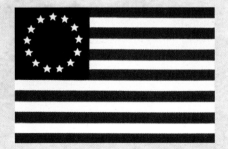

The first true American flag, the 1775 Grand Union flag (at left) or Continental flag eventually evolved into the familiar star-spangled banner that flew over

that were sent to New Orleans and twenty-seven more flags for the Indian Department.

When Betsy Ross died in 1836, at age eighty-four, the flag still had not yet taken its place of honor. While "The Star-Spangled Banner" had been written by Francis Scott Key in 1814 as he watched the flag sewn by another Philadelphia seamstress flying over Fort McHenry, it did not become popular until just before the Civil War when patriotism first began surging, and it was not adopted as our national anthem until 1931.

The historical claim for Betsy Ross sewing the flag actually was made for the first time by her grandson, William Canby, in 1870, ninety-four years after it supposedly took place—and at the same time several other families were asserting that their relatives had produced it. Canby admitted he could not produce any diaries, journals, congressional records, or other documents corroborating his claim, although other members of his family supported him. Canby's story was published in the popular magazine *Harper's New Monthly Magazine* in 1873 and was accepted by elementary school teachers who began including this tale in their history curriculum, giving it the appearance of reality. Over time it took on the appearance of settled truth, even though there is little evidence to support it, and it has become an important part of the American mythology.

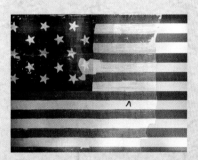

Fort McHenry in September 1814, inspiring Francis Scott Key to write our national anthem.

ACKNOWLEDGMENTS

Writing, illustrating, and publishing a book like this one requires the best work of many people, and I am grateful to everyone who participated. I especially would like to thank the people at the N. S. Bienstock Agency, in particular the founders, Richard Leibner and Carol Cooper, whom I greatly admire for their achievements and the way they work every day, in every way, to make the world a better place. I also greatly appreciate the work of Paul Fedorko, who runs Bienstock's literary department and does so with complete professionalism and the necessary mischievous glint in his eye!

It is always a pleasure to work with Henry Holt's editor in chief, the unflappable and always supportive Gillian Blake, who deals with every one of the many issues involved in this complex project with calmness and wisdom. Editorial Assistant Eleanor Embry successfully keeps all of us on track and does so with a minimum of drama. The design of this book, which personally I love, is the work of Nancy Singer, who successfully re-creates each period with the assistance of Liz Seramur, who collects the images and deals with all the headaches that go with that.

I relied on several people to point me in the right directions, but none more than my friend David Malinsky, who has a passion for this period and has written about it himself. I also relied on Casson Masters's masterful transcription service Scribecorps, as I always do, and I could not recommend them more highly.

I also would especially like to acknowledge the contribution of well respected author Don N. Hagist, Editor, *Journal of the American Revolution*;

the story of the Revolution is replete with heroics, legends, and lies, and separating them can be very difficult, and without his efforts this book would be considerably less accurate.

Finally, as always, my appreciation and my love to my wife, Laura Fisher, who makes the often difficult job of being the wife of a writer seem a lot easier than it actually is. I know what she does for me every single day and I enjoy the opportunity to sing her praises in front of other people. I also need to thank our two boys, Taylor and Beau, for their continued support and for not crashing the cars near deadlines. Finally, our dog Willow Bay, is always there when I need her, and for her I want to thank the North Shore Animal Shelter.

BIBLIOGRAPHY

I have also consulted several websites to gather, compare, and confirm information. The following sites proved to be especially valuable, providing useful material as well as directing me to additional sources:

AllThingsLiberty.com/: Journal of the American Revolution online

AlphaHistory.com/americanrevolution

Biography.com

Books.Google.com

ConstitutionFacts.com

EyeWitnessToHistory.com

History.com

HistoryIsFun.org

HudsonRiverValley.com

MassHist.org: Massachusetts Historical Society

NSA.gov/cryptologichistory: The Center for Cryptologic History (CCH)

OurAmericanRevolution.org

PBS.org

SmithsonianMag.com

USHistory.org

Wikipedia.org

Allbray, Nedda C. *Flatbush: The Heart of Brooklyn*. Charleston, SC: Arcadia Publishing, 2004.

Andrlik, Todd, ed. *Journal of the American Revolution, Annual Volume 2015*. Yardley, PA: Westholme Publishing, 2015.

Arnold, Samuel Greene. *History of the State of Rhode Island and the Providence Plantations, Volume 2*. New York: D. Appleton & Company, 1859.

Barefoot, Daniel W. *Touring South Carolina's Revolutionary War Sites*. Winston-Salem, NC: John F. Blair Publisher, 1999.

Breen, T. H. *American Insurgents, American Patriots: The Revolution of the People*. New York: Hill and Wang, 2010.

Burr, Aaron, and Matthew L. Davis. *Memoirs of Aaron Burr*. New York: Harper & Brothers, 1837.

Carr, J. Revell. *Seeds of Discontent: The Deep Roots of the American Revolution, 1650–1750*. New York: Walker & Company, 2008.

Curran, John J. *Peekskill's African American History: A Hudson Valley Community's Untold Story*. Charleston, SC: History Press, 2008.

Dann, John C., ed. *The Revolution Remembered: Eyewitness Accounts of the War for Independence*. Chicago: University of Chicago Press, 1980.

Ellis, Joseph J. *Founding Brothers: The Revolutionary Generation*. New York: Alfred A. Knopf, 2000.

———. *His Excellency: George Washington*. New York: Alfred A. Knopf, 2004.

Frothingham, Richard. *History of the Siege of Boston, and of the Battles of Lexington, Concord, and Bunker Hill*. Boston: C. C. Little and J. Brown, 1851.

Guthrie, James M. *Campfires of the Afro-American: or, The Colored Man as a Patriot*. Philadelphia: Afro-American Publishing Company, 1899.

Hsiung, David C. "Food, Fuel, and the New England Environment in the War for Independence, 1775–1776." *New England Quarterly* 80, no. 4 (December 2007): 614–54.

Isaacson, Walter. *Benjamin Franklin: An American Life*. New York: Simon & Schuster, 2003.

Kiernan, Denise, and Joseph D'Agnese. *Signing Away Their Lives: The Fame and Misfortune of the Men Who Signed the Declaration of Independence*. Philadelphia: Quirk Books, 2009.

Kozuskanich, Nathan. *Benjamin Franklin: American Founder, Atlantic Citizen*. New York: Routledge, 2015.

Lecky, William E. H. *A History of England in the Eighteenth Century*. New York: D. Appleton, 1892–93.

Malcolm, Joyce L. *Peter's War: A New England Slave Boy and the American Revolution*. New Haven, CT: Yale University Press, 2009.

Mark, Steven Paul. "For Sale: West Point." Journal of the American Revolution Online Magazine, May 2014.

McCullough, David G. *John Adams*. New York: Simon & Schuster, 2001.

Moore, Horatio N. *The Life and Times of Gen. Francis Marion*. Philadelphia: J. B. Perry, 1845.

Nash, Gary B. *The Unknown American Revolution: The Unruly Birth of Democracy and the Struggle to Create America*. New York: Viking, 2005.

Nelson, James L. *With Fire and Sword: The Battle of Bunker Hill and the Beginning of the American Revolution*. New York: Thomas Dunne Books, 2011.

Phelps, M. William. *Nathan Hale: The Life and Death of America's First Spy*. New York: Thomas Dunne Books, 2008.

Puls, Mark. *Samuel Adams: Father of the American Revolution*. New York: Palgrave Macmillan, 2006.

Skemp, Sheila L. *Benjamin and William Franklin: Father and Son, Patriot and Loyalist*. Boston: Bedford Books of St. Martin's Press, 1994.

———. *The Making of a Patriot: Benjamin Franklin at the Cockpit*. New York: Oxford University Press, 2013.

Sparks, Jared. *The Life of Washington*. Boston: Little, Brown, 1852.

Williams, Catherine Read. *Biography of Revolutionary Heroes, Containing the Life of Brigadier Gen. William Barton*. Providence, RI: Published by the author, 1839.

Winfield, Charles H. *History of the County of Hudson, New Jersey: From Its Earliest Settlement to the Present Time*. New York: Kennard & Hay Stationery Manufacturing and Printing Company, 1874.

Winter, Claudia Bell. "The Aaron Burr Trial." PhD diss., University of Richmond, 1967.

Wood, Gordon S. *The American Revolution: A History*. New York: Modern Library, 2002.

INDEX

CREDITS

Page iii: Background and title logo courtesy of FOX NEWS CHANNEL. Page 2: Courtesy of the Library of Congress, LC-DIG-pga-02468. Page 2: Peter Newark American Pictures/Bridgeman Images. Page 6: Stock Montage/Getty Images. Page 9: Historical Society of Pennsylvania. Pages 10–11: Universal History Archive/UIG. Page 13: © Massachusetts Historical Society/Bridgeman Images. Page 13: Museum of Fine Arts, Boston/Carolyn A. and Peter S. Lynch Gallery (Gallery 132)/Bridgeman Images. Page 14: American Antiquarian Society/Bridgeman Images. Page 17: Courtesy of the Library of Congress, LC-DIG-ppmsca-37946. Page 17: American Antiquarian Society/Bridgeman Images. Page 19: Bridgeman Images. Page 22: Peter Newark American Pictures/Bridgeman Images. Page 25: American Antiquarian Society/Bridgeman Images. Page 26: Museum of Fine Arts, Boston/Gift by Subscription and Francis Bartlett Fund/Bridgeman Images. Page 27: Courtesy of the Library of Congress, LC-DIG-ppmsca-01657. Page 28: Granger, NYC—All rights reserved. Page 31: Courtesy of Swann Auction Galleries/Bridgeman Images. Page 32: Courtesy of the Library of Congress, LC-USZ62-45586. Page 37: Peter Newark American Pictures/Bridgeman Images. Page 38: American Antiquarian Society/Bridgeman Images. Page 40: Courtesy of the Library of Congress, LC-DIG-ds-03379. Page 41: National Trust Photographic Library/Bridgeman Images. Page 42: © Philadelphia History Museum at the Atwater Kent/Courtesy of Historical Society of Pennsylvania Collection/Bridgeman. Page 45: Courtesy of the Library of Congress, LC-USZC2-2452. Page 46: Peter Newark American Pictures/Bridgeman Images. Page 49: Courtesy Crocker Art Museum. Page 49: Courtesy of the Evanston History Center. Page 49: John Singleton Copley, American, 1738–1815, *Paul Revere*, 1768 (detail). Photograph © 2016 Museum of Fine Arts, Boston. Page 51: Bridgeman Images. Page 52–53: Granger, NYC—All rights reserved. Page 54: Bridgeman Images. Page 56: © Chicago History Museum, USA/Bridgeman Images. Page 59: Bridgeman Images. Page 61: Peter Newark American Pictures/Bridgeman Images. Page 63: Peter Newark American Pictures/Bridgeman Images. Page 65: Universal History Archive/UIG/Bridgeman Images. Page 67: SuperStock. Page 68: © Massachusetts Historical Society, Boston, MA, USA/Bridgeman Images. Page 69: Bridgeman Images. Page 71: Courtesy of the Library of Congress, G3764.B6S31775.J4. Page 74: Courtesy of the Library of Congress, LC-USZ62-45535. Page 78: Peter Newark American Pictures/Bridgeman Images. Page 82: Courtesy of the Library of Congress, LC-USZ62-78928. Page 84: Yale University Art Gallery, New Haven, CT, USA/Bridgeman Images. Page 87: Pennsylvania Academy of the Fine Arts, Philadelphia, USA/Bridgeman Images. Page 90: Peter Newark Western Americana/Bridgeman Images. Page 92: Photo © PVDE/Bridgeman Images. Page 93: © Collection of the New-York Historical Society, USA/Bridgeman Images. Page 97: Map © 2013 Jeffrey L. Ward. Used by permission. Page 98: Courtesy of the Library of Congress, LC-USZC4-9060. Pages 100–101: Photo © Liszt Collection/Bridgeman Images. Page 103: Peter Newark American Pictures/Bridgeman Images. Page 104: Brown University Library, Providence, RI, USA/Bridgeman Images. Page 106: Peter Newark Pictures/Bridgeman Images. Page 109: © charistoone-images/Alamy Stock Photo. Page 110: akg-images/ullstein bild. Page 112: S Capitol Collection, Washington D.C., USA/Photograph © Boltin Picture Library/Bridgeman Images. Page 115: Granger, NYC—All rights reserved. Page 117: Huntington Library and Art Gallery, San Marino, CA, USA/© The Huntington Library, Art Collections & Botanical Gardens/Bridgeman Images. Page 117: Courtesy of the Library of Congress, E211.J44 E187.C72 vol. 12, no. 2. Page 118: Granger, NYC—All rights reserved. Page 119: Photo © Tarker/Bridgeman Images. Page 120: Granger, NYC—All rights reserved. Page 123: The Heckscher

Museum of Art, Huntington, NY, USA/August Heckscher Collection/Bridgeman Images. Page 126: Courtesy of the Library of Congress, LC-USZ62-43020. Page 127: Ken Welsh/Bridgeman Images. Page 129: The Stapleton Collection/Bridgeman Images. Page 130: Courtesy of the Library of Congress, LC-USZ62-111795 (b&w). Page 131: Granger, NYC—All rights reserved. Page 136: Map © 2002 Jeffrey L. Ward. Used by permission. Page 138: Bridgeman Images. Page 140: Granger, NYC—All rights reserved. Page 143: Metropolitan Museum of Art, New York, USA/Bridgeman Images. Page 146: Museum of Fine Arts, Boston, MA, USA/Gift of the Owners of the old Boston Museum/Bridgeman Images. Page 148: Brown University Library, Providence, RI, USA/Bridgeman Images. Page 150: Courtesy of the Library of Congress, LC-DIG-ppmsca-19163. Page 152: Bettman/CORBIS. Page 158: Courtesy of the Library of Congress, LC-USZ62-108232. Page 161: Courtesy of the Library of Congress, LC-USZC4-2912. Page 163: Granger, NYC—All rights reserved. Page 164: Granger, NYC—All rights reserved. Page 167: Courtesy of the Library of Congress, LC G3804.W53S31779.S5. Page 168: Granger, NYC—All rights reserved. Page 170: Courtesy of the Library of Congress, LC-USZC4-2396. Page 175: Courtesy of the Library of Congress, LC-USZC4-6877. Page 177: Pennsylvania State Capitol, PA, USA/Bridgeman Images. Page 181: Courtesy of the Library of Congress, LC-DIG-pga-01392. Page 182: Peter Newark American Pictures/Bridgeman Images. Page 185: © North Wind Picture Archives. Page 185: National Gallery, London, UK/Bridgeman Images. Page 187: Courtesy of the Library of Congress, G3913.C3P5178-.P5. Pages 188–189: Granger, NYC—All rights reserved. Page 191: Brown University Library, Providence, RI, USA/Bridgeman Images. Page 193: De Agostini Picture Library/Bridgeman Images. Page 197: Brown University Library, Providence, RI, USA/Bridgeman Images. Page 201: Universal History Archive/UIG/Bridgeman Images. Page 201: Ken Welsh/ Bridgeman Images. Page 202: Brown University Library, Providence, RI, USA/Bridgeman Images. Page 206: New York Public Library, USA/Bridgeman Images. Page 207: Peter Newark American Pictures/Bridgeman Images. Page 209: Photo © Christie's Images/Bridgeman Images. Page 212: Metropolitan Museum of Art, New York, USA/Bridgeman Images. Page 214: © Look and Learn/Bridgeman Images. Page 215: © Boston Athenaeum, USA/Bridgeman Images. Page 217: © CORBIS. Page 218: Image copyright © The Metropolitan Museum of Art. Image source: Art Resource, NY. Page 219: © Massachusetts Historical Society, Boston, MA, USA/Bridgeman Images. Page 221: Yale University Art Gallery, New Haven, CT, USA/Bridgeman Images. Page 223: Bridgeman Images. Page 224: Brown University Library, Providence, RI, USA/Bridgeman Images. Page 228: Musee de la Ville de Paris, Musee Carnavalet, Paris, France/Archives Charmet/Bridgeman Images. Page 235: Photograph © Christie's Images/Bridgeman Images/Printed by permission of the Norman Rockwell Family Agency/Copyright © 2016 the Norman Rockwell Family Entities. Page 236: Brown University Library, Providence, RI, USA/Bridgeman Images. Page 237: Bridgeman Images. Page 238: Bridgeman Images. Page 241: © Chicago History Museum, USA/Bridgeman Images. Page 242: Bridgeman Images. Page 245: Courtesy of the Library of Congress, LC-DIG-ppmsca-17522. Page 245: Granger, NYC—All rights reserved. Page 246: Courtesy of the Library of Congress, LC-USZ62-77992. Page 246: Bridgeman Images. Page 248: Granger, NYC—All rights reserved. Page 252: Courtesy of the National Archives. Page 255: Granger, NYC—All rights reserved. Page 255: Granger, NYC—All rights reserved. Page 259: Peter Newark American Pictures/Bridgeman Images. Page 260: Courtesy of the Library of Congress, LC-USZ62-54169. Page 261: Independence Hall, Philadelphia, PA, USA/Bridgeman Images. Page 264: De Agostini Picture Library/W. Buss/Bridgeman Images. Page 267: © Look and Learn/Bridgeman Images. Page 268: Courtesy of the Library of Congress, LC-DIG-ppmsca-19356. Page 271: © Collection of the New-York Historical Society, USA/Bridgeman Images. Page 274: Peter Newark American Pictures/Bridgeman Images. Page 275: © Collection of the New-York Historical Society, USA/Bridgeman Images. Page 275: © Chicago History Museum, USA/Bridgeman Images. Pages 276–277: Musee Franco-Americaine, Blerancourt, Chauny, France/Roger-Viollet, Paris/Bridgeman Images. Page 280: © Look and Learn/Bridgeman Images. Page 283: Granger, NYC—All rights reserved. Page 285: Granger, NYC—All rights reserved. Page 290: Archives Charmet/Bridgeman Images. Page 290: Granger, NYC—All rights reserved. Page: 291: Granger, NYC—All rights reserved. Page 291: Granger, NYC—All rights reserved.

NORTH DAKOTA
MINNESOTA
WISCONSIN
Little Bighorn
Minneapolis
Mississippi River
Deadwood
Pierre
Northfield
Rapid City
SOUTH DAKOTA
le-in-the-Wall
French Creek
Madison
WYOMING
BLACK HILLS
sper
IOWA
NEBRASKA
Adair
Des Moines
Wilcox
N. Platte River
Omaha
Cheyenne
Platte River
Rock Creek
ILLINOIS
S. Platte River
North Platte
Missouri River
Republican River
St. Joseph
Liberty
Centralia massacre
Denver
Fort Leavenworth
Kansas City
St. Louis
KANSAS
Colorado Springs
Hays City
Lawrence
Abilene
COLORADO
MISSOURI
Wichita
Dodge City
Springfield
ROCKY MOUNTAINS
Arkansas River
INDIAN TERRITORY
ARKANSAS
Mississippi River
TN
Santa Fe
Canadian River
Custer massacre
Oklahoma City
Little Rock
Washita River
Albuquerque
Fort Sumner
OKLAHOMA
LINCOLN COUNTY
Lincoln
Dallas
Shreveport
NEW MEXICO
Sabine River
MS
Red River
Pecos River
TEXAS
El Paso
Brazos River
LOUISIANA
Rio Grande
Austin
Colorado River
Houston
The Alamo/ San Antonio
ICO
Gulf of Mexico

BILL O'REILLY'S

LEGENDS & LIES

BILL O'REILLY'S

& LEGENDS LIES

THE REAL WEST

WRITTEN BY DAVID FISHER

Henry Holt and Company, LLC
Publishers since 1866
175 Fifth Avenue
New York, New York 10010
www.henryholt.com

Henry Holt® and ⬛® are registered trademarks of Henry Holt and Company, LLC.
Copyright © 2015 by Warm Springs Productions, LLC and Life of O'Reilly Productions
All rights reserved.
Distributed in Canada by Raincoast Book Distribution Limited
Library of Congress Cataloging-in-Publication Data is available
ISBN: 978-1-62779-507-4

Henry Holt books are available for special promotions and premiums.
For details contact: Director, Special Markets.

First Edition 2015

Interior Design by Nancy Singer
Endpaper map by Jeffrey L. Ward

Photo research and editing provided by Liz Seramur, with assistance from Nancy Singer,
Emily Vinson, and Adam Vietenheimer

Jacket art credits: Background and title logo courtesy of FOX NEWS CHANNEL;
Denver Public Library, Western History Collection/Bridgeman Images; Chappel, Alonzo
(1828–87) (after)/Private Collection/Ken Welsh/Bridgeman Images; Private Collection/
Peter Newark Western Americana/Bridgeman Images; Private Collection/Bridgeman
Images; Universal History Archive/UIG/Bridgeman Images

Interior art credits appear on pages 293–94.

Printed in the United States of America

10 9 8 7 6 5 4 3 2 1

CONTENTS

KIT CARSON
1809–1868

DANIEL BOONE
1734–1820

WILD BILL HICKOK
1837–1876

BLACK BART
1829–?

BASS REEVES
1838–1910

DAVID CROCKETT
1786–1836

GEORGE ARMSTRONG
CUSTER
1839–1876

JESSE JAMES
1847–1882

BILLY THE KID
1859–1881

DOC HOLLIDAY
1852–1887

BUFFALO BILL AND
ANNIE OAKLEY
1846/1860–1917/1926

BUTCH CASSIDY
1866–1908

BILL O'REILLY'S

LEGENDS & LIES

INTRODUCTION

The classroom was filled with bored faces. About forty of them. All staring at a young history teacher fresh out of college who, at age twenty-one, was just a few years older than his students. What had I gotten myself into?

My initial task was to get these teenagers interested in things that had happened in America hundreds of years ago, events they thought had little or no meaning in their current lives.

It wasn't easy.

While I taught, I learned. There was a way to spread historical information around so that the urchins would not nod off. But it involved energy and thought, not just standing there pontificating. I learned back then that in order for people to enjoy history, you have to make it come alive in a vivid way. My students were taught to put themselves into the historical fray by visualizing themselves in the action. Those who did that learned about America in an unforgettable way.

Enter this book, *Legends & Lies*. It is based upon my high school teaching techniques that cut through the clutter to tell amazing stories. Want specifics? How about this: Evidence suggests that the real Lone

Ranger was a black man! You'll ride with him through a series of harrowing adventures that few Americans know about.

What you will read in this book is the truth about some very famous people. It's not always pretty, and it's definitely not the stuff they taught you in school. No, these pages are filled with facts and personalities, many of them disturbing. But we have made them all real people on the page because they were real people in life. Folks who did extraordinary things. A guy like Kit Carson, traveling thousands of miles through the freezing Rocky Mountains and then over the scorching-hot Arizona desert. At least Carson had a horse—the bandit Black Bart was afraid of horses and actually walked from Illinois to Montana! Don't believe me? Read the book. Walk alongside him.

America has a tendency to glamorize its past, creating myths instead of reporting truth. Let's take the Old West, for example. Our image of that time is John Wayne, Marshal Matt Dillon in *Gunsmoke*, and maybe a squinting, grizzled Clint Eastwood mowing down bad guys in a dusty town. But the truth about the West is far different from *Rio Bravo* or *Stagecoach* or *The Good, the Bad and the Ugly*. This was a place where brutality ruled, and life expectancy was measured in months. If you lived to be forty, you were way ahead. Some famous western men and women were both heroes and villains, split personalities. The dangers they faced were unrelenting.

Did you know that some Indians were more civilized than the settlers they encountered? But other Native Americans would torture in ways that are nearly inconceivable. Some out-laws, such as Butch Cassidy and Black Bart, were almost noble in their outlook. Some law-men, such as Pat Garrett, were not. It is these stories that we will relate to you in this book, and after reading them, you will know the truth about America's lively and unique past. You will have also learned about some lies that still circulate today. Debunking falsehoods is a major theme here.

As in my previous history books, *Killing Lincoln, Killing Kennedy, Killing Jesus,* and *Killing Patton*, we will put you on the scene as historical events unfold. You will be in the room and on the trail with Jesse James, Wyatt Earp, Wild Bill Hickok, and many other legendary figures. You will vividly see these men live and sometimes die. While reading this book, you will experience history rather than be numbed by it. Some say that after reading the Killing series, they understand the towering figures in history in a unique way. Each of those books has sold millions of copies.

When I engaged my students all those years ago, I painted a verbal picture for them of times past. Billy the Kid, for example, was a lot like they were, a confused teenager who chose the wrong road and paid the ultimate price. Or did he? There's always a bit more to the story if you dig deep enough. In *Legends & Lies*, you will see that the Kid's fate may have turned out far differently than many believe or the press reported.

And that's the fun of these pages. We dig deep, uncovering facts that illuminate the legends and debunk the lies that have somehow become folklore. History can be thrilling, and America's past is full of tremendous characters whose exploits can enrich our own lives today. It took me a while to convince my students of that, but I did it, and my history classes rocked, according to their own reviews (conducted each year at the school's behest).

Now it's your turn, and as a plus, there's no homework! Enjoy the exciting journey, and thanks for reading the book!

Bill O'Reilly
January 2015

DANIEL BOONE

Traitor or Patriot?

As Daniel Boone approached his log cabin one October day in 1778, carrying fur and meat to take his family through the winter, he probably guessed something was wrong. Keenly perceptive and attuned to the rhythms of nature, he would have sensed the discord. His family came out to greet him, followed almost immediately by several stern-looking men. As Boone dismounted, one of them handed him a subpoena. Another man stepped forward, unrolled a scroll, and announced, "Daniel Boone, you are hereby formally charged with treason and shall face a court-martial . . ."

No one embodied the spirit of the frontier more than Daniel Boone, who faced and defeated countless natural and man-made dangers to literally hand cut the trail west through the wilderness. He marched with then colonel George Washington in the French and Indian War, established one of the most important trading posts in the West, served three terms in the Virginia Assembly, and fought in the Revolution. His exploits made him world famous; he served as the model for James Fenimore Cooper's Leatherstocking Tales and numerous other pioneer stories. He was so well known and respected that even Lord Byron, in his epic poem *Don Juan*, wrote, "Of the great names which in our faces stare, The General Boon, back-woodsman of Kentucky, Was happiest amongst mortals anywhere . . ."

And yet he was accused of treason—betraying his country—the most foul of all crimes at the time. What really happened to bring him to that courtroom? And was the verdict reached there correct?

Daniel Boone was born in Pennsylvania in 1734, the sixth child of Quakers Sarah and Squire Boone. His father had come to America from England in 1713. The Boones were known as thrifty, prosperous people. His cousin, James Boone, had a knack for numbers and eventually became known as "Boone, the Mathematician." But Daniel Boone did not find comfort in the classroom or with books. He had enough schooling to know how to sign his name, but his real education was learning the skills of survival on the frontier: He became an expert hunter, tracker, trapper, marksman, and trailblazer. It was said that no Indian could aim his rifle,

Born in 1734 in Birdsboro,
Pennsylvania, Daniel Boone
was the seventh of twelve
children.

find his way through a pathless forest, or search out game better than young Daniel Boone. He was hard to pin down to any one place; he always loved being on his own, away from the clatter of the cities.

When Squire Boone was "disowned" by the Quaker meeting for allowing his children to "marry out of unity"—meaning to marry non-Quakers—he moved his family to North Carolina. The Boones had only just settled there when the French and Indian War began in 1754. Young Daniel Boone served as a wagoneer in British major Edward Dobb's North Carolina militia. He marched with Lieutenant Colonel George Washington under the despised General Braddock in his disastrous effort to capture Fort Duquesne. When Braddock was killed in the Battle of the Wilderness, Washington took command and began building his heroic reputation. During the war, Boone first heard tell of a place the Indians called the Dark and Bloody Ground, a paradise that some people called Kentucke. An Indian trader named John Finlay had actually been there and was determined to get back. At that time, very little about the lands south of the Ohio River was known to the British, and Boone listened to these stories with excitement, his heart making the decision that he would go there.

A small group of extraordinarily courageous men risked their lives exploring and settling the American frontier. They were people who felt an urgent pull to see what lay beyond the next mountain and depended on their skills, wits, and sometimes just plain luck to reach the next summit. They were most at home in foreign and wild places, living off God's bounty. Many of these early American pioneers are forgotten, but through hundreds of years of American history, Daniel Boone has stood for them all.

It took Boone twelve more years to finally get to Kentucke, and by that time he had married his neighbor's daughter, Rebecca Bryan, and they'd had four children, in addition to taking in several nieces and nephews. He'd also explored the area called Florida (he reportedly bought land near Pensacola but elected not to settle there), as well as the unspoiled wilderness of the Alleghenies, the Cumberlands, and the Shenandoah Valley. In 1851, author Henry Howe described Boone's arrival in Kentucke, writing that his party, "after a long and fatiguing march, over a mountainous and pathless wilderness, arrived on the Red River. Here, from the top of an eminence, Boone and his companions first beheld a distant view of the beautiful lands of Kentucky. The plains and forests abounded with wild beasts of every kind;

Thomas Cole's *Daniel Boone Sitting at the Door of His Cabin on the Great Osage Lake, Kentucky*, 1826

deer and elk were common; the buffalo were seen in herds and the plains covered with the richest verdure . . . this newly discovered Paradise of the West." Daniel Boone was the first settler to set his eyes and bestow a name on many of the now familiar features of Kentucky. Like many frontiersmen of the time, as Boone explored, he carved his name into the trees to show he had been there, and a beech tree on the Watauga River in Tennessee still bears the inscription D. BOON CILLED A. BAR ON TREE IN THE YEAR 1760.

His first time in Kentucke, he stayed only long enough to know that he'd found the open spaces in which he wanted to raise his family. He returned in 1769 with five other men, blazing the first trail from North Carolina into eastern Tennessee. During that expedition, he spent two years there, twice being captured by Indians; the first time, he was set free, the next time, he escaped. As he later wrote, the Indians "had kept us in confinement seven days, treating us with common savage usage . . . in the dead of the night, as we lay in a thick cane-break by a large fire, when sleep had locked up their senses, my situation not disposing me for rest, I touched my companion, and gentle awoke him. We improved this favorable opportunity, and departed, leaving them to take their rest, and speedily directed our course towards our old camp." His companion was his brother-in-law, John Stewart, who had been captured with him both times, but eventually Stewart's luck ran out. While out hunting one day, he was shot by an Indian raiding party and took refuge in a hollowed-out tree, where he bled to death; his body was found there almost five years later.

Boone would spend his winters hunting beaver and otter, and in the spring sell or trade the furs he had collected. In the summers he would farm and hunt deer, gathering meat for the winter and deerskins for trade. The value of these deerskins, or buckskins, fluctuated against the British pound and later the American dollar, and eventually *buck* became an acceptable slang term for "dollar."

Boone also made his clothes from the skins of the animals, and his buckskin shirt and leggings, moccasins, and beaver cap were the accepted dress of the frontiersmen.

In 1773, Boone decided it was time to move his family to Kentucke. He sold his farm and all his possessions and agreed to lead the first group of about fifty British colonists into the new territory. On the journey west, his son James trailed behind, bringing cattle and supplies to the settlements. On October 9, James Boone's small group was camped along Wallen Creek when Indians attacked. They had failed to take the necessary precautions and were defenseless. James and several others were brutally tortured and killed. Although Boone urged the rest of the settlers to push forward, this deadly attack frightened them into returning to civilization in Virginia and Carolina. He had no choice but to go back with them.

Early American history has been told—and often exaggerated—by the pen and the paintbrush. Daniel Boone's fame as a bear hunter is depicted by Severino Baraldi (*above*), while this portrait of the lone woodsman was painted by Robert Lindneux.

Boone blazing the trail west in George Caleb Bingham's 1851–52 oil painting, *Daniel Boone Escorting Settlers through the Cumberland Gap*

Boone was not a man who relished a fight, but he never backed away from one, either. In 1774, he led the defense of three forts along Virginia's Clinch River from Shawnee attacks and, as a result, earned a promotion to captain in the militia—as well as the respect of his men. While Boone proved to be one of the settlers' most ferocious fighters, he did understand the reason for the Indians' resistance and perhaps even sympathized with them, admitting that the war against them was intended to "dispossess them of their desirable habitations"— in simpler words, take their land.

His reputation was growing, the word spread by his admirers, who never hesitated to tell stories of his courage, even if some were a bit exaggerated. In 1775, the Transylvania Company, which had purchased from the Cherokees all the land lying between the Cumberland Mountains, the Cumberland River, and the Kentucky River, south of the Ohio, hired Boone to lead the expedition of axmen that carved the three-hundred-mile-long Wilderness Road through three states and the Cumberland Gap. It was this trail that opened up the frontier to the many thousands of settlers who would follow.

When Boone's men finally reached Kentucke, he laid out the town and fort of Boonesborough. During that journey, four men were killed and five were wounded by the increasingly hostile Shawnees. But Boonesborough and Harrodsburg, wrote Henry Howe, "became the nucleus and support of emigration and settlement in Kentucky." The settlers, including Boone's wife and their children, raced to erect fortifications strong enough to resist Indian attacks, and on May 23, 1776, the Shawnees attacked Boonesborough. They were repelled, but they would come back, and everybody knew it.

Less than two weeks later, the Continental Congress, meeting in Philadelphia, signed the Declaration of Independence. It would take more than a month for the settlers to learn of it.

On April 1, 1775, Boone and thirty axmen began construction of Fort Boonesborough, choosing a location in a defensible field "about 60 yards from the river, and a little over 200 yards from a salt lick."

The coming war for independence did not really affect or concern them; they were already too busy fighting a war for their own survival. Boone was not a political man and did not strongly support either the Revolutionaries or the British. That was not a luxury he had time for. Life on the frontier was always a daily life-or-death struggle. Just about a week after the noble document was signed, for example, Boone's daughter, Jemima, and two other young girls were kidnapped by a Shawnee-Cherokee raiding party. He immediately gathered nine men and set off after them.

From all accounts, Daniel Boone was not a man of exuberant emotions. He kept his feelings contained and was respected for his cunning and his steadfast leadership. He was not a man who ever asked another to take a risk in his place. When a task needed to be done, he took the lead. The rescuers pursued the Indians for three days, finally sneaking up on them as they sat by a breakfast fire. Their first shot wounded a guard and alerted the others to escape. Two of the Indians were killed, and the three girls were freed without harm. This kidnapping and rescue later served as an inspiration for James Fenimore Cooper, who included a similar incident in *The Last of the Mohicans*, with the character Hawkeye modeled after Boone.

The Revolutionary War just brushed the frontier, and rather than facing the redcoats, the pioneers fought Native Americans supplied and supported by British forces headquartered in Detroit. It was questionable whether the Indians were actually fighting to protect the Empire or to maintain their own rights to live and hunt on the land. By 1777, Indians were focusing their attacks on Boonesborough, forcing the settlers to stay close to the fort. One afternoon, Boone was outside the perimeter when the Shawnees attacked. As Boone took up his long gun to return fire, a bullet smashed into his ankle and sent him to the ground. He was carried through the closing gate as Indian bullets ripped into the wooden walls.

The constant pressure of attacks kept the settlers confined, and by the end of the year, supplies were running low. In early February, Boone was asked to lead a twenty-seven-man expedition to the Blue Licks, a salt lick located several miles away. It was a very risky mission: Several weeks earlier, three Shawnee chiefs in captivity at Fort Randolph had been killed, and the tribe was seeking revenge. As Boone's men were gathering vital salt, he was alone, hunting for provisions— and he was surprised and captured by a Shawnee war party. More than one hundred warriors were led by Chief Blackfish, a man Boone had met decades earlier while serving in Braddock's campaign. Blackfish apparently respected Boone as the chief of his people and told him he intended to avenge the murders of the three Indian chiefs by killing everyone in the salt-gathering party, then destroying Boonesborough. Boone negotiated with him, finally offering to arrange the peaceful surrender of his men, who would then go north with the tribe. Chief Blackfish agreed.

As this G. W. Fasel lithograph depicts, when Boone's daughter and two friends were kidnapped by Indians in 1776, he tracked them down and rescued them—an episode that served as an inspiration for James Fenimore Cooper's *Last of the Mohicans*.

Boone was reputed to be the young nation's
greatest Indian fighter, as shown in this Baraldi
painting of an attack on Boonesborough.

Boone led the Shawnees to his hunting party—and when his men saw him with the Indians, they suspected that he had betrayed them and prepared to fight for their lives. "Don't fire!" Boone warned them. "If you do they will massacre all of us." He put his reputation on the line, ordering his men to stack their arms and surrender. In the confusion, some men escaped and hurried back to warn the settlers.

Daniel Boone and the remaining members of the expedition went north with the Shawnees to the village of Chillicothe, where there was great debate on how to treat the prisoners: Some of the braves wanted to kill them, but apparently Boone convinced them otherwise. As the weeks went by, he actually was adopted into the tribe and given the Indian name Sheltowee, or "Big Turtle." He was known to hunt and fish and play sports with the tribe, and there were even some stories that he took a bride. The Shawnees trusted him enough to take him to Detroit, where he met with the British governor Hamilton. But when he returned to Chillicothe, he found more than four hundred fifty armed and painted braves preparing to attack Boonesborough. He feared that the unprepared settlers would be slaughtered. Boone waited for the right opportunity, and in the confusion of a wild-turkey hunt, he managed to slip away.

He raced 160 miles in less than five days, on foot and horseback. He paused only one time for a meal. He reached Boonesborough still dressed in Indian garb, and his warning was met with great suspicion. The men who had escaped the original attack cautioned that he was cooperating with the Shawnees, pointing out that he had lived safely among the tribe for months and that he had returned while many of their relations remained captives. Finally Boone was able to convince the settlers to strengthen their wooden fortifications and, in an effort to prove his loyalty, suggested that instead of waiting for the attack, they take the offensive.

He and his friend John Logan led a thirty-man raiding party to the Shawnee village of Paint Creek on the Scioto River. After a trek of several days, they found it abandoned—meaning the main Indian force, then under the command of the Canadian captain Duquesne, was already on its way to the settlement. The raiding party made it back safely, and the cattle and horses were brought into the fort, which was made as secure as possible. Soon Boonesborough was surrounded by as many as five hundred Shawnee braves. British colors were displayed, and the settlers were told to either surrender, with a promise of good treatment, or fight and face the hatchet. Rather than fighting, Boone asked Captain Duquesne for a parley.

Boone and eight other men met with the Indians in a meadow beyond the settlement's walls. Eventually they reached an agreement: The Ohio River would be the boundary between the settlers and the tribes. As they shook hands, the Indians tried to grab Boonesborough's leaders and drag them away, but carefully hidden sharpshooters opened fire. Boone and his men retreated, and an eleven-day siege began. The enemy made several efforts to break into the fort, but riflemen inside the garrison released a steady stream of accurate fire on anyone who came within range. When the Indian force broke off the attack, thirty-seven braves had been killed and many more wounded, while inside the walls only two settlers had died and two were wounded. The resistance, led by Daniel Boone, had saved the settlement.

But within weeks, Boone was accused of treason. Two militia officers—whose kin had been taken on the salt-lick expedition and were still being held captive in Detroit—claimed he had been collaborating with the Indians and the British. He was accused of surrendering the original expedition at the salt flats, consorting with the British in Detroit in their plan to capture the settlement, intentionally weakening Boonesborough's defense by taking thirty men on the "foolish raid" on Paint Creek, and leaving the fort vulnerable by bringing its leadership outside to negotiate with Blackfish. The penalty for treason was death by hanging.

Boone's trial was held at another settlement, Logan's Station. With few records available, it is difficult to reconstruct events. His accusers were Richard Callaway and Benjamin Logan. Callaway testified, "Boone was in favor of the British government and all his conduct proved it."

Boone insisted on representing himself rather than retaining a lawyer. He testified that both his salt expedition and the settlement were outmanned and outgunned, and neither of them was strong enough to survive a surprise attack. To prevent a massacre, he had been forced to "use some stratagem," telling the Indians "tales to fool them." After hearing his testimony, and perhaps taking into account his good name, the judges found him not guilty—then promoted him to the rank of major.

Boone accepted the acquittal but could not forgive the insult, so he left Boonesborough and founded a new settlement in an area known as Upper Louisiana, which actually was in present-day Missouri. When asked why he'd left Kentucke, he replied, "I want more elbow room." In recognition of his accomplishments, the Spanish governor of that region granted him 850 acres and appointed him commandant. He settled there with his family but couldn't stay settled long.

Perhaps still angry about the false accusations, in 1780 he finally joined the Revolution, acting as a guide for George Rogers Clark's militia as they attacked and defeated a joint British and Indian force in Ohio. In that attack, his brother Ned was shot and killed. Apparently believing they had killed the great Daniel Boone, the Shawnees beheaded Ned Boone and took his head home as a trophy.

This Currier and Ives hand-colored
lithograph by Fannie Flora Palmer, *The
Rocky Mountains—Emigrants Crossing the
Plains*, 1866, illustrates the barren beauty
of the frontier—although Palmer never
left New York.

A year later, Daniel Boone stood for election to the Virginia Assembly. He would be elected to that body three times.

Two years later, at the Battle of Blue Licks, the then lieutenant colonel Daniel Boone warned his commanding officer that the militia was being led into an Indian trap. He explained that the Indians had left a broad and obvious trail, which was contrary to their

custom and "manifested a willingness to be pursued." Boone believed that "an ambuscade was formed at the distance of a mile in advance" and urged him not to cross the Licking River until the area could be properly scouted or reinforcements known to be marching toward them arrived. But as the commanders debated their strategy, a headstrong young Major McGary ignored Boone's advice and instead mounted and charged the enemy. When he was in the middle of the stream, he paused, waved his hat over his head, and shouted, "Let all who are not cowards follow me!" As the rest of the men cheered and followed, Boone supposedly said, "We are all slaughtered men," but still joined the attack. As pioneer historian Howe described it, "The action became warm and bloody . . . the slaughter was great in the river." When the trap was sprung, as Boone had warned, he fought courageously and helped organize the militia's retreat. Boone himself was in desperate trouble: Several hundred Indians were between him and the main force. Howe wrote, "Being intimately acquainted with the ground, he, together with a few friends, dashed into the ravine which the Indians had occupied, but

which most of them had now left to join the pursuit. After sustaining one or two heavy fires, and baffling one or two small parties, who pursued him for a short distance, he crossed the river below the ford, by swimming, and entering the wood at a point where there was no pursuit, returned by a circuitous route. . . ."

Unfortunately, as he made this miraculous escape, Boone's twenty-three-year-old son, Israel, was shot and became one of sixty men killed in the battle. It was the worst defeat the Kentuckians were to suffer in the long war against the Indians—and it came weeks after the Revolution had ended in the East.

After the war, Boone settled in Limestone, Kentucky, a booming town on the Ohio River. He worked there as the deputy surveyor of Lincoln County, a horse trader, and a land speculator—as well as owning a small trading house.

By the time America became an independent nation in 1783, Daniel Boone was one of its most famous citizens. That fame was magnified a year later during the celebration of his fiftieth birthday, with the publication of historian John Filson's book, *The Discovery, Settlement,*

This fanciful hand-colored lithograph by Henry Schile (c. 1874), *Daniel Boone Protects His Family*, probably best captures the enduring image of the legendary frontiersman.

and Present State of Kentucke, with an appendix entitled "The Adventures of Col. Daniel Boon, One of the First Settlers." The book, published both in the United States and England, was a great success and guaranteed Boone's place in history. A year later, *The Adventures of Colonel Boone* was published by itself, further spreading Boone's fame. The image of Boone exploring the frontier, dressed in deerskin, fighting Indians, stood for all of the men—and women— who settled the West. Although the book supposedly included words that came "out of his own mouth," the sometimes exaggerated tales caused Boone to admit later, "Many heroic actions and chivalrous adventures are related of me which exist only in the regions of fancy. With me the world has taken great liberties, and yet I have been but a common man."

Boone's battles were not yet completely done. The Revolution was over, but the Indians north of the Ohio River had not given up fighting for their land. Battle hardened and desperate, they continued to raid settlements, killing and kidnapping people or stealing their livestock. In 1786, a war party of more than four hundred fifty braves had come into the Cumberland region and announced their intention to kill all the Americans. Mingo, Chickamauga, and Shawnee warriors had raided several settlements and murdered a number of people. In response, Benjamin Logan put together an army of 888 men and rode into the Mad River Valley to find and punish the tribes. Boone served as one of the commanders of the raiding party. Unfortunately, it proved far easier to find innocent Indians than those who had staged the attacks, and Logan's men burned seven villages and destroyed the food supply of mostly peaceful natives. Among those taken prisoner were the Shawnee chief Moluntha, who believed he had made peace with the Americans. When he was brought to see Colonel Logan, he carried with him an American flag and a copy of the treaty he had signed at Fort Finney declaring he would fight no longer. He had proudly honored that agreement. However, while he was there he was accosted by the now colonel McGary—the same officer who had ignored Boone's advice about riding into the Indian trap—who demanded to know if he had been present at the Battle of the Blue Licks. Although Moluntha had not fought in that battle, McGary did not believe his claim and clubbed him to death with a tomahawk. In an incredible twist, Logan adopted the chief's son and raised him to become an honored American soldier.

Boone, too, was greatly chagrined by the vengeance taken on innocent Indians. He brought several Shawnees back with him to Limestone, where he fed and cared for them until a truce could be negotiated and a prisoner exchange arranged. Although he was already in his fifties, quite an old age at that time, he still had one more fight left in him. During a 1787 Indian raid in Kanawha Valley, a settler named John Flinn and his wife were killed, and their young daughter, Chloe, was kidnapped. Boone happened to be nearby and quickly organized a party to pursue the Indians. Boone's men caught up with them and killed them, rescuing the child—who was watched over by Boone for the remainder of his years.

Like many other men of action, Daniel Boone was not especially successful when it came to business, and most of his enterprises eventually failed. He made and lost large amounts of money speculating in Kentucke land, buying and selling claims to vast tracts. For a brief time, he was rich and owned seven slaves, which some believed to be the most of any one master in the entire territory of Kentucke. His common decency was his greatest business flaw, as he was too often reluctant to enforce a claim to the detriment of others. He said he just didn't like the feeling of profiting from another man's loss. The respect he gained was paid for in the dollars he forfeited. Ironically, in 1798, a court in Mason County issued a warrant for his arrest for his failure to testify in a court case, while later that same year, Kentucke honored him by naming a large region of the state Boone County.

But what pressed on him most was a large debt he spent much of his later life repaying: While sleeping in a Richmond tavern on his way to Williamsburg in 1780, he was robbed of twenty thousand dollars in depreciated scrip and land certificates that had been entrusted to him by settlers to purchase supplies and buy land claims from the Virginia government. Although some of the settlers forgave him, he vowed to pay all of them back completely. It took him more than thirty years to do so, which he finally did by selling off most of the lands he had been awarded in 1815 by President James Monroe. After making the final repayment, it was said he was left with fifty cents.

His wife, Rebecca, died in 1813 after nearly fifty-seven years of marriage. She was buried on a knoll along Tuque Creek in Missouri, in the shade of large apple trees that had been grown from seeds Daniel had brought with him from Kentucke.

In spirit, as well as body, Daniel Boone never really left the wilderness, continuing to hunt and fish well into his older years. There is some evidence that he went hunting up the Missouri all the way to the Yellowstone River in his eighty-first year. He spent the last years of his life living in the large stone house his son Nathan had built on the land originally given to Boone by the Spanish in the town of Booneslick, Missouri, where Kit Carson would grow up years later. In 1820, secure in his status as an American hero, he said simply, "My time has come," and died. He was two and a half months short of his eighty-sixth birthday.

In all those years after he had left Kentucke, Boone had rarely, if ever, spoken about the court-martial. Certainly any question about his allegiance had been answered decades earlier when he fought for the patriot cause. That the state of Kentucky had chosen to honor him

The only portrait of Daniel Boone painted from life, Chester Harding's oil painting was done in 1820, only a few months before Boone's death.

by naming a county after him and President Monroe publicly recognized his service to the new country by awarding him a large tract of land settled any doubts about his loyalty. In *The Adventures of Colonel Boone*, the accusations were dismissed without being directly addressed: "My footsteps have often been marked with blood, and therefore I can truly subscribe to its original name [The Dark and Bloody Ground]. Two darling sons, and a brother, have I lost by savage hands, which have also taken from me forty valuable horses, and abundance of cattle."

Near the end of his life, he was able to look back on the many sacrifices he had made to help settle the nation. He said, "Many dark and sleepless nights have I been a companion for owls, separated from the cheerful society of men, scorched by the summer's sun, and pinched by the winter's cold, an instrument ordained to settle the wilderness. But now the scene is changed: peace crowns the sylvan shade."

DAVID CROCKETT

★ CAPITOL ★ HILLBILLY ★

uring David Crockett's first visit to Washington, D.C., in 1827, the newly elected congressman from Tennessee was stopped by a man who loudly proclaimed his support for President John Quincy Adams. When Crockett responded angrily, "You had better hurrah for hell and praise your own country," the man demanded to know who was speaking. Crockett stood tall and replied, "I'm that same David Crockett, fresh from the backwoods, half horse, half alligator, a little touched with the snapping turtle; can wade the Mississippi, leap the Ohio, ride upon a streak of lightning and slip without a scratch down a honey locust; can whip my weight in wildcats and, if any gentleman pleases, for a ten dollar bill he may throw in a panther . . ."

Davy Crockett, who lives in American legend as "the King of the Wild Frontier," was celebrated during his lifetime as "the Coonskin Congressman," a backwoodsman who had "kilt bears" and fought Indians, then went to Congress to fight for the rights of the hardworking settlers. He was among the most popular people in the country; his autobiography was so successful that he followed it with two more books. A play based on his exploits entitled *The Lion in the West* was a hit in New York in 1831, and marching bands would often greet him when he arrived in a city. He was so admired, in fact, that a faction of the Whig Party supported him for the presidency before the campaign of 1836.

But instead of going to the White House, on March 6, 1836, Crockett and about one hundred courageous Texans trapped in a century-old mission in San Antonio known as the Alamo were overwhelmed and killed by more than a thousand Mexican troops under the command of General Santa Anna. "Never in the world's history had defense been more heroic," reported an 1851 book entitled *The Great West*. "It has scarce been equaled, save at the Pass of Thermopylae."

Crockett was the rare American who went from the quagmire of American politics to the real battlefields of freedom. People have long wondered—and speculated—how this national hero ended up dying at the Alamo. Others have taken the question even further and wondered if he did actually die there.

David Crockett, as he liked to be called, was a true child of the American frontier. His great-grandparents immigrated to America from Ireland in the early 1700s. His father, John Crockett, was born in 1753 in Virginia and was one of the Overmountain Men—patriots living west of the Appalachians—who fought in the Revolutionary War. Several members of the Crockett family were killed or captured and enslaved by Cherokees and Creek Indians in 1777. Davy Crockett was born in 1786, near the Nolichucky River in Tennessee. As did all children growing up on the frontier, Davy learned how to track, hunt, and shoot fast and straight, and was always comfortable in the backwoods. His father worked various jobs, from operating a gristmill to running a tavern, but struggled to support his family. When David Crockett was twelve years old, he was leased out as a bound boy to settle his father's debt, tending cattle on a four-hundred-mile cattle drive. When he returned home, he was enrolled in Benjamin Kitchen's school—and just four days later, after whupping the tar out of a bully, he took off from home to avoid his father's wrath. His real knowledge came from practical lessons on how to survive on his own in the world.

After spending three years on the trail, finding work wherever it was offered as a hand, a drover, a teamster, and even a hatter, or simply hunting his food when it became necessary, he arrived back at the Crockett Tavern. It has been suggested that his adventures during these years, as he related them in his autobiography, served as a model for Mark Twain's *Huckleberry Finn*. And Twain did acknowledge reading Crockett's tales.

He took several jobs to settle the rest of his father's debts; he worked for six months at a neighbor's tavern, where, he wrote, "a heap of bad company meet to drink and gamble." And when that note was satisfied, he began working for another neighbor, a farmer named John Canady. Crockett spent four years on the Canady farm, staying on for pay long after the debt was settled. During that period, the plain-speaking personality that was to prove so politically appealing years later first began to emerge. Upon meeting a lovely young girl, for example, he wrote that his heart "would flutter like a duck in a puddle, and if I tried to outdo it and speak, it would get right smack up in my throat, and choke me like a cold potato."

It was on the Canady farm that he got his first real taste of book learning, using the money he earned to pay Canady's son for reading lessons, and after several months' hard studying, "I learned to read a little in my primer, to write my own name, and to cypher some in the first three rules in figures."

David Crockett also began growing himself a reputation, not only as a straight talker but also as a straight shooter. The practice in shooting matches at the time was to split a beef carcass into four quarters, with contestants competing separately for each one. Entry was twenty cents a shot. At one of those events, Crockett not only won the whole cow, he also won the "fifth quarter"—the hide, horns, and tallow.

Before his twentieth birthday in 1806, he married and settled on a rented farm with the former Miss Polly Finley, a lovely girl he'd met at a harvest festival. He hunted bear and fowl, trapped forest animals, cleared acreage and planted crops, and fathered two boys, but there was a pull inside him that he couldn't ignore. When war was declared against Great Britain in 1812, most of the Indian tribes sided with the British, believing their victory would end American expansion into the West. Tribes that had lived peacefully with settlers for decades suddenly went on the warpath. In August 1813, a thousand Red Sticks, as Alabama Creek Indian warriors were known, attacked Fort Mims and massacred as many as five hundred people. Crockett answered the call for help, signing up as a scout for Colonel Andrew Jackson's militia army, which was marching south to avenge that attack.

Although Davy Crockett might well have seen it as his duty to fight for his country,

After the largest massacre of settlers in the South at Fort Mims, Davy Crockett volunteered to fight for Colonel Andrew Jackson.

he had other reasons for wanting to go. It's possible he recognized an opportunity to make his name—and perhaps avenge the earlier murders of his kin. His farm was struggling, the money he would earn was desperately needed, and his unique skills would be very valuable during a war and just might secure his future. Polly begged him not to go, but he told her, "If every man would wait till his wife got willing for him to go to war, there would be no fighting done till we all got killed in our own house."

He quickly established himself as a reliable scout—although even he admitted his sense of direction was woefully lacking. Once, while hunting, he realized he was lost, and "set out the way I thought [home] was, but it turned out with me, as it always does a lost man, I took the contrary direction from the right one."

No one knows how a man will react to battle until lead is flying, and Davy Crockett turned out to be a courageous soldier. In early November, General John Coffee, under the command of Andrew Jackson, led about a thousand dragoons in an attack on the Alabama Creek village of Tallushatchee. An estimated two hundred warriors were killed in the brief battle. At the Battle of Talladega a week later, Coffee's men killed an additional 299 Creeks.

But Crockett also learned that war was a lot more complicated than he had anticipated. He found that he admired the courage of his enemies, and whenever it was possible, he avoided confrontations with them. At the same time, he grew to despise Andrew Jackson for the way he treated his men. "Old Hickory" was a brutal leader, who seemed not to care about his troops' welfare. Although Crockett and other scouts did their best to hunt wild game for the militia, because of lack of food and supplies, countless men just got on their horses and rode home. Davy Crockett's enmity toward Jackson that began during this campaign would follow the two men throughout their political careers—and spark Crockett's ride to the Alamo.

Although Crockett earned his reputation as a frontiersman, it was his engaging personality that attracted people to him. He was a great storyteller, with a lively wit and an appealing aw-shucks personality. For many other men, lack of an education might have proved a barrier to a political career, but he learned how to use it to his advantage. Later on, he often reminded voters that he wasn't one of those fancy men from back east who were always changing their minds to please their supporters, but just a regular man trying to do the best he could for his people. His political philosophy wasn't particularly sophisticated: He stood up for what he believed, he didn't seem to care if his positions were popular, and he wasn't afraid to confront the most powerful men in the nation. He articulated his credo this way: "Be always sure you're right, then go ahead."

I leave this rule, for others when I am dead
Be always sure, you are right, then go a head

David Crockett

Colonel David Crockett,
painted by A. L. DeRose,
engraved by Asher B. Durand

Davy Crockett's political career began when his former commanding officer, Captain Matthews, was a candidate for the office of lieutenant colonel of the Fifty-Seventh Regiment of the Tennessee Militia and asked Crockett to run for major. Initially Crockett turned him down, explaining that he'd done his share of fighting, but the captain insisted. Finally, Crockett agreed. Only when it came time to make his campaign speech did he learn that his opponent would be Captain Matthews's son. The meaning was clear to him: Matthews thought that running an unqualified hayseed against his son would guarantee victory. That insult got Crockett fired up, and he decided that if he was going to run, he should run against Matthews himself, for colonel. He stood on a tree stump and "told the people the cause of my opposing him, remarking that as I had the whole family to run against any way, I was determined to levy on the head of the mess."

His audience, presumably delighted by the honesty of this speech, elected him to run the militia. Ironically, he became Colonel Crockett on the campaign trail rather than on the battlefield.

Crockett found that politics fit him well. But he didn't forget where he came from. Consciously or not, he always advertised his frontier background, from the buckskin clothes he wore to the way he spoke to the political positions he supported. His greatest political strength was that ordinary people believed he understood their needs—the key requirement for a populist politician.

His wife Polly had died giving birth to their daughter, and he had remarried—to a woman with an eight-hundred-dollar dowry, so for the first time in his life he didn't have to struggle to earn his keep. After moving to Lawrence County in 1817, he served as a town commissioner and helped draw the new county's borders, then accepted an appointment as the local justice of

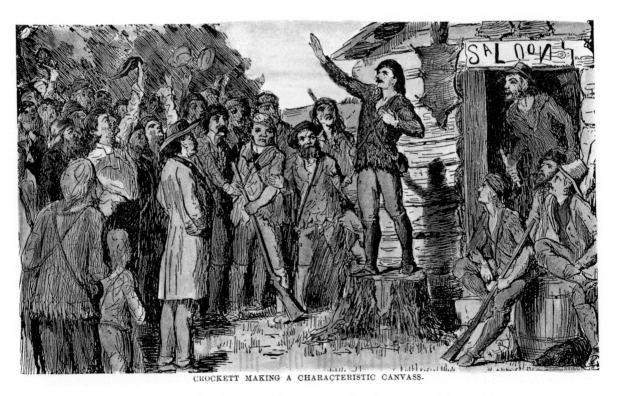

CROCKETT MAKING A CHARACTERISTIC CANVASS.

On the campaign stump, Crockett would sometimes finish his speech by inviting everyone to join him for a drink, leaving his opponent to address a reduced crowd.

the peace. In 1821, his friends and supporters urged him to run for the Tennessee legislature, representing the counties of Lawrence and Hickman. As he remembered, "It now became necessary that I should tell the people something about the government, and an eternal sight of other things that I knowed nothing more about than I did about Latin, and law."

His opponent, he recalled, "didn't think he was in any danger from an ignorant backwoods bear hunter." Crockett stood up on the stump and told people that he had come for their votes, and that if they didn't watch mighty close, he'd get them. In one campaign appearance, he told his listeners the story of a traveler who saw somebody beating on an empty barrel. When asked what he was doing, the man explained that just a few days earlier there had been cider in there and he was trying to get it out. Then Crockett added, "there had been a little bit of a speech in me a while ago, but I believed I can't get it out." The crowd laughed, and as he finished, he told them it was time to wet their whistles and led them to the liquor stand—leaving only a sparse few people to listen to his frustrated opponent.

Crockett won his first election, receiving more than twice as many votes as his rival. Although other members of the legislature referred to him derisively as "the Gentleman from the Cane"—meaning from the uncivilized backwoods—he stood up to the wealthy and powerful. His staunch support for the struggling west Tennessee farmers and local folk made him so popular that a year after his election his constituents presented him with a .40-caliber flintlock with the motto GO AHEAD inscribed in silver near the sight. He named this beautiful hunting rifle Old Betsy, in honor of his oldest sister.

When he was not doing the people's work, he was building a new cabin for his family in the wilds of the Obion River, relying on Old Betsy to keep his family fed and warm. On one hunt, he brought down a six-hundred-pound bear, although he admitted that it took three shots. That he chose to live in the wilderness, where a man survived by his wits rather than his wallet, reinforced his growing reputation as a man of the people. Although he did not intend to stand for reelection in 1823, when a newspaper article appeared to lampoon him, he changed his mind. His opponent, Dr. William Butler, was Andrew Jackson's nephew-in-law. It proved to be one of the most memorable populist campaigns ever run. On the stump, Crockett confessed that his campaign was financed by the raccoon pelts and wolf scalps his children and hunting dogs had gathered, and he reckoned after visiting Dr. Butler's impressive home that he walked on fancier materials on his floor than most people's wives wore on their backs. Crockett wore his buckskin shirt with extra-large pockets—for a twist of tobacky and a bottle of hooch—and won the election by 247 votes.

At this same time, Andrew Jackson's political fortunes were skyrocketing. The military hero, who had defeated the British in the Battle of New Orleans and led the nation to victory in both the War of 1812 and the First Seminole War, was a nominee for the presidency in 1824. Although Jackson won the popular vote, the close election was thrown into the House of Representatives, which chose John Quincy Adams. But Tennessee senator Jackson had established himself as a formidable politician and kept his sights firmly on the White House.

Crockett had aroused Jackson's anger by supporting the candidate running against Old Hickory's handpicked choice for governor in 1821, personally defeating his relation two years later, and backing Jackson's opponent when he ran for the Senate. In fact, Crockett called his vote against Jackson "the best vote I ever gave."

When his supporters urged him to run for Congress in 1825, Crockett accepted their nomination, then lost a woefully underfinanced campaign to the incumbent by 267 votes. But his reputation continued to grow, and it was known that in the winter of 1826, he and his hunting buddies accounted for 105 dead bears. Supposedly he had killed 47 of them himself.

Crockett lived a life of adventure—but one fraught with danger. He almost died twice from malaria, suffered near-fatal hypothermia, and was mauled by a bear. He had cheated death so often that his family refused to believe he had been killed at the Alamo and sent young John Crockett to verify it. Once, while he was earning his living cutting and selling barrel staves, his barge got caught in the rapids and he was trapped in its tiny cabin as it flooded. He struggled to escape through a small window and got stuck, urging rescuers to pull him out no matter what it required, "neck or nothing, come out or sink." Indeed, they got him out, but he suffered serious injuries. Among the rescuers was a wealthy businessman and politician, Memphis mayor Marcus Brutus Winchester, who would take to Crockett and financially support his successful run for Congress in 1827.

Crockett's homespun appeal attracted considerable attention in Washington, even before he arrived there. He was introduced by letter to Henry Clay, "the Great Compromiser," who was preparing to run for the presidency, by Clay's son-in-law, James Irwin, as an uncouth, loud talker, who was "independent and fearless and has a popularity at home that is unaccountable."

Even nearly two centuries ago, a backwoodsman who often dressed in hand-sewn buckskin was considered out of place in the nation's increasingly sophisticated and dignified capital. However, that worked in Crockett's favor politically. Although he belonged to no political party, the Whigs saw great potential in him and helped build on the myths about him that were already spreading. More than a century later, Crockett would be celebrated on television by the Disney company as a man who wrestled alligators and "kilt him a bear when he was only three," but the foundations of his legend were laid not in Hollywood but while he was in Congress.

In Congress, Crockett never wavered from his support for the rights of the poor. During his first term, he opposed a land bill because it might result in squatters being driven off their farms, pointing out, "The rich require but little legislation. We should at least occasionally legislate for the poor." Although he had ended up supporting Andrew Jackson in Old Hickory's victorious run for the White House in 1828, he didn't hesitate to fight hard against him—as well as other members of the Tennessee delegation—when the land bill again was proposed in 1830. He answered to a higher power than Washington politicians, he explained: the people who put him in office; the kind of people whose children "never saw the inside of a college, and never are likely to do so."

Crockett was becoming a problem for Jackson. He was an extraordinarily popular

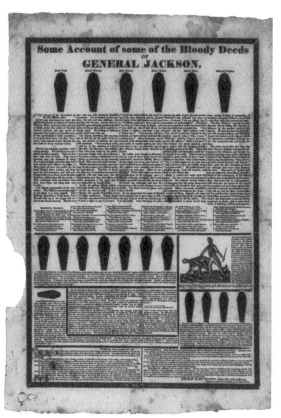

Crockett's biggest political rival was Andrew Jackson, seen in this 1860 portrait by D. M. Carter, who was charged with extraordinary "bloody deeds" in this 1828 "coffin" handbill.

politician who too often opposed him. Their biggest fight came when Jackson introduced the Indian Removal Act in 1829, which proposed granting to the tribes the unsettled lands west of the Mississippi River, where they would be taught "the arts of civilization," in exchange for their land within existing state borders. Jackson believed this separation of whites and Indians was the only way to ensure peace and was the most humane way of dealing with the Indian problem. Crockett opposed him; he had lived among Indians his whole life and believed they should be left in peace on their own lands. Describing it as "a wicked, unjust measure," he voted against it and said bitterly, "I gave a good honest vote, and one that I believe will not make me ashamed on the day of judgment." The bill passed, but the Cherokee chief sent a letter to Crockett thanking him for his vote.

When Crockett stood for reelection in 1831, Jackson personally recruited a man named William Fitzgerald to run against him. It was going to be a difficult campaign for Crockett because the majority of people in his district had supported the Removal Act. Fitzgerald ran a dirty campaign, accusing Crockett of being a violent drunk and a gambling man who cheated on his wife. His men would post signs advertising a Crockett appearance that Crockett knew nothing about—but when he failed to show up, he was the one who was blamed. The tensest moment of the campaign came during a debate in Nashville. As the *Nashville Banner* reported,

> Fitzgerald spoke first. Upon mounting the stand he was noticed to lay something on the pine table in front of him, wrapped in his handkerchief.
>
> He commenced his speech. . . . When Fitzgerald reached the objectionable point, Crockett arose from his seat in the audience and advanced toward the stand. When he was within three or four feet of it, Fitzgerald suddenly removed a pistol from his handkerchief and, covering Colonel Crockett's breast, warned him that a step further and he would fire.
>
> Crockett hesitated a second, turned around and resumed his seat.

The episode caused a stir, but Jackson was well liked in Tennessee, and Crockett lost the election. To pay off all his campaign debts, he had to sell his land, and with the assistance of someone who knew how to spell, a man named Matthew St. Clair Clarke, he "wrote" *The Life and Adventures of Colonel David Crockett of West Tennessee*, one of the first campaign biographies. It marked the beginning of his transformation from David Crockett to Davy Crockett, King of the Wild Frontier. It described his life-threatening adventures and his good character while vilifying Andrew Jackson—and was an immediate success. Two years later, after he defeated Fitzgerald to regain his seat in Congress, his official autobiography was published—partially to correct some of the taller tales told in that first book—and caused such a great stir that a segment of Whigs began suggesting he would be the perfect candidate to succeed Jackson in the White House.

Ironically, considering his feelings about Jackson—in 1833 he told reporters, "Look at my neck and you will not find any collar with a label, 'My Dog, Andrew Jackson'"—he actually helped the president survive the first presidential assassination attempt in American history. On the afternoon of January 30, 1835, an unemployed house painter named Richard Lawrence, who believed he was King Richard III, approached Jackson as he left the capitol, drew his pistol and, at point-blank range, pulled the trigger. Incredibly luckily for the president, the gun misfired. The sixty-seven-year-old Jackson began hitting his attacker with his cane. Crockett and several other men leaped on Lawrence and dragged him to the ground. In the melee, the madman managed to pull a second pistol from under his coat and fire at Jackson from inches away—and that gun also misfired! Thanks to Crockett, several other men, and amazing good fortune, the president's life was saved—although no one ever has been able to figure out why either gun, much less both of them, misfired. Lawrence spent the rest of his life in an asylum.

To reinforce his growing reputation, Crockett "authored" another book, *A Narrative of the Life of David Crockett, written by Himself,* and for the only time in his life visited the Northeast, on what arguably was one of the first celebrity publicity tours. He traveled from Baltimore to Philadelphia by steamboat and train, the first time he had ridden on the latter. The Whigs had gathered a large, enthusiastic crowd to greet him when he arrived in Philadelphia, which he described as "the whole face of the earth covered with people." From there he went to New York, where, once again, delighted crowds turned out to see him. He spent an evening at the theater and toured the roughest area of the city, a pro-Jackson slum known as Five Points. It was so filthy, he remarked, that the people there were "too mean to swab hell's kitchen," a phrase that later coined the nickname for an uptown slum. When he reached Boston, again the welcoming crowds turned out, and he toured Faneuil Hall and visited various factories. He dined at the leading restaurants and sipped champagne "foaming up as if you were supping fog out of speaking trumpets."

Although his congressional district had been gerrymandered by the pro-Jackson legislature in 1833, he had still managed to win that election. But the frontier was moving westward, and Tennessee was being settled by people who didn't know Crockett and instead were vocal in their admiration for President Jackson. In the congressional election of 1835,

Crockett's opponent, Adam Huntsman, who had lost a leg in the Creek War, made Crockett's inability to get a land bill passed by Congress in three terms a major issue in the campaign. Huntsman was supported by both President Jackson and Tennessee's Governor Carroll and beat Crockett by 230 votes.

During the campaign, Crockett had promised several times to move to Texas if he was defeated or if Jackson's vice president, Martin van Buren, was elected president. What probably surprised everyone was that this was a campaign promise Crockett intended to keep. On November 1, 1835, dressed in his hunting suit and wearing a coonskin cap, he gave Old Betsy to his son John Wesley Crockett and, following the trail blazed by his friend Sam Houston, set out for Texas with three friends, telling his constituents, "Since you have chosen to elect a man with a timber toe to succeed me, you may all go to hell and I will go to Texas."

Many have speculated on the real reasons he went to Texas. *Texas* is an Indian word, meaning "friends," but for hundreds of years it had been unsettled by whites. The territory had been claimed by France and Spain, then became Mexico's when it won its independence from Spain in 1821. The Mexican government initially had welcomed American settlers to the territory, believing they would control the Indians living there. But by 1826, the Anglos wanted to rid themselves of Mexican control and establish an independent state that they intended to name Fredonia. The leader of the original settlers, Stephen Austin, went to Mexico City to petition for recognition as a separate Mexican state, with the right to form its own legislature. Instead, he was arrested and thrown into a dungeon.

But the spirit of independence had caught hold. In 1835, seventeen thousand of the twenty thousand people living in Texas were Americans. Austin returned to Texas after spending eight months in prison and immediately began forming militias to fight for Anglo rights under the Mexican constitution. Mexican leader Santa Anna threatened an invasion to quell the uprising. The Texas War for Independence began at the battle of Gonzales in October 1835. A month later, Texas declared its independence, naming Sam Houston its commander in chief. It was a situation ripe for heroics.

Davy Crockett did not go to Texas to die at the Alamo but rather to live in a country he described in a letter to his children as "the garden spot of the world. The best land and the best prospects for health I ever saw, and I do believe it is a fortune to any man to come here." There obviously were many reasons for him to leave Tennessee: He had been defeated by the Jacksonians and abandoned by the Whigs; he was separated from his wife; he was in debt and had no source of income; and for a man who had spent much of his life pursuing adventure, he lacked any current challenges. It also was the right place to reestablish his reputation:

The Alamo, Midnight, lithograph by Frank Callcott

Many people had begun wondering if all the attention and publicity had changed him. His exploits had been so obviously exaggerated that some doubted there was much truth to any of them. And it was not in his nature to back away from a fight.

It's impossible to know what his expectations were when he rode to Texas. Although it's clear that he intended to become a land speculator and perhaps make "a fortune yet for my family, bad as my prospect has been," some historians believe he planned to become involved in the politics of the new republic, maybe even run for president. He did write that he expected to be elected to the planned constitutional convention. When he learned the provisional government was offering 4,600 acres of good growing land to any man willing to fight for Texas's freedom, he announced, "As the country no longer requires my services, I have made up my mind to go to Texas. I start anew upon my own hook, and may God grant that it be strong enough to support the weight that may be hung upon it."

When he finally reached Nacogdoches in January 1836, he received a "harty [*sic*] welcome to the country," which included a cannon salute and invitations to social events held in his honor. In Nacogdoches, with sixty-five other men, he volunteered with the Texas Volunteer Auxiliary Corps, taking an oath to fight for six months in return for 4,600 acres. Before signing the oath, he insisted the word *republican* be inserted to ensure he would not be obliged to serve a dictatorship. In early February, provisional government president Sam Houston ordered him to lead a squad of expert riflemen to reinforce San Antonio de Bexar.

Until the preceding December, San Antonio had been occupied by more than a thousand Mexican soldiers. But after a five-day battle, the Mexican army had been defeated and had surrendered all property, guns, and ammunition to the Texans. The furious Santa Anna was determined to demonstrate to the settlers that resistance to Mexican rule was futile by retaking San Antonio—whatever the cost. He made it clear that there would be no quarter given, no prisoners taken; this would be a lesson the Texans would never forget. When 1,800 Mexican troops arrived in San Antonio on February 23, the 145 Texans—among them Davy Crockett—moved into the fortified mission called the Alamo.

Historians have been studying—and debating—the details of the battle for the Alamo for years without reaching agreement as to precisely how it unfolded. Apparently Sam Houston initially told his commander in San Antonio, Colonel William B. Travis, to destroy the mission and withdraw, believing his troops lacked the manpower and supplies necessary to defend it. Had Travis been able to comply with those instructions, most of the garrison could have survived, but he allowed his men to vote on whether to stay—and rather than retreat, they elected to stay and fight. When Santa Anna arrived and demanded their surrender, Travis responded with a cannon shot.

The Alamo was a small fortress, protected by limestone-block walls eight feet high and about three feet thick. Santa Anna's army immediately began bombarding the mission, his artillery moving closer each day. On the twenty-fifth, an estimated three hundred Mexican troops crossed the San Antonio River and reached a line of abandoned shacks less than one hundred yards from the walls. It was an important strategic position from which to launch an assault; the Texans had to dislodge them. While the Alamo's cannons and Crockett's marksmen provided cover, a small group of volunteers reached the shacks and burned them down.

Travis pleaded for reinforcements, warning that his troops were running out of ammunition and supplies. On the twenty-sixth, 420 men with four artillery pieces set out from the fort at Goliad to relieve the garrison. When this force was unable to successfully ford the San Antonio River, they turned back, although about twenty men volunteered to try to reach the Alamo.

"The enemy . . . treated the bodies with brutal indignation." They were thrown onto a pile and burned. The remains are believed to be in this casket in San Antonio's San Fernando Cathedral.

Little is known about what was going on inside the Alamo during the siege, although one of the few survivors of the battle, a woman named Susanna Dickinson, wrote that Davy Crockett had entertained the garrison with his violin and storytelling. In records found after the massacre, Colonel Travis wrote of observing Crockett everywhere in the Alamo "animating men to do their duty." It was also reported that Crockett had killed five Mexicans in succession as they tried to fire a cannon at the walls, and some claimed that he came within a whisker of killing Santa Anna, who had wandered into rifle range. There is some evidence that Crockett had managed to sneak out through Mexican lines to locate the small band of reinforcements waiting at Cibolo Creek and guide them into the Alamo. Several months after the battle, the *Arkansas Gazette* reported, "Col. Crockett, with about 50 resolute volunteers had cut their way into the garrison through the Mexican troops only a few days before the fall of San Antonio." The meaning of that is clear, and it erases any doubts about his courage and

The map shows:

Batería del Ejército Mexicano

ALAMO

Fuerte del Alamo

a	Entrada	g	Parque
b	Habitaciones de Oficiales	h	Foso interior
c	Cuerpo de Guardia	i	Caballero alto
d	Comandancia de Artillería	j	Batería a barbeta
e	Cuartel de Artillería	k	Batería atronada
f	Cuarteles	l	Fosos exteriores

VILLITA

Río de San Antonio

BEJAR

Campo Santo

Camino de Río Grande

"Remember the Alamo" was the battle cry that led Sam Houston's troops to victory at the Battle of San Jacinto six weeks later—and Americans have never forgotten the sacrifices made there. *Above*, a map of the Alamo based on Santa Anna's battlefield map; *opposite, top left*, Newell Convers Wyeth's *Last Stand at the Alamo*; *top right*, an imagined Crockett fighting his last battle; *bottom*, William H. Brooker's engraving *Siege of the Alamo, March 6, 1836*

FLAGS IN AMERICA'S HISTORY

THE LAST STAND AT THE ALAMO.

THE ALAMO FLAG

SIEGE OF THE ALAMO. MARCH 6, 1836.

his integrity: Crockett had made his way out of what appeared to be a hopeless situation and could have escaped. Instead, he fought his way back inside to make a final stand with his men.

Santa Anna's army, which had been reinforced and numbered four thousand troops, attacked before dawn on March 6, advancing, according to Henry Howe in *The Great West*, "amid the discharge of musketry and cannon, and were twice repulsed in their attempt to scale the walls." Susanna Dickinson later testified that when the attack began, Crockett had paused briefly to pray, then started fighting. After a fierce battle, Mexican troops breached the north outer walls. Although most of the defenders withdrew to the barracks and chapel, Crockett and his men stood in the open and fought. They fired their weapons until they were out of ammunition, then used their rifles as clubs and knives until they were overwhelmed.

It isn't known how Davy Crockett died. There are several conflicting reports. A slave named Ben, who also survived the battle, claimed he had seen Crockett's body surrounded by "no less than 16 Mexican corpses," including one with Crockett's knife still buried in it. Henry Howe reported, just fifteen years after the battle, that "David Crockett was found dead surrounded by a pile of the enemy, who had fallen beneath his powerful arm." Most historians believe he was killed by a bayonet as he clubbed attackers with his rifle. He was forty-nine years old.

As happens often when heroes die without witnesses, alternative stories have persisted. One claims that Crockett and several other men either surrendered or were captured and brought before Santa Anna, who ordered their immediate execution. The purported eyewitness to that, a Mexican lieutenant named José Enrique de la Peña, supposedly wrote in a diary, found and published almost one hundred fifty years later, that Crockett had been executed, and "these unfortunates died without complaining and without humiliating themselves before their torturers."

There were only three survivors: Susanna Dickinson and her young child and the black slave, Ben. "The enemy," wrote Howe, "exasperated to the highest degree by this desperate resistance, treated the bodies with brutal indignation." Although there were some reports of mutilation, it is generally agreed that the bodies were thrown onto a pile and burned. The number of Mexicans who died in the attack is estimated at between six hundred and sixteen hundred men. Texans were shocked by the massacre. Almost immediately, "Remember the Alamo" became the rallying cry of the Texas army of independence. Less than two months later, on April 21, General Sam Houston's army captured Santa Anna at the Battle of San Jacinto, and the Republic of Texas was born.

The legend of Davy Crockett grew even larger after his death. A book entitled *Col. Crockett's Exploits and Adventures in Texas . . . Written by Himself* was published the summer after his death and, while clearly a work of fiction, served to reinforce his heroic sacrifice. Another story circulated claiming that Crockett was last seen standing at his post swinging his rifle as Mexican troops poured through a break in the walls. The memoir of Santa Anna's personal secretary, Ramón Martínez Caro, published in 1837 in Mexico, reported, "Among the 183 killed there were five who were discovered by General Castrillón hiding after the assault. He took them immediately to the presence of His Excellency who had come up by this time. When he presented the prisoners, he was severely reprimanded for not having killed them on the spot, after which he turned his back upon Castrillón while the soldiers stepped out of their ranks and set upon the prisoners until they were all killed." Although this was purportedly an eyewitness account, there is no direct evidence that Crockett was one of these men.

Crockett became a symbol of the spirit of Texas and America, a man who willingly gave his life for freedom. His last known words, written to his daughter weeks before his death, have often been quoted: "I am rejoiced at my fate. I would rather be in my present situation than be elected to a seat in Congress for life. Do not be uneasy about me, I am with my friends . . . Farewell, David Crockett."

His son John Wesley Crockett served two terms in Congress and finally was able to pass an amended version of the land bill that his father had initially introduced. Like so many others, he spent years trying to uncover the facts of his father's death—but in his lifetime no reliable witnesses stepped forward.

More than one hundred twenty years later, the larger-than-life character Davy Crockett, the King of the Wild Frontier, was introduced to a new generation of young people in a television series—coonskin cap, tall tales, and all—that captivated the nation and had millions of Americans singing his praises, saluting his courage, and romanticizing the frontier way of life.

KIT CARSON

Duty Before Honor

any years later, in the warmth of his own memories, Kit Carson would describe what happened at the rendezvous in Green River as an "affair of honor." Although few mountain trappers took much note of the year, Carson put it at the summer of 1835. For those men, who mostly lived in small roaming bands, a rendezvous was an important event. Hundreds of mountain men and natives from local tribes would camp together for a month or, as he wrote in his autobiography, "as long as the money and credit of the trappers last" to trade goods and tales. Coffee, sugar, and flour, then considered luxuries, sold for two dollars a pint, and ordinary blankets for as much as twenty-five dollars apiece. There were daily contests, including shooting, archery, and knife and tomahawk throwing; there was fiddling and dancing; there was drinking and revelry; and, naturally, there was gambling and brawling. The laws of these camps were whatever the strongest men could enforce, and arguments often were settled with rifles at twenty paces. Among the people at this particular meeting on the Green River in Wyoming was an especially disagreeable French Canadian trapper named Joseph Chouinard, who was said to be "exceedingly overbearing" and who, "upon the slightest pretext . . . was sure to endeavor to involve some of the trappers in a quarrel." Other trappers avoided him, until one day he violently grabbed a beautiful young Arapaho woman named Singing Grass. Holding tightly on to her arms, he began kissing her and rubbing himself against her.

That was finally enough for Kit Carson. He was small in stature, no more than five feet four, but large in courage. Brandishing his hunting knife, he warned Chouinard to let go of the Indian woman. "I assume the responsibility of ordering you to cease your threats," he said, "or I will be under the necessity of killing you."

It was a challenge Chouinard could not turn down. He released the girl and angrily walked off toward his own lodge. Minutes later, the two men faced each other on horseback, as knights had done hundreds of years earlier. The French Canadian carried a rifle; Kit Carson was armed with a single-barrel dragoon pistol. At the mark, they raced toward each other. When they were only a few feet apart, both men fired; Carson's shot ripped

Kit Carson earned his reputation among mountain men when he stood up to the bully Chouinard at the 1835 rendezvous, as seen in this 1858 woodcut.

into Chouinard's right forearm, throwing off his aim so that, as Carson later recalled, "[H]is ball passed my head, cutting my hair and the powder burning my eye. . . . During our stay in camp we had no more trouble with the bully Frenchman."

As the trappers cheered him, Carson walked off with Singing Grass.

Christopher Carson was born in Madison County, Kentucky, on Christmas Eve 1809, the eleventh of fifteen children. It was the same year Abraham Lincoln was born, the year in which James Madison succeeded Thomas Jefferson as president of the seventeen newly United States. His father was a celebrated hunter and farmer who had fought in the Revolution. Within a year of Kit's birth, his father moved his family to the frontier settlement of Cooper's Fort in Boonslick Country, Missouri. This was considered the edge of the civilized nation. Most of the land stretching from there all the way to the Pacific Ocean was wilderness, with occasional settlements inhabited by the native peoples who were fighting to protect their territory, their food sources, and their way of life. It took great skill and daunting courage to survive in these dangerous lands. Those who took the risk were the mountain men, the trappers, the explorers, and the soldiers who went into the unknown in search of adventure. As the author Henry Howe wrote in his classic volume *The Great West* more than one hundred fifty years ago, "From the Mississippi to the mouth of the Colorado, from the frozen regions of the North to Gila in Mexico, the beaver trapper has set his traps in every stream. Most of this country, but for their daring enterprise, would be, even now, a terra incognita to geographers. . . . These alone are the hardy pioneers who braved the way for the settlement of the western country."

Carson was loosely related to the legendary frontiersman and trailblazer Daniel Boone—Boone's daughter was married to Carson's uncle—and there is no doubt that Boone served as young Kit Carson's role model. Missouri had been part of the 1803 Louisiana Purchase—bought for about four cents an acre—and quickly became the jumping-off place for expeditions going west, where life was a constant battle for survival against nature—and the native tribes. Carson became a man in that wilderness, learning how to track and shoot and, when necessary, fight Indians.

Carson's father died when Kit was only nine years old; some histories report that he was killed by Indians, while others claim that a large branch from a burning tree fell on him. His mother remarried, but Kit never got along with his stepfather. When he was fourteen years old, his stepfather apprenticed him to a harness and saddle maker named David Workman, during which time Kit heard the exciting stories told by mountain men returning from the West, stories that captured his imagination. After his second year, he couldn't wait any longer. "[B]eing anxious to travel for the purpose of seeing different countries," he ran away, joining a wagon-train expedition to the Rocky Mountains. Workman placed a notice in the newspaper, offering a one-cent reward for the return of his apprentice.

During the next years, Carson tasted adventure, working as a cook for trapper and fur trader Ewing Young, as a teamster in the copper mines near Rio Gila, and as an interpreter along the Chihuahua Trail into Mexico. He'd dropped out of school before learning to read or write, but he learned to speak Spanish and eight Indian languages from a mountaineer named Kincard. He trapped beaver, traded furs, and, when it became necessary, fought Indians.

His first recorded battle with Indians came in 1829, when one of Ewing Young's trading parties was attacked by Navajos. Young was determined to get vengeance and organized his own raiding party, which trailed the Indians to the head of the Salt River and waited. When the Navajos spotted a small band of trappers, they attacked—and rode into Young's ambush. His men—young Kit Carson among them—opened fire and killed fifteen Indians.

A rendezvous near Green River, Oregon, about 1835

Eventually Carson would become one of history's most renowned Indian fighters, but he acquired this reputation only out of necessity. The mountain men lived by a warrior's code that required an eye for an eye, a scalp for a scalp. When one member of your tribe was killed, that score had to be settled. A warrior who showed great courage in battle, who got close enough to physically touch his enemy, was said to be "counting coup," and this was the highest honor he could achieve. Carson recounted one story in which he was awakened by a Blackfoot brave counting coup—literally prodding him with a knife. The band of Indians had snuck into camp to steal horses. Carson kicked him away, scrambled to his feet while grabbing his own knife, and fatally stabbed his attacker.

In 1839, Carson led a party of forty-three mountaineers in an attack on the Blackfeet who had been raiding their camp. They charged into the Blackfeet village, quickly killing ten warriors. The battle raged for more than three hours. During the action, a mountaineer named Cotton was trapped beneath his horse after it was shot from underneath him. Six warriors raced forward to take his scalp. Carson leaped from his saddle, steadied his hand,

and shot the leader through his heart. Three more Indians were shot down by other shooters before they could reach cover, enabling Cotton to get loose and make his way to safety.

Kit Carson believed totally in the warrior's code—but he also spent many years living peacefully among the tribes. After his encounter with Chouinard, he took Singing Grass as his wife and settled in her village. When Singing Grass died giving birth to their second child, he married a Cheyenne maiden named Making-Out-Road. He was considered an honored guest in the lodges of the Arapahos, Cheyennes, Kiowas, and Comanches. Even his favorite horse was proudly named Apache. He lived so easily among the tribes that he once remembered, "For many consecutive years I never slept under the roof of a house or gazed upon the face of a white woman. . . . My rifle furnished nearly every particle of food on which I lived."

Carson had earned a fine reputation as a hunter and trapper, becoming known as "the Monarch of the Prairies" and "the Nestor of the Rocky Mountains," Nestor being a mythical Greek king known for his bravery. His word was said to be "as sure as the sun comin' up," and his skills enabled him to hire on in the 1840s as "hunter to the fort," meaning he was responsible for supplying all the food for the forty-man garrison at Bent's Fort, the only trading post on the Santa Fe Trail between Missouri and Mexico. Ultimately, though, Carson and his fellow trappers proved so proficient at their trade that by the time of the last rendezvous in 1840, the beaver had been hunted almost to extinction.

Yet during his years on the frontier, as Charles Burdett wrote in his *Life of Kit Carson*, "his curiosity, as well as care to preserve the knowledge for future use, led him to note in memory every feature of the wild landscape, its mountain chains, its desert prairies . . ." and prepared him to play a very special role in the settling of the West.

The concept of Manifest Destiny, the dream of a nation that stretched across the continent from the Atlantic to the Pacific, was beginning to take hold. At his inauguration in 1845, President James K. Polk prophesized, "It is confidently believed that our system may be safely extended to the utmost bounds of our territorial limits, and that as it shall be extended the bonds of our union, so far from being weakened, will become stronger . . ."

Kit Carson proved to be extraordinarily important in the fulfillment of that dream. In 1842, after sixteen years on the frontier, he brought his four-year-old daughter, Adaline, to live with his sister in St. Louis, where she could receive the proper education he never had. From St. Louis he boarded the first steamboat at work on the great Missouri River, intending to return to his family homestead. Also on that boat was Lieutenant John C. Frémont of the Army Corps of Topographical Engineers, who coincidentally was looking to hire an experienced guide to lead him to Wyoming, where he was to survey the South Pass, the most

Kit Carson (*left*) and John Frémont came from completely different backgrounds, but their adventures introduced America to the possibilities of the great West.

popular route across the Continental Divide, and measure the height of the mountains. After introducing himself to Frémont, Carson explained, "I have been some time in the mountains and I think I can guide you to any point there you wish to reach." After making inquiries, Frémont hired Carson to guide the expedition at a salary of one hundred dollars a month.

The two men hardly could have been more different. While the rough-hewn Carson had never learned to read or write, Frémont was a polished, ambitious mathematics teacher who was married to the daughter of powerful United States senator Thomas Hart Benton. Senator Benton, the political champion of Manifest Destiny, apparently had helped his son-in-law get his army commission, then convinced Congress to support his explorations.

The twenty-eight-man party that would eventually make both Frémont and Carson national heroes departed St. Louis on June 10, 1842. Several of Carson's closest friends had joined the expedition, mountain men he respected and trusted, men he wanted to have by his side in a fight. When they reached Fort Laramie, Wyoming, they learned that almost a thousand Sioux had attacked a party of trappers and Snake Indians and were still in the region.

Carson and Frémont would save each other's lives
as they fought Indians, outlaws, Mexicans, and the
elements to survey the western wilderness.

The expedition was advised to turn back or risk being massacred. Frémont refused, replying that his government had directed him to perform a certain duty and he intended to do so. If he perished in the effort, he was confident his government would avenge his death. Carson admired the Southerner's fortitude and courage, and that helped cement their friendship.

The expedition accomplished each of its objectives, and Frémont's beautifully written reports, which were reprinted in newspapers throughout the country, thrilled Americans with their vivid descriptions of a magnificent landscape and vast regions waiting for settlement. Frémont was celebrated as "the Pathfinder," and Kit Carson was credited as his trusted scout. While Frémont returned to Washington to lay plans for a second expedition, Kit Carson married for the third time—his second wife having left him to join the migration of her tribe—this time to a Mexican, Senora Josefa Jaramilla, with whom he would have three children. To appease her family he agreed to convert to Catholicism.

Frémont and Carson's second expedition, intended to map the remainder of the Oregon Trail, began in the summer of 1843 and eventually brought them in sight of the magnificent Cascade Range. During their return journey, they became snowbound in the Sierra Nevada and faced starvation. Food was so scarce that their half-starved mules "ate one another's tails and the leather of the pack saddles," and Frémont gave his men permission to eat their dogs. Somehow Carson managed to scrounge enough food for them to survive. During the trek through the deep snow, Frémont and Carson left their party to scout for a path over a raging, icy river. As Frémont wrote, "Carson sprang over, clear across a place where the stream was

Josefa Jaramilla-Carson with
Kit Carson Jr.

compressed . . ." but when Frémont tried to follow, his moccasins slipped on an icy rock and he fell into the river. "It was some few seconds before I could recover myself in the current, and Carson, thinking me hurt, jumped in after me, and we both had an icy bath."

After spending the winter at Sutter's Fort in California, the expedition set out for home. To get there, they had to go through the Mojave Desert. In addition to heat and thirst, they had to endure several Indian attacks. After Indians stampeded their livestock, Carson took off after them. As Frémont later described it, "Carson may be considered among the boldest. . . . Two men, in a savage desert, pursue day and night an unknown body of Indians into the defiles of an unknown mountain—attack them on sight, without counting numbers, and defeat them in an instant."

As they made their way out of the Mojave, they encountered a Mexican man and boy, survivors of an Indian attack. They had been ambushed by an estimated thirty Indians, they said; two men had been killed in the attack, their two female cooks had been captured, and twenty horses had been stolen. Carson and his friend Richard Godey volunteered to go after the captured women. The two men tracked the Indians for two nights and found them at dawn. They silently crawled into the camp, hiding among the stolen horses. When the horses stirred, alerting the Indians, Carson and Godey had no choice but to attack. They raced into the camp. Carson raised his rifle and shot the leader dead. Godey's first shot missed, but his second shot killed his target. The Indians hesitated to respond, believing the two men must be the point of a much larger group waiting in ambush.

Carson and Godey recovered fifteen horses and then began searching for the captured women. Instead, they found the bodies of the two Mexican men who had been killed, staked to the ground and mutilated. In response they "took the hair" of the Indians they had shot, honoring the counting-coup tradition.

Frémont's reports transformed Kit Carson into a frontier legend, the brave tracker who saved the expedition in the snowbound mountains, then practically single-handedly attacked and defeated thirty wild Indians. While the true story was amazing enough, reporters and dime novelists exaggerated it even further, attributing to Kit Carson all the ideal traits—humility, loyalty, and bravery—characteristic of this new country. The first of these "blood and thunders," as these books were known, *Kit Carson: Prince of the Gold Hunters*, told the fictional story of Carson rescuing a kidnapped young girl from the Indians. Carson, who didn't know how to read, had to have these stories read to him.

Frémont's third expedition left St. Louis in the summer of 1845, initially intending to map the source of the Arkansas River. But when the expedition accomplished this objective, he continued on to California, which was still Mexican territory, to support the growing number of American settlers there who wanted to join the United States. The superior number of Mexican troops forced Frémont to go north, making camp at Klamath Lake, Oregon. One night in May 1846, as the party slept, Indians crept into camp and killed Carson's friend Basil Lajeunesse with a single hatchet blow to his head. In the ensuing battle, two more of Frémont's men were killed. Several attackers also died and, as Frémont later reported, the enraged Carson continued to pummel the body of one of them, beating his face into pulp.

THE YOUTH'S COMPANION HISTORIC MILESTONES

KIT CARSON ·· HUNTER AND TRAPPER ·· IMPLACABLE FOE OF HOSTILE INDIANS BUT FRIEND AND PROTECTOR OF THOSE THAT WERE PEACEFUL ·· TRAIL MAKER · PATHFINDER · GUIDE ·· INCOMPARABLE SCOUT AND LOYAL AND EFFICIENT SOLDIER ·· THE LAST OF THE OLD FRONTIERS-MEN AND ONE OF THE GREATEST

For more than a century, *The Youth's Companion* was one of the country's most popular magazines for children. This heroic illustration was published in about 1922.

That wasn't enough to satisfy him, though; to avenge Lajeunesse's death, he led an attack on a Klamath tribe fishing village where 150 braves lived. When Carson's rifle misfired during the battle, a Klamath warrior took aim at him with a poisoned arrow. Frémont acted instantly to save his life—"he plunged the rowels of his spurs deep into his horse" and trampled the enemy warrior. By the end of the day, in what became known as the Klamath Lake Massacre, most of the Indians had been killed and their village had been burned to the ground. Only later was it discovered that this tribe probably was not involved in the initial attack.

Coincidentally, on the day of the massacre, President Polk called on Congress to declare war on Mexico. Frémont's mapping party was almost instantly transformed into a fighting force called the California Battalion. Carson was given the rank of lieutenant. Returning to California, Frémont led a successful insurrection and declared himself military governor of the new American territory. Carson was dispatched to Washington, D.C., to inform President Polk of the victory, a cross-country journey he promised to make in sixty days. His planned route would take him through Taos, where he hoped to spend at least a brief time with his wife, whom he hadn't seen in more than a year. But when he was only days from home, he encountered General Stephen Kearny and his Army of the West, which had successfully seized New Mexico for the United States, and was en route to California. Kearny ordered Carson to turn around and guide him to San Diego and to send Frémont's dispatches to President Polk with another rider. Although he was only one long ride from his wife, he responded, "As the General thinks best," and joined his troops.

By the time Kearny's one hundred dragoons got to California, the situation there had changed drastically. The Mexicans had counterattacked, and Frémont was besieged by Californios, Mexican troops carrying eight-foot-long lances. Kearny clearly underestimated the Mexican troops when he launched an attack on the village of San Pasqual. By the end of the second day of fighting, almost fifty of Kearny's vastly outnumbered Americans had been killed or wounded, and the survivors were trapped on a hilltop without sufficient food, water, or ammunition. If they were not quickly reinforced, they would face annihilation. During the night, Kit Carson and Navy Lieutenant Beale removed their shoes and silently slipped through enemy lines, coming so close to being caught that Carson later claimed that "he could distinctly hear Lt. Beale's heart pulsate." Knowing they could not risk using the trails, the two men ran, walked, and crawled almost thirty miles barefoot through the sagebrush and cactus of the rocky terrain, the prickly pears digging into their bare feet. They raced through two nights without food or water until they finally reached American lines in San Diego. Carson had chosen the more difficult terrain to cover so arrived after Lieutenant Beale. Kearny's troops

When General S. W. Kearny's troops were surrounded and greatly outnumbered by Mexican forces, Carson and Navy Lieutenant Beale crawled through enemy lines, then ran almost thirty miles barefoot to save the besieged soldiers.

were preparing to make a final, desperate attempt to break out when the two hundred American reinforcements sent by Carson and Beale reached them. The Mexican army withdrew and the remnant of Kearny's battalion was saved. It took Lieutenant Beale more than a year to recover fully from this experience.

When the war ended, Commodore Stockton, who had been involved in the American revolt, declared Frémont governor of California. Six weeks later, General Kearny, claiming to be acting on government orders, charged Frémont with insubordination, a serious military offense, and named himself acting governor. Frémont immediately dispatched Carson to Washington to plead his case before President Polk. While in the capital, Carson stayed in Frémont's home, choosing to sleep outside on the porch rather than in a stuffy bedroom. Frontiersman Kit Carson was a sensation in Washington, though there was little about his physical appearance that reflected his exploits. The blood-and-thunder books had depicted him as a giant, America's first action hero, so people were greatly surprised that in the flesh this living legend actually was a small, stoop-shouldered, bowlegged, and freckled man, and that he responded to questions with simple, often one-word answers and spoke in a voice "as soft and gentle as a woman's." His appearance was so different from expectations that one man who had traveled a long distance to meet the great Indian fighter looked him up and down and said, "You ain't the kind of Kit Carson I am looking for." In fact, Carson's fame was so great across the country that there was a lively business in Kit Carson imposters.

The real Kit Carson was not impressed by his own celebrity. In fact, after making four more trips across the country as President Polk's personal courier, Carson happily mounted up and headed home.

At this point in his life, Carson and one of the men he'd traveled with, Lucien Maxwell, decided to build a real homestead in the Rayado valley, about fifty miles east of Taos. "We had been leading a roving life long enough and now, if ever, was the time to make a home for ourselves," he explained. "We were getting old and could not expect much longer to continue to be able to gain a livelihood as we had been doing for many years. . . . We commenced building and were soon on our way to prosperity."

It was impossible for him to stop adventuring, though, and he continued to accept commissions from the government. He led other survey teams into the Rockies; he drove

The 1847 Battle of Buena Vista was one of the bloodiest fights of the Mexican-American War. More than 3,400 Mexican troops and 650 Americans under the command of General Zachary Taylor were killed or wounded before Santa Anna withdrew in the night.

a herd of 6,500 sheep from New Mexico to the markets of California, where they sold for $5.50 per head; and at times he pursued Indians and outlaws. Not long after he had settled down with his third wife, "Little Jo," he learned that a Jicarilla (Apache) Indian raiding party had attacked a small group riding toward Santa Fe, killing merchant James White and another man and taking his wife, daughter, and a black female slave captive. The Jicarillas had then killed the child with one blow of a tomahawk and thrown her body into the Red River. Carson couldn't let this stand. He saddled up and joined the posse headed by an army major. They tracked the Indians for twelve days over harsh terrain. In camps along the way they found scraps of Mrs. White's dress and some of her possessions. When they finally found the Indian band with their captives, Carson wanted to attack immediately, but the major insisted that they instead parley with them and try to arrange a trade for the women. Carson was furious, knowing that the Indians had no interest in talk, but he was a man who followed orders. As the major waited, a single rifle shot rang out from the Indian camp, striking that officer squarely in the chest. In an incredible coincidence, only minutes earlier he had taken off his buckskin gauntlets and put them in his breast pocket. The buckskin had saved his life.

The outnumbered Indians scattered, leaving behind their belongings, but the major's order to charge came too late. They found Mrs. White's body and determined "her soul had but just flown to heaven." She had been shot through her heart with an arrow only minutes earlier. Then Carson found something he would never forget. According to his biographer,

> Among the trinkets and baggage found in the [Indians'] camp there was a novel, which described Kit Carson as a great hero, who was able to slay Indians by scores. This book was shown to Kit and, he later wrote, "It was the first of the kind I had ever seen . . . in which I was made a great hero, slaying Indians by the hundreds. . . . I have often thought that perhaps Mrs. White, to whom it belonged, read the same and knowing that I lived not very far off, had prayed to have me make an appearance and assist in freeing her. I consoled myself with the knowledge that I had performed my duty."

The ride home had been difficult. The posse was caught in a blizzard and one of their men froze to death. Later Carson learned that the Jicarilla had been caught in the same storm. And he shed no tears when he learned that without the furs and blankets that they had been forced to leave behind in the camp, many of them had frozen to death as well.

Sometime in 1849, Carson was told about a plot to murder two merchants. A man appropriately named Fox had hired on to guide the merchants on a trip to buy goods they

Kit Carson fought Indians, then went to Washington to fight for those same peoples, but his actions eventually caused him to be reviled by the tribes of the Southwest.

would use for trade. To accomplish that, they were carrying a large sum of money. In fact, Fox intended to kill them on the trail and then leave the bodies in the wilderness. Fox made the mistake of trying to enlist a shady character living in Rayado to help him. This man turned down the offer and, when Fox went back out on the trail, told the story to the local army post commander. When Carson learned of it, he gathered a small posse and raced almost three hundred miles through Indian territory to catch up with the party, arriving just in time to save the two merchants. Although they offered Carson a substantial reward, he refused to accept even one penny and instead took Fox back with him to jail.

As the American frontier moved steadily westward, Indian resistance to the settlers increased. The pioneers lived in fear of sudden and deadly attacks. Few people dared leave a settlement without first making careful preparations. It would be impossible to determine how many encounters Kit Carson had with the tribes, but it is accurate to state that precious few men could match that number. He had come to be known as the greatest Indian fighter in the West. No man was more qualified or better prepared to deal with the tribes, whether the encounter required words spoken over a shared peace pipe or the skilled use of a rifle, knife, or hatchet.

In 1865, Kit Carson, the nation's most famous Indian fighter, told a congressional committee, "I came to this country in 1826 and since then have become pretty well acquainted with the Indian tribes, both in peace and at war. I think, as a general thing, the difficulties arise from aggressions on the part of the whites."

But Carson avoided violence when possible. For instance, in the summer of 1851 he went east to St. Louis to visit his daughter and buy provisions for the winter, and on his way back, a few miles after crossing the Arkansas River, he encountered a band of Cheyennes. Carson could not have known these Cheyennes were on the warpath; a chief had been flogged by an American officer and they were out for revenge. Carson knew his party was too small and ill equipped to outrun them; he ordered the wagons to stay close and told his men to have their rifles ready. The Indians' war party shadowed them for more than twenty miles. When the caravan made camp for the night, Carson invited the advance party to join him for a talk and a smoke.

These young braves did not recognize Carson. Although they would have recognized his name, they would not have known what he looked like. So they certainly did not suspect that this white man spoke their language. As the pipe was passed, the Indians began speaking to each other in the Sioux language, so that if any of the white men escaped this trap, the Sioux would be blamed for the attack. It was not an unusual ruse. But as they continued smoking into the night, they eventually resorted to their own tongue. Finally they revealed their plan: When the pipe was next passed to Carson, he would have to lay down his weapon to take it, and at that moment they would attack and kill him. Then they would kill the other members of the party.

Carson understood every word, and he waited. When it was his turn, rather than taking the pipe, he grabbed his rifle and stood in the center of the circle, ordering his men to ready their weapons. The Cheyennes were stunned. Speaking to them in their own language, Carson demanded to know why they wanted his scalp. He had never been guilty of a single wrong to the Cheyennes, he said, and in fact their elders would tell them that he was a friend. Finally he ordered them out of his camp, warning that anyone who refused to leave would be shot and that if they returned, they would "be received with a volley of bullets."

Carson knew his threat would not stop the Indians indefinitely, but it would buy time. At the darkest point of that night, he took a young Mexican runner aside and instructed him to run as fast as possible to Rayado and return with soldiers. Their lives depended on him, he whispered. The boy was long gone by sunrise. It was said that young runners could cover more than fifty miles in a day. Almost a full day passed before the Cheyennes reappeared. They were wearing their war paint. As their braves approached, Carson warned them that a scout had been sent ahead for help. If they attacked, he admitted to them, the Cheyennes would suffer large casualties but eventually they would win. He knew that. But he had many friends among the soldiers and they would know which people had committed this crime "and would be sure to visit upon the perpetrators a terrible retribution."

Indian scouts found the boy's footprints, but with his long lead time they knew he could not be caught. Reluctantly, the war party withdrew. Two days later an army patrol under the command of Major James Henry Carleton arrived to escort Carson's party safely to Rayado.

As ruthlessly as Kit Carson often fought against the Indians, he also fought for them. In the early 1850s, he became the Indian agent—the government's representative to the tribe—for the Mohauche Utes, or Utahs, and several Apache tribes. While the Apaches continued to fight, initially the Utes remained at peace with the white man. Carson worked for the best interests of the tribe and at times fought doggedly with officials in Washington. He even requested permission to live with the Utes on their reservation, which was denied. Utes came almost daily to his ranch for food and tobacco, which he had paid for himself and happily supplied to them. He was so respected by the tribe that he became known as "Father Kit," and General Sherman once remarked, "Why his integrity is simply perfect. They [the Utes] know it, and they would believe him and trust him any day before me."

Unfortunately, when many Utes died from smallpox after receiving blankets from the government's Indian supervisor, the tribe joined the Apaches on the warpath. Eventually this uprising was smothered, but Carson's relationship with the tribes of New Mexico never completely recovered. The days when the Indians had freely roamed the plains were ending. During the gold rush, more than a hundred thousand people flocked to the West, and the Indians were pushed off their traditional lands onto reservations. Carson watched this clash of civilizations from his ranch and eventually began to believe that the two peoples could not live together peacefully and that it was best for the Indians to live far away from the white settlers.

In 1868, Carson led a delegation of Utes to Washington, where he negotiated the "Kit Carson Treaty" that guaranteed peace, territory, and government assistance to the tribe.

By 1860, the issue of slavery had raised passions in the West, although in that region slaves were mostly Mexican and Indian. While many people in New Mexico sympathized with the Confederacy, Carson remained loyal to the Union. When the Civil War began in 1861, he was appointed a colonel in the First New Mexico Volunteer Infantry. Years earlier, young Kit Carson had walked into the wilderness to live by wit and skill, and finally civilization, or at least the shadow of it, had caught up with him. He moved his family to Albuquerque and went to war.

Carson's first engagement was the 1862 battle of Val Verde, in which both Union and Confederate troops suffered large casualties but neither side declared victory. After two days' hard fighting, the Union troops withdrew and the Rebels made a wide swing around the garrison at Fort Craig and proceeded up the Rio Grande toward Albuquerque and Santa Fe. After that battle, Kit Carson spent the rest of the war once again fighting Indians. His commanding officer for much of that time, coincidentally, was General James Carleton, the same man who while a major had rescued Carson's caravan from the Cheyennes. After the Confederate attempt to capture New Mexico had been repulsed, Carleton took aim at the Indian tribes—in particular, the Navajos. Navajo raiding parties had taken advantage of the war to become a serious threat to settlers, a threat that Carleton, who didn't share Colonel Carson's respect for the native tribes, was determined to remove.

In 1862, Carleton ordered the Mescalero Apaches moved from their lands in the Sacramento Mountains to newly constructed Fort Sumner and the Bosque Redondo, the Round Forest, on the Pecos River. He issued an order: "All Indian men of that tribe are to be killed whenever and wherever you can find them. . . . If the Indians send in a flag of truce say to the bearer . . . that you have been sent to punish them for their treachery and their crimes. That you have no power to make peace, that you are there to kill them wherever you can find them."

Carson was appalled. He had lived his life with honor, and now he was being forced to choose between disobeying a direct order, which would mean facing a court-martial, and committing despicable acts. No one knows what went on his mind, but he might well have realized that even if he refused the order, the man who replaced him would not—and that man probably would not understand the tribes as he did. While he accepted the command to force the Apaches into confinement, he refused to follow the rest of General Carleton's orders. Instead he met with the elders of the tribe and convinced them to surrender. Within a few months, he brought four hundred Apaches to Bosque Redondo.

The Mescalero campaign was simply the beginning. Carleton then gave Carson command of two thousand troops and ordered him to capture the Navajos and imprison them on the

During his campaign against the Navajos, Carson's commanding officer, the brutal general James Carleton, told his troops that Indians "must be whipped and fear us before they will cease killing and robbing the people."

same reservation as their enemy, the Apaches. "You have deceived us too often," Carleton warned the Navajos, "and robbed and murdered our people too long, to trust you again at large in your own country. This war shall be pursued against you if it takes years, now that we have begun, until you cease to exist or move. There can be no other talk on the subject."

That was too much for Carson. He resigned his commission, stating, "By serving in the Army, I have proven my devotion to that government which was established by my ancestors. . . . At present, I feel that my duty as well as happiness directs me to my home and family and trusts that the General will accept my resignation."

The reason for what happened next will never be known, but the result has caused the name Kit Carson to be reviled by the tribes of the Southwest from that time forward in history. Carleton somehow convinced Carson to change his mind. Some historians believe General Carleton gave him assurances that once the Navajos were on the reservation they would be allowed to live peacefully. It also is true that Carson had come to believe that Indians and settlers could never live peacefully together and urged their separation. He may well have believed that by carrying out this policy he actually was ensuring the safety of both the Native Americans and the new Americans. Whatever the cause, Carson agreed to round up the Navajos.

Copyright 1904
By E S Curtis
x 1013

By the turn of the nineteenth century, the Navajos, here crossing Canyon de Chelly in northeastern Arizona, had settled peacefully on this land, as negotiated by Carson.

Rather than standing and fighting the army, the Indians dispersed and fled into the hills. The army retaliated by burning their crops and orchards, their cornfields and bean patches, their fruit trees and melon fields. Guards were posted by sources of salt and water, and Carleton authorized a fee to be paid to soldiers for each Indian animal they captured or killed. The army invaded the Navajos' main hunting grounds and camp, Canyon de Chelly, and destroyed it, burning it as completely as Sherman would level Atlanta. Without a single major battle being fought, almost ten thousand Navajos surrendered to Carson's troops. It was the largest number of Indians ever captured, and back east it added to the legend of Kit Carson.

In April 1864, the army led these captives on a forced march of more than three hundred miles to Fort Sumner. Hundreds of Indians died on "the Long Walk," as it is known in tribal history. Although Carson was not riding with his troops, as their commander he was responsible for their actions. Captives died from sickness, starvation, and exposure to the cold. Some of those who could not keep up were shot by soldiers. When they reached the reservation, conditions were not much better. Many more of the native peoples died during their four years of captivity. Eventually the Apaches escaped and disappeared into the hills, while the Navajos, after signing a treaty in 1868 with General Sherman, were moved to a portion of their traditional lands, where they have remained.

For his service, Kit Carson was promoted to the rank of general.

In late 1864, General Carson was sent to west Texas with 325 soldiers and 75 Ute scouts to subdue the Indians there. Kiowas, Comanches, and Cheyennes were known to be in that area. Carson headed toward the ruins of Adobe Walls, which he remembered from his scouting days two decades earlier. On November 25, his troops attacked a Kiowa village estimated to include 176 lodges. But the scouts failed to discover that this was one of the smallest of many villages in the area. The Kiowas fled from the attack but began gathering a massive Indian force. Within hours, about fourteen hundred warriors attacked. It was similar to the situation in which General Custer would find himself a few months later. One of the men with Carson later described the initial counterattack, writing that the Indians charged "mounted and covered with paint and feathers . . . charging backwards and forwards . . . their bodies thrown over the sides of their horses, at a full run, and shooting occasionally under their horses." Carson's men dug into the ruins of Adobe Walls. Unlike Custer, Carson had brought with him twin howitzers, big guns, and used them to his advantage. But he was greatly outnumbered. Backfires and the howitzers kept the Indians at a distance until Carson was able to effect a retreat. Carson suffered 6 dead and 125 wounded, while the tribes suffered many times that. Both the army and the tribes declared victory, the Kiowas calling it "the time when the Kiowas repelled Kit Carson."

When fifty-nine-year-old Kit Carson died in May 1868, he had become
among the most famous and respected men in the nation.

At the end of the Civil War, Carson was given command of Fort Garland, in the Colorado
Territory. It was the proper choice, wrote General John Pope, because "Carson is the best man
in the country to control these Indians and prevent war. . . . He is personally known and liked
by every Indian . . . no man is so certain to insure it as Kit Carson."

When he finally left the army in 1867, he resumed fighting to protect the Utes, whom
he had long embraced as friends. Although his health was failing, he returned to Washington

with several chiefs to negotiate a fair treaty, which guaranteed to that tribe peace, territory, and assistance. Carson and the Ute chiefs met with President Grant, and eventually a treaty was signed. Then he went home to be with his wife Josefa and their seven children. It was time for him to rest.

He had become one of the most honored men in American history. More than fifty blood-and-thunder novels had been written about him; Herman Melville compared him to Hercules in his novel *Moby-Dick*. He had been instrumental in the creation of an America that would eventually reach from ocean to ocean. But now he was suffering. In 1860, in the San Juan Mountains, he had been leading his horse down a steep hill when the animal slipped and fell on him; Carson became entangled in the lead rope and was dragged for some distance. The internal injuries he suffered caused chest pains, a persistent cough, and breathing difficulty, which plagued him for the rest of his life. In April 1868, Josefa died giving birth to his eighth child. Some believe his spirit died with her. Within weeks he was in bed in the quarters of the assistant surgeon general of the army, just outside Fort Lyon, Colorado. He had been diagnosed with a heart aneurysm, an enlargement of an artery, also believed to have been caused by that fall. As a legendary scout, he knew what lay ahead. Several times coughing attacks threatened his life, and the surgeon, H. R. Tilton, saved it by giving him chloroform. He wrote his will and made arrangements for his children. On May 23, almost exactly one month after his wife's death, Kit Carson smoked his pipe, ate his favorite meal, and lay down. Late in the afternoon, as the doctor read to him, he suddenly called out, "Doctor, compadre. Adios," and died.

Applying our moral standards to a man who lived in and helped shape a different time in our history is an impossible chore. Perhaps the only conclusion to reach is that by his courage and character he helped create this nation. Upon his death, an army officer who had served with him wrote what is perhaps the most fitting description: "Kit was particular to himself. No such combination ever existed in a man before . . . he united the courage of a Coeur de Leon, the utmost firmness, the strongest will and the best of common sense. He could weep at the misfortunes or sufferings of a fellow creature, but could punish with strictest rigor a culprit who justly deserved it."

BLACK BART

Gentleman
Bandit

The Wells Fargo & Company stagecoach was rumbling down the rugged Siskiyou Trail in November 1883, making about ten miles an hour. As the stage slowed to begin the steep climb up Funk Hill, not far from the aptly named copper-mining town of Copperopolis, a man dressed in a long white linen duster and a bowler hat, his face covered with a flour sack with holes cut out for his eyes and mouth, similar sacks covering his feet, and holding a double-barreled twelve-gauge shotgun, stepped out from behind a rock onto the trail. The driver, Reason McConnell, immediately began reining in his team. He knew instantly what was going on: He was being held up by the most famous stagecoach robber in the West, Black Bart.

The robber blocked the coach wheels with rocks to prevent the driver from making a run for it, then ordered McConnell to throw down the strongbox, a big, green, locked wooden box with metal bands around it, which often carried gold or coins from miners. On this trip, the Wells Fargo stage was transporting 228 ounces of silver and mercury amalgam, worth about four thousand dollars, and five hundred dollars in gold dust and coins. McConnell replied that he couldn't throw down the box because the company had begun bolting it to the floor inside the stage to prevent robberies. Black Bart told the driver to climb down from his seat, then made him unhitch the horses and walk them down the hill. By the time McConnell was several hundred yards down the trail, the robber was hacking at the box with an ax.

What Bart did not know was that McConnell had been carrying a passenger, nineteen-year-old Jimmy Rolleri, whom he had dropped at the bottom of Funk Hill to do some hunting while the stage made the difficult climb. Rolleri was planning to catch up at the other end. McConnell found Rolleri and told him the stage was being robbed. The two men hustled back up to the top of the hill just in time to see the robber Black Bart climbing out of the stage lugging the strongbox. Grabbing Rolleri's rifle, McConnell began firing. Once! Twice! He missed. Missed again! Bart raced for the thicket. Rolleri reclaimed his rifle and fired into the undergrowth. Twice more. This time, the robber stumbled. He was hit. He regained his footing and disappeared into the thick brush. The two men followed cautiously, knowing an armed and wounded bandit was dangerous. They pursued a trail of bloody droplets until it disappeared. Once again, Black Bart was gone.

But this time he had made a mistake.

Between 1875 and 1883 the mysterious rogue known across the nation as Black Bart, "the Gentleman Bandit," held up twenty-eight Wells Fargo stagecoaches in northern California. His pattern never varied: He robbed only Wells Fargo coaches, he was always alone, he never fired a shot or made threats, and he always escaped on foot.

When the stagecoach robber Black Bart was finally identified and arrested by detective James B. Hume in 1883, he turned out to be a most unlikely suspect. The story begins in John Sutter's sawmill, on the south fork of the American River in northern California, when Sutter's partner, James Marshall, discovered a few flakes of gold. That marked the beginning of the American gold rush, and during the next seven years more than three hundred thousand men caught gold fever and rushed to the area to find their fortunes. Among them was twenty-one-year-old Charles Bowles, who had been born in Norfolk, England, and brought to America as a young child. Bowles and his two brothers had left their home in upstate New York and crossed the continent to pan for gold. At just about the same time, young James Hume and his brother left their home—coincidentally also in upstate New York—carrying with them the same dreams as Bowles. The difference was that Charles Bowles failed completely—and both of his brothers died in the effort—while Hume was able to eke out a living from his claim.

By 1860, Bowles had married and was living on a small farm in Illinois. In 1862, he volunteered with the 116th Illinois Regiment and ended up serving for three years under General William T. Sherman in the March to the Sea. Although many soldiers served in the cavalry, that was not the right assignment for him: "Whistling Charlie," as he was known, was evidently afraid of horses. He apparently served with valor, seeing action in numerous battles, including the bloody Battle of Vicksburg—where he reportedly was seriously wounded—and by the time he was discharged in 1865 he had risen to the rank of lieutenant.

Like so many other soldiers who came home from the war, he found it difficult to return to life on the farm. In 1862, miners working Grasshopper Creek in Montana made a major strike. At the end of the war, a second gold rush began, and once again Bowles couldn't resist it. Apparently he set out on foot for the West, covering as many as forty miles a day, walking all the way to Montana. When he finally got there, he staked a claim and began panning along a creek. On occasion he would write letters to his wife, but he eventually stopped writing, and after several months without any contact at all, she concluded that he had died.

That misconception might have marked the beginning of Charles Bowles's life of grand deception—and retribution. There is much about Bowles that isn't known, but historians have been able to put together a plausible explanation for his hatred of Wells Fargo & Company. To work his claim in Montana, he built a wooden contraption known as a "tom," a device able to separate nuggets from rocks and sand. But, as with most forms of panning, it required a steady flow of water. His claim was promising, and eventually two men approached him and offered to buy the property. When he rejected their offer, they purchased the land above him and shut off the flow of water, making his claim worthless. Apparently these men were affiliated in some way with Wells Fargo, which had been buying substantial amounts of land around mining towns. Bowles considered their depriving him of water an act of economic war and set out to get even. One way or another, he was going to get his gold.

James Hume, after earning a decent living, also turned to the world of crime—but he took the side of the law and became a detective. In the early 1860s, he was appointed city

Under the name Black Bart, Charles Earl Bowles committed twenty-eight stagecoach robberies between 1875 and 1883—without a single person being injured.

marshal and chief of police of Placerville, California, a gold rush settlement better known as Hangtown. At that time, little "detection" actually occurred. It was extremely difficult to connect a person to a crime through the use of evidence: It would be several decades before law enforcement appreciated the value of fingerprints, for example. And photography was a recent invention of little use to detectives. In most cases, witness testimony comprised almost all the evidence.

But Hume set out to change that. He was among the very first detectives known to carefully explore crime scenes, searching for clues. He dug buckshot out of animals and walls to be used for comparisons. He analyzed footprints. He searched for connections between the smallest pieces of evidence and a suspect. In 1872, his stellar reputation earned him the job of Wells Fargo's first chief detective. Hume was comfortably settled into his job when the bandit who would become known as Black Bart struck for the first time.

Wells Fargo had been founded in San Francisco in 1852, offering both banking and express services to miners. It used every possible means of transportation—stagecoach, railroad, Pony Express, and steamship—to carry property, mail, and money in its many forms across the West, and by 1866 its stagecoaches covered more than three thousand miles from California to Nebraska. Their famous green strongboxes, usually carried under the driver's seat, weighed as much as 150 pounds and often held thousands of dollars' worth of gold dust, gold bars, gold coins, checks, drafts, and currency. The long, hard, and isolated trails these coaches traveled made them desirable prey for bandits. In 1874, the Jesse James Gang committed its first stagecoach robbery, getting away with more than three thousand dollars in gold, cash, and jewels, a fortune at that time.

The legend of Black Bart began at the summit on Funk Hill on July 26, 1875, when a man stepped out from behind some rocks and ordered driver John Shine to halt. The bandit was dressed in a linen coat, had a bowler on his head, and, Shine noticed, wore rags on his feet to obscure his footprints. When the coach stopped, the robber shouted loudly to other members of his gang, "If he dares shoot give him a solid volley, boys!" Looking around, Shine saw what appeared to be the long barrels of six rifles pointing at him from behind nearby boulders. Shine didn't argue; he tossed down the strongbox, which contained about two hundred dollars—the equivalent of about four thousand dollars today—and warned his ten passengers to stay quiet. According to the legend, one panicked woman threw her purse out the window, but rather than taking it, the bandit handed it back to her, explaining, "Madam, I do not wish to take your money. In that respect I honor only the good office of Wells Fargo."

Black Bart sent the coach on its way. The last time Shine saw him, he was on the ground, breaking the chest open. The driver stopped his coach at the bottom of the hill and walked back to retrieve the broken box. The robber was gone without a trace—but Shine was shocked to see that the rest of his gang hadn't moved from their positions behind the rocks. Curious, he moved closer and discovered that the "rifles" were actually sticks that had been placed there.

With the proceeds from this robbery, Charles Bowles settled in San Francisco, where he lived under the name Charles Bolton. It was the perfect disguise: He was hiding in plain sight, enjoying the life of a city gentleman. He lived in grand hotels, dined daily at fine restaurants, and dressed to fit the role. Perfectly groomed, he carried a short cane and favored diamonds in his lapel. He was welcome among the swells of the city. When asked, he described himself as a mining engineer, a profession that required him to take frequent business trips.

No one ever figured out that each of those trips coincided with another stagecoach robbery. In fact, there was not a lot of sympathy for Wells Fargo. Many people believed it was just another big company taking advantage of hardworking people. Some stagecoach robbers were glamorized; they were seen as brave bandits robbing the rich and . . . well, robbing the rich.

Bowles often waited months before staging another heist. Later he claimed that he stole only "what was needed when it was needed." Those robberies took careful planning: Because he was afraid of horses, he couldn't ride, so he had to walk to the scene and then walk away

Black Bart's success in robbing Wells Fargo stagecoaches eventually led the company to offer a reward—and when that failed, the company hired private detective Harry Morse, "the Bloodhound of the West," to track down the bandit.

after the job was done. The robberies almost always took place on the uphill side of a mountain, because the horses had to slow to pull the load. And although no one knew it at the time, the rifle he carried was old and rusted and probably wouldn't have fired even if he had loaded it, which he did not.

The second robbery took place more than five months after the holdup on Funk Hill. Once again, the driver reported a lone holdup man, with three armed accomplices hiding among the rocks. When investigators arrived at the scene, they found the sticks still in position.

Almost eighteen months passed before Bowles's next crime. In the interim, he had accepted a teaching position in Sierra County. At that time the school year was only about three months long, and that job probably provided an acceptable diversion for him. Supposedly he was well liked by his students; he was known for reciting poetry and quoting Shakespeare, especially *Henry V*.

When not robbing stages, Bowles lived as a socialite in San Francisco.

At first, Detective Hume was so busy with other matters that he took little notice of these sporadic holdups. But that changed after Black Bart's fourth crime, on October 2, 1878. His method hadn't changed, but for the first time he left a clue. Investigators found a poem in the broken strongbox:

> *I've labored long and hard for bread,*
> *For honor and for riches*
> *But on my corns too long you've tread*
> *You fine-haired sons-of-bitches*

It was signed *Black Bart, the P o 8.*
A day later another stage was robbed. Once again a poem was left at the scene:

> *Here I lay me down to sleep*
> *To wait the coming morrow*
> *Perhaps success, perhaps defeat*
> *And everlasting sorrow*
>
> *Yet come what will, I'll try it once*
> *My conditions can't be worse*
> *And if there's money in that box*
> *'Tis money in my purse*

Once again, it was signed *Black Bart, the P o 8.*

The audacity of the robber who left poems at the scene quickly attracted the attention of newspaper editors and dime novelists, and Black Bart, the Gentleman Bandit, captured the fancy of the American public. All this publicity naturally brought him to the attention of James Hume. Wells Fargo's analysis of the handwriting suggested a man who had long been employed in clerical work. An eight-hundred-dollar reward was posted for information leading to his capture, and detectives confidently announced he would soon be brought to justice. But the robberies continued without indication that detectives were closing in.

In 1880, Hume finally made an arrest in the case, but it was quickly discovered that the man they arrested actually had the perfect alibi—he had been in prison when several of the robberies occurred.

I rob the rich to feed the poor
Which chardly is a sin,
A widow ne'er knocked at my door
But what I let her in,
So blame me not for what I've done
I dont deserve your curses
And if for any, cause I'm hung
Let it be for my verses

Black Bart
The po8

The fact that Black Bart left his own poems, signed "the P o 8," at the scenes of his crimes attracted national attention—although his reason for doing so was never determined.

In fact, no one had the slightest idea why this bandit left poems at these crime scenes, nor why had decided to call himself Black Bart, nor even what his signature, "the P o 8," meant. Only years later was it revealed that the name had been taken from a dime novel published in 1871 entitled *The Case of Summerfield*. The book, which had been reprinted in the *Sacramento Union* soon after its initial publication, featured a robber named Black Bart, a villain who dressed all in black, had long, wild, black hair, and robbed Wells Fargo stagecoaches. Supposedly the story was based on the true exploits of Captain Henry Ingraham's Raiders, a group of Confederate soldiers who robbed Wells Fargo's Placerville stage of as much as twenty thousand dollars to purchase uniforms for new recruits—and left a receipt for the theft. There is some evidence that James Hume was involved in tracking down those soldiers and arresting them. If it was true that Hume was involved in that case, then Bowles might have picked that name to taunt him: *You caught them but you can't catch me.*

Bowles never revealed the meaning of his signature, "the P o 8." Some historians believe it meant simply "the poet," honoring Bowles's love of poetry, while others suggest it referred to "pieces of eight," meaning booty taken by pirates, and was meant to honor the greatest pirate of the Caribbean, Bartholomew "Black Bart" Roberts, who captured more than four hundred ships before being killed in battle.

For more than a century, criminologists have debated why Black Bart left the poems. Maybe the best explanation is that he wanted people to know that he had outsmarted the great Wells Fargo; he wanted to rub the company's nose in the dirt trails used by their stages. At the same time, he apparently took pride in the fact that no one ever got hurt during his holdups. He was the perfect gentleman robber: He was unfailingly polite, he never took anything from passengers, and he never used foul language. In fact, to reassure their passengers, Wells Fargo issued a statement pointing out that "[he] has never manifested any viciousness and there is reason to believe he is averse to taking human life. He is polite to all passengers, and especially to ladies. He comes and goes from the scene of the robbery on foot; seems to be a thorough mountaineer and a good walker," then added, "[I]t is most probable he is considered entirely respectable wherever he may reside." Although that statement may well have calmed passengers, it also helped to make Charles Bowles's Black Bart into a romantic legend.

It was after his fifth robbery that authorities discovered their first real lead. Investigators found out that following the holdup, a stranger on foot had stopped at a farm and paid for a meal. The farmer's teenage daughter described him as having "[g]raying brown hair, missing two of his front teeth, deep-set piercing blue eyes under heavy eyebrows. Slender hands in conversation, well-flavored with polite jokes." It wasn't much, but for the clue-collecting Hume it was a beginning.

The robberies continued through the early 1880s. Several stagecoach drivers reported actually having pleasant conversations with the bandit during the holdups. In 1881, for example, Horace Williams asked him, "How much did you make?" to which he replied, "Not very much for the chances I take."

That so many people considered this thief a hero continued to rankle Detective Hume, and he committed considerable resources to the job of catching the elusive robber. He hired the sixty-man detective agency run by the renowned San Francisco detective Harry Morse, "the Bloodhound of the West," and assigned that company to work on this case. Hume also personally visited the sites of many robberies and diligently scoured the area, looking for the smallest clues. At several of the locations, Hume's team found the robber's abandoned camp, which indicated he had waited there patiently, sometimes for several days, for the stage to arrive.

Bowles's first close call came near Strawberry, California, in July 1882, when he attempted the biggest job of his career. The Oroville stage was carrying more than eighteen thousand dollars in gold bullion, although it isn't known whether he was aware of that. But perhaps because that

gold was on board, Hume had assigned a shotgun-armed guard to ride next to the driver. Black Bart suddenly appeared in the middle of the trail and took hold of the horse, which bolted, and the coach ran off the road. The robber's attention was diverted, so he failed to see armed guard George Hackett lift his shotgun and let loose a volley. The buckshot lifted Bowles's bowler off his head, grazing his scalp. Bowles had no desire—or ability—to shoot back; instead, he disappeared into the brush, leaving his bloodied hat lying in the dirt. The robbery had failed, but he had escaped. By the time a posse got there, he was long gone and had left no other evidence.

Bowles continued to lead two completely different lives: one in San Francisco, where he was Charles Bolton, a man of leisure and wealth, a socialite who slept comfortably on clean sheets and was always welcomed in the better establishments of the city; the other in the wilderness, where he camped alone as he waited for the next stage, sleeping on the hard ground, confronting the elements, eating sardines out of tin cans. Although he subsisted mostly on his ill-gotten gains, he did invest some money in several small businesses that apparently returned a small profit.

It probably isn't accurate to claim that Hume pursued Black Bart with the same diligence and ferocity with which Victor Hugo's classic Inspector Javert hunted for Jean Valjean, but his pursuit lasted more than eight years. Hume was head of investigations for a large company and responsible for solving many cases, but clearly this was the big one. From his investigations he began to develop a theory that was considered radical at the time—criminals will often return to the scene of their crimes. This was especially true of Black Bart, who required a specific set of circumstances for his crimes to succeed: Because he was on foot, he couldn't pursue a stage, so he needed a secluded place where the stage was already moving slowly and thick foliage nearby through which he could make his escape without fear of pursuit. There were only a limited number of such locations, which made Hume believe he was destined to use the same site more than once.

And indeed, Black Bart's end came in the place where he had begun, the summit of Funk Hill. On November 3, 1883, driver Reason McConnell and Jimmy Rolleri pegged four shots at the bandit. Although the first three shots missed, the fourth shot nicked Bowles's hand. The robber ran about a quarter of a mile, then stopped and wrapped a handkerchief around his knuckles to stem the bleeding. He hid the four thousand dollars he'd grabbed in a rotten log and kept the five hundred dollars in coins, put his rifle inside a hollow tree, and made his walkaway. He covered the hundred miles back to the city in three days, then went by train to Reno to lie low for several more.

Hume and Morse rode to the scene of the crime as quickly as their horses would take them. The driver McConnell was certain he'd hit the robber; he'd heard him yelping. The two detectives carefully searched the entire area and eventually found several items that had been left behind in haste, including a derby hat, size 7¼; a tin of supplies, including sugar, coffee, and crackers; a belt; a binocular case; a magnifying glass; a razor; two flour sacks—and a bloodied handkerchief with the laundry mark "F.X.0.7."

A century later, the DNA in the blood might have enabled Hume to identify his man, but in 1883, something much less scientific caught his attention—the laundry mark. In those days, many men had at most only two shirts or handkerchiefs, and few workingmen could afford to send them out to a laundry to be cleaned. Certainly, few common stagecoach bandits sent their shirts out to be laundered. Clearly Black Bart was not the type of holdup man Hume had imagined him to be. From that clue, Hume deduced that Black Bart was living in a big city, and the only big city within walking distance was San Francisco.

Harry Morse's men began visiting each of the more than ninety laundries in San Francisco, trying to associate "F.X.0.7" with a specific person. It took more than a week, but eventually

Thomas Ware, the proprietor of the California Laundry on Stevenson Street, only a few blocks from the Wells Fargo office, identified the laundry mark. The handkerchief belonged to one of his better customers, he said, a Mr. Charles E. Bolton, the mining engineer who lived at the Webb House, a hotel on Second Street.

When Morse investigated further, he found that people spoke highly of this Charles Bolton. He was "an ideal tenant," his landlady explained, "so quiet, so respectable and punctual with his room rent." He was a fine fellow, others said.

Morse assigned several detectives to stake out the hotel. About a week later his men spotted the nattily dressed Mr. Bolton emerging from his rooms. They noted that he appeared to have a wound on his hand. Morse took charge: One afternoon, as his suspect sauntered down the street carrying a fancy cane, Morse successfully made his acquaintance. He had been told that Bolton was a mining engineer, he explained, then asked for his assistance. He had in his possession several pieces of ore that needed to be identified. Perhaps Mr. Bolton would be so kind as to do so?

Remembering this event years later, the detective Morse wrote, "One would have taken him for a gentleman who had made a fortune and was enjoying it. He looked anything but a robber."

Perhaps sensing a business opportunity, Bowles agreed and walked with Morse to the nearby Wells Fargo office, completely unaware that the man who had spent the past eight and a half years trying to capture him was waiting there. It was there that James Hume introduced himself to Charles Bowles and arrested him for the robberies committed by the bandit Black Bart. Bowles by this time had perfected his acting skills and appeared genuinely surprised by the accusation, continuing to insist that a mistake had been made, that he was a fifty-six-year-old mining engineer named Charles Bolton. The handkerchief? Perhaps he'd dropped it and the real Black Bart had picked it up. But any doubt that another mistake had been made was erased after Morse searched his rooms. There he found letters written in the same hand as the two poems left by Black Bart, as well as several shirts bearing the laundry mark "F.X.0.7."

Bowles was taken to Stockton and arraigned. Although he continued to maintain his innocence, at one point he did ask if a man who confessed to a robbery and returned all the proceeds might avoid going to prison. That wouldn't be possible, he was informed, but it was probable that a judge would look kindly upon a man who confessed to his robberies and had never hurt a soul. Finally Bowles/Bolton/Black Bart confessed—to the final robbery. He took authorities to the top of Funk Hill and handed over all the loot.

His arrest took place while San Francisco's newspapers were fighting for circulation, and they all wanted Black Bart's story. Late one night, *Examiner* reporter Josiah Ward got into Bowles's cell. He watched as Bowles entertained a series of visitors, including his landlady, who dabbed the prisoner's eyes as he cried. Eventually Bowles agreed to be interviewed. Ward's article reported him as saying, "I never drink and I don't smoke. All my friends are gentlemen and I never associated with other than gentlemen. I can't claim to be perfect. They do say I will rob a stage occasionally. But no one can say that I ever raised my hand to do any harm. I merely carried a gun to intimidate the driver. As for using it—why for all the gold that road ever carried I would not shoot a man."

In the middle of November, Bowles was convicted of only one robbery—the final job—and sentenced to six years in San Quentin prison. While he was imprisoned, the dime novel *The Gold Dragon; or, The California Bloodhound: The Story of PO8, the Lone Highwayman* was published, adding to his nationwide fame. He never admitted in court that he was Black Bart; he never confessed to another robbery or returned any of the stolen money. It was never determined exactly how much he stole, with estimates ranging between twenty thousand and one hundred thousand dollars, or about three million dollars in today's money.

He was released in January 1888, an event covered by all the newspapers. He had served four and a half years and was released for good behavior. His eyesight was failing, he said, and he had gone deaf in one ear. Asked by a reporter if he intended to return to his "profession," he smiled and said, "No, gentlemen. I'm through with crime." When another reporter followed up by asking if he might write more poetry, he shook his head. "Now, didn't you hear me say that I am through with crime?"

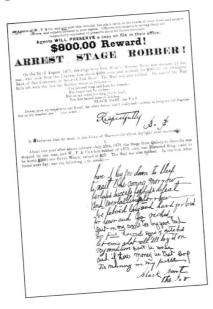

Detective James Hume, who established Wells Fargo's own special-agent operation, relentlessly pursued the famous stage robber for eight years.

Wells Fargo agents followed him for several weeks as he moved from town to town, but in February he walked out of the Palace Hotel in Visalia and was never seen or heard from again.

Or was he? In November later that year, a Wells Fargo stagecoach was held up by a masked highwayman in a manner reminiscent of Black Bart. After he escaped, a poem was found:

> *So here I've stood while wind and rain*
> *Have set the trees a–sobbin*
> *And risked my life for that box,*
> *That wasn't worth the robbin.*

The note was sent to Detective Hume for examination. He compared it to the original poems known to have been written by Bowles and announced that this holdup was committed by a copycat.

However, for several years, rumors of Bowles's activities and whereabouts continued to surface. William Randolph Hearst's *San Francisco Examiner* claimed that after a few robberies in northern California, Wells Fargo had agreed to give Bowles some sort of "pension" in exchange for his promise to never rob another stage, with the figure varying between $125 and $250 a month.

Although the company firmly denied having struck any deal, it did continue to list the newly released "Bolton" as a suspect in several stage holdups, describing him as "a thorough mountaineer, a remarkable walker, and claims he cannot be excelled in making quick transits over mountains and grades," concluding that he was "a cool self-contained talker with waggish tendencies; and since his arrest . . . has exhibited genuine wit under most trying circumstances."

Other stories of his fate speculated that he lived the rest of his life in luxury in Mexico or New York or St. Louis with the proceeds he had secreted from his life of crime. A thief arrested outside Kansas City was identified by local authorities as Black Bart, but one of Hume's men identified him as a different Wells Fargo robber who had served time in Folsom Prison. That same detective claimed he had discovered what had actually happened to Bowles—he had sailed to Japan on the *Empress of China* and was living there happily. One newspaper reported he had been killed holding up a stage from Virginia City to Reno and had been buried in a shallow grave at the side of the road. Detective Hume once said he'd heard that Bowles died while hunting game in the high Sierra. He was supposedly seen in the Klondike after the gold strike of 1896 in the Yukon. Reporter Josiah Ward wrote that Bowles had indeed been hired by Wells Fargo—to ride shotgun on stages, and eventually "saved and bought a ranch where he abode in peace and quiet until he died." Finally, in 1917, *The New York Times* printed the obituary of Civil War veteran Charles E. Boles [*sic*], although no mention was made of another career. If that was Black Bart—and there is no compelling evidence to either confirm or deny that—he would have been eighty-eight years old.

Perhaps it's appropriate that his fate remains unknown; the Gentleman Bandit Black Bart had effectively escaped again, living out the rest of his life in obscurity. No one would ever break his record of twenty-nine stagecoach robberies. Henry Ford introduced his Model T in 1908, thus putting an end to the profession of stagecoach robber forever.

After serving four years and two months in San Quentin, Black Bart was released and supposedly disappeared—although a year later, Wells Fargo issued his last Wanted poster, accusing him of committing two more robberies.

THE DIME NOVELS

The image of the rip-roaring, hard-riding, two-fisted, straight-shooting cowboy, standing up for Old West justice against villainous varmints was initially the creation of small paper books known as dime novels. Although the real skills and courage of the men who tamed the American frontier could often be awe inspiring, these very popular novels successfully turned these men into the near superheroes that have become a staple of popular culture.

There has always been something magical about the exploits of these brave men, but beginning with the minstrel shows and popular music of the mid-1800s, their feats of derring-do were greatly exaggerated. P. T. Barnum might have been the first to exploit the fascination with the frontier, when he presented live Indians as a curiosity at his New York City museum in the 1840s. But the real effort to make the West wilder began in June 1860, when *Malaeska, the Indian Wife of the White Hunter* was published by the New York printing firm Beadle and Adams.

Technological advances in printing in the 1840s had made it possible to inexpensively produce numerous copies of a book. Cheap and easily carried, dime novels were extremely popular among Civil War soldiers looking for any diversion, and soon people everywhere were seeking them out.

The initial success of Beadle's books caused competitors to rush to publish their own, which often were stories that previously had been

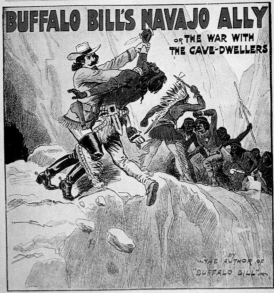

Although inexpensive "yellow-backed" paper books had been published earlier, dime novels—and the nickel or "half-dime" novels that followed—generally were published as numbered volumes in series that featured recognizable characters. More than 40,000 different titles were published, many of them by Beadle and Adams, who warned potential authors, "We prohibit what cannot be read with satisfaction by every right-minded person—old and young alike."

serialized in three-penny dailies or story newspapers. Although these books were called dime novels, some of them sold for a nickel or less. The character of the virtuous cowboy fighting vicious Indians and ruthless outlaws grew out of the early stories of heroic frontiersmen, in particular, James Fenimore Cooper's Leatherstocking Tales. To compete, authors had to continuously up the ante, putting their characters into increasingly dangerous situations and then giving them the almost superhuman skills needed to survive for another book. These sensationalized action-adventure stories often were based extremely loosely on real events and used real names—and turned men and women such as Buffalo Bill, Wild Bill Hickok, Bat Masterson, Calamity Jane, and even Belle Starr into American celebrities.

These books were the original pulp fiction, written to be devoured in one gulp and quickly forgotten. Millions of copies were sold. Edward Judson, writing as Ned Buntline, could write a book in a few days and published more than four hundred of them, transforming Buffalo Bill into a legendary figure. The most successful dime novelist was probably Edward Ellis, whose *Seth Jones; or, the Captives of the Frontier*, sold six hundred thousand copies in six languages.

By the time dime novels disappeared early in the twentieth century, the character of the valiant cowboy defeating evil at the last possible moment was forever enshrined in our culture and had become the symbol of the Old West recognized throughout the world. The movies picked it up from there, and the rest has become history!

WILD BILL
HICKOK

Plains Justice

In the settling heat of an early summer evening, at six o'clock on the twenty-first of July, 1865, Wild Bill Hickok stood calmly in the center of the Springfield, Missouri, town square, his Colt Navy revolvers resting easy in a red sash tied around his waist, their ivory handles turned forward. About seventy-five yards away, the gambling man Davis K. Tutt stepped out of the old courthouse, where he'd been settling some fines. The two men stared at each other. Even at that distance, Wild Bill could see the old Johnny Reb Tutt slowly pull a gold watch out of his vest pocket and glance nonchalantly at the time—the very watch that Hickok had warned him not to display. Hickok yelled to him, "Don't you cross the square with my watch!" Tutt responded by slipping the watch back into his pocket and stepping out into the middle of the square. Neither man was the type to back down from a challenge. They faced each other: Dave Tutt turned to his side; Wild Bill squared his shoulders and stood facing straight ahead. For a few seconds, nothing happened. Then they went for their guns.

This story of the first showdown in the Old West has been carried by the winds for one hundred fifty years, and in all that time the details tend to get a bit murky. According to legend, the two men had met the night before at the Lyon House Hotel, where Tutt had demanded that Hickok settle a $35 debt. Hickok insisted that he owed the man only $25, but until the debt could be settled, Tutt took Hickok's gold watch as collateral. Hickok accepted the deal but warned Tutt not to embarrass him by flaunting that watch in public. There was nothing wrong with losing at the table and paying your debts, he knew, but he was not a man who stood by quietly when held up for ridicule.

Legend has it that Tutt wasn't too interested in the correct time when he pulled it out of his vest; he was instead calling Hickok's bluff.

But others claim that the real reason for this feud was lady troubles. Some said that when Hickok had a falling-out with a woman he was courting named Susannah Moore, Dave Tutt had taken advantage of the situation and waltzed in between them. In response, Hickok had struck up a relationship with Tutt's sister. Whatever the reason, there was bad blood between the two men and it was going to end that afternoon. Contrary to the movies and TV Westerns, quick-draw showdowns on main streets were very rare. This was the first one, and it appears that a lot of the townspeople turned out to watch it.

Most reports claim that both men pulled their guns evenly, but, rather than firing wildly, they took their time to aim—then fired simultaneously, their respective volleys sounding like a single shot. "Tutt was a famous shot," said an observer, known in those parts as Captain Honesty, "but he missed this time; the ball from his pistol went over Bill's head . . . Bill never shoots twice at the same man, and his ball went through Dave's heart."

Tutt shouted to bystanders, "Boys, I'm killed!" then fell dead.

After he'd fired, Hickok whirled to face Tutt's men, who were standing nearby and looked ready to draw. "Put up your shootin' irons," he warned, "or there'll be more dead men here."

They reluctantly put down their weapons. And the legend of Wild Bill Hickok, "the Prince of Pistoleers," already well established, began to grow. James Butler Hickok was the most famous gunslinger of the Old West; a man known to be reluctant to shoot, but when it became necessary, his draw was "as quick as thought" and his aim was always true. He was the man boys grew up wanting to become; a man of courage and honor whom other men proudly stepped aside for, then bragged they'd met; a man of such grace and bearing that he made women swoon. The fetching Libbie Custer, General Custer's widow, with whom Hickok may have dallied, wrote of him,

> Physically, he was a delight to look upon. Tall, lithe and free in every motion, he rode and walked as if every muscle was perfection, and the careless swing of his body as he moved seemed perfectly in keeping with the man, the country and the time in which he lived. . . . [H]e carried two pistols. He wore top-boots, riding breeches and dark blue flannel shirt, with scarlet set in front. A loose neck handkerchief left his fine firm throat free [and] the frank, manly expression of his fearless eyes and his courteous manner gave one a feeling of confidence in his word and in his undaunted courage.

Fame sometimes has a lot of sharp edges and has to be handled carefully. Hickok's reputation as a deadly gun followed him throughout his life, wherever he traveled, and brought with it some heavy challenges. And some people wonder if, on his last day, it was that fame that caused his demise.

In his lifetime, Hickok became the embodiment of all the virtues attributed to the great

This was the image of the gunfighter Wild Bill Hickok that thrilled Americans: "'Wild Bill' Hickok (1837–76) demonstrates his marksmanship with his Colt Navy model revolver."

men who fought to settle the West, a man who stood up for what was right. He was born in 1837, in the frontier town of Homer, Illinois. His parents, William Alonzo and Polly Butler Hickok, were abolitionists who risked their lives by turning their home into a station on the Underground Railroad. The Hickok family often hid slaves in cubbyholes dug out under their floorboards and, when necessary, carried them to the next station in their wagon. It was said that the Hickoks provided for dozens, maybe even hundreds, of escaping slaves.

Even as a young man, Hickok was known to be a sure shot, and when he was still a teenager he rode with the Jayhawkers, an antislavery militia fighting in the Kansas Territory. There he became known as Shanghai Bill because of his height and his slim frame, but the name didn't stick. It was there that he purportedly first met his lifelong friend William Cody,

a twelve-year-old boy who years later would gain fame as Buffalo Bill, but who was then scouting for the army. The way Cody told the story, he was being bullied by some local toughs and Hickok stepped into the situation and walked him out.

William Hickok's legend had its origins in the summer of 1861 at the Pony Express station in Rock Creek, Nebraska. Speculation abounds concerning what actually happened there, and over time the tales have gotten taller. The twenty-four-year-old Hickok had been driving freight wagons and coaches along the Santa Fe Trail for Russell, Majors, & Waddell, the parent company of the Pony Express, until he got into a tussle with a bear; when his shot ricocheted off the bear's head, Hickok rassled it and cut its throat, but not before that bear inflicted some serious damage. While recuperating, Hickok did odd jobs at the relay station, tending to horses and wagons for station manager Horace Wellman. Hickok lived with Wellman and Wellman's wife, Jane, in the station's small cabin, which had been built on land Wellman purchased from a local rancher named David C. McCanles. McCanles was an ornery fellow, who insisted on derisively calling Hickok "Duck Bill," supposedly a reference to his large, narrow nose and protruding lips—and another name that didn't stick. Naturally, being made fun of did not sit well with Hickok. One day McCanles showed up at the station with his son, Monroe, and two members of his gang, demanding his land back because Wellman was late on his payments. But, once again, another version of the story says that the real reason McCanles showed up concerned the affections of a young woman who had taken a liking to Hickok.

McCanles stood outside the cabin and began haranguing Hickok and the Wellmans, possibly ordering them off his land. A blanket had been hung inside the cabin, most likely to provide some privacy, and both Hickok and Wellman stepped behind it. One of them—it never was quite clear which—took a Hawken rifle off the wall and fired once through the blanket into McCanles's chest; he fell dead on the ground. McCanles's men, James Woods and James Roberts, went for their guns. Woods rushed the cabin, but Hickok pulled his Colt and wounded him, allowing Jane Wellman to finish him off with her sharpened garden hoe. Hickok fired again through the door, this time hitting Roberts, who stumbled off into the woods. Hickok pursued him and came out alone. Monroe McCanles ran off untouched.

Civilization was coming to the West, and three dead men now required a legal hearing. Four days after the shoot-out, Hickok and Horace Wellman were on trial. McCanles had

⌖ This was the first published image of Wild Bill Hickok, Alfred Waud's lithograph, as it appeared in *Harper's Magazine*, 1867.

come to Nebraska from North Carolina, so, in addition to being a bully, he was thought to be pro-Confederate. Wellman and Hickok claimed they had been defending company property, and the circuit judge agreed with them. But as soon as the verdict was rendered, Hickok packed his saddlebags and left Rock Creek to join the war. The first battle of the Civil War, First Bull Run, had just begun at Manassas, Virginia.

By 1867, stories of derring-do in the West were thrilling readers in the big cities. In February of that year, journalist George Ward Nichols published a long, illustrated article entitled "Wild Bill" in the popular *Harper's New Monthly Magazine.* In this wildly exaggerated article, McCanles showed up at the station with his gang of "reckless, blood-thirsty devils, who would fight as long as they had the strength to pull the trigger." By the time the shooting ended, Hickok had dispatched McCanles and ten of his men. The hair-raising story introduced a fighting man to a post–Civil War American public searching desperately for a hero. Nichols created a larger-than-real-life character, a living legend, Wild Bill Hickok. "You would not believe that you were looking into the eyes that have pointed the way to death to hundreds of men," he wrote. "Yes, Wild Bill with his own hands has killed hundreds of men. Of that I have no doubt. He shoots to kill as they say on the border."

Hickok wasn't the first Wild Bill, but when the name finally fell to him, he quickly became the one and the only. Another story that helped build his legend occurred when he enlisted in the Union army and was tasked with spying on the Rebels, scouting, and acting as a provost, or military policeman. One night he came upon a large group of troublemakers, probably fueled by drink, roughing up a bartender outside a saloon. There had been a fair fight, which the bartender had won, but the toughs came back with friends. They had dragged the bartender outside and were beating on him, threatening a hanging. Hickok didn't hesitate, putting himself between the bartender and the mob. "How 'bout we make this a fair fight," he said, glaring at them with his steel-blue eyes. Two men reached for their guns. But before they could clear their holsters, Hickok had drawn both his ivory-handled revolvers and had both men in his sights. They stopped and took their hands away from their weapons. Hickok nodded appreciatively, pointed his guns over their heads, and shot out a kerosene light. "That'll be enough," he was reported to have said. And as the crowd began dissipating, a woman called out, "My God, ain't he wild!"

Wild Bill could indeed be a wild man: He drank, he brawled, he loved the cards and the ladies and treated them both with respect; he could be a gentleman or a cold-blooded shooter, depending on the occasion. He wasn't just passing through life, he was taking thrilled Americans with him on his adventures as the cowboys and gunslingers and lawmen fought to tame the Wild West.

Hickok's exaggerated exploits quickly made him a living legend. In this Hays City brawl, Sheriff Hickok supposedly faced fifteen Seventh Cavalry soldiers—killing two of them and shooting several more.

His legendary skills as a horseman and sure shot served him well during the Civil War. While many fighting men preferred to carry a long gun, Hickok was a pistoleer. He became well known for carrying two ivory-handled Colts, tucked handles-out into a sash or wide belt, which enabled his quick draw. Gunslingers were particular about the way they drew their weapons; a split second could mean the difference between life and death, and Hickok favored the lightning-quick cross-draw in which he'd reach across his body with both hands and pull out his guns. It was a unique style and required a hard twist of the wrist. Some said he'd based it on the technique used by military officers to draw their swords, but others believed it was his lifelong choice from early on. It was also during the war that he became known for wearing a broad-brimmed hat, his long, drooping mustache, and flowing hair.

More stories about Wild Bill's Civil War exploits circulated: During one battle he worked as a sniper and supposedly shot thirty-five men. Hickok himself years later told a story of working as a spy behind Confederate lines at the Battle of Westport, an important fight that took place near where Kansas City now stands. Apparently a skirmish broke out across the Sugar Creek River, with the Union and Confederate troops close enough to see the expressions on their enemies' faces. One of the bluecoats suddenly recognized Hickok behind gray lines. "Bully for Wild Bill!" he shouted, catching the attention of a Rebel sergeant, who suddenly realized there was a spy in the ranks. He reached for his pistol, but Hickok beat him to the draw and drilled him in the chest; then, as Hickok remembered it, "As he rolled out of his saddle, I took his horse by the bit and dashed into the water as quick as I could. . . . The minute I shot the sergeant our boys set up a tremendous shout, and opened a smashing fire on the Rebs who had commenced popping at me. But I had got into deep water, and had slipped off my horse over his back, and steered him for the opposite bank by holding onto his tail with one hand, while I held the bridle rein of the sergeant's horse in the other hand." Wild Bill then crossed the river to safety.

After that escape, Hickok delivered his intelligence to General Curtis, information that may well have aided the Union troops in their victory at what became known as "the Gettysburg of the West" and ended with the Rebels being driven out of Missouri.

Hickok's bravery and success as a scout attracted the attention of Union commanders, and when the war ended, General William Tecumseh Sherman employed him as a guide to take his party to Fort Kearny, Nebraska. He also scouted in the West for General Winfield Scott Hancock and Lieutenant Colonel George Armstrong Custer. In Custer's 1874 book, *My Life on the Plains*, he wrote of Hickok, "Of his courage there could be no question. His skill in the use of the rifle and pistol was unerring. His deportment was entirely free of bravado. . . . His influence among frontiersmen was unbounded, his word was law, and many are the personal quarrels and disturbances which he had checked among his comrades. . . . I have a personal knowledge of at least half a dozen men whom he has at various times killed, others have been seriously wounded—yet he always escaped unhurt in every encounter."

The great respect in which Hickok was held made him the perfect lawman. His presence alone, often without a word or warning spoken, was known to quiet a combustible situation. At the end of the war, he raised his right hand and became a US deputy marshal at Fort Riley, Kansas, while also hiring on as a scout in the Indian Territory for George Custer's Seventh Cavalry. The Indian tribes were seen as an obstacle to the spirit of Manifest Destiny, the belief that America would someday stretch across the continent from the Atlantic to the Pacific, as ordained by God. Agreements were reached with several tribes, granting them reservations, but other tribes decided to stand and fight for their traditional lands. In May 1867, while based in Fort Harker, Kansas, Hickok reported being attacked by a large Indian

Rincon train station, New Mexico, 1883

band, successfully driving them off by killing two of them. Two months later, he led a patrol in pursuit of Indians who had attacked a homestead near the fort and killed four men. Although some stories claim Wild Bill's patrol returned to the fort with five prisoners after killing ten more, others say they returned to Fort Harker without ever having seen an Indian.

Hickok worked out of Hays City, Kansas, and as US deputy marshal tracked down deserters, horse and mule thieves, counterfeiters, and everyone else who ran afoul of the law. In 1868, he worked with his old friend, then government detective William F. Cody, to transport eleven Union deserters from Fort Hays to Topeka for trial.

After the fanciful *Harper's* article spread Hickok's fame throughout the West, he was faced with the downside of being a legend: He had to live up to it every day. People expected to see him regularly perform the kind of feats they'd read about. There was also the continual threat of yet another lowlife trying to earn his spurs by standing up to Wild Bill Hickok.

In 1869, Hickok won a special election to finish the term of the sheriff of Ellis County and marshal of Hays City. Hays needed him. It was a boomtown built out of the tumbleweeds to be the jumping-off point for teamsters carrying freight brought by the Kansas Pacific railroad from back east down to all the towns along the Smoky Hill and Santa Fe Trails. An endless stream of land speculators, tradesmen, storekeepers, and clerks, and sometimes their families, came roaring into town, followed by the buffalo hunters, the cattlemen, the adventurers, the Civil War veterans, and all the others looking for a place to stay a night or settle for a time. To satisfy these transients' social needs, twenty-three saloons and gambling dens were built practically overnight, and the prostitutes and the card sharks and the cattle rustlers and the con artists followed the money. Within a year or so, Hays City had become the largest city in northwest Kansas—as well as the wickedest. It was a lawless place. One writer even referred to it as "the Sodom of the plains."

Hickok quickly made his presence known. As author and historian Lieutenant Dan Marcou explained, "He would not walk down the sidewalk, he would walk down the middle of the street, his eyes were always searching. He was looking for trouble and when he found it he rushed in. His trademark entry to a saloon was to slam the saloon doors open all the way to the wall, both to let it be known he was there and make certain no one was hiding behind them. Then he announced his presence and, in most cases, Wild Bill coming through the door was all that was necessary."

Trouble came to Hays City in all kinds of ways, and Hickok always responded. As one young mother wrote in a letter, she had entrusted her baby to a friend for a few moments so she could get her chores done, but somehow this man's attention wandered, and when she looked out from the shop, she was stunned to see her child crawling in the dusty street as horses and wagons whizzed by. Almost simultaneously she saw Hickok race into the street and rescue the baby—and, after making sure the child was safe, pummel the man responsible.

Hickok was not a man to draw his guns easily, but when it became necessary he was the fastest draw around. In the summer of 1869, a drunken cowboy named Bill Mulvey came bursting out of Tommy Drum's Saloon and began shooting out lamps and windows. Hickok tried to calm him down peacefully, but Mulvey somehow got the drop on him. Thinking quickly, Hickok looked over Mulvey's shoulder and yelled, "Don't shoot him in the back, he's drunk!" Mulvey hesitated—just long enough for Wild Bill to draw his gun and drill the cowboy in his chest.

Only weeks later, a drunken teamster named Sam Strawhun and about eighteen of his buddies began shooting up John Bittles Beer Saloon. Strawhun had been chased out of town several weeks earlier after attacking a member of the town's Vigilance Committee, a group

Martha Cannary, the fabled Calamity Jane, circa 1895

of citizens trying to bring order to Hays City. He'd come back with vengeance on his mind and was heard to promise, "I shall kill someone tonight, just for luck." Hickok managed to get Strawhun and his men out into the street, then collected their beer mugs, which he brought back inside. Strawhun followed, looking for a fight; he threatened to tear up the place. "Do it," Hickok was said to warn, "and they will carry you out."

Strawhun went for his gun. Hickok was faster, drawing his Colts and putting two bullets into Strawhun's head before he could pull the trigger. At the inquest, a jury determined that Hickok had been trying to restore peace and that his actions were justifiable. Although the local newspaper wrote, "Hays City under the guardian care of Wild Bill is quiet and doing well," two killings in only a few months stirred the town, and in the next election Hickok was defeated by his own deputy, Peter Lanihan. Some questions about misconduct and irregularities were raised during the election.

After that, Wild Bill drifted in and out of Hays City, sometimes working with Lanihan to enforce the law. From all reports, Hickok enjoyed all the delights of the place and could often be found sitting back against the wall at a poker table in one of its many saloons. He was also known to enjoy the company of the dance-hall girls, although stories that he dallied there with Martha Jane Cannary, who gained her own fame as the sharpshooting Calamity Jane, probably aren't true. The two legends crossed paths in Hays City, but there is no evidence they ever were involved romantically.

Hickok's stay in Hays City ended abruptly in July 1870, when he was confronted by Jeremiah Lonergan and John Kyle, two privates from Custer's Seventh Cavalry. Animosity between Hickok and the troopers from Fort Hays had been building for a long time. Some of the veterans still resented the fact that Hickok had been paid as much as five dollars a day as a scout during the war while they were doing tougher duty and earning substantially less. More recently, it seemed as if every time they rode into town to blow off some steam, Hickok was waiting there to restrain them. With Lonergan, though, it was personal. His military career had been marked by both desertions and courage, and at some point he'd lost a tussle to Hickok. Lonergan and Kyle reportedly had been drinking the night they decided it was high time to deal with Wild Bill. Witnesses say Hickok was leaning against Tommy Drum's bar, quite probably having enjoyed several whiskeys himself. The saloon was filled with other troops from Custer's command when the two soldiers came in. Lonergan apparently came up behind him and, without one word of warning, grabbed hold of his arms and slammed him down to the floor. The two men wrestled, and when the fight turned in Hickok's favor, Kyle pulled his .44 Remington pistol, put the barrel into Hickok's ear, and squeezed the trigger.

Longhorn cattle drive from Texas to Abilene, Kansas

The gun misfired.

Before Kyle could load a dry charge, Hickok managed to get one hand free, pulled out his Colt, and fired it, his first shot hitting Kyle in the wrist. Kyle's gun clattered to the floor. Hickok fired again, this time striking Kyle in the stomach. As Kyle fell, mortally wounded, Wild Bill got off another shot, his bullet smashing into Lonergan's knee; Lonergan screamed and rolled off Hickok. Wild Bill knew he had only seconds before other cavalrymen in the area heard about the fight and came to settle the score, so he scrambled to his feet and dived through the saloon's glass window. He went back to his rented room to retrieve his Winchester rifle and at least one hundred rounds of ammunition. If a fight was coming, he was going to be ready for it. He walked up to Boot Hill, the cemetery and the highest point in the town, and took his position, waiting for them to come.

Fate had smiled on Wild Bill Hickok. This was the closest he had come to being killed in his career, and his life had been saved only because the black powder cartridges used by Kyle's Remington were notorious for absorbing moisture, causing them to jam. Kyle was considerably less fortunate; he died in the post hospital the next day, joining the growing list of outlaws and troublemakers brought to final justice by Wild Bill Hickok. History records no legal hearings held about this matter, but clearly Wild Bill understood that Hays City was no longer a safe place for him.

Each of these tales was reported in the newspapers back east, where readers were riveted by the adventures of brave Americans taming the Wild West. The stories piled up as competing newspapers and the publishers of the popular dime novels fought for readers, and as a result Wild Bill Hickok became one of the best-known men in America. Some said he was even more famous than the president of the United States.

Hickok's celebrity brought him to the attention of the town elders in Abilene, Kansas, known to be the rowdiest cow town in the West. Abilene had suddenly and unexpectedly found itself in need of a new marshal when Tom "Bear River" Smith was shot and nearly decapitated with an ax during a dispute with a local cattle rancher. For Hickok, Hays City was fine preparation for Abilene.

Abilene was the railhead at the end of the Chisholm Trail. Cowboys drove their herds all the way up from San Antonio, and from there the cattle were shipped back east. But it was a difficult place to pursue a civilized life. The citizens lived in fear each time a large herd arrived. The Texas cowboys, after months on the trail and with a payoff in their pockets, intended to have fun—and there were plenty of disreputable men and fancy women anxious to help them do it. Neither side was about to let the honest citizens stop them. So in April 1871, Abilene mayor Joseph G. McCoy offered Hickok a badge and $150 a month, plus 25 percent of the fines received from the people Hickok arrested.

Hickok began by offering some strong advice to potential troublemakers: "Leave town on the eastbound train, the westbound train, or go North in the morning"—"North" meaning Boot Hill, and no one doubted his words. Hickok and his three deputies began cleaning up the town by closing down the houses of ill repute and warning the saloon keepers against employing card sharks and con men. He stood up to the bullies and the drunkards and enforced ordinances against carrying guns in town. He employed all the legal powers given to him, and if at times he found it necessary to exceed those boundaries, nobody much objected—and it didn't seem that anyone defied him twice. Mayor McCoy once said, "He was the squarest [most honest] man I ever saw."

As always, Hickok backed down from no man. Among the gunslingers who came to town was the outlaw John Wesley Hardin. While working along the Chisholm Trail, he supposedly killed seven men, and then between one and three more in Abilene, before Hickok pinned on the badge. Hickok finally confronted the eighteen-year-old Hardin—although at that time the marshal had no knowledge that he was a wanted man—and ordered him to hand over his guns for the duration of his stay in town. Many years later, Hardin bragged in his autobiography that he'd offered them to Hickok butt-end first and then, as the marshal moved to take them, employed the "road agents spin," in which he twirled the guns in his own hands, ready to fire them. That statement is tough to believe, as that's an old trick and Hickok certainly would have known about it, and Hardin never made the claim until long after Hickok's death. The more likely story is that he simply handed them over.

At some point much later, while trying to get some shut-eye in his apartment at the American House Hotel, Hardin became irate because his roommate's loud snoring was making that impossible—so he fired several shots through the wall into the next room to get the man's attention. Unfortunately, one of those bullets hit the man in the head, killing him instantly. When Hickok responded to reports of gunfire in town, Hardin climbed out a window and hid in a haystack, later writing, "I believed that if Wild Bill found me in a defenseless condition he would take no explanation, but would kill me to add to his reputation." Instead of standing up to the marshal, Hardin stole a horse and hightailed it out of town.

Hickok also found time to do some courting. Only a few months after he moved to Abilene, "the Hippo-Olympiad and Mammoth Circus," starring the beautiful Agnes Thatcher Lake, came to town, and Hickok took up with the leading lady. Agnes Lake was a well-known dancer, tightrope walker, lion tamer, and horsewoman, who had toured Europe and even spoke several languages. Wild Bill was smitten but was convinced that she would eventually return to the East Coast.

Until that time, another gal, Jessie Hazell, the proprietor of a popular brothel, had held his attention. But the "Veritable Vixen," as the successful businesswoman was known in Abilene, instead had returned the affection of another suitor, Phil Coe. Coe was a gambler who co-owned the Bull's Head Tavern with gunfighter Ben Thompson. Even before their romantic competition, Hickok and Coe had built a strong dislike for each other. Not only had Hickok's rules been bad for Coe's business, but the marshal had embarrassed Coe by personally taking a paintbrush and covering the Bull's Head's finest advertisement: a painting of a bull with a large erect penis that adorned the side of the building. In response, Coe reportedly promised that he was going to kill Hickok "before the frost," claiming that he was such a sure shot that he could "kill a crow on the wing."

The famous story goes that when Hickok heard that, he replied, "Did the crow have a pistol? Was he shooting back? I will be."

This feud finally erupted into gunplay on the cool night of October 5. It is generally agreed that Coe, who might have been drunk, announced his intentions by firing several shots into the air, in violation of the law. Hearing the shots, Hickok told his close friend and deputy, Mike Williams, to stay put while he investigated. Wild Bill found Coe and a large number of his supporters waiting for him in front of the Alamo Saloon. Coe told the marshal he'd fired at a stray dog. Hickok responded by ordering Coe and his men to hand over their guns and get out of town.

This was the moment Coe had been waiting for. Hickok was alone on a dark street, completely surrounded by men who hated him and his laws. Coe fired twice; both shots missed. Hickok returned the fire and he did not miss. Both shots hit Coe in the stomach.

Suddenly, from the corner of his eye, Wild Bill saw another man with a revolver charging at him out of the shadows. He whirled and fired twice more. The man went down in the dirt. It was probably only seconds later that Hickok realized that he'd killed his deputy, Mike Williams, who had heard the four shots and come running to stand with him.

Hickok turned on the mob, reportedly warning, "Do any of you fellows want the rest of these bullets?" They saw the anguish and the anger on his face and drifted away. Williams's body was carried into the Alamo and laid on a billiard table. It was said that Hickok wept.

After that night, he was a changed man. He'd spent his life killing men who had deserved it, but this was different. He had reacted too quickly and his friend had paid the ultimate price. There were so many things Wild Bill Hickok was good at, but finding a way to forgive himself was not among them. His anger had been unleashed; it seemed like he was out of control. Within months the town had turned on him; a newspaper editorial declared that "gallows and penitentiary are the places to tame such blood thirsty wretches as 'Wild Bill.'" In December, Abilene relieved him of his duties, and Wild Bill Hickok rode out of town.

His prospects were limited. Because of his work, and that of others like him, the West had become considerably less wild. He'd worked his way out of a job. He returned to Springfield and set out to earn his keep gambling. Historians report that he drank too much and won too little. It was there that Buffalo Bill found him.

The one thing Hickok had left was his reputation. People would pay to see him—pay a lot. He had dipped his toe into show business earlier, partnering with Colonel Sidney Barnett of Niagara Falls, New York, to produce a show called *The Daring Buffalo Chase of the Plains*, but the buffalo did not like being roped and the show had failed. Meanwhile, the showbiz bug had bitten Buffalo Bill Cody, who was producing *Scouts of the Plains; or, On the Trail*, a

Legends (*from left*) Wild Bill Hickok, Texas Jack Omohundro, and Buffalo Bill Cody in an 1874 promotional photo for Cody's show *Scouts of the Plains*

Hickok spent one winter performing in Cody's show, and when he went back out west, Cody and Texas Jack Omohundro each gave him five hundred dollars and a pistol, urging him to "make good use of it among the Reds."

precursor to his famous *Wild West Show*. He offered Hickok a fair salary to star in the show. Hickok had little choice but to accept the offer.

Hickok apparently was terrible onstage. Worse, he knew it and was said to spend much of his time between performances presiding over a card game and a stream of liquor bottles. Legend has it that while the show was playing in New York City he walked into a poolroom to find a fair game. The players didn't recognize him and began making fun of his long hair and western clothes. There was no one left standing when he walked out the door. Later he explained, "I got lost among the hostiles."

Few doubt that Hickok could have spent the rest of his days trading on his fame, earning a living simply by showing up and telling his stories to awed crowds in the concert saloons and variety halls of the new entertainment called vaudeville. But that wasn't right for him; he never quite embraced or fully accepted his celebrity. Perhaps that was due to his personality, which always chose action over words, or to his knowledge that so many of the tales written about him had been exaggerated or simply made up. He had accomplished a great deal, but no one could have done all the things with which he was credited.

Finally he could take it no more and left Cody's show, going back out west where he belonged, eventually settling in Cheyenne, Wyoming, in 1876. His reasons for landing in Cheyenne aren't known, but one may have been that Agnes Lake was staying there with friends. It was the first time they'd seen each other since Abilene, though they had continued to correspond through the years. They took up quickly, though, and were married within months. The local newspaper noted, "Wild Bill of western fame has conquered numerous Indians, outlaws, bears and buffalos, but a charming widow has stolen the magic wand . . . he has shuffled off the coil of bachelorhood."

Hickok still needed to figure out how to earn a living. His once-legendary eyesight appeared to be diminished and his bankroll was thin. Two years earlier, an expedition led by General Custer had discovered gold in the Dakotas, setting off a gold rush. Shortly after his marriage, Hickok gathered a group of men and set out for the Black Hills. Although people generally believe that he was going there to prospect, there also is the possibility that he was hoping to be hired on as marshal of the boomtown of Deadwood, giving him a chance to relive the great days of his life and to tame one last town.

Deadwood was no different than all the other towns that sprang up to support gold strikes. Money came hard, and the law was whatever the toughest men in town decided it was. Hickok mined during the day and played cards at night, trying to win enough of a stake to bring Agnes out there. He wrote to his new wife often, promising her, "We will have a home yet, then we will be so happy." But there were also signs that he sensed real danger around him, and in his last letter to her he promised, "Agnes darling, if such should be we never meet again, while firing my last shot, I will gently breathe the name of my wife, Agnes, and with wishes even for my enemies I will make the plunge and try to swim to the other shore."

Some historians believe Hickok was resigned to his fate and had even predicted it, supposedly telling a friend, "I have a hunch that I am in my last camp and will never leave this gulch alive . . . something tells me my time is up. But where it is coming from I do not know."

On August 2, 1876, Hickok strolled into Nutter and Mann's Saloon, looking for a game of poker. Historians have speculated that he went to the saloon directly from a local opium den. Three men he knew were seated around a table, the only empty chair facing a wall. Hickok never sat with his back to a door; he wanted to see trouble when it walked in. Sitting in the available seat made it impossible for him to watch the rear entrance. He twice asked the other players to change seats with him, but both requests were refused. That these men felt comfortable turning down the great Hickok is an indication of how far his stock had fallen. Only a few years earlier, almost everyone would gladly have given up his seat for an opportunity to play cards with the famous Wild Bill Hickok. Reluctantly Hickok sat down in that chair and put his chips on the table.

The night before, he had played poker with a former buffalo hunter and gambler, Jack

McCall, known as Crooked Nose Jack; Hickok had cleaned him out, then offered him some money for breakfast. Some saw that as an insult. But McCall was back the next day, standing at the bar when Hickok walked into Nutter and Mann's. If they acknowledged each other at all, no one ever spoke of it. Wild Bill's game of five-card draw had been in progress for some time when McCall got up from his bar stool and walked past Hickok toward the back door—then stopped suddenly about three feet away from him and turned. Hickok had been winning and had just been dealt a pleasing hand—black aces and black eights. He had discarded his fifth card and was waiting for his next card—legend claims it was the jack of diamonds—when McCall suddenly pulled out his double-action Colt .45 six-shooter, shouted, "Damn you! Take that!" and fired one shot into the back of Hickok's head at point-blank range. The bullet tore through his skull, emerging from his cheek and striking another player in the wrist. Wild Bill Hickok died instantly.

McCall reportedly pulled the trigger several more times, but his gun failed to fire. It was later determined that all six chambers were loaded, but only one bullet fired—the shot that killed Hickok. McCall raced outside and jumped on his horse, but his cinch was loose and the saddle slipped. He ran into a butcher's shop, where he was quickly captured by the sheriff.

A satisfactory explanation for the assassination has never been found. McCall might have been avenging the "insult" from the previous night. But during his trial, he claimed that Hickok had killed his brother and he was avenging that shooting, although there is no evidence that he even had a brother. There were rumors that he had been paid to assassinate Hickok, and there is always the possibility that he simply wanted to kill the famous Wild Bill.

A trial was held in Deadwood the next day, and McCall, claiming he was entitled to avenge his brother's death, was acquitted. The local newspaper derided the verdict, suggesting, "Should it ever be our misfortune to kill a man . . . we would simply ask that our trial may take place in some of the mining camps of these hills."

McCall left town. When he reached Yankton, capital of the Dakota Territory, he was arrested once again. His acquittal in the first trial was set aside because Deadwood was not yet a legally recognized town. McCall was tried a second time—and during this trial it was suggested that he had been hired to commit the killing by gamblers who feared that Hickok, "a champion of law and order," was about to be appointed town marshal. This time the jury convicted McCall, and he was sentenced to death. He was hanged on March 1, 1877.

The cards Wild Bill Hickok were holding when he was shot, black aces and eights, have been forever immortalized in poker lore as the famed "dead man's hand."

Since Hickok's death almost one hundred fifty years ago, a question has remained

ASSASSINATION OF WILD BILL (J. B. HICKOK) BY JACK McCALL, AT DEADWOOD CITY, D. T.

During the assassin Jack McCall's first trial, Hickok was described as a "shootist," who "was quick in using the pistol and never missed his man, and had killed quite a number of persons in different parts of the country."

unanswered: Why did he agree to take a seat with his back to a door? No one will ever know for sure, but since that fateful day, many have wondered if Hickok was simply tired of life. In many ways, he had become a captive of his fame: Although he no longer was capable of living up to it, the great expectations remained. Wild Bill might well have moved to Deadwood, a wild place where reputations didn't hold much water and where what mattered was only what happened yesterday, to escape his own legend. But on that fateful August day in 1876, it finally caught up with him.

At his death, he was credited with thirty-six righteous shootings. And his friend Captain Jack Crawford, who had scouted the trails of the Old West with him, probably described him best when he recalled, "He was loyal in his friendship, generous to a fault, and invariably espoused the cause of the weaker against the stronger one in a quarrel."

UP AND DOWN TOWNS

As tens of thousands of settlers raced to find their fortunes in the West, countless boomtowns suddenly burst out of the sagebrush. Many of these towns, which usually were dirty, poorly built, and often lawless, existed for only a brief time, until the mines gave out, the cattle drives ended, or the railroad crews set down somewhere else; then they quickly became ghost towns. But whether a town struggled on or ceased to exist, the events that took place there—and their subsequent appearance in numerous movies and TV shows—made the names Dodge City, Deadwood, and Tombstone legendary.

Dodge City, Kansas, came into existence in 1871, when a rancher settled there to run his operation. Originally named Buffalo City, until someone discovered there already was a place by that name, it was perfectly located just a whisker west of Fort Dodge and near the Santa Fe Trail and Arkansas River. It boomed a year later, with the coming of the Santa Fe railroad and the opening of the first saloon. The railhead allowed cowboys to ship buffalo hides and, within a few years, longhorn cattle driven up on the Chisholm Trail from Texas to points north and east. Then they would stay awhile to brush off the trail dust and spend their earnings. "The streets of Dodge were lined with wagons," wrote one city elder. "I have been to several mining camps where rich strikes had been made, but I never saw any town to equal Dodge." "The Queen of the Cow Towns," as it was called, offered a wide choice of saloons—including the famous Long

Branch—gambling dens, brothels, and even, for a brief period, a bullring. The hardest men in the West—cowboys off the trail, buffalo hunters, bull whackers, and muleteers—would ride in rich, ready for a good time, and ride out a few days later poor but happy. For a time, Dodge really was as wild as its legend. It welcomed more gunslingers than any other city, and

Dodge City's Long Branch Saloon, which was built in 1874 and burned down in 1885, probably is best remembered as Miss Kitty's place, where Marshal Matt Dillon would "set a spell" in the TV series *Gunsmoke*. The saloon was the center of entertainment in western towns. In addition to serving "firewater," it might feature professional gamblers playing faro, Brag, three-card monte, poker, and dice games, or dancing, billiards, or even bowling. Many of them never closed, and a few didn't even have a front door.

several of the great lawmen tried to calm it down, among them Wyatt Earp, Bat Masterson, and Bill Tilghman. But it was actually the Kansas state legislature that caused Dodge's demise, when it extended an existing cattle quarantine across the state in 1886 and shut down the end of the trail. With that, the fast money disappeared, and most of the population realized it was time to "get out of Dodge."

Deadwood, South Dakota, sprang up almost overnight after gold was discovered, first by General Custer in the Black Hills, then quickly by a miner in Deadwood Gulch in 1875. Because by treaty this was Indian land, the army tried to keep out the prospectors, so it took tough men to settle it. Fortunes were made, mostly by the saloon keepers, gamblers, opium dealers, and ladies of the evening, who had followed the gold diggers. Its reputation as a lawless town was sealed when Wild Bill Hickok was shot in the back of the head there in 1876, and for a while, Deadwood averaged one murder per day. Hickok and Calamity Jane had ridden in together as guards escorting a wagon train bringing prostitutes and gamblers from Cheyenne, and both of them were buried on Deadwood's Boot Hill. Only three years later, in 1879, a massive fire destroyed almost three hundred buildings; by that time, new gold claims were pretty much played out, people were ready to move on to the next boomtown, and Deadwood settled down.

Miners pulled the modern-day equivalent of almost $1.5 billion in silver from the mines near Tombstone, Arizona, between 1877 and 1890, and within a few years, its population exploded, from about one hundred

After being founded in 1879 when silver was discovered nearby, in less than seven years, the town of Tombstone grew from one hundred people to fourteen thousand. An 1886 fire destroyed the expensive pumping plant, and the population dwindled to a few hundred, turning it into a ghost town. It exists today as a tourist destination, the once-wild city where the legendary gunfight at the O.K. Corral took place.

to fourteen thousand. It got its name because its founder, Ed Schieffelin, had been warned that the Apaches didn't cotton much to prospectors and that the only thing he'd find in the hills there was his own tombstone. For several years, there were few more dangerous towns on the frontier; "the town too tough to die," as it was known, was close enough to the Mexican border for rustlers to use as their base of operations. Eventually there were more saloons, gambling houses, and brothels there than in any town in the

Southwest. When the Cowboys gang met the Earp brothers at the O.K. Corral, Tombstone's place in history, and in the movies, was ensured.

Numerous other violent boomtowns eventually became ghost towns. Canyon Diablo, Arizona, for example, was created when railroad workers had to wait for a bridge to be built, and within months fourteen saloons and ten gambling houses faced one another on Hell Street. The first sheriff was dead five hours after he pinned on his badge, and none of the five men who followed lived more than a month. When the bridge was finally completed ten years later, most people got on the train and left.

Gold was discovered in Bodie, California, in the Sierra Nevada in 1859, and before the vein dried up a decade later, the population had grown to ten thousand people. There is a long list of towns that boomed briefly, from Fort Griffin, Texas, to Leadville, Colorado (originally known as Slabville). However, throughout the country, it was believed that "the roughest, toughest town west of Chicago" was Palisades, Nevada, which had more than a thousand showdowns, bank robberies, and Indian raids in about three years in the mid-1870s. Although no one is quite sure how it began, each day as the railroad arrived, townspeople would stage a fake showdown or holdup and getaway for the benefit of the "dudes" from back east. Apparently this was done for entertainment rather than profit, as no money changed hands. The terrified passengers, who were never let in on the joke, would tell stories of their encounters with outlaws to newspapers back home. The stories were printed or otherwise passed along, allowing Palisades to gain its notorious reputation.

BASS REEVES

★ The Real Lone Ranger ★

On Monday night, January 30, 1933, racing to the unmistakable beats of Rossini's *William Tell* Overture, a new hero rode into American cultural history.

American families struggling through the Great Depression gathered around the radio every night for a few hours of escape and entertainment. On that winter's night, they were introduced to a remarkable character who would take Americans with him on his adventures into the next century. In a mellifluous voice resonating with awe, the announcer introduced the Superman of the Old West:

> A fiery horse, with a speed of light—a cloud of dust, a hearty laugh, The Lone Ranger is perhaps the most attractive figure ever to come out of the West. Through his daring, his riding, and his shooting, this mystery rider won the respect of the entire Golden Coast—the West of the old days, where every man carried his heart on his sleeve and only the fittest remained to make history. Many are the stories that are told by the lights of the Western campfire concerning this romantic figure. Some thought he was on the side of the outlaw, but many knew that he was a lone rider, dealing out justice to the law abiding citizenry. Though the Lone Ranger was known in seven states, he earned his greatest reputation in Texas. None knew where he came from and none knew where he went.

And then, as thunder boomed in the background, the story began: "Old Jeb Langworth lived alone in his small shack just outside the wide open community of Red Rock. One evening as he was watching the coffee boil and the bacon sizzle in the pan, and thinking of how snug his cabin was, with the storm raging outside, there came a knock on the door . . ."

A masked man riding the range with his trusty sidekick, the Indian brave Tonto, protecting the weak, righting wrongs, and dispensing Old West justice with his blazing guns, the Lone Ranger was the perfect hero.

No one knew his real name or where he came from, only that he left his calling card, a silver bullet, when he uttered his famous parting words, "Hi-Yo, Silver—away!" then disappeared into the wilderness until the next episode. The Lone Ranger eventually became one of the most iconic figures in American media, a star of radio, television, movies, novels, and comic books.

But what has been almost completely forgotten is that the character of the Lone Ranger was likely based on the life of a real person, whose true story is even more incredible than the fictitious adventures of the masked man.

Bass Reeves was a black American, born into slavery in Crawford County, Arkansas, in 1838, but came of age in Grayson, Texas. He was the property of William S. Reeves, but apparently early in his life was given to Reeves's son George. While growing up, Bass Reeves never learned to read or write, but his mother taught him the Bible, and he was known to recite verses from memory. He was such a good marksman that his master entered him in shooting contests. When George Reeves eventually became the county sheriff and tax collector, he undoubtedly was pleased to have his sharpshooting servant at his side. Unfortunately, the history of black men in America around that time is difficult to reconstruct. Reeves would later claim to have fought in the Civil War battles of Chickamauga and Missionary Ridge under Colonel George Reeves and earned his freedom on the battlefield, but another story claims that he attacked his master when they argued over a card game and knocked him out, a crime punishable by death in Texas, so he was forced to flee into Indian Territory. Whatever the truth about his early years, Bass was twenty-two years old in 1863 when Abraham Lincoln issued the Emancipation Proclamation and he became a freeman.

He eventually settled in the Indian Territory, which included present-day Oklahoma, and lived there peacefully among the tribes, the white squatters, and the white criminals escaping justice. He learned to speak the languages of "the five civilized tribes" (the Choctaws, Chickasaws, Seminoles, Creeks, and Cherokees) and gained a reputation as a skilled tracker, horseman, and deadeye shot—both right- and left-handed, and with both pistols and long guns. Bass Reeves was a big man, described as being six feet two and a muscular two hundred pounds, with a big, bushy mustache and piercing eyes that could a freeze a man before he made a foolhardy move. At first, as a freeman, he made his living working on farms, but his knowledge of the Territory "like a cook knows her kitchen," as he once put it, enabled him to become a trusted guide and interpreter for the US marshals riding that range.

At the time, it was well known that "There is no God west of Fort Smith." Indian Territory was one of the most dangerous places in the world. The murder rate rivaled that of the worst cities in the country; people were killed over anything from a horse to a coarse

The Lone Ranger became one of America's most popular characters. In addition to 2,956 radio shows, he was the protagonist of motion pictures and animated features, books, a syndicated comic strip and comic books, 221 half-hour television episodes, and even a video game.

word. The outlaw Dick Glass once killed a man in a dispute over an ear of corn. It was once estimated that out of the twenty-two thousand white men living in the Territory, seventeen thousand were criminals on the lam. While tribal courts had jurisdiction over the Indians, white criminals had to be taken to Fort Smith, Arkansas, or Paris, Texas, for trial. The only law enforcement was the few US deputy marshals working out of Fort Smith. There often wasn't a lawman to be found within two hundred miles, leaving plenty of room for vigilante justice.

It was a good place for a freeman, because it might have been the most racially and ethnically integrated area in the United States. Few people had the time or the inclination for racism. Everybody pretty much lived together and suffered equally. Even the outlaw gangs were integrated. Dick Glass, for example, who ran one of the most vicious gangs in the

Territory, was himself half-black and half–Creek Indian, and his gang consisted of five black men, four Indians, and two white men.

Bass Reeves was living on his own farm in Van Buren, Arkansas, with his wife, Jinnie, their three children, his mother, and his sister in 1875, when President Ulysses S. Grant appointed Judge Isaac Parker to bring law and order to the Western District of Arkansas. This included all of western Arkansas and the Indian Territory, seventy-four thousand lawless square miles. It was considered a safe place for every type of criminal on the prairie to hide out: the murderers, rapists, cattle robbers, and thieves; the bootleggers selling to the Indians; and the con men. Parker, who was to gain fame as "the Hanging Judge," was given permission to hire two hundred new deputies. Having heard that Reeves could speak the Indian languages and had often assisted marshals, he offered him a permanent position as a US deputy marshal. Legend has it that when Reeves was asked by a family member why he was willing to risk his life enforcing "white man's law," he replied, "Maybe the law ain't perfect, but it's the only one we got, and without it we got nuthin'."

The United States Marshals Service was founded in 1789, created in the Judiciary Act by the First Congress. It was established to be the law-enforcement arm of the federal judicial system. US marshals, and the deputies they legally appointed to assist them, were empowered to serve the subpoenas, summonses, writs, warrants, and other legal documents issued by the

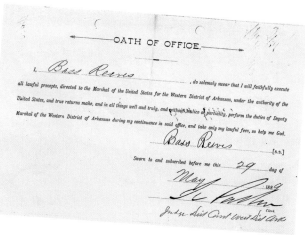

Judge Issac Parker appointed Bass Reeves a deputy US marshal in 1879. In the Hanging Judge's twenty-one years on the bench, he tried 13,490 cases—and saw seventy-nine people hanged.

federal courts, make all arrests, and handle prisoners anywhere in the country. Unlike local law enforcement, their jurisdiction was not limited by borders. They were paid for the work they did, meaning they earned a fee for each wanted man they brought to justice. But it was incredibly dangerous work. More than 130 deputies were killed in the Territory before Oklahoma became a state in 1907.

Although Reeves was not the first black US deputy marshal, he quickly became the best known, and several of his characteristics would later come to be associated with the Lone Ranger. In those days, when a deputy went out on the trail after outlaws, he would take a wagon (in which to bring back the fugitives he caught), a cook, and a posse man (a deputy who would work with him). Reeves's posse man was often an Indian from the tribal Lighthorse, which is what the five tribes called their mounted police force. Although Reeves worked with many different Indian officers, apparently there was one man that he chose to ride with whenever possible. His name is lost to history, but he in all probability served as the model for the Lone Ranger's faithful sidekick, Tonto. Also, later in Reeves's fabled career, he was known for giving a silver dollar to those people who helped him, which obviously is close to the concept of the Lone Ranger leaving a silver bullet.

Among the many virtues the Lone Ranger shared with Reeves was a great sense of fair play and a desire to bring 'em back alive. Almost immediately after accepting the job, Reeves's respect for the law became clear. According to legend, one afternoon out on the trail he spotted a group of men holding a lynching party and rode over to them. Lost to history is whether the prisoner was a horse thief or a cattle thief, but apparently he'd been caught dead-to-rights and the penalty for that crime was well known. The suspect was sitting on a horse, his hands tied behind his back, a noose around his neck. When Reeves was told what had happened, he showed the group his badge and explained that in this part of the world, he was the law and he intended to take this man back to Fort Smith. Sitting tall on his own horse, showing his two pistols and complete confidence, he presented a figure nobody seemed anxious to challenge. He cut the noose and rode away with the suspect. As far as he was concerned, that man's fate needed to be in the hands of Judge Parker, not a mob out on the prairie. Nobody dared try to stop him.

He also believed in bringing prisoners back alive, although he didn't hesitate to shoot when it became necessary. During a tense confrontation with a horse thief named John Cudgo, he laid out his philosophy. In 1890, Reeves went to Cudgo's spread on the Seminole Nation to arrest him for larceny. The two men had known each other for almost a decade. As Reeves approached Cudgo's house, the outlaw suddenly popped out from beneath his front

Bass Reeves (*far left*) had served as a deputy marshal for twenty-eight years when this "family photo" was taken in 1907—the year Oklahoma entered the Union and instituted the Jim Crow laws that forced him to end his federal law-enforcement career.

porch, holding his Winchester. Reeves ordered him to surrender and he refused, warning that no marshal was taking him back to Fort Smith—especially not Reeves. He then asked Reeves to send his posse men away so that the two of them might talk. When the men were gone, Cudgo cocked his rifle and said he wanted to be allowed to die in the house he'd built, trying to provoke Reeves into shooting him. Reeves shook his head and told him, "Government law didn't send me out here to kill people, but to arrest them." Hours later, Cudgo surrendered without a single shot being fired.

As for his integrity, few tasks could possibly be more difficult for a lawman than having to arrest his own son, and that was the situation Reeves faced in 1902 when his son Bennie was accused of fatally shooting his wife when he caught her cheating on him. After the murder, Bennie Reeves had fled into the Territory. When the district marshal initially gave the warrant to another deputy, Reeves supposedly insisted that he be the man to serve it, explaining, "There's no sense in nobody else getting hurt over my son. I'll bring him in." He tracked Bennie to a small town. Nobody knows what took place between the two of them, but Reeves brought his son to justice. Bennie Reeves was convicted of the crime and sentenced to life imprisonment at Fort Leavenworth, Kansas, but was released for good behavior after ten years.

Reeves also arrested his own minister for selling whiskey. Reeves himself served as a deacon of his church in Van Buren, Arkansas, and it was said that some nights while on the trail he would chain captured fugitives to a log and preach the Gospel to them, asking them to confess their sins and repent.

Bass Reeves served as a US deputy marshal for thirty-three years. Although the precise number of men he tracked down and brought to justice isn't known, he is credited with more than three thousand arrests. The number of men he shot or killed also isn't known, although newspapers reported that he had killed twenty men. Outlaws used to say that drawing on Bass Reeves was as good as committing suicide. Whatever the number, by the time he retired he had become a legend, and songs were being written about him. It was said that when the famous outlaw Belle Starr heard that Reeves had been given the warrant for her arrest, she actually walked into Fort Smith and surrendered.

Just like the Lone Ranger, Reeves would travel light and move as quickly as possible. Because he couldn't read the warrants, when getting ready to go out on the trail he would have someone read as many as thirty of them to him. He would memorize each one, including the crime and the description of the wanted man, and was said to have perfect recall. He usually traveled with a wagon driven by his cook, one posse man, and a long chain. He often traveled with two horses; if he had to work in disguise he didn't want his good riding horse attracting attention. His posse would stay on the trail for several weeks, sometimes months, and the wanted men he captured would be chained to the rear axle of the wagon, usually in pairs, until he'd caught his fill and decided to bring them all back to Judge Parker's court. Other deputies were bringing in five or six men at a time; on one trip Reeves returned with sixteen

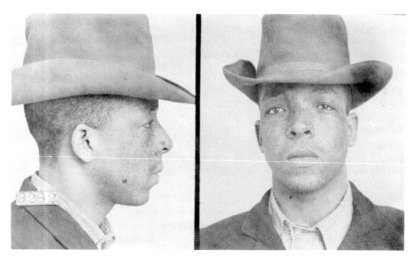

In 1902, Reeves went into the Indian Territory and captured his son, Bennie, who had shot his wife. Ben Reeves served ten years before being released for good behavior.

men and collected seven hundred dollars in fines; he always claimed that the largest number he brought in at one time was nineteen horse thieves, for which he was paid nine hundred dollars. On occasion he was also known to pack his bedroll and go out into the wilderness by himself, an image of the lone deputy that easily can be seen as inspiration for the Lone Ranger.

Among his most famous arrests was the nefarious Seminole To-Sa-Lo-Nah, also known as Greenleaf, who was wanted for the brutal murders of at least seven people, as well as for selling whiskey to the tribes. Four of his victims were Indians who had worked with deputies as posse men to try to capture him—he had shot the last one, in fact, twenty-four times. That made it very difficult to find an Indian tracker who would even speak his name. Greenleaf had successfully eluded capture for eighteen years when Reeves got the warrant for his arrest. Reeves used his own network of informants, men who trusted him to protect them, and one of them got word to him that Greenleaf had recently brought a wagonload of whiskey into the area. In the middle of the night, Reeves and his posse man crawled close enough to the house in which Greenleaf was staying to hear him whooping and shouting. When the house finally grew quiet, Reeves led his posse in an assault, jumping over a fence and getting the drop on the killer before he could go for his gun. After Reeves had put the cuffs on Greenleaf, a steady stream of people came to look at the vicious killer long believed to be uncatchable, now in chains.

Perhaps the Lone Ranger's most instantly identifiable feature was the black mask he wore to disguise his true identity. Although Reeves didn't wear a mask, like the fictional character he did sometimes use disguises to help him draw close to dangerous criminals. He was known to impersonate preachers, cowboys, hobos, farmers—whatever seemed suitable for the situation. Once, for example, he was tracking two brothers who had a five-thousand-dollar bounty on their heads. No one had been able to get near them. Knowing that the two men had remained in contact with their mother, Reeves supposedly shot two holes through an old hat, put it on along with ragged clothes and shoes with broken heels, hid his pistol and handcuffs under his clothes—then walked twenty miles to the mother's home. He arrived there filthy, sweating, and thirsty and pleaded with her for water and a square meal, complaining that he was on the run from a posse. The woman invited him in and permitted him to stay the night, telling him that her two boys were also on the run and suggesting they might work together. After dark the two fugitives snuck into the house. While they were sleeping, Reeves snapped his cuffs on both of them. When he marched them out in the morning, their mother is said to have walked with them for the first several miles, yelling and cursing at Reeves every single step of the way.

In another case, he learned that two wanted men were traveling on a certain road. Cutting across the brush to get ahead of them, he ran his wagon into a ditch. When the two men rode by, they saw a lone black man struggling to get his wagon back on the trail. They offered to help him, and when they placed their hands on the wagon, he revealed his identity and took them into custody.

Perhaps his best-known deception led to the capture of the killer Jim Webb in 1883. Webb was foreman of the Washington and McLish Ranch on the Chickasaw Nation. A black minister, Reverend William Steward, owned a piece of adjoining land. When Steward set a controlled fire to burn some brush on his property, it got out of control and burned off feed grass on Bill Washington's spread. Washington sent his foreman to see Steward and set things right, but their conversation grew heated and Webb killed him. Reeves was given the warrant for his arrest.

Reeves and his posse man, Floyd Wilson, rode up to the ranch pretending to be cowboys looking for work. As they approached, they saw Webb and one of his ranch hands, a man named Frank Smith, sitting on the veranda with their pistols ready in their laps. Reeves explained that they had been riding for a spell and were hoping to get some breakfast and feed for their horses. Webb told them to take the horses over to the stable, but as they did he kept a wary eye on them. As the horses watered, Bass took his Winchester from his saddle and stood it up against a wall, hoping to calm any suspicions Webb might hold. Then Reeves and Wilson sat down for breakfast. There was a mirror in the bunkhouse, and in the reflection Reeves saw Webb and Smith having a serious discussion, seemingly about them. Reeves told his man that when he gave the sign, he would grab Webb, and Wilson needed to take down Smith.

After the meal, the deputy and his posse man sat down with Webb and Smith, supposedly to have a friendly chat about possible employment. Something happened during the conversation to convince Reeves that Webb was on to him. He reacted just like the Lone Ranger would have done on the radio or in the early years of television: He grabbed Webb by the throat and started squeezing. His posse man was too stunned to move, and Smith raised his pistol. Before he could take aim, Reeves, still holding Webb tightly by the throat, drew his own six-gun and fired. Smith reeled backward, mortally wounded.

Wilson slipped the irons on Webb's wrists and they got him out of there quickly. Webb was delivered to the court to be tried for the murder of Reverend Steward. Somewhat surprisingly, he was released on seventeen thousand dollars' bail, truly a small fortune, supposedly put up by Bill Washington. As soon as Webb was released, he took off. The bail was forfeited.

He wasn't heard from for more than two years, when Reeves suddenly got word that he'd returned to the ranch. Reeves had no intention of letting Webb get away a second time.

Reeves and posse man John Cantrell headed back into the Territory, where they learned that Webb had recently been seen at Bywater's General Store. When they got to the store, Reeves sent Cantrell ahead to scout out the situation. Webb was there, sitting by a window—and he spotted the two men as they rode up. He jumped out a side window and made for his horse. Reeves cut off his escape. Webb turned and started running for the brush. He had his pistol and Winchester with him. As Reeves closed in on him, Webb spun around and pegged several shots at him. At least one of those shots took a button off Reeves's coat; another supposedly knocked his hat off his head. Reeves reined in his horse and jumped off. Taking his own Winchester out of its scabbard, he aimed and fired twice. Historians put the distance between them anywhere between two hundred and five hundred yards. Both of Reeves's shots found their mark, ripping into Webb's chest; he fell in his tracks.

Reeves, Cantrell, and Jim Bywater approached Webb carefully. Playing possum was a well-known trick, and Reeves wasn't about to fall for it. But when they came closer they saw the blood flowing from Webb's wounds. He was still alive, a revolver in his hand, but his injuries were bad. Reeves didn't take any chances; holding his gun on Webb, he ordered him to throw away his weapon. Webb tossed it into the bushes, then asked Reeves to come close. Bywater later reported that with his dying breath, Webb said to Reeves, "You are a brave man. I want you to accept my revolver and holster as a present. Take it, for with it I have killed eleven men, four of them in Indian Territory. I expected you would be number twelve, but you were too good for me."

No one was too surprised that Reeves was able to put two slugs into Webb at more than two hundred yards. Hitting a running target at several hundred feet wasn't extraordinary for him. Reeves's training growing up as a slave had enabled him to become, just like the fictional Lone Ranger, a crack shot. Historians tell several amazing stories about his proficiency with guns. He wore two Colt revolvers butt-forward for a quick draw, and he carried a Winchester in his saddle. Historian Art Burton, the author of the Reeves biography *Black Gun, Silver Star*, once interviewed an elderly man who many years earlier had worked for the legendary deputy James Bud Ledbetter. Ledbetter was renowned as a crack shot himself, one time killing five men in a gunfight without being so much as scratched. This elderly man had been riding with Ledbetter when they tracked down a wanted man. He had holed himself up well, and Ledbetter's posse couldn't get close; they'd spent the afternoon throwing lead at him but hadn't come close to hitting anything. Finally Ledbetter got angry because all they were doing was wasting his ammunition inventory, so he sent a man back to Muskogee to get Bass Reeves. The sun was just starting to set when Reeves arrived. Whether the desperado knew that Reeves was there or just grew tired of being shot at, he suddenly took off across a field. The posse opened up on him, but he was at least a quarter mile away, out of range of their pistols. Finally Ledbetter yelled above the din, "Get 'im, Bass!"

Bass responded very calmly and cooly, promising, "I will break his neck." He put his Winchester to his shoulder, took aim, and fired a single shot—right through the outlaw's throat. Then he slipped his rifle back into its scabbard, got on his horse, and rode away.

The Lone Ranger was a fictional character; Reeves was not. But some of the stories told about his shooting skills made him appear larger than life. Supposedly, for example, a desperado was hiding behind the thick trunk of a large tree. It seemed impossible to dislodge him. Somehow, Reeves fired a shot that ricocheted between branches to bring down the outlaw. On another occasion he purportedly rode over a rise and saw six wolves pulling down a steer. Shooting from a moving horse, he killed all six wolves with only eight shots—it took eight shots because two of his first shots were gut shots, so he had to shoot those wolves a second time!

Perhaps because he had spent so much time living and working with Indians, Bass Reeves also was considered the best manhunter among the marshals. When he got on a man's trail, he wouldn't quit until he brought him in. At one point, Reeves was tracking an outlaw named Bob Dozier, a successful rancher who had turned to crime; he was a cattle thief and a bank robber; he held up stagecoaches and bushwhacked travelers going through the Territory; he was a con man and a fence; and it was rumored that he tortured people for information before he killed them. He had successfully eluded deputies—until Reeves picked up his scent.

Because Dozier was known to keep moving, Reeves knew it would be easier to pursue him alone or, at times, with just one posse man. Reeves chased him for months without laying eyes on him. But he wouldn't give up. When Dozier found out that the great Bass Reeves was on his trail, he sent word that if Reeves didn't stop he would be obliged to kill him. Apparently Reeves sent his own return message to the outlaw: To make that play, Dozier would have to stop running, and Reeves made it clear he would welcome that confrontation.

Reeves and his posse man pursued Dozier into the Cherokee Hills, eventually picking up fresh tracks. The outlaw was riding with one other man, and they had only a few hours' lead. A fierce lightning storm erupted, washing out the tracks, and Reeves decided to bed down. As Reeves and his posse man rode into a ravine, Dozier opened up on him. A shot whizzed right by his head. The two lawmen made for cover, successfully putting timber between themselves and the ambush. Reeves finally found a safe place behind a tree and didn't move. Several quiet minutes passed; then Reeves spotted a shadow moving between trees, trying to circle around on him. He waited. The next time that man moved, Reeves stepped out from behind the tree and fired twice, bringing down that shadow.

However, he had been forced to reveal himself, and the second outlaw opened up on him. Reeves stood upright—then fell facedown in the brush. He lay there motionless, his eyes wide open, his Colt cocked and ready. After a few minutes, the shooter stepped out from behind a tree. He waited, watching and listening. Finally he took a couple of wary steps toward the prone figure, probably assuming Reeves was dead and his posse man had fled, knowing he was no match for an experienced hand.

As the gunman came closer, Reeves was probably smiling. When Dozier was only a few yards away, Reeves suddenly raised his Colt and shouted at him to throw away his gun. Dozier dived for the good earth but he wasn't quick enough. Reeves put his first shot through the outlaw's neck. They had finally reached the end of the trail.

One man did get away from Reeves, though: the legendary Indian Ned Christie. His place in history remains unsettled: To some he was a vicious outlaw; to others he was a warrior fighting the railroads for the rights of Indians. At one point Reeves believed he had trapped Ned Christie in his impregnable cabin, so he burned it down. Christie wasn't there. Later it was reported that Christie had killed Reeves, causing the *Eufaula Indian Journal* to report in 1891, "Deputy Marshall [*sic*] Bass Reeves lacks lots of being dead as was reported recently from Muskogee to the Dallas News. He turned up Saturday from west with two wagons of prisoners going to Ft. Smith. He had twelve prisoners in all; Eight for whisky vending, three for larceny and one for murder." Christie eventually was trapped in his "mountain fort" by a sixteen-man posse and died there.

It might be that the Lone Ranger's greatest attribute was his courage. As every red-blooded American boy knew, no matter what the odds, the Lone Ranger sat tall in the saddle. The same was true of Reeves: Historians wrote that he had no fear of anything that walked the face of the earth. In the Territory, outlaws were known to post notes on trees in an area known as "the dead line," warning deputies that if they crossed that line they would be killed. Several of those notes were addressed specifically to Reeves; at his retirement, in fact, Reeves claimed to have made a nice collection of them.

It was said that Reeves never blinked, even when he was looking danger in the eye. Among the many stories admirers told to illustrate his bravery was of the day the murderous Brunter brothers got the drop on him. One of the three brothers had his pistol aimed right at Reeves's chest and ordered him off his horse. "What are you doing here?" he asked Reeves.

"Why, I've come to arrest you," Reeves replied. He then asked the date, explaining that by law he had to write down the date of the arrest on the warrant. The brothers apparently found that amusing, considering that they were holding him at gunpoint. "Here, look at this," Reeves continued, handing over the warrant to the outlaw holding the gun. As the man glanced at it, his two brothers moved closer to look at it over his shoulders—and while their attention was diverted, Reeves grabbed the barrel of the gun and pushed it away, holding on to it while the man wasted three shots. At the same time, he drew his own gun with his other hand, shot a second brother, slammed the third brother over the head with his pistol, then stuck the barrel in the first outlaw's stomach.

His career wasn't without controversy. In 1886, he was arrested for the murder of his trail cook, William Leech, and eventually tried by Judge Parker. Although Parker is remembered in history as the Hanging Judge, he was in fact respected for running a strict but fair courtroom. While it's probable that no deputy kept Parker's courtroom more crowded than Reeves, and the two men were said to be on friendly terms, this was a fair trial. In the courtroom of Judge

Judge Parker's ornate courtroom in Fort Smith, Arkansas, about 1890. When Reeves was tried for the shooting of his trail cook several years earlier, Judge Parker had presided in a courtroom located in a converted military barracks.

Isaac Parker, the law was respected. Reeves testified that his rifle had gone off accidentally while he was cleaning it, striking Leech in the neck. Initially the wound was not considered serious and Reeves immediately tried to get medical help, but eventually the cook took a turn for the worse and died. However, nine people testified against Reeves—every one of them a fugitive he had captured and was bringing to Fort Smith. They testified that there was bad blood between the two men, and that when the cook fed boiling oil to Reeves's dog, the deputy had lost his temper and shot him.

The case against Reeves pretty much fell apart when another witness testified that all those men actually had been chained in the prisoners' tent at the time of the shooting and couldn't have seen it happen. After deliberating for a full day, the jury found Reeves not guilty.

Although racism really wasn't an issue during most of Reeves's career, it ironically became important at the end of it. Judge Parker died in 1896, and two years later Reeves was transferred to Muskogee, in the Northern District of the federal court. He worked there until 1907, when Oklahoma was admitted to the Union and immediately instituted a series of harsh Jim Crow laws. Although these laws made Indians "honorary whites," they were specifically designed to keep the races apart. That made it almost impossible for a black man

Judge Isaac Parker, shortly
before his death in 1896.

After Judge Parker's death, Reeves transferred to Muskogee, in the Indian Territory, where this photo of federal marshals and local police officers was taken in about 1900.

such as Reeves to enforce the law on white people. Rather than retiring, the sixty-seven-year-old Bass Reeves joined the Muskogee police department and actually walked a beat—with the help of a cane—for two more years, until a lifetime of adventure caught up with him. He died in 1910, and as institutionalized racism became part of American culture, he was mostly lost to history. In fact, it isn't even known where he is buried.

As this country has begun recovering that history, the fact and legend of Bass Reeves has emerged. Did he serve as the model for the Lone Ranger? There is no specific evidence that he did, and the men credited with creating the character in 1933 never spoke about it. But the parallels between the real Bass Reeves and the fictional Lone Ranger are too strong to ignore. If the character was not based on Reeves, the coincidences would be almost as impossible to believe as the facts of Bass Reeves's extraordinary life.

GEORGE ARMSTRONG CUSTER

A General's Reckoning

n the hot sunny afternoon of June 25, 1876, Lieutenant Colonel George Armstrong Custer, his younger brother Tom Custer, and two other men brought their mounts to a halt atop the Crow's Nest, a bluff above the Little Bighorn River in the Montana Territory. Custer raised his binoculars and looked into the distance—and what he saw must have taken his breath away. Nestled in a valley almost fifteen miles distant was the largest Indian encampment he had ever seen. He knew immediately that he had found Sitting Bull and Crazy Horse. There was little visible activity in the village, leading Colonel Custer to believe he had caught them by surprise. That was an extraordinary bit of good luck. "We've caught them napping," he said. He immediately sent a note to Captain Frederick Benteen, an experienced officer commanding a nearby battalion. "Come on," the note read. "Big village. Be quick. Bring packs."

Custer knew he had come upon the main Cheyenne and Lakota Sioux camp. One of his scouts reportedly told him, "General, I have been with these Indians for thirty years, and this is the largest village I have ever heard of." Based on the best available intelligence, Custer assumed there would be no more than two thousand hostiles in the camp. His strategy was clear. As he had written just two years earlier in his well-received book, *My Life on the Plains*, "Indians contemplating a battle . . . are always anxious to have their women and children removed from all danger. . . . [T]heir necessary exposure in case of conflict, would operate as a powerful argument in favor of peace."

Although his force of seven hundred troopers was outnumbered, it appeared that Custer intended to apply the same strategy he had previously used with great success: He would capture the Indian women, children, and elderly and use them as hostages and human shields. If his troops could occupy the village before the Indians organized their resistance, the warriors would be forced to surrender or shoot their own people. Initially, Custer planned to wait until the following morning to launch his attack, but when he received a report that hostiles had been seen on his trail, he feared losing the advantage of surprise. He had no way of knowing that those warriors had come out of the village and were riding away when they were spotted.

Had Custer waited through that night, it is quite possible that his scouts would have discovered the truth: What he had seen through his binoculars was only one end of a massive encampment that stretched for several miles along the river. Although the actual number of warriors has never been determined, it was many thousands more than he had estimated, and they were well armed with modern weaponry.

Custer split his force into three battalions. Major Marcus Reno's second detachment was to lead the charge into the village from the south to create a diversion; then, while the hostiles rushed to meet this attack, Custer's men would come down into the valley from the hills and take hostages. The Indians would be forced to kill their own families or surrender.

At noon, Custer ordered the attack to begin. Reno's men crossed the Little Bighorn and charged—and were stunned to discover that the village was much larger than anyone had

Custer expected the Indians to flee Major Reno's diversionary attack. Instead, according to brave Flying Hawk, as seen in this illustration by Amos Bad Heart Buffalo, "The dust was thick and we could hardly see. We got right among the soldiers and killed a lot with our bows and arrows and tomahawks. Crazy Horse was ahead of all, and he killed a lot of them with his war club."

realized. Hundreds of armed warriors, rather than dispersing as Custer believed they would, instead began fighting back. Reno had led his men into a trap. His charge was halted almost a mile from the village, and the Indians counterattacked his exposed flank with a force more than five times his. Furthermore, unlike his troops, most of whom were armed with single-shot rifles, many of the Indians carried repeaters. Reno was forced to fall back into the woods, telling his men, "All those who wish to make their escape take your pistols and follow me." After holding there briefly, he led a chaotic retreat to the top of the bluff, losing about a third of his men, where he was reinforced by the three companies commanded by Captain Benteen. Their fortunate arrival may well have saved Reno's troops from annihilation, but the combined forces were pinned down for crucial minutes in that position and could not move to help Custer.

When Custer first came upon the camp, it is probable that he envisioned an illustrious future. He was already a well-known soldier and Indian fighter, having been the youngest

Two great warriors, Colonel Custer and Crazy Horse, meet in this allegorical drawing by Kills Two.

Although, according to the Cheyenne chief Two Moons, the battle at Little Bighorn
lasted only "as long as it takes for a hungry man to eat his dinner," it will forever be part of
American folklore. The chaos of those brief moments was depicted by Charles M. Russell in
his 1903 painting *The Custer Fight*.

brevet—or, temporarily appointed—brigadier general in the Union army at twenty-three years old. He had been present at Lee's surrender at Appomattox and had later toured the South with President Andrew Johnson. This final victory over Crazy Horse in the Great Sioux War would raise his status to that of an American hero. He was hard on the path to glory. Even the presidency was possible.

When Colonel Custer heard gunfire, indicating Reno's troops had engaged the Indians, he turned in his saddle to face his men. "Courage, boys!" he yelled. "We've got them. We'll finish them off and then go home to our station." He did not know that Reno's attack had failed.

Then he raised his hand in the air and began his charge into history.

Custer's men were massacred. After forcing Reno to retreat, the main contingent of Lakota and Cheyenne warriors had turned to meet Custer. They surrounded his force and tightened the ring. Every soldier was killed, 210 men, and many of their bodies mutilated. There was no one left alive to report exactly what had happened. While the native peoples told the story from their point of view, their many versions were confused and contradictory. Countless historians have investigated and written about it, but the actual details of the battle will never be fully known. "Custer's Last Stand," as this worst defeat in American military history quickly became known, has become part of American mythology. Custer himself has become a historical enigma, as often praised for his courage in giving up his life for his country as he is vilified for his impetuousness in leading his men to slaughter. His name has become synonymous with defeat, and his actions that day have been cited as the ultimate example of hubris; his ego and ambition have been blamed for the decisions that resulted in the tragic loss of so many lives. Although several books published in the aftermath of the battle portrayed him as heroic, President U. S. Grant purportedly told a reporter for the *New York Herald*, "I regard Custer's Massacre as a sacrifice of troops, brought on by Custer himself; that was wholly unnecessary—wholly unnecessary."

Was Custer at fault, as Grant believed, for splitting his forces or for engaging the enemy without sufficient intelligence? Or, as many other people believe, was he betrayed by Major Reno and Captain Benteen, who were known to dislike him and were later accused of cowardice?

There is no question that George Armstrong Custer's contributions to the victories in the Civil War and the Indian wars have been largely forgotten, and instead he is remembered almost exclusively for this devastating defeat. This is not the end that anyone would have expected.

George Custer was born in the small town of New Rumley, Ohio, in 1839. His father, a farmer and a blacksmith, belonged to the New Rumley Invincibles, the local militia, and often brought his son to their meetings. Dressed in a Daniel Boone outfit made for him by his mother, Autie (as he was called) loved the ceremony of those meetings, and by the time he was four he could execute the entire manual of arms—using a wooden stick. When war against Mexico was being debated in 1846, he stunned the corps of Invincibles by waving a small flag and declaring, "My voice for war!"

His passion for the military never wavered. Although, at that time, most of the cadets at the US Military Academy at West Point came from wealthy and well-connected families, Custer managed to convince a congressman to sponsor him for the Class of 1862. He managed to get into plenty of trouble at West Point. Each cadet was permitted 100 demerits every six months and, every six months, Cinnamon, as he was nicknamed because he would use sweet-smelling cinnamon oils on his unusually long blond hair, would manage to get close to that limit before the period ended and the clock started again. His infractions were always minor: He'd be late for supper, his long blond hair would be out of place, he'd swing his arms while marching, or he'd get into a snowball fight. His mischievous personality just couldn't conform to the strict code of conduct. In his career at the Point he compiled 726 total demerits, which still ranks as one of the worst conduct records in Academy history. He was quite popular with his classmates, though. Once, in Spanish class, he asked the instructor how to say "Class dismissed" in Spanish. When the instructor replied, everybody stood up and walked out—another incident that helped him set that record.

Unfortunately, he wasn't a good student, either. When the Civil War started in 1861, more than a third of his class dropped out to join the Confederacy. The rest of the class was graduated a year early to serve in the war—and academically he finished at the very bottom of the remaining thirty-four students. Ironically, he received his worst grades in Cavalry Tactics.

Few people would have predicted that a poor student who wouldn't follow orders would soon distinguish himself on the battlefield, but as it turned out, George Custer proved to be a natural leader, a man of great courage, who—unlike many fellow officers—always rode at the front of his force when his men charged into battle. Those other officers might have found him arrogant and vain, but no one questioned his bravery.

When he graduated, he was offered a cushy and safe assignment or the opportunity to go right into combat. He chose to go to war; when he was told they didn't have a mount for him, he managed to find his own horse. Second Lieutenant Custer joined the Second Cavalry in time to fight in the First Battle of Bull Run. He began distinguishing himself as a staff

Custer distinguished himself in battle during the Civil War, and he is shown in this 1864 engraving presenting captured battle flags to the US war department.

officer for General George McClellan during the Union army's first attempt to capture the Confederate capital, Richmond. At one point during their march south, McClellan's men were trying to find a safe place to cross the Chickahominy River, which was at flood tide. When Custer overheard General Joe Johnson complaining to his staff that he wished he knew how deep the river was, Custer, with typical bravado, spurred his horse into the middle of it, continuing even as the water rose up to his neck, then turned and announced, "This is how deep it is, General." McClellan then assigned Custer to lead four companies of the Fourth Michigan Infantry into battle. Custer's force captured fifty prisoners—and the first Rebel battle flag of the war. McClellan described Custer as "a reckless, gallant boy, undeterred by fatigue, unconscious of fear," and promoted him to the rank of captain.

Custer had learned the value of self-promotion and rarely hesitated to set himself apart from other officers. Following the example of his commander, General Alfred Pleasonton, he began wearing extravagant, customized uniforms. Cavalry captain James Kidd described him as "[a]n officer superbly mounted, who sat on his charger as if to the manor born." He wore

Known by his troops
for wearing flamboyant
uniforms, Custer posed
for this 1865 portrait in
the traditional Union
blues.

a black velvet jacket trimmed with gold lace and brass buttons, a wide-brimmed hat turned down on one side, a sword and belt, and gilt spurs on high-top boots. And around his neck was "a necktie of brilliant crimson tied in a graceful knot at the throat, the lower ends falling carelessly in front," which stood out brightly against his blond mustache and flowing blond hair.

Another officer wrote that Custer "is one of the funniest-looking beings you ever saw, and looks like a circus rider gone mad."

Custer contended that there was a good reason for his choice of uniform. "I want my men to recognize me on any part of the field," he wrote. And, given the smoke and confusion of close combat, that made a lot of sense. If initially turned off by his flamboyant style, his troops were won over by his aggressive tactics and his willingness to lead attacks. There are reports that he had as many as a dozen horses shot out from under him during the Civil War, proof that he was usually in the thick of the action. Eventually his men began wearing similar red kerchiefs as a matter of pride.

Throughout his career, however, Custer was criticized for his seemingly endless pursuit of attention and recognition. At times, he would allow reporters to go out with his men on patrols. Some people believed that need for recognition caused him to behave recklessly.

It was at Gettysburg that George Custer became nationally famous. Three days before the battle began, he was promoted to brigadier general of volunteers, a temporary rank, and given command of the newly formed Michigan Brigade. At twenty-three years old, he was the youngest general in the army, but almost immediately, he showed his grit. At Hunterstown, on the road to Gettysburg, he led a charge into the mouth of Jeb Stuart's troops. When his horse was shot and fell, he was nearly captured but was saved when a heroic private galloped forward and swooped him up, while at the same time shooting at least one Confederate soldier.

When Stuart attempted to flank the Union's lines and attack the rear, he found Custer waiting for him at a place called Two Taverns. Ordered to counterattack, Custer stood before his troops, drew his saber, shouted "Come on, you Wolverines!" and raced into the action. He was said to be a veritable demon in the heat of battle, striking ceaselessly with any weapon available to him—slashing with his sword, firing his pistol—constantly urging his men forward, always forward. Within minutes, his horse was shot, but he commandeered a bugler's horse and continued the fight. Seven hundred men clashed along a fence line, fighting for victory and their lives in close quarters. The sounds of battle were described as louder than a collision of giants; a relentless roar of men and horses, of carbines and pistols firing, of metal sabers clashing, and the cries of the wounded. And in the middle of it all was Custer. When he lost a second mount, he found another and never left the battlefield. His ability to stay in the middle of every fight without being wounded, even as one horse after the next was shot out from under him, became known far beyond his Wolverines as "Custer's Luck."

Finally Stuart withdrew; it was the first time in the war that his cavalry had been stopped. In his report, Custer wrote, "I challenge the annals of warfare to produce a more brilliant or successful charge of cavalry." There were 254 Union casualties—219 of them were Custer's men. Reporting Custer's actions at Gettysburg, the *New York Herald* called him "the boy General with his flowing yellow curls."

The public—and the newspapers—took notice. As Custer continued to distinguish himself throughout the remainder of the war, the media reported each success in increasingly larger headlines. His unusual manner of dress, his brilliant tactical maneuvers, his bravery, and the resulting victories made him great copy. Marching with General Philip Sheridan, Custer's Third Division contributed to the victory in the 1864 Valley Campaign. In the battle of Yellow Tavern he led a saber charge into Jeb Stuart's cannon, "advancing boldly," he reported, "and when within 200 yards of the battery, charged it with a yell which spread terror before them. Two pieces of cannon, two limbers . . . and a large number of prisoners were among the results of this charge." Although he did not report it, supposedly his troops moved so quickly that they captured Jeb Stuart's dinner.

Two weeks later, after the Wolverines had routed the Rebels at Haws Shop, an officer serving under Custer wrote in awe, "For all this Brigade has accomplished all praise is due to Gen. Custer. So brave a man I never saw and as competent as brave. Under him a man is ashamed to be cowardly. Under him our men can achieve wonders."

Custer's wedding in 1864 to Elizabeth Bacon, the daughter of a politically powerful judge, was a major social event attended by hundreds of prominent guests. Unlike most military wives, Libbie Custer became known for camping with her husband in the field whenever it was deemed safe, explaining years later, "It is infinitely worse to be left behind, a prey to all the horrors of imagining what may be happening to one we love."

Custer's lovely wife, Libbie, seen here with her husband (seated) and his brother Tom Custer (a two-time Medal of Honor recipient who also perished at Little Bighorn), often traveled with her husband on the frontier.

In the final battle of the Civil War, when Robert E. Lee began his retreat at Appomattox Station, Custer's division cut off his last route of escape, then captured and secured supplies that Lee's troops needed desperately. He received the first truce flag from a Confederate force. The newly appointed major general of temporary volunteers was in attendance at the Appomattox Court House when Lee offered his sword in surrender to Grant. In recognition of Custer's valor, his commander, General Sheridan, purchased the table on which the surrender document was signed and presented it as a gift to Libbie Custer.

George Custer emerged from the Civil War as a national hero, although at the conclusion of hostilities, his temporary promotion to general of the volunteers ended and he was returned to his permanent rank, once again becoming Captain Custer. Beginning with George Washington, America had rewarded victorious military leaders with political office. General U. S. Grant was already on his way to becoming president, and Custer certainly could have moved into business or politics and transformed his fame into a safe and financially secure life. Railroad and mining companies offered him jobs. He might have accepted the offer to become adjutant general of the army of Mexican president Benito Juárez, which would have put him right back in the middle of battle, this time fighting Emperor Maximilian. But the army refused to give him the year's leave he requested, meaning he would have had to resign his commission if he wanted to fight for Mexican freedom. He considered running for Congress from Michigan but decided against it, telling Libbie that the political world had surprised him. "I dare not write all that goes on underhand," he said.

When President Andrew Johnson toured the country, trying to build support for his Reconstruction policies, he brought George and Libbie Custer with him, knowing that even those who opposed him would turn out to cheer the Custers. Captain Custer's admittedly large ego was probably bursting from all the attention. He considered all the offers, but in the end, he was a soldier. He loved the challenges of leadership, he loved being with his men on a campaign, he loved the planning and the execution of strategy, but most of all he loved the taste of battle.

There was only one war left to fight. The Plains Indians were on the warpath.

Since the beginning of American westward expansion, the native tribes had been continuously pushed into smaller and smaller areas. Those tribes that had tried to fight back were eventually defeated, often at great cost. By the end of the Civil War, only a few tribes—the Sioux, Cheyennes, Arapahos, Kiowas, and Comanches—had the will and the resources to fight for their land and their traditions. The army was sent west to subdue those tribes and force them onto reservations.

This 1865 *Harper's Weekly* photograph
shows General Philip Sheridan (*second
from left*) with his generals—Wesley
Merritt, George Crook, James William
Forsyth, and George Armstrong
Custer—around a table examining a
document.

When Congress created four cavalry units to fight the Indians on the western frontier,
Custer used his political contacts to secure an appointment as lieutenant colonel of the
Seventh Cavalry. Obtaining this command had not been easy; while in Washington, he had
become involved in a complicated political situation. He had testified in a corruption hearing
against the secretary of war, angering President Grant. Generals Sherman and Sheridan had
interceded successfully on his behalf, but certainly there was additional pressure on him to
bring back some victories. As General William T. Sherman wrote, Custer "came to duty
immediately upon being appointed . . . and is ready and willing now to fight the Indians."

Custer probably discovered rather quickly that the tactics he had mastered against the
Confederacy had little value on the Great Plains. The Civil War had been fought in proper
military fashion by two great armies that stood face-to-face and battled until one side was
decimated. In that type of warfare, Custer's chosen strategy of attacking ferociously and
hitting the enemy before they were prepared for the fight often proved decisive. But the
Indians did not fight static battles. Frequently outnumbered and fighting a better-equipped
enemy, they had mastered the art of guerrilla warfare. Rather than fighting as one army with
a centralized command structure, they would travel and live in small groups. Rather than
trying to take and hold territory, raiding parties would attack isolated targets—wagon trains

or settlers, for example—then disappear. And rather than fighting a pitched battle when attacked, they would fade into the protective hills and forests.

Custer found himself chasing an elusive enemy. By the time he would be notified of an attack, homesteads would already have been burned to the ground, victims slaughtered, and the Indians long gone. Through the summer of 1867, Custer's Seventh Cavalry was reduced to providing limited security when possible, but mostly chasing ghosts. His biggest enemy turned out to be his own growing frustration and anger.

Any doubts his troops might have begun harboring about his leadership ability were reinforced one day when he spotted a herd of antelope far in the distance. He released the pack of dogs he brought along to track Indians to pursue the herd—and then suddenly took off after them. He rode so fast and so hard that he almost lost sight of his column. He was about to turn back when he saw the first buffalo he had ever laid eyes on and raced toward them. He brought his horse alongside one and ran gloriously at full speed next to this huge animal—and when he finally moved to shoot it with his pistol, the buffalo jostled him, causing him to shoot his own horse in the head. He was thrown into the dirt, but except for some bruises, he was uninjured. Only then did he realize that he was lost and alone on the vast prairie. As he would describe this incident, "How far I had traveled, or in what direction from the column, I was at a loss to know . . . I had lost all reckoning."

Once again, Custer was very lucky: Several hours later his men found him—before the Indians did.

The Indians were there; the Seventh Cavalry just couldn't find them. Instead they kept coming upon the ruins of their attacks. Although Custer had seen many men killed, wounded, and horribly disfigured during the war, this was the first time he had seen evidence of the Indians' brutality. "I discovered the bodies of the three station-keepers, so mangled and burned as to be barely recognizable as human beings. The Indians have evidently tortured them . . ." It was determined they had been killed by Sioux and Cheyennes.

Custer pushed his men hard, and they began to resent him for it. They also resented that Seventh Cavalry officers continued to eat well, while their rations included old bread and maggot-infested meat. In the heat of battle, Custer had been able to mold his troops, but in the summer heat of the plains, he was losing control. To maintain discipline he began tightening his rules. After gold was discovered in the region, thirty-five soldiers deserted and set out to seek their fortunes in the mines. In response, Custer issued a harsh and highly controversial order: Catch them and shoot them. He was reported to have said, loudly enough for all his men to hear, "Don't bring one back alive."

There were alternative punishments—military regulations also permitted him to whip or tattoo them—but he chose the harshest sentence. Three of those deserters were dealt with according to his orders; two of them died of their wounds. By the middle of the summer, his men were on the verge of mutiny. Frustrated, tired, and lonely, Custer made a rash and inexplicable decision: He took seventy-six men with him and rode to eastern Kansas to be with his wife. He deserted his command, and that mistake was compounded when, during the three-day ride, two of his men were picked off by a band of about twenty-five Indians—and still he kept going. Soon after reuniting with Libbie, he was arrested for being absent without leave and for ordering deserters shot without a trial. His court-martial lasted a month, and only a few officers—including his brother Tom—testified on his behalf. The court found him guilty as charged and suspended him from duty without pay for a year. His fall from the heights had been brutally quick; his once-promising career was shattered.

George Custer had been prepared to deal with pretty much anything—except failure. He had always been able to skirt the rules and get away with it, but not this time. He spent that year trying to rehabilitate his reputation, writing magazine articles detailing his Civil War exploits and justifying the actions for which he had been suspended.

Meanwhile, the Indians grew bolder. During the summer of 1868, for example, they killed 110 settlers, raped thirteen women, and stole more than a thousand head of cattle. General Sheridan was made commander of the Department of Missouri, a huge area encompassing parts of six future states and the Indian Territory. At his request, Custer's suspension was ended several months early and he was given orders to "march my command in search of the winter hiding places of the hostile Indians, and wherever found to administer such punishment for past deprecations as my force was able to." He was ordered to "destroy their villages and ponies, to kill or hang all warriors, and bring back the women and children."

Custer was extremely pleased to be recalled, and he had every intention of fulfilling those orders. He knew his career depended on it. On November 26, 1868, Colonel Custer's scouts located a large Cheyenne village near the Washita River in what is now Oklahoma. The Indians had camped there for the winter. Fearful that his presence would be discovered, Custer decided not to wait for his scouts to gather intelligence. Instead, he planned his attack. Had he waited, he would have learned that the people in this village had nothing to do with attacks on settlers: This was a peaceful camp located on reservation land, where they had settled after the government guaranteed their safety to the chief Black Kettle. A white flag actually was flying from a large teepee, further evidence that this tribe had given up the fight.

Custer also would have discovered this was simply the westernmost village of a huge

Indian camp stretching more than ten miles along the river. In addition to the estimated 250 people in this village, more than six thousand native people from many tribes had made camp there for the winter.

But even that knowledge might not have discouraged his attack. His determination was so strong that when an aide wondered aloud if there might be more Indians in the camp than was believed, Custer replied firmly, "All I'm afraid of is we won't find enough. There aren't enough Indians in the world to defeat the Seventh Cavalry."

Custer's reputation as an Indian fighter was established in his 1868 attack on a large Cheyenne village on the Washita River, where he first employed the tactics that would doom his troops on the Little Bighorn.

He divided his 720 men into four elements and, at dawn, attacked from four positions. The signal to attack was the unit band striking up the song "Garry Owens." The unprepared Cheyennes were unable to mount any kind of defense and instead dispersed into the surrounding hills and foliage. The chief, Black Kettle, and his wife were killed in the first moments of the fighting. While Custer later reported killing 103 Cheyennes, that figure is generally accepted to be greatly exaggerated, with the actual number being closer to fifty. But that number included many noncombatants—women and even children. The Seventh Cavalry also took fifty-three hostages, who were put on horses and dispersed among the troops. But in the midst of the battle, several warriors reached their horses and escaped. Major Joel Elliott, Custer's second in command, took seventeen men and raced downstream in pursuit.

As the battle raged, Custer must have been stunned when he looked up at the top of the rise and saw as many as a thousand warriors "armed and caparisoned in full war costume" looking down upon his force. "[T]his seemed inexplicable," he wrote later. "Who could these new parties be, and from whence came they?" It was only after the battle that he learned the true size of the camp. However, his desperate strategy had been successful—it would have been impossible for those warriors to attack without risking the lives of the hostages. Custer feigned an advance, and rather than engaging him, the Indians dispersed.

Fully aware that he was outnumbered, Custer waited for nightfall and then ordered his troops to burn the village to the ground, destroy the herd of horses, and withdraw—without waiting for Major Elliott and his men to return or sending out scouts to find him. Many of his men considered leaving troops behind on the battlefield an unpardonable sin, among them Elliott's close friend, H Company captain Frederick Benteen. Custer claimed that he had ordered the withdrawal to prevent additional casualties and that he was confident that Elliott would return on his own.

Elliott and all his men seemed to have disappeared. Two weeks after the battle, Custer returned to the river with a large force, and, as he described, "We suddenly came upon the stark, stiff, naked and horribly mutilated bodies of our dead comrades. . . . Undoubtedly numbered more than one hundred to one, Elliott dismounted his men, tied their horses together and prepared to sell their lives as dearly as possible. . . . The bodies of Elliott and his band . . . were found lying within a circle not exceeding twenty yards." Major Elliott's force had been wiped out, apparently in a single charge.

Although it would have been impossible for Custer to know it, as he bent over the bodies of his men, he was looking at his own future.

Despite this loss, the media celebrated the battle of Washita as the first major victory of this frustrating campaign, helping to at least partially restore Custer's tarnished reputation. He became known as a great Indian fighter. And his innovative strategy of taking hostages to prevent Indian counterattacks was replicated successfully by other commanders. At the battle of North Fork three years later, the 284 men of Colonel Ranald Mackenzie's Fourth Cavalry defeated 500 Comanche warriors by taking 130 women and children to shield their withdrawal and used those hostages to force the tribe to return to the reservation and release its white prisoners.

But there were rumblings of dissent. As the public learned the details of the attack on a peaceful tribe, some insisted that it was a massacre of innocents rather than a great victory. Then *The New York Times* published an anonymous letter accusing Custer of abandoning Elliott's men in the field. The irate Custer responded by meeting with his officers and demanding to know who had written it, threatening to horsewhip that person. However, when Captain Benteen stepped forward and admitted it was his work, Custer backed off, although clearly from that point forward there was bitterness between the two officers.

To protect himself from further criticism, Custer surrounded himself with family members, close friends, and proven supporters, including his brother Tom—a two-time Medal of Honor winner—his brother Boston, and his brother-in-law James Calhoun.

Soldiers are prone to dehumanize the enemy during wartime, but Custer's feelings about the Indians were ambivalent. On one hand, he wrote that hunting buffalo was as exciting as hunting Indians. On the other, he showed great sympathy for the tribes in his book, even suggesting that if he had been treated as unfairly as the government had dealt with the Indians, he might have rebelled, too. Earlier in his life he had learned sign language to teach deaf children and had also studied Spanish at West Point, which made him one of the few officers able to communicate with the Plains Indians in the sign-language Spanish that the tribes used. And finally, there are accounts that he had a long-term relationship with an Indian woman named Spring Grass, who had been taken as a hostage at the Washita River. She was "an exceedingly comely squaw," he wrote, "possessing a bright cheery face [and] a countenance beaming with intelligence." According to Captain Benteen, Custer shared his tent with her both in camp and during his campaigns, when she served as a translator. Spring Grass eventually bore two children, although rumors hinted strongly that their father was Tom Custer, because George Custer suffered from gonorrhea contracted during his time at West Point.

The army's inability to gain control over all the tribes eventually led to a change in strategy. Rather than capturing the Indians, the army would destroy their source of food—the Plains buffalo. The government planned to starve the Indians onto reservations. Unlike the Indians,

The ambitious George Custer clearly understood the value of publicity, often allowing reporters to ride with his troops. This portrait seems to illustrate the no-nonsense attitude that caused him to reject a cautious approach when his scouts discovered the encampment at Little Bighorn.

buffalo were a very easy target. It is estimated that more than four and a half million buffalo were killed by 1872.

Colonel Custer remained a valuable public-relations tool for the government during this period. When Grand Duke Alexis of Russia wanted to tour the West and see wild Indians, for example, Custer and Buffalo Bill Cody were assigned to make all the arrangements. To ensure the grand duke's safety, Custer supposedly recruited some reservation Indians to "attack" the train, with all the requisite whooping and hollering. Before this event began, these Indians were given a considerable amount of beer; so much beer, in fact, that those show Indians got carried away and seemed to actually be attacking the train. Alexis was so convinced the attack was real that he had to be restrained from shooting at them.

To an ambitious man like Custer, who lived for the battle—and for the acclaim that came with victory—these assignments must have been terribly boring. But Custer's Luck held once again—and he managed to turn a mundane task into career gold: The military was needed to protect the men who were building America's railroads as they expanded into Indian lands. In 1873, the Northern Pacific approached the Black Hills, the sacred lands promised to the Sioux forever in the Fort Laramie treaty of 1868. That expansion came to an unexpected halt when the company went bankrupt, taking with it numerous other businesses and precipitating the Panic of 1873, the worst economic crisis in the early history of America. Unemployment skyrocketed and the government became desperate to find new sources of revenue. For several years, there had been rumors of vast gold deposits in the Black Hills—exactly what was needed to restore the failing economy. On July 2, 1874, Custer led a thousand troops out of Fort Rice on the Missouri River into the Black Hills to protect the surveyors searching for gold.

Naturally, accompanying this expedition were eager young newspapermen from New York and Philadelphia anxious to report the news of a new American gold rush—and to bestow the proper credit on the stalwart Colonel Custer, who was leading the way into the future.

On July 27, the first strike was reported on French Creek. In what can accurately be described as a masterstroke of public relations, somehow George Custer, a military officer who had never touched a shovel, managed to receive at least partial credit for the gold strike. Within days, the *Bismarck Tribune* reported, "Gold in the Grass Roots and in Every Panful of Earth Below: Anybody Can Find It—No Former Experience Necessary."

For Custer, the timing seemed perfect: Within months, his colorful autobiography, *My Life on the Plains*, was published. This supposedly true tale of the adventures of a fighting man on the frontier sold well and was met with critical acclaim, going a long way toward restoring his image. Only those who were with him during those times knew the truth, and the increasingly bitter Benteen suggested the book might more accurately be titled *My Lie on the Plains*.

Within a year, more than fifteen thousand miners raced west to the Black Hills to find their fortunes. Initially, the government attempted to lease or even buy this land from the Sioux, but the tribe rejected every offer. There was no price for sacred land. Fighting for the last part of their traditional lands that they still held, bands of Sioux warriors began attacking prospectors. The government ordered the Sioux to return to their reservation within sixty days, warning that if they resisted, force would be brought against them. When the Indians refused, General Sheridan ordered three battalions—one of them Custer's Seventh Cavalry—to find and surround the Indian camps and round them up—or wipe them out.

For the Indian fighter George Custer, this was an opportunity to get back in the saddle and ride to what he must have believed would be the greatest victory of his career. He was so confident, that when he was offered additional troops and two Gatling guns—essentially machine guns and the most fearsome weapon on the Plains—he turned them down, believing those weapons weren't needed and would only slow down his advance. The possibility that his mostly inexperienced and undertrained troops might be outnumbered did not shake him; the Plains Indians had never defeated a force the size of his Seventh Cavalry.

Custer simply did not appreciate the determination of the tribes camped on the banks of the Little Bighorn River. This was not only a battle for their sacred land, but their last chance to protect their way of life. Freedom to roam the plains was being taken from them. They weren't fighting for something; they were fighting for everything. Sitting Bull was their great chief, which meant he was in charge of the civil affairs, including all negotiations with the United States government, but when the fighting began, Crazy Horse was in command. Crazy Horse was himself a great warrior, a veteran of many indigenous battles, and an excellent tactician. He is credited with devising some of the basic strategies of guerrilla warfare on which special operations are still based. And in his daring and bravery, he was at least the equal of Custer.

Both sides seemed to know this battle was coming. As Custer prepared to mount up and leave, Libbie had a nightmare that he would die in battle and be scalped, so she pleaded with him to cut his long golden hair. To please her, he did. And during a sacred ceremony, a Sun Dance, Sitting Bull too had a vision: He had seen soldiers and their horses falling upside down from the sky like grasshoppers into his camp. This, he told his people, meant there would be a great victory.

Historians also wonder about one additional premonition: The night before the battle, Custer supposedly ordered his men to finish their whiskey rations, perhaps trying to help his raw troops find their courage; or, as some have suggested, he knew what was waiting for him.

There is no question that when planning his attack, Custer drew on his success at the Washita River. He divided his forces into three components; he commanded the largest force, while Major Reno and Captain Benteen were in charge of smaller units. He might not have liked Benteen, but obviously he thought him a capable officer. Reno was ordered to charge into the village, presumably to create the diversion that would allow Custer to take hostages. Custer and Reno anticipated that the Indians would flee when attacked, as they had done previously; this was a grievous miscalculation. The warriors so outnumbered Reno's troops that rather than flee, they initiated their own counterattack, trapping Reno.

Custer had dressed in a white buckskin suit with a bright red tie around his neck for the battle. As Reno's troops swept down on the camp, Custer waved his gray hat at him in approval. But by the time Reno's advance had been stopped and his troops were in retreat, Custer was moving along the ridgeline to launch his own attack and was not aware of what was happening.

After Benteen received Custer's message, "Come quick," he moved forward with his supply train, but when he reached the battlefield, the besieged Reno ordered him to stay there

Custer often wore a fringed white buckskin jacket, like this one in the Smithsonian, reportedly so that his troops could easily identify him during a battle.

 CUSTER'S LAST FIGHT.

The Original Painting has been Presented to the Seventh Regiment U.S. Cavalry

BY **ANHEUSER BUSCH BREWING ASSOCIATION,**

Although the massacre shocked the nation in the midst of its centennial celebration, by 1889, Custer's heroic last fight was being celebrated in one of the very first beer advertisements, a colored lithograph that hung in saloons throughout the country and helped create the enduring image of the brave soldiers. Many of the details are wrong. The original painting, donated to the Seventh Cavalry, was destroyed in a barracks fire.

and reinforce his troops. The appearance of these reinforcements forced the native warriors to cease their attack. But rather than trying to ascertain Custer's situation and perhaps provide the timely assistance that might have saved him, Reno and Benteen remained in their defensive position much too long. Late in the battle, an officer in Reno's command, Captain Weir, insisted that they find Custer. When Reno refused, Weir took the initiative and led his company toward Custer's position. Far away in the swirling dust he saw riders and got ready to attack—and then he realized that all those riders were Indians and they were riding in a circle, shooting at the ground. Reno and Benteen had followed Weir, but when they discovered it was too late, they retreated to their defensive position and fought it out for the rest of the day.

It will never be known whether Custer fully understood Reno's predicament. But at some point, he must have realized that his only hope of victory lay in taking sufficient hostages to force the warriors to lay down their weapons. When it became apparent that Sioux warriors blocked his path, it was no longer a matter of victory—he was fighting for survival. He retreated up the slope, trying to reach high ground. There was no cover for his troops, so he ordered them to kill their horses to provide some defense. But it was hopeless. His soldiers were rapidly overwhelmed by a massive force attacking with guns, arrows, clubs, and lances. Custer was shot in his breast, and then in his temple, the second shot killing him.

In about twenty minutes, all 225 of Custer's men were dead. Sitting Bull supposedly once told an interviewer that Custer laughed in the last moment of his life, although that's doubtful, because evidence indicates that the Indians were not even aware that Custer was among the dead. In addition to George Custer, his brothers Tom and Boston and his nephew Henry Reed died on what has become known as Last Stand Hill. An Associated Press reporter sent to cover Custer's victory was the first AP reporter to die in combat. His notes were found on his body, concluding, "I go with Custer and will be at the death."

The nation, celebrating its centennial, was stunned and shaken by the unexpected news of Custer's Last Stand. It was said that America's heart was broken. The day after the battle, the Indians packed up their camp and began moving. But this great victory soon proved to be the last major battle of the Indian wars: The defeat caused the army to increase its efforts to subdue the tribes, and within five years, almost all Sioux and Cheyennes would be settled on reservations.

The nation replayed the battle of Little Bighorn for many years, trying to understand how one of its most brilliant leaders had been so brutally slaughtered. Benteen was criticized for reinforcing Reno rather than Custer, and people wondered if the animosity between the two men had played any role in his decision. But, in fact, he had little choice: Reno was his commanding officer and had ordered him to stay. Reno himself was accused of both cowardice

Painted only six years after the battle, this lithograph already demonstrates
the esteem with which the heroic Custer, standing taller than all his men, a
pistol in one hand and a sword in the other, was being portrayed.

and drunkenness at Little Bighorn. He demanded a court of inquiry be convened; while it
did not sustain the charges, it also offered no rebuttals to the claims made against him. But
as William Taylor, a soldier who served at Little Bighorn under Reno, later wrote bitterly,
"Reno proved incompetent and Benteen showed his indifference—I will not use the uglier
words that have often been in my mind. Both failed Custer and he had to fight it out alone."

Did General Custer's hubris cause him to underestimate his enemy and lead his men into
a massacre? Although no one ever questioned George Custer's bravery, military historians
have been critical of Custer's tactical decisions, from his initial refusal to accept additional
men and weapons to his choice to split up his already outnumbered force and attack without
sufficient intelligence.

Years earlier, Custer had written, "My every thought was ambitious. I desired to link
my name with acts and men, and in such a manner as to be a mark of honor, not only to
the present but to future generations." Although he achieved his aim to be remembered in
history, it is not as he had hoped, because the name George Armstrong Custer will always be
associated with one of the most devastating defeats in American history.

THE REALITY OF AN "INDIAN SUMMER"

Few things are as welcome as an Indian summer, that sudden and unexpected change in the fall weather after the first frost that brings a brief return to the balmy temperatures of summer. But originally, rather than being welcomed, the possibility of an Indian summer was absolutely

Unlike the mood depicted in this pastoral watercolor of Indians camping outside Fort Laramie in about 1860, the early settlers lived in terror of Indian raids.

MASSACRE OF SETTLERS.

When the early settlers tried to bring European values to the Native Americans, the Indians resisted. The first recorded Indian attack took place in March 1622, when Powhatans killed 347 men, women, and children in Jamestown in their houses and fields.

terrifying. In the early days of the West, the fear of Indian raids forced settlers to live together in walled forts from spring through the early fall. At the first frost, the Indians would pack up, leave their villages, and move to their winter camping grounds. When they were gone, the settlers would return to their homesteads and make preparations for the winter. For those settlers, after spending months in crowded, confined surroundings, it was like being released from prison. They actually looked forward to the cold of winter.

But as sometimes happened, the weather would turn once again, bringing back the warm sun to melt the snows—and with it would come the Indians. "Indian summer" meant Indian attack. As Henry Howe wrote, "The melting of the snow saddened every countenance and the general warmth of the sun filled every heart with horror. The apprehension of another visit from the Indians, and being driven back to the detested fort, was painful in the highest degree."

But as the country grew and the Indians were forced onto reservations, these fears diminished, and over time the term evolved to refer solely to the delightful change in the weather, as it does today.

BUFFALO BILL AND

AND

ANNIE OAKLEY

The Radical Opportunists

The Deadwood stage was bouncing over rough terrain, trying to make time. Inside the coach, five very important men were holding on to the straps for dear life. Up on the box, the driver and shotgun were nervously craning their necks, scanning the horizon for any sign of trouble. They'd heard tell that Indians had been seen in these parts and feared an attack. The driver whipped his team, trying to coax a little more speed out of them—and then they heard the first terrible cry.

Indians were closing in fast from both sides, screaming their blood-curdling war whoops, firing their weapons, and waving their war lances as they raced in for the kill. The driver whipped his team again. The guard turned in his seat and counted six pursuers. He let loose with his first volley, knocking one of the attackers right out of his saddle. The coach was bouncing crazily over the hard ground. "Hold tight," the driver shouted to his passengers, "and keep your heads down!"

The Indians were shooting back; the driver hunched low in his seat. The guard had reloaded and fired again. A second attacker went sprawling. For a few seconds, the Indians seemed to be closing the gap, but by then the stage was up to full speed, spewing clouds of dust. The driver whipped his horses again and again. With one last *Hey-yaa!* from the driver, the stage pulled away. The Indians pulled up short. One of them angrily stabbed his long lance into the ground, and then they turned and trotted back from where they had come, leaving the banners on the lance ruffling in the wind.

After a few seconds of silence, all twenty thousand people in the audience began cheering. The driver, Buffalo Bill, spun the stagecoach around, creating a dust devil, and brought it to a stop directly in front of the grandstand. He hopped down and opened the door, and the king of Denmark, the king of Belgium, the king of Greece, and the king of Saxony—all in London to celebrate Queen Victoria's jubilee—climbed out to the loud hurrahs of the audience and waved, and then a mighty roar erupted as the future king, Edward, Prince of Wales, emerged. When the cheering stopped, he said to Bill Cody, in a voice loud enough for all to hear, "Colonel, you never held four kings like these before, have you?"

For more than three decades, Buffalo Bill's Wild West shows thrilled America and Europe, as seen in this 1907 reenactment of a battle from the Indian wars.

Buffalo Bill responded, just as loudly, "I've held four kings, but four kings and the Prince of Wales makes a royal flush such as no man has ever held before!" And with a great wave of his hat, Bill Cody ended the show.

Some courageous men explored and settled the West, and other brave settlers fought the Native American warriors for the right to live there, but William "Buffalo Bill" Cody, with important assistance from Annie Oakley, Sitting Bull, and Geronimo, successfully merchandised it. For three decades, Buffalo Bill Cody's *Wild West* brought the spirit and the adventure of life on the frontier to audiences around the world, successfully creating the romantic, rip-roaring image of the Old West that persists to this day. Presidents, kings, Queen Victoria, and Pope Leo XIII were all captivated by the action-packed performance.

In addition to the Indian attack on the Deadwood stage—and Cody actually had purchased the old Deadwood stage for this scene—the show included, among many other en-

The attempted robbery of the original Deadwood stage was a highlight of the show, and Cody would invite local dignitaries to participate as passengers.

tertainments, pioneers defending their homestead against an Indian attack; a stage or train robbery; Indians attacking a wagon train; races between Pony Express riders and between an Indian on foot and a pony; buffalo hunting; displays of roping and riding, bulldogging and sharpshooting; and even a sad reenactment of General Custer's Last Stand. Buffalo Bill and his cast of hundreds of "authentic Red Indians" brought the Old West to life for tens of thousands of people and, in so doing, made himself the most famous American in the whole world.

While most people loved the show, few of them ever wondered how accurate it was—or whether Buffalo Bill and Annie Oakley had ever played a real role in the Old West. Were those two legendary figures true survivors of a time gone by, or were they simply entertainers earning a fine living from the exploitation of a myth? Ironically, Buffalo Bill Cody is probably remembered more for the amazing shows he created than for his very real accomplishments riding the ranges of the West.

After a parade down Fifth Avenue, the *Wild West Show* settled into Madison Square Garden for the winter of 1886. As more than five thousand spectators—including General Sherman—watched on opening night, "One big bull elk forgot his cue, [and] sauntered slowly down the arena, inspecting the pretty girls in the boxes with critical stares and gazing at the rest of the spectators in a tired way."

William Cody was born in rural Iowa in 1846 to educated parents. When he was seven years old, Isaac and Mary Ann Cody sold their farm and moved to Fort Leavenworth, Kansas, arriving in the middle of the raging debate over slavery. In that part of the state, Isaac Cody's antislavery sentiments were not popular, and eventually he was stabbed while giving an impassioned speech. He died a few years later while trying to bring antislavery settlers from Ohio into the state, leaving his family close to ruin. To support them, young Bill Cody took an assortment of jobs, including "boy extra" on wagon trains, teamster, bull whacker on cattle drives, and, finally, army scout. How he developed his renowned tracking and shooting skills isn't known.

As he wrote in his autobiography, *Buffalo Bill's Own Story*, his first encounter with Indians occurred while he was scouting for the army. Soldiers were trying to quash a threatened Mormon rebellion in Salt Lake City. "Presently the moon rose," he wrote, "dead ahead of me; and painted boldly across its face was the figure of an Indian. He wore this war-bonnet of the Sioux, at his shoulder was a rifle pointed at someone in the river-bottom 30 feet below; in another second he would drop one of my friends. I raised my old muzzle-loader and fired. The figure collapsed, tumbled down the bank and landed with a splash in the water. . . . So began my career as an Indian fighter."

Almost as if in preparation for the spectacular shows he would eventually produce, Cody had a range of real-life experiences in most of the situations his performers would later replicate. When out trapping with a friend, he had slipped and broken his leg; his friend left to get help to bring him home, and Cody was discovered by a band of Indians, who spared his life only because he was just a "papoose," as he heard them describe him, and because he had previously met their leader, Chief Rain-in-the-Face. On another hunt, he ran across a band of murderous outlaws and was forced to shoot one of them to make his escape.

Bill Cody was only thirteen years old when he headed west to mine for gold but instead signed on with the Pony Express. After building and tending stations, he became one of the youngest riders on that trail—or, as he later would portray it, a lone figure dashing across the stormy prairies carrying the mail! In his autobiography, he claimed to have made the longest Pony Express journey ever, 322 miles round-trip. He also recalled, "Being jumped by a band of Sioux Indians . . . but it fortunately happened I was mounted on the fleetest horse belonging to the Express company. . . . Being cut off from retreat back to Horse Shoe, I put spurs to my horse, and lying flat on his back, kept straight for Sweetwater."

It was while working as a rider that he began to gain fame as an Indian fighter. At one point, the Indians had become so troublesome that all service had to stop, so Cody joined Wild Bill Hickok and twenty or more other men to look for a horse herd that had been stolen. They found the Indians, who had "never before been followed into their own country by white men," camped by a river. Led by Hickok, they attacked, capturing not just their own horses but more than a hundred Indian ponies.

How many of these tales told by Cody in his bestselling autobiography are accurate will never be known, because so much is impossible to verify. But when it was originally published in 1879, his biographers believed that most of it was true, and none of the people he depicted ever contradicted his version of events.

At the beginning of the Civil War, he rode with Chandler's Jayhawkers, an abolitionist militia that he joined happily to "retaliate upon the Missourians for the brutal manner in which they had treated and robbed my family." He awoke one day and found himself enlisted in the Seventh Kansas Cavalry, although he claimed no memory of exactly how that happened. His most notable service was acting as a courier for Hickok, who was operating as a spy within the Confederate army, gathering important intelligence that affected the battles in Missouri.

After the war, Bill Cody continued scouting for the army, serving in '67 as a guide for Brevet Major General George Custer, and later fighting the Plains tribes himself in many death-defying encounters. During this tour of duty, he took part in sixteen battles, including the 1869 fight against the Cheyennes at Summit Springs, Colorado. He fancied himself an expert Indian fighter, and in his autobiography he sometimes described braves he had killed as "good Indians." The irony of that statement would be evident several years later. As his fame spread on the Plains, the army assigned him to work with Custer, guiding wealthy dignitaries on western hunting expeditions, mostly Europeans such as Grand Duke Alexis of Russia, who wanted the excitement of seeing a real wild Indian. For his service, in 1872 he became one of only four civilian scouts ever awarded the Medal of Honor, which, although not yet the rarely awarded medal it would become, was even then held in great esteem and given only to those who served with honor and valor.

In the late 1860s, he took up a challenge from a renowned scout and buffalo hunter named Billy Comstock to see which of them could kill the most buffalo in eight hours. This was another area of his expertise: In addition to scouting, he earned his living supplying buffalo to feed the crews building the Kansas Pacific Railway—a lot of buffalo. He once claimed he'd killed 4,280 head in seventeen months. The wager with Comstock was five hundred dollars. More than a hundred spectators turned out to see the contest. Using Lucretia, as he affectionately named his breech-loading Springfield rifle, he killed 69 to Comstock's 46 and, in addition to winning the bet, became known from that day forward as the one and only Buffalo Bill.

By the time he had acquired that nickname, a young woman named Phoebe Ann Cates was already astounding people with her uncanny marksmanship. Born in a rural Ohio cabin in 1860, she often said, "I was eight years old when I made my first shot," describing shooting a squirrel in the head to preserve its meat for the stew pot. At the time, ladies of any age were not known for their marksmanship; in fact, most of them didn't even shoot guns. Although "Annie" apparently could perform all the standard "womanly" tasks, such as cooking, sewing, and embroidering, she also could outshoot pretty much any man. As a teenager, she supported her family by selling game she had hunted and trapped to local hotels and restaurants, and she claimed she had earned enough to pay off the mortgage on the family farm.

While she was still a very young woman, one of her regular customers, enterprising Cincinnati hotel owner Jack Frost, arranged a one-hundred-dollar betting match between Frank E. Butler, the star and owner of the Baughman & Butler traveling marksmen show, and five-foot-tall Annie Cates. Through twenty-four rounds of live-bird trapshooting, they matched each other shot for shot, but after he missed his twenty-fifth shot, she successfully hit the bird and won the match. Rather than being upset about losing to a young girl, Frank Butler

Annie Oakley at work in 1892

fell in love with her. Within a year, she had become the star of Butler's show and, at some point soon after, also became his wife. Their marriage lasted fifty years. It's generally accepted that she adopted the name Oakley from the Cincinnati neighborhood in which they briefly lived.

Frank Butler understood the appeal of a small, lovely, and very feminine woman who could outshoot any he-man who challenged her, and he essentially retired to manage her career. Billing her as "Little Sure Shot," he promoted her as the sharpest shooter in the world, "the peerless wing and rifle shot"—and routinely risked his life to prove it: Holding a lit cigarette between his lips, he would let her shoot it out of his mouth. Using a rifle, a shotgun, and a handgun, she could extinguish a candle at thirty paces, split a playing card facing her sideways from ninety feet away, hit dimes tossed into the air, and riddle dropped playing cards with numerous shots before they hit the ground.

For several years, they toured the new vaudeville circuit in an act that included their dog, who sat patiently and still and allowed Annie to shoot an apple off his head. In 1885, she accepted an offer to join the new *Buffalo Bill's Wild West* extravaganza, and within a year had become the second most popular performer in the show, second only to Buffalo Bill himself.

Although popular fiction plots of the day often turned on fortuitous and unexpected meetings, such was exactly the case when Bill Cody met Edward Judson in 1869. Cody had been ordered to scout for an expedition hunting a band of Sioux that had attacked Union Pacific workers near O'Fallon's Station in Nebraska and was told Judson would be riding along. Judson turned out to be an extraordinarily eccentric character, at the time becoming quite famous under the pseudonym Ned Buntline. Buntline was a writer, journalist, and publicist, a man known for delivering passionate temperance lectures—after which he would often go out and celebrate by getting drunk. It was Buntline who introduced Bill Cody to the art of selling the West and introduced Buffalo Bill to the world. Buntline understood that Americans were thrilled by the hair-raising stories of cowboys and Indians in the Old West and set out to profit from it. After meeting Cody and hearing his stories, Buntline wrote an adventure serial for Street and Smith's *New York Weekly* entitled "Buffalo Bill, the King of the Border Men." The popularity of that story convinced Buntline to write and publish the first of dozens of dime novels featuring Cody's exploits: *Buffalo Bill, The Scouts of the Plains; or, Red Deviltry as It Is*. These action-packed adventure stories of a heroic Buffalo Bill defending his life and his honor against the most evil villains of the West became tremendously popular, turning Cody into a national hero. Taking advantage of this fame, Buntline convinced Cody to star in a rousing play he had written and was producing entitled *The Scouts of the Plains*. "There's money in it," Cody reported being told by Buntline, "and you will prove a big card, as your character is a novelty on stage."

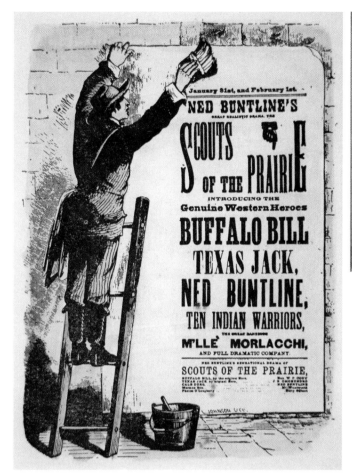

Ned Buntline's 1872 show set the stage for the creation of the western myth. Although the Chicago *Times* called it a "combination of incongruous drama, execrable acting, renowned performers, mixed audience, intolerable stench, scalping, blood and thunder," audiences loved it.

Cody decided, "A fortune is what we're after, and we'll at least give the wheel a turn or two to see what luck we have." Starring Cody, Texas Jack Omohundro, a young Italian actress playing an Indian maiden, and eventually Wild Bill Hickok, the play toured eastern cities for years. As Cody described it, "[T]here were between forty and fifty 'supers' dressed as Indians. . . . We blazed away at each other with blank cartridges . . . We would kill them all off in one act, but they would come up again ready for business in the next."

What the play lacked in dramatic conventions, it made up for in exuberance. "An extraordinary production," wrote the *Boston Journal*, "with more wild Indians, scalping knives

Buffalo Bill was already America's first matinee idol when he added to his legend by killing Cheyenne chief Yellow Hair and claiming, "The first scalp for Custer!"

and gun powder to the square inch than any drama ever before heard of." The *Norfolk Journal* reported that "one of the largest audiences ever assembled within [Opera House] walls" saw "the crowning piece of the night . . . which excited juveniles to the wildest demonstrations of delight . . . whenever Texas Jack and Buffalo Bill appeared on stage the audience cheered . . ."

A different type of entertainment apparently was taking place backstage as men accustomed to a rougher type of living adjusted to show business. There were stories of all-night card games, brawls, wrecked furniture, and the occasional arrest. But for Cody, the lines between reality and theater truly became blurred when the army called him into service to scout for the Fifth Cavalry in the Sioux Wars after his friend, Colonel George Custer, was killed and his troops massacred at Little Bighorn.

A legendary story Bill Cody told in his memoirs perfectly illustrated how he straddled the line between real life and entertainment: By mid-July 1876, the Fifth Cavalry had been chasing the Cheyennes for more than a week, intent on avenging Custer's death. When Cody awoke on the morning of July 17, he sensed there would be a fight that day. So he dressed for the battle carefully, putting on the scouting costume he wore in Buntline's show: a red silk shirt with billowing sleeves and decorative silver buttons, flared black pants with gold cross braiding embroidered on the thighs and held in place by a broad leather belt with a large rectangular metal buckle, a well-worn leather vest, comfortable boots, and a sombrero-like brown hat with the brim pushed up in front.

At daybreak, the Fifth Cavalry finally spotted the Cheyennes, who were getting ready to attack two couriers. Cody led fifteen men to cut them off. Then the Indian chief, who later was identified as Yellow Hair, "sang out to me, in his own tongue, 'I know you Pa-he-haska; if you want to fight, come ahead and fight me.'" They raced toward each other; the chief's shot missed, but Cody's shot struck the Indian's horse and it went down. An instant later, Cody's horse stepped in a gopher hole and stumbled. Cody fell off but scrambled to his feet; he was about twenty paces from the chief. They fired again: "My usual luck did not desert me on this occasion, for his bullet missed me, while mine struck him in the breast." Cody was on top of him in an instant: "Jerking his war bonnet off, I scientifically scalped him in about five seconds. . . . I swung the Indian chieftain's top-knot and bonnet in the air and shouted—'The first scalp for Custer!'"

How much of what he wrote was accurate and how much was entertainment has been debated almost since that time, although there is no doubt that Chief Yellow Hair was killed in that battle. What also became clear is that Buffalo Bill Cody had successfully made the transition from performance to performer. And when the two overlapped, it was even better.

Naturally, when Cody returned to the stage at the end of that campaign, this scene was incorporated into a show entitled *Buffalo Bill's First Scalp for Custer*. That show, as Cody admitted, "[a]fforded us ample opportunity to give a noisy, rattling, gunpowder entertainment, and to present a succession of scenes in the late Indian war."

For Cody, this brought a whole new meaning to the western concept of being "on a stage." After becoming comfortable in front of audiences, Cody struck off on his own, organizing "dramatic combinations," as he referred to them, while also appearing on the vaudeville circuit to spread the legend of Buffalo Bill. These shows often introduced genuine frontier characters such as Wild Bill Hickok to the stage, as well as real Indians in their actual war bonnets, fancy shooting and roping, and even some horse tricks. There was no shortage anywhere in the country of people wanting to experience even a small taste of Old West authenticity, and his stage shows proved very successful.

In 1883, Buffalo Bill decided to create a new type of entertainment, a Wild West show that would be bigger and more action-packed than anything anyone had previously done. As he later remembered, "I conceived the idea of organizing a large company of Indians, cowboys, Mexican vaqueros, famous riders and expert lasso throwers, with accessories of stage coach, emigrant wagons, bucking horses and a herd of buffalos, with which to give a realistic entertainment of wild life on the plains." It would be more like a circus than a play, performed outdoors with many individual scenes and exhibitions rather than following a single story line. It was to be a highly stylized dramatization of the settling of the West.

The first such extravaganza was presented as part of a Fourth of July celebration in North Platte, Nebraska, entitled *Wild West, Rocky Mountain and Prairie Exhibition*. The success of that event led him to create *Buffalo Bill's Wild West*. The three-hour-long show thrilled audiences, and Cody proved to be quite a creative showman. He tried for three years to hire his former adversary, the great Sioux chief Sitting Bull. Initially the government refused to allow it, insisting that the Sioux stay on the Pine Ridge reservation rather than "visiting places where they would naturally come in contact with evil associates and degrading immoralities." Finally, the secretary of the interior approved the request in 1885. Less than a decade after defeating Custer at Little Bighorn, Sitting Bull would endure being taunted and booed by the same audiences that also paid him well to sign photographs of himself afterward.

That was the same year that Annie Oakley joined the troupe, performing tricks such as sighting a target in a mirror and shooting over her shoulder. Although by this time there were other female sharpshooters, Annie's conservative and feminine style set her apart. Women loved watching her best men in contests—and do so in a very ladylike fashion.

Chief Sitting Bull toured with the *Wild West Show* for four months in 1875. During that time, he befriended Annie Oakley, calling her Watanya Cicilia, which translated to Little Sure Shot.

While giving an exhibition a year earlier, she had met Sitting Bull, who noted that she was about the same age his own daughter would have been if she had survived the Indian wars and gave her the name Watanya Cicilia, which in Lakota means Little Sure Shot. During the time they spent together traveling with Buffalo Bill's show, they became close, and he adopted her into the Hunkpapa Lakota tribe, an honor that she took seriously.

In 1886, the show set down for the entire summer on New York's Staten Island, drawing almost 336,000 spectators to that season's production, "The Drama of Civilization." Many patrons traveled by ferry from Manhattan, passing the newly installed Statue of Liberty, then taking a four-mile ride on the new rail line. When the weather turned cold, the show moved inside, to Madison Square Garden. Bringing the Wild West to sophisticated New York caused a sensation, resulting in a great deal of national publicity for Annie Oakley. Her ability to drill bullet holes in falling cards was the inspiration for a common slang term for a free or complimentary ticket to an event—an "Annie Oakley"—because holes had already been punched in it.

That same season, Buffalo Bill added to his cast fifteen-year-old sharpshooter Lillian Smith, "the Champion Girl Shot," who quickly developed a rivalry with Annie Oakley.

The popularity of the show led Mark Twain to encourage Cody to take it to Europe, to bring the epic story of the settlement of the West to the celebration of Queen Victoria's fiftieth year on the throne: "It is often said on the other side of the water that none of the exhibitions which we send to England are purely and distinctly American. If you will take the Wild West show over there you can remove that reproach." Cody packed 300 performers, including 97 Indians, 18 buffalo, 181 horses, 10 elk, 4 donkeys, 5 Texas longhorns, 2 deer, 10 mules, and the Deadwood stage on several ships and sailed to England. The troupe toured for six months, often drawing crowds of more than thirty thousand people. This glamorized version of the American West became the accepted European version of life on the frontier. Although the image of the cowboy became symbolic of the brave-if-not-so-sophisticated nation, Cody's Indians also created a fervor, and Europeans rushed to touch them when a rumor spread in France that brief contact with an Indian assured fertility.

The show gave two command performances for Queen Victoria, one of them causing a sensation. As Cody wrote, "When the standard bearer passed the royal box with Old Glory her Majesty arose, bowed deeply and impressively to the banner, and the entire court party came up standing . . . and all, saluted." This marked the first time in history that a British monarch had saluted the American flag.

As soon as the show returned from its triumphant tour, Annie Oakley resigned. Various reasons were given but they all centered on the same issue: She just didn't like Lillian Smith. She resumed touring as a solo act, briefly joined a competing Wild West show, and even appeared onstage in a trifle called *Deadwood Dick*. Smith eventually fell in love with a cowboy and left the show as well, darkening her skin and touring in *Mexican Joe's Wild West* show as Princess Winona, the Indian Girl Shot. Her departure allowed Annie Oakley to rejoin Cody's show in time for another long tour of Europe.

The show became part of the Paris Exposition, staged to commemorate the one hundredth anniversary of the French Revolution. Oakley became the sensation of Europe: She reportedly took part in the lighting ceremony of the newly built Eiffel Tower; the president of France offered her a commission in the French army; the king of Senegal wanted to buy her so she might kill the tigers then terrorizing his country; and she nearly created a scandal when she ignored protocol and shook hands with the Princess of Wales.

When *Buffalo Bill's Wild West* set up in Italy, Cody and Sitting Bull visited Rome on a tour personally conducted by Pope Leo XIII. To promote the show, an Indian village was built

Buffalo Bill's shows were wildly successful throughout Europe, creating the romanticized impression of the American West that has become accepted as reality.

inside the Colosseum, and a mock shoot-out between cowboys and Indians was staged in St. Peter's Square—followed by a sharpshooting demonstration from Annie Oakley. And the show's concessionaires introduced another American creation to Italian audiences—popcorn!

While the show was wowing Europe, at home the United States Census Bureau officially declared the frontier settled. The dream of a nation stretching from ocean to ocean had come true. The Indian wars were over and most tribes were settled on reservations; the majority of the land had been explored and opened for settlement; the great buffalo herds were mostly gone; railroads crisscrossed the continent; and people were even talking to one another on the telephone. When Cody had first opened his show, it reflected current events, but within a decade, it was presenting a sometimes nostalgic look at a rapidly vanishing era of our history. The reality had been transformed into myth. And crowds loved it. In 1890, the show drew six million people and reported a million-dollar profit. Buffalo Bill Cody and Annie Oakley had become among the best-known Americans in the world. Bill Cody was consulted by presidents on just about all matters concerning the West, and among his friends were the most celebrated writers, painters, and inventors of the time.

Producing a show of that size was an enormous undertaking and required ingenuity to set up and move quickly from place to place at minimal cost. In 1899, for example, the show gave 341 performances in 200 days across 11,000 miles. To accomplish that, the troupe had to carry its own bleacher seating and canopies, electrical generators, and kitchens, and under the direction of James Bailey of the Barnum & Bailey Circus, they revolutionized methods of rapidly and safely loading and unloading railway flatcars.

Among the people who delighted in the performance was the inventor of the electric light, Thomas Edison, who in fact did light the show brightly, enabling it to become one of the first entertainments to be staged in the relative coolness of the night. Oakley and Edison had met in Paris at the 1889 exposition, where he was demonstrating his phonograph. In 1894, he invited her to the Black Maria, which is what he called his photo studio, where he used his kinetograph, the earliest movie camera, to capture the smoke as she fired her guns— as well as visually recording glass balls shattering when she hit them. The "moving pictures" he shot eventually were shown in Kinetoscope parlors and cost five cents to view, causing these halls to become known as *nickelodeons*—and turning Annie Oakley into one of the world's first "movie" stars. After proving he could capture rising smoke on film, Edison also brought Buffalo Bill and several Indians to his West Orange, New Jersey, studio and recorded them.

The success of the *Wild West Show* found Cody in the odd position of being the employer and, at times, the guardian of the same Indians whose tribes he had been at war with only years earlier. It is possible he had even fought some of these specific individuals in battle. But Buffalo Bill proved to be an enlightened employer, paying his cast equal wages and treating all of them—including Indians, black cowboys, and women—with great respect. Indians, in particular, earned a much better wage than would have been possible on a reservation and were able to make their case for fair treatment in show programs and when speaking to newspapers. Cody's abolitionist upbringing transformed easily into common decency, and he was said to be respected by all the people he dealt with. He was known to be an advocate for women's suffrage and at every opportunity fought for fair treatment of Native Americans.

Annie Oakley and Frank Butler had left the show at the beginning of the new century, and Oakley once again took to the stage, starring as *The Western Girl*, a play written for her that involved her using a pistol, rifle, and rope to vanquish the bad guys. A story published in William Randolph Hearst's newspapers in 1904 accused her of being addicted to cocaine and claimed she had been arrested. Outraged by that attack, she sued fifty-six newspapers for libel—winning fifty-five of those cases and restoring her reputation.

The Butlers never quite mastered the art of settling down: building then selling houses in several places, preferring to stay at resorts or in a New York City apartment. Annie Oakley was quoted as admitting, "I went all to pieces under the care of a home." She retired from touring in 1913.

Toward the end of his life, Cody explained, "[T]he west of the old times, with its strong characters, its stern battles and its tremendous stretches of loneliness, can never be blotted from my mind."

By then, *Buffalo Bill's Wild West* had lost its luster. Through the years, several others had attempted to launch competitive Wild West shows, although none of them had been able to survive more than a few seasons. But in 1903, *The Great Train Robbery*, the first Western motion picture, had been released. It was a huge success and further established the Western as a popular cultural form—and cut deeply into the audiences for live shows.

Buffalo Bill had earned a fortune bringing the Wild West to the East Coast and Europe. He'd invested those profits in everything from Arizona mines to filmmaking, publishing, and even a crazy idea about selling fresh spring water all over the country, but in the end, he had little money to show for it. In '08, he'd sold a substantial interest in the show to *Pawnee Bill's Wild West and Great Far East Show* but continued starring in it. In 1910, he began a three-year farewell tour, and the show finally closed forever in 1913.

Buffalo Bill immediately secured backing to produce a five-reel Western picture, *The Indian Wars*. He toured with other shows for another two years, until his health failed. When his death was reported, quite prematurely, he remarked, "I have yet a great life work to complete before I pass over the river. I have been supervising the taking of motion pictures. These start with the opening of the west . . ."

In 1915, Frank and Annie Butler drove their car to visit him while he was appearing in a show entitled *Sells Floto Circus & Buffalo Bill Himself*. That was the last time they were together. When he died at home in 1917, the nation mourned. As the respected western historian and writer William Lightfoot Visscher wrote, "Prominent men and women from many states and civilized nations journeyed to Denver to attend his funeral. Cities did him honor and legislatures adjourned for the obsequies . . ."

From Pine Ridge, the Oglala Sioux sent a telegram, part of which read, "Know that the Oglalas found in Buffalo Bill a warm and lasting friend; that our hearts are heavy from the burden of his passing . . ." It was signed *Chief Jack Red Cloud*.

And Annie Oakley said simply, "He was the kindest hearted, broadest minded, simpliest [*sic*] most loyal man I ever knew. He was in very fact the personification of those sturdy and lovable qualities that really made the West . . ."

Annie Oakley continued to give occasional performances for charity and was especially active raising money to aid the war effort throughout World War I. A strong supporter of women's suffrage, she offered to raise an entire regiment of women capable of fighting in that war. She was sixty-six years old when she died in November 1926, and only three weeks later, Frank Butler, her husband of fifty years, also died.

But both Buffalo Bill and Annie Oakley have lived on in the legends they helped create.

Annie Oakley would be remembered in numerous movies, beginning with the 1935 film *Annie Oakley*, and most successfully in Irving Berlin's Broadway musical and subsequent hit film *Annie Get Your Gun*; while the story of Buffalo Bill has been told in numerous entertainment formats, and he has been played by numerous actors, from Roy Rogers to Paul Newman.

Buffalo Bill and Annie Oakley created the passion for western entertainment that remains so firmly embedded in American culture. Annie Oakley, for all her talent with a gun, never set foot in the Old West. William Cody, on the other hand, played an important role not only in settling the West but also in creating the myths that would end up at least partially obscuring what really happened in this exciting but dangerous time. It was his vision that laid the foundation for all the wonderful storytellers who would follow him, who would turn the hardest days in the Old West into one of the world's most popular entertainment subjects.

While honoring Bill Cody, the state legislature of California properly noted, "[I]n his death that romantic and stirring chapter in our national history that began with Daniel Boone is forever closed."

THE AMERICAN INDIAN: WITH NO RESERVATIONS

Lonesome Dove author Larry McMurtry wrote, "Most of the traditions which we associate with the American West were invented by pulp writers, poster artists, impresarios and advertising men." And without question, at the heart of that invention is the American Indian.

The Indians played an essential role in the actual settling of the West and then played an even larger role in all the glorified stories told about it. The actual relationship between the white settlers and the several hundred different tribes that had lived on the land for thousands of years is extraordinarily complex, but in the legends it generally has been described as an almost continuous battle between mostly innocent settlers wanting to live in peace and the warlike Indians who slaughtered them.

Actually, the many millions of Indians living on the North American continent when Europeans arrived generally left the newcomers alone. In fact, an early problem faced by settlers was that too many of them wanted to leave the settlements and live among the tribes. Ben Franklin said, "No European who has tasted Savage life can afterwards bear to live in our societies."

Most of the tribes didn't care very much about the settlers; they were too busy fighting other tribes. In some ways, theirs was a relatively sophisticated society: Hundreds of years before the American Constitution was written, the Iroquois Great Law of Peace apparently included the freedoms of speech and religion, a separation of powers in government, and the right of women to participate in government. Prior to the American Revolution, the relationship between the largest tribes and the British was good; the Indians even adopted some elements of the British lifestyle and

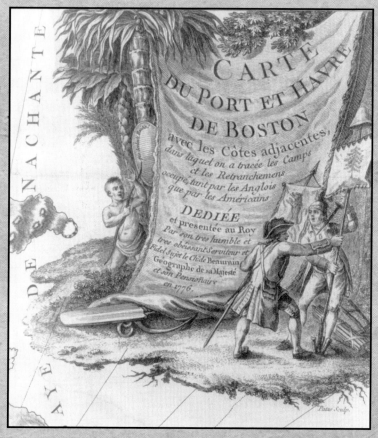

This 1776 illustration depicts a British Loyalist and American colonist fighting over a banner, while a Native American watches what he believed to be a battle over Indian lands. The Indians sided with the British, anticipating that a British victory would end westward expansion.

farming techniques. And when that war erupted, they fought alongside the British to maintain that relationship.

Following the Revolution, the question that was to shape this new nation—Who owned the land on which the Indians lived?—was strongly debated. George Washington's secretary of war, Henry Knox, believed that "the Indians being the prior occupants, possess the right of the soil."

Responding to President Monroe's attempts to buy their land, a Choctaw chief laid out the Indians' desire: "We wish to remain here, where we have grown up as the herbs of the woods; and do not wish to be transplanted into another soil."

The Indian wars that would spring up like brush fires across the continent for most of the nineteenth century began in the Southeast after the British surrender at Yorktown. But by 1830, all the tribes east of the Mississippi had been pacified, and those tribes were "removed" into the Indian Territory. Andrew Jackson had promised the Indians that the land would be theirs "as long as grass will grow green and the river waters will flow." In actuality, within a decade, more than four million white settlers had crossed the Appalachians into the vast Mississippi valley.

The government negotiated several treaties with the Indians, then proceeded to break those pacts when the land became valuable. The terrifying—then, years later, thrilling—fighting began with the discovery of gold in the Dakotas in 1849 and the decision to build a transcontinental railroad. Great Plains tribes such as the Lakota Sioux, Navajos, Cheyennes,

Comanches, Apaches, Kiowas, and Arapahos lived and hunted on those lands and fought to protect their way of life. But mostly they fought soldiers, not settlers. Although attacks on wagon trains were common in dime novels, Wild West shows, and movies, they were uncommon in real life. It's estimated that fewer than four hundred settlers were killed in Indian attacks, and the settlers probably killed an equal number of Indians. Settlers were much more likely to hire Indians as guides or trade with them than fight them.

As the tribes settled on reservations, government Indian agents and traders arrived, both to provide assistance and to exploit them whenever it was possible.

The Dawes Act of 1887 and ensuing legislation allowed the federal government to sell lands to white settlers that had already been granted by treaty to the tribes. This 1911 poster offers settlers "fine lands in the West" for easy payments.

But the fighting between the army and the Plains Indians was brutal. General Sherman gave his troops orders to kill all Indians—and even their dogs—and burn their villages to the ground. When that failed, the cavalry killed the buffalo to starve the Indians into submission. In 1890, the Census Bureau estimated that in the forty different Indian wars, nineteen thousand white men, women, and children had been killed, along with at least thirty thousand Indians. But the real number of Indian dead is likely in the hundreds of thousands, as countless more tens of thousands died of disease and other factors during long forced marches to designated lands.

Although it is understood that the victors get to write the history, in recent years, Americans have reassessed the country's victory in the Indian wars. Many people have gained a greater understanding of the Indian point of view, perhaps best explained by Chief Black Hawk, who said, upon his surrender in 1832, "We told them to leave us alone, and keep away from us; they followed on, and beset our paths, and they coiled themselves among us, like the snake. They poisoned us by their touch."

JESSE JAMES

 BLOODY POLITICS

O n December 7, 1869, "a mist like pall" hung over the small town of Gallatin, Missouri. "The city," reported the *Booneville Weekly Adventures,* "was veiled from sight by the dense fog that prevailed, and an unusual stillness and quiet pervaded every quarter of the little city." Out of that fog and into legend rode the outlaw brothers Jesse and Frank James.

They dismounted and hitched their horses at the water trough in front of the Daviess County Savings Association. At twenty-six, Frank was four years older than Jesse; both brothers had ridden hard through the Civil War and its aftermath. And they hadn't forgotten for a bit what they'd seen and who had done them wrong. They intended to steal the money in this bank, no question about that, but that was not their main reason for being there. They had come to avenge the killing of a friend.

The owner of the bank, former Union captain John W. Sheets, was sitting at his desk in conversation with lawyer William McDonald when the James brothers walked through the door. As Sheets got up to greet these customers, McDonald started to leave. The two men cornered Sheets and pulled their six-shooters. They told him why he was about to die: He had caused the death of their former commander and good friend, "Bloody Bill" Anderson, and they were bound by oath to avenge it. The James brothers then shot him twice, once in the head and once in the heart. When the lawyer McDonald started running, they winged him in his arm, but he got away. Then they grabbed several hundred dollars from the safe and till and took off. A posse pursued them out of town and shots were exchanged. One of the James brothers fell from his horse, which galloped away, but the other brother grabbed his arm and swung him up onto *his* horse, and they outraced their pursuers. As the *Kansas City Daily Journal* reported, "There is a boldness and recklessness about this robbery and murder that is almost beyond belief."

It turned out that Jesse and Frank James had made a mistake—they had killed the wrong man. Although Sheets had been on the team that tracked down and ambushed the murderous Anderson, in fact, it was Major Samuel Cox who deserved credit for bringing an end to Bloody

Bill's reign of terror. Not that the James brothers cared particularly; killing came pretty easily to them. And the result of this bank robbery was far greater than they could have imagined: It made Jesse James famous.

Although bank robberies weren't uncommon, this was such a cold-blooded killing that Missouri governor Thomas T. Crittenden offered the largest reward in state history, ten thousand dollars, for the capture of the outlaws. Among those who read the breathless newspaper account was the founder and editor of the *Kansas City Times*, John Newman Edwards.

In Jesse James, John Edwards found the man he had been looking for. During the war, the James brothers had served with Bloody Bill, who commanded one of the Confederacy's most successful—and vicious—guerrilla units. As an element of Quantrill's Raiders, they had participated in the Centralia massacre, in which more than a hundred Union troops had been slaughtered. After the war, Jesse and Frank James essentially refused to surrender, instead hitting the outlaw trail.

Brothers Frank and Jesse James in about 1870, just after they had become infamous bank robbers

The former colonel John Edwards also had been a proud Confederate. He had served as adjutant to General Joseph Shelby, commanding a division and organizing an extremely successful intelligence operation. Rather than surrender at the conclusion of the war, Edwards fled to Mexico with Shelby and about a thousand men and remained there for several years. When amnesty was granted to most Confederate soldiers, he returned and founded the *Kansas City Times*, a highly political newspaper that championed former Rebel leaders. In its pages, he railed against the corruption, oppression, and criminality of the Republican government, urging ex-Confederates to fight for political power.

Edwards's objective was to restore a sense of pride in the defeated Rebels, and Jesse James proved the perfect symbol for him. As he once wrote of James, "We called him outlaw, and he was—but fate made him so. When the war closed Jesse James had no home . . . hunted, shot, driven away . . . a price upon his head—what else could a man do . . . except what he did? When he was hunted he turned savagely about and hunted his hunters," adding at another time, "They are outlaws through no fault or crime other than participating in a civil war that was not successful. [They are] now so wantonly and unjustly hunted and denounced by all who have partisan passions to gratify."

According to Edwards's newspaper, and the other journals that joined him, rather than a bank robber, train robber, thug, and killer, Jesse James was a political symbol: He was the courageous representative of the defiant South; a man so noble in defeat that he might have "sat with Arthur at the Round Table"; a man of the Confederacy who struck back against the excesses of the carpetbaggers by robbing their banks and their trains—but was careful not to

The journalist John Edwards, whose purple prose transformed the bank robber Jesse James into a Southern hero

trouble innocent people. It worked: The general public had no love for either the banks or the railroads, which were controlled by fat cats in the North and the East who cared not at all for the troubles of the poor workingman. All Jesse James was doing was fighting back for all the people who had no fight left in them. He became the nation's most revered outlaw.

Jesse James readily accepted the mythical role that Edwards had created for him, regularly writing letters to the paper claiming to be innocent of the crimes he was accused of committing, describing his latest exploits, and even leaving press releases at the scenes of his crimes. His tawdry life has been romanticized in literature, theater, and music, and it is accurate to claim that Jesse James wrote the first chapter in the colorful history of American outlaws.

But the question remains: How accurate—if at all—was Edwards's portrayal? Was there, in reality, any political motivation behind James's life of crime, or was he simply a bad guy who served a symbolic purpose? Was he a hero of the downtrodden South, or was he the same person once described by Robert Pinkerton as "the worst man, without any exception, in America. He is utterly devoid of fear and has no more compunction about cold blooded murder than he has about eating his breakfast"?

He certainly was a son of the Old South. Jesse Woodson James was born in Clay County, Missouri, an area known as "Little Dixie," in 1847. His father, Robert James, was a farmer and Baptist minister who was prosperous enough to own six slaves. But the lure of gold drew

Jesse James's father, Baptist minister Robert S. James, was a founder of William Jewell College in Liberty, Missouri, while his mother, Zerelda, was a strong woman who eventually sold pebbles from her son's grave site as souvenirs.

him to California, where he died. It appears that the James boys got their character from their mother, Zerelda James, who hardly fit the definition of a genteel Southern belle. She was a big woman, strong both physically and in temperament. After her husband's death, she married twice more, the second time to Dr. Reuben Samuel, with whom she had four children and owned seven slaves. Zerelda was a practical woman; after Jesse was killed, for example, she profited by selling pebbles off his grave as souvenirs—being careful to replenish those stones each morning so as not to disappoint her customers.

She also was a staunch supporter of the Confederacy. Missouri was a border state, and in the years before war erupted, it was bitterly divided between abolitionists and the proslavery faction—which included Zerelda James and her family. As part of the Missouri Compromise, Missouri had been admitted to the Union as a slave state in 1820, while Maine was admitted as a free state. In 1854, the Kansas-Nebraska Act opened up those two Indian territories to settlers, ruling that the people who lived there would vote on whether these territories would permit slavery. In Kansas, each side set up a state government—and then organized militias to protect its supporters and enforce its orders. In a prelude to the Civil War, the free-state Kansas Jayhawkers and the mostly proslavery Missouri bushwhackers fought a vicious war. Although these two groups supposedly were fighting for their political beliefs, many of the men on both sides were just bandits who used these ideals as an excuse for arson, looting, beatings, and even wholesale murder.

When the Civil War began in April 1861, Missouri officially remained in the Union and declared itself neutral but actually sent troops and supplies to both sides. With Zerelda's encouragement—and wearing the clothes she'd sewn for him—eighteen-year-old Frank James set off to join the Rebels. After he was captured and sent home by Union troops, the local militia forced him to sign an oath swearing loyalty to the Republic. Instead of honoring that oath, he hooked up with Quantrill's Raiders, an especially violent group of bushwhackers. Utilizing guerrilla tactics tailored to each situation, small bands of William Quantrill's men attacked Jayhawkers, Union troops, and pro-Union civilians, in an attempt to drive them out of the territory. They were known to use disguises—including dressing in Union uniforms to infiltrate their ranks—and to organize well-planned attacks and stage ambushes. And, like regular military units, on occasion they did not hesitate to attack towns and kill civilians.

Frank James was an intelligent young man who loved Shakespeare and had once dreamed of going to college and becoming a teacher; instead, he earned a reputation as a fearsome guerrilla fighter. Between raids, he would return to the family farm and regale his relatives with tales of his attacks on Yankees. Jesse certainly listened in awe to his older brother's

The young guns: portraits of twenty-one-year-old Frank and sixteen-year-old Jesse taken during the Civil War

stories—and although he had hoped to follow his father into the ministry, he instead began dreaming of joining his brother in the fight to preserve their way of life.

Attempting to stop these hit-and-run raids, Union troops arrested anyone who had aided or abetted the Raiders, especially the female relatives of known guerrilla fighters. They were held in a three-story house in Kansas City. Four of these women were killed and others were badly injured when the building collapsed in August 1863. Quantrill retaliated by bringing all of his small bands together—an estimated four hundred men—and attacking the town of Lawrence, Kansas. Frank James joined this massacre, which resulted in at least a quarter of the town being burned to the ground and the cold-blooded murders of 150 men and boys. Irate Union troops set out to find and punish the killers.

Jesse James was plowing the family's fields when a Union patrol arrived and demanded to know where his brother was hiding. Sixteen-year-old Jesse refused to answer—and was beaten and horsewhipped. His stepfather Reuben Samuel was tortured, suspended from a tree, then dropped several times until he gave up the information. He barely survived. Apparently the bluecoats found Frank James's band, but he managed to escape. When he rejoined the militia, his younger brother was riding with him.

After the Lawrence massacre, Quantrill's Raiders split into three large bands, and Frank and Jesse James rode with Bloody Bill Anderson's eighty-man army. The savage lessons they learned fighting with Anderson would be put to use after the war ended.

Anderson had joined Quantrill after Union militiamen had hanged his father and uncle. His three sisters were among the Kansas City hostages; in the collapse, one of them died and the other two suffered injuries that would plague them for the rest of their lives. Whatever humanity Anderson had at that point disappeared, and as he once said, "I ask no quarter and give none." He was known to torture captives, scalping them and cutting off their ears. Anderson and his teenage lieutenant, Archie Clement, who became known to authorities as "Bill Anderson's scalper and head devil," served as young Jesse James's mentors. "Little Arch," as the latter was known, was only a bit over five feet tall and was full-up angry at the world.

Jesse James was with them when they rode into the town of Centralia, Missouri, in

Bloody Bill Anderson became a guerrilla in 1862 after Jayhawkers hanged his father and his uncle, stole all their possessions, and burned their home to the ground.

September 1864, a few weeks after six of Anderson's men had been killed and scalped by federal troops. Bloody Bill's men stopped a train and captured twenty-two of General Sherman's soldiers on their way home on furlough. They were stripped, lined up, and shot numerous times; then their bodies were mutilated. A witness described the event as "a carnival of blood." About one hundred fifty Union soldiers were sent to track Anderson down; instead, his men ambushed the patrol and killed every member of it, even the wounded. Jesse James received credit for killing the patrol's commander, Major A. V. E. Johnson. Then, in a truly mad frenzy, the Raiders disemboweled, scalped, crushed, and decapitated the bodies of their victims.

At sixteen, Jesse James was probably the youngest participant in these atrocities. A month after the Centralia massacre, three hundred men of the Missouri state militia, led by Major Samuel P. Cox, found Anderson's camp near Orrick, Missouri. In the ensuing gun battle, Anderson was shot twice in the back of his head. Among his possessions was a rope in which he had tied a knot for each man he killed personally; Cox's men counted fifty-four knots. After Anderson's body was photographed as evidence of his death, his head was severed and mounted on top of a telegraph pole.

The James brothers managed to get away, eventually rejoining Quantrill in an ill-fated attempt to ride to Washington and kill President Lincoln. Several weeks after General Lee's surrender at Appomattox, a militia force surprised Quantrill's men near Taylorsville, Kentucky; Quantrill was shot and died a month later of his wounds. There are conflicting reports about exactly what happened next. According to T. J. Stiles, author of the acclaimed biography *Jesse James: Last Rebel of the Civil War*, James was captured by Union forces and held prisoner in a hotel that had been used as a hospital, where he was forced to surrender. But according to Judge Thomas Shouse, who had been friends with both James brothers, Jesse told him that he had been shot in his right lung by a "mini-ball" fired by drunken Union soldiers as he rode into Lexington, Missouri, carrying a white flag of surrender, prepared to sign the Union's loyalty oath. He claimed that was the seventh time he had been wounded. His horse was killed, and as he later wrote, "I ran through the woods pursued by two men on horseback. . . . I was near a creek. I lay in the water all night, it seemed that my body was on fire." A farmer plowing nearby helped him, and eventually he made it back to his family, who by then were living in Rulo, Nebraska. For eight weeks he hovered between life and death, at one point telling his mother, "I don't want to die in a northern state." Among the women who nursed him back to health was his lovely cousin Zerelda "Zee" Mimms, whom he would later marry.

He later claimed that while he was recovering, five militiamen came to his house, prepared to kill him. It was fight or die, he later wrote: "Surrender had played out for me." He struggled to get out of bed, fired once through the front door, then flung it open, and with a pistol in each hand, commenced firing, bringing down four of them. He knew then that he would never be allowed to live peacefully.

At the end of the war, Frank James surrendered in Kentucky, then violated postwar regulations by sneaking home. On his dangerous journey, he got into a gunfight with four Union soldiers; he killed two of them and wounded a third, and a bullet nipped him in the left hip. He made it home, but he couldn't stay there. For men like the James brothers, returning to any kind of normal civilian life proved impossible. The war had transformed them into different people; after what they had seen, after what they had done, after all the destruction the war caused, there was nothing for them to go back to. And, in addition, as Jesse had learned, Union militiamen weren't about to forgive them, no matter what Lincoln and Grant had promised.

In addition to Frank and Jesse James, among the people permanently scarred by the war were Cole and James Younger. They were farm boys from Kansas, two of the fourteen children of Henry Washington Younger. Although a slave owner, Henry was a Union sympathizer, as was his whole family. But when Jayhawkers began raiding the family farm, stealing livestock

The outlaw Cole Younger in 1903; after serving twenty-five years in prison, he published his autobiography and partnered with Frank James to create a Wild West show.

and destroying property, Cole Younger turned against them and eventually joined Quantrill's Raiders. Any ambivalence he might have felt disappeared when Union militiamen killed his father. Cole rode into Lawrence, Kansas, with Quantrill and Frank James, and when they rode out a day later, all of them would be bonded forever.

Cole's little brother James also joined Quantrill and stayed with the Raiders when Cole joined the regular Confederate army and, as a captain, led troops into Louisiana and California. When the Younger brothers finally made it home after the war, the family farm was a ruin.

Several of the former guerrillas stayed loosely together during Reconstruction under the leadership of Little Arch Clement, who is generally believed to have turned them into outlaws. On the cold morning of February 13, 1866, they began to show the world the valuable lessons they had learned, when about thirteen of them rode into Liberty, Missouri, dressed in the long blue coats of the Union soldiers. There were only a few people on the street, and no one suspected that this was the beginning of a bank robbery—because never before in peacetime had a bank robbery taken place in the light of day.

There is no record of exactly whose idea it was to hold up the Clay County Savings Bank in broad daylight, but several important facts linked the plan directly to the James brothers: The bank was owned by a man named Greenup Bird, who years earlier had been especially harsh on Reuben Samuel in negotiations over a debt. Also, disguising themselves as Union soldiers was an old Raiders trick. And, finally, the bank was filled with Yankee dollars.

Using the same raiding tactics they had perfected during the war, the men dismounted and took their assigned positions, creating a series of perimeters around the bank. Jesse wasn't among them, because he was still recovering from his chest wound and unable to ride, although it is believed that he helped plan the job. Frank James and Cole Younger entered the bank and pulled their pistols. The only other person in the bank was Bird's son. He and his father put all the bank's money into a large grain sack. The robbers escaped with $58,072.64, the modern-day equivalent of almost a million dollars.

No one had been hurt during the robbery, but the gang made its escape a-whoopin' and a-hollerin' out of town—and wildly firing guns in the air. As the men raced down the main street, two other young men watched them—and for no reason anyone could ever figure, Arch Clement took aim and shot one of them dead. As was later remarked, Arch just liked killing. A few days after the robbery, the victim's family reportedly received a letter signed by a man no one had ever heard of at the time named Jesse James, who apologized for the murder and stated that the gang had not intended to kill anyone.

The take was so large that if money had been the motivation, most members of that crew could have quit robbing right then and lived comfortably for the rest of their lives. Some of them did, in fact, but not the James boys, nor the Youngers. For them, this was just the beginning of a crime spree that would last almost two decades and grow to include dozens of bank, train, and stagecoach robberies.

The first robbery in which Jesse was believed to be an active participant took place at the end of October, when bandits stole $2,011.50 from the Alexander Mitchell and Company bank in Lexington, Missouri. The robbers followed a pattern that was to become familiar: One man would ask a clerk to change a large bill, and then at least one other "customer" would pull his gun and announce the holdup. Six weeks after this job, the state militia caught up with Arch Clement, drinking in a Lexington saloon. Clement got on his horse and tried to ride his way out of it, but he was shot in the chest. A second shot knocked him off his horse. As he lay dying in the dirt, trying to cock his revolver with his teeth, he said, "I've done what I've always said I would do . . . die before I'd surrender."

In the months following Clement's death, several members of his gang either were caught and hanged or just had enough and rode off, leaving the core crew that gained renown as the James-Younger Gang. Due primarily to the eventual notoriety of Jesse James, it became the best-known gang in the Old West, though there are historians who doubt it deserves that recognition.

As bank robbing became a more popular crime, it became more and more difficult to pin any holdup on a specific gang, and even when the gang could be identified, it was almost impossible to know who exactly was riding with it at that point. The better known the James-Younger Gang became, for example, the more robberies were attributed to it, as if there were some status attached to being held up by Jesse James and Cole Younger. The next job attributed to them—that they may or may not have pulled off—was the Hughes and Wasson Bank in Richmond, Missouri; fourteen robbers stole about thirty-five hundred dollars—and killed three men who got in their way. Four former bushwhackers were eventually caught and lynched for this robbery.

But there is no doubt that Jesse James and Cole Younger led eight men into Russellville, Kentucky, on May 20, 1868, and rode out with exactly $9,035.92. As the gang made its escape, shooting into the air to discourage gawkers, one member shot at the metal fish weather vane atop the courthouse, sending it spinning. Almost a century later, that historic weather vane, with a bullet hole through it, could still be seen on the roof of the new courthouse, where it had been placed to honor the town's history. One man was eventually convicted for that robbery, for which he served three years in prison.

As the robberies continued, the fame—and fear—spread. On June 3, 1871, a gang of men rode into Corydon, Iowa, intending to rob the county treasurer of tax receipts. As usual, they began by asking to change a large bill. But before they pulled their guns, they were informed that the safe was time locked. The kindly clerk suggested they could get change at the Ocobock Brothers Bank, which was opening that very day. They thanked the man and helped celebrate the new bank's opening by stealing about six thousand dollars. Following this robbery, authorities hired the famed Pinkerton detective agency, renowned as the best modern crime solvers in the world, to finally bring this gang to justice.

The banks began falling like targets in a shooting gallery, and the gang began expanding its efforts. In 1872, the men stole the cash box from the Kansas City Exposition. Although most reports claim they got almost ten thousand dollars, the treasurer later claimed it was only $998. Shots were fired while they were making their getaway, and a young girl was slightly wounded. Soon afterward, an anonymous letter published in the *Kansas City Weekly Times* admitted, "It is true I shot a little girl, though it was not intentional; and if the parents will give me their address through the columns of [this newspaper] I will send them money to pay her doctor's bill."

In July 1873, the gang pulled off its first train robbery outside Adair, Iowa. The men removed a track rail, believing that this would force the Chicago, Rock Island & Pacific conductor to stop the train. Unfortunately, the train derailed, killing the engineer and injuring many passengers. The gang boarded the train dressed in the white sheets of Ku Klux Klan members and stole $2,337. During the holdup, Jesse supposedly told the passengers that the gang was stealing from the rich to help the poor. The railroad immediately offered a $5,500 reward for the conviction of these robbers. Six months later, the gang robbed its first stagecoach, this time wearing Union army blue coats and getting away with anywhere between one thousand and eight thousand dollars—but returning a purse untouched to a man who claimed to have fought for the Confederacy.

At the end of January 1874, the gang stopped an Iron Mountain Railway express near Gads Hill, Missouri. For the first time, the men robbed train passengers—asking each person to hold out his hands for inspection, permitting workingmen with calluses to keep their money. They took $10,000 from the safe and $3,400 from passengers. As they were making their escape, one of the robbers, later identified by his handwriting as Jesse James, left a note reading, "The most daring robbery on record! The southbound train on the Iron Mountain Railroad was stopped here this evening by five heavily armed men and robbed of _____ dollars. . . . The robbers were all large men, none of them under six feet tall. They were masked . . ."

The fame of the James-Younger Gang resulted in individual *cartes-de-visite*, collectible business-card-size portraits, of the best-known members. This 1876 composite includes the eight most infamous outlaws and their final victim.

A magazine illustration showing Frank and Jesse James holding up the Chicago & Alton Railroad in 1879—escaping with six thousand dollars

The gang followed no discernible pattern and stayed on the move. Its reputation continued to grow throughout the country, but especially throughout the former Confederacy, where sympathizers helped the men evade the law. At times they lived a reasonably normal life, at least for robbers and killers. Within months of each other early in 1874, for example, both Jesse and Frank married and set up households.

Their fame was such that almost every crime in the region initially was attributed to them. Jesse's audacious scheme of leaving notes at robberies helped the newspapers create his populist image. Some Southern newspapers began to portray him in almost heroic terms, repeating the completely untrue claim that he robbed from the rich and gave to the poor. In actuality, the gang robbed from pretty much everybody, and kept all of it.

In March 1874, Pinkerton operative Joseph Whicher arrived in Clay County, intending to go out to the James farm disguised as a fugitive from justice and confront Jesse and Frank.

One day later, his body was discovered with three bullet holes in it. By the time the body was found, the pigs had gotten to it. At just about the same time, three Pinkertons went to St. Clair County, Missouri, to deal with the Youngers. In a shoot-out, John Younger and two of the Pinks were killed.

For reasons obvious and personal, the founder of Pinkerton's, Allan Pinkerton, responded harshly to the murder of his three men. On the night of January 25, 1875, as Reuben and Zerelda Samuel and their nine-year-old son, Archie, slept, Pinks silently surrounded the farmhouse. One of them hurled an incendiary device through the window. Reuben found a shovel and pushed it into the fireplace—and seconds later it exploded. Zerelda's arm was so badly ripped apart that it had to be amputated; shrapnel tore into Archie Samuel's body and killed him. Eight Pinks were indicted for murder, although none was ever tried for the crime. The Pinkertons, facing the unenviable task of pursuing popular criminals living in an environment supportive of them and hostile to the detectives, dropped the case. The gang had defeated the best law-enforcement agency in the country.

John Edwards used his editorial pages to raise both fury at the carpetbaggers and sympathy for the people who fought them, causing the Missouri legislature to propose a bill granting amnesty to the James-Younger Gang. But when Daniel Askew, a local farmer who was believed to have helped the Pinkertons plan their raid, was murdered on April 12, that offer was rescinded.

After the disastrous attempt to rob the Northfield, Minnesota, bank, this posse pursued the three Younger brothers for almost three weeks before capturing them in a swamp.

It's doubtful Jesse would have accepted it, anyway. The killing of his half brother and maiming of his mother pushed Jesse James far beyond any possibility of redemption. His only purpose in life was to punish the North. To build support, Jesse routinely wrote letters to newspapers, claiming as he did in the *Nashville Banner*, "[F]or 10 years the radical papers in Mo. and other states have charged nearly every daring robbery in America to the James and Youngers. It is enough persecution for the northern papers to persecute us without the papers in the south persecuting us, the land we fought for four years to save from northern tyranny . . ." In a postscript to this letter, the obviously proud James asks that a copy of it be sent to his mother in Clay County.

Perhaps believing the tales that made it appear invincible, the gang made the fatal decision to move north for its next caper, far from the friendly surroundings that provided cover for it. The men chose the First National Bank of Northfield, Minnesota, supposedly because of its connection to two Union generals, Benjamin Butler and Adelbert Ames. Ames was believed to have recently made a fifty-thousand-dollar deposit. They planned the job for weeks but failed to take into account the very different environment in Minnesota. Northfield was a small town of hardworking, tough people and farmers who dressed plainly, and the only weapons they carried were long guns. Many of the residents had seen action with the First Minnesota during the war. From the moment the robbers rode into town, dressed in linen dusters and carrying pistols, they attracted suspicion. Three members of the gang went into the bank, while five men waited outside, several of whom began riding up and down Division Street, firing their weapons into the air, attempting to scare people off the streets.

The First National Bank of Northfield, Minnesota, was the last robbery of the infamous James-Younger Gang. Every gang member was wounded, two of them were killed, and the three Younger brothers were captured—for bags of nickels.

These people didn't scare easily. Instead, one man peered into the bank through a window and began shouting, "They're robbing the bank, boys! Go get your guns!"

The robbery went wrong from the beginning. When a cashier refused to open the safe, he was killed. Rather than the fifty thousand, the gang found only bags of nickels worth about twenty-three dollars. Townspeople reached for their guns and started firing while the robbers were still inside the bank. The *Sunday Times* of Chicago praised them: "The robbers did not get into the vault, nor did they find the cashier's drawer, except the nickel drawer, and the handful of nickels taken from it was thrown to the floor. The citizens of Northfield behaved like old veterans, as many of them are." The proprietor of the local hardware store initially believed the robbery was a promotional stunt for a local theater company, but when he realized it was for real, he picked up a single-shot Remington and took aim. Other people threw rocks at them, or fired bird shot from shotguns. Soon deadly fire was coming from every direction as the gang tried to make its escape. Two members of the gang were killed, and every other member was wounded as they made their getaway. Frank James was shot in his right leg; Jesse was hit in his thigh. In addition to the cashier, one local citizen was killed in the gunfight. The men split up when they got out of town in an attempt to evade the posses they knew would be coming for them. Supposedly they burned fourteen mills in the county to create a distraction. While the James brothers successfully evaded the estimated thousand men searching for them, somehow making it safely into the Dakotas, two weeks after the raid, all three Younger brothers were captured in a swamp. Cole Younger had been shot eleven times but survived. Rather than face execution, they pleaded guilty and were sentenced to life imprisonment. Bob Younger died in prison of tuberculosis in 1889, but Cole and Jim were paroled after serving twenty-five years. That Northfield raid marked the bloody end of the legendary James-Younger Gang.

For the next three years, Frank and Jesse lay low. They supposedly spent almost two years hiding out in Mexico until some of the heat was off, then returned. "Those years," Frank James said, "of quiet, upright life, were the happiest I have spent since my boyhood. My old life grew more detestable the further I got away from it." Jesse and Zee lived under the name Howard, and until the day Jesse died, his two surviving children did not know their real last name or their father's identity. Although Frank had decided he was done with the criminal life and wanted to live peacefully, Jesse clearly harbored other ideas.

The times had changed. The hatreds instilled by the war were calming. People had moved on, and the support that Jesse had once enjoyed was gone. Even the newspaperman Edwards would no longer publish his letters. But James had become addicted to danger and fame, and apparently also to laudanum, an opiate that dulled the senses and was often used as a painkiller.

Supposedly, while visiting the boomtown of Las Vegas to see if his family might settle there, Jesse encountered Billy the Kid and unsuccessfully attempted to persuade him to ride to Tennessee with him. When his brother Frank refused to return to a life of crime, Jesse recruited a new band of outlaws. Among them was his first cousin Wood Hite, who had also ridden with Bloody Bill during the war, and an alcoholic gunfighter, a horse thief, a slow-witted farmer, and the younger brother of an old friend. Jesse James was now the sole leader of this motley gang, in charge of making all the plans.

They struck first in October 1879, rolling a boulder across railroad tracks and stopping a Chicago & Alton Railroad express at Glendale, Missouri. They got away clean with six thousand dollars. Jesse James was back in business.

A month later, a Kansas City newspaper reported that a former member of the James-Younger Gang had killed Jesse. The story got a lot of coverage, but it was quickly proven false, although no one figured out why the claim had been made. Meanwhile, Jesse had used his share of the loot to buy a racehorse. The horse won enough races to show some early promise, but when Jesse took him to Atlanta and bet heavily on him, he lost, forcing Jesse to sell him to have enough money to get home.

That Jesse's new gang lacked the loyalty of his first gang, loyalty that had been forged in common experience, became obvious when Jesse got into an argument with one of his new members and shot him dead. The gang also lacked the ambition of the early days, settling for robbing a tourist stagecoach of two thousand dollars, then missing a coal-mine payroll and instead getting away with a paltry thirteen. In March 1881, they robbed a courier carrying the payroll for workers digging a canal at Muscle Shoals, Alabama. They took the five-thousand-dollar payroll but let the paymaster keep the fifty dollars in his own wallet.

By that point, disintegrating loyalties had put everyone at risk, including Frank James, who was afraid his new identity and location would be exposed. For reasons that have never been determined, although he simply might have needed money, Frank James decided to rejoin the outfit. Where once Frank had been in command and Jesse dutifully followed his older brother's orders, now Jesse was clearly the leader and decision maker. Under his leadership, the James brothers returned to their old ways, jumping aboard and stopping a Chicago, Rock Island & Pacific Railroad train at Winston, Missouri, on July 15, 1881. During the robbery, Jesse decided that the conductor was the man who had assisted the Pinkertons when they had bombed his parents' home, and he apparently shot him in the back without warning. When a passenger came to the conductor's assistance, he was also shot and killed, and it is generally believed that Frank James pulled the trigger. The gang netted only $650.

Public opinion had turned completely against the James brothers. Even residents of their hometown, who had once celebrated them, admitted that they needed to be stopped. It was commonly accepted that their continued presence in the area gave the whole of Missouri a poor reputation, limiting immigration and economic expansion. In Governor Crittenden's 1881 inaugural address, he stated that capturing the James brothers was his top priority and that he was not going to allow political considerations to get in the way, proclaiming, "Missouri cannot be the home and abiding place of lawlessness of any character." Laws passed when the James-Younger Gang enjoyed popular support prevented the governor from offering a sizeable reward, but after the murders in Winston, he convinced the railroad to put up a reward of ten thousand dollars each (the equivalent of about a quarter million dollars today) for the capture of Frank and Jesse James.

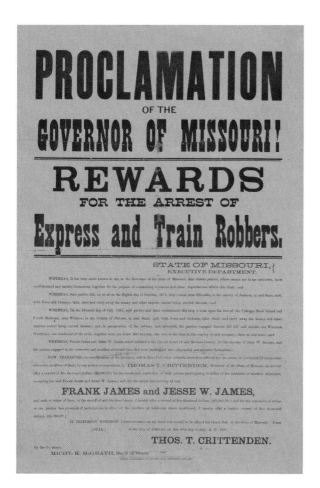

Missouri governor Crittenden offered five thousand dollars for the arrest and conviction of the men who had robbed two trains—but offered double that reward each for Frank and Jesse James.

In early September 1881, the James Gang, now including newcomer Charley Ford, flagged down a St. Louis, Alton & Chicago Railroad train as it slowed to go through an area known as the Blue Cut in Glendale, Missouri. Although five of the robbers were masked, Jesse James was not and actually told passengers who was holding them up. The train's safe was almost empty, so the gang relieved the passengers of their money, watches, and jewelry, fleeing with about a thousand dollars. As it turned out, this was Jesse James's last robbery.

That ten-thousand-dollar reward stirred up a lot of interest. Jesse was no longer that larger-than-life character whose name alone evoked terror. Realizing that there were now few people he could trust, Jesse settled with his family in St. Joseph, Missouri, living there under the name of Thomas Howard.

To keep his gang close, Jesse let Charley and his younger brother Bob Ford stay with him. The rest of his gang was scattered nearby: His cousin Wood Hite was staying with another gang member, Dick Liddil, at the home of Charley Ford's sister Martha Bolton. Apparently Martha was a lovely woman, as both Hite and Liddil were said to be smitten with her. There were even some reports that Jesse also had cast his eyes in her direction. But something happened in that house in early December. There already was some bad blood between Hite and Liddil about the split on the Blue Cut job, but the tension erupted one morning and they

Robert Ford was twenty years old when he shot unarmed Jesse James in the back of the head. He later reenacted the deed onstage in the play *How I Killed Jesse James*—but most people condemned his cowardly action and the play failed.

In death, Jesse James's celebrity grew. Only Buffalo Bill appeared as a hero in more dime novels, in addition to numerous "true accounts" and even touring stage shows.

took to shooting at each other. Both men were wounded, but probably not seriously. Then Martha and Bob Ford came upon the scene, and the twenty-one-year-old Bob Ford shot Hite once in the head, settling the dispute. Jesse James's cousin was buried in a shallow grave on the property. Liddil and Ford knew they had a serious problem: No one wanted to hazard a guess at what actions Jesse might take when he learned his cousin had been killed.

Charley and Bob Ford were looking for a way out of this mess, and in January they found it. They met secretly with Governor Crittenden and the Clay County sheriff and were not at all surprised to discover they shared some goals, the foremost of which was to rid Missouri, and perhaps the world, of Jesse James. In addition to the ten-thousand-dollar reward, the Ford brothers wanted a blanket pardon for all their crimes, including the murder they were about to commit, as well as a pardon for Liddil. The governor apparently was amenable, although the extent of that amenability would later be debated. Several days later, Liddil surrendered to the sheriff, although no announcement was made to the press so as not to alert Jesse.

Sometime in March 1882, Jesse began planning his next stickup, finally deciding to rob the bank in Platte City, Missouri. To pull it off, though, he told Charley Ford, he needed some other people. Ford suggested his brother Bob. Preparations were stepped up in late March. The robbery was planned for the first week in April.

At breakfast on the morning of April 3, Jesse was surprised to find an article in the local newspaper reporting that Liddil had surrendered. Word had leaked out. Oddly, he didn't ask the Ford brothers if they knew anything about this, a natural question, and the fact that he didn't ask made them very nervous. Instead, he cursed Liddil as a traitor and declared that he deserved to hang. After breakfast, Jesse had some chores to do. It was a warm day, so he took off his coat. Jesse always wore his guns, but he also wore a coat so no one would wonder why a peaceful man named Tom Howard was carrying two six-shooters. When he took off his coat, he also took off his gun belt and laid his guns on the bed. This was very unusual for him, as he was never to be found without his guns at arms' length. It was the opportunity the Fords had been waiting for. As they were talking, Jesse suddenly noticed that a picture hanging on the wall was askew and did something completely out of character. He stood on a chair, turned his back to the Fords, and started straightening the picture, or dusting it.

Bob Ford shot him dead. Both Ford brothers had pulled their weapons; there were reports that Charley fired too and missed. But Bob Ford's one shot hit Jesse James under his right ear, and he fell. He was thirty-four years old when he died.

Bob Ford sent wires to the governor and the sheriff, claiming the reward, then both brothers surrendered to the local marshal. As word spread that Thomas Howard was actually

The assassination of Jesse James made national headlines. The popular *Police Gazette* immediately published this fanciful illustration (*above left*). The photo of the outlaw in death became a national sensation, and crowds flocked to see the house in St. Joseph where he was murdered.

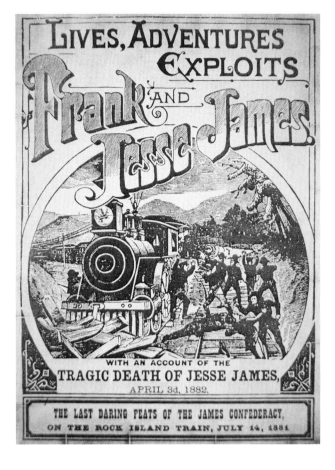

This softcover edition from Chicago's Stein Publishing House was typical of the numerous books rushed into print after James's murder.

the feared killer Jesse James, the people of St. Joseph rushed to the house to catch a glimpse of his body, stunned to discover that the most wanted man in the country had been living comfortably among them.

The Fords were arrested. Two weeks later, within hours, both men were indicted for the murder of Jesse James, pleaded guilty, were sentenced to hang, were pardoned by Governor Crittenden, and walked out of the prison free men. Rather than the ten-thousand-dollar reward, they ended up with about six hundred, as the governor divided the money among many deserving parties—himself included. And, rather than being acclaimed for finally bringing Jesse James to eternal justice, the Fords were scorned as cowards for shooting him in the back.

Within a month of Jesse's death, the newspaperman John Edwards began corresponding with the governor to arrange Frank James's surrender. For the next three years, Frank fought charges accusing him of committing numerous crimes in several states. He was tried on only two of the murder-robberies and was acquitted. Many respectable men testified to his good character. In February 1885, he was cleared of all charges. For him, the Civil War and all the battles that followed finally were over.

Charley and Bob Ford toured in a theater production entitled *The Brother's Vow; or, the Bandit's Revenge*, in which they reenacted the murder of Jesse James. Initially it was quite successful, but over time audiences lost interest, and it closed, leaving them almost broke. In 1884, Charley Ford, addicted to morphine and suffering from tuberculosis, and distraught at being considered a coward, committed suicide. Bob Ford held several jobs, earning some money posing for photographs with rubes in dime museums, billed as "the man who killed Jesse James." By 1892, he was running a tent saloon in Creede, Colorado. A man named Ed O'Kelley shot and killed him there after an argument.

Frank James held several jobs, even touring with Cole Younger for a bit in a theatrical production called *The Great Cole Younger and Frank James Historical Wild West Show*. Frank James died of a heart attack in 1915.

The legend of Jesse James has been told in almost every American cultural medium—but two often-asked questions have never been satisfactorily answered. One: Was Jesse James a hero of the Old South, fighting against the evils of Reconstruction and the carpetbaggers' intent to profit from the destruction of war, or was he an outlaw who took advantage of the political situation? When he raged, "Just let a party of men commit a bold robbery, and the cry is hang them, but [President] Grant and his party can steal millions, and it is all right," was he simply an actor playing a role created for him by John Edwards, or did he really mean it? The answer, most probably, is a bit of both. He started out with a set of skills perfected in the war; then he clearly embraced and enjoyed playing the noble character fighting for Southern dignity, and perhaps at times he truly meant it. But even after that was no longer relevant, he continued robbing and killing. He knew no other way.

The second and equally intriguing question is, Why would he take off his guns and turn his back on two men he did not know especially well and probably didn't trust? He never went anywhere without his guns. Historians have offered a variety of explanations, describing the act as everything from foolhardy to courageous. Bob Ford once said he thought it was a trick: that Jesse wanted to make it appear that he trusted them so that he might later take action against them. Others have suggested that perhaps Jesse was tired and careless and willing to let fate play its hand. As he himself once wrote, "Justice is slow but sure, and there is a just God that will bring all to justice."

DOC HOLLIDAY

🔫 🔫 *Desperate Measures* 🔫 🔫

lthough it reads like an advertisement for a movie, this is a true story: The gunslinger Doc Holliday spent most of his life preparing to die, until he finally found a reason to live—and it almost killed him.

Without a doubt, John Henry Holliday was the meanest, toughest, and probably the most violent dentist in American history; although, truth be told, he definitely could fill a cavity. His close friend Wyatt Earp described him as "a philosopher whom life had made a caustic wit . . . the most skillful gambler, and the nerviest, fastest, deadliest man with a six gun I ever saw."

Unlike the other famous gunslingers of the Old West, John Holliday was a wealthy, well-educated man. His father, Henry Holliday, was a soldier, druggist, and planter who had fought the Indians in 1838, the Mexicans in 1846, and the Union army in 1861, rising to the rank of major before being forced by illness to resign his commission. His mother, Alice, was a classic Southern belle. His cousin, Mattie Holliday, who lived to be one hundred, served as the model for the character Melanie in Margaret Mitchell's *Gone With the Wind*. John Henry was born in Griffin, Georgia, in 1852, but a decade later, the family, fleeing General Sherman's March to the Sea, moved to Valdosta, Georgia, where Henry Holliday eventually was elected mayor. When John Henry was fifteen years old, his mother died of tuberculosis, the same disease that would later kill his adopted brother and shape the course of his own life.

Nothing about his childhood suggested that he would one day wind up in the most famous gunfight in American history, the showdown at the O.K. Corral. John Henry received a classical education, studying grammar, mathematics, French, Latin, and ancient Greek. When it came time for him to pick a career, dentistry seemed an appropriate path to follow; his cousin had founded Philadelphia's Pennsylvania College of Dental Surgery. He graduated from there in 1872, after writing a thesis on diseases of the teeth, and joined a practice in Atlanta. Under normal circumstances, he would have gone on to have a fine life: He would have married a genteel woman and started a family; at night, he would sit by the parlor fire in his comfortable Georgia home; and he would die in old age, surrounded by loved ones.

Instead, he started coughing.

In 1873, when he was only twenty-two years old, John Holliday was diagnosed with tuberculosis, at that time a fatal disease. The cause wasn't known, and there was no cure. He consulted the best doctors in Atlanta, and their opinion was unanimous: The only treatment was to move to a drier climate, which was believed to prolong life. As it turned out, he might well have had another reason to leave Georgia: It's possible that he had shot his first victim.

According to the story, written years later by lawman-turned-journalist Bat Masterson, John Henry and some friends came upon a group of black teenagers enjoying a popular swimming hole on the Withlacoochee River. Supposedly the two groups got into an argument, and Holliday produced a double-barreled shotgun. He shot and killed two of them and wounded several others, although his family insisted the story wasn't true and he had simply fired over their heads to scare them away.

Legends are born of reality, which is exaggerated and embellished until it shines brightly. Although the actual facts of that day are hazy, the meaning is clear: Even at a young age, there was a dark and dangerous side to John Henry Holliday.

Whatever the reason, Holliday moved to Dallas and opened a dental practice. His skills were obvious: At the Dallas County Fair, he won several awards, including "best set of teeth in gold." Dallas was a booming cow town, the railroad making it a hub for shipping grain, cotton, and buffalo hides. It might have been a smart place for a skilled dentist to set up shop, but not too many people there were willing to risk their lives visiting a dentist infected with consumption. As he soon discovered, though, there was another trade at which he excelled: John Holliday was a gambling man. As Masterson wrote, "Gambling was not only the principal and best-paying industry of the town at the time, but it was also reckoned among its most respectable."

The cards loved him. He possessed two traits that were essential for any gambler: intelligence and a poker face. If there was a single benefit to living with a death sentence, this was it: Nothing seemed to really make a difference to him. Win or lose, he was going to be dead in a few years. That knowledge made it easy for him to hide his emotions and draw the next card—or, when necessary, draw his gun.

When money and alcohol are put on the same table, tempers can get mighty thin. The first time a gambling man backed down in the Old West, he might just as well keep moving, because people would learn about it and wouldn't hesitate to take advantage. In 1875, Holliday was arrested after trading wild shots with saloon keeper Charles Austin. He was acquitted but, supposedly, a few days later, got into another gunfight and this time killed "a prominent citizen." There is at least some evidence that this incident was just a story Holliday concocted to impress people. Apparently it worked, because by the time he settled in Jacksboro, Texas, in 1876, he was said to be carrying two guns and a knife and had become known as "the Deadly Dentist"! Allegedly he had to hightail it out of Jacksboro after killing a black soldier from nearby Fort Richardson—with the army, the Texas Rangers, the US marshal, the local sheriff, and a posse of citizens in hot pursuit, trying to collect the reward placed on his head. There actually may be some truth to that one, as there is a record of a Private Jacob Smith being shot around that time by an "unknown assailant."

Gamblers are always chasing the next big pot, and Holliday moved often, usually carrying with him some tale of violence for which there was little evidence. Supposedly, for example, while dealing faro in Denver under the alias Tom Mackey in 1875, he slashed the throat of a bully named Buddy Ryan. He also is credited with three killings in Cheyenne. It is possible; Masterson was blunt in his assessment, pointing out, "Holliday had a mean disposition and an ungovernable temper, and under the influence of liquor was a most dangerous man." True or not, these stories served a purpose: Holliday had figured out pretty quickly that a reputation for being good with a gun would often make people hesitate before drawing on you.

While on the trail, John Henry hadn't forgotten his dental training, and when he found himself staying in one place for more than a short spell, he'd hang out his shingle, which gave him the nickname by which he would eventually gain renown, "Doc" Holliday.

A gambler's place of work is the saloon, and nobody ever claimed that Doc Holliday didn't enjoy a drink or two or several more. Why not—one thing he knew for sure was that it wasn't the whiskey that was going to kill him. He was what we'd now call a functioning alcoholic, with a hair-trigger temper. In a barroom fight in Breckenridge, Texas, he beat a gambler named Henry Kahn with his walking stick. Kahn returned later that day and shot Holliday. His wounds were so serious that the *Dallas Weekly Herald* quite prematurely reported his death. Upon his recovery, he settled in the rowdy town of Fort Griffin, where only a few years earlier a band of Kiowas had attacked a wagon train and killed seven men. But for Doc Holliday, that's where the tall tales ended and his life as an American western legend took root.

While working as a card dealer at the pugilist John Shanssey's saloon in 1877, he met a truly formidable woman named Mary Katherine Horony, a curvaceous twenty-six-year-old dance-hall girl and sometime prostitute better known as "Big Nose Kate," who would be his primary female companion for the rest of his life. The Hungarian-born, well-bred, and well-educated Kate was a fine match for him: She didn't seem to give two hoots about very much, either, especially what people thought of her. She was tough, stubborn, and hot tempered

This portrait of thirty-one-year-old
Doc Holliday was taken only months
after the shoot-out at the O.K. Corral.

and often told people that she belonged to no man, nor to any madam—she worked as a prostitute because she liked both the benefits and the freedom. And, ironically, she had already been married once—to a dentist, who had died.

Soon after Holliday and Kate got together, she had an opportunity to show how much she cared for him: She got to break him out of prison. In one version of the story, Doc had been playing poker with a gambler named Ed Bailey, who insisted on sifting through the discards in violation of the rules of Western Poker. Doc finally had had enough and claimed the pot. Bailey pulled his revolver, but before he could fire, Holliday whipped out his knife and gutted him. In another version, Doc was actually arrested for "illegal gambling." Whatever the reason for his arrest, he was put under guard in a locked hotel room because the town didn't have a jail. In the first version, a lynch mob was forming, and Kate was forced to take action to save his life. In both stories, she set fire to an old shed behind the hotel. When the fire threatened to engulf the town, everyone rushed to fight it. With their attention diverted, Kate broke Doc out of the hotel. Some say she pulled two six-shooters on the jailer and forced him to open the door. Guns or no, she got him out, and they took off for Dodge City.

John Shanssey also introduced Doc Holliday to deputy US marshal Wyatt Earp. Shanssey and Earp had met several years earlier, when the future lawman had refereed one of the future saloon man's bouts. This time, Earp had come to "the Flats," as the town near Fort Griffin was called, hunting a train robber named "Dirty Dave" Rudabaugh. Perhaps at Shanssey's request, Doc told Earp what he knew: While playing cards with Rudabaugh a few days earlier, he'd heard the man say something about going back to Dodge City. Earp sent that information by telegraph to Dodge City's assistant deputy, Bat Masterson, who eventually made the arrest. But that encounter marked the beginning of the most important relationship of Doc Holliday's life.

Wyatt Earp was himself an ornery character. He'd been a boxer and a gambler; he'd worked on the railroads, as a constable, and as a horse thief. There were a lot of men like him in the Old West, people who just flowed with the opportunities life presented to them. For the previous few years, he'd been working mostly as a strongman, keeping the peace in brothels. He'd moved to Wichita in '74 to keep the peace in his brother Virgil's house of ill repute, while also working as a part-time peace officer for the city. When Earp first crossed paths with Doc Holliday in '77, he had recently been named Dodge City's chief deputy marshal.

Presumably, Earp welcomed the Doc and Kate, who found lodging at Deacon Cox's boardinghouse when they arrived in Dodge. If it wasn't the roughest town in the West, it definitely was high on the list. As a letter that appeared in the *Washington Evening Star* complained, "Dodge City is a wicked little town. Its character is so clearly and egregiously bad that one might conclude . . . that it was marked for special Providential punishment."

The night on which Holliday and Earp forged the friendship that would last for the rest of their lives began when as many as fifty cowboys just off the trail came galloping down Front Street, raising a holy ruckus. After shooting out most of the shop windows, they ended up at the Long Branch Saloon, where Doc was in the back room, quietly tending to his nightly business. There is no record of how the cards were treating him that night. Soon Deputy Earp walked through the swinging doors, not having the slightest idea what was waiting inside for him. The cowboys were led by Tobe Driskill and Ed Morrison, a man who had been humiliated by Wyatt in Wichita several years earlier and had been itching to get even. Earp

In 1883, the Dodge City Peace Commission ended the Dodge City War without a shot being fired.

pushed open the door and found fifty pistols and rifles pointed at him. As Wyatt Earp told the story years later, Morrison warned him, "Pray and jerk your gun. Your time has come, Earp!"

Before anyone could make a move, Holliday got up from his table quickly and quietly, pulled his own gun, and aimed it squarely at the back of Morrison's head. "No, friend," he said. "You draw or throw your hands up. Any of you bastards pulls a gun and your leader loses what's left of his brains." Fifty guns hit the floor. Earp punctuated the stand-down by slamming Morrison over his head with his Colt before taking him and Driskill to jail. As he later wrote, "The only way anyone could have appreciated the feeling I had for Doc after the

Driskill-Morrison business would have been to have stood in my boots at the time Doc came through the Long Branch doorway."

Word spreads lickety-split when one man stands up to a saloon full of armed cowhands. Doc Holliday earned himself a reputation that night. People might have wondered if he had been drunk or crazy, but after that, no one ever doubted his courage.

Not surprisingly, Doc and Kate had a tumultuous relationship, breaking up and getting back together several times. Neither one of them liked to stay still for too long. When she took off on him in '78, Doc decided to join the Earp brothers, Wyatt, Morgan, and Virgil, in Tombstone, Arizona. Tombstone was one of the West's last mining boomtowns, built on a mesa above the Tough Nut Silver Mine. By the time Doc Holliday rode into Tombstone in 1880, the town already had an estimated 110 saloons, 14 gambling halls, a plentiful number of brothels, and 1 bowling alley.

Supposedly he'd left several bodies along the trail between Dodge and Tombstone. In Las Vegas, then part of the New Mexico Territory, for example, he got into a shoot-out with an old army scout named Mike Gordon. When Gordon's former girlfriend, one of the saloon girls, refused to leave town with him, he'd started shooting up the place. As Holliday tried to get out of there, Gordon pegged a shot at him. Doc put two shots into his chest. Likely it was considered self-defense, as the coroner's jury ruled that Gordon's fatal wounds "had been inflicted by some person unknown to that jury."

Doc almost settled another score before heading for Tombstone, trading shots with bartender Charlie White in Vegas's Plaza Hotel saloon. This feud had started in Dodge. According to the future governor of New Mexico, Miguel Antonio Otero, who was a witness to this duel, "The two men faced each other and began shooting. They shoot and shoot with no one scoring a hit. Finally, Charlie White is down!" A scalp wound had stunned him senseless, but he recovered and left town.

A bad situation was already brewing in Tombstone when Holliday rode into town. Until the Earps arrived there, Tombstone had pretty much been run by a loosely knit gang known as the Cowboys. Mostly ranchers and cowboys who had been living there before the big mining companies came in and staked their claims, the Cowboys consisted of men like the Clantons, the McLaury brothers, Curly Bill Brocius, and Johnny Ringo, all of them known to be handy with a six-shooter. As long as they limited their activities to running across the border into Sonora and rustling Mexican cattle, nobody paid them too much mind, but after the Mexican government had gotten involved, making that too risky, the gang began stealing US cavalry beef. The Earps had been brought in to tame the town and had done a pretty good job of it. As the *Tombstone Daily Epitaph* reported, "Since the retirement of Ben Sippy as marshal and the appointment of V.W. Earp to fill the vacancy the town has been noted for its quietness and good order. The fractious and much dreaded cowboys when they came to town were upon their good behavior and no unseemly brawls were indulged in, and it was hoped by our citizens that no more such deeds would occur as led to the killing of Marshal White one year ago."

Hostility simmered between the lawmen and the Cowboys. The county sheriff, John Behan, stood between them, although he tended to lean toward the gang. Doc made his presence known soon after arriving, getting into a drunken brawl with another gambler in the

Tombstone, Arizona, in 1881 had a population of 4,000, 600 dwellings—and 2 churches. The large building in the foreground (*opposite*) is the Tough Nut mine hoisting works.

Oriental Saloon. Milt Joyce, the saloon's owner, had disarmed Doc, and when he refused to return his gun, Holliday got himself another weapon and walked in shooting. Joyce raised his gun to shoot back, and Holliday shot the weapon out of his hand, then shot the bartender in the toe. When Doc's attention was diverted, Joyce picked up his gun and whomped Holliday over the head with it, knocking him out cold. Holliday was arrested. He was found guilty of assault and battery and fined $20, plus $11.25 in court costs.

By this time, Doc's consumption had taken hold and was beginning to affect him. He'd lost considerable weight and ended most nights drunk. He was on a sure path to a sorry end. It turned out, though, that the Cowboys thought they might help that along just a bit. On

the Ides of March (March 15) 1881, four masked bandits held up the Kinnear & Company stagecoach. The driver and one passenger were killed during the robbery. The Cowboys claimed Doc Holliday had been one of the bandits, and as evidence, they offered an affidavit that had been signed by a very drunk Big Nose Kate during one of their fights. On July 5, Doc Holliday was arrested and charged with murder and stage robbery; Wyatt Earp and a local saloon keeper put up his five-thousand-dollar bail, then set out to prove his innocence. When Kate sobered up, she insisted that Sheriff Behan and Milt Joyce had supplied the drink as well as the pen and paper and that she hadn't known what she was signing. Other people testified that they had been with Holliday at the time of the robbery. After hearing all the evidence, the district attorney called the charges "ridiculous," and Holliday was released from bond. It didn't take Doc long to find out that Cowboy Ike Clanton was behind the ruse. He knew that one day soon, they would be settling up.

Ike Clanton knew that the real killers were some of the boys he was riding with. Wyatt Earp was especially interested in putting the cuffs on them; the election for sheriff was coming up, and he intended to replace the slippery Behan in that job, which paid a handsome sum. The story is that Wyatt made a deal with Clanton: If Clanton told him where the robbers were hiding out, Wyatt would let him keep the whole $3,600 reward, content in the knowledge that capturing those killers would just about guarantee his election. Ike Clanton agreed and provided the information, but before Earp could act, three of those men were caught rustling cattle and killed. That set Ike on edge; he began getting paranoid that Earp might reveal his double-dealing, which for him would be a death sentence.

In July, several Mexican smugglers were attacked and killed in Skeleton Canyon, and the silver they were carrying was stolen. The perpetrators were never identified, but Mexicans living near the border felt sure this was the work of the Cowboys.

A month later, the head of the Cowboys and Ike's father, Newman Haynes Clanton, better known as Old Man Clanton, and six of his men were driving a herd to market in Tombstone through Guadalupe Canyon, the main smuggling route over the border. After making camp, they were ambushed; five men died, including Old Man Clanton. Although the evidence pointed to Mexicans seeking retribution for the Skeleton Canyon attack, the Cowboys believed the Earps and Doc Holliday were somehow involved. It was not an unreasonable assumption: Wyatt Earp and Doc Holliday eventually showed up in town wounded, Doc using a cane.

By the fall, the relationship between the law and the Cowboys was about as dangerous as tinder in a drought, just waiting for a spark. The Cowboys were openly threatening to "clean out the Earps," along with Holliday, if they didn't clear out of town. Ironically, in his friendship with the Earps—especially with Wyatt and Morgan—Doc Holliday had finally found the thing worth living for, and for which he was willing to put his life on the line.

The gunfight at the O.K. Corral took place on October 26, 1881. It took about thirty seconds to write a chapter in American history that will never be forgotten. As the *Epitaph* reported the next day, "Stormy as were the early days of Tombstone nothing ever occurred equal to the event of yesterday."

The stage had been set the night before outside the Alhambra Saloon, when Ike Clanton and Doc Holliday, both having far exceeded their alcohol limit, staggered around threatening to kill each other. Clanton supposedly promised that he was going to kill an Earp, and allegedly Doc responded by claiming to have killed Old Man Clanton and to be looking forward to adding Ike to his count. Virgil Earp had broken up the fight.

The thirty-second-long gunfight at the O.K. Corral has been the subject of numerous books, pieces of art, television shows, and Hollywood films in which Doc Holliday was played by Walter Huston, Stacy Keach, Victor Mature, Kirk Douglas, Jason Robards, Val Kilmer, and Dennis Quaid.

Meanwhile, Clanton had met up with Wyatt and supposedly told him flat out, "Your consumptive friend . . . he's a dead man tomorrow."

To which Earp responded, "Don't you tangle with Doc Holliday. He'll kill you before you've begun."

The morning of the twenty-sixth was gray and windy. Ike Clanton showed up early at Fly's Boardinghouse, demanding to see Holliday. Doc wasn't there, but later, when Big Nose Kate told him about Clanton's visit, he responded, "If God will let me live long enough, he will see me."

About one o'clock in the afternoon, tired of his threats, Virgil and Morgan Earp went looking for Ike Clanton. They found him walking on Fourth Street, carrying a Winchester rifle with a revolver on his hip. Virgil Earp approached him cautiously, then banged him on his head, taking both his weapons. He hauled him off to Judge Albert O. Wallace's courtroom. Wyatt found Clanton there and warned him: "You damn dirty cow thief. You have been threatening our lives, and I know it. I think I would be justified in shooting you down any place I would meet you. But if you are anxious to make a fight, I will go anywhere on earth to make a fight with you."

"Fight is my racket, and all I want is four feet of ground," Clanton supposedly replied. But he backed down from a fight right there, making it clear he didn't like the odds. Instead he was fined $27.50 and released.

As Wyatt Earp was leaving the courtroom, he bumped right into one of the Cowboys, Tom McLaury, at the front door. Earp apologized, but when McLaury bad-mouthed him, Earp smashed him in the head with his pistol.

With trouble brewing, marshal Virgil Earp swore in Morgan Earp and Doc Holliday, giving them the legal authority granted to all US deputy marshals: They could shoot to kill.

Almost two hours later, a local man named R. F. Coleman saw Ike and Billy Clanton and Frank and Tom McLaury in Dunbar's corral. At some point, they were joined by another one of the Cowboys, Billy Claibourne. The speculation is that they were planning to ambush Doc Holliday, who normally passed that way each morning. Coleman claimed that he found Sheriff Behan, warning him that those boys were looking for trouble and that it was his duty to disarm them.

Everybody in town knew what was coming: a showdown. Apparently several members of Tombstone's Citizens Committee volunteered to walk with the Earps. Wyatt turned them down, explaining that it was his responsibility to enforce the law and that's what he intended to do. But he did allow Doc Holliday to join him. The long trail Doc had been traveling for so many years had led him to this point. There is some evidence that at first Wyatt told Holliday that this wasn't his affair. But the result of that conversation was that Virgil Earp gave Holliday a ten-gauge shotgun, the type of double-barreled gun carried by coachmen, which he secreted under his greatcoat. In return, Doc handed Virgil his cane. Virgil planned to carry it as a way of making clear to the Cowboys that he wasn't armed and, if possible, of preventing bloodshed.

The four lawmen started walking shoulder-to-shoulder down the center of Fremont Street. Officially, they intended to enforce the law prohibiting people from carrying guns within Tombstone, but in fact they were going to get this thing settled. The Earps were dressed all in black; Doc Holliday was wearing gray. Sheriff Behan tried to derail them, apparently telling them that the Cowboys weren't armed. In response, Wyatt suggested that Behan go with him to talk to the boys. Supposedly Behan laughed and told him, "Hell, this is your fight, not mine."

Doc Holliday and the Earp brothers confronted the Clantons and McLaurys in a narrow fifteen-foot-wide space behind the O.K. Corral, between Fly's Photograph Gallery and Jersey's Livery Stable. For some reason, Claibourne had left the gang. The men faced one another for a few long seconds, then Virgil Earp shouted, "Give up your arms or throw up your arms!"

Another second passed; then it started. Billy Clanton and Frank McLaury went for their guns. Virgil warned them, "Hold on, I don't want that." But it was too late.

As eyewitness R. F. Coleman described it to a reporter the next day,

> There was some reply made by Frank McLaury, when firing became general, over thirty shots being fired. Tom McLaury fell first, but raised and fired again before he died. Bill Clanton fell next, and raised to fire again when Mr. Fly took his revolver from him. Frank McLaury ran a few rods and fell. Morgan Earp was shot through and fell. Doc Holliday was hit in the left hip but kept on firing. Virgil Earp was hit in the third or fourth fire, in the leg which staggered him but he kept up his effective work. Wyatt Earp stood up and fired in rapid succession, as cool as a cucumber, and was not hit.
>
> Doc Holliday was as calm as though at target practice and fired rapidly.

Thirty shots were fired in thirty seconds; then it was over. Tom McLaury, Frank McLaury, and Billy Clanton were dead. Doc Holliday was credited by the *Tombstone Nugget* with killing both McLaurys—he blew Tom McLaury away with both barrels at close range—and possibly wounding Billy Clanton. Ike Clanton, who took off running when the shooting started, survived. Morgan Earp was seriously wounded, but he would survive. And, as the *Epitaph* concluded, "Doc Holliday was hit upon the scabbard of his pistol, the leather breaking the force of the ball so that no material damage was done other than to make him limp a little in his walk."

When the smoke cleared, the mine whistles started whining. The miners rose to the surface, armed themselves, and raced into town to preserve law and order. Armed guards surrounded the jail and would remain there throughout the night. Sheriff Behan approached Wyatt Earp and told him boldly, "I'll have to arrest you."

Earp shook his head. "I won't be arrested today," he said. "I am right here and am not going away. You have deceived me. You told me these men were disarmed; I went to disarm them."

Tom and Frank McLaury and Billy Clanton were buried in the same grave. The *Tombstone Epitaph* reported, "The funeral . . . procession headed by the Tombstone band, moved down Allen street and thence to the cemetery. The sidewalks were densely packed for three or four blocks. It was a most impressive and saddening sight and such a one as it is to be hoped may never occur again in this community."

Big Nose Kate said later that Doc Holliday returned to their room, sat on the bed, and wept. "That was awful," he said. "Awful."

Three days later, Ike Clanton filed charges, and Wyatt and Doc were arrested. An inquest into the shootings lasting almost a month concluded, "The defendants were fully justified in committing these homicides, that it was a necessary act done in the discharge of official duty."

The gunfight turned out to be only the beginning of the bloodletting. Two months later, marshal Virgil Earp was ambushed by three men with shotguns on his way to the Crystal Palace. He was hit twice and suffered permanent injury. The Cowboys believed to be responsible were arrested, but other members of the gang swore that these men were with them at the time of the attack, and they were acquitted.

In March of the following year, Morgan Earp was shot and killed while playing pool at Hatch's Saloon and Billiard Parlor. When Doc learned that the cowards had shot Morgan in the back, he apparently went ripping through the town, kicking open locked doors, hunting the killers. But they'd gotten away. Morgan was laid to rest wearing one of Doc's finest blue suits. The Doc and the Earps now understood that they could not depend on the law to protect them. That was the beginning of what has become known as "the Vendetta Ride."

Tombstone had become much too dangerous for the Earp family. All the women and children were packed up and, along with Morgan Earp's body, put on a train for California. Doc, Wyatt, and several others rode along to protect them. As the train pulled into Tucson, a lookout spotted Ike Clanton and Frank Stilwell, believed to be lying in wait to finish the job on Virgil. Stilwell had been bragging that he had fired the fatal shot into Morgan Earp's back, so no one was much surprised the next morning when Stilwell's thoroughly ventilated body was found lying in the dirt near the tracks. As the newspapers reported, he was buried the next day "unfollowed by a single mourner." Doc and Wyatt were named as his killers but suffered no repercussions for that act.

The bodies continued to pile up. Deputy Wyatt Earp's posse heard that some of the Cowboys were in the Dragoon Mountains; they found one of the gang, Florentino Cruz, and dispensed western justice upon him. Two days later, nine Cowboys led by Curly Bill Brocius ambushed the posse. Doc was quoted as telling a newspaperman, ". . . eight rustlers rose up from behind the bank and poured from thirty-five to forty shots at us. Our escape was miraculous. The shots cut our clothes and saddles and killed one horse, but did not hit us. I think we would have been killed if God Almighty wasn't on our side. Wyatt Earp turned loose with a shotgun and killed Curley Bill." After that, it turned out to be open season on the Cowboys: Johnny Barnes, who was also involved in the attack on Virgil, suffered wounds that eventually would kill him. A couple of months later, the body of Johnny Ringo—with a bullet hole in his right temple and his gun dangling from one finger—was found propped up in the trunk of a large tree in West Turkey Creek Canyon, Arizona Territory. Local authorities speculated that it might have been suicide, but there were serious hints that it was the work of Wyatt Earp. Within a year after the murder of Morgan Earp, at least five more Cowboys were killed by people unknown. The gang was decimated.

Doc Holliday was arrested in Denver, although once again, no charges stuck. Reporting his arrest, the *Denver Republican* wrote, "Holliday has a big reputation as a fighter, and has probably put more rustlers and cowboys under the sod than any other one man in the west. He had been the terror of the lawless element in Arizona, and with the Earps was the only man brave enough to face the bloodthirsty crowd which has made the name of Arizona a stench in the nostrils of decent men."

In 1883, Holliday settled in the mining town of Leadville, Colorado, the highest city above sea level in the country and a questionable place for a man with tuberculosis. The British writer Oscar Wilde had visited it a year earlier on his national lecture tour and remarked that it was there that he saw the only rational method of art criticism he'd ever encountered, on a notice hung in a saloon. It read, "Please do not shoot the pianist. He is doing his best." Although some believed Doc Holliday was completely broke and given to borrowing money, he worked as a faro dealer at the Board of Trade Saloon, drawing players from all around who wanted to say that they'd sat at the table with the great Doc Holliday.

Holliday spent a good deal of his time fighting reality with alcohol and the opiate laudanum. In 1884, he was involved in one of the last gunfights of his storied career, when a kid named Johnny Allen challenged him. Apparently Holliday ignored him as long as he could, but when Allen drew on him in Hyman's Saloon, Doc fired twice, hitting the kid in the arm. The bartender jumped on him to prevent him from shooting again. That was the seventeenth and final arrest of his life. A jury found him not guilty of attempted murder.

In the winter of '86, Doc Holliday and Wyatt Earp met for the last time, in the lobby of Denver's Windsor Hotel. Wyatt's wife, Josephine, wrote that the two men sat together and laughed and cried, and that she had rarely seen a man as happy as Doc Holliday was that day. She described him as frail, unsteady on his feet with a persistent cough.

Holliday eventually made it to the sulfurous Yampah Hot Springs near Glenwood Springs, Colorado, a place that supposedly had healing powers. But the tuberculosis had him wrapped. He spent the last two months of his life in bed, delirious at least some of the time. Doc had always told people that he intended to die with his boots on, the western way of saying he was going to

Doc Holliday's grave in Glenwood Springs, Colorado, has become a popular tourist destination. To his own surprise, and perhaps disappointment, he died in bed, with his boots off.

die fighting, but in fact his boots were off as he lay in bed. On November 8, 1887, he supposedly awoke and asked in a clear voice for a glass of whiskey. Like so much else in his life, some reports say the nurse gave it to him; other reports claim she refused. But it is generally believed that he sighed, looked down at his bare feet, and commented, "Damn, this is funny," and died.

After years of gunfights in which he was responsible for piling up a slew of bodies, Doc Holliday died with his boots off—but his reputation as a man who had found a friendship worth living and fighting for was intact. A few days after he was buried, the Leadville *Carbonate Chronicle* printed his obituary, which read in part, "There is scarcely one in the country who had acquired a greater notoriety than Doc Holliday, who enjoyed the reputation of being one of the most fearless men on the frontier, and whose devotion to his friends in the climax of the fiercest ordeal was inextinguishable. It was this, more than any other faculty that secured for him the reverence of a large circle who were prepared on the shortest notice to rally to his relief."

SHOOTING DOWN A LEGEND

Among the most common icons of the American West is the quick-drawing, sharpshooting sheriff, facing down an outlaw at high noon on a dusty street as the anxious folks take cover. Indeed, most western tales seem to end with guns blazing, and when the smoke clears, only the good guys are left standing.

It is generally believed that six-shooters tamed the West, that a man couldn't safely walk the streets without his Colt resting easily on his hip, and that the background music in most western towns was church bells and gunshots. The heroes were the men who shot quickest and straightest.

Contrary to the legend, not every man in the West carried a six-gun or was quick to draw. Gunfights were rare and mostly avoided if possible. As Doc Holliday learned, a big reputation was often more valuable than a gunslinger's skill, because it prevented people from drawing on you—or, just as likely, shooting you in the back. In fact, in most towns, once they had been settled for a few years, it actually was illegal to carry a gun. In most places, people were much more likely to be carrying a shotgun or a rifle than a pistol, because they were much more likely to need a gun for hunting than for protection. The heyday of the gunfighter (or the pistolero, as he was often called) began after the Civil War, when many

thousands of men came home with weapons and experience in using them. There actually were very few real showdowns, where two men faced each other a few feet apart and drew; they were so rare, in fact, that killing Davis Tutt on a street in Springfield, Missouri, made Wild Bill Hickok a national celebrity. And even in those few real duels, it rarely mattered who fired the quickest, but rather, whose aim was true. Most times, shooters would just keep firing until—or if—someone got hit. Weapons and bullets at the time were notoriously unreliable. As Buffalo Bill Cody once admitted, "We did the best we could, with the tools we had."

So, while quick draws were impressive in the movies, in real life, they rarely made any difference in the outcome. In fact, as Wyatt Earp once explained, "The most important lesson I learned . . . was that the winner of a gunplay usually was the one who took his time."

The notion of a fair fight was also mostly a Hollywood creation. Because it was a matter of survival rather than honor, in many shootings, the winner was simply the guy who got the drop on his opponent. Some

Charles Marion Russell, "the Cowboy Artist," tells an Old West story in his oil painting *Death of a Gambler:* Cards, alcohol, and guns all come together in a saloon and lead to an inevitable result.

men carried a pistol on their hip, knowing it would attract attention—but when necessary, they'd pull their serious weapon, often a small derringer, from under a coat or shirtsleeve and fire before their startled opponent could respond. It has been estimated that as many three out of four people who died from gunshots were killed by concealed second weapons. When gunfights did take place, they generally happened on the spur of the moment, sometimes breaking out when people were liquored up and angry, and the shooters, rather than standing at a distance from each other, were only a few feet apart.

Most guns used the "cap and ball" system, exploding black powder-propelled "bullets" little bigger than a marble that were accurate only to about fifty feet. Bat Masterson was quoted as advising, "If you want to hit a man in his chest, aim for his groin." If more than one person was involved, the situation quickly became chaotic: After the first few shots, the black smoke would have obscured everybody's vision for several seconds, making it even more difficult to fire rapidly and hit a target with the next shots.

The truth is that guns and rifles were common and absolutely necessary in the West, but they were used more for hunting and protection than for two-gun shoot-outs.

BILLY THE KID

Escape Artist

t about nine o'clock on the warm moonlit night of July 14, 1881, the sheriff of Lincoln County, New Mexico, Pat Garrett, rode out to old Fort Sumner with deputies John W. Poe and Kip McKinney. The famous fort had been abandoned by the army after the Civil War, and cattle baron Lucien Maxwell had transformed it into a beautiful hacienda. His family now lived in the officers' quarters, while Mexicans occupied many of the outer buildings. Lucien himself had died, and his son Pete was now running the compound. Garrett had received some reliable information that the outlaw Billy the Kid had holed up there with his girlfriend. He and his deputies would need to be quiet and careful: Billy the Kid was a cold-blooded killer. Garrett knew that better than most: He had captured the Kid just six months earlier, only to have the outlaw escape the noose by killing two of his deputies—while still wearing chains.

The weather was pleasant as the three lawmen unsaddled their horses outside the compound and entered the peach orchard on foot. They saw people sitting around evening campfires in the yard, conversing mostly in Spanish. Somebody was strumming a guitar. Garrett and his men stayed silently in the shadows, watching, without knowing exactly what they were looking for. The sheriff intended to have a private conversation with Pete Maxwell, who was a law-abiding citizen. As they lingered, a man stood up, hopped over a low fence, and walked directly toward Maxwell's house. In the firelight, they saw that he was wearing a broad-brimmed sombrero and a dark vest and pants; he was not wearing boots. They couldn't see his face and didn't pay him much attention.

To avoid being noticed, just in case the Kid was there, Garrett and his men backed up and took a safer path to the house. Around midnight, the sheriff placed Poe and McKinney on the porch, about twenty feet from the open door, and eased himself into Maxwell's dark bedroom. Garrett sat down at the head of the bed and shook Maxwell awake. Speaking in a whisper, he asked him if he knew the whereabouts of the Kid. Maxwell was not pleased to have been woken, but he told Garrett that the outlaw had indeed been there for a spell. Whether he was still there, he did not know.

As they conversed, they heard a man's voice outside demanding, "*¿Quien es?*" ("Who are you?") A split second later, a thin figure appeared in the doorway. Looking back outside, the man asked again, "*¿Quien es?*" Even in the dim light, Garrett could see that the man was holding a revolver in his right hand and a butcher knife in his left.

The man moved cautiously into the bedroom. Garrett guessed he was Pete Maxwell's brother-in-law, who had probably seen two men on the porch and wanted to know what was going on. The sheriff also knew he had a big advantage: The thin man didn't know he was there, and it would take a few seconds for his eyes to adjust to the dark. The man walked toward the bed, leaned down, and asked Maxwell in a soft voice, "*¿Quienes so esos hombres afuera, Pedro?*" ("Who are those men outside, Peter?")

It's impossible to know what Maxwell was thinking at that moment, but just above a whisper, he said to Garrett, "That's him."

The thin man stood up and started backing out of the room. He raised his gun and pointed it into the darkness. As Garrett later remembered, "Quickly as possible I drew my revolver and fired, threw my body aside and fired again." Garrett and Maxwell heard the man fall to the floor. Not knowing how badly he was hit, they scrambled out of the room. The Mexicans had heard the shots and were running toward Maxwell's place. Safely outside, Garrett waited to see if anyone else came out. No one did. "I think I got him," Garrett said finally.

They waited a bit longer, then Pete Maxwell put a lit candle in the window. In the flickering light, they saw the lifeless body of Billy the Kid sprawled on the floor. Garrett had shot him dead just above his heart. As Garrett concluded, "[T]he Kid was with his many victims." The legendary outlaw was twenty-one years old when he was killed that night.

If he actually *was* killed that night.

No one disagrees that Billy the Kid was one of the most ruthless outlaws to roam the Old West. As the *Spartanburg Herald* reported, "He was the perfect example of the real bad man, and his memory is respected accordingly by the few surviving friends and foes of his time, who knew the counterfeit bad man from the genuine." But since that night, when sheriff Pat Garrett fired two shots into the darkness, people have wondered who actually died on Pete Maxwell's floor.

Few names are better known in American folklore than Billy the Kid. Although his life as an outlaw lasted only four or five years, he accomplished enough during that brief span to ensure that he would be remembered forever. The only authentic photograph of the Kid, a two-by-three-inch ferrotype, was sold at auction in 2011 for $2.3 million, at that time making it the fourth most valuable photograph in the world. It was a tribute to his notoriety.

Perhaps surprising for someone so well known, there are very few verifiable facts about his life. It's generally believed that his name was William Henry McCarty Jr.—or, as he called himself, William H. Bonney—and that he was born about 1859, probably in New York City. He was the son of Irish immigrants who came to America to escape the Potato Famine. His father was long gone by the time his mother and stepfather opened a boardinghouse in Silver City, New Mexico. His mother, Catherine, tried to raise him right: He could read well and write in a legible hand; he was known to be polite and well mannered. But the New Mexico Territory was a hard place to grow up; gunplay was common, and the murder rate was high. The people who stayed at the family boardinghouse were on the move: miners, gamblers, merchants, women of pleasure, teamsters, and toughs. From these people, the impressionable boy learned the skills of survival. His proudest possession was a deck of Mexican cards; by the time he was eight, he could deal monte, and within a few years, he was said to be as skillful with cards as any of the gamblers in the local saloons.

Whatever chance Billy Bonney might have had for a decent life ended when he was fourteen years old and his mother died of tuberculosis. He stayed in Silver City for a short time after that, cleaning and washing dishes for neighbors who owned a hotel. His life was pretty much a scuffle; he didn't appear to have any particular destination. Although he didn't show much promise, he also didn't appear to be a bad sort. He fell in with the Mexican community and fully embraced its vibrant culture. Like most young men, he loved to dance and party. On occasion, he displayed a temper. The Mexicans called him El Chivato, "the Rascal." He committed the sort of minor offenses that have long been associated with teenagers: Once he was caught stealing cheese; another time, he was arrested for holding shirts a friend of his known as "Sombrero Jack" had stolen from the Chinese laundry run by Charley Sun and Sam Chung. Sheriff Harvey Whitehill put him in jail for that, figuring he'd give him a good scare, but instead he shimmied up and out of the jailhouse chimney and took off for a sorry future.

He kicked around the area, finding work as a ranch hand and shepherd until he fell in with John R. Mackie, a small-time criminal whose gang consisted mostly of teenage boys. Mackie might have recognized the possibilities in the young man: Billy Bonney had a slight build and a winning way about him. People took to him easily; his smallish stature was nonthreatening, and his easy smile was reassuring. But when it was necessary, he was quick on the draw and known to be an accurate shot. The gang stole horses and cattle from the government in Arizona and sold it to the government in New Mexico; then they would steal stock in New Mexico and take it to Arizona. However, on the night of August 17, 1877, seventeen-year-old Billy Bonney's life of crime took a more dangerous turn.

He was playing cards in George Atkin's cantina in Camp Grant, Arizona, with a blacksmith named Frank Cahill. Cahill's big mouth, which had earned him the nickname Windy, was working hard that night, throwing a string of insults at Bonney. Cahill was a small man with blacksmith's muscles and a mean temper. In some stories, the fight started because of a gambling disagreement; in others, as the result of drink; and in still others, Cahill called Billy a pimp, and Bonney responded by calling him a son of a bitch. Whatever the cause, suddenly Windy Cahill grabbed Bonney and threw him hard to the floor. The Kid got up, and Cahill pushed him down again. Billy got up once more, and Cahill shoved him a third time, but this time Cahill jumped on top of him and pinned his shoulders to the floor. Then he started punching him, again and again. The Kid had no chance of winning this fistfight, but somehow he managed to pull out the peacemaker he carried, a Colt .45, and fired one shot into Cahill's chest. Cahill slumped over and died the next day. Billy was locked up in the camp's guardhouse.

William Henry Bonney likely earned his nickname Billy the Kid after this shooting. It obviously was based on his youthful appearance. Fully grown, Billy Bonney stood five-foot-seven and weighed no more than 135 pounds; he was described by newsmen as "slender and slight, a hard rider and active as a cat." Other reports described him as "quite a handsome looking fellow, the only imperfection being two prominent front teeth slightly protruding like a squirrel's teeth." Although the shooting of Cahill appeared to be a case of self-defense, the Kid didn't wait around for the law's decision. Instead, he slipped out of the guardhouse and took off for New Mexico. That turned out to be the right move. After hearing the evidence, a coroner's jury ruled that because Cahill wasn't armed, the shooting was "criminal and unjustifiable." Billy the Kid was wanted for murder.

He stopped running when he reached Lincoln County and hired on with merchants and cattle ranchers Major Lawrence G. Murphy and James J. Dolan. Lincoln County consisted of thirty thousand square acres of some of the best cattle-grazing land in the country. Murphy and Dolan ran a large mercantile business, known as "the House" in honor of the mansion that served as their office. They were in fierce competition with newcomers Alexander McSween and John Tunstall, who were backed by the legendary cattle baron John Chisum. Their rivalry involved much more than money: The Irishmen Murphy and Dolan did not take kindly to the Englishman Tunstall trying to cut into their business. The fight between these two factions was known as the Lincoln County War, and Billy the Kid found himself right in the middle of it.

Initially he joined a gang of mostly teenage cattle rustlers run by gunman Jesse Evans; they called themselves "the Boys." It was a rough group, known to have committed several murders. The Boys had been hired by the House to steal cattle from Chisum's Jinglebob Ranch, which would then be sold to Mexicans and Indians. At first, McSween and Tunstall tried to fight back legally, but when the law failed them, they hired their own guns.

Somehow John Tunstall recruited Billy onto his side; one story claims that Billy was caught stealing a horse or cattle belonging to Tunstall and was arrested. Rather than put him in prison, Tunstall offered him a choice. If he agreed to testify against other members of the Boys, Tunstall would give him a job. It was a chance to make an honest living. Tunstall wasn't much more than a kid himself, being about twenty-four, and most reports indicate that he and Billy took a strong liking to each other. Apparently Tunstall once said, "That's the finest

When William Bonney reached Lincoln County, he hired on as a hand with merchants and cattlemen James Dolan and Major Lawrence Murphy, who ran their operation out of this mansion, known as the House.

Eventually Billy went to work for John
Tunstall, whose efforts to compete with the
House led to the Lincoln County War. When
Tunstall was murdered, the Kid declared his
own personal war on the House.

lad I ever met. He's a revelation to me everyday and would do anything to please me. I'm
going to make a man out of that boy yet."

He never got the chance to do that. On February 18, 1878, Tunstall and several hands—Billy
might have been among them—were driving nine horses to Lincoln on the Rio Feliz when they
were cut off by a posse that had been deputized by Lincoln sheriff William Brady and included
several members of the Boys. These killers now had the law backing their moves. At first, the
Boys claimed the horses had been stolen, but clearly that was only a ruse. Three of them managed
to isolate Tunstall in the brush, and when the shooting stopped, Tunstall's body was found lying
in the dirt next to his buckboard, one shot in his breast and a second shot in the back of his head.

When Billy the Kid learned of the murder, he said, "He was the only man that ever
treated me kindly, like I was born free and white," and then vowed, "I'll get every son of a
bitch who helped kill John if it's the last thing I ever do."

Lincoln County justice of the peace "Squire" John Wilson swore in a posse of special
constables, headed by ranch owner—and Tunstall's foreman—Dick Brewer, to arrest Tunstall's
killers. Billy the Kid joined this group, "the Regulators," as they became known, when they set

off to dispense justice. It was a very strange situation, two legally deputized posses hunting each other. The Regulators struck first, arresting two of the House's men and then killing them, allegedly as they tried to escape. The escalating war reached a new level about a month later, when Billy the Kid and five other Regulators ambushed and killed Sheriff Brady and his deputy as they walked down the street in Lincoln. Billy was slightly wounded in the gunfight. Although Brady was known to be sympathetic to the House, killing a lawman was serious business, even in a lawless environment, and people turned away from the Regulators, believing them to be no different than Murphy and Dolan's men.

Over the next months, both sides lost men. Dick Brewer was killed during a shoot-out at Blazer's Saw Mill, in which House man Buckshot Roberts also died. Frank McNab, who replaced Brewer as captain of the Regulators, was killed a month later; in return, Manuel Segovia, who was believed to have murdered McNab, was tracked down and killed, again allegedly trying to escape. The US cavalry joined the fight on the side of the House, giving

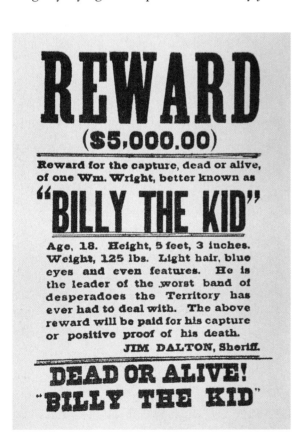

Although there is a lively market in Billy the Kid Wanted posters, most of them were created to take advantage of his fame after his death. The facts here are accurate, but the only verified "poster" was a reward notice published in the *Las Vegas Gazette*.

This 1880 illustration from the *Police Gazette* portrays Billy the Kid killing a man in a saloon, probably referring to the shooting of Joe Grant. The *Police Gazette* was known for its illustrations and photographs of popular criminals and scantily clad women.

their gunmen both legal cover and added firepower. Although nobody knows if Billy the Kid actually did any of the killing, it was agreed that he never held back.

The Lincoln County War came to a head at the five-day-long battle of Lincoln. On July 15, about forty of Dolan's men laid siege to McSween's house, where he was holed up with at least fifteen men. Supposedly, during a lull in the fighting, a House man called out to Billy to surrender, claiming he had a warrant for his arrest for the murder of Sheriff Brady and his deputy. Billy was said to reply, "We too have warrants for you and all your gang which we will serve on you hot from the muzzle of our guns!"

For three days, the town was a battlefield; then a column from Fort Stanton under the command of Colonel Nathan Dudley joined the fight on the side of the Dolans. Two days later, McSween's house went up in flames. McSween stepped out into his yard and was shot nine times. Several Regulators were killed attempting to escape the fire. But Billy Bonney was among the Regulators who slipped out the back and made it across the river.

News of the Lincoln County War was reported throughout the nation, and Billy the Kid—the murderous teenager—quickly caught the fancy of the public. In those stories, he was given credit for even more killings than he was known to be responsible for, ensuring his reputation while selling newspapers and novels.

McSween's death marked the end of the war. In total, twenty-two men had died. At the time, President Rutherford B. Hayes appointed Civil War general Lew Wallace governor of the New Mexico Territory. Determined to end the bitterness, Wallace offered amnesty to everyone who had fought in the war—except those indicted for murder. Because there was a warrant out for Billy the Kid for the murder of Sheriff Brady, he did not qualify for forgiveness. But Billy, being a bright sort, had a plan. He had witnessed James Dolan and two other men murder a Las Vegas lawyer, Huston Chapman. The Kid was hoping to arrange a deal; he wrote a letter to the new governor, stating that he would agree to testify against those three men in exchange for the same amnesty granted other Regulators. "I was present when Mr. Chapman was murdered," he wrote. "I know who did it. . . . If it is in your power to annully [*sic*] those indictments I hope you will do so as to give me a chance to explain. . . . I have no wish to fight any more indeed I have not raised an arm since your proclamation."

Meeting face-to-face with a feared killer was not out of the question for Governor Wallace. In addition to fighting in the war and trying to bring peace to a violent region, he was writing a novel that would become part of American literary history, *Ben-Hur*. On March 17, 1879, Wallace and Billy the Kid met in the home of a man named John Wilson. Billy carried his pistol in one hand and his Winchester in the other. Wallace agreed to Bonney's terms, but only if Bonney would submit to a token arrest and stay in jail until his testimony was completed. Billy was leery, supposedly telling Wallace, "There's no justice for me in the courts of this country. I've gone too far," but agreed to think it over. It was said that Wallace promised that if Bonney gave himself up, the governor would set him "scot free with a pardon in your pocket for all your misdeeds," but Bonney insisted that rather than his being "captured," he wanted it reported that he had surrendered. Two days after the meeting, he accepted the deal and surrendered to authorities.

He was held in a makeshift cell in the back of a store. His testimony helped to convict Dolan, but the local district attorney reneged on the deal; rather than letting him go, he

Lincoln, March 15. 1879.

W. H. Bonney.

Come to the house of old Squire Wilson (not the lawyer) at nine (9) o'clock next Monday night alone. I don't mean his office, but his residence. Follow along the foot of the mountain south of the town, come in on that side, and knock at the east door. I have authority to exempt you from prosecution, if you will testify to what you say you know.

The object of the meeting at Squire Wilson's is to arrange the matter in a way to make your life safe. To do that the utmost secrecy is to be used. So come alone. Don't tell anybody — not a living soul — where you are coming or the object. If you could trust Jesse Evans, you can trust me.

Lew. Wallace.

Billy the Kid's unusual correspondence with Governor Lew Wallace led to the wanted fugitive actually meeting face-to-face with the future author of the classic *Ben-Hur*. Billy believed they had worked out a deal that would result in his pardon, but when he was betrayed he escaped from prison and shot his way into legend.

Santa Fe Jail New Mex
March 2d 1881

Gov. Lew Wallace
　　　Dear Sir
　　I wish you would come down to
the jail and see me. it will be to
your interest to come and see me, I have
Some letters which date back two
Years. and there are Parties who
are very anxious to get them
, but I Shall not dispose of them
until I See You. that is if you
will come imediatly
　　　　Yours Respect
　　　　Wm H Bonney

"Billy the Kid"

Pat Garrett became famous for
supposedly killing Billy the Kid.
But his account has long been
disputed. Inconsistencies in his
story led to him becoming a
controversial figure. Although he
did not receive the reward money,
citizens who felt threatened by
the Kid collected the equivalent of
twenty thousand dollars for him.

decided to bring him to trial for Sheriff Brady's killing. After three months sitting in his cell and with his own trial for murder now scheduled, Billy did what came naturally—he slipped out. He probably could have found safety and a long life across the border in Mexico, but he'd grown sweet on Pete Maxwell's younger sister, Paulita, so instead he rode for Fort Sumner, where he believed he could live among his Mexican friends.

Among the people he surely got to know around Fort Sumner at that time was a former buffalo hunter and cowpuncher by the name of Pat Garrett, who had part ownership of Beaver Smith's Saloon. Depending on which story you choose to believe, Pat Garrett and Billy the Kid either barely knew each other or had become such close friends and gambling buddies that they were called Big Casino and Little Casino.

It is possible that Billy the Kid might have settled down with Pete Maxwell's comely sister, but the sad truth is that he was in too deep. Although Bonney was a wanted man, it wasn't a big secret that he had been seen around Fort Sumner. In January 1880, Billy met a man named Joe Grant in a local saloon. They got to drinking, and Grant confided in him that he aimed to become famous by killing the outlaw Billy the Kid as soon as he could find him. Grant wasn't the first man to make that boast, but he made the mistake of picking the wrong man to make it to. Billy asked to see his six-shooter, then managed to either empty the shells or set it on an empty cylinder. He handed it back and then admitted that, in fact, he was the very man that Grant was seeking. In some tellings, he then got up and walked out of the saloon. Grant fired at him; his gun clicked on the empty chamber. Billy dispatched him with a single shot. "It was a game for two," he later explained, "and I got there first."

To survive, Billy organized his own gang, which became known as "the Rustlers," or Billy the Kid's Gang. There was no lack of young men willing to ride with the famous outlaw, among them Tom O'Folliard, Charlie Bowdre, Tom Pickett, and Dirty Dave Rudabaugh. As their name suggests, they rustled cattle and stole horses, just as Billy had done years earlier.

The presence of a famous outlaw who had escaped justice riding the range with impunity finally got the attention of Governor Wallace. In November, he appointed Pat Garrett sheriff of Lincoln County. He might have received that badge because he promised to bring law and order to the county, but many people believed it was because he had been friends with Billy Bonney and knew where he was most likely to be found.

In late November, the gang stole sixteen horses from Padre Polaco and headed out to White Oaks to sell them. On the way they stopped at "Whisky Jim" Greathouse's ranch and way station and sold him four. Billy the Kid also intended to meet with his lawyer in White Oaks to see if there was any way of making a deal with the government. White Oaks deputy Will Hudgens raised a posse and tracked the fugitives to the Greathouse Ranch. Hudgens sent a note inside, informing the outlaws that they were surrounded and demanding their surrender. Jim Greathouse personally delivered their refusal. Apparently stalling until it got dark enough for them to make their escape, the gang agreed to allow the blacksmith Jimmy Carlyle, who was trusted by both sides, to come inside and discuss the terms of surrender. Greathouse agreed to stay with the posse as a voluntary hostage to ensure Carlyle's safety.

The Rustlers passed the day drinking. When Carlyle failed to return, the posse threatened to shoot Greathouse. As it grew dark, a member of the posse accidentally fired his weapon. Hearing that shot, Carlyle believed that the posse had shot Greathouse and that therefore his own life was suddenly in great jeopardy. He made a run for it, leaping out of a window into the snow. Billy the Kid later wrote to Governor Wallace to explain what happened that day: "In a short time a shot was fired on the outside and Carlyle thinking Greathouse was killed, jumped through the window, breaking the sash as he went and was killed by his own party they thinking it was me trying to make my escape." Members of the posse swore that the

Sheriff Pat Garrett's posse pursued Billy the Kid for four days before trapping him in Stinking Springs. This 1880 photograph shows the posse arriving in Santa Fe with its captives.

shots came from inside and specifically blamed the Kid. It made no difference to Carlyle how it happened: Somebody shot him dead.

The posse opened up on the house, firing as many as seventy shots without nicking anyone. When night fell, the posse gave up and rode back to White Oaks, allowing the gang to make tracks. Three days later, the Greathouse Ranch burned to the ground. The arsonists were never found.

The killing of Jim Carlyle outraged the public. The *Las Vegas Gazette* railed in an editorial, "the gang is under the leadership of Billy the Kid, a desperate cuss, who is eligible for the post of captain of any crowd, no matter how mean or lawless. . . . Are the people of San Miguel

County to stand this any longer?" This editorial might well have been the first time the entire nickname "Billy the Kid" was used; until this point he was generally known as simply "the Kid."

In response, Governor Wallace posted a notice in that paper, announcing, "I will pay $500 reward to any person or persons who will capture William Bonny [*sic*], alias The Kid, and deliver him to any sheriff of New Mexico."

Sheriff Garrett knew his success in his job would be measured by his ability to bring Billy the Kid to justice. He organized a posse and quickly picked up Bonney's trail. On December 18, he learned that the gang was coming into Fort Sumner, and he beat them there and lay in wait for them. Around midnight, the posse heard horses coming into town. Tom O'Folliard was riding point. The posse opened fire, hitting O'Folliard, who screamed, "Don't shoot, I'm killed!" and died minutes later. The gunfire alerted the rest of the gang to the ambush and allowed them to make a getaway.

But the posse stayed on their trail, catching up with them four days later in Stinking Springs. They quietly surrounded the Kid and his men, who were asleep in an abandoned stone building. Just after sunrise, Charlie Bowdre went outside to feed the horses. The posse evidently mistook him for the Kid and shot him down. Then the posse shot a horse, which fell and blocked the only exit, trapping the gang inside without food or water and little ammo. The standoff lasted almost two days, during which Garrett's men cooked their meals over an open fire and screamed invitations to the gang to join them. At one point, the Kid challenged Garrett to "[c]ome up like a man and give us a fair fight." When Garrett responded that he didn't aim to do that, Billy chided him: "That's what I thought of you, you old long legged son of a bitch."

Finally, realizing that it was out of options, the gang surrendered. The men were taken to Las Vegas, where a large crowd gathered to see them. As Billy the Kid told a reporter from the *Gazette*, "If it hadn't been for that dead horse in the doorway I wouldn't be here today. I would have ridden out on my bay mare and taken my chances. . . . We could have stayed in that house but they . . . would have starved us out. I thought it was better to come out and get a good square meal."

Billy the Kid was locked up in the prison in Santa Fe to await trial. During that time, he wrote several letters to Governor Wallace, pleading for the governor to intercede. "I expect you have forgotten what you promised me, this month two years ago, but I have not and I think you ought to have come and seen me. . . . I have done everything that I promised you I would and you have done nothing that you promised me." The governor did not respond.

While pleading for a pardon, Billy and his men planned an escape and began to dig their way out of the prison. When this tunnel was discovered, the Kid was put in solitary confinement, chained to the floor of his cell.

In April, he was taken to Mesilla, a town to the south of Santa Fe, and tried for the murders of Buckshot Roberts and Sheriff William Brady. He was acquitted of the Roberts killing on a technicality, his attorney arguing successfully that Roberts was not shot on federal property, and therefore the federal court had no jurisdiction. However, Billy was not as fortunate in his second trial. After hearing one day of testimony, Judge Warren Bristol pronounced him guilty, then sentenced him to "hang, until you are dead, dead, dead."

It is said that the Kid responded by telling the judge, "You can go to hell, hell, hell."

Billy the Kid was the only man convicted of a crime committed during the Lincoln County War, which he believed to be patently unfair. His only hope, he understood, was that the governor would honor the agreement they had made. As he told a reporter, "I think he [Wallace] ought to pardon me. . . . Think it hard that I should be the only one to suffer the extreme penalties of the law." On April 16, he was taken by wagon to Lincoln, where he was scheduled to be hanged on May 13, between the hours of nine a.m. and three p.m. Among the seven men who guarded him during that five-day trip was an old enemy, Bob Olinger, who had fought for Dolan in the war and, from all accounts, was especially hard on the Kid. It was reported that more than once he poked him with his shotgun and dared him to try to escape so that he could shoot him in the back, "Just like you did Brady."

In Lincoln, the Kid was shackled to the floor on the second story of a merchant building, guarded by Olinger and deputy James W. Bell. On the evening of April 28, Olinger went across the street to get some dinner, leaving the Kid alone with Deputy Bell. People have always said Bell was a decent man who was just in the wrong place at the wrong time. There are several versions of what happened next, but they all usually begin with Billy asking the deputy to take him outside to the privy. Perhaps Billy shoved Deputy Bell down the steps, then hobbled into the gun room and grabbed a pistol. Maybe he bludgeoned Deputy Bell with his chains and grabbed his gun. Or perhaps Billy never touched Deputy Bell but instead retrieved a pistol that had been planted for him in the latrine. However it happened, Billy the Kid added to his legend by obtaining a gun and shooting Deputy Bell, who staggered into the street and died. Then, still in chains, Billy managed to get into the armory and grab Olinger's double-barreled shotgun, the very gun with which he had been poked and taunted. He then stood at the window, patiently awaiting the return of Robert Olinger.

It was not a long wait. Hearing the shots, Olinger raced from the hotel dining room. A passerby warned him, "Bob, the Kid has killed Bell." And, at that moment, Olinger saw the

Billy the Kid escapes from prison by killing deputy Robert Olinger.

Kid framed in the window only a few feet away, holding a shotgun. "Hello, Bob," Billy is reputed to have said.

Olinger accepted his fate and has been quoted as saying, "Yes, and he's killed me, too."

Billy the Kid fired both barrels; Olinger died without another word. With the help of people who were never identified, he was able to sever his chains, arm himself, and then steal a horse and ride out of town.

Pat Garrett had been in White Oaks when the daring escape took place. He assumed that Billy would head immediately for the Mexican border. So he bided his time, waiting until the following July, when he heard that Billy the Kid might be visiting a lady friend out at Pete Maxwell's place. He rode out there that night with his two deputies. Not surprising, there are other versions of the final confrontation between Pat Garrett and Billy the Kid. In one, Garrett tied up and gagged Paulita Maxwell, and when the Kid came in to see her, Garrett let loose with both barrels of his shotgun. There is no argument, though, that Pat Garrett shot and killed a man at Pete Maxwell's ranch on the night of July 14. The man believed to be Billy the Kid was buried by his Mexican friends on the Maxwell Ranch. A white wooden cross marked his grave, and inscribed on it were the words DUERME BIEN, QUERIDO ("Sleep well, beloved").

Almost immediately, souvenir hunters started pulling at the grave site, so within days, his body was moved to the nearby Fort Sumner military cemetery and buried next to his friends Tom O'Folliard and Charlie Bowdre. The inscription on their stone reads simply, PALS, then identifies the three men.

Pat Garrett did not receive the attention he had hoped for, and in fact, many people believed he had shot the Kid in the back in a cowardly manner. At an inquest, Garrett stated, "He came there armed with a pistol and a knife expressly to kill me if he could. I had no alternative but to kill him or suffer death at his hands." The coroner's jury ruled it a justifiable homicide. To profit from his success in tracking down the outlaw Billy the Kid, Garrett published a ghostwritten book in 1882 entitled *The Authentic Life of Billy, the Kid*. It was moderately successful but served primarily to embellish the growing legend of William H. Bonney. When Garrett ran for sheriff in the next election, he was defeated. In 1884, he ran for the New Mexico state senate, was also defeated, and left New Mexico for Texas. In 1908, he was shot to death outside Las Cruces, New Mexico, allegedly during an argument about goats grazing on his land without permission. His body was found lying by the side of the road.

In his twenty-one years, Billy the Kid was credited with killing twenty-one men, but as with so much else about his life, that number certainly is exaggerated. It is known that he

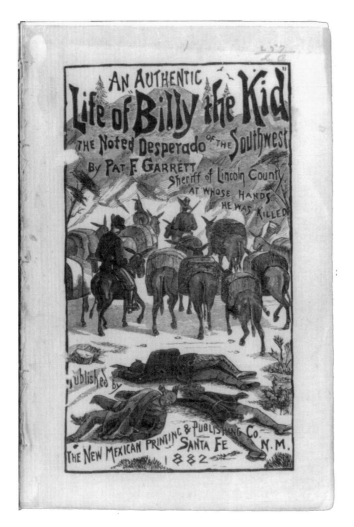

Months after he had shot Billy the Kid, Pat Garrett published this ghostwritten book, which did more to support the growing legend of Billy the Kid than benefit the sheriff.

killed at least four men himself and was involved in five more fatal shootings. That's nine. As for the others, no one will ever know how many notches were on his gun.

And as with other notorious outlaws, the story doesn't end in that hacienda. Legends take on a life of their own, and people wanted to believe that the Kid who'd pulled off so many daring feats and escapes had executed just one more. Rumors quickly surfaced that Billy the Kid did not die that night. To support these claims, people have pointed out that

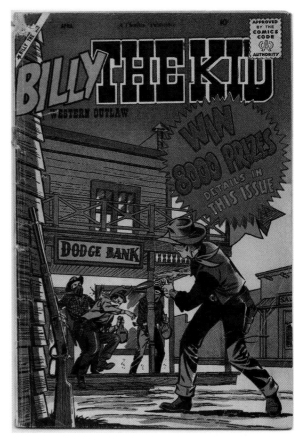

Although only twenty-one years old when he died, Billy the Kid had shot his way into American history. His legend has been celebrated in dime novels, books, comics, plays, songs, poems, and even an Aaron Copeland ballet. He has been portrayed more often in film and television than any other person, by actors including Paul Newman, Kris Kristofferson, and Marlon Brando.

no photographs of the body exist, no death certificate was ever issued, Pat Garrett was never paid the reward, and the three coroner's jury reports contained conflicting testimony and were signed by people who admitted they did not witness the shooting. In fact, beyond Pat Garrett's claims, there is little evidence that the victim was Billy the Kid.

Is it possible that Billy the Kid actually survived that night? According to one version, he was badly wounded, but the Mexican women of the hacienda saved his life, then substituted the body of a man who had died naturally that night; Bonney then lived the rest of his life peacefully under the name John Miller. Another version claims that Garrett and the Kid had become close friends years earlier in Beaver Smith's Saloon and that Garrett had helped set up this elaborate ploy, to enable Billy to live the rest of his life in peace. And from time to time, through the succeeding years, men would show up in the saloons of the Old West claiming to be Billy the Kid, saying they'd miraculously escaped death at the end of Pat Garrett's six-shooter that night—*And, by the way, would you buy me a drink?*

The most publicized claim was made in 1949, when a ninety-year-old man from Hamilton County, Texas, William H. "Brushy Bill" Roberts, stated that his true identity was, in fact, Billy the Kid. The man killed that night in 1881, he said, was a friend of his, known as Billy Barlow. He himself had lived in Mexico until things cooled down, then led a life of adventure. He'd served with Pancho Villa in the Mexican Revolution, worked in *Buffalo Bill's Wild West Show*, joined Teddy Roosevelt's Rough Riders and fought in Cuba, and even served as a US marshal while marrying four times and living under a dozen aliases. Although Roberts died of a heart attack in 1950, the book detailing his story, *Alias Billy the Kid,* was published in 1955. Although it was generally dismissed at that time, years later, the full transcripts of interviews conducted before his death seemed to make a much more convincing case.

Brushy Bill told an entertaining story. Although there was compelling evidence that "Brushy Bill" was actually a man named Oliver P. Roberts, who was born in 1879, other evidence seems to indicate that William Roberts had intimate knowledge of Lincoln City and many of the events that took place there. In face, there is more hard evidence to support the claim that William H. Roberts was indeed Billy the Kid than there is evidence that Pat Garrett actually killed the Kid the night of July 14, 1881.

In 2007, a legal effort was launched to settle the story once and for all by exhuming the remains in Billy Bonney's grave and attempting to match the DNA to that of his mother. That request was denied. Although it is still generally accepted that the legendary life of William H. Bonney, alias Billy the Kid, ended in the darkness of Pete Maxwell's bedroom, there remain enough unanswered questions to make this one of the Wild West's most compelling mysteries.

BUTCH CASSIDY

THE LAST MAN STANDING

utch Cassidy slowly pulled back a corner of the white lace curtain and looked out the broken windowpane. The plaza seemed deserted. But from behind every barrier, he saw the long barrel of a rifle pointed directly at him. Without counting, he figured at least three dozen Bolivian soldiers were drawing a bead on the house at that very moment. From the back of the darkened room, the wounded Sundance Kid asked evenly, "So, what do you think?"

"Looks like rain," Butch replied casually. "Now's probably not a good time to go for a stroll."

"Yeah, that's just what I was thinking." After a brief pause, Sundance said, "Hey, I got an idea; when it clears up, let's go watch one of those newfangled moving pictures."

Butch sparked at that thought, then smiled broadly. "Hey, maybe they'll make one of them about us sometime. You know, the story of two good-natured fellas just trying to make a decent living in a quick-changing world?"

Sundance laughed. "More likely, people'll be walking on the moon."

And then another shot shattered the remains of the window.

Did that conversation ever take place? Of course not. But it may be about as accurate as most of the stories that have been told about Butch Cassidy and the Sundance Kid and the gang they rode with, the Wild Bunch. Those oft-told tales, culminating in the award-winning 1969 film starring Paul Newman and Robert Redford, have ensured that the two robbers and the last gang to roam the Old West will live forever in American folklore. Although the movie purportedly told the "true story" of these outlaws, in this case, the word *true* was defined pretty loosely.

According to that history, after a successful life of crime in the United States, Butch and Sundance fled to South America, where they were eventually trapped by soldiers in a small house in San Vicente, Bolivia. The ambiguous ending of that classic movie left open the possibility that Butch and Sundance somehow managed to survive that last gunfight. And, in the century since that 1908 shoot-out, several intriguing stories would actually seem to support that contention. Although the fate of all the other members of the Wild Bunch is well known and accepted without question, some people do wonder if it is possible that Butch and Sundance somehow escaped.

Robert Leroy Parker was born in April 1866, the first of thirteen children, and grew up in Circleville, Utah. As a teenager, he worked briefly as a butcher, supposedly cutting up rustled cattle, then rode for a time with rancher and cattle and horse thief Mike Cassidy, which led to him being nicknamed Butch Cassidy.

Harry Alonzo Longabaugh was born a year later in Mont Clare, Pennsylvania. As a twenty-year-old, he was caught stealing a gun, a horse, and a saddle from a ranch in Sundance, Wyoming. While serving eighteen months in jail there, he picked up the nickname by which he gained fame, "the Sundance Kid."

A loosely knit association of various gangs, operating mostly out of the Hole-in-the-Wall hideout in Wyoming's Bighorn Mountains, the Wild Bunch pulled off the longest string of bank and train robberies in American history. In addition to Butch and Sundance, the primary members included Elzy Lay, Kid Curry Logan, News Carver, Tall Texan Kilpatrick, Matt Warner, Butch's brother Dan Parker, Flat Nose Currie, and Harry Bass. From 1889 through the turn of the century, the Wild Bunch purportedly stole the modern-day equivalent of about $2.5 million, before each of its members was caught or killed, one by one.

Robert Leroy Parker, who became the famed Butch Cassidy.

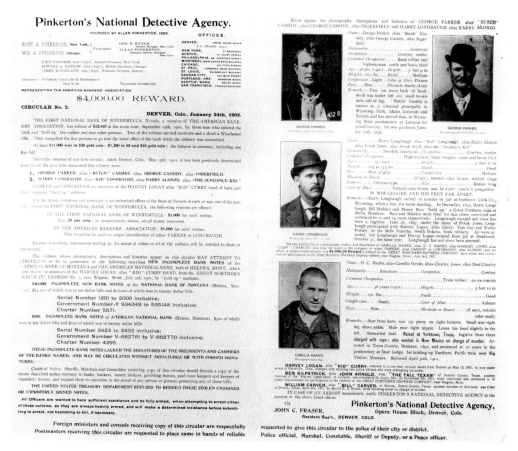

After Butch and Sundance held up the First National Bank of Winnemucca, Nevada, and got away with $32,640, the Pinkertons issued this Wanted poster, in which Cassidy was described as a "known criminal in Wyoming, Utah, Idaho, Colorado and Nevada," and it was pointed out that the Kid "is bow-legged and his feet far apart."

Butch Cassidy committed his first bank job in 1889, when he and several other masked men held up the San Miguel Valley Bank in Telluride, Colorado, riding away with about twenty thousand dollars. It was a transitional time for a region once known as the Wild West. Civilization was encroaching quickly, brought in by the 164,000 miles of railroad track that now stretched from the Atlantic to the Pacific, with trains that ran on a schedule. People were talking to friends miles away on the candlestick telephone. They were driving crazy fast in horseless carriages; in fact, only a year earlier, one of them had raced from Green Bay to

A 1901 formal portrait of Sundance taken in New York City

Madison, Wisconsin, in just thirty-three hours, almost as fast as the stage. In cities, people were speeding over paved streets on bicycles with pneumatic tires. And instead of living in fear of Indians and highwaymen, for only a few cents people could watch reenactments of Indian attacks on wagon trains and stagecoach robberies—and even behold the actual Sitting Bull and twenty of his warriors, when *Buffalo Bill's Wild West* and its "Congress of Rough Riders of the World," just back from Paris, came to town.

It took a while for Butch and Sundance to meet up, and by the time they did, both of them were fiercely committed to a life of larceny. Butch Cassidy had no formal education, learning the necessities of his trade from outlaw Mike Cassidy. By the time Mike Cassidy had killed a Wyoming rancher and taken off for parts unknown, Bob Parker could outride a posse and shoot well enough to hit a playing card dead center at fifty paces. It was said that he could ride around a tree trunk full tilt and put all six shots from his revolver into a three-inch circle. But in addition to outlaw skills, he also was said to have a pleasing way with words, a sense of fairness, and a quick wit. His first train robbery took place outside Grand Junction, Colorado, when his gang forced the Denver and Rio Grande Express to stop by blocking the tracks with a small mountain of stones. Guns drawn, the gang climbed aboard and ordered the guard to open the safe. He refused, claiming he did not have the combination. Butch's partner in that crime, a gunman named Bill McCarty, put his revolver to the guard's head, cocked it, and asked, "Should we kill him?"

After a pause, Butch suggested, "Let's vote!" He then persuaded the rest of the bandits to leave the guard alone. They collected about one hundred forty dollars from the passengers and rode away.

That wicked sense of humor was also present when he robbed the First National Bank of Denver. He approached the president of that institution and blurted out breathlessly, "Sir! I just overheard a plot to rob this bank!"

The bank president froze in his tracks. "Oh, Lord!" he supposedly said. "How did you learn of this plot?"

Cassidy smiled. "I planned it. Put up your hands!"

Sundance had spent several years working as a ranch hand, committing the occasional crime, when he joined Bill Madden and Henry Bass and held up the Great Northern westbound number 23 train near Malta, Montana, in 1892. This robbery was even less successful than Cassidy's attempt: Although he got away with about twenty-five dollars, his accomplices were caught and implicated him. Within days, the railroad issued Wanted posters bearing an accurate description of him and offering a five-hundred-dollar reward for his capture. A similar Wanted poster issued years later described his nose as "rather long," his hair as "brown, may be dyed, combs it pompadour," and notes that he "is bow-legged and his feet far apart." Madden was sentenced to ten years, Bass got fourteen, and Sundance spent the rest of his life as a fugitive.

It isn't known precisely when or how Butch and Sundance met, but in those days, after pulling a job, desperadoes were known to retreat to hideouts until things cooled down. As the *St. George Union* wrote in 1897, "The outlaws live among 'breakes,' the wildest, most rugged and inaccessible except to the initiated anywhere under the blue firmament. In recesses cut into the side of those yawning chasms, two or three men are able to hold an army at bay. To such places all who have stolen, robbed or murdered are welcomed so that the gangs are becoming augmented steadily as time goes on . . . There is no use attempting to dislodge them by force . . . the only way would be to starve them out and it is questionable if that is feasible."

These places had many advantages: They offered a clear view of all approaches, they were hard to find and get into, and if it became necessary, they were easy to defend. Pretty much anyone on the run was welcome in these hideouts. For example, young Bob Parker allegedly spent a lot of time in Brown's Park (or Brown's Hole, as it also was known), an isolated valley along the Green River, stretching between Colorado and Utah, when he was riding with Mike Cassidy. The Wild Bunch, or, as it originally was called, the Hole-in-the-Wall Gang, was formed by Butch Cassidy and his best friend at that time, rustler and holdup man Elzy Lay, while they were lying low in Robbers Roost, a hideout in southeastern Utah. (The gang also called itself, with a wink, the Train Robbers Syndicate.) When lawmen discovered the location of the Roost, the Wild Bunch departed for the famous Hole-in-the-Wall, a natural fortress atop a plateau in Carbon County, Wyoming, used by numerous gangs, a redoubt that could be reached only by squeezing through narrow passes and which was said to be so secure that a dozen men could defend it against a hundred.

Many plans were hatched and relationships formed along the well-known "outlaw trail." Membership in a gang was fluid; people would ride with several other bandits for a limited time or for a specific job, then move along. Several dozen men participated in at least one of the more than two dozen holdups believed to have been committed by the Wild Bunch. It's likely that Butch and Sundance crossed paths during one of these robberies.

By the turn of the twentieth century, it was becoming difficult to make a decent living cattle rustling or horse thieving, but it was a good time to be a bank or train robber. The West

Only outlaws on the run were welcomed at the easily defended Hole-in-the-Wall in Wyoming and at Brown's Park, or Brown's Hole, in Colorado (*inset*).

was being tamed. New towns were springing up all over the prairie; most of them had banks, while few of them could afford sufficient law enforcement. The iron horse was replacing the stagecoach, carrying money and mail vast distances, often with very little security on board.

Butch Cassidy was a new kind of bank robber. He treated robbing as his profession rather than as a dangerous hobby. Instead of just bursting into a place and waving guns around, he spent considerable time planning his jobs. Before proceeding, he gathered intelligence: By the time he was ready to move forward, he knew how he intended to get into and out of the town, how many lawmen might be on the job, and, most important, how much money was in the safe.

Even more crucial, he planned his escapes. For example, his men would climb poles and cut the town's telegraph lines to prevent the sheriff from contacting nearby law enforcement for help. They would leave horses waiting a good distance from a town, and if they were pursued by a posse of lawmen, they would ride hard to that place and change mounts, so that they would be riding fresh horses while the posse's would be wearing out. Sometimes all that planning wasn't really necessary. In 1896, Cassidy, recently released after serving eighteen months of a two-year sentence for stealing a horse, learned along with Elzy Lay and Bob Meeks that the town of Montpelier, Idaho, had only a part-time deputy who was paid a paltry ten dollars a month—and that he had neither a horse nor a gun.

But the town did have a bank.

They rode out of Montpelier with $7,165 in cash, gold, and silver—a fortune at the time—pursued by part-time deputy sheriff Fred Cruikshank, frantically pedaling his bicycle. When the word of that job spread, seasoned bandits began offering to ride with Butch Cassidy's Wild Bunch.

Sundance probably joined him right around that time. In April 1897, after cutting the telegraph wires in Castle Gate, Utah, the gang got away with the Pleasant Valley Coal Company's $9,860 payroll. In response, the company paymaster handed out checks to miners, informing them, "Paymaster Cassidy of Robbers Roost will honor the paper." As in almost all of Cassidy's heists, no shots had been fired. Butch Cassidy wasn't exactly nonviolent, but he definitely was averse to unnecessary bloodshed. He and his gang weren't in the robbing business to hurt people, just the banks, the railroads, and the large cattle owners who were putting up fences across the once-open ranges. The most dangerous member of the gang was Kid Curry, who was described by the *Anaconda Standard* as being "fond of dress and his taste in that direction is rather flashy. He is absolutely reckless and careless, and since he has been an outlaw has been known to take the most desperate chances. . . . A dead shot with a revolver and rifle, he will be a hard man to capture."

The "wildest of the Wild Bunch" was Harvey Logan, known as Kid Curry, who was credited with killing eleven men. He is shown here with his girlfriend, prostitute Annie Rogers, also known as Della Moore.

With each successful Wild Bunch robbery, Butch Cassidy's reputation spread. In 1898, a Chicago newspaper declared him "King of the Bandits," reporting that he was "the worst man" in Utah, Colorado, Wyoming, and Idaho. The article claimed that he had five hundred outlaws working for him, "subdivided into five gangs." The daring exploits and well-planned heists of the Wild Bunch made headlines and sold newspapers throughout the country. The gang did give newspapermen plenty to write about: They were committing crimes in five states, the named four plus South Dakota, in robberies that netted as much as seventy thousand dollars.

Although the size of the gang was obviously exaggerated, the "King of the Bandits" story was accurate on one important point: Butch did run the operation. He was known for teaching the other outlaws the proper way to plan and carry out a job and was the acknowledged mastermind behind many of the robberies—even if he didn't personally participate in them. Occasionally, something would go wrong. In July 1899, Elzy Lay was riding with a group of train robbers known as the Ketchum Gang. They held up the Colorado & Southern number 1 train outside Folsom, New Mexico, getting away with fifty thousand dollars. They didn't get far, though; the railroads had gotten a lot smarter and were hiring their own guns for protection. The Ketchum Gang was surprised by a determined posse, which lit out after it. They tracked it for several days, and in the running gun battles, two members of the posse were killed, including sheriff Edward Farr, and one man was wounded. One of the bandits died of his wounds, another man escaped, and Elzy Lay was wounded and captured. He recovered well enough to spend the rest of his life in prison.

The loss of his best friend left an empty saddle next to Butch Cassidy, and the Sundance Kid stepped up to fill it. For a time after Lay's incarceration, Butch Cassidy softened and considered leaving the profession. There are reports that he tried to make a deal with the railroads: If they agreed to let him be, he would leave their safes alone. He might even agree to consult for them as a security specialist—preventing train robberies. Any possibility of that deal ended near Wilcox, Wyoming, when the Wild Bunch took an estimated thirty thousand dollars in gold, cash, jewelry, and banknotes from the Union Pacific Overland Flyer number 1 train. According to a message sent by Union Pacific executives to the Laramie County sheriff, "[A] party of six masked robbers held up the first section of train number one . . . and after dynamiting bridges, mail and express cars and robbing the latter, disappeared." There is some evidence that this robbery served as the inspiration for the famous 1903 silent moving picture, *The Great Train Robbery*, and later for a memorable scene in the 1969 classic film *Butch Cassidy and the Sundance Kid*.

Blowing things up proved to be a bit of a problem for the gang. It turned out that the use of dynamite wasn't one of their areas of expertise. Because no crew member aboard this train was given the combination to the safe carried in the baggage car, the outlaws reacted by attempting to blow it open. Apparently they used considerably more dynamite than was necessary, blowing up the entire railway car, down to the frame. Some of the money was scorched in the explosion or stained by raspberries, also being transported in that car. Thus, the Wilcox robbery might be considered a failed experiment. As the *Rawlins Semi-Weekly Republican* reported, the robbers "wrecked the car, blowing the roof off and sides out, portions of the car being blown 150 yards." The safe, according to the *Laramie Daily Boomerang*, was blown "out of all semblance to the original self."

After the robbery, members of the train crew complimented the manners of the thieves, one of them telling reporters that he had asked for a chew of tobacco, which was given to him by one of the robbers. Another crew member said the bandits had reassured him, "Now boys, don't get scared. You're just as safe here as you would be in Cheyenne."

The robbers split up to make their getaway. Posses eventually including several hundred

A classic scene from the movie *Butch Cassidy and the Sundance Kid* recreated the 1899 robbery of the Union Pacific Overland Flyer near Wilcox, Wyoming: Attempting to blow open the safe, the gang mistakenly used enough dynamite to blow up the entire railroad car.

In an attempt to catch the Wild Bunch, the Union Pacific created a special car for mounted rangers and their horses, enabling them to instantly pursue the robbers.

men, some of them using bloodhounds brought in all the way from Beatrice, Nebraska, for the task, pursued the bandits for several weeks. Converse County sheriff Josiah Hazen's posse eventually caught up to Sundance, Kid Curry Logan, and Flat Nose Currie near Castle Creek, Wyoming, and in a gunfight, Kid Curry shot and killed the sheriff. As the *Boomerang* related, "It was rough and broken country, and the outlaws had the advantage of knowing every inch of it. From behind boulder and brushwood they held off the posse—five men against two hundred. Hazen exposed himself and the next moment reeled back with a bullet through his heart. Darkness fell . . ." Eventually the bandits escaped into Hole-in-the-Wall territory.

The *New York Herald* reported, "They were lawless men who have lived long in the crags and become like eagles." Although in fact these were killers and robbers, people had already begun romanticizing the Wild Bunch. But this robbery put a quick stop to that.

Killing the sheriff and stealing gold that was to be used to pay American boys fighting in the Spanish-American War proved to be the beginning of the gang's downfall. The Union Pacific offered an eighteen-thousand-dollar bounty for the capture of the outlaws—dead or alive. It also hired armed guards, Rangers, to protect their trains, warning, "They ride on the engine. In the baggage car, on the dry coaches, or in the sleepers, being instructed not to stay always at one point of the train. Any gang of bandits attacking a Union Pacific train now will know it has to reckon on a stiff fight, for not only is each train guarded, but somewhere up or down the line is the patrol body of rangers, ready to be shipped to the danger zone as fast as steam can carry them."

Equally significant, the railroad also hired the Pinkertons to once and for all put the gang out of the stealing business. The Pinks represented the largest and toughest private security company in America. In fact, the Pinkerton agency was the only truly national law-enforcement operation; by the 1870s, there were more Pinkerton men than there were soldiers in the American army. They were known to be relentless in their pursuit, professional and thorough in their investigations, and as tough as necessary in their enforcement methods. Without question, they brought scientific detection techniques to American law enforcement, and they were the first to employ mug shots, fingerprints, and undercover agents. But they also were well known to rely on their own interpretation of the law to accomplish their objectives—even when it required bloodshed.

Following the Wilcox robbery, the Pinkertons picked up the trail of the Wild Bunch. And once they had it, they never let it go. By tracing scorched and stained banknotes, they tracked Kid Curry's brother, Lonnie Logan, and Bob Lee to Cripple Creek, Colorado. Lee eventually was captured and sentenced to ten years in prison. Pinkerton operatives caught

Hole in Wall S. H.

The Hole-in-the-Wall in the Bighorn Mountains of northern Wyoming, where the Wild Bunch was formed, was a full day's ride from civilization. Although outlaws were well protected, life was hard there. Each gang was responsible for its own cabins, livestock, and provisions. There was no leader, no structure—and almost no rules. Among the few prohibited acts were murder and stealing another gang's supplies.

up with Lonnie Logan in a rural farmhouse, and when he attempted to escape into the nearby woods, they shot him dead. Almost two years later, Pinkertons caught Kid Curry in Knoxville, Tennessee. After a trial, he was sentenced to 20 to 130 years in federal prison. He escaped less than a year later. In 1904, a posse caught up with him again after a train robbery near Parachute, Colorado. He was wounded in the shoot-out, and rather than surrender and be sent back to prison, he shouted to his companions, "I'm hit! Don't wait for me, boys. I'm all in. Good-bye!" Then he put his gun to his head and committed suicide.

Although the Pinks were successfully dismantling the Wild Bunch man by man, their real target remained the most wanted man in the West, Butch Cassidy. The reward offered for his capture or death was raised to ten thousand dollars. However, the fact that the greatest law-enforcement organization in the world was on his tail didn't appear to worry him much. On August 29, 1900, a masked robber boarded Union Pacific's Overland Flyer number 3 outside Tipton, Wyoming, put a pistol to the conductor's head, and ordered him to stop the train when it reached a campfire by the side of the road. The Wild Bunch had yet to master the art of dynamite and once again blew the baggage car to smithereens, causing a rain of bills estimated at fifty-five thousand dollars. The gang was polite about it, though: After the robbery, a member of the train's crew complimented the robbers on their courtesy, explaining that one of the holdup men told him the gang really didn't want to hurt anyone and had made a pact that anyone who killed without reason would be executed. And the bandits said "so long" as they rode away. In a sign of the changing times, a member of the train crew used a pay phone to report the robbery. A posse pursued the Wild Bunch for more than a week, but eventually, as the *Salt Lake Herald* reported, "All hope of capturing the four men who held up, dynamited and robbed the overland express train at Tipton three weeks ago has been given up . . . the route of the robbers was well chosen and was through a wild and uninhabited country. . . . The crimes go on record as one of the most successful and daring robberies in the history of the west."

Less than a month later, members of the gang were credited with looting the First National Bank in Winnemucca, Nevada, of $32,640. These robbers were not as polite, however, threatening to cut the cashier's throat if he refused to open the safe. Announcing their presence, one robber pulled a pair of .45s and warned, "Stick 'em up, Slim, or I'll make you look like a naval target," adding minutes later, "Just feel how fine and soft the atmosphere is above your head, feel it with both hands at once."

Although it's impossible to even roughly estimate the total amount of money stolen by the Wild Bunch—because no one knows how many robberies they actually pulled off—without question, they got away with today's equivalent of millions of dollars. Most of the

After Butch and Sundance stopped the Great Northern Express near Wagner, Montana, in 1901, they cut loose the express car, blew up the safe, and escaped with forty thousand dollars. In those days, different organizations offered rewards—including a percentage of the money recovered—so it's impossible to know the total amount of the bounty on the heads of the robbers.

money was spent on fast living, although stories are told about Cassidy handing out cash to people who needed it or refusing to steal money from civilians. He also was known to be meticulous about paying his debts. A man named John Kelly, who had worked with "Roy Parker" as a ranch hand, once lent him twenty-five dollars, "so he could get out of Butte, Montana." Several years later, Kelly unexpectedly received a letter from Parker, and when he opened it, one hundred dollars fell out. The enclosed note read, "If you don't know how I got this, you will soon learn someday."

It is possible that some of the loot ended up in the hands of women. Butch was a handsome man; his Wanted poster in 1900 described him as five feet nine inches tall with a medium build, a light complexion, flaxen hair, and blue eyes. His face was square and young-looking, and he bore a naturally inviting, bemused smile. When he was imprisoned in Wyoming, in addition to his physical description, his record noted, "Habits of Life: Intemperate." He appeared to enjoy the company of the ladies as much as they liked being with him, and it was said that he knew how to treat a woman properly.

Sundance was about the same height and weight, but on his Wanted posters, he was said to have "a dark complexion, black hair, black eyes" and "Grecian features." The Pinkertons added that he was a fast draw who "drinks very little, if any, and is believed to be involved with a school m'arm known only as Etta Place."

Little is known about Etta Place, not even her real name. Place was the maiden name of Sundance's mother. And Etta might actually have been "Ethel." It isn't even known if she really was a teacher; she also has been described as a saloon girl and as a prostitute who met both Butch and Sundance while working in a brothel, possibly Fannie Porter's Sporting Parlor in San Antonio. She was about ten years younger than Sundance and had, according to the Pinkertons, "classic good looks . . . and she appears to be a refined type." Other people described her as one of the most beautiful women they had ever seen, and men who later knew her in South America said, "She was a goddess—everyone was enamored of her." Whether Sundance and Etta were legally married isn't known, but she wore engagement and wedding rings, and they referred to each other as husband and wife.

It does seem that the core members of the Wild Bunch truly were friends in addition to being business associates. Less than three months after the Tipton heist, for instance, several members of the gang found themselves living the sporting life in the cattle boomtown of Fort Worth, Texas. For reasons that will never be understood, five members of the gang—Butch and Sundance, Kid Curry, News Carver, and Tall Texan Kilpatrick—walked into the photography shop of John Swartz, dressed in the dandy-wear of bankers and railroad executives, and posed for a formal picture. This iconic photograph eventually became known as "The Ft. Worth Five," the most famous mug shot in western history.

The proud photographer was so pleased with his work that he enlarged a copy and placed it on an easel in his front window as an advertisement. Among the people who admired the portrait was a Pinkerton agent who happened to be in town on an assignment and immediately recognized the gang. Within days, it was hanging in every post office, train station, Wells Fargo outlet, and law-enforcement office in the country.

Things were beginning to heat up in early 1901 when Cassidy and Sundance decided to make good their final escape. Although they had only done two or three jobs together, they had become close. Life on the run could wear a man down; as gang member Matt Warner once said, "You'll never know what it means to be hunted. You can never sleep. You've always got to listen with one ear and keep one eye open. After awhile, you almost go crazy. No sleep! No sleep! Even when you know you're perfectly safe, you can't sleep. Every pissant under your pillow sounds like a posse of sheriffs coming to get you!"

"The Ft. Worth Five"

Their challenge was to find a place where they weren't known. After the "Ft. Worth Five" picture had been circulated, no place in America was safe for them—unless they intended to spend the rest of their lives in some forsaken hideout. Fortunately, a lot of Wyoming ranchers were then moving to South America, in particular Argentina and Bolivia, where the weather was good, land was cheap and plentiful, and nobody asked a lot of embarrassing questions. Oh, and the nearest Pinkertons were more than five thousand miles away.

Obviously, they weren't in a big hurry. After welcoming the New Year 1901 in New Orleans, then traveling by train to Niagara Falls, Butch, Sundance, and the lovely and mysterious Etta Place visited one of the most populous places on earth, New York City. While there, Butch bought a gold watch and Sundance and Etta purchased a lapel watch and stickpin at the fashionable jewelry store Tiffany's, and the winsome couple posed for a "wedding portrait" at the De Young Photography Studio in Union Square. On the twentieth of January, Mr. and Mrs. Longabaugh, accompanied by her "brother," "James Ryan," set sail for Buenos Aires aboard the British steamer *Herminius*.

Without their leadership, the remains of the Wild Bunch scattered and by 1905 had passed into Old West history. Historians attribute more than twenty murders to gang members

during its roughly fifteen years in existence. Fifteen members of the gang died with their boots on, and another three committed suicide. Six of them were caught and went to prison—and were killed when they got out. Elzy Lay was believed to be the last survivor. He was pardoned and released from prison in 1906 for saving the warden's wife and daughter during a prison uprising and lived quietly in Los Angeles until his death—from natural causes—in 1934.

Retirement proved to be only temporary for Butch and Sundance. Upon their arrival in Buenos Aires, Sundance deposited $12,500 in an Argentinean bank. Then the three of them traveled by steamer to Cholila, a small frontier town in the sparsely populated region of Patagonia, where they lived for a time as Mr. and Mrs. Harry "Enrique" Place and James "Santiago" Ryan. Under the terms of an 1884 law, passed to encourage immigration, they were given fifteen thousand acres to develop. A portion of those lands actually belonged to Place, making her the first woman in Argentina to receive land under this law. They built a four-room cabin on the east bank of the Blanco River, with the snowcapped Andes in the distance, and started a ranching operation. It grew to a decent size, according to a letter Cassidy wrote to a friend in Vernal, Utah. The estancia had 300 head of cattle, 1,500 sheep, and 25 horses. Their closest neighbor was almost a day's ride away.

Sundance and Etta returned to the United States for brief visits in 1902 and again in 1904. During those trips, the tourists visited sites including Coney Island in Brooklyn and the St. Louis World's Fair, but they also saw several doctors, and the speculation is that both of them were suffering from venereal disease.

The Pinkertons had not let go of their pursuit. By intercepting letters Sundance had written to his family in Pennsylvania, they learned that the bandits were living in Argentina. In 1903, agent Frank Dimaio traveled to Buenos Aires and from there traced them to Cholila. Supposedly the onset of the rainy season prevented him from reaching the ranch, but there is a story that Butch and Sundance killed a Pink sometime that year and buried the body, which, in a quite embarrassing episode, was later dug up by Etta Place's dog while they were entertaining dinner guests.

Whatever actually took place, it did not appear to alarm the trio, because early in 1904, the territorial governor spent a night as a guest in their cabin, dancing with Etta as Sundance played a samba on his guitar.

Maybe their money was running out, or perhaps they just missed the excitement, but in February 1905, English-speaking bandits later identified as Butch and Sundance held up the

❦ The "wedding portrait" of Harry Longabaugh, the Sundance Kid, and the beautiful Etta Place, taken in New York City in 1901, shortly before they departed for South America

Banco de Tarapaca y Argentina and got away with the modern-day equivalent of about $100,000. Supposedly Etta had assisted in the planning by talking her way into the vault to case the layout of the bank, and later in the actual robbery by dressing in men's clothing and waiting outside, holding the horses. A story often told in Argentina asserts that she was such a good markswoman that as they made their escape, she was able to split the telegraph wire with a single rifle shot.

There remains some question regarding whether they actually pulled this job. An official of the Argentinean government claimed to be with them on their ranch the day after the robbery, which, if true, was essentially an unbreakable alibi. True or not, governor Julio Lazana signed a warrant for their arrest, but they learned about it days before it could be executed and immediately sold part of their land for eighteen thousand pesos and ordered their foreman to liquidate the rest of their property, before sailing to Puerto Montt, Chile.

Sundance and Etta later left Chile for a trip to San Francisco, but upon their return, the three of them went back to work, holding up the Banco de la Nacion in Villa Mercedes, Argentina, and escaping with today's equivalent of about $135,000. When the bank manager resisted, he was, depending on reports, either pistol-whipped or shot by an unknown third "man." That third "man" could have been Etta, who had cut her hair short and had previously been described by a Buenos Aires newspaper as "an interesting woman . . . who wears male clothing with total correctness" and was also a "fine rider" who knew how to handle "all classes of firearms." Posses chased them into the Andes before losing their trail, but now they were on the run, and they would never stop.

At some point that summer, Sundance and Etta Place again traveled to San Francisco, but this time Sundance returned alone. There is some evidence that she had an operation in Denver for appendicitis or a gall-bladder problem, but the woman known in history as Etta Place was never heard from again.

The trail tends to get a little murky from then on. It's likely that Butch and Sundance found jobs at the Concordia Tin Mine in the Bolivian Andes—ironically enough, guarding the mine payroll. What better way for robbers to hide in plain sight than to protect a payroll? They probably were looking for the big score, that one legendary robbery large enough to support them for the rest of their lives. There were scattered reports of smaller heists that took place while they were living in that region, successful robberies attributed to "Yankees," but there is no real evidence linking Butch and Sundance to them.

Eventually they appeared to focus on the bank in the mining area of Tupiza. For several weeks, while casing the bank, they bunked with a British engineer named A. G. Francis in a small town about fifteen miles south of the city. Butch regularly went into Tupiza to study the bank operations. He discovered that a detachment of soldiers from an elite Bolivian unit was quartered in a hotel across the town square from the bank—much too close—and it didn't appear as if they were leaving anytime soon.

But while there, Butch discovered an even softer target, the Aramayo family mining interests. The family owned and operated several tin mines in the area, and the payrolls for all of them passed through their main office in Tupiza. Butch learned that an Aramayo manager named Carlos Peró would be transporting an eighty-thousand-peso payroll, about half a million in today's dollars, from Tupiza to Quechisla—by mule. On foot. Unarmed. And without any guards.

On November 4, 1908, as Peró, his young son, and a peon who was assisting him walked up Dead Cow Hill, they were confronted by two men. Bandanas covered their faces, and their hat brims were turned down so that only their eyes were visible. They were wearing dark-red corduroy suits and cartridge belts bulging with ammunition. Each man held a Mauser carbine and had a Colt revolver tucked in his holster. One of them stepped close and told Peró he wanted the eighty thousand pesos, and he wanted it quick. Peró apologized profusely. That payroll was being carried the next week, he explained, but this week he had only fifteen thousand pesos (about ninety thousand dollars). Obviously Butch and Sundance would not be coming back the following week, so they took the smaller payroll and a dark brown mule, then disappeared into the Bolivian wilderness.

Within a day, *la guardia*, military patrols, and armed miners were watching every town and village, every ravine and culvert, every train station and horse ranch, looking for two gringos with a dark brown mule.

Butch and Sundance had made it back to Francis's place. They leveled with him, then spent the night ruminating about what might have been. Francis recalled Cassidy telling him that he'd wanted to live a law-abiding life, but that each time he tried, the Pinks had shown up and forced him to return to the outlaw road. Cassidy told him he'd never hurt or killed a man except in self-defense—making him unique among western outlaws—and had robbed only rich corporations.

Fearing that an army patrol would find them, Butch and Sundance departed very early the next morning, taking Francis with them as a guide. A day later they released him. At sundown on November 6, they rode cautiously into the mining village of San Vicente, one of them astride a dark brown mule. The *corregidor*, a local magistrate named Cleto Bellot, welcomed the strangers and inquired as to their business. They were on their way to Santa Catalina, they explained, and asked for supplies and directions. Bellot offered his assistance, then found them lodging for the night in a thatched adobe house at the end of a walled alley.

After Bellot left them there for the night, he went right to the place where a four-man posse, consisting of soldiers and *la guardia*, was staying and told them where they would find the outlaws. As the four men approached the adobe house at the end of the alley, a man later identified as Butch Cassidy stepped into the open doorway and began firing his pistol at them. The soldier Vincent Lopez was struck in the neck and would die there. The posse took up defensive positions and began firing into the house. One of them went to seek armed friends who would guard the rear and the roof to prevent an escape. Unlike in the final scene in the wonderful movie that would be made about the outlaws sixty years later, only a few anxious men surrounded the house. And there was no cascade of bullets, only several shots. Within several minutes, though, three loud screams came from the house, and then there was no more shooting.

In the early light of the next morning, the soldiers entered the house. Both Yankees were dead: Butch Cassidy was lying on the floor, a bullet in his arm and a bullet in his temple. The Sundance Kid was still sitting on a bench behind the door, his arms wrapped around a large ceramic jar, with several shots in his body and one shot in the center of his forehead. To knowledgeable people, it looked as if Butch had finished off his wounded friend, Sundance, then killed himself.

The payroll was still in their saddlebags. No one knew their names, but Peró identified them as the men who had held him up. They were buried in San Vicente.

That's the whole story, except that the ending has long been questioned.

Several different versions of the climactic shoot-out were reported to have taken place in several different cities. One such version, written by missionary and explorer Hiram Bingham, who had coincidentally arrived in Tupiza two weeks after the shooting, was published in 1911. Bingham wrote, ". . . a party of 50 Bolivian soldiers went on the trail of the robbers, who were found lunching in an Indian hut. They had carelessly left their mules and rifles several yards from the door of the hut and were unable to escape. After a fight, in which three or four soldiers were killed and as many more wounded, the thatch roof of the hut was set on fire and the bandits forced out into the open where they finally fell, each with half a dozen bullets in his body."

Although these bodies were positively identified as those of the bandits who had robbed the Aramayo payroll, there was no evidence that they were Butch and Sundance. The Pinkertons were not convinced of their identity; William A. Pinkerton himself dismissed "the whole story as a fake," and the agency never officially ended its search for the outlaws. In fact, Pinkerton supposedly confided to an operative, "The last we heard of Longabaugh he was in jail in Peru for an attempted bank robbery. Cassidy had been with him but got away."

Many people later claimed to have met or spent time with both men in many different places, long after their deaths had been reported. Even Bingham concluded his story by admitting, "We received a call from two rough-looking Anglo-Saxons who told us hair raising stories of dangers on the Bolivian roads where highway robbers driven out of the United States . . . and hounded to death by Pinkerton detectives, had found a pleasant place to pursue their chosen occupation. . . . We found out afterwards that one of our informants was one of this damn gang of robbers."

Cassidy's sister Lula Betenson claimed that her brother had visited her in 1925 and related yet another version of the story. Two men were indeed killed that night in San Vicente, but they were identified as Cassidy and Sundance by a friend of theirs from the Concordia Tin Mines named Percy Seibert, who did it to allow his friends to start a new life without living in fear of the law.

The bodies of the two men who died that night have been lost to history, so DNA testing can't be conducted, ensuring that the question of who really did die in that small Bolivian village will never be definitively answered. For the many people enamored with the romantic tale of the gentlemen train robbers and the beautiful Etta Place, who want to believe that Butch and Sundance lived long lives under assumed names, this is a perfect ending.

Paul Newman as Butch Cassidy and Robert Redford as the Sundance Kid depicted the legendary friendship between the outlaws in the classic 1969 movie. Nominated for seven Academy Awards, winning four, it guaranteed that Butch, Sundance, Etta Place, and the Hole-in-the-Wall Gang would live forever in the legends of the Old West.

A MOVING IMAGE:
CREATING THE WILD WEST
ON FILM

No medium has done more to shape our image of the Old West than the motion-picture industry. It was a fortunate coincidence that moving pictures became easily accessible to most Americans at just about the same time in our history that the Wild West became settled. Western stories were perfect for the rudimentary technology then available: The large cameras required a lot of light, so most films had to be shot outdoors. Because there was no sound, plots had to be uncomplicated, and it had to be easy for the audience to instantly tell the good guys from the bad guys. A new genre was created, a world of adventure and suspense in which a man's character could be determined by the color of his hat.

Movies were pure entertainment; they were not intended to be history. The real challenges faced and conquered by the explorers and homesteaders of the West lacked the instant excitement of stagecoaches being chased by outlaws, settlers fighting Indians, and quick-draw shoot-outs, so those and other similar elements were magnified and exaggerated and very rapidly came to define the West in the minds of moviegoers.

Although Edwin Porter's 1903 ten-minute-long *Great Train*

Robbery is usually cited as the first Western, in fact, Thomas Edison was experimenting with films such as *Sioux Ghost Dance* a decade earlier. Ironically, those early Westerns were filmed in New York and New Jersey and featured lush landscapes replete with lakes, streams, and forests rather than the vast plains that would later become the easily recognizable West. And in many of those early films, Indians were noble and trustworthy people who guided whites through perilous adventures, often having to save their lives; it would be another decade before Indians morphed into the cunning and heartless enemy. Brave cowboys such as "Broncho Billy" Anderson and Tom Mix, with his "wonder horse," Tony, were the first movie stars.

By the 1920s, Westerns had evolved from inexpensive one-reelers shown in nickelodeons to epic films. The most popular film of 1923, *The Covered Wagon*, was based on a dime novel. In 1924, director John Ford, who probably did more than any other person to create and shape the myth of the Old West, filmed *The Iron Horse*, which featured an army cavalry regiment, 3,000 railroad workmen, 1,000 Chinese laborers, 800 Indians, 2,800 horses, 1,300 buffalo, and 10,000 cattle.

It was the necessity of filming outdoors that eventually caused the motion-picture industry to move west for the year-round sunny skies of Hollywood. America's passion for movies sparked another kind of California gold rush, and the studios began producing countless low-budget B movies. Inexpensive western series and serials, with their

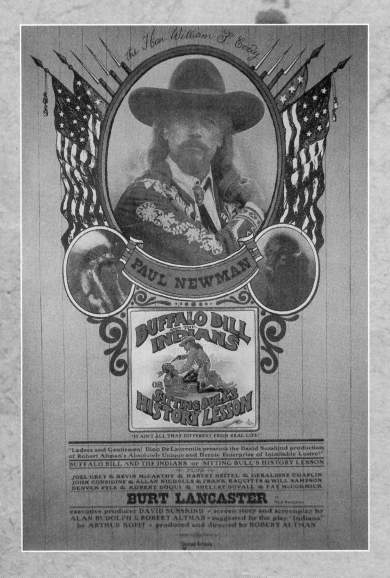

Since the founding of the motion-picture industry, the incredible true-life adventures of the men who tamed the West have served as source material— which was then turned into the larger-than-real-life legends we celebrate.

formulaic plots, usually including deception, betrayal, stampedes, and showdowns—and just a hint of romance—filled theaters around the country, spreading the gospel of the straight-shooting cowboy defending the weak and exploited against unscrupulous outlaws and untamed Indians.

In the 1950s, television created a whole new audience for these films, further guaranteeing the survival of this mythical vision of the West. When those studios moved from showing their old movies to producing new western TV series, they stayed true to the myths, portraying real men such as Davy Crockett, Wild Bill Hickok, Bat Masterson, and Wyatt Earp as mostly fictionalized characters. By 1958, eight of the ten most popular shows were Westerns, and the three networks were broadcasting forty-eight different western series, thirty of them in prime-time hours.

Unable to compete with the action-packed series, the movie studios began using the western backdrop to tell deeper human stories. In 1953, for example, the allegorical Western *High Noon* was nominated for seven Oscars, winning four of them. In movie history, only sixteen Westerns have even been nominated for Best Picture, and three of them—*Cimarron* (1931), *Dances with Wolves* (1990), and *Unforgiven* (1992)—have won.

Awards or no, the motion-picture industry molded the image of the Wild West that has become so much a part of American history.

ACKNOWLEDGMENTS

There are many people whose efforts made this project possible. I would like to express my appreciation to our editorial director, Gillian Blake, whose calm management of a complex project under difficult conditions has been superb. Literary agent Paul Fedorko of N.S. Bienstock brought all the disparate pieces together and was always there with a solution when difficulties arose. And as Paul will happily admit, he could not have done so without his assistant, Sammy Bina.

Coordinating this book with the television series being created by Warm Springs Productions of Missoula, Montana, has been made easy by line producer Bridger Pierce, whose enthusiasm for telling this wonderful story resonates on every page, and among the many people who have assisted him are Keith Palmer, Ajax Broome, and Jason Broome.

The beautiful illustrations that bring to life this colorful period in our history were cultivated and selected by Liz Seramur, Emily Vinson, and Adam Vietenheimer, along with Nancy Singer, who also created the book's artful and complementary design. The following people provided invaluable assistance in finding the images: John Waggener and Victoria Allen, American Heritage Center, University of Wyoming; Alyssa Bentz, Wells Fargo Corporate Archives; Jeff Corrigan, the State Historical Society of Missouri; Eileen Price, Center for Southwest Research, University of New Mexico; Hayes Scriven, Northfield Historical Society; Loren McLane, Fort Smith Historic Site; Stephen Spence, National Archives at Kansas City; Jacquelyn Slater Reese, Western History Collections, University of Oklahoma; Gregory M. Walz, Utah State Archives and Utah State History; Karen Douglas, Kit Carson Home; Thomas Haggerty and Wendy Zieger, Bridgeman Collection; Glenn Bradie and Alison Rigney, Everett Collection; Brandt Buell and Michelle Graham, Getty Images; Sarah Steele and Silka Quintero, Granger Collection; Ashley Morton and Joergen Birman, National Geographic Creative; Peter Rohowsky and Jennifer Belt, Art Resource; Dave Alexander, Legends of America. A very special thanks to copy editor deluxe Jane Hardick, whose passion for clarity and accuracy has made a huge difference.

Several people assisted me with my research, including Rob Farwell, Dusty Pendleton, and Steve Boynton, whose efforts I truly appreciate.

Completing a project like this requires continued support through long days and nights, which I always get from my beautiful wife (and America's finest yoga instructor!), Laura Stevens, and the small but confident dog who shared those hours with me, Willy.

And finally, I would also like to express my deepest appreciation to Bill O'Reilly for making it possible for me to participate in this project.

BIBLIOGRAPHY

The following books were excellent sources for general background on the Old West.

Calloway, Colin G. *New Worlds for All: Indians, Europeans and Remaking of Early America.* Baltimore: Johns Hopkins University Press, 2005.

Cody, William F. *An Autobiography of Buffalo Bill.* New York: Farrar and Rinehart, 1920.

Custer, George Armstrong. *My Life on the Plains; or, Personal Experiences with Indians.* New York: Sheldon & Company, 1876.

Howe, Henry. *The Great West.* Cincinnati: Henry Howe Publishing, 1851.

O'Neal, Bill. *Encyclopedia of Western Gunslingers.* Norman: University of Oklahoma Press, 1979.

Wright, Robert M. *Dodge City, the Cowboy Capital, and the Great Southwest.* Wichita, KS: Wichita Eagle Press, 1913.

Zinn, Howard. *A People's History of the United States.* New York: HarperCollins, 2005.

I have also consulted several websites to gather, compare, and confirm information. The following sites proved to be especially trustworthy and provided useful material, as well as directing me to additional sources:

Books.Google.com
EyewitnesstoHistory.com
History.com
legendsofamerica.com
PBS.org
Project Gutenberg (gutenberg.org)
Truewestmagazine.com
Wikipedia.org

The following resources provided information on the specific subjects profiled in this book.

Daniel Boone

Bakeless, John. *Daniel Boone, Master of the Wilderness.* 1939. Reprint, Lincoln: University of Nebraska Press, 1989.

Boone, Daniel. *The Adventures of Colonel Boone, Formerly a Hunter, Containing a Narrative of the Wars of Kentucky, Written by Himself.* John Filson, 1823.

Filson, John. *The Discovery, Settlement, and Present State of Kentucke.* Includes an appendix, "The Adventures of Col. Daniel Boon, One of the First Settlers." John Filson, 1784.

Fort Boonesborough Living History, "Daniel Boone and the History of Fort Boonesborough," http://www .fortboonesboroughlivinghistory.org/html/daniel_boone.html.

Hawks, Francis Lister. *The Adventures of Daniel Boone, the Kentucky Rifleman.* New York: D. Appleton, 1843.

Lord Byron. *Don Juan.* Reprint of the 1837 Halifax, Nova Scotia, edition, Project Gutenberg, 2007. http://www .gutenberg.org/files/21700/21700-h/21700-h.htm.

David Crockett

Akenson, Donald Harman. *Irish History of Civilization.* Volume 1. London: Granta Books, 2005.

Clarke, Matthew St. Clair. *The Life and Adventures of Colonel David Crockett of West Tennessee.* 1833.

Crockett, David, E. L. Carey, and A. Hart. *A Narrative of the Life of David Crockett, written by Himself.* Philadel- phia: E. L. Carey and A. Hart, 1834.

de la Peña, José Enrique. *The Memoirs of Lt. Col. José Enrique de la Peña.* College Station: Texas A&M University Press, 1975.

Editors of *True West* Magazine. "How Did Davy Really Die?" In *True Tales and Amazing Legends of the Old West: From* True West *Magazine.* New York: Crown, 2005.

Jones, Randell. *In the Footsteps of Davy Crockett.* Winston-Salem, NC: John F. Blair, 2006.

Legends of America, "Davy Crockett," http://www.legendsofamerica.com/we-davycrockettoutlaw.html.

Kit Carson

Burdett, Charles. *Life of Kit Carson.* Philadelphia: Porter and Coates, 1869.

Frémont, John C. *Report of the Exploring Exhibition to the Rocky Mountains, and to Oregon & California in the Years 1843–'44.* Washington, DC: Gales and Seaton, 1845.

Peters, DeWitt C. *The Life and Adventures of Kit Carson, the Nestor of the Rocky Mountains, from Facts Narrated by Himself.* New York: W. H. Tinson, 1858. Published as *Pioneer Life & Frontier Adventures of Kit Carson.* Boston: Estes & Lauriat, 1883.

Sides, Hampton. *Blood and Thunder.* New York: Doubleday, 2006.

Black Bart

"Black Bart: California's Infamous Stage Robber," http://www.BlackBart.com.

Hoeper, George. *Black Bart: Boulevardier Bandit.* Sanger, CA: Word Dancer Press, 1995.

Jackson, Joseph Henry. *Bad Company: The Story of California's Legendary and Actual Stage Robbers, Bandits, High- waymen and Outlaws from the Fifties to the Eighties.* Lincoln: University of Nebraska Press, 1977. First pub- lished 1949 by Harcourt Brace.

Nolan, Frederick. *The Wild West: History, Myth and the Making of America.* London: Arcturus, 2003.

Pryor, Alton. *Outlaws and Gunslingers.* Roseville, CA: Stagecoach Publishing, 2001.

Wild Bill Hickok

Black Plains Pioneer, August 5, 1876.

Cheyenne Daily Sun, March 8, 1876.

Hardin, John Wesley. *The Life of John Wesley Hardin as Written by Himself.* 1896. Reprint, Norman: University of Oklahoma Press, 1977.

Nichols, George Ward. "Wild Bill." *Harper's New Monthly Magazine,* February 1867.

Rosa, Joseph G. *They Called Him Wild Bill: The Life and Adventures of James Butler Hickok.* Norman: University of Oklahoma Press, 1979.

Topeka Daily Commonwealth, November 3, 1869.

Bass Reeves

Burton, Art T. *Black Gun, Silver Star: The Life and Legend of Frontier Marshal Bass Reeves*. Lincoln: University of Nebraska Press, 2006.

Fischer, Ron W. *The Tombstone News* (2006): "Bass Reeves: He Set a Timeless Example," http://www.TheTombstone News.com.

Generic Radio Workshop Script Library, "The Lone Ranger, episode 1," http://www.genericradio.com/show .php?id=1975f5a375929e64.

Legends of America, "Old West Legends: Bass Reeves; Black Hero Marshal," http://www.legendsofamerica.com/ we-bassreeves.html.

Nelson, Vaundra Micheaux. *Bad News for Outlaws: The Remarkable Life of Bass Reeves, U.S. Marshal*. Minneapolis: Lerner Publishing Group, 2009.

United States Marshals Service. "U.S. Marshal Bass Reeves," http://www.usmarshals.gov/news/chron/2011/ 111611.htm.

George Armstrong Custer

Ambrose, Stephen E. *Crazy Horse and Custer: The Parallel Lives of Two American Warriors*. New York: Random House, 1996.

Bismarck Tribune, September 2, 1874.

Connell, Evan. *Son of the Morning Star*. New York: North Point Press, 1984.

Lehman, Tim. *Bloodshed at Little Bighorn: Sitting Bull, Custer, and the Destinies of Nations*. Baltimore: Johns Hopkins University Press, 2010.

Buffalo Bill and Annie Oakley

Boston Journal, March 4, 1872.

Bridger, Bobby. *Buffalo Bill and Sitting Bull: Inventing the Wild West*. College Station: University of Texas Press, 2002.

Cody, William F., and Frank E. Bliss. *Life of Honorable William F. Cody, known as Buffalo Bill, the Famous Hunter*. Hartford, CT: Frank E. Bliss, 1879.

Cody, William F., and William Lightfoot Visscher. *Buffalo Bill's Own Story of His Life and Deeds*. Chicago: Homewood Press, 1917.

Gilbert, Sara. *Annie Oakley*. Mankato, MN: Creative Education, 2006. http://www.annieoakleycenterfoundation .com.

Norfolk Journal, May 18, 1873.

Russell, Don. *Lives and Legends of Buffalo Bill*. Norman: University of Oklahoma Press, 1960.

Rydell, Robert, and Rob Kroes. *Buffalo Bill in Bologna: The Americanization of the World 1869–1922*. Chicago: University of Chicago Press, 2005.

Jesse James

Daviess County Historical Society. http://daviesscountyhistoricalsociety.com/modules.php?op=modload&name =News&file=article&sid=384.

Kansas City Times, August 18, 1876.

Love, Robertus. *The Rise and Fall of Jesse James*. New York: G. P. Putnam, 1926.

Stiles, T. J. *Jesse James: The Last Rebel of the Civil War*. New York: Knopf, 2002.

Sunday Times of Chicago, September 10, 1876.

Yeatman, Ted P. *Frank and Jesse James: The Story Behind the Legend*. Nashville, TN: Cumberland House, 2003.

Doc Holliday

Denver Republican, May 22, 1882.

Herda, D. J. *They Call Me Doc: The Story Behind the Legend of John Henry Holliday*. Guilford, CT: Globe Pequot, 2011.

Leadville Carbonate Chronicle, November 14, 1887.

Masterson, W. R. Bat. "Doc Holliday," *Human Life Magazine*, 1907.

Otero, Miguel Antonio. *My Life on the Frontier*. New York: Press of the Pioneers, 1935.

Rewin, Richard E. *The Truth About Wyatt Earp*. Bloomington, IN: iUniverse, 2000.

Roberts, Gary L. *Doc Holliday: The Life and Legend*. Hoboken, NJ: John Wiley and Sons, 2006.

Tombstone Daily Epitaph, October 27, 1881.

Washington, D.C., Evening Star, January 1, 1878.

Billy the Kid

Garrett, Pat Floyd. *The Authentic Life of Billy, the Kid: The Noted Desperado of the Southwest*. Santa Fe: New Mexican Printing and Publishing, 1881.

Las Vegas Gazette, December 23, 1889.

Metz, Leon Claire. *Pat Garrett: The Story of a Western Lawman*. Norman: University of Oklahoma Press, 1983.

Nolan, Frederick. *The Billy the Kid Reader*. Norman: University of Oklahoma Press, 2007.

Pryor, Alton. *Outlaws and Gunslingers*. Roseville, CA: Stagecoach Publishing, 2001.

Siringo, Charles. *History of Billy the Kid*. Taos, NM: Charles Siringo, 1923.

Utley, Robert M. *Billy the Kid: A Short and Violent Life*. Lincoln: University of Nebraska Press, 1991.

Butch Cassidy

Anaconda Standard, July 14, 1901.

Descriptions of outlaw hideouts, http://www.wyostatearchives.wordpress.com.

Editors of *True West* Magazine. *True Tales and Amazing Legends of the Old West*. New York: Crown, 2005.

Fulton County News, April 26, 1905.

Garcia, Vince. "The Wild Bunch Chronicles: A Timeline from 1890–1910." http://www.centralcal.com/timeline.htm.

Kelly, Charles. *The Outlaw Trail: A History of Butch Cassidy and His Wild Bunch*. Lincoln: University of Nebraska Press, 1996.

Laramie Daily Boomerang, June 4, 1899.

Ogden Standard, June 3, 1898.

Patterson, Richard. *Butch Cassidy: A Biography*. Lincoln: University of Nebraska Press, 1990.

Pointer, Larry. *In Search of Butch Cassidy*. Norman: University of Oklahoma Press, 1977.

Raine, William MacLeod. "Guarding a Railroad in the Bandit Belt," *Wide World Magazine*, November 1904.

Rawlins Semi-Weekly Republican, June 3, 1899.

St. George Union, April 24, 1897.

Salt Lake Herald, September 17, 1900.

CREDITS

Page iii: Background and title logo courtesy of FOX NEWS CHANNEL. Page vi: Chappel, Alonzo (1828–87) (after)/Private Collection/Ken Welsh/Bridgeman Images; Courtesy Library of Congress, LC-DIG-pga-04179; Courtesy Kit Carson House and Museum; Mary Evans Picture Library/Everett Collection; Private Collection/Peter Newark American Pictures/Bridgeman Images; LegendsOfAmerica.com. Page vii: Courtesy Library of Congress, LC-DIG-ppmsca-33129; Universal History Archive/UIG/Bridgeman Images; Private Collection/Peter Newark American Pictures/Bridgeman Images; Courtesy Library of Congress, LC-USZ62-3854; LegendsOfAmerica.com; Courtesy National Archives, Photo no. 406-NSB-011-Billykid; Courtesy Library of Congress, LC-DIG-ppmsca-10772. Page 4: Chappel, Alonzo (1828–87) (after)/Private Collection/Ken Welsh/Bridgeman Images. Page 6: Library of Congress, Prints & Photographs Division, HABS PA, 6-BAUM.V, 1–5. Page 7: Cole, Thomas (1801–48)/Mead Art Museum, Amherst College, MA, USA/Museum purchase/Bridgeman Images. Page 9: Baraldi, Severino (b. 1930)/Private Collection/© Look and Learn/Bridgeman Images; Lindneux, Robert Ottokar (1871–1970)/Private Collection/Peter Newark American Pictures/Bridgeman Images. Page 10: Bingham, George Caleb (1811–79)/Washington University, St. Louis, USA/Bridgeman Images. Page 11: American School (20th century)/Private Collection/Peter Newark American Pictures/Bridgeman Images. Page 13: MPI/Getty Images. Page 14: Baraldi, Severino (b. 1930)/Private Collection/© Look and Learn/Bridgeman Images. Page 17: Private Collection/Peter Newark American Pictures/Bridgeman Images. Pages 18–19: The Print Collector/Print Collector/Getty Images. Page 20: Courtesy Library of Congress, LC-DIG-pga-02659. Page 23: Daniel Boone, 1820 (oil on canvas), Harding, Chester (1792–1866)/© Massachusetts Historical Society, Boston, MA, USA/Bridgeman Images. Page 24: Courtesy Library of Congress, LC-DIG-pga-04179. Page 27: Private Collection/Peter Newark American Pictures/Bridgeman Images. Page 29: Courtesy Library of Congress, LC-USZ62-7368. Page 30: Granger, NYC—All rights reserved. Page 33: Courtesy Library of Congress, LC-USZ62-43901; Courtesy Library of Congress, LC-DIG-pga-02501. Page 37: Callcott, Frank C. (1891–1979)/Dallas Museum of Art, Texas, USA/gift of Professor Dudley F. McCollum/Bridgeman Images. Page 39: Stephen St. John/National Geographic Creative. Page 40: Private Collection/Peter Newark American Pictures/Bridgeman Images. Page 41: Wyeth, Newell Convers (1882–1945)/Private Collection/Bridgeman Images; Private Collection/© Look and Learn/Bridgeman Images; Private Collection/Bridgeman Images. Page 44: Courtesy Kit Carson House and Museum. Page 46: Granger, NYC—All rights reserved. Pages 48–49: University of Wyoming, American Heritage Center, Everett D. Graff Collection, Accession Number 4912. Page 51: 000-742-0217, William A. Keleher Pictorial Collection, Center for Southwest Research, University Libraries, University of New Mexico. Page 52: The New York Public Library/Art Resource, NY. Page 53: Courtesy Kit Carson House and Museum. Page 55: Courtesy Library of Congress, LC-USZC4-2631. Page 57: 000-742-0067, William A. Keleher Pictorial Collection, Center for Southwest Research, University Libraries, University of New Mexico; Vector Graphic by Retro Design Elements. Page 58: Courtesy Library of Congress, LC-DIG-hec-13449. Page 60: Granger, NYC—All rights reserved. Page 61: Return of scouts—Cheyenne 1910 (photo)/Universal History Archive/UIG/Bridgeman Images. Page 63: Denver Public Library, Western History Collection/Bridgeman Images. Page 65: Courtesy Library of Congress LC-DIG-cwpb-07381. Page 66: Courtesy Library of Congress, LC-USZC4-11256. Page 68: Courtesy Library of Congress, LC-BH83-1371. Page 70: Mary Evans Picture Library/Everett Collection. Page 73: Private Collection/Peter Newark American Pictures/Bridgeman Images. Page 75: Private Collection/Peter Newark Western Americana/Bridgeman Images; De Agostini Picture Library/Bridgeman Images. Page 76: Private Collection/Ken Welsh/Bridgeman Images. Page 78: Private Collection/Peter Newark American Pictures/Bridgeman Images. Pages 80–81: Courtesy Library of Congress, LC-DIG-pga-01018. Page 84: Wells Fargo Corporate Archives. Page 86: Granger, NYC—All rights reserved; Vector Graphic by Retro Design Elements. Pages 88, 90, 93: Private Collection/Peter Newark American Pictures/Bridgeman Images. Page 94: Private Collection/Peter Newark Western Americana/Bridgeman Images. Page 97: Stock Montage/Getty Images. Pages 98–99: Private Collection/Peter Newark American Pictures/Bridgeman Images. Page 101: Courtesy Library of Congress, LC-USZ62-50004. Page 103: Collection/Peter Newark American Pictures/Bridgeman Images. Page 107: American Photographer (19th century)/Private Collection/Peter Newark American Pictures/Bridgeman Images. Pages 108, 111: Private Collection/Peter Newark American Pictures/Bridgeman Images. Page 114: Peter Newark American Pictures/Bridgeman Images. Page 116: Courtesy Library of Congress, LC-USF34-016687-C. Page 118: LegendsOfAmerica.com. Page 121: Courtesy Everett Collection. Page 122: Courtesy National Archives, photo no. 111-B-3202 and record no. 6851120. Page 124: Western History Collections, University of Oklahoma Libraries, Twine Family 61. Page 125: Courtesy National Archives at Kansas City, Records of the Bureau of Prisons, RG 129. Pages 131, 132, 133: Courtesy the Fort Smith National Historic Site. Page 134: Courtesy Library of Congress, LC-DIG-ppmsca-33129. Page 136: Amos Bad Heart Buffalo (1869–1913)/Private

Collection/The Stapleton Collection/Bridgeman Images. Page 137: Kills Two (Nupa Kte) (1969–1927)/Private Collection/The Stapleton Collection/Bridgeman Images. Page 138: Courtesy Library of Congress, LC-USZC4-7160. Pages 141, 142: De Agostini Picture Library/Bridgeman Images. Page 144: Courtesy Library of Congress, LC-USZ62-114798. Page 146: Courtesy Library of Congress, LC-DIG-ppmsca-24021. Page 149: De Agostini Picture Library/Bridgeman Images. Page 152: Courtesy Library of Congress, LC-BH831-365. Page 155: National Museum of American History, Smithsonian Institution, USA/ Bridgeman Images. Page 156: Becker, Otto (fl. 1895) (after)/Private Collection/Peter Newark American Pictures/Bridgeman Images. Page 158: Private Collection/Bridgeman Images. Page 159: Miller, Alfred Jacob (1810–74)/© Walters Art Museum, Baltimore, USA/Bridgeman Images. Page 160: Peter Newark Pictures/Bridgeman Images. Page 162: Universal History Archive/ UIG/Bridgeman Images; Private Collection/Peter Newark American Pictures/Bridgeman Images. Page 164: American Photographer, (20th century)/Private Collection/Peter Newark American Pictures/Bridgeman Images. Page 165: Private Collection/Peter Newark Western Americana/Bridgeman Images. Page 166: American School/Private Collection/Bridgeman Images. Page 169: Denver Public Library, Western History Collection/Bridgeman Images. Page 171: Private Collection/Peter Newark American Pictures/Bridgeman Images; Private Collection/Peter Newark Western Americana/Bridgeman Images. Page 172: Newberry Library, Chicago, Illinois, USA/Bridgeman Images. Page 175: Courtesy Library of Congress, LC-USZ62-21207 and LC-DIG-ppmsca-24362. Page 177: Private Collection/© Look and Learn/Peter Jackson Collection/Bridgeman Images. Page 179: The Illustrated London News Picture Library, London, UK/Bridgeman Images. Page 181: Private Collection/© Look and Learn/Bridgeman Images. Page 183: Courtesy Library of Congress, LC-USZ62-46076. Page 185: Underwood Archives/ UIG/Bridgeman Images. Page 186: Private Collection/Peter Newark American Pictures/Bridgeman Images. Page 188: Courtesy Library of Congress, LC-USZ62-3854. Page 190: Private Collection/Peter Newark American Pictures/Bridgeman Images. Pages 191, 192: Used with permission of The State Historical Society of Missouri. Page 194: Used with permission of The State Historical Society of Missouri; Courtesy Library of Congress, LC-USZ62-3855. Page 195: Used with permission of The State Historical Society of Missouri. Page 197: Courtesy Library of Congress, LC-USZ62-3855. Page 201: Everitt, Elias Foster (1837–1928)/Private Collection/Courtesy of Swann Auction Galleries/Bridgeman Images. Page 202: Private Collection/Peter Newark American Pictures/Bridgeman Images. Pages 203, 204: Northfield Historical Society. Page 207: Used with permission of The State Historical Society of Missouri. Page 208: LegendsOfAmerica.com. Page 209: Private Collection/Photo © Barbara Singer/Bridgeman Images. Page 211: Private Collection/Bridgeman Images; Private Collection/Peter Newark American Pictures/Bridgeman Images; Courtesy Library of Congress LC-USZ62-4049. Page 212: Private Collection/Peter Newark American Pictures/Bridgeman Images. Page 214: LegendsOfAmerica.com. Page 218: Private Collection/Peter Newark Western Americana/Bridgeman Images. Page 220: The Stapleton Collection/Bridgeman Images. Pages 222–23: LegendsOfAmerica. com. Page 225: Private Collection/Bridgeman Images. Page 228: Private Collection/Peter Newark American Pictures/ Bridgeman Images; Courtesy Library of Congress, LC-USF33-012679-M4. Page 231: The Denver Post via Getty Images. Page 233: Courtesy Library of Congress, LC-USZ62-50009 and LC-USZ62-50007. Page 234: Private Collection/Peter Newark American Pictures/Bridgeman Images. Page 236: Courtesy National Archives, Photo no. 406-NSB-011-Billykid. Page 241: 000-118-0017 and 000-742-0111, William A. Keleher Pictorial Collection, Center for Southwest Research, University Libraries, University of New Mexico; LegendsOfAmerica.com. Page 242: 000-742-0151, William A. Keleher Pictorial Collection, Center for Southwest Research, University Libraries, University of New Mexico. Page 243: Private Collection/Peter Newark Western Americana/Bridgeman Images. Page 244: American School (19th century)/Private Collection/Peter Newark Western Americana/Bridgeman Images. Page 246: Wallace, Lew (1827–1905)/© Collection of the New-York Historical Society, USA/Bridgeman Images. Page 247: AP photo/Fray Angelico Chavez History Library. Page 248: Courtesy Everett Collection. Page 250: Private Collection/Bridgeman Images. Page 253: Courtesy Everett Collection. Page 255: Courtesy Library of Congress, LC-USZ62-87581. Page 256: Charlton Comics, http://digitalcomicmuseum.com. Page 258: Courtesy Library of Congress, LC-DIG-ppmsca-10772. Page 260: University of Wyoming, American Heritage Center, Everett D. Graff Collection, Accession Number ah101308. Page 261: Used by permission, Utah State Historical Society. Page 262: Courtesy Library of Congress, LC-DIG-ppmsca-10770. Pages 264–65: University of Wyoming, American Heritage Center, Everett D. Graff Collection, Accession Number ah01053_0946. Page 265: Courtesy Library of Congress, LC-DIG-ppmsca-11844. Page 267: Courtesy Library of Congress, LC-DIG-ppmsca-07624. Page 269: University of Wyoming, American Heritage Center, Everett D. Graff Collection, Accession Numbers ah00176_0285, ah00176_0283, and ah-2995. Page 270: Underwood Archives/UIG/ Bridgeman Images. Page 271: University of Wyoming, American Heritage Center, Everett D. Graff Collection, Accession Number ah01053_0918. Page 273: Private Collection/Peter Newark American Pictures/Bridgeman Images; University of Wyoming, American Heritage Center, Everett D. Graff Collection, Accession Number ah001401. Page 275: University of Wyoming, American Heritage Center, Everett D. Graff Collection, Accession Number ah002690. Page 276: Courtesy Library of Congress, LC-USZ620132506; Vector Graphic by Vector Open Stock. Page 281: ©20thCentFox/Courtesy Everett Collection. Page 284: Private Collection/Peter Newark American Pictures/Bridgeman Images.

THE LANDS OF
Legends & Lies

© 2015 Jeffrey L. Ward

KEY
- ------- Wilderness Road, 1796 *(inset)*
- – – – Santa Fe Trail, 1821
- – – Frémont's expedition, 1842
- – – Oregon Trail, 1842
- – – Wells Fargo Overland, 1852
- ---- Pony Express Trail, 1860
- — — "The Long Walk," 1864
- ---- Chisholm Trail, 1867
- ┼┼┼ Transcontinental Railroad, 1869

OREGON

MONTANA

Yellowstone Ri...

Boise

IDAHO

Snake River

ROCKY MOUNTAINS

Great Salt Lake

Salt Lake City

Brown's Hole

UTAH

Green River

Robbers Roost

Sacramento River

Sacramento

Carson City

◆ *Sutter's Mill*

◆ *Funk Hill*

San Joaquin River

NEVADA

Pacific Ocean

San Francisco

◆ *Gold Rush*

SIERRA NEVADA

Las Vegas

MISSOURI COMPROMISE LINE

Fort Defiance ◆

CALIFORNIA

Colorado River

•Flagstaff

• Los Angeles

ARIZONA

Phoenix

San Diego

Gila River

Tucson ◆

Tombstone ◆

0 Miles 100 200

0 Kilometers 200

(inset map)

IL

IN

OH

Ohio River

MO

Boonesborough

WV

KENTUCKY

VA

Cumberland Gap

APPALACHIAN MTNS

NC

AR

TENNESSEE

LAWRENCE COUNTY

SC

Mississippi River

MS

AL

GA